PUBLIC ADMINISTRATION

Concepts and Cases

SIXTH EDITION

Richard J. Stillman II
University of Colorado

Houghton Mifflin Company   **Boston**   **Toronto**

Geneva, Illinois   Palo Alto   Princeton, New Jersey

Editor in Chief: Jean Woy
Senior Associate Editor: Fran Gay
Senior Project Editor: Susan Westendorf
Senior Production/Design Coordinator: Jill Haber
Senior Manufacturing Coordinator: Priscilla Bailey
Marketing Manager: Clint Crockett

For my wife, Kathleen
my daughter, Shannon Marie
my son, Richard J. III

Printed in the U.S.A.

Library of Congress Catalog Card Number: 95-76990

ISBN: 0-395-75492-5

CDEFGHIJ—QM—99 98 97 96

Contents

Preface

The publication of this sixth edition marks the twentieth anniversary of this text's first appearance in print. At that time, I hoped that this text would offer an improved way to teach the "basics" of public administration that would be both exciting and challenging for students. Over the intervening two decades it has succeeded more than I could have imagined. I hope that readers of this sixth edition will find that this edition continues to meet their needs for a different and better way of introducing the field of public administration to both new students and "old hands."

Format and Approach

The methodological format and design of the first five editions remain intact in the sixth edition. The approach seeks to interrelate many of the authoritative conceptual works in public administration with contemporary case studies.

By pairing a reading with a case study in each chapter, the text serves four important purposes:

1. The concept-case study method permits students to read firsthand the work of leading administrative theorists who have shaped the modern study of public administration. This method aims at developing in students a critical appreciation of the classic administrative ideas that are the basis of modern public administration.
2. The text encourages a careful examination of practical administrative problems through the presentation of contemporary cases—often involving major national events—that demonstrate the complexity, the centrality, and the challenge of the current administrative processes of public organizations.
3. The book seeks to promote a deeper understanding of the relationship between the theory and practice of public administration by allowing readers to test for themselves the validity of major ideas about public administration in the context of actual situations.
4. Finally, the concept-case method develops a keener appreciation of the eclectic breadth and interdisciplinary dimensions of public administration by presenting articles—both conceptual and case writings—from a wide variety of sources, using many materials not available in the average library.

The immense quantity of literature in the field has always made selecting the writings a challenge. My final choice of writings is based on affirmative answers to the following four central questions:

1. Do the writings focus on the central issues confronting public administrators?
2. Do the writings, individually and collectively, give a realistic view of the contemporary practice of public administration?
3. Do the individual conceptual readings and case studies relate logically to one another?

4. Are the writings interesting and long enough to convey the true sense and spirit intended by the authors?

The arrangement of the selections follows an order of topics used by many instructors in the field, moving from a definition of public administration to increasingly specific issues and problems. Many subjects (such as headquarters-field relationships, position classification, enforcement, government regulation, productivity, and personnel recruitment), though not treated separately, are discussed within various chapters under other headings (refer to the topic index for additional cross-references).

This diagram may help readers to understand the design of the book more clearly.

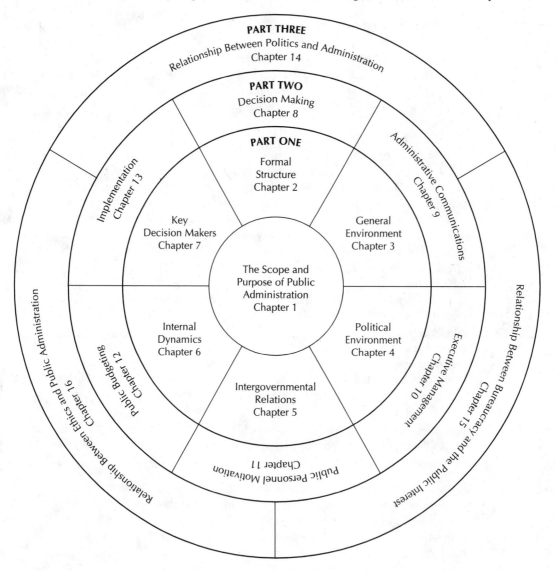

At the center of this schematic figure is Chapter 1, which discusses "The Scope and Purpose of Public Administration," perhaps the most difficult, central intellectual problem in public administration today. The first ring outward is Part One, "The Pattern of Public Administration in America." These six chapters present concepts and cases pertaining to the broad environment surrounding public administration and the work of public administrators. The second ring is Part Two, "The Multiple Functions of Public Administrators." These six chapters focus on the major activities, roles, and responsibilities of practicing administrators in the public sector. The exterior ring is Part Three; these three chapters discuss "Enduring and Unresolved Relationships" in public administration, ones especially critical during the last decade of the 20th century for the field as a whole.

New Material in the Sixth Edition

Readings and cases have been carefully selected with an eye to readability and contemporary appeal to ensure that the text stays current and continues to reflect the ideas and events shaping public administration today. In this edition, special attention has been paid to ensuring the accessibility of writings for students: contemporary topics and issues that students want and need to know about make up more than half (17 of 32) of the new selections.

Seven new readings appear in this edition:

Reading 1.2: "The Refounding Movement in American Public Administration" (Richard J. Stillman II)

Reading 5: "American Intergovernmental Relations: An Overview" (Laurence J. O'Toole, Jr.)

Reading 7: "Inside Public Bureaucracy" (Richard J. Stillman II)

Reading 11: "The Motivational Bases of Public Service" (James L. Perry and Lois Recascino Wise)

Reading 13: "The Conditions of Effective Implementation" (Paul Sabatier and Daniel Mazmanian)

Reading 15: "Bureaucracy and the Public Interest" (James Q. Wilson)

Reading 16: "Public Administration and Ethics: A Prologue to a Preface" (Dwight Waldo)

Ten case studies are also new to this edition:

Case Study 2: "How Kristin Died" (George Lardner, Jr.)

Case Study 4: "The Last Flight of the Space Shuttle Challenger" (Michael T. Charles)

Case Study 5: "Wichita Confronts Contamination" (Susan Rosegrant)

Case Study 7: "Twisting in the Wind? Ambassador Glaspie and the Persian Gulf Crisis" (Jillian P. Dickert)

Revised and expanded introductions, alerting students to the main ideas that follow, open each selection. Also updated are the review questions, key terms, and suggestions for further reading that conclude each chapter, as well as the subject and topic indexes.

The Instructor's Guide

The *Instructor's Guide* complements the text by offering insights, practical suggestions, and resources for teaching introductory and graduate students. The guide is organized as a set of memoranda from myself to the instructor. Each memo addresses a separate important topic, such as "How to use case studies in the classroom." The guide also includes sample quizzes, exams, and course evaluation forms. Appendices include the Federalist Papers, nos. 10 and 51, the Declaration of Independence, and the Constitution.

Acknowledgments

Various people have contributed to this book either by helping to shape its focus in the early stages or by reviewing the finished manuscript. Special thanks are due: James M. Banovetz, Northern Illinois University; James L. Garnett, Rutgers University at Camden; John E. Moore, University of California, Santa Barbara; Michael Munger, University of North Carolina at Chapel Hill; Laurence J. O'Toole, Jr., University of Georgia; Alan Shank, State University of New York—Geneseo; and Edward M. Wheat, University of Southern Mississippi.

Thanks must also go to my editors at Houghton Mifflin for their generous support and enthusiastic encouragement throughout this difficult writing and editing assignment, particularly Jean Woy, Fran Gay, and Susan Westendorf. My graduate assistant at the University of Colorado, Lynn Nestingen, was invaluable in preparing the sixth edition and I owe her considerable thanks as well. The students, both graduate and undergraduate, whom I have taught over the last two and a half decades have shaped this text in more ways than I can calculate—or thank them for: To these and many others, I owe a debt of gratitude for their assistance.

R.J.S. II

CHAPTER 1

The Search for the Scope and Purpose of Public Administration

*O*ur *own politics must be the touchstone for all theories. The principles on which to base a science of administration for America must be principles which have democratic policy very much at heart.*

Woodrow Wilson

READING 1.1

Introduction

A definition of the parameters of a field of study, that is, the boundaries, landmarks, and terrain that distinguish it from other scientific and humanistic disciplines, is normally considered a good place to begin any academic subject. Unfortunately, as yet, no one has produced a simple definition of the study of public administration—at least one on which most practitioners and scholars agree. Attempting to define the core values and focus of twentieth-century public administration provides lively debates and even deep divisions among students of the field.

A major difficulty in arriving at a precise and universally acceptable definition arises in part from the rapid growth in the twentieth century of public administration, which today seems to be all-encompassing. Public administrators are engaged in technical, although not necessarily mundane details: they prepare budgets for a city government, classify jobs in a post office, have potholes patched and mail delivered, or evaluate the performance of a city's drug treatment centers. At the same time, they are also concerned with the major goals of society and with the development of resources for achieving those goals within the context of a rapidly changing political environment. For instance, if an engineering staff of a state agency proposes to build a highway, this decision appears at first glance to be a purely administrative activity. However, it involves a wide range of social values related to pressing concerns such as community land-use patterns, energy consumption, pollution control, and mass transit planning. Race relations, the general economic well-being of a community, and the allocation of scarce physical and human resources affect even simple administrative decisions about highway construction.

Public administration does not operate in a vacuum but is deeply intertwined with the critical dilemmas confronting an entire society. The issue then becomes: How can a theorist reasonably and concisely define a field so interrelated with all of society?

The rapidly increasing number and scope of activities involving public administration have led theorists to develop a variety of definitions. Consider ten offered during the last decade by leading textbook writers:

> Public Administration is the production of goods and services designed to serve the needs of citizens-consumers.
>
> Marshall Dimock, Gladys Dimock, and Douglas Fox,
> *Public Administration* (Fifth Edition, 1983)

> We suggest a new conceptual framework that emphasizes the perception of public administration as *design,* with attendant emphasis on participative decision making and learning, purpose and action, innovation, imagination and creativity, and social interaction and "coproduction."
>
> Jong S. Jun,
> *Public Administration* (1986)

> In ordinary usage, public administration is a generic expression for the entire bundle of activities that are involved in the establishment and implementation of public policies.
>
> Cole Blease Graham, Jr., and
> Steven W. Hays,
> *Managing the Public Organization* (1986)

> Traditionally, public administration is thought of as the accomplishing side of government. It is supposed to comprise all those activities involved in carrying out the policies of elected officials and some activities associated with the development of those policies. Public administration is . . . all that comes after the last campaign promise and election-night cheer.
>
> Grover Starling,
> *Managing the Public Sector* (Third Edition, 1986)

> Public administration:
> 1. is a cooperative group effort in a public setting.
> 2. covers all three branches—executive, legislative, and judicial—and their interrelationships.
> 3. has an important role in the formulation of public policy, and is thus part of the political process.
> 4. is different in significant ways from private administration.
> 5. is closely associated with numerous private groups and individuals in providing services to the community.
>
> Felix A. Nigro and Lloyd G. Nigro,
> *Modern Public Administration* (Seventh Edition, 1989)

Public administration is the use of managerial, political, and legal theories and processes to fulfill legislative, executive, and judicial governmental mandates for the provision of regulatory and service functions for the society as a whole or for some segments of it.

David H. Rosenbloom and Deborah D. Goldman,
Public Administration: Understanding Management, Politics, and Law in the Public Sector (Second Edition, 1989)

. . . public administration is centrally concerned with the organization of government policies and programs as well as the behavior of officials (usually nonelected) formally responsible for their conduct.

Charles H. Levine, B. Guy Peters, and Frank J. Thompson,
Public Administration: Challenges, Choices, Consequences (1990)

The practice of public administration involves the dynamic reconciliation of various forces in government's efforts to manage public policies and programs.

Melvin J. Dubnick and Barbara S. Romzek,
American Public Administration: Politics and the Management of Expectations (1991)

Public administration is concerned with the management of public programs.

Robert B. Denhardt,
Public Administration: An Action Orientation (1995)

Public administration may be defined as all processes, organizations, and individuals (the latter acting in official positions and roles) associated with carrying out laws and other rules adopted or issued by legislatures, executives, and courts.

George J. Gordon and Michael E. Milakovich,
Public Administration in America (1995).

Generally, these attempts at defining public administration seem to identify it with the following: (1) the executive branch of government (yet it is related in important ways to the legislative and judicial branches); (2) the formulation and implementation of public policies; (3) the involvement in a considerable range of problems concerning human behavior and cooperative human effort; (4) a field that can be differentiated in several ways from private administration; (5) the production of public goods and services; and (6) rooted in the law as well as concerned with carrying out laws. However, trying to pin down public administration in more specific detail becomes, according to specialists such as Harold Stein, a fruitless endeavor. The many variables and complexities of public administration make almost every administrative situation a unique event, eluding any highly systematic categorization. As Harold Stein writes: "public administration is a field in which every man is his own codifier and categorizer and the categories adopted must be looked on as relatively evanescent."[1]

---

[1]Harold Stein, Public Administration and Policy Development: A Case Book (New York: Harcourt Brace Jovanovich, 1952), p. xxv.

For some writers like Frederick C. Mosher, the elusiveness of a disciplinary core for public administration gives the subject its strength and fascination, for students must draw upon many fields and disciplines, as well as their own resources, to solve a particular administrative problem. As Mosher writes: "Perhaps it is best that it [public administration] not be defined. It is more an area of interest than a discipline, more a focus than a separate science. . . . It is necessarily cross-disciplinary. The overlapping and vague boundaries should be viewed as a resource, even though they are irritating to some with orderly minds."[2]

But for others like Robert S. Parker, the frustrations of dealing with such a disorderly discipline mitigate against its being a mature, rewarding academic field of study. "There is really no such subject as 'public administration,' " writes Parker. "No science or art can be identified by this title, least of all any single skill or coherent intellectual discipline. The term has no relation to the world of systematic thought. . . . It does not, in itself, offer any promising opportunity to widen or make more precise any single aspect of scientific knowledge."[3]

Despite Parker's pessimistic assessment of the present and future status of public administration, the search for a commonly accepted definition of the field, both in its academic and professional applications, continues by many scholars.

Indeed, defining public administration—its boundaries, scope, and purpose—has become, in recent decades, a preoccupation and difficulty confronting public administration theorists. The field's "identity crisis," as Dwight Waldo once labeled the dilemma, has now become especially acute because a plethora of models, approaches, and theories now purport to define what public administration is all about.

To help us understand public administration today, it is useful to study the rationale for creating this field, as outlined in an essay written in 1887 by Woodrow Wilson, a young political scientist at the time. Wilson (1856–1924) is better known as the twenty-eighth President of the United States (1913–1921), father of the League of Nations, Commander-in-Chief during World War I, and author of much of the "New Freedom" progressive reform legislation. Wilson is also credited by scholars with writing the first essay on public administration in the United States and therefore is considered by many as its American founder. His short but distinguished essay, "The Study of Administration," was published a century after the U.S. Constitution's birth. Wilson had just begun his academic career, teaching political science at Bryn Mawr College in Pennsylvania, after earning his Ph.D. at Johns Hopkins University. The editor of a new journal *(Political Science Quarterly)* asked Wilson to contribute an essay on this developing subject. At that time, public administration had been a well-established discipline in Europe, but was largely unknown in America.

Geographic isolation, agrarian self-sufficiency, the absence of threats to national security, and limited demands for public services, among other things, had allowed the United States to get along reasonably well during its first century of existence without the self-conscious study of public administration. However, many events were forcing

---

[2]Frederick C. Mosher, "Research in Public Administration," Public Administration Review, 16 (Summer 1956), p. 177.

[3]Robert S. Parker, "The End of Public Administration," Public Administration, 34 (June 1965), p. 99.

Americans to take notice of the need for public administration. By the late nineteenth century, technologic innovations such as the automobile, telephone, and light bulb and growing international involvement in the Spanish-American War, combined with increasing public participation in a democratic government, created urgent needs for expanded, effective administrative services. As a consequence, we also required an established field of administrative study. Wilson wrote his essay at the time when civil service reform had been instituted in the federal government (the Civil Service Act or "the Pendleton Act," named for its legislative sponsor, had been passed in 1883). Much of Wilson's centennial essay was, not surprisingly, a plea for recognizing the central importance of administrative machinery, especially a well-trained civil service based on merit, rather than politics, to operate a modern democratic government.

Just as the *Federalist Papers,* authored by James Madison, Alexander Hamilton, and John Jay had a century before advocated the passage of the U.S. Constitution, Wilson called in 1887 for the necessity of this new field "to run a constitution" during its second century. His essay strived to encourage the development of public administration and to underscore the importance of effective administration for the Constitution's survival in the future.

But how could Americans graft public administration into their Constitution, which had not mentioned this subject? For Wilson—and modern students of the field—this was the critical issue. In developing public administration—both practically and academically—Wilson's basic difficulty was to reconcile the notions of constitutional democracy with inherent concerns for popular control and participation with theories of efficient, professional administration, and their stress on systematic rules and internal procedures as distinct from democratic oversight and influence. For Wilson, this inevitable conflict could be settled by dividing government into two spheres—"politics," in which choices regarding what government should do are determined by a majority of elected representatives, and "administration," which serves to carry out the dictates of the populace through efficient procedures relatively free from political meddling.

Although modern administrative scholars generally reject the possibility or desirability of drawing any hard-or-fast line between politics and administration, or what most call "the politics-administration dichotomy," the issues Wilson raised are enduring and important. Read the essay for yourself and see how you judge the validity of Wilson's arguments.

How did Wilson define public administration and why did he believe it was so critical to the future of the United States? Are his arguments for its basic rationale and value still valid?

Why did Wilson distinguish between "politics" and "administration" as important terms for creating public administration? In your opinion, is such a "politics-administration dichotomy" practical and workable? What are the advantages and disadvantages of using such a dichotomy today as a way to advance this field of study?

What sources did Wilson believe the U.S. should draw on in developing this new field? And what sources should Americans avoid in shaping their administrative enterprise? And why?

What issues and challenges did Wilson pose for administrative study and practice? Are these still priorities today?

The Study of Administration

WOODROW WILSON

I suppose that no practical science is ever studied where there is no need to know it. The very fact, therefore, that the eminently practical science of administration is finding its way into college courses in this country would prove that this country needs to know more about administration, were such proof of the fact required to make out a case. It need not be said, however, that we do not look into college programmes for proof of this fact. It is a thing almost taken for granted among us, that the present movement called civil service reform must, after the accomplishment of its first purpose, expand into efforts to improve, not the *personnel* only, but also the organization and methods of our government offices: because it is plain that their organization and methods need improvement only less than their *personnel*. It is the object of administrative study to discover, first, what government can properly and successfully do, and, secondly, how it can do these proper things with the utmost possible efficiency and at the least possible cost either of money or of energy. On both these points there is obviously much need of light among us; and only careful study can supply that light.

Before entering on that study, however, it is needful:

I. To take some account of what others have done in the same line; that is to say, of the history of the study.
II. To ascertain just what is its subject-matter.

Reprinted with permission from *Political Science Quarterly,* 2 (June 1887): 197–222.

III. To determine just what are the best methods by which to develop it, and the most clarifying political conceptions to carry with us into it.

Unless we know and settle these things, we shall set out without chart or compass.

I.

The science of administration is the latest fruit of that study of the science of politics which was begun some twenty-two hundred years ago. It is a birth of our own century, almost of our own generation.

Why was it so late in coming? Why did it wait till this too busy century of ours to demand attention for itself? Administration is the most obvious part of government; it is government in action; it is the executive, the operative, the most visible side of government, and is of course as old as government itself. It is government in action, and one might very naturally expect to find that government in action had arrested the attention and provoked the scrutiny of writers of politics very early in the history of systematic thought.

But such was not the case. No one wrote systematically of administration as a branch of the science of government until the present century had passed its first youth and had begun to put forth its characteristic flower of systematic knowledge. Up to our own day all the political writers whom we now read had thought, argued, dogmatized only about the *constitution* of government;

about the nature of the state, the essence and seat of sovereignty, popular power and kingly prerogative; about the greatest meanings lying at the heart of government, and the high ends set before the purpose of government by man's nature and man's aims. The central field of controversy was that great field of theory in which monarchy rode tilt against democracy, in which oligarchy would have built for itself strongholds of privilege, and in which tyranny sought opportunity to make good its claim to receive submission from all competitors. Amidst this high warfare of principles, administration could command no pause for its own consideration. The question was always: Who shall make law, and what shall that law be? The other question, how law should be administered with enlightenment, with equity, with speed, and without friction, was put aside as "practical detail" which clerks could arrange after doctors had agreed upon principles.

That political philosophy took this direction was of course no accident, no chance preference or perverse whim of political philosophers. The philosophy of any time is, as Hegel says, "nothing but the spirit of that time expressed in abstract thought"; and political philosophy, like philosophy of every other kind, has only held up the mirror to contemporary affairs. The trouble in early times was almost altogether about the constitution of government; and consequently that was what engrossed men's thoughts. There was little or no trouble about administration,—at least little that was heeded by administrators. The functions of government were simple, because life itself was simple. Government went about imperatively and compelled men, without thought of consulting their wishes. There was no complex system of public revenues and public debts to puzzle financiers; there were, consequently, no financiers to be puzzled. No one who possessed power was long at a loss how to use it. The great and only question was: Who shall possess it? Populations were of manageable numbers; property was of simple sorts. There were plenty of farms, but no stocks and bonds; more cattle than vested interests.

• • •

There is scarcely a single duty of government which was once simple which is not now complex; government once had but a few masters; it now has scores of masters. Majorities formerly only underwent government; they now conduct government. Where government once might follow the whims of a court, it must now follow the views of a nation.

And those views are steadily widening to new conceptions of state duty; so that, at the same time that the functions of government are every day becoming more complex and difficult, they are also vastly multiplying in number. Administration is everywhere putting its hands to new undertakings. The utility, cheapness, and success of the government's postal service, for instance, point towards the early establishment of governmental control of the telegraph system. Or, even if our government is not to follow the lead of the governments of Europe in buying or building both telegraph and railroad lines, no one can doubt that in some way it must make itself master of masterful corporations. The creation of national commissioners of railroads, in addition to the older state commissions, involves a very important and delicate extension of administrative functions. Whatever hold of authority state or federal governments are to take upon corporations, there must follow cares and responsibilities which will require not a little wisdom, knowledge, and experience. Such things must be studied in order to be well done. And these, as I have said, are only a few of the doors which are being opened to offices of government. The idea of the state and the consequent ideal of its duty are undergoing noteworthy change; and "the idea of the state is the conscience of administration." Seeing every day new things which the state ought to do, the next thing is to see clearly how it ought to do them.

This is why there should be a science of administration which shall seek to straighten the paths of government, to make its business less unbusinesslike; to strengthen and purify its organization, and to crown its duties with dutifulness. This is one reason why there is such a science.

But where has this science grown up? Surely not on this side of the sea. Not much impartial scientific method is to be discerned in our administrative practices. The poisonous atmosphere of city government, the crooked secrets of state administration, the confusion, sinecurism, and corruption ever and again discovered in the bureaus at Washington forbid us to believe that any clear conceptions of what constitutes good administration are as yet very widely current in the United States. No; American writers have hitherto taken no very important part in the advancement of this science. It has found its doctors in Europe. It is not of our making; it is a foreign science, speaking very little of the language of English or American principle. It employs only foreign tongues; it utters none but what are to our minds alien ideas. Its aims, its examples, its conditions, are almost exclusively grounded in the histories of foreign races, in the precedents of foreign systems, in the lessons of foreign revolutions. It has been developed by French and German professors, and is consequently in all parts adapted to the needs of a compact state, and made to fit highly centralized forms of government; whereas, to answer our purposes, it must be adapted, not to a simple and compact, but to a complex and multiform state, and made to fit highly decentralized forms of government. If we would employ it, we must Americanize it, and that not formally, in language merely, but radically, in thought, principle, and aim as well. It must learn our constitutions by heart; must get the bureaucratic fever out of its veins; must inhale much free American air.

If an explanation be sought why a science manifestly so susceptible of being made useful to all governments alike should have received attention first in Europe, where government has long been a monopoly, rather than in England or the United States, where government has long been a common franchise, the reason will doubtless be found to be twofold: first, that in Europe, just because government was independent of popular assent, there was more governing to be done; and, second, that the desire to keep government a monopoly made the monopolists interested in discovering the least irritating means of governing. They were, besides, few enough to adopt means promptly.

• • •

The English race . . . has long and successfully studied the art of curbing executive power to the constant neglect of the art of perfecting executive methods. It has exercised itself much more in controlling than in energizing government. It has been more concerned to render government just and moderate than to make it facile, well-ordered, and effective. English and American political history has been a history, not of administrative development, but of legislative oversight,—not of progress in governmental organization, but of advance in law-making and political criticism. Consequently, we have reached a time when administrative study and creation are imperatively necessary to the well-being of our governments saddled with the habits of a long period of constitution-making. That period has practically closed, so far as the establishment of essential principles is concerned, but we cannot shake off its atmosphere. We go on criticizing when we ought to be creating. We have reached the third of the periods I have mentioned,—the period, namely, when the people have to develop administration in accordance with the constitutions they won for themselves in a previous period of struggle with absolute power; but we are not prepared for the tasks of the new period.

Such an explanation seems to afford the only escape from blank astonishment at the fact that, in spite of our vast advantages in point of political liberty, and above all in point of practical political skill and sagacity, so many nations are ahead of us in administrative organization and administrative skill. Why, for instance, have we but just begun purifying a civil service which was rotten full fifty years ago? To say that slavery diverted us is but to repeat what I have said—that flaws in our Constitution delayed us.

Of course all reasonable preference would declare for this English and American course of politics rather than for that of any European country. We should not like to have had Prussia's history for the sake of having Prussia's administrative skill; and Prussia's particular system of administration would quite suffocate us. It is better to be untrained and free than to be servile and systematic. Still there is no denying that it would be better yet to be both free in spirit and proficient in practice. It is this even more reasonable preference which impels us to discover what there may be to hinder or delay us in naturalizing this much-to-be desired science of administration.

What, then, is there to prevent?

Well, principally, popular sovereignty. It is harder for democracy to organize administration than for monarchy. The very completeness of our most cherished political successes in the past embarrasses us. We have enthroned public opinion; and it is forbidden us to hope during its reign for any quick schooling of the sovereign in executive expertness or in the conditions of perfect functional balance in government. The very fact that we have realized popular rule in its fullness has made the task of *organizing* that rule just so much the more difficult. In order to make any advance at all we must instruct and persuade a multitudinous monarch called public opinion,—a much less feasible undertaking than to influence a single monarch called a king. An individual sovereign will adopt a simple plan and carry it out directly; he will have but one opinion, and he will embody that one opinion in one command. But this other sovereign, the people, will have a score of differing opinions. They can agree upon nothing simple: advance must be made through compromise, by a compounding of differences, by a trimming of plans and a suppression of too straightforward principles. There will be a succession of resolves running through a course of years, a dropping fire of commands running through a whole gamut of modifications.

In government, as in virtue, the hardest of hard things is to make progress. Formerly the reason for this was that the single person who was sovereign was generally either selfish, ignorant, timid, or a fool,—albeit there was now and again one who was wise. Nowadays the reason is that the many, the people, who are sovereign have no single ear which one can approach, and are selfish, ignorant, timid, stubborn, or foolish with the selfishnesses, the ignorances, the stubbornnesses, the timidities, or the follies of several thousand persons,—albeit there are hundreds who are wise. Once the advan-

tage of the reformer was that the sovereign's mind had a definite locality, that it was contained in one man's head, and that consequently it could be gotten at; though it was his disadvantage that that mind learned only reluctantly or only in small quantities, or was under the influence of someone who let it learn only the wrong things. Now, on the contrary, the reformer is bewildered by the fact that the sovereign's mind has no definite locality, but is contained in a voting majority of several million heads; and embarrassed by the fact that the mind of this sovereign also is under the influence of favorites, who are none the less favorites in a good old-fashioned sense of the word because they are not persons but preconceived opinions; *i.e.,* prejudices which are not to be reasoned with because they are not the children of reason.

Wherever regard for public opinion is a first principle of government, practical reform must be slow and all reform must be full of compromises. For wherever public opinion exists it must rule. This is now an axiom half the world over, and will presently come to be believed even in Russia. Whoever would effect a change in a modern constitutional government must first educate his fellow-citizens to want *some* change. That done, he must persuade them to want the particular change he wants. He must first make public opinion willing to listen and then see to it that it listen to the right things. He must stir it up to search for an opinion, and then manage to put the right opinion in its way.

The first step is not less difficult than the second. With opinions, possession is more than nine points of the law. It is next to impossible to dislodge them. Institutions which one generation regards as only a makeshift approximation to the realization of a principle, the next generation honors as the nearest possible approximation to that principle, and the next worships as the principle itself. It takes scarcely three generations for the apotheosis. The grandson accepts his grandfather's hesitating experiment as an integral part of the fixed constitution of nature.

Even if we had clear insight into all the political past, and could form out of perfectly instructed heads a few steady, infallible, placidly wise maxims of government into which all sound political doctrine would be ultimately resolvable, *would the country act on them?* That is the question. The bulk of mankind is rigidly unphilosophical, and nowadays the bulk of mankind votes. A truth must become not only plain but also commonplace before it will be seen by the people who go to their work very early in the morning; and not to act upon it must involve great and pinching inconveniences before these same people will make up their minds to act upon it.

And where is this unphilosophical bulk of mankind more multifarious in its composition than in the United States? To know the public mind of this country, one must know the mind, not of Americans of the older stocks only, but also of Irishmen, of Germans, of Negroes. In order to get a footing for new doctrine, one must influence minds cast in every mould of race, minds inheriting every bias of environment, warped by the histories of a score of different nations, warmed or chilled, closed or expanded by almost every climate of the globe.

• • •

II.

The field of administration is a field of business. It is removed from the hurry and strife of politics; it at most points stands apart even from the debatable ground of constitutional study. It is a part of political life only as the methods of the counting-house are a part of the life of society; only as machinery is part of the manufactured product. But it is, at the same time, raised very far above the dull level of mere technical detail by the fact that through its greater principles it is directly connected with the lasting maxims of political wisdom, the permanent truths of political progress.

The object of administrative study is to rescue executive methods from the confusion and costliness of empirical experiment and set them upon foundations laid deep in stable principle.

It is for this reason that we must regard civil service reform in its present stages as but a prelude to a fuller administrative reform. We are now rectifying methods of appointment; we must go on to adjust executive functions more fitly and to prescribe better methods of executive organization and action. Civil service reform is thus but a moral preparation for what is to follow. It is clearing the moral atmosphere of official life by establishing the sanctity of public office as a public trust, and, by making the service unpartisan, it is opening the way for making it businesslike. By sweetening its motives it is rendering it capable of improving its methods of work.

Let me expand a little what I have said of the province of administration. Most important to be observed is the truth already so much and so fortunately insisted upon by our civil service reformers; namely, that administration lies outside the proper sphere of *politics.* Administrative questions are not political questions. Although politics sets the tasks for administration, it should not be suffered to manipulate its offices.

This is distinction of high authority; eminent German writers insist upon it as of course. Bluntschli, for instance, bids us separate administration alike from politics and from law. Politics, he says, is state activity "in things great and universal," while "administration, on the other hand," is "the activity of the state in individual and small things. Politics is thus the special province of the statesman, administration of the technical official." "Policy does nothing without the aid of administration"; but administration is not therefore politics. But we do not require German authority for this position; this discrimination between administration and politics is now, happily, too obvious to need further discussion.

There is another distinction which must be worked into all our conclusions, which, though but another side of that between administration and politics, is not quite so easy to keep sight of; I mean the distinction between *constitutional* and administrative questions, between those governmental adjustments which are essential to constitutional principle and those which are merely instrumental to the possibly changing purposes of a wisely adapting convenience.

One cannot easily make clear to every one just where administration resides in the various departments of any practicable government without entering upon particulars so numerous as to confuse and distinctions so minute as to distract. No lines of demarcation, setting apart administrative from non-administrative functions, can be run between this and that department of government without being run up hill and down dale, over dizzy heights of distinction and through dense jungles of statutory enactment, hither and thither around "its" and "buts," "whens" and "howevers," until they become altogether lost to the common eye not accustomed to this sort of surveying, and consequently not acquainted with the use of the theodolite of logical discernment. A great deal of administration goes about *incognito* to most of the world, being confounded now with political "management," and again with constitutional principle.

Perhaps this case of confusion may explain such utterances as that of Niebuhr's: "Liberty," he says, "depends incomparably more upon administration than upon constitution." At first sight this appears to be largely true. Apparently facility in the actual exercise of liberty does depend more upon administrative arrangements than upon constitutional guarantees; although constitutional guarantees alone secure the existence of liberty. But—upon second thought—is even so much as this true? Liberty no more consists in easy functional movement than intelligence consists in the ease and vigor with which the limbs of a strong man move. The principles that rule within the man, or the constitution, are the vital springs of liberty or servitude. Because dependence and subjection are without chains, are lightened by every easy-working device of considerate, paternal government, they are not thereby transformed into liberty. Liberty cannot live apart from constitutional principle; and no administration, however perfect and liberal its methods, can give men more than a poor counterfeit of liberty if it rest upon illiberal principles of government.

A clear view of the difference between the province of constitutional law and the province of administrative function ought to leave no room for misconception; and it is possible to name some roughly definite criteria upon which such a view can be built. Public administration is detailed and systematic execution of public law. Every particular application of general law is an act of administration. The assessment and raising of taxes, for instance, the hanging of a criminal, the transportation and delivery of the mails, the equipment and recruiting of the army and navy, etc., are all obviously acts of administration; but the general laws which direct these things to be done are as obviously outside of and above administration. The broad plans of governmental action are not administrative; the detailed execution of such plans is administrative. Constitutions, therefore, properly concern themselves only with those instrumentalities of government which are to control general law. Our federal Constitution observes this principle in saying nothing of even the greatest of the purely executive offices, and speaking only of that President of the Union who was to share the legislative and policy-making functions of government, only of those judges of highest jurisdiction who were to interpret and guard its principles, and not of those who were merely to give utterance to them.

This is not quite the distinction between Will and answering Deed, because the administrator should have and does have a will of his own in the choice of means for accomplishing his work. He is not and ought not to be a mere passive instrument. The distinction is between general plans and special means.

There is, indeed, one point at which administrative studies trench on constitutional ground—or at least upon what seems constitutional ground. The study of administration, philosophically viewed, is closely connected with the study of the proper distribution of constitutional authority. To be efficient it must discover the simplest arrangements by which responsibility can be unmistakably fixed upon officials; the best way of dividing authority without hampering it, and responsibility without obscuring it. And this question of the distribution of authority, when taken into the sphere of the higher, the originating functions of government, is obviously a central constitutional question.

If administrative study can discover the best principles upon which to base such distributions, it will have done constitutional study an invaluable service. Montesquieu did not, I am convinced, say the last word on this head.

To discover the best principle for the distribution of authority is of greater importance, possibly, under a democratic system, where officials serve many matters, than under others where they serve but a few. All sovereigns are suspicious of their servants, and the sovereign people is no exception to the rule; but how is its suspicion to be allayed by *knowledge*? If that suspicion could but be clarified into wise vigilance, it would be altogether salutary; if that vigilance could be aided by the unmistakable placing of responsibility, it would be altogether beneficent. Suspicion in itself is never healthful either in the private or in the public mind. *Trust is strength* in all relations of life; and, as it is the office of the constitutional reformer to create conditions of trustfulness, so it is the office of the administrative organizer to fit administration with conditions of clear-cut responsibility which shall insure trustworthiness.

And let me say that large powers and unhampered discretion seem to me the indispensable conditions of responsibility. Public attention must be easily directed, in each case of good or bad administration, to just the man deserving of praise or blame. There is no danger in power, if only it be not irresponsible. If it be divided, dealt only in shares to many, it is obscured; and if it be obscured, it is made irresponsible. But if it be centred in heads of the service and in heads of branches of the service, it is easily watched and brought to book. If to keep his office a man must achieve open and honest success, and if at the same time he feels himself entrusted with large freedom of discretion, the greater his power the less likely is he to abuse it, the more is he nerved and sobered and elevated by it. The less his power, the more safely obscure and unnoticed does he feel his position to be, and the more readily does he relapse into remissness.

Just here we manifestly emerge upon the field of that still larger question,—the proper relations between public opinion and administration.

To whom is official trustworthiness to be disclosed, and by whom is it to be rewarded? Is the official to look to the public for his meed of praise and his push of promotion, or only to his superior in office? Are the people to be called in to settle administrative discipline as they are called in to settle constitutional principles? These questions evidently find their root in what is undoubtedly the fundamental problem of this whole study. That problem is: What part shall public opinion take in the conduct of administration?

The right answer seems to be, that public opinion shall play the part of authoritative critic.

But the *method* by which its authority shall be made to tell? Our peculiar American difficulty in organizing administration is not the danger of losing liberty, but the danger of not being able or willing to separate its essentials from its accidents. Our success is made doubtful by that besetting error of ours, the error of trying to do too much by vote. Self-government does not consist in having a hand in everything, any more than housekeeping consists necessarily in cooking dinner with one's own hands. The cook must be trusted with a large discretion as to the management of the fires and the ovens.

In those countries in which public opinion has yet to be instructed in its privileges, yet to be accustomed to having its own way, this question as to the province of public opinion is much more readily soluble than in this country, where public opinion is wide awake and quite intent upon having its own way anyhow. It is pathetic to see a whole book written by a German professor of political science for the purpose of saying to his countrymen, "Please try to have an opinion about national affairs"; but a public which is so modest may at least be expected to be very docile and acquiescent in learning what things it has *not* a right to think and speak about imperatively. It may be sluggish, but it will not be meddlesome. It will submit to be instructed before it tries to instruct. Its political education will come before its political activity. In trying to instruct our own public opinion, we are dealing with a pupil apt to think itself quite sufficiently instructed beforehand.

The problem is to make public opinion efficient without suffering it to be meddlesome. Directly exercised, in the oversight of the daily details and in the choice of the daily means of government, public criticism is of course a clumsy nuisance, a rustic handling delicate machinery. But as superintending the greater forces of formative policy alike in politics and administration, public criticism is altogether safe and beneficent, altogether indispensable. Let administrative study find the best means for giving public criticism this control and for shutting it out from all other interference.

But is the whole duty of administrative study done when it has taught the people what sort of administration to desire and demand, and how to get what they demand? Ought it not to go on to drill candidates for the public service?

There is an admirable movement towards universal political education now afoot in this country. The time will soon come when no college of respectability can afford to do without a well-filled chair of political science. But the education thus imparted will go but a certain length. It will multiply the number of intelligent critics of government, but it will create no competent body of administrators. It will prepare the way for the development of a sure-footed understanding of the general principles of government, but it will not necessarily foster skill in conducting government. It is an education which will equip legislators, perhaps, but not executive officials. If we are to improve public opinion, which is the motive power of government, we must prepare better officials as the *apparatus* of government. If we are to put in new boilers and to mend the fires which drive our governmental machinery, we must not leave the old wheels and joints and valves and bands to creak and buzz and clatter on as the best they may at bidding of the new force. We must put in new running parts wherever there is the least lack of strength or adjustment. It will be necessary to organize democracy by sending up to the competitive examinations for the civil service men definitely prepared for standing liberal tests as to technical knowledge. A technically schooled civil service will presently have become indispensable.

I know that a corps of civil servants prepared by a special schooling and drilled, after appointment, into a perfected organization, with appropriate hierarchy and characteristic discipline, seems to a great many very thoughtful persons to contain elements which might combine to make an offensive official class,—a distinct, semi-corporate body with sympathies divorced from those of a progressive, free-spirited people, and with hearts narrowed to the meanness of a bigoted officialism. Certainly such a class would be altogether hateful and harmful in the United States. Any measures calculated to produce it would for us be measures of reaction and of folly.

But to fear the creation of a domineering, illiberal officialism as a result of the studies I am here proposing is to miss altogether the principle upon which I wish most to insist. That principle is, that administration in the United States must be at all points sensitive to public opinion. A body of thoroughly trained officials serving during good behavior we must have in any case: that is a plain business necessity. But the apprehension that such a body will be anything un-American clears away the moment it is asked, What is to constitute good behavior? For that question obviously carries its own answer on its face. Steady, hearty allegiance to the policy of the government they serve will constitute good behavior. That *policy* will have no taint of officialism about it. It will not be the creation of permanent officials, but of statesmen whose responsibility to public opinion will be direct and inevitable. Bureaucracy can exist only where the whole service of the state is removed from the common political life of the people, its chiefs as well as its rank and file. Its motives, its objects, its policy, its standards, must be bureaucratic. It would be difficult to point out any examples of impudent exclusiveness and arbitrariness on the part of officials doing service under a chief of department who really served the people, as all our chiefs of departments must be made to do.

• • •

The ideal for us is a civil service cultured and self-sufficient enough to act with sense and vigor, and yet so intimately connected with the popular thought, by means of elections and constant public counsel, as to find arbitrariness or class spirit quite out of the question.

III.

Having thus viewed in some sort the subject-matter and the objects of this study of administration, what are we to conclude as to the methods best suited to it—the points of view most advantageous for it?

Government is so near us, as much a thing of our daily familiar handling, that we can with difficulty see the need of any philosophical study of it, or the exact point of such study, should it be undertaken. We have been on our feet too long to study now the art of walking. We are a practical people, made so apt, so adept in self-government by centuries of experimental drill that we are scarcely any longer capable of perceiving the awkwardness of the particular system we may be using, just because it is so easy for us to use any system. We do not study the art of governing: we govern. But mere unschooled genius for affairs will not save us from sad blunders in administration. Though democrats by long inheritance and repeated choice, we are still rather crude democrats. Old as democracy is, its organization on a basis of modern ideas and conditions is still an unaccomplished work. The democratic state has yet to be equipped for carrying those enormous burdens of administration which the needs of this industrial and trading age are so fast accumulating. Without comparative studies in government we cannot rid ourselves of the misconception that administration stands upon an essentially different basis in a democratic state from that on which it stands in a non-democratic state.

After such study we could grant democracy the sufficient honor of ultimately determining by debate all essential questions affecting the public weal, of basing all structures of policy upon the major will; but we would have found but one rule of good administration for all governments alike. So far as administrative functions are concerned, all governments have a strong structural likeness; more than that, if they are to be uniformly useful and efficient, they *must* have a strong structural likeness. A free man has the same bodily organs, the same executive parts, as the slave, however different may be his motives, his services, his energies. Monarchies and democracies, radically different as they are in other respects, have in reality much the same business to look to.

It is abundantly safe nowadays to insist upon this actual likeness of all governments, because these are days when abuses of power are easily exposed and arrested, in countries like our own, by a bold, alert, inquisitive, detective public thought and a sturdy popular self-dependence such as never existed before. We are slow to appreciate this; but it is easy to appreciate it. Try to imagine personal government in the United States. It is like trying to imagine a national worship of Zeus. Our imaginations are too modern for the feat.

But, besides being safe, it is necessary to see that for all governments alike the legitimate ends of administration are the same, in order not to be frightened at the idea of looking into foreign systems of administration for instruction and suggestion; in order to get rid of the apprehension that we might perchance blindly borrow something incompatible with our principles. That man is blindly astray who denounces attempts to transplant foreign systems into this country. It is impossible: they simply would not grow here. But why should we not use such parts of foreign contrivances as we want, if they be in any way serviceable? We are in no danger of using them in a foreign way. We borrowed rice, but we do not eat it with chopsticks. We borrowed our whole political language from England, but we leave the words "king" and "lords" out of it. What did we ever originate, except the action of the federal government upon individuals and some of the functions of the federal supreme court?

We can borrow the science of administration with safety and profit if only we read all fundamental differences of condition into its essential tenets. We have only to filter it through our constitutions, only to put it over a slow fire of criticism and distill away its foreign gases.

● ● ●

Let it be noted that it is the distinction, already drawn, between administration and politics which makes the comparative method so safe in the field of administration. When we study the administrative systems of France and Germany, knowing that we are not in search of *political* principles, we need not care a peppercorn for the constitutional or political reasons which Frenchmen or Germans give for their practices when explaining them to us. If I see a murderous fellow sharpening a knife cleverly, I can borrow his way of sharpening the knife without borrowing his probable intention to commit murder with it; and so, if I see a monarchist dyed in the wool managing a public bureau well, I can learn his business methods without changing one of my republican spots. He may serve his king; I will continue to serve the people; but I should like to serve my sovereign as well as he serves his. By keeping this distinction in view,—that is, by studying administration as a means of putting our own politics into convenient practice, as a means of making what is democratically politic towards all administratively possible towards each,—we are on perfectly safe ground, and can learn without error what foreign systems have to teach us. We thus devise an adjusted weight for our comparative method of study. We can thus scrutinize the anatomy of foreign governments without fear of getting any of their diseases into our veins; dissect alien systems without apprehension of blood-poisoning.

Our own politics must be the touchstone for all theories. The principles on which to base a science of administration for America must be principles which have democratic policy very much at heart. And, to suit American habit, all general theories must, as theories, keep modestly in the background, not in open argument only, but even in our own minds,—lest opinions satisfactory only to the standards of the library should be dogmatically used, as if they must be quite as satisfactory to the standards of practical politics as well. Doctrinaire devices must be postponed to tested practices. Arrangements not only sanctioned by conclusive experience elsewhere but also congenial to Amer-

ican habit must be preferred without hesitation to theoretical perfection. In a word, steady, practical statesmanship must come first, closet doctrine second. The cosmopolitan what-to-do must always be commanded by the American how-to-do-it.

Our duty is, to supply the best possible life to a *federal* organization, to systems within systems; to make town, city, county, state, and federal governments live with a like strength and an equally assured healthfulness, keeping each unquestionably its own master and yet making all interdependent and cooperative, combining independence with mutual helpfulness. The task is great and important enough to attract the best minds.

This interlacing of local self-government with federal self-government is quite a modern conception. It is not like the arrangements of imperial federation in Germany. There local government is not yet, fully, local *self*-government. The bureaucrat is everywhere busy. His efficiency springs out of *esprit de corps,* out of care to make ingratiating obeisance to the authority of a superior, or, at best, out of the soil of a sensitive conscience. He serves, not the public, but an irresponsible minister. The question for us is, how shall our series of governments within governments be so administered that it shall always be to the interest of the public officer to serve, not his superior alone but the community also, with the best efforts of his talents and the soberest service of his conscience? How shall such service be made to his commonest interest by contributing abundantly to his sustenance, to his dearest interest by furthering his ambition, and to his highest interest by advancing his honor and establishing his character? And how shall this be done alike for the local part and for the national whole?

If we solve this problem we shall again pilot the world. There is a tendency—is there not?—a tendency as yet dim, but already steadily impulsive and clearly destined to prevail, towards, first the confederation of parts of empires like the British, and finally of great states themselves. Instead of centralization of power, there is to be wide union with tolerated divisions of prerogative. This is a tendency towards the American type—of governments joined with governments for the pursuit of common purposes, in honorary equality and honorable subordination. Like principles of civil liberty are everywhere fostering like methods of government; and if comparative studies of the ways and means of government should enable us to offer suggestions which will practically combine openness and vigor in the administration of such governments with ready docility to all serious, well-sustained public criticism, they will have approved themselves worthy to be ranked among the highest and most fruitful of the great departments of political study. That they will issue in such suggestions I confidently hope.

▨▨▨▨ READING 1.2

Introduction

Before going on to the case study, as normally happens in this text's concept-case methodology, which pairs concepts with cases throughout this book, let's look at one more conceptual overview that attempts to define what is the nature and substance of public administration. Unlike the Wilson essay, the following piece by the author of this textbook tries to sketch the contemporary academic study of public administration in the 1990s. He argues that public administration as a field of study is currently involved in what he labels, "The Refounding Movement," which is searching for new answers to old issues such as the meaning of community, citizenship, accountability, centralization *vs.* decentralization, effectiveness, efficiency, economy, and so on. In part, this intensive preoccupation with "refounding the field" comes as a response to the rapidly changing socio-political-economic environment of the late 20th century due to the end of the Cold War, the rise of new global economies, the challenges of new technologies, changing demographics, and voter dissatisfaction.

The author outlines the six major schools of thought that have emerged in the 1990s at the forefront of this refounding effort: 1) "The Reinventors," 2) "The Communitarians," 3) "The VPI Refounders," 4) "The Interpretists" and "Postmoderns," 5) "The Tools Approach," and 6) "New Bureaucratic Perspectives." The essay sums up the "plus-sides" and "down-sides" of each school and argues the general thesis that the "Refounding Movement" as a whole is attempting to correct, at least in part, the more "rabid anti-statism" exhibited by leading theorists in the field during the past two decades. However, the field still fails to come to grips with the meaning and purpose of "the administrative state" as the essential prerequisite for defining and legitimizing its role within society today.

Because much of the following essay attempts to define the field of American Public Administration in the 1990s by arguing that its outlook and values are still pervasively dominated by anti-statism, it is worth briefly defining "statism" and "anti-statism" as an introduction to this essay. What do those two terms mean?

As one leading expert on this topic recently defined "state":

A state is any set of relatively differentiated organizations that claims sovereignty and coercive control over a territory and its population, defending and perhaps extending that claim in competition with other states. The core organizations that make up a state include administrative, judicial, and policing organizations that collect and dispense revenues, enforce the constitutive rules of the state and society, and maintain some modicum of domestic order, especially to protect the state's own claims and activities.[1]

"Statism" therefore are doctrines and ideas that advocate strengthening the role and sovereignty of the state institutions in society. "Anti-statism" is the opposite, namely ideas and doctrines expressly hostile to these central governing institutions in society, which argue for reducing, limiting, even eliminating their role(s) and activities.

As you study this "dragnet overview" of the study of public administration today, you might ask yourself these questions:

How does the field define itself today in contrast with Wilson's 1887 perspective? What are its basic values and outlooks?

What are the central problems public administration is trying to address now in comparison to Wilson's era?

How does the field today view the problem of relating politics and administration, by contrast to Wilson's essay?

Do you agree that "The Refounding Movement" is the correct label for what is happening within public administration in the 1990s? If so, what are the implications for the *practice* of public administration?

THE REFOUNDING MOVEMENT IN AMERICAN PUBLIC ADMINISTRATION: From "Rabid" Anti-Statism to "Mere" Anti-Statism in the 1990s

RICHARD J. STILLMAN II

Rejection of statism has deep roots in American public administration, but no era in U.S. administrative science's history witnessed such an intense outpouring of anti-statist literature as the late 1960s and early 1970s. The reasons for this outbreak of rabid anti-statism remain unclear even today: perhaps it was due to the Vietnam War? Watergate? The growth of "the counter-culture"? Reactions to the Great Society? Whatever the causes, the two most prominent examples were The Minnowbrook Conference, whose proceedings were published in Frank Marini's (ed.), *Toward a New Public Administration: The Minnowbrook Perspective* (1971) and Vincent Ostrom's *The Intellectual Crisis in American Public Administration* (1973, rev. 1974).

[1]Theda Skocpol, *Protecting Soldiers and Mothers: The Political Origins of Social Policy in the United States* (Cambridge, MA: Harvard University Press), p. 43. Skocpol's conceptualization of "state," as she indicates in a footnote, draws heavily from the writings of Max Weber and Otto Hintz.

"The Refounding Movement in American Public Administration" by Richard J. Stillman II from *Administration Theory & Praxis,* 17(1): 29–45, 1995. Copyright © 1995 by Public Administration Theory Network (PAT-Net). Reprinted by permission.

Both books hotly repudiated statism and argued for forging new foundations for the field, though by means of fundamentally differing methodologies.

The 1968 Minnowbrook Conference, made up of mostly under-thirty-year-old scholars from political science, argued for fresh beginnings for American administrative sciences based upon ideals of participation, consensus-building, sharing ideas, mutual trust and even "love of mankind." They exhibited particular hostility towards traditional state-building models such as POSDCORB or techno-professional expertise such as embodied in systems theory or "hard" quantitative, rational planning (Marini, 1971).

Other books during the 1970s echoed and elaborated upon the Minnowbrookian "slash and burn" anti-statism to perhaps extreme, radical 16th century Digger and Leveller positions. Frederick C. Thayer, *An End to Hierarchy! An End to Competition!* (1973) saw bureaucratic hierarchy and its related problem of competition as the root of social evil in the modern world. "Hierarchy," wrote Thayer, "actually is the fundamental problem of human society, competition merely the most unfortunate result of an attempt to escape from hierarchy." Thayer advocated the elimination of both in order to return to "the genuine community of mankind," or in his words, one that is "cognitive, collective, and non hierarchical . . . on a global basis" (1973, p. 133).

Likewise, William G. Scott and David K. Hart's *Organizational America* (1979) sought the return to small, natural communities, free of artificially erected statism. "The modern organization," they wrote, "is an essential feature of totalitarianism because it is the primary means of control" (1979, p. 16). This control-orientation fosters a relentless competition and drive for national wealth, or what the authors called, "the organizational imperative," which in turn created uniformity, sterility, commercialization, inequality, the loss of personal freedom and dignity in our modern culture. For Scott and Hart, nothing short of a total social revolution, led by "a vanguard of professionals" could smash "the organizational imperative" and bring about a

new humane world order without bureaucracy. The return to the small, harmonious natural community was a compelling vision within Minnowbrookian-inspired literature of the 1960s and 1970s.

By contrast, Ostrom's *Intellectual Crisis* introduced "public choice doctrines" to assault frontally older state-building doctrines which the author labelled as "The Wilson-Weber Paradigm," and castigated as "single-centered administration," "hierarchical structures," with "sharp separation of politics from administration." Based on a rereading of the *Federalist Papers,* and Alexis de Tocqueville's *Democracy in America,* as well as public choice economics, Ostrom advocated a radically anti-statist replacement or what he called, "The Democratic Administrative Paradigm," with diverse "decision-making centers," "popular participation," "fragmented, overlapping, decentralized jurisdictions," or the very reverse of the Wilson-Weber Paradigm (Ostrom, 1973). In brief, Ostrom sought "public choice" (read: "individual choice") as a "new model," for American administrative sciences.

Mingling with the public choice doctrines in the 1960s and 1970s were broader "neo-conservative beliefs" spawned by social scientists such as Irving Kristol, Aaron Wildavsky, James Q. Wilson and others associated with *The Public Interest* journal, who collectively fostered widespread intellectual hostility towards big government and advocated various techniques to cut, trim and squeeze the state. A typical example in this era was Aaron Wildavsky's book, *How to Limit Government Spending* (1980) that argued for a constitutional balanced budget amendment. He believed it would help to redress the mix of public vs. private expenditures which he saw as "out of balance." "Big government," contended Wildavsky, "is no bargain. Doing what comes naturally it will (with consent, to be sure) eat us out of house and home" (1980, p. 6). A balanced budget amendment, in his view, would limit the increase of the federal expenditures to the proportional rise in the Gross National Product, hence, the size of the public sector would not be allowed to grow any faster than the private sector. It could stimulate investment, protect the market economy and keep big government "off our backs." Other neo-conservatives such as E.S. Savas pressed for micro-surgery of the state apparatus in his *Privatizing the Public Sector* (1982), which proposed a broad range of specific cuts in big government. Savas saw public bureaucracy, much like a monopolistic business, in which its operations were largely run inefficiently and wastefully because of the absence of market competition. The alternative was, according to Savas, to "privatize government," either by returning its activities entirely to business or operating those activities within government as closely as possible to free market competition through a variety of arrangements such as "load-shedding," "franchising," "contracting-out," "voucher systems" and the like (Savas, 1982). Individually and collectively, neo-conservatives, like public choice advocates, in the tradition of Adam Smith, wanted ideally public administration as supporting a "minimalist state role" throughout society, merely tending to the bare-bones of national security, the courts and few other activities, leaving the rest to private markets.

Both Minnowbrook and public choice/neo-conservative views were widely discussed and found support within American administrative sciences at the time of their publication. Today "the new public administration" is largely manifest in the work of the "phenomenologists, critical theorists, interpretive theorists and postmodernists," identified as the fourth reform movement late in this essay. Public choice and neo-conservatism doctrines à la Vincent Ostrom, William Niskanen, James Buchanan, Irving Kristol and others continue to find broad public appeal as well as sustained academic interest. Throughout the 1980s and continuing in the 1990s, their doctrines have translated into numerous applied reforms in government such as: deregulation of business, "sunshine laws," term limits, balanced budget amendments, tax limits, cutback management and the like. Academic centers such as Indiana University and George Mason University as well as think tanks like Washington, D.C.'s American Enterprise Institute, the CATO Institute, and the Heritage Foundation or the editorial pages of the *Wall Street Journal* continue as stout advocates of various

shades of public choice and neo-conservatism. Their ideas have even found their way into the 1994 Republican "Contract with America" political platform.

Thus the intellectual roots of today's popular visions of "good public administration" date back more than two decades and are by and large predicated on value premises that favor:

- extensive popular participation throughout the administrative enterprise, especially mass, voluntary involvement (as opposed to staffing administration with paid, full-time professionals);
- maximum decentralization of administrative functions (in order to cut back federal activities and enhance local discretion and scrutiny over public programs);
- operational simplicity and fiscal economy ("simplicity" so that administrative activities can be easily understood by the average citizen and "economy" so that they will not become fiscally burdensome);
- a thoroughly "economized" public administration (which translates into every public program as far as feasible being measured by "its bottom line" as opposed to "promoting the public good," "social equity," etc.);
- strict legal limits on public spending, administrative discretion and organizational purposes (in order to restrict the expansion of the public sector and thereby promote free market economics);
- weak leadership roles for public administrators, essentially defining their functions as mainly specialists or technicians (as opposed to broadly trained professionals with advanced degrees and widely respected discretionary authority);
- little or no concern for national planning, long-term operational stability, effective program implementation to promote national goals (except for defense and social security).

However, during the 1990s American administrative sciences have seen a new counter movement grow to correct, in part, some of the excesses of the past two decades, a movement that perhaps is best loosely termed, "a refounding movement." It includes recent efforts by numerous serious administrative scholars to reconsider fundamental issues in the field and pose new answers to old administrative questions such as: what is public administration? the meaning of the good life? who should govern? the criteria for action? the nature of community? should administration be centralized or decentralized? redefinitions of old concepts like citizenship, the public interest, accountability and responsibility? The field right now is therefore in the midst of a yeasty debate over these and other seminal administrative issues. To be sure, there are no settled "answers" but at least six prominent schools of thought can be identified as being currently at the forefront of the refounding movement.

"The Reinventors"

First, and perhaps the most influential, is the "reinventing government school" which is most directly associated with David Osborne and Ted Gaebler's *Reinventing Government: How the Entrepreneurial Spirit is Transforming the Public Sector* (1992). Few books about public administration in the 1990s have received such widespread publicity—and sales. The back cover of the book attests to its unusual popularity by the prominent names asserting the value of the book's ideas. From leaders "on the right" like Republican Governor William Weld to leaders of "the left" like President Bill Clinton, all say they find this book invaluable for reforming government today. The power of this book's appeal is reflected by the fact that it served as the basic framework for Vice President Gore's *National Performance Review* (1993), which set forth proposals designed to "reinvent" the federal government, roughly along the lines recommended by Osborne and Gaebler's formula.

The general thesis, outlined in the "Introduction: An American Perestroika," argues that neither the old style 1930s New Deal "big bureaucratic or-

ganization" nor the 1980s Reagan-Bush era free-market or public choice approaches to government work effectively today. The authors instead propose a "third way" that neither relies on traditional big government nor dismantling government, a third way which they describe as already being put into practice throughout American Government. At the heart of their text, its ten of eleven chapters outline the basic transformations presently taking place which can be summed up as essentially building entrepreneurial incentives within government or as its subtitle emphasizes, "How the Entrepreneurial Spirit is Transforming the Public Sector." Chapter by chapter the book outlines how this "reinvention" occurs as well as *should* occur: namely by government "steering rather than rowing," "encouraging competition rather than monopolies," "being mission-driven rather than rule-driven," "meeting the needs of the customer not the bureaucracy," "focusing on investing not spending," "decentralizing authority not centralizing power," and so forth. Graphic examples from all levels of U.S. government are included within each chapter to underscore in practical ways how these trends are indeed "reinventing government" (Osborn & Gaebler, 1992, p. 192).

The authors attempt to chart "a middle way" between the extremes of statism and laissez fairism. They lambaste both, but do they offer a convincing alternative? There is much fadishness in their nostrums that mix a confusion of prescription and description—what should be *and* what is?—as well as clumsily put together an awkward set of reform ideas, some old and some new, that don't really fit neatly as a whole. But reformist ideas seldom are logical, and perhaps for that reason alone they sell well today in many quarters.

The themes of *Reinventing Government* and its clone, *The National Performance Review,* stand squarely within the long-reformist traditions of public administration, but unlike past administrative reformist literature, neither sets forth an explicit theoretical view of government reorganization. Perhaps this was because public administration scholars were not involved. Indeed when asked if any scholars served as advisors in preparing the *National Performance Review,* Vice President Gore is reported to have said curtly, "No." This approach stands in marked contrast to prior major reorganization efforts such as the Brownlow Commission (1937), first Hoover Report (1949) or Ash Commission (1971) in which academics from public administration played prominent roles and theoretical underpinnings were explicit: *i.e.,* strengthen executive leadership, improve public accountability, professionalize the public service and develop clear lines of communication and coordination.

There is no talk of "such stuff" by the "Reinventors." Rather the entire thrust is to "put customers first," "cut red tape," "empower employees" and thereby create "entrepreneurial organizations" (Gore, 1993). Business values of entrepreneurialism and a customer-focused bottom-line should—ought?—replace general responsiveness to "the public interest" for strengthening public administration in the 1990s. By making "this new customer service contract with the American people," in the words of The Gore Report, it is hoped to close the "trust deficit" and to restore confidence in government. The administrative state, envisioned by these writers, thus would persist, though it would be sustained and perhaps legitimized largely by satisfying little markets of customers throughout society. The U.S. Government as a McDonald's franchise? Indeed both Osborne and Gaebler acknowledge in their book's credits none other than Peter Drucker, the business guru of the Fortune 500, as the single most influential theorist in shaping their viewpoints.

Of course, the central problem of adopting the Druckerian perspective, like numerous reformers who have advocated turning government into a business enterprise, is quite simply—how can a public agency become a business without a measurable bottom-line? Business success—or failure—is judged by its profits, sales or market shares. Yet, what is the bottom line of the Defense Department? Winning wars? Or, the local welfare agency? Numbers of impoverished clients put to work? Or, for the police? Crimes prevented? How can one measure such things, at least in meaningful ways? Slogans like "cutting red tape" may have a nice ring for voters, but in practice how is "it" actually accomplished? "Red tape" may mean excessive rules and procedures for some, but for others, rules and procedures may very well protect minority rights, constitutional due process, social welfare and equity.

There is also a not-so-apparent slight-of-hand in the choice of examples the "Reinventors" use to support their case. The illustrations designed "to prove" their thesis are mainly drawn from reform-oriented communities or organizations like Sunnyvale, California; Phoenix, Arizona; or large federal agencies like the Department of Defense where the "ends" are largely agreed upon and choices are reduced to questions of "what's the most efficient means." Missing are examples from New York, Detroit or Boston where bare-knuckle Hobbesian politics prevail and "ends" really do matter!

Do the "Reinventor's" recipes for success work in even small homogeneous communities? A recent article in *Governing* magazine pointed out that the "E word" (entrepreneurialism) is not used much these days around Visalia, California, the small town where Ted Gaebler, the book's coauthor, was until recently its city manager. It seems that Mr. Gaebler had certainly played the "entrepreneur" in attracting a new Radisson Hotel to redevelop the downtown, but today it stands as a major money-losing "white elephant" for the community (Gurwitt, 1994). The lesson that should not be lost here is—public administrators' careers will be short-lived if they operate with only *one* value in mind, like customer-driven entrepreneurialism. Unless of course, they leave town and co-author best-selling books. The reality of their line of work must be, must always be, to continually juggle several, often competing values such as efficiency, economy, effectiveness, administrative compliance, and so on, if they plan to survive in the public sector. And that is certainly the way the Founding Fathers of 1787 designed the U.S. Constitution with competing power centers, protection of individual rights, regular elections, federalism, and separation of powers. No *one* value or interest was meant to reign supreme, no matter how worthy it may be—even a customer-oriented public service. "Government is different," as Paul Appleby said long ago (1945).

The Communitarians

A second school of thought within the refounding movement that has also gained a degree of public prominence is communitarianism. It includes the writings drawn mainly from sociologists such as William Galston, Amitai Etzioni, David Chrislip and Philip Selznick (unlike the consultants and practitioners that largely inhabit the ranks of "the Reinventors"). Since the late 1980s these scholars have produced a noteworthy spate of books, articles, even a new journal and annual conferences generally concerning themes of balancing rights and responsibilities, nurturing moral ties of family, neighborhood, work place and citizenship as the basis for bringing about a better society. Like "the Reinventors," the "Communitarians" seek to curb the excesses of the Reagan-Bush free market, economic-driven conservatism, where only the bottom line counted, at least in their view. For them, primary importance should be placed upon collective responsibility and moral values of citizenship which translate into specific policy proposals such as national public service programs, improved crime control, health care, job retraining, child day care for working mothers, welfare reform, and the like.

If all that agenda sounds familiar—and it should because it is part and parcel of President Clinton's first two years' domestic policies—the "charge" has been made that Clinton is "a communitarian" (which he would no doubt deny in the wake of the post-November 1994 election). Whether or not he adopts the formal label, Clinton's deputy domestic affairs advisor is William Galston, a card-carrying communitarian, and so communitarian influence has been pervasive within the Clinton administration.

While "restoring community," "less crime," and other communitarian ideas sound appealing, "high policy" however does not necessarily translate easily into "lowly administrative sciences" in America. Indeed the two operate seemingly often in distinctively bifurcated worlds. This is true especially of communitarians where their writings rarely "touch down" to the mundane world of administrative reality, let alone administrative sciences. Hence, there is something of an air of unreality, at least for public administrators, to much of their lofty discussions about morality, rights, responsibilities and community. Their unstated assumption seems to be that the world works without an administrative state, a point of view that borders on the airy-fairy notions of medieval scholastics debating the number of angels dancing on the head of a pin. What is ironic is that many of these same writers—Etzioni and Selznick in particular—have contributed major classic pieces to American administrative sciences in the past. Thus, their neglect of public administration is especially puzzling.

Perhaps the main cause of the absence of reference to "public administration" throughout their voluminous writings is due to their basic philosophical conception (or misconception?) of community. Communitarians premise their writings largely upon a rejection of both individualist and pluralist paradigms in which rights of individuals, excessively, in their view, outweigh a sense of responsibility to community. It is a movement, in the words of Amitai Etzioni, "aiming at shoring up the moral, social and political environment" (1993, p. 247). Where they chiefly draw their intellectual inspiration for conceptualizing "community" is from 18th century republicanism thought—a cluster of ideas in which citizenship and public virtue were valued for their own sake, in which active participation in public affairs was encouraged and in which people displayed a deep, abiding sense of obligation toward the common good and protection of liberty.

As Gordon Wood and other historians remind us, this very republicanism served for the Founding Fathers as the intellectual framework for the American Constitution as well as the revolutionary foil with which to fight against the British Monarchy, or what was then viewed as "a corrupt state." So no wonder that ideals of republicanism (with a small "r") should be revived and find respectability today in the ranks of a homegrown American movement to restore community? There remains nostalgia for "res republica" in late 20th century America, for a time before big interest groups, widespread democracy, urbanization, technological change, international commitments, industrialization and the large American State—and, yes, public administration—sprang into existence. The 18th century was a time when institutions were valued for their capacity to promote direct participation and engage in the words of Robert Reich, "civic discovery," or as Philip Selznick calls, "a moral ideal and a road to community." Indeed Selznick titles his communitarian magnum opus, *The Moral Commonwealth* (1992), in the true spirit of 18th century republicanism.

In keeping with their republican ideals, the moral purpose for communitarians is not achieved via coercion of impersonal organizations or a big state apparatus but rather in the words of the *Responsive Communitarian Platform,* "mainly through education and persuasion . . ." (p. 2). Nor can it be an individual endeavor, but is rather a product of a collective group activity in small, informal settings with an emphasis on applied practice and socialization where morality can be infused and inculcated throughout society. In the process, society then itself will, in the view of the communitarians, become both a "tolerant" and "good society." In their view, ". . . this important moral realm, which is neither one of random choice, nor of government control has been much neglected . . ." (p. 2). The kind of republican world that communitarians envision—or want to inhabit—is best summed up by Etzioni's new book, *The Spirit of Community,* where: ". . . people [are] committed to creating a new moral social and public order based on restored communities, without allowing puritanism or oppression" (Etzioni, 1993).

If communitarianism sounds like the Declaration of Independence, the U.S. Constitution, the Gettysburg Address all rolled together, it certainly

fits—fits well with the basic faith and tenets of 18th century republicanism upon which America was founded. Yet, what these communitarians fail to address, despite all their learned and weighty tomes, is how can a modern community operate successfully—or at all—*without the prerequisites of public administration*? Or, how in the late 20th century can America return to an essentially small, rural agrarian—*and above all, elitist*—society that served as preconditions to the creation of past republican virtues? The reality of American life today is the reverse: today we exist as a massive, urban, pluralist, technological administrative state. Is it possible to turn back the clock?

The VPI "Refounders"

By contrast, "the VPI refounding school" of authors is a third identifiable group within the contemporary "refounding movement," largely made up of academics closely connected throughout their careers with American administrative sciences. Perhaps the most prominent of these writings is the book, *Refounding Public Administration* (1990), by Gary L. Wamsley, Robert N. Bacher, Charles T. Goodsell, Philip S. Kronenberg, John A. Rohr, Camilla M. Stivers, Orion F. White, and James F. Wolf—all respected members of America's public administration educational fraternity. Originally developed from their "1982 Blacksburg Manifesto," as a response to the excesses of "bureaucrat-bashing" in the early Reagan Administration, this Virginia Polytechnic Institute initiative subsequently grew into a book of essays that elaborated on the Blacksburg Manifesto thesis.

Their general conclusions, which are often contradictory and complex to follow, as in the case of most multi-authored books, are, in brief, that: 1) public administration should be viewed as broadly involving "governance rather than merely management or administration of the public sector," 2) an agency perspective should serve "as an institutional grounding point for the practicing public administrator," 3) the concepts of citizenship and the public interest should be revived, revitalized *and* become the central normative guideposts for the field, 4) public administration should be linked to the purposes and processes of constitutional government and 5) thus be legitimized within the U.S. Constitutional framework. There are a number of other issues touched upon by these authors but their central purpose is none other than "refounding public administration" by developing "a normative theory of American public administration and . . . a theory of the American state . . ." (Wamsley, et al., 1990, p. 16). No small task, but something that these writers see as missing from current American administrative sciences and the chief cause of its present, and past, dilemmas in finding a legitimate role within American government.

This book deserves attention because it is a product of serious scholars who are attempting to grapple with major issues facing the field today. These authors are at least attempting to come to grips with many central issues, such as legitimacy, accountability, and definition of state. However, there are inherent theoretical problems with this text. For one, it assumes that the field, both its theory and practice, needs to be "refounded." In fact, the field in America was "founded" nearly a century ago and its record of accomplishments are not all that bad. American public administration, for example, can boast that it successfully fought two world wars as well as the Cold War, operates today as the last global superpower, "cured" a Great Depression in the 1930s, built a massive highway network, sent men and women into space, everyday pumps clean water and removes sewage from homes, educates millions of kids from the most diverse social backgrounds of any culture, and so on. The point is: at least compared to other nations, America's administrative state has achieved quite a lot and so the question that the "Refounders" must answer in some way first of all is—why should American public administration be refounded? In other words, *some* justification for fundamental redesign is essential to "prove" their case. Of course, they may rightly suggest that what was "good" for the past is not necessarily all that

"good" for the future, but still the rationale for any reform belongs squarely with those who propose it.

Nor do the authors address satisfactorily the "who elected them?" issue. Clearly the "Refounders," individually and collectively, favor a stronger, more central, legitimate role for bureaucracy and bureaucrats within the American governmental system. Though where in the U.S. Constitution, the primary founding document of the Republic, is "bureaucracy," "civil service," "public service" or for that matter anything about public administration mentioned? The Founders of the Great Charter of 1787 instead did everything to insure that America would *not* be governed by a European-style state; certainly they did everything possible to check its development. Granted, one author, John Rohr, stresses that election is not essential to legitimacy and that "at least 22 ways have been or still are approved for holding office under the Constitution." True enough, but still the Constitution gives no hint of elevating the status of bureaucrats and bureaucracy to the degree proposed by the "Refounders."

In connection with the VPI Refounders, James Stever's *The End of Public Administration* (1988) deserves mention. Much like the VPI Refounders (though he is not teaching at VPI), Stever's book addresses many of the same issues such as legitimacy and seeks ultimately a stronger, more positive role for an administrative state, though from a different perspective. His text begins with what he views as a fundamental "contradiction within American Culture," namely a fear of bureaucracy, on one hand, and "an affinity for the programs and goals that generate increasing amounts of public administration." At the outset, Stever outlines three alternatives to resolve this contradiction: 1) let the contradiction continue which he believes would be "risky"; 2) reduce the dependency upon government which Stever says is "infeasible and somewhat romantic"; and 3) "embark on the arduous task of enhancing the status of public administration in American Culture" (1988, p. 6), which Stever views as the best alternative.

Essentially the object of this third strategy, that

Stever endorses, entails nothing less than positively legitimizing public administration. He adds further complications by rejecting at the outset what he calls, "negative legitimizing strategies" or those methods that support public administration through reactive or restrictive means such as supervision by elected officials or emphasis upon procedural rules. Rather, Stever opts for the more difficult and complex strategy of "positive legitimization." To accomplish this objective, Stever suggests we must transcend "the neo-Weberian skeptics" who see public administration as a threat to liberal American democracy. The bulk of his book is a historical review of "three contributing failures" in the so-far failed attempt to make public administration legitimate within the United States. One occurred after World War I, an era Stever labels the "post-progressive era," in which public administration greatly expanded in size and complexity, with the resulting loss of integrity and increased intellectual fragmentation. A second involved the rise during this period of entrepreneurial values that substituted for neutral expertise and that led to the infiltration of "alien business values into the public sector." A third was "the inability to develop institutional integrity and institutional vitality" which left the public sector to become diffuse, sprawling and blurred with private sector roles.

"Visible, legible authority is vital for the positive legitimation of public administration" (1988, p. 20) argues Stever. In his last chapter, he outlines an agenda to legitimize positively public administration through its becoming "a polity profession." He advances the argument:

> If public administration is to develop as a profession there are certain necessary conditions that must be present: 1) a theoretical, scientific and technical base, 2) training in the theories, science, and techniques of administration, 3) a "calling to service" attitude on the part of individuals recruited into the profession, 4) an institutional network, and 5) the exercise of control over practice. Beyond these necessary conditions there is one sufficient condition.

Public administration must appear to both elected officials and the public as a crucial function to the maintenance of society. Furthermore, the civil servant must acquire a certain mystique in the performance of these crucial functions (p. 171).

Stever presents a stimulating argument that addresses, like the VPI Refounders, a central—perhaps *the* central—dilemma for the field today, namely its very legitimacy. Ominously, the book is entitled, *The End of Public Administration,* which Stever sees as a distinct possibility, unless its underpinnings are legitimized. Though his answer: turning the field into "a polity profession" runs squarely into the quandary faced by the VPI Refounders, namely how within the context of the U.S. Constitution can public administration be elevated to such a lofty status? Again, short of fundamental constitutional reform, how can Stever's "cure" be achieved? Even if amending the Constitution were possible, is the professionalization the best route to follow? Certainly professionalization is a highly nebulous and contentious construct (one on which few modern scholars can agree) upon which to model the entire field—let alone redesign the U.S. Constitution around. Questions and more questions.

Interpretive Theorists and *Postmodernists*

This group of theorists comprise a fourth significant group within the refounding movement in the 1990s. They are the direct heirs of the "New Public Administration" movement. "Interpretive Theorists" draw their intellectual thinking from a reaction to positivist and functionalist "objective" approaches in social science in the 1960s and 1970s. They are oriented toward phenomenology, an understanding of the "subjective-intersubjective" relationship that girds the construction of any social reality, and toward exploring and articulating the difficult, profound ontological and epistemological issues that ground the study of public administration as a way of framing a new intellectual basis for the field. This orientation influenced noteworthy American administrative scholarship during the past decade or so such as Robert B. Denhardt's *In the Shadow of the Organization* (1981), Michael M. Harmon's *Action Theory for Public Administration* (1981), Ralph P. Hummel's *The Bureaucratic Experience* (4th edition, 1994) or Jong S. Jun's *Public Administration: Design and Problem Solving* (1986). These theorists in the 1990s are well represented in the Public Administration Theory Network (PAT-Net). PAT-Net has developed its own peer-reviewed journal, *Administrative Theory and Praxis,* and sponsors well-attended annual conferences, and a SAGE book series. The essential ideas of these theorists are reflected in the curriculum of a major academic program at California State University-Hayward. The Department has become an important "refounding force" within American administrative theory.

Possibly, the best representative of contemporary interpretative theory within American administrative sciences is Henry D. Kass and Bayard L. Catron's *Images and Identities in Public Administration* (1990). Sixteen leading theorists are included in this collection of essays which, like the "VPI Refounders," explores alternative bases upon which to legitimize American public administration. Yet, unlike the "VPI Refounders," who tend to emphasize reform through institutional methods, these theorists see the problems with field as rooted in fundamentally the wrong images by which it was created. Therefore, these writers argue for "the need to develop legitimacy concepts for public administration that can send their roots deep into the soil of American political culture" (Kass & Catron, 1990, p. 10). As a result, the bulk of the text explores, as its title underscores, new varieties of "images and identities in public administration." An innovative array of alternative "images and identities" are presented in the text through what is termed, "imagizing" or "thinking and rethinking the implications of a variety of possible images (metaphors) for a

phenomenon (public administration)." Michael Harmon's essay advances "a tortured soul" concept; Ralph Hummel's "circle and pyramid" images; Orion White and Cynthia McSwain's "phoenix project," Henry Kass's "stewardship," or Douglas Morgan's "phronemos" (practical reasoner). Some of these new images or identities for the field are presented as descriptive reality, Kass's "stewards" for example; some are prescriptive in nature, for example, White and McSwain's "phoenix project" that proposes nothing less than "a rebirth of the field." These writings are by no means easy to read—or comprehend. They sometimes invent new terminology and metaphors that are highly abstract, but they are worth studying with care because they reflect some of the most avant-garde thinking within American administrative sciences in the 1990s.

These writers, by proposing the subjective process of "imagizing," seek, like the VPI Refounders, none other than a new legitimate basis for the field. As the conclusion emphasizes:

> What can be inferred from the spate of images about the identity of public administration? As the chapters selected for this volume reveal, a common concern for the identity of public administration also entailed a search for its nature and legitimacy (Kass & Catron, 1990, p. 242).

Generally throughout this book, critical theorists reject mechanical "positivist" images and favor more creative "subjective" alternatives to define the field's nature and legitimacy. As its Preface reminds the reader,

> . . . when we talk about organizations, it's usually the mechanical version, typified in the process of bureaucracy, that usually comes to mind. To break free of this conception . . . there may be merit in replacing the concept of organization with that of *imagination*. The purpose—to recognize that organization is a creative activity that can be developed and understood in many creative ways (Kass & Catron, 1990, p. 7).

A related but different and equally interesting cluster of scholars are the "postmodernists" who are less interested in problem-solving and change and are exploring the ways we think about the field by the very language we use. They are followers of postmodern philosophers like Foucault, Derida, Lyotard and Rorty. A new book by a prominent postmodernist scholar, Camilla Stivers' *Gender Images in Public Administration* (1993), examines the way we use language as a basis for our understanding of public administration and its problems today. Her thesis is:

> . . . the images of expertise, leadership and virtue that mark the defense of administrative power contain dilemmas of gender. They not only have masculine power features but help to keep in place or bestow political and economic privilege on the bearers of culturally masculine qualities at the expense of those who display culturally feminine ones. . . . The characteristic of masculinity of public administration is systemic: it contributes and sustains power relationships in society (p. 4).

Much like Frederick Taylor nearly a century ago, Stivers issues a call for "a mental revolution," but here one having to do with the very language that the field uses to define itself, which she argues is "gender-bound," or rather, bound to one gender. A new legitimacy for the field thereby is discovered via creating a more inclusive language for public administration, or as she writes: "If we keep seeing Public Administration as genderless, we risk either continuing masculination of administration or marginalizing 'others' " (p. 10).

Though like the other schools of thought "interpretive theory" and "postmodernists" have their "down-sides." Fundamentally, most of these authors assume that there is "one best way" to knowing "the truth," namely most assume that knowledge is a product of images, or rather, "imagizing" or through the language we use. In other words, truth is simply derived by "what's in our heads," and therefore we merely by our intellects manufacture "reality." A nice thought,

but hardly "true" when it comes to comprehending—or reforming—public administration. Our massive administrative state is hardly a fairy tale like "Snow White." It regrettably has a very real capacity to kill or maim millions instantly with a flip of a switch. In short, reimaging or revising the language can be stimulating intellectual exercises that can expand our creative thought but not necessarily something that squares with reality—or has *any* hope for changing reality. To repeat an old saw, "wishing it so, ain't going to make it so."

Furthermore, these writers, individually and collectively, simply ignore history, or read it very poorly. American public administration was not made just yesterday but rather was and is a product of more than two hundred years of history. This historic past cannot be created or recreated overnight, no matter how worthy the cause. To overlook this slow evolutionary aspect of American institutional and intellectual development is simplistic, at best; perilous, at worst. It can lead to serious, if not massive misconceptions about human abilities to effect change. Much the same could be said about their flawed views of the American Constitution, even politics, law, and cultural values that they so earnestly propose to reform, or rather "reimage." Perhaps these theorists should learn a lesson or two from the great German military theorist, Karl von Clausewitz: one should know the foe well in order to defeat him. One senses that these theorists know their foe—but not well.

Finally, while these writers advance our understanding in several heretofore unexplored or underexplored areas of the subjective unconscious, the significance of human nature and even the language we use in public administration, ultimately they seem to envision a sort of "therapeutic state" with public administrators as "the chief therapists." But is that the end-goal of public administration—or should it be? Like the "Reinventors" who favor entrepreneuralism above all other values, perhaps so too do the "interpretive" and "postmodernist" theorists run the risk of reification of "the subjective" over many values? Thereby possibly marginalizing others deemed central to the study and practice of the field?

The "Tools Approach"

The "tools approach" offers a fifth alternative redefinition and reconstruction of American public administration. Technologists' perspectives have a long and rich tradition within U.S. administrative sciences, starting from Frederick Taylor's "scientific management," through POSDCORB, cost-benefit analysis, PPBS, MBO and many other purportedly "one-best-ways" to do public administration. America's innovative culture of "hard" technologies throughout the 20th century "inspired" a vast array of "soft" administrative technologies to achieve the most economy, the most efficiency, the most effectiveness, or what not. A recent *and* sophisticated version of American technicalism applied to administrative sciences can be found in Lester M. Salamon (ed.), *Beyond Privatization: The Tools of Government Action* (1989). As Salamon underscores in his opening chapter, "The tools approach grew out of dissatisfaction with the research paradigms dominant in the field of public administration." In a nutshell, according to Salamon and his co-authors, traditional public administration does not adequately explain nor address the realities of running and implementing contemporary public sector programs. This is due, as numerous scholars have pointed out, to the transformation that has occurred in the federal government since World War II, in part caused by the massive increase in size and scale of government and the proliferation of new tools the public sector uses to achieve its purposes. As Salamon emphasizes, today "various government programs embody significantly different instruments of public action" (p. 8) and so there is no longer one best way to manage the public sector. Rather, at the federal level there is an enormous range and complexity of operating agency activities. Increasingly they rely upon "third parties" to carry out public actions which only complicates public policy making and its implementation. This factor,

as Salamon suggests, ". . . puts government in the position of operating by remote control, relying on other entities to deliver the services that government has authorized."

The bulk of this book focuses, chapter by chapter, on an analysis of the various major alternative "tools" of service delivery: *i.e.,* direction action, grants-in-aid, loan guarantees, tax incentives, social regulations and government corporations. In chapter two, the book outlines the basic analytics which lays out a framework that sees "no-one-best-way" but rather "many-ways" for carrying out public policies—each with their own strengths and weaknesses concerning: 1) administrative feasibility, 2) political support, 3) securing equity, 4) achieving efficiency and 5) overall program effectiveness. There is no *one* solution but instead, as Harvey Sherman once said, "it all depends" (1966) on the situation and goals being pursued for implementing public policy. Here, in other words, is a new political-economizing methodology that grew out of the frustrations of Salamon and his co-authors to select a way to implement federal policies. Traditional public administration concepts proved unhelpful in making such choices. Hence, this Urban Institute book about rethinking and reconceptualizing the field came as a result of a lack of any available conceptual framework.

Overall, the book is a thoughtful, well-reasoned, empirically grounded approach (unlike the prior four approaches). Therefore, Salamon presents no simplistic technocratic perspective, yet its examples and applications are entirely confined to the federal level, which makes its generalizations questionable when applied to state or local-levels that now encompass roughly sixty percent of American public service. With the federal sector being "down-sized" radically in the 1990s, the bulk of government activities *and* workforce may increasingly devolve to sub-federal levels which, in turn, makes "lessons" from this book of limited value to public administration as a whole. Nor, has academic consensus been reached on the definition or classifications of the "tools," that Salamon outlines even at the federal level, which further complicates the applications of this book to the field as a whole.

Moreover, the book assumes at the federal level that there is choice(s) available to policy makers in carrying out public programs. As the recent American health care debate underscored all too clearly, and perhaps tragically, rational choice of alternative "tools" have little to do with the modern reality of federal policy-making in which powerful interest groups "muscle" their preferences over what to do—or not to do. Politics matters; maybe it is the only thing that matters within the federal arena, which leaves "the tools approach" in a questionable if not limited role today.

Finally, on the intellectual level, can—should?—administrative sciences be reduced to merely a set of tools or techniques for making choices over implementation issues? Granted, again Salamon is offering us no simplistic Taylorist technicism, but his analysis dramatically constricts the scope and substance of what is traditionally viewed as American administrative sciences to "choice questions" over program implementation. In practice *or* theory is that all public administration encompasses? Most public administrators who are on-the-firing-line would probably respond that this work in fact makes up a very limited aspect of their job. And for most, those issues are not even within their purview but are instead subject only to elected officials or top political appointees' decisions. Thus, by adopting this new version of "a tools approach," does the field run the risk of "marching out" of public administration large "bread and butter" issues such as motivation questions, communications issues, program direction, staffing and other "mainline" administrative science concerns? Like adopting any other one-best-way methodology, does the field risk overlooking wider constitutional, ethical and value issues?

New Bureaucratic Perspectives

Finally, a vibrant, rich literature on public bureaucracy continues to contribute to the advancement of administrative sciences in the United States.

Drawn from the social sciences, largely from the pens of political scientists, these writings focus on issues such as the place of bureaucracy in a democracy, methods of oversight and control, the reality of the internal dynamics and the influence of the "pluralistic forces" on shaping bureaucracy. One can find the legacy and voices of the great 20th century social scientists like Max Weber, Robert Merton, Carl Friedrich, E. Pendleton Herring, Norton Long, and Robert Michels in these writings, but addressed to problems of the 1990s and using diverse, innovative empirical methodologies.

In one of the more interesting bureaucratic studies to appear in the 1990s, Gerald Garvey's *Facing the Bureaucracy* (1993), utilizes a "participant-observer" approach to view from within the dynamics of organizational change and development of a government bureaucracy, The Federal Energy Regulatory Commission (FERC). As he writes, "I have tried . . . to present some glimpses of the lived experience of bureaucracy . . . that experience is untidy, with ambiguity and personal conflicts" (p. xii). In an extended study of his own involvement with FERC as a consultant, Garvey recounts the internal dynamics of change within this government agency as it is pulled and hauled through various changing political appointees, with differing agendas, within a rapidly shifting external political environment of competing powerful special interests. What emerges is a portrait of how difficult and complex it becomes to achieve bureaucratic change and innovation within a modern federal agency. The odds are stacked against effective reforms from taking place due to rigid rules, procedures, inertia of the bureaucratic culture and the strong incentives for civil servants to prefer the status quo over reform. But change can occur, as Garvey writes:

When bureaucracy works, it is usually because an opportunistic leader sees a way through the obstacles and presses an agenda to its limit: Seek the chance, take the risk, push the project. But the concept of the limit is as important as is that of the venture itself. Opportunistic management is visionary leadership tempered by realism. It is what remains after the would-be radical transformer of structures or processes reckons with the constraints of public sector management (p. 212).

What emerges from this tale is an argument against what Garvey calls "the Old Theory of Public Administration," or the well-known top-down Weberian Rational Model, and instead for an "opportunistic management" approach that encourages risk-taking and strategizing or what Garvey refers to as "transactional manipulation in day-to-day operations," using whatever and wherever the resources happen to be on hand. It is often a messy and uncertain process, but it is one that Garvey sees as potentially an effective alternative to achieving fundamental change and innovation within often highly structured, rule-bound organizations.

Likewise, B. Dan Wood and Richard W. Waterman's *Bureaucratic Dynamics* (1994) attempts to look carefully at the realities of modern public administration. However, rather than "a participant-observer" point of view, their book offers an abstract, empirical study, based upon data drawn from eight federal agencies, and using a far more rigorous quantitative methodology than other studies to appear in book-form the 1990s on this topic. The authors' findings by means of their analysis contradict the popular notions that bureaucracy is "out of control" or "unresponsive" and instead see public agencies as highly dynamic, open to change and democratically responsive. Generally, this study presents public bureaucracies in a positive light, for as the authors conclude:

There is reason for optimism about bureaucratic democracy because public organizations are eminently moldable by U.S. political institutions. Agencies respond systematically to changes in political leadership, as manifested through appointments, changing budgets, reorganizations, and various other tools of administrative control (p. 151).

The picture that unfolds from these recent stud-

ies paints a far more optimistic view of bureaucracy: one that is open to leadership, responsive to democratic oversight, accountable to the public interest, flexible, pluralist, fluid and adaptive to change, and hardly a threat to American society. But is this message all that new? A new language, new examples, even new intellectual perspectives with greater empirical rigor may be evidenced here, but many of these "bottom line findings" have been argued before by Hugh Heclo, David Truman, Wallace Sayre, Herbert Kaufman and other post-World War II political scientists. One senses these writers are simply rediscovering the old "positivists" pluralist paradigm and not working towards a fundamentally new definition of the field. Though certainly reconfirmation of old conclusions matters—still.

A Conclusion, of Sorts . . .

To sum up, other schools of thought could be added to this American Refounding Movement in the 1990s—such as "neo-institutionalism," "chaos theory," and the like. The contemporary administrative literature in the U.S.A. is rich and diverse and perhaps this review does not do adequate justice to its impressive size, range and depth of ideas. Even the label "Refounding Movement" may not properly describe the many contradictory trends and diverse directions now occurring and flowing out of so many intellectual sources. Yet these aforementioned six are some of the most influential today, at least as judged by the attention they are currently receiving from both practitioners and educators in the field.

What conclusions then can be drawn from this "dragnet review"? First, the "Refounding Movement" today, much like those of yesterday, POSDCORB in the 1930s·or Behaviorism in the 1950s, is influenced by its external environment. The rapid changes in the American scene in the 1990s, *i.e.,* the end of the cold war, fierce global economic competition, voter dissatisfaction with government, demographic shifts, technological innovations, and so forth, are compelling the field, both on institutional and intellectual levels, to "refound itself." The porous nature of the field, its very openness to outside trends, encourages, indeed invites, new thinking from different sources. The six schools discussed in this review bring genuinely important intellectual perspectives to the field, such as new ideas about "community" from the "communitarians" or new methods of decision analysis from the "tools approach."

Second, the diversity of external "impacts" may largely be the source of its rejection of "one best way solutions" to cope with the external changes. Even the "tools approach" presents an intellectual framework for the field that offers no simple "technologist solution" such as scientific management or POSDCORB once did. Easy prescriptions for "refounding the field" based on *single* disciplines such as economics, law, or sociology, unlike in prior decades, seem to find little favor among those concerned with building a new intellectual framework for public administration in the 1990s.

Third, though *single* disciplinary "solutions" seem to find little support today, the refounding movement in the 1990s is largely a product of separate clusters of experts with their own expertise, who often do not talk with one another, or even know one another, using different languages and metaphors to speak about "the problem." The "reinventors" consciously exclude "academics" from their ranks (at least in *The Gore Report*), whereas the "communitarians" are largely confined "sociologists" who have not included many "public administrationists." Likewise, other clusters of scholars seem to operate "on-to-themselves," or in the words of Gabriel Almond, "sit at separate tables," thereby inhibiting dialogue and advancement toward a common intellectual framework for the field.

Fourth, and finally, all put forward fundamental conceptualizations or reconceptualizations of public administration and are, collectively and individually, attempting by different routes to move the field away from the extreme anti-statism of the past two decades. Though none advocate a strong administrative state, nor even define a "state" in the

European tradition of state theory. There are no European strong-state Bodins, no Hobbes, no Von Steins, no Schmitts here. All these refounders still remain squarely within the American liberal, anti-state or "stateless" tradition. The "reinventors" are hardly "statists," given their apparent enthusiasm for spreading the gospel of entrepreneurialism throughout government. The "communitarians" neglect the administrative state altogether and "the interpretative and postmodern theorists," while eager to "reimage" it or change its language, avoid "positivist" prescriptions that would strengthen "state" within society. The "tools advocates" use a reductionist logic that defines the field so narrowly in terms of "choice mechanisms" that "big" questions of political-constitutional-state matters become simply "non-issues." The "new bureaucratic perspectives" see it largely as an interplay of pluralistic political forces and fail to define what "it" is or even if "it" exists. Only the "VPI Refounders" try to address this topic, but despite their impressive effort to wrestle with and "levitate" public administration to a central if not commanding position in American Government, their formulas remain unconvincing—at least at this stage of development.

So here may be the critical theoretical problem facing the future development of the field. Today American administrative sciences, unlike its counterparts in Europe, ignore or avoid the concept of an administrative state possibly because Americans never have had much of a "state tradition" to identify with or possibly because the "state" deals with broad philosophical ends or goals of society that are so contentious, transient and diverse that they seem impossible to confront, or best be left to others to decide. Rather, pragmatic Americans find it far easier to identify public administration with means, processes and methods, as in the case of "the reinventors," "the tools approach" or "new bureaucratic perspectives." Even the "communitarians" and "interpretive theorists" talk of "community" and "reimaging" more as means rather than purposes. In some ways, the 1990s administrative sciences are curiously recreating the politics-administrative dichotomy by leaving to others the questions of purpose while public administration is being defined mostly as "the doing" activities. Yet, as the Dutch Scholar Mark Rutgers reminds us, ". . . we cannot do without an integrative concept of state in the study of public administration so as to define its nature and thereby enable us to select and integrate relevant knowledge . . ." (p. 409).

Nonetheless, an integrative framework may be too much to expect of American administrative sciences to discover and adopt, at least at this stage. Maybe all we should look toward or hope to work for is something more modest, as Dwight Waldo wisely suggested a few years ago:

> . . . I do not believe the hoped-for integrated framework of or for public administration will be achieved unless and until the framing circumstances change significantly. This does not mean that public administration as a function and activity will end—unless government ends. Or that public administration as a self-aware enterprise—doctrines, techniques, curricula, etc.—will end; though much is "down," much is "up."

> I think we *should* work toward the desired harmonious landscape—a road here, a bridge there, a grove of trees another place. Maybe I am wrong about what is possible. I *hope* I am wrong (pp. 931–2).

References

Appleby, Paul H. (1945). *Big Democracy.* New York: Knopf.

Etzioni, Amitai. (1993). *The Spirit of Community: Rights, Responsibilities and the Communitarian Agenda.* New York: Crown Books.

Gore, Al. (1993). *Creating a Government That Works Better and Costs Less: Report of the National Performance Review.* Washington, DC: USGPO.

Gurwitt, Rob. (1994, May). Entrepreneurial government: The morning after. *Governing,* pp. 34–40.

Kass, Henry D. & Catron, Bayard L. (Eds.). (1990). *Images and Identities in Public Administration.* Newbury Park, CA: Sage Publications.

Marini, Frank (Ed.). (1971). *Toward a New Public Administration: The Minnowbrook Perspective.* Scranton, PA: Chandler.

Osborne, David & Gaebler, Ted. (1992). *Reinventing Government: How the Entrepreneurial Spirit Is Transforming the Public Sector from Schoolhouse to State House, City Hall to the Pentagon.* Reading, MA: Addison-Wesley.

Ostrom, Vincent. (1974). *The Intellectual Crisis in American Public Administration* (Revised). Tuscaloosa, AL: University of Alabama Press.

Responsive Communitarian Platform, The. (1991). Washington, DC: The Communitarian Network.

Rutgers, Mark R. (1994, September). Can the study of public administration do with a concept of the state? *Administration and Society,* 26(3), p. 409.

Salamon, Lester M. (Ed.) with Lund, Michael S. (1989). *Beyond Privatization: The Tools of Government Action.* Washington, DC: The Urban Institute Press.

Savas, E.S. (1982). *Privatizing the Public Sector.* Chatham, NJ: Chatham House.

Scott, William G. & Hart, David K. (1979). *Organizational America: Can Individual Freedom Survive Within the Security It Promises?* Boston, MA: Houghton Mifflin.

Selznick, Philip. (1992). *The Moral Commonwealth: Social Theory and the Promise of Community.* Berkeley, CA: University of California Press.

Sherman, Harvey. (1966). *It All Depends—A Pragmatic Approach to Organization.* University: University of Alabama Press.

Stever, James A. (1988). *The End of Public Administration: Problems of the Profession in the Post-Progressive Era.* Dobbs Ferry, NY: Transnational Publishers.

Stivers, Camilla M. (1993). *Gender Images in Public Administration: Legitimacy and the Administrative State.* Newbury Park, CA: Sage Publications.

Thayer, Frederick C. (1973). *An End to Hierarchy! An End to Competition.* New York: New Viewpoints.

Waldo, Dwight. (1988, September/October). The end of public administration? *Public Administration Review,* 38(5), pp. 931–932.

Wamsley, Gary L., Bacher, Robert N., Goodsell,

Charles T., Kronenberg, Phillip S., Rohr, John A. Stivers, Camilla M., White, Orion F., & Wolf, James F. (1990). *Refounding Public Administration.* Newbury Park, CA: Sage Publications.

Wildavsky, Aaron. (1980). *How to Limit Government Spending.* Berkeley, CA: University of California Press.

Wood, B. Dan & Waterman, Richard W. (1994). *Bureaucratic Dynamics: The Role of Bureaucracy in a Democracy.* Boulder, CO: Westview Press.

☐ CASE STUDY 1

Introduction

The following story may shed some further insight into the role of public administration in modern society. The story, "The Blast in Centralia No. 5: A Mine Disaster No One Stopped," is an excellent account of a mine disaster that occurred a generation ago in Centralia, Illinois, killing 111 miners. This article is an unusual case study in public administration; not only does the author, John Bartlow Martin, carefully recount the facts of the catastrophe, but he also attempts to understand the reasons behind the disaster. In his search for clues, the writer reveals much about the inner complexities of the administrative framework of our modern society—a coal company sensitive only to profit incentives; state regulatory agencies inadequately enforcing mine safety legislation; federal officials and mine unions complacent about a growing problem; and the miners incapable of protecting themselves against the impending disaster.

This is an example of administrative reality that, for some, will only confirm their suspicions about the inherent corruption of modern administrative enterprises. The victims died, they might argue, because the mine owners were only interested in profits, not in human lives. But is this the correct interpretation? Martin does not blame any one individual or even a group of individuals but stresses the ineffectiveness of the administrative structure on which all the disaster victims were dependent for survival.

After reading this story you will probably be struck by how much modern society depends on the proper functioning of unseen administrative arrangements—for safeguarding our environment; for protecting the purity of our food; for transporting us safely by road, rail, or air; for sending us our mail; or for negotiating an arms limitations agreement at some distant diplomatic conference. All of us, like the miners in Centralia No. 5, rely throughout our lives on the immovable juggernaut of impersonal administrative systems. A functioning, ordered public administration, as this story illustrates, is an inescapable necessity for maintaining the requisites of a civilized modern society.

As you read this selection, keep the following questions in mind:

What does this case study tell us are the central problems and issues facing public administrators in their work? Why is government administration such a complex and difficult task according to this study?

Given the themes and problems in this case study, how would you frame a suitable definition of the field of public administration? Does it "square" with Woodrow Wilson's or any of the more recent theories put forth in Stillman's prior essay?

What does the case say about the special *public* obligations of public administrators compared to the obligations of those engaged in private administration?

Finally, if you had actually been one of the leading administrative officials in the case—Driscoll O. Scanlan, Dwight Green, or Robert Medill—what would have been your view of public administration, and how might such a perspective on administration have helped to shape the outcome of the story?

The Blast in Centralia No. 5: A Mine Disaster No One Stopped

JOHN BARTLOW MARTIN

Already the crowd had gathered. Cars clogged the short, black rock road from the highway to the mine, cars bearing curious spectators and relatives and friends of the men entombed. State troopers and deputy sheriffs and the prosecuting attorney came, and officials from the company, the Federal Bureau of Mines, the Illinois Department of Mines and Minerals. Ambulances arrived, and doctors and nurses and Red Cross workers and soldiers with stretchers from Scott Field. Mine rescue teams came, and a federal rescue unit, experts burdened with masks and oxygen tanks and other awkward paraphernalia of disaster. . . .

One hundred and eleven men were killed in that explosion. Killed needlessly, for almost everybody concerned had known for months, even years, that the mine was dangerous. Yet nobody had done any-

thing effective about it. Why not? Let us examine the background of the explosion. Let us study the mine and the miners, Joe Bryant and Bill Rowekamp and some others, and also the numerous people who might have saved the miners' lives but did not. The miners had appealed in various directions for help but got none, not from their state government nor their federal government nor their employer nor their own union. (In threading the maze of officialdom we must bear in mind four agencies in authority: The State of Illinois, the United States Government, the Centralia Coal Company, and the United Mine Workers of America, that is, the UMWA of John L. Lewis.) Let us seek to fix responsibility for the disaster. . . .

The Centralia Mine No. 5 was opened two miles south of Centralia in 1907. Because of its age, its maze of underground workings is extensive, covering perhaps six square miles, but it is regarded as a medium-small mine since it employs but 250 men and produces but 2,000 tons of coal daily. It was owned by the Centralia Coal Company, an appendage of the Bell & Zoller empire, one of the Big

Six among Illinois coal operators. . . . The Bell & Zoller home office was in Chicago (most of the big coal operators' home offices are in Chicago or St. Louis); no Bell & Zoller officers or directors lived at Centralia.

There are in coal mines two main explosion hazards—coal dust and gas. Coal dust is unhealthy to breathe and highly explosive. Some of the dust raised by machines in cutting and loading coal stays in suspension in the air. Some subsides to the floor and walls of the tunnels, and a local explosion will kick it back into the air where it will explode and, in turn, throw more dust into the air, which will explode; and as this chain reaction continues the explosion will propagate throughout the mine or until it reaches something that will stop it.

The best method of stopping it, a method in use for some twenty-five years, is rock dusting. Rock dusting is simply applying pulverized stone to the walls and roof of the passageways; when a local explosion occurs it will throw a cloud of rock dust into the air along with the coal dust, and since rock dust is incombustible the explosion will die. Rock dusting will not prevent an explosion but it will localize one. Illinois law requires rock dusting in a dangerously dusty mine. Authorities disagreed as to whether the Centralia mine was gassy but everyone agreed it was exceedingly dry and dusty. The men who worked in it had been complaining about the dust for a long time—one recalls "the dust was over your shoetops," another that "I used to cough up chunks of coal dust like walnuts after work"—and indeed by 1944, more than two years before the disaster, so widespread had dissatisfaction become that William Rowekamp, as recording secretary of Local Union 52, prepared an official complaint. But even earlier, both state and federal inspectors had recognized the danger.

Let us trace the history of these warnings of disaster to come. For in the end it was this dust which did explode and kill one hundred and eleven men, and seldom has a major catastrophe of any kind been blueprinted so accurately so far in advance.

Driscoll O. Scanlan (who led the rescue work after the disaster) went to work in a mine near Centralia when he was 16, studied engineering at night school, and worked 13 years as a mine examiner for a coal company until, in 1941, he was appointed one of 16 Illinois state mine inspectors by Governor

Green upon recommendation of the state representative from Scanlan's district. Speaking broadly, the job of a state inspector is to police the mine operators—to see that they comply with the state mining law, including its numerous safety provisions. But an inspector's job is a political patronage job. Coal has always been deeply enmeshed in Illinois politics.

Dwight H. Green, running for Governor the preceding fall, had promised the miners that he would enforce the mining laws "to the letter of the law," and however far below this lofty aim his administration fell (as we shall see), Scanlan apparently took the promise literally. Scanlan is a stubborn, righteous, zealous man of fierce integrity. Other inspectors, arriving to inspect a mine, would go into the office and chat with the company officials. Not Scanlan; he waited outside, and down in the mine he talked with the miners, not the bosses. Other inspectors, emerging, would write their reports in the company office at the company typewriter. Not Scanlan; he wrote on a portable in his car. Widespread rumor had it that some inspectors spent most of their inspection visits drinking amiably with company officials in the hotel in town. Not Scanlan. Other inspectors wrote the briefest reports possible, making few recommendations and enumerating only major violations of the mining law. Scanlan's reports were longer than any others (owing in part to a prolix prose style), he listed every violation however minor, and he made numerous recommendations for improvements even though they were not explicitly required by law.

Scanlan came to consider the Centralia No. 5 mine the worst in his district. In his first report on it he made numerous recommendations, including these: "That haulage roads be cleaned and sprinkled. . . . That tamping of shots with coal dust be discontinued and that clay be used. . . ." Remember those criticisms, for they were made February 7, 1942, more than five years before the mine blew up as a result (at least in part) of those very malpractices.

Every three months throughout 1942, 1943, and 1944 Scanlan inspected the mine and repeated his recommendations, adding new ones: "That the mine be sufficiently rock dusted." And what became of his reports? He mailed them to the Department of Mines and Minerals at Springfield, the agency which supervises coal mines and miners. Springfield is dominated by the Statehouse, an ancient structure of spires and towers and balconies, of colonnades and domes; on its broad front steps Lincoln stands in stone. Inside all is gloom and shabby gilt. The Department of Mines and Minerals occupies three high-ceilinged rooms in a back corner of the second floor. The Director of the Department uses the small, comfortable, innermost office, its windows brushed by the leaves of trees on the Statehouse lawn, and here too the Mining Board meets. In theory, the Mining Board makes policy to implement the mining law, the Director executes its dictates; in practice, the Director possesses considerable discretionary power of his own.

In 1941 Governor Green appointed as Director Robert M. Medill, a genial, paunchy, red-faced man of about sixty-five. Medill had gone to work in a mine at sixteen; he rose rapidly in management. He had a talent for making money and he enjoyed spending it. He entered Republican politics in 1920, served a few years as director of the Department of Mines and Minerals, then returned to business (mostly managing mines); and then, after working for Green's election in 1940, was rewarded once more with the directorship. Green reappointed him in 1944 with, says Medill, the approval of "a multitude of bankers and business men all over the state. And miners. I had the endorsement of all four factions." By this he means the United Mine Workers and its smaller rival, the Progressive Mine Workers, and the two associations of big and little operators; to obtain the endorsement of all four of these jealous, power-seeking groups is no small feat. As Director, Medill received $6,000 a year (since raised to $8,000) plus expenses of $300 or $400 a month. He lived in a sizable country house at Lake Springfield, with spacious grounds and a tree-lined driveway.

To Medill's department, then, came Driscoll Scanlan's inspection reports on Centralia Mine No. 5. Medill, however, did not see the first thirteen reports (1942–44); they were handled as "routine" by Robert Weir, an unimaginative, harassed little man who had come up through the ranks of the miners' union and on recommendation of the union had been appointed Assistant Director of the Department by Green (at $4,000 a year, now $5,200). When the mail brought an inspector's report, it went first to Medill's secretary who shared the office next to Medill's with Weir. She stamped the report [with

date of receipt] . . . and put it on Weir's desk. Sometimes, but by no means always, Weir read the report. He gave it to one of a half-dozen girl typists in the large outer office. She edited the inspector's recommendations for errors in grammar and spelling, and incorporated them into a form letter to the owner of the mine, closing:

"The Department endorses the recommendations made by Inspector Scanlan and requests that you comply with same.

"Will you please advise the Department upon the completion of the recommendations set forth above?

"Thanking you . . ."

When the typist placed this letter upon his desk, Weir signed it and it was mailed to the mine operator.

But the Centralia company did not comply with the major recommendations Scanlan made. In fact, it did not even bother to answer Weir's thirteen letters based on Scanlan's reports. And Weir did nothing about this. Once, early in the game, Weir considered the dusty condition of the mine so serious that he requested the company to correct it within ten days; but there is no evidence that the company even replied.

This continued for nearly three years. And during the same period the federal government entered the picture. In 1941 Congress authorized the U.S. Bureau of Mines to make periodic inspections of coal mines. But the federal government had no enforcement power whatever; the inspections served only research. The first federal inspection of Centralia Mine No. 5 was made in September of 1942. In general, the federal recommendations duplicated Scanlan's—rock dusting, improving ventilation, wetting the coal to reduce dust—and the federal inspectors noted that "coal dust . . . at this mine is highly explosive, and would readily propagate an explosion." In all, they made 106 recommendations, including 33 "major" ones (a government official has defined a "major" hazard as one that "could . . . result in a disaster"). Four months passed before a copy of this report filtered through the administrative machinery at Washington and reached the Illinois Department at Springfield, but this mattered little: the Department did nothing anyway. Subsequent federal reports in 1943 and 1944 showed that the "major" recommendations had not been complied with. The federal bureau lacked the power to force compliance;

the Illinois Department possessed the power but failed to act.

What of the men working in the mine during these three years? On November 4, 1944, on instructions from Local 52 at Centralia, William Rowekamp, the recording secretary, composed a letter to Medill: "At the present the condition of those roadways are very dirty and dusty . . . they are getting dangerous. . . . But the Coal Co. has ignored [Scanlan's recommendations]. And we beg your prompt action on this matter."

The Department received this letter November 6, and four days later Weir sent Inspector Scanlan to investigate. Scanlan reported immediately:

"The haulage roads in this mine are awful dusty, and much dust is kept in suspension all day. . . . The miners have complained to me . . . and I have wrote it up pretty strong on my inspection reports. . . . But to date they have not done any adequate sprinkling. . . . Today . . . [Superintendent Norman] Prudent said he would fix the water tank and sprinkle the roads within a week, said that he would have had this work done sooner, but that they have 20 to 30 men absent each day." (This last is a claim by the company that its cleanup efforts were handicapped by a wartime manpower shortage. This is controversial. Men of fifty-nine—the average wartime age at the mine—do not feel like spending weekends removing coal dust or rock dusting, a disagreeable task; winter colds caused absenteeism and miners are always laying off anyway. On the other hand, the company was interested in production and profits: as Mine Manager Brown has said, "In the winter you can sell all the coal you can get out. So you want top production, you don't want to stop to rock dust.")

At any rate, Rowekamp's complaint got results. On December 2, 1944, he wrote Scanlan: "Well I am proud to tell you that they have sprinkled the 18th North Entry & 21st So. Entry and the main haulage road. . . . Myself and the Members of Local Union #52 appreciate it very much what you have done for us." It is apparent from this first direct move by Local 52 that Scanlan was working pretty closely with the Local to get something done.

But by the end of that month, December 1944, the mine once more had become so dirty that Scanlan ended his regular inspection report, ". . . if necessary the mine should discontinue hoisting coal for a few days until the [cleanup] work can be done."

But all Weir said to the company was the routine "The Department endorses. . . ."

Early in 1945 it appeared that something might be accomplished. Scanlan, emerging from his regular inspection, took the unusual step of telephoning Medill at Springfield. Medill told him to write him a letter so Scanlan did:

"The haulage roads in this mine are in a terrible condition. If a person did not see it he would not believe. . . . Two months ago . . . the local officers [of Local Union 52] told me that . . . if [the mine manager] did not clean the mine up they were going to prefer charges against him before the mining board and have his certificate canceled. I talked them out of it and told them I thought we could get them to clean up the mine. But on this inspection I find that practically nothing has been done. . . . The mine should discontinue hoisting coal . . . until the mine is placed in a safe condition. . . . The coal dust in this mine is highly explosive. . . ."

This stiff letter was duly stamped "Received" at Springfield on February 23, 1945. A few days earlier a bad report had come in from Federal Inspector Perz. And now at last Medill himself entered the picture. What did he do? The Superintendent at Centralia had told Scanlan that, in order to clean up the mine, he would have to stop producing coal, a step he was not empowered to take. So Medill bypassed him, forwarding Scanlan's letter and report to William P. Young, Bell & Zoller's operating vice-president at Chicago: "Dear Bill. . . . Please let me have any comments you wish to make. . . . Very kindest personal regards." From his quiet, well-furnished office near the top of the Bell Building overlooking Michigan Avenue, Young replied immediately to "Dear Bob" [Medill]: "As you know we have been working under a very severe handicap for the past months. The war demand for coal . . . we are short of men. . . . I am hopeful that the urgent demand of coal will ease up in another month so that we may have available both the time and labor to give proper attention to the recommendations of Inspector Scanlan. With kindest personal regards. . . ."

A week later, on March 7, 1945, Medill forwarded copies of this correspondence to Scanlan, adding: "I also talked with Mr. Young on the phone, and I feel quite sure that he is ready and willing. . . . I would suggest that you ask the mine committee [of

Local 52] to be patient a little longer, inasmuch as the coal is badly needed at this time."

The miners told Scanlan they'd wait till the first of April but no longer. On March 14 Medill was to attend a safety meeting in Belleville. Scanlan went there to discuss Centralia No. 5 with him. According to Scanlan, "When I went up to his room he was surrounded with coal operators . . . all having whiskey, drinking, having a good time, and I couldn't talk to him then, and we attended the safety meeting [then] went . . . down to Otis Miller's saloon, and I stayed in the background drinking a few cokes and waited until the crowd thinned out, and went back up to his hotel room with him. . . . I told him that the mine was in such condition that if the dust became ignited that it would sweep from one end of the mine to the other and probably kill every man in the mine, and his reply to me was, 'We will just have to take that chance.' " (Medill has denied these words but not the meeting.)

On the first of April the president of Local Union 52 asked Scanlan to attend the Local's meeting on April 4. The miners complained that the company had not cleaned up the mine and, further, that one of the face bosses, or foreman, had fired explosive charges while the entire shift of men was in the mine. There can be little doubt that to fire explosives on-shift in a mine so dusty was to invite trouble—in fact, this turned out to be what later caused the disaster—and now in April 1945 the union filed charges against Mine Manager Brown, asking the State Mining Board to revoke his certificate of competency (this would cost him his job and prevent his getting another in Illinois as a mine manager). Rowekamp wrote up the charges: ". . . And being the Mine is so dry and dusty it could of caused an explosion. . . ."

Weir went to Centralia on April 17, 1945, but only to investigate the charges against Brown, not to inquire into the condition of the mine. He told the miners they should have taken their charges to the state's attorney. Nearly a month passed before, on May 11, Weir wrote a memorandum to the Mining Board saying that the company's superintendent had admitted the shots had been fired on-shift but that this was done "in an emergency" and it wouldn't happen again; and the Board refused to revoke Manager Brown's certificate.

Meanwhile, on April 12 and 13, Scanlan had made his regular inspection and found conditions worse than in February. He told the Superintendent: "Now, Norman, you claim Chicago won't give you the time to shut your mine down and clean it up. Now, I am going to get you some time," and he gave him the choice of shutting the mine down completely or spending three days a week cleaning up. The Superintendent, he said, replied that he didn't know, he'd have to "contact Chicago," but Scanlan replied: "I can't possibly wait for you to contact Chicago. It is about time that you fellows who operate the mines get big enough to operate your mines without contacting Chicago." So on Scanlan's recommendation the mine produced coal only four days a week and spent the remaining days cleaning up. For a time Scanlan was well satisfied with the results, but by June 25 he was again reporting excessive dust and Federal Inspector Perz was concurring: "No means are used to allay the dust." Following his October inspection Scanlan once more was moved to write a letter to Medill; but the only result was another routine letter from Weir to the company, unanswered.

Now, one must understand that, to be effective, both rock dusting and cleanup work must be maintained continuously. They were not at Centralia No. 5. By December of 1945 matters again came to a head. Scanlan wrote to Medill, saying that Local 52 wanted a sprinkling system installed to wet the coal, that Mine Manager Brown had said he could not order so "unusual" an expenditure, and that Brown's superior, Superintendent Prudent, "would not talk to me about it, walked away and left me standing." And Local 52 again attempted to take matters into its own hands. At a special meeting on December 12 the membership voted to prefer charges against both Mine Manager Brown and Superintendent Prudent. Rowekamp's official charge, typed on stationery of the Local, was followed next day by a letter, written in longhand on two sheets of dime-store notepaper, and signed by 28 miners. . . . At Springfield this communication too was duly stamped "Received." And another Scanlan report arrived.

Confronted with so many documents, Medill called a meeting of the Mining Board on December 21. Moreover, he called Scanlan to Springfield and told him to go early to the Leland Hotel, the gathering place of Republican politicians, and see Ben H. Schull, a coal operator and one of the operators' two men on the Mining Board. In his hotel room, Schull (according to Scanlan) said he wanted to discuss privately Scanlan's report on Centralia No. 5, tried to persuade him to withdraw his recommendation of a sprinkling system, and, when Scanlan refused, told him, "you can come before the board." But when the Mining Board met in Medill's inner office, Scanlan was not called before it though he waited all day, and after the meeting he was told that the Board was appointing a special commission to go to Centralia and investigate.

On this commission were Weir, two state inspectors, and two members of the Mining Board itself, Schull and Murrell Reak. Reak, a miner himself, represented the United Mine Workers of America on the Mining Board. And Weir, too, owed his job to the UMWA but, oddly, he had worked for Bell & Zoller for twenty years before joining the Department, the last three as a boss, so his position was rather ambiguous. In fact, so unanimous were the rulings of the Mining Board that one cannot discern any management-labor cleavage at all but only what would be called in party politics bipartisan deals.

The commission had before it a letter from Superintendent Prudent and Manager Brown setting forth in detail the company's "absentee experience" and concluding with a veiled suggestion that the mine might be forced to close for good (once before, according to an inspector, the same company had abandoned a mine rather than go to the expense entailed in an inspector's safety recommendation). Weir wrote to Prudent, notifying him that the commission would visit Centralia on December 28 to investigate the charges against him and Brown; Medill wrote to the company's vice-president, Young, at Chicago ("You are being notified of this date so that you will have an opportunity to be present or designate some member of your staff to be present"); but Medill only told Rowekamp, "The committee has been appointed and after the investigation you will be advised of their findings and the action of the board"—he did not tell the Local when the commission would visit Centralia nor offer it opportunity to prove its charges.

Rowekamp, a motorman, recalls how he first learned of the special commission's visit. He was working in the mine and "Prudent told me to set out an empty and I did and they rode out." Prudent—remember, the commission was investigating charges against Prudent—led the commission through the mine. Rowekamp says, "They didn't see nothing. They didn't get back in the buggy runs where the dust was the worst; they stayed on the mainline." Even there they rode, they did not walk through the dust. Riding in a mine car, one must keep one's head down. In the washhouse that afternoon the men were angry. They waited a week or two, then wrote to Medill asking what had been done. On January 22, 1946, Medill replied: the Mining Board, adopting the views of the special commission, had found "insufficient evidence" to revoke the certificates of Prudent and Brown.

He did not elaborate. Next day, however, he sent to Scanlan a copy of the commission's report. It listed several important violations of the mining law: inadequate rock dusting, illegal practice in opening rooms, insufficient or improperly placed telephones, more than a hundred men working on a single split, or current, of air. In fact, the commission generally concurred with Scanlan, except that it did not emphasize dust nor recommend a sprinkling system. Thus in effect it overruled Scanlan on his sprinkling recommendation, a point to remember. It did find that the law was being violated yet it refused to revoke the certificates of the Superintendent and the Mine Manager, another point to remember. Weir has explained that the board felt that improvements requiring construction, such as splitting the airstream, would be made and that anyway "conditions there were no different than at most mines in the state." And this is a refrain that the company and the Department repeated in extenuation after the disaster. But actually could anything be more damning? The mine was no worse than most others; the mine blew up; therefore any might blow up!

The miners at Centralia were not satisfied. "It come up at the meeting," Rowekamp recalls. Local 52 met two Wednesday nights a month in its bare upstairs hall. The officers sat at a big heavy table up front; the members faced them, sitting on folding chairs which the Local had bought second-hand from an undertaker. Attendance was heavier now than usual, the men were aroused, some were even telling their wives that the mine was dangerous. They wanted to do something. But what? The state had rebuffed them. Well, why did they not go now to the higher officials of their own union, the UMWA? Why not to John L. Lewis himself?

One of them has said, "You have to go through

the real procedure to get to the right man, you got to start at the bottom and start climbing up, you see? If we write to Lewis, he'll refer us right back to Spud White." Spud White is Hugh White, the thick-necked president of the UMWA in Illinois (District 12), appointed by Lewis. Now, Lewis had suspended District 12's right to elect its own officers during the bloody strife of the early 1930s, when the members, disgusted with what they called his "dictator" methods and complaining of secret payrolls, expulsions, missing funds, stolen ballots, and leaders who turned up on operators' payrolls, had rebelled; in the end the Progressive Mine Workers was formed and Lewis retained tight control of the UMWA. A decade later the Illinois officers of UMWA demanded that he restore their self-government, but Lewis managed to replace them with his own men, including Spud White. By 1946 President White, a coal miner from the South, was consulting at high levels with Lewis, he was receiving $10,000 a year plus expenses (which usually equal salary), and he was maintaining a spacious house on a winding lane in the finest residential suburb of Springfield, a white house reached by a circular drive through weeping willows and evergreens.

Evidently the perplexed miners at Centralia already had appealed to District 12 for help, that is to White. Certainly Murrell Reak, the UMWA's man on the Mining Board and a close associate of White's, had asked Weir to furnish him with a copy of the findings of the special commission: "I want them so I may show the district UMWA. So they in turn may write Local Union down there, and show them that their charges are unfounded or rather not of a nature as to warrant the revocation of mine mgr. Certificate. . . ." Jack Ripon, the bulky vice-president of District 12 and White's right-hand man, said recently, "We heard there'd been complaints but we couldn't do a thing about it; it was up to the Mining Department to take care of it."

And yet in the past the UMWA has stepped in when the state failed to act. One unionist has said, "White could have closed that mine in twenty-four hours. All he'd have had to do was call up Medill and tell him he was going to pull every miner in the state if they didn't clean it up. It's the union's basic responsibility—if you don't protect your own wife and daughter, your neighbor down the street's not going to do it."

Perhaps the miners of Local 52 knew they must go it alone. They continued to address their official complaints to the State of Illinois. On February 26 Rowekamp wrote once more to Medill: "Dear Sir: At our regular meeting of Local Union 52. Motion made and second which carried for rec. secy. write you that the members of local union 52 are dissatisfied with the report of the special investigation commission. . . ." No answer. And so the members of Local 52 instructed Rowekamp to write to higher authority, to their Governor, Dwight H. Green.

It took him a long time. Elmer Moss kept asking if he'd finished it and Rowekamp recalls, "I'd tell him, Elmer, I can't do that fast, that's a serious letter, that'll take me a while." He wrote it out first in pencil and showed it to a couple of the boys and they thought it sounded fine. Then, sitting big and awkward at his cluttered little oak desk in the living room of his home outside town, he typed it, slowly and carefully—"anything important as that I take my time so I don't make mistakes, it looks too sloppified." He used the official stationery of the Local, bearing in one corner the device of the union—crossed shovels and picks—and in the other "Our Motto—Justice for One and All." He impressed upon it the official seal—"I can write a letter on my own hook but I dassen't use the seal without it's official"—and in the washhouse the Local officers signed it. Rowekamp made a special trip to the post office to mail it. It was a two-page letter saying, in part:

> Dear Governor Green:
>   We, the officers of Local Union No. 52, U. M. W. of A., have been instructed by the members . . . to write a letter to you in protest against the negligence and unfair practices of your department of mines and minerals . . . we want you to know that this is not a protest against Mr. Driscoll Scanlan . . . the best inspector that ever came to our mine. . . . But your mining board will not let him enforce the law or take the necessary action to protect our lives and health. This protest is against the men above Mr. Scanlan in your department of mines and minerals. In fact, Governor Green this is a plea to you, to please save our lives, to please make the department of mines and minerals enforce the laws at the No. 5 mine of the Centralia Coal Co. . . . before we have a dust explosion at this mine like just happened in

Kentucky and West Virginia. For the last couple of years the policy of the department of mines and minerals toward us has been one of ignoring us. [The letter then recited the story of the useless special commission.] We are writing you, Governor Green, because we believe you want to give the people an honest administration and that you do not know how unfair your mining department is toward the men in this mine. Several years ago after a disaster at Gillespie we seen your pictures in the papers going down in the mine to make a personal investigation of the accident. We are giving you a chance to correct the conditions at this time that may cause a much worse disaster. . . . We will appreciate an early personal reply from you, stating your position in regard to the above and the enforcement of the state mining laws.

The letter closed "Very respectfully yours" and was signed by Jake Schmidt, president; Rowekamp, recording secretary; and Thomas Bush and Elmer Moss, mine committee. Today, of these, only Rowekamp is alive; all the others were killed in the disaster they foretold.

And now let us trace the remarkable course of this letter at Springfield. It was stamped in red ink "Received March 9, 1946, Governor's Office." In his ornate thick-carpeted offices, Governor Green has three male secretaries (each of whom in turn has a secretary) and it was one of these, John William Chapman, that the "save our lives" letter, as it came to be called, was routed. Two days later Chapman dictated a memorandum to Medill: ". . . it is my opinion that the Governor may be subjected to very severe criticism in the event that the facts complained of are true and that as a result of this condition some serious accident occurs at the mine. Will you kindly have this complaint carefully investigated so I can call the report of the investigation to the Governor's attention at the same time I show him this letter?" Chapman fastened this small yellow memo to the miners' letter and sent both to Medill. Although Medill's office is only about sixty yards from the Governor's, the message consumed two days in traversing the distance.

The messenger arrived at the Department of Mines and Minerals at 9:00 a.m. on March 13 and handed the "save our lives" letter and Chapman's

memorandum to Medill's secretary. She duly stamped both "Received" and handed them to Medill. He and Weir discussed the matter, then Medill sent the original letter back to the Governor's office and dictated his reply to Chapman, blaming the war, recounting the activities of the special commission, saying: "The complaint sounds a good deal worse than it really is. The present condition at the mine is not any different than it has been during the past ten or fifteen years. . . . I would suggest the Governor advise Local Union No. 52, U. M. W. of A., that he is calling the matter to the attention of the State Mining Board with instructions that it be given full and complete consideration at their next meeting."

This apparently satisfied Chapman for, in the Governor's name, he dictated a letter to Rowekamp and Schmidt: "I [i.e., Governor Green] am calling your letter to the attention of the Director of the Department of Mines and Minerals with the request that he see that your complaint is taken up at the next meeting of the State Mining Board. . . ." This was signed with Governor Green's name but it is probable that Green himself never saw the "save our lives" letter until after the disaster more than a year later. Nor is there any evidence that the Mining Board ever considered the letter. In fact, nothing further came of it.

One of the most remarkable aspects of the whole affair was this: An aggrieved party (the miners) accused a second party (Medill's department) of acting wrongfully, and the higher authority to which it addressed its grievance simply, in effect, asked the accused if he were guilty and, when he replied he was not, dropped the matter. A logic, the logic of the administrative mind, attaches to Chapman's sending the complaint to the Department—the administrative mind has a pigeonhole for everything, matters which relate to law go to the Attorney General, matters which relate to mines go to the Department of Mines and Minerals, and that is that—but it is scarcely a useful logic when one of the agencies is itself accused of malfunction. Apparently it did not occur to Chapman to consult Inspector Scanlan or to make any other independent investigation.

And Jack Ripon, Spud White's second-in-command at the District UMWA, said recently, "If I get a letter here I turn it over to the department that's supposed to take care of it, and the same with Governor Green—he got some damn bad publicity he shouldn't have had, he can't know everything that's going on." Ripon's sympathy with Green is understandable—he must have known how Green felt, for he and Spud White received a copy of the same letter. Ripon says, "Oh, we got a copy of it. But it wasn't none of ours, it didn't tell us to do anything. So our hands was tied. What'd we do with it? I think we gave it to Reak." Perhaps Murrell Reak, the UMWA's man on the Mining Board, felt he already had dealt with this matter (it was Reak who, to Scanlan's astonishment, had joined the other members of the special commission in upholding the Superintendent and Mine Manager in their violations of the law and then had been so anxious to help White convince the members of Local 52 "that their charges are unfounded"). At any rate, Reak apparently did not call the Board's attention to the "save our lives" letter, even though it was a local of his own union which felt itself aggrieved. And White took no action either.

As for Medill, on the day he received the letter he called Scanlan to Springfield and, says Scanlan, "severely reprimanded" him. According to Scanlan, Medill "ordered me to cut down the size of my inspection report," because Medill thought that such long reports might alarm the miners, "those damn hunks" who couldn't read English (Medill denied the phrase); but Scanlan took this order to mean that Medill wanted him to "go easy" on the operators— "it is the same thing as ordering you to pass up certain things." And one day during this long controversy, Medill buttonholed Scanlan's political sponsor in a corridor of the Statehouse and said he intended to fire Scanlan; Scanlan's sponsor refused to sanction it and but for this, Scanlan was convinced, he would surely have lost his job.

But now hundreds of miles away larger events were occurring which were to affect the fate of the miners at Centralia. In Washington, D.C., John L. Lewis and the nation's bituminous coal operators failed to reach an agreement and the miners struck, and on May 21, 1946, President Truman ordered the mines seized for government operation. Eight days later Lewis and Julius A. Krug, Secretary of the Interior, signed the famous Krug-Lewis Agreement. Despite strenuous protests by the operators, this agreement included a federal safety code. It was drawn up by the Bureau of Mines (a part of the U.S. Department of the Interior). And now for the first time in history the federal government could exercise police power over coal mine safety.

Thus far the efforts of the miners of Local 52 to thread the administrative maze in their own state had produced nothing but a snowfall of memoranda, reports, letters, and special findings. Let us now observe this new federal machinery in action. We shall learn nothing about how to prevent a disaster but we may learn a good deal about the administrative process.

"Government operation of the mines" meant simply that the operators bossed their own mines for their own profit as usual but the UMWA had a work contract with the government, not the operators. To keep the 2,500 mines running, Secretary Krug created a new agency, the Coal Mines Administration. CMA was staffed with only 245 persons, nearly all naval personnel ignorant of coal mining. Theirs was paper work. For technical advice they relied upon the Bureau of Mines plus a handful of outside experts. More than two months passed before the code was put into effect, on July 29, 1946, and not until November 4 did Federal Inspector Perz reach Centralia to make his first enforceable inspection of Centralia No. 5. Observe, now, the results.

After three days at the mine, Perz went home and wrote out a "preliminary report" on a mimeographed form, listing 13 "major violations" of the safety code. He mailed this to the regional office of the Bureau of Mines at Vincennes, Indiana. There it was corrected for grammar, spelling, etc., and typed; copies then were mailed out to the Superintendent of the mine (to be posted on the bulletin board), the CMA in Washington, the CMA's regional office at Chicago, the District 12 office of the UMWA at Springfield, the UMWA international headquarters at Washington, the Bureau of Mines in Washington, and the Illinois Department at Springfield. While all this was going on, Perz was at home, preparing his final report, a lengthy document listing 57 violations of the safety code, 21 of them major and 36 minor. This handwritten final report likewise went to the Bureau at Vincennes where it was corrected, typed, and forwarded to the Bureau's office in College Park, Maryland. Here the report was "reviewed," then sent to the Director of the Bureau at Washington. He made any changes he deemed necessary, approved it, and ordered it processed. Copies were then distributed to the same seven places that had received the preliminary report, except that the UMWA at Springfield received two copies so that it could forward one to Local 52. (All this was so complicated that the Bureau devised a "flow sheet" to keep track of the report's passage from hand to hand.)

We must not lose sight of the fact that in the end everybody involved was apprised of Perz's findings: that the Centralia Company was violating the safety code and that hazards resulted. The company, the state, and the union had known this all along and done nothing, but what action now did the new enforcing agency take, the CMA?

Naval Captain N. H. Collison, the Coal Mines Administrator, said that the copy of the inspector's preliminary report was received at his office in Washington "by the head of the Production and Operations Department of my headquarters staff . . . Lieutenant Commander Stull. . . . Lieutenant Commander Stull would review such a report, discuss the matter with the Bureau of Mines as to the importance of the findings, and then . . . await the final report"— unless the preliminary report showed that "imminent danger" existed, in which case he would go immediately to Captain Collison and, presumably, take "immediate action." And during all this activity in Washington, out in Chicago at the CMA's area office a Captain Yates also "would receive a copy of the report. His duty would be to acquaint himself with the findings there. If there was a red check mark indicating it fell within one of the three categories which I shall discuss later, he would detail a man immediately to the mine. If it indicated imminent danger . . . he would move immediately." The three categories deemed sufficiently important to be marked with "a red check mark" were all major hazards but the one which killed 111 men at Centralia No. 5 was not among them.

These, of course, were only CMA's first moves as it bestirred itself. But to encompass all its procedures is almost beyond the mind of man. Let us skip a few and see what actually resulted. The CMA in Washington received Perz's preliminary report November 14. Eleven days later it wrote to the company ordering it to correct one of the 13 major violations Perz found (why it said nothing about the others is not clear). On November 26 the CMA received Perz's final report and on November 29 it again wrote to the company, ordering it to correct

promptly all violations and sending copies of the directive to the Bureau of Mines and the UMWA. Almost simultaneously it received from Superintendent Niermann a reply to its first order (Niermann had replaced Prudent, who had left the company's employ): "Dear Sir: In answer to your CMA8-gz of November 25, 1946, work has been started to correct the violation of article 5, section 3c, of the Federal Mine Safety Code, but has been discontinued, due to . . . a strike. . . ." This of course did not answer the CMA's second letter ordering correction of all 57 violations, nor was any answer forthcoming, but not until two months later, on January 29, 1947, did the CMA repeat its order and tell the company to report its progress by February 14.

This brought a reply from the company official who had been designated "operating manager" during the period of government operation, H. F. McDonald. McDonald, whose office was in Chicago, had risen to the presidency of the Centralia Coal Company and of the Bell & Zoller Coal Company through the sales department; after the Centralia disaster he told a reporter, "Hell, I don't know anything about a coal mine." Now he reported to CMA that "a substantial number of reported violations have been corrected and others are receiving our attention and should be corrected as materials and manpower become available." For obvious reasons, CMA considered this reply inadequate and on February 21 told McDonald to supply detailed information. Three days later McDonald replied ("Re file CMA81-swr"): He submitted a detailed report—he got it from Vice-President Young, who got it from the new General Superintendent, Walter J. Johnson—but McDonald told the CMA that this report was a couple of weeks old and he promised to furnish further details as soon as he could get them. The CMA on March 7 acknowledged this promise but before any other correspondence arrived to enrich file CMA81-swr, the mine blew up.

Now, the Krug-Lewis Agreement set up two methods of circumventing this cumbersome administrative machinery. If Inspector Perz had found what the legalese of the Agreement called "imminent danger," he could have ordered the men removed from the mine immediately (this power was weakened since it was also vested in the Coal Mines Administrator, the same division of authority that hobbled the state enforcers). But Perz did not report "imminent danger." And indeed how could he? The same hazardous conditions had obtained for perhaps twenty years and the mine hadn't blown up. The phrase is stultifying.

In addition, the Krug-Lewis Agreement provided for a safety committee of miners, selected by each local union and empowered to inspect the mine, to make safety recommendations to the management, and, again in case of "an immediate danger," to order the men out of the mine (subject to CMA review). But at Centralia No. 5 several months elapsed before Local 52 so much as appointed a safety committee, and even after the disaster the only surviving member of the committee didn't know what his powers were. The UMWA District officers at Springfield had failed to instruct their Locals in the rights which had been won for them. And confusion was compounded because two separate sets of safety rules were in use—the federal and the state—and in some instances one was the more stringent, in other instances, the other.

Meanwhile another faraway event laid another burden upon the men in the mine. John L. Lewis' combat with Secretary Krug. It ended, as everyone knows, in a federal injunction sought at President Truman's order and upheld by the U.S. Supreme Court, which forbade Lewis to order his miners to strike while the government was operating the mines. (Subsequently Lewis and the UMWA were fined heavily.) The members of Local 52 thought, correctly or not, that the injunction deprived them of their last weapon in their fight to get the mine cleaned up—a wildcat strike. A leader of Local 52 has said, "Sure we could've wildcatted it—and we'd have had the Supreme Court and the government and the whole public down on our necks."

The miners tried the state once more: Medill received a letter December 10, 1946, from an individual miner who charged that the company's mine examiner (a safety man) was not doing what the law required. Earlier Medill had ignored Scanlan's complaint about this but now he sent a department investigator, who reported that the charges were true and that Mine Manager Brown knew it, that Superintendent Niermann promised to consult Vice-President Young in Chicago, that other hazards existed, including dust. Weir wrote a routine letter and this time Niermann replied: The examiner would do his job properly. He said nothing about dust. This let-

ter and one other about the same time, plus Young's earlier equivocal response to Medill's direct appeal, are the only company compliance letters on record.

There was yet time for the miners to make one more try. On February 24, 1947, the safety committee, composed of three miners, wrote a short letter to the Chicago area office of the Coal Mines Administration: "The biggest grievance is dust. . . ." It was written in longhand by Paul Compers (or so it is believed: Compers and one of the two other committee members were killed in the disaster a month later) and Compers handed it to Mine Manager Brown on February 27. But Brown did not forward it to the CMA; in fact he did nothing at all about it.

And now almost at the last moment, only six days before the mine blew up, some wholly new facts transpired. Throughout this whole history one thing has seemed inexplicable: the weakness of the pressure put on the company by Medill's Department of Mines and Minerals. On March 19, 1947, the St. Louis *Post-Dispatch* broke a story that seemed to throw some light upon it. An Illinois coal operator had been told by the state inspector who inspected his mine that Medill had instructed him to solicit money for the Republican Chicago mayoralty campaign. And soon more facts became known about this political shakedown.

Governor Dwight H. Green, a handsome, likeable politician, had first made his reputation as the young man who prosecuted Al Capone. By 1940 he looked like the white hope of Illinois Republicans. Campaigning for the governorship, Green promised to rid the state of the Democratic machine ("there will never be a Green machine"). He polled more votes in Illinois than Roosevelt; national Republican leaders began to watch him. Forthwith he set about building one of the most formidable machines in the nation. This task, together with the concomitant plans of Colonel Robert R. McCormick of the Chicago *Tribune* and others to make him President or Vice-President, has kept him occupied ever since. He has governed but little, permitting subordinates to run things. Reelected in 1944, he reached the peak of his power in 1946 when his machine succeeded in reducing the control of the Democratic machine over Chicago. Jubilant, Governor Green handpicked a ward leader to run for mayor in April of 1947 and backed him hard.

And it was only natural that Green's henchmen

helped. Among these was Medill. "Somebody," says Medill, told him he was expected to raise "$15,000 or $20,000." On January 31, 1947, he called all his mine inspectors to the state mine rescue station in Springfield (at state expense), and told them—according to Inspector Scanlan who was present—that the money must be raised among the coal operators "and that he had called up four operators the previous day and two of them had already come through with a thousand dollars . . . and that he was going to contact the major companies, and we was to contact the independent companies and the small companies." Medill's version varied slightly: he said he told the inspectors that, as a republican, he was interested in defeating the Democrats in Washington and Chicago, that if they found anybody of like mind it would be all right to tell them where to send their money, that all contributions must be voluntary.

After the meeting Scanlan felt like resigning but he thought perhaps Governor Green did not know about the plan and he recalled that once he had received a letter from Green (as did all state employees) asking his aid in giving the people an honest administration: Scanlan had replied to the Governor "that I had always been opposed to corrupt, grafting politicians and that I wasn't going to be one myself; and I received a nice acknowledgement . . . the Governor . . . told me that it was such letters as mine that gave him courage to carry on. . . ." Scanlan solicited no contributions from the coal operators.

But other inspectors did, and so did a party leader in Chicago. So did Medill: he says that his old friend David H. Devonald, operating vice-president of the huge Peabody Coal Company, gave him $1,000 and John E. Jones, a leading safety engineer, contributed $50 (Jones works for another of the Big Six operators and of him more later). No accounting ever has been made of the total collected. The shakedown did not last long. According to Medill, another of Governor Green's "close advisers" told Medill that the coal operators were complaining that he and his inspectors were putting pressure on them for donations and if so he'd better stop it. He did, at another conference of the inspectors on March 7.

Since no Illinois law forbids a company or an individual to contribute secretly to a political campaign, we are dealing with a question of political morality, not legality. The Department of Mines and Minerals long has been a political agency. An inspector is a political appointee and during campaigns he is expected to contribute personally, tack up candidates' posters, and haul voters to the polls. Should he refuse, his local political boss would have him fired. (Soliciting money from the coal operators, however, apparently was something new for inspectors.) Today sympathetic Springfield politicians say: "Medill was just doing what every other department was doing and always has done, but he got a tough break." But one must point out that Medill's inspectors were charged with safeguarding lives, a more serious duty than that of most state employees, and that in order to perform this duty they had to police the coal operators, and that it was from these very operators that Medill suggested they might obtain money. A United States Senator who investigated the affair termed it "reprehensible."

What bearing, now, did this have on the Centralia disaster? Nobody, probably, collected from the Centralia Coal Company. But the shakedown is one more proof—stronger than most—that Governor Green's department had reason to stay on friendly terms with the coal operators when, as their policemen, it should have been aloof. As a miner at Centralia said recently: "If a coal company gives you a thousand dollars, they're gonna expect something in return."

Here lies Green's responsibility—not that, through a secretary's fumble, he failed to act on the miners' appeal to "save our lives" but rather that, while the kingmakers were shunting him around the nation making speeches, back home his loyal followers were busier building a rich political machine for him than in administering the state for him. Moreover, enriching the Green machine dovetailed nicely with the personal ambitions of Medill and others, and Green did not restrain them. By getting along with his old friends, the wealthy operators, Medill enhanced his personal standing. Evidence exists that Bell & Zoller had had a hand in getting him appointed Director, and remember, Weir had worked as a Bell & Zoller boss. By nature Medill was no zealous enforcer of laws. As for the inspectors, few of them went out of their way to look for trouble; some inspectors after leaving the Department have obtained good jobs as coal company executives. Anyway, as one inspector has said, "If you tried to ride 'em, they'd laugh at you and say, 'Go ahead, I'll just call up Springfield.' " As one man has said, "It was a cozy combination that worked for everybody's benefit, everybody except the miners." And the miners' man on the Board, Murrell Reak of the UMWA, did not oppose the combination. Nor did Green question it.

As the Chicago campaign ground to a close, down at Centralia on March 18 Federal Inspector Perz was making another routine inspection. General Superintendent Johnson told him the company had ordered pipe for a sprinkler system months earlier but it hadn't arrived, "that there would be a large expenditure involved there . . . they had no definite arrangements just yet . . . but he would take it up with the higher officials of the company" in Chicago. Scanlan and Superintendent Niermann were there too; they stayed in the bare little mine office, with its rickety furniture and torn window shades, till 7:30 that night. No rock dusting had been done for nearly a year but now the company had a carload of rock dust underground and Scanlan got the impression it would be applied over the next weekend. (It wasn't.) Perz, too, thought Johnson "very conscientious . . . very competent." Scanlan typed out his report—he had resorted wearily to listing a few major recommendations and adding that previous recommendations "should be complied with"—and mailed it to Springfield. Perz went home and wrote out his own report, acknowledging that 17 hazards had been corrected but making 52 recommendations most of which he had made in November (the company and the CMA were still corresponding over that November report). Perz finished writing on Saturday morning and mailed the report to the Vincennes office, which presumably began processing it Monday.

The wheels had been turning at Springfield, too, and on Tuesday, March 25, Weir signed a form letter to Brown setting forth Scanlan's latest recommendations: "The Department endorses. . . ." But that day, at 3:26 p.m., before the outgoing-mail box in the Department was emptied, Centralia Mine No. 5 blew up. . . .

The last of the bodies was recovered at 5:30 a.m. on the fifth day after the explosion. On "Black Monday" the flag on the new city hall flew at half staff and all the businesses in town closed. Already the funerals had begun, 111 of them. John L. Lewis cried that the 111 were "murdered by the criminal negligence" of Secretary Krug and declared a national six-day "mourning period" during this Holy Week, and

though some said he was only achieving by subterfuge what the courts had forbidden him—a strike and defiance of Krug—nonetheless he made the point that in the entire nation only two soft coal mines had been complying with the safety code; and so Krug closed the mines.

Six separate investigations began, two to determine what had happened, and four to find out why. Federal and state experts agreed, in general, that the ignition probably had occurred at the extreme end, or face, of the First West Entry, that it was strictly a coal-dust explosion, that the dust probably was ignited by an explosive charge which had been tamped and fired in a dangerous manner—fired by an openflame fuse, tamped with coal dust—and that the resulting local explosion was propagated by coal dust throughout four working sections of the mine, subsiding when it reached rock-dusted areas. . . .

And what resulted from all the investigations into the Centralia disaster? The Washington County Grand Jury returned no-bills—that is, refused to indict Inspector Scanlan and five company officials ranging upward in authority through Brown, Niermann, Johnson, Young, and McDonald. The Grand Jury did indict the Centralia Coal Company, as a corporation, on two counts of "willful neglect" to comply with the mining law—failing to rock dust and working more than 100 men on a single split of air—and it also indicted Medill and Weir for "palpable omission of duty." The company pleaded nolo contendere—it did not wish to dispute the charge—and was fined the maximum: $300 on each count, a total of $1,000 (or less than $10 per miner's life lost). The law also provides a jail sentence of up to six months but of course you can't put a corporation in jail.

At this writing the indictments against Medill and Weir are still pending, and amid interesting circumstances. Bail for Medill was provided by Charles E. Jones, John W. Spence, G. C. Curtis, and H. B. Thompson; and all of these men, oddly enough, are connected with the oil and gas division of the Department from which Medill was fired. And one of them is also one of Medill's defense attorneys. But this is not all. Medill and Weir filed a petition for a change of venue, supported by numerous affidavits of Washington County residents that prejudice existed. These affidavits were collected by three inspectors for the oil and gas division. They succeeded in getting the trial transferred to Wayne County, which is dominated by a segment of Governor Green's political organization led locally by one of these men, Spence. Not in recent memory in Illinois has the conviction of a Department head on a similar charge been sustained, and there is little reason to suppose that Medill or Weir will be convicted. Medill performed an act of great political loyalty when he shouldered most of the blame at Centralia, in effect stopping the investigation before it reached others above him, and this may be his reward.

Why did nobody close the Centralia mine before it exploded? A difficult question. Medill's position (and some investigators') was that Inspector Scanlan could have closed it. And, legally, this is true: The mining law expressly provided that an inspector could close a mine which persisted in violating the law. But inspectors have done so very rarely, only in exceptional circumstances, and almost always in consultation with the Department. Scanlan felt that had he closed the Centralia mine Medill simply would have fired him and appointed a more tractable inspector. Moreover, the power to close was not his exclusively: it also belonged to the Mining Board. (And is not this divided authority one of the chief factors that produced the disaster?) Robert Weir has said, "We honestly didn't think the mine was dangerous enough to close." This seems fantastic, yet one must credit it. For if Scanlan really had thought so, surely he would have closed it, even though a more pliable inspector reopened it. So would the federal authorities, Medill, or the company itself. And surely the miners would not have gone to work in it.

Governor Green's own fact-finding committee laid blame for the disaster upon the Department, Scanlan, and the company. The Democrats in the Illinois joint legislative committee submitted a minority report blaming the company, Medill, Weir, and Green's administration for "the industrial and political crime . . ."; the Republican majority confessed itself unable to fix blame. After a tremendous pulling and hauling by every special interest, some new state legislation was passed as a result of the accident, but nothing to put teeth into the laws: violations still are misdemeanors (except campaign solicitation by inspectors, a felony); it is scarcely a serious blow to a million-dollar corporation to be fined $1,000. Nor does the law yet charge specific officers of the companies—rather than the abstract corporations—with legal responsibility, so it is still easy for a company official to hide behind a nebulous chain of command reaching up to the stratosphere of corporate finance in Chicago or St. Louis. It is hard to believe that compliance with any law can be enforced unless violators can be jailed.

As for the Congress of the United States, it did next to nothing. The Senate subcommittee recommended that Congress raise safety standards and give the federal government power to enforce that standard—"Immediate and affirmative action is imperative." But Congress only ordered the Bureau of Mines to report next session on whether mine operators were complying voluntarily with federal inspectors' recommendations. . . .

After the Centralia disaster each man responsible had his private hell, and to escape it each found his private scapegoat—the wartime manpower shortage, the material shortage, another official, the miners, or, in the most pitiable cases, "human frailty." Surely a strange destiny took Dwight Green from a federal courtroom where, a young crusader, he overthrew Capone to a hotel in Centralia where, fifteen years older, he came face to face with William Rowekamp, who wanted to know why Green had done nothing about the miners' plea to "save our lives." But actually responsibility here transcends individuals. The miners at Centralia, seeking somebody who would heed their conviction that their lives were in danger, found themselves confronted with officialdom, a huge organism scarcely mortal. The State Inspector, the Federal Inspector, the State Board, the Federal CMA, the company officials—all these forever invoked "higher authority," they forever passed from hand to hand a stream of memoranda and letters, decisions and laws and rulings, and they lost their own identities. As one strives to fix responsibility for the disaster, again and again one is confronted, as were the miners, not with any individual but with a host of individuals fused into a vast, unapproachable, insensate organism. Perhaps this immovable juggernaut is the true villain in the piece. Certainly all those in authority were too remote from the persons whose lives they controlled. And this is only to confess once more that in making our society complex we have made it unmanageable.

Epilogue*

Illinois Governor Dwight Green was ruined politically by the Centralia disaster. He had been mentioned as a possible Republican vice-presidential candidate in 1948 and had all the makings of a successful national political figure, but in 1948 he even lost his bid for reelection to the governorship. One of the issues that his opponent, Adlai Stevenson, raised during the campaign was mine safety. Governor Stevenson eventually became a national political figure, running twice—unsuccessfully—for U.S. president in 1952 and 1956.

Robert M. Medill, director of the Illinois Bureau of Mines and Minerals, was asked to resign his post and did so, April 1, 1947. His assistant, Robert Weir, though indicted, remained in his post until his retirement.

The mine owners, Bell and Zoller Coal Company, paid the fine of $1000, but none of the company's officers were indicted or imprisoned.

Despite the six separate investigations of the disaster that were undertaken by various state and federal authorities, neither the state of Illinois nor the federal government changed its mine safety laws or enforcement policies. Only after the 1952 West Frankfurt, Kentucky, coal mine disaster was a stricter federal mine safety code enacted and enforcement procedures improved.

The Centralia blast created 99 widows and 76 fatherless children under the age of 18, which prompted the United Mine Workers Union to change its welfare death benefits from lump sum payouts to monthly stipends. The union used the disaster to press for higher wages and benefits for miners elsewhere.

The Centralia Mine was sold to the Peabody Coal Company and reopened on July 21, 1947, with sixty miners, including many of the survivors, but was closed in two years due to the high costs of production. The mine was abandoned and sealed with concrete. In 1980 a solid waste disposal company bought the property, bulldozed the remaining buildings and plans someday to grind up solid waste and deposit it in the mine shafts. Today coal fragments and slate can be found around the grounds, along with foundations of the old mine and rusting equipment overgrown with weeds. In the nearby Centralia Foundation Park and in the Village of Wamac, plaques recently were dedicated to the miners who lost their lives in Centralia.

*Note: Written by Richard Stillman.

Chapter 1 Review Questions

1. How did Woodrow Wilson justify the creation of the new field of public administration? Why does he view public administration as being so critical to the future of the United States? Do you agree? What does Wilson conclude are the best ways to develop this new field? Are these ideas still valid? By contrast, based on your reading of Stillman's essay, how is the field evolving today? Is it evolving along the lines Wilson's essay envisioned?

2. Why does Wilson stress throughout his essay the importance of finding the appropriate relationship between democracy and public administration? What does he mean by that? For example? According to Stillman's essay, how does the field in the 1990s deal with this issue?

3. Did the case, "The Blast in Centralia No. 5," help you to formulate your own view of what the scope and purpose of the field are or should be today? Does the case contradict or support the conclusions about the importance of this field made in the Wilson essay? Or in Stillman's essay?

4. Based on your reading of the case, what do you see as the central causes of the tragedy in "The Blast in Centralia No. 5"? Why did these problems develop?

5. What reforms would you recommend to prevent the tragedy from reoccurring elsewhere? How could such reforms be implemented? Do the 1990s writings offer any solutions according to the Stillman essay?

6. Based on your analysis of "The Blast in Centralia No. 5," can you generalize about the importance of public administration for society? Can you list some of the pros *and* cons of having a strong and effective administrative system to perform essential services in society?

Key Terms

public administration	public opinion
politics-administration dichotomy	civil service
"The Reinventors"	The "VPI Refounders"
"The Communitarians"	The "Tools Approach"
"The Refounding Movement"	"Anti-statism"

Suggestions for Further Reading

The seminal book on the origins and growth of public administration in America remains Dwight Waldo, *The Administrative State: A Study of the Political Theory of American Public Administration* (New York: Ronald Press, 1948), which has been reissued in 1984, with a new preface, by Holmes and Meier Publishers. For other writings by Waldo, see "The Administrative State Revisited," *Public Administration Review,* 25 (March 1965), pp. 5–37, and *The Enterprise of Public Administration: A Summary View* (Navato, Calif.: Chandler and Sharp Publishers, 1980). For a helpful commentary on Waldo's ideas and career, see Brack Brown and Richard J. Stillman II, *A Search for Public Administration* (College Station: Texas A&M University Press, 1986). Also for insightful review of Dwight Waldo's contributions, read Frank Marini, "Leaders in the Field: Dwight Waldo," *Public Administration Review,* 53 (Sept./Oct. 1993), pp. 409–18. For two excellent reassessments of Woodrow Wilson and his influence on the field, read Paul P. Van Riper, ed., *The Wilson Influence on Public Administration: From Theory to Practice* (Washington, D.C.: American Society for Public Administration, 1990); and

Daniel W. Martin, "The Fading Legacy of Woodrow Wilson," *Public Administration Review* (March/April 1988), pp. 631–636.

Much can be learned from the writings of important contributors to the field, like Woodrow Wilson, Frederick Taylor, Luther Gulick, Louis Brownlow, Herbert Simon, and Charles Lindblom. For an excellent collection of many of those classic writings with insightful commentary, see Frederick C. Mosher, ed., *Basic Literature of American Public Administration 1787–1950* (New York: Holmes and Meier, 1981), and for a recent selection of key theorists, read Frederick S. Lane, ed., *Current Issues in Public Administration,* Fifth Edition (New York: St. Martin's Press, 1993). Equally valuable is the four-volume history of public administration prior to 1900 by Leonard D. White: *The Federalists* (1948); *The Jeffersonians* (1951); *The Jacksonians* (1954); and *The Republican Era* (1958), all published by Macmillan. Michael W. Spicer, *The Founders, the Constitution, and Public Administration: A Conflict in World Views* (Washington, D.C.: Georgetown Press, 1995), offers a recent study of the constitutional origins of the field. Some of the important books that document the rise of public administration in the twentieth century are Jane Dahlberg, *The New York Bureau of Municipal Research* (New York: New York University Press, 1966); Robert H. Wiebe, *The Search for Order, 1877–1920* (New York: Hill & Wang, 1967); Don K. Price, *America's Unwritten Constitution* (Baton Rouge, La.: Louisiana State University Press, 1983); John A. Rohr, *To Run a Constitution: The Legitimacy of the Administrative State* (Lawrence: University of Kansas Press, 1986); Barry Karl, *Executive Reorganization and Reform in the New Deal* (Cambridge, Mass.: Harvard University Press, 1963); and Stephen Skowronek, *Building a New American State: The Expansion of National Administrative Capacities, 1877–1920* (New York: Cambridge University Press, 1982). Because Frederick Taylor was so critical to the early development of the field, a noteworthy biography of his life and work is Hindy Lauer Schachter, *Frederick Taylor and the Public Administration Community: A Reevaluation* (Albany, N.Y.: State University of New York Press, 1989). For a broader biographical treatment of the field's major figures, see Brian R. Fry, *Mastering Public Administration: From Max Weber to Dwight Waldo* (Chatham, N.Y.: Chatham House, 1989).

In addition, several other impressive retrospectives on key founders of the field have appeared in recent years: James A. Stever, "Marshall Dimock: An Intellectual Portrait," *Public Administration Review,* 50 (Nov./Dec. 1990), pp. 615–622; Lyle C. Fitch, "Luther Gulick," *Public Administration Review,* 50 (November/December 1990), pp. 604–638; Max O. Stephenson, Jr., and Jeremy F. Plant, "The Legacy of Frederick C. Mosher," *Public Administration Review,* 51 (March/April 1991), pp. 97–113; L. R. Jones, "Aaron Wildavsky: A Man and Scholar for All Seasons," *Public Administration Review,* 55, (January/February 1995), pp. 3–16, as well as the entire issue of the *Public Administration Quarterly* (Fall 1988) devoted to an appraisal of Herbert Simon's work. For excellent insights into Simon's life and work, read his autobiography: Herbert A. Simon, *Models of My Life* (New York: Basic Books, 1991).

The three best journals that cover administrative theory today are the *Public Administration Review, Administrative Theory and Praxis*, and *Administration and Society.*

Numerous shorter interpretative essays on the development of the field include Herbert Kaufman, "Emerging Conflicts in the Doctrines of Public Administration," *American Political Science Review* (December 1956), pp. 1057–1073; David H. Rosenbloom, "Public Administration Theory and the Separation of Powers," *Public Administration Review,* 43 (May/June 1983), pp. 213–227; Luther H. Gulick, "Reflections on Public Administration, Past and Present," *Public Administration Review,* 50 (November/December 1990), pp. 599–603; Gregory A. Daneke, "A Science of Public Administration?" *Public Administration Review,* 50 (May/June 1990), pp. 383–392; Laurence J. O'Toole, Jr., "Harry F. Byrd, Sr. and the New York Bureau of Municipal Research: Lessons from an Ironic Alliance," *Public Administration Review,* 46 (March/April 1986), pp. 113–123; Donald F. Kettl, "The Perils—and Prospects—of Public Administration," *Public Administration Review,* 50 (July/August 1990), pp. 411–419; Richard T. Green, Laurence F. Keller, and Gary L. Wamsley, "Reconstituting a Profession for American Public Administration," *Public Administration Review,* 53 (November/December 1993), pp. 516–524; Lynton K. Caldwell, "Novus Ordo Seclorum: The Heritage of American Public Administration," and Barry Karl, "Public Administration and American History: A Century of Professionalism"—both appeared in *Public Administration Review,* 36 (September/October 1976), pp. 476–505. Several excellent essays are also found in Frederick C. Mosher, ed., *American Public Administration: Past, Present, Future* (University, Ala.: University of Alabama Press, 1975); Ralph Clark Chandler, ed., *A Centennial History of the American Administrative State* (New York: Free Press, 1987); the bicentennial issue of the *Public Administration Review* (January/February 1987), entitled, "The American Constitution and Administrative State," edited by Richard J. Stillman II, as well as Jack Robin and Thomas Vocino, eds., "A Special Issue:

Foundations of Public Administration," *International Journal of Public Administration,* 16, no. 2 (1992), entire issue.

The past decade has witnessed an outpouring of new, rich, and diverse perspectives on what public administration is and ought to be. Among the recent, more challenging points of view, which attempt to "reformulate the basics" of the field, are: James A. Stever, *The End of Public Administration: Problems of the Profession in the Post-Progressive Era* (Ardley-on-the-Hudson, N.Y.: Transnational Publishers, 1988); "Minnowbrook II," by H. George Frederickson and Richard T Mayer, eds., *Public Administration Review* (March/April 1989), entire issue; Naomi B. Lynn and Aaron Wildavsky, eds., *Public Administration: The State of the Discipline* (Chatham, N.J.: Chatham House, 1990); Gary L. Wamsley et al., *Refounding Public Administration* (Newberry Park, Calif.: Sage, 1990); Henry D. Kass and Bayard L. Catron, eds., *Images and Identities in Public Administration* (Newberry Park, Calif.: Sage, 1990); Richard J. Stillman II, *Preface to Public Administration: A Search for Themes and Direction* (New York: St. Martin's Press, 1991); Camilla Stivers, *Gender Images in Public Administration: Legitimacy and the Administrative State* (Newbury Park, Calif.: Sage, 1993); Charles J. Fox and Hugh T. Miller, *Postmodern Public Administration: Toward a Discourse* (Newbury Park, Calif.: Sage, 1995); Jong S. Jun, *Philosophy of Administration* (Seoul, Korea: Daeyoung Moonhwa International, 1994); and Jay D. White and Guy B. Adams, eds., *Research in Public Administration* (Newbury Park, Calif.: Sage, 1994). Also, the entire 50th anniversary issue of the *Public Administration Review* (March/April, 1990) contains several fine reflective essays on the current status of the field. For useful comprehensive guides to public administration literature, see Howard E. McCurdy, *Public Administration: A Bibliographic Guide to the Literature* (New York: Marcel Dekker, 1986); Daniel W. Martin, *The Guide to the Foundations of Public Administration* (New York: Marcel Dekker, 1989); and Donald F. Kettl, "Public Administration," in Ada F. Finifter, ed., *Political Science: The State of the Discipline II* (Washington D.C.: APSA, 1993), pp. 407–430.

PART ONE

The Pattern of Public Administration in America: Its Environment, Structure, and People

Public administrators are surrounded by multiple environments that serve to shape decisively what they do and how well (or how poorly) they do it. Part One discusses the major conceptual ideas about the key environmental factors that profoundly influence the nature, scope, and direction of contemporary public administration. Each reading in Part One outlines one of these important environmental concepts, and each case study illustrates that concept. The significant environmental concepts featured in Part One include:

CHAPTER 2
The Formal Structure: *The Concept of Bureaucracy*
What are the formal elements of the bureaucratic structure that serve as core building blocks in the administrative processes?

CHAPTER 3
The General Environment: *The Concept of Ecology*
How does the general administrative environment significantly influence the formulation, implementation, and outcomes of public programs?

CHAPTER 4
The Political Environment: *The Concept of Administrative Power*   What is the nature of the political landscape in which public agencies operate, and why is administrative power key to their survival, growth, or demise?

CHAPTER 5
Intergovernmental Relations (IGR): *The Concept of IGR as Interdependence, Complexity, and Bargaining*   Why do intergovernmental relationships create complex problems for modern American public administrators? What is the structure of these relationships in the 1990s?

CHAPTER 6
Internal Dynamics: *The Concept of the Informal Group*   How does the internal environment of organizations affect the "outcomes" of the administrative processes? How can administrators assess and cope with "internal groups"?

CHAPTER 7
Key Decision Makers in Public Administration: *The Concept of Competing Bureaucratic Subsystems*
Who are the key decision makers in public agencies today? Why are they so vital to shaping public policy?

CHAPTER 2

The Formal Structure: The Concept of Bureaucracy

*U*nder normal conditions, the power position of a fully developed bureaucracy is always overtowering. The 'political master' finds himself in the position of the 'dilettante' who stands opposite the 'expert.' . . .

Max Weber

▬▬▬ READING 2

Introduction

To most Americans, "bureaucracy" is a fighting word. Few things are more disliked
than bureaucracy, few occupations held in lower esteem than the bureaucrat. Both are
subjected to repeated criticism in the press and damned regularly by political soap box
orators and ordinary citizens. "Inefficiency," "red tape," "stupidity," "secrecy," "smug-
ness," "aggressiveness," and "self-interest" are only a few of the emotionally charged
words used to castigate bureaucrats.

There may be considerable truth to our dim view of bureaucrats. We also may be
justified in venting our spleens occasionally at the irritating aspects of bureaucracy
that arise almost daily—we may even experience a healthy catharsis in the process.
But this understandably testy outlook should not prevent us from grasping the central importance and meaning of this phenomenon of bureaucracy.

From the standpoint of public administration and social science literature in general, "bureaucracy" means much more than the various bothersome characteristics of
modern organizations. The term in serious administrative literature denotes the general, formal structural elements of a type of human organization, particularly a governmental organization. In this sense bureaucracy has both good *and* bad qualities; it
is a neutral term rather than one referring to only the negative traits of organizations.
It is a lens through which we may dispassionately view what Carl Friedrich has appropriately tagged "the core of modern government."

The German social scientist, Max Weber (1864–1920), is generally acknowledged
to have developed the most comprehensive classic formulation of the characteristics
of bureaucracy. Weber not only pioneered ideas about bureaucracy but ranged across
a whole spectrum of historical, political, economic, and social thought. As Reinhard

Bendix observed, Weber was "like a man of the Renaissance who took in all humanity for his province." In his study of Hindu religion, Old Testament theology, ancient Roman land surveying, Junker politics, medieval trading companies, and the Chinese civil service, he sought to analyze objectively the nature of human institutions and to show how ideas are linked with the evolution of political, economic, and social systems. One of his best works, *The Protestant Ethic and the Spirit of Capitalism,* established the critical intellectual ties between the rise of Protestantism and capitalism in the sixteenth and seventeenth centuries. He constantly pressed for answers to enormously complex problems. What is the interplay between ideas and institutions? What distinguishes the Western culture and its ideas? Why has a particular society evolved the way it has?

We cannot summarize here the numerous ideas formulated by Max Weber's fertile mind, but we can examine a few aspects of his thought that bear directly on his conception of bureaucracy. Weber believed that civilization evolved from the primitive and mystical to the rational and complex. He thought that human nature progressed slowly from primitive religions and mythologies to an increasing theoretical and technical sophistication. World evolution was a one-way street in Weber's nineteenth-century view: he visualized a progressive "demystification" of humanity and humanity's ideas about the surrounding environment.

In keeping with his demystification view of progress, Weber describes three "ideal-types" of authority that explain why individuals throughout history have obeyed their rulers. One of the earliest, the "traditional" authority of primitive societies, rested on the established belief in the sanctity of tradition. Because a family of rulers has always ruled, people judge them to be just and right and obey them. Time, precedent, and tradition gave rulers their legitimacy in the eyes of the ruled.

A second ideal-type of authority, according to Weber, is "charismatic" authority, which is based on the personal qualities and the attractiveness of leaders. Charismatic figures are self-appointed leaders who inspire belief because of their extraordinary, almost superhuman, qualifications. Military leaders, warrior chiefs, popular party leaders, and founders of religions are examples of individuals whose heroic feats or miracles attract followers.

Weber postulated a third ideal-type of authority that is the foundation of modern civilizations, namely, "legal-rational" authority. It is based on "a belief in the legitimacy of the pattern of normative rules and the rights of those elevated to authority under such rules to issue commands." Obedience is owed to a legally established, impersonal set of rules, rather than to a personal ruler. Legal-rational authority vests power in the office rather than in the person who occupies the office; thus anyone can rule as long as he or she comes to office "according to the rules."

This third type of authority forms the basis for Weber's concept of bureaucracy. According to Weber, bureaucracy is the normal way that "legal-rational" authority appears in institutional form; it holds a central role in ordering and controlling modern societies. "It is," says Weber, "superior to any other form in precision, in stability, in stringency of its discipline, and in its reliability. It thus makes possible a particularly high degree of calculability of results for the heads of organizations and for those acting in relation to it." It is finally superior in its operational efficiency and "is formally capable of application to all kinds of administrative tasks." For Weber, bureaucracy is indispensable to maintaining civilization in modern society. In his view, "however much people may complain about the evils of bureaucracy it would be sheer illusion to think for a moment that continuous administrative work can be carried out in any field except by means of officials working in offices."

A great deal of Weber's analysis of bureaucracy dealt with its historical development. According to Weber, modern bureaucracy in the Western world arose during the Middle Ages when royal domains grew and required bodies of officials to oversee them. Out of necessity, princes devised rational administrative techniques to extend their authority, frequently borrowing ideas from the church, whose territories at that time encompassed most of Europe. "The proper soil for bureaucratization of administration," writes Weber, "has always been the development of administrative tasks." Bureaucracy grew because society needed to do things—to build roads, to educate students, to collect taxes, to fight battles, and to dispense justice. Work was divided and specialized to achieve the goals of a society.

Weber also identified a monied economy as an important ingredient for the development of bureaucracy. "Bureaucracy as a permanent structure is knit to the presupposition of a constant income for maintenancy. . . . A stable system of taxation is the precondition for the permanent existence of bureaucratic administration." Other cultural factors contributing to the rise of highly structured bureaucracies were the growth of education, the development of higher religions, and the burgeoning of science and rationality.

Weber listed in a detailed fashion the major elements of the formal structure of bureaucracy. Three of the most important attributes in his concept of bureaucracy were the division of labor, hierarchical order, and impersonal rules—keystones to any functioning bureaucracy. The first, specialization of labor, meant that all work in a bureaucracy is rationally divided into units that can be undertaken by an individual or group of individuals competent to perform those tasks. Unlike traditional rulers, workers do not *own* their offices in bureaucracy but enjoy tenure based on their abilities to perform the work assigned. Second, the hierarchical order of bureaucracy separates superiors from subordinates; on the basis of this hierarchy, remuneration for work is dispensed, authority recognized, privileges allotted, and promotions awarded. Finally, impersonal rules form the life-blood of the bureaucratic world. Bureaucrats, according to Weber, are not free to act in any way they please because their choices are confined to prescribed patterns of conduct imposed by legal rules. In contrast to "traditional" or "charismatic" authority, bureaucratic rules provide for the systematic control of subordinates by superiors, thus limiting the opportunities for arbitrariness and personal favoritism.

Weber theorized that the only way for a modern society to operate effectively was by organizing expertly trained, functional specialists in bureaucracies. Although Max Weber saw bureaucracy as permanent and indispensable in the modern world, he was horrified by what he believed was an irreversible trend toward loss of human freedom and dignity:

It is horrible to think that the world could one day be filled with nothing but those little cogs, little men clinging to little jobs and striving towards bigger ones—a state of affairs which is to be seen once more, as in the Egyptian records, playing an ever-increasing part in the spirit of our present administrative system and especially of its offspring, the students. This passion for bureaucracy . . . is enough to drive one to despair.[1]

And although he despaired over the increasing trend toward bureaucratization in the modern world, Weber also observed the leveling or democratizing effect of bureaucracy on society. As Reinhard Bendix wrote of Weber's idea: "The development of bureaucracy does away with . . . plutocratic privileges, replacing unpaid, avocational administration by notables with paid, full-time administration by professionals, regardless of their social and economic position. . . . Authority is exercised in accordance with rules, and everyone subject to that authority is legally equal."[2]

Over the last fifty years, certain elements in Max Weber's conception of bureaucracy have fueled repeated academic debate and scholarly criticism.[3] There are those social scientists who criticize his "ideal-type" formulations as misleading. They contend that it offers neither a desirable state *nor* an empirical reality. Others suggest that he overemphasizes the *formal* elements of bureaucracy—i.e., specialization, hierarchy, rules, division of labor, etc.—and does not appreciate the *informal* dimensions— such as human relationships, leadership, communication networks, etc.—as equally, if not more important, for influencing bureaucratic performance and efficiency. Still others say that Weber neglects the deficiencies of large-scale bureaucracies that can encourage alienation of workers and citizens alike, in contrast to the stimulating creativity that small, fluid networks of specialists can enhance. Some scholars charge Weber's concept as being both time-bound and culture-bound to the late nineteenth and early twentieth century German "scientific" heritage. They say he idealized the German bureaucratic state that dominated that era. This list of social science criticisms could go on, and they are all to some degree telling criticisms.

Nevertheless, the main outline of Weber's classic formulation is generally accepted as true and significant. For students of public administration, his concept forms one of the essential intellectual building blocks in our understanding of the formal institutional structure of public administration.

As you read this selection, keep the following questions in mind:

Where can you see evidence of Weber's concept of bureaucracy within familiar organizations?

In what respects does Weber's characterization of bureaucracy as a theoretical

---

[1] As quoted in Reinhard Bendix, *Max Weber: An Intellectual Portrait* (New York: Doubleday and Co., 1960), p. 464.

[2] Ibid., p. 429.

[3] For an excellent discussion of general academic criticism and revision of Weber's ideas, read either Alfred Diamant, "The Bureaucratic Model: Max Weber Rejected, Rediscovered, Reformed," in Ferrel Heady and Sybil L. Stokes, *Papers in Comparative Public Administration* (Ann Arbor, Mich.: Institute of Public Administration, 1962), or Peter M. Blau and Marshall W. Meyer, *Bureaucracy in Modern Society* (New York: Random House, 1971). For a recent bold and different interpretation of Weber, see the essay on Weber by Robert Leivesley, Adrian Carr, and Alexander Kauzmin, in Ali Farazmand, ed., *Handbook of Bureaucracy* (New York: Marcel Dekker, 1994).

"ideal-type" miss the mark in describing the practical reality? In what respects is it on target?

How is Weber's bureaucratic model relevant to the previous case, "The Blast in Centralia No. 5"? On the basis of that case as well as your own observations, can you describe some positive and negative features of modern bureaucracy?

Bureaucracy[1]

MAX WEBER

1. Characteristics of Bureaucracy

Modern officialdom functions in the following specific manner:

I. There is the principle of fixed and official jurisdictional areas, which are generally ordered by rules, that is, by laws or administrative regulations.

1. The regular activities required for the purposes of the bureaucratically governed structure are distributed in a fixed way as official duties.
2. The authority to give the commands required for the discharge of these duties is distributed in a stable way and is strictly delimited by rules concerning the coercive means, physical, sacerdotal, or otherwise, which may be placed at the disposal of officials.
3. Methodical provision is made for the regular and continuous fulfilment of these duties and for the execution of the corresponding rights; only persons who have the generally regulated qualifications to serve are employed.

In public and lawful government these three elements constitute 'bureaucratic authority.' In private economic domination, they constitute bureaucratic 'management.' Bureaucracy, thus understood, is fully developed in political and ecclesiastical communities only in the modern state, and, in the private economy, only in the most advanced institutions of capitalism. Permanent and public office authority, with fixed jurisdiction, is not the historical rule but rather the exception. This is so even in large political structures such as those of the ancient Orient, the Germanic and Mongolian empires of conquest, or of many feudal structures of state. In all these cases, the ruler executes the most important measures through personal trustees, table-companions, or court-servants. Their commissions and authority are not precisely delimited and are temporarily called into being for each case.

II. The principles of office hierarchy and of levels of graded authority mean a firmly ordered system of super- and subordination in which there is a supervision of the lower offices by the higher ones. Such a system offers the governed the possibility of appealing the decision of a lower office to its higher authority, in a definitely regulated manner. With the full development of the bureaucratic type, the office hierarchy is monocratically organized. The principle of hierarchical office authority is found in all bureaucratic structures: in state and ecclesiastical structures as well as in large party organizations and private enterprises. It does

From Max Weber: Essays in Sociology, translated and edited by H. H. Gerth and C. Wright Mills. Copyright © 1946 by Oxford University Press, Inc. Renewed copyright 1973 by Hans H. Gerth. Reprinted by permission of the publisher.

[1]*Wirtschaft und Gesellschaft,* part III, chap. 6, pp. 650–78.

not matter for the character of bureaucracy whether its authority is called 'private' or 'public.'

When the principle of jurisdictional 'competency' is fully carried through, hierarchical subordination—at least in public office—does not mean that the 'higher' authority is simply authorized to take over the business of the 'lower.' Indeed, the opposite is the rule. Once established and having fulfilled its task, an office tends to continue in existence and be held by another incumbent.

III. The management of the modern office is based upon written documents ('the files'), which are preserved in their original or draught form. There is, therefore, a staff of subaltern officials and scribes of all sorts. The body of officials actively engaged in a 'public' office, along with the respective apparatus of material implements and the files, make up a 'bureau.' In private enterprise, 'the bureau' is often called 'the office.'

In principle, the modern organization of the civil service separates the bureau from the private domicile of the official, and, in general, bureaucracy segregates official activity as something distinct from the sphere of private life. Public monies and equipment are divorced from the private property of the official. This condition is everywhere the product of a long development. Nowadays, it is found in public as well as in private enterprises; in the latter, the principle extends even to the leading entrepreneur. In principle, the executive office is separated from the household, business from private correspondence, and business assets from private fortunes. The more consistently the modern type of business management has been carried through the more are these separations the case. The beginnings of this process are to be found as early as the Middle Ages.

It is the peculiarity of the modern entrepreneur that he conducts himself as the 'first official' of his enterprise, in the very same way in which the ruler of a specifically modern bureaucratic state spoke of himself as 'the first servant' of the state. The idea that the bureau activities of the state are intrinsically different in character from the management of private economic offices is a continental European notion and, by way of contrast, is totally foreign to the American way.

IV. Office management, at least all specialized office management—and such management is distinctly modern—usually presupposes thorough and expert training. This increasingly holds for the modern executive and employee of private enterprises, in the same manner as it holds for the state official.

V. When the office is fully developed, official activity demands the full working capacity of the official, irrespective of the fact that his obligatory time in the bureau may be firmly delimited. In the normal case, this is only the product of a long development, in the public as well as in the private office. Formerly, in all cases, the normal state of affairs was reversed: official business was discharged as a secondary activity.

VI. The management of the office follows general rules, which are more or less stable, more or less exhaustive, and which can be learned. Knowledge of these rules represents a special technical learning which the officials possess. It involves jurisprudence, or administrative or business management.

The reduction of modern office management to rules is deeply embedded in its very nature. The theory of modern public administration, for instance, assumes that the authority to order certain matters by decree—which has been legally granted to public authorities—does not entitle the bureau to regulate the matter by commands given for each case, but only to regulate the matter abstractly. This stands in extreme contrast to the regulation of all relationships through individual privileges and bestowals of favor, which is absolutely dominant in patrimonialism, at least in so far as such relationships are not fixed by sacred tradition.

2. The Position of the Official

All this results in the following for the internal and external position of the official:

I. Office holding is a 'vocation.' This is shown, first, in the requirement of a firmly prescribed course of training, which demands the entire capacity for work for a long period of time, and in the generally prescribed and special examinations which are prerequisites of employment. Furthermore, the position of the official is in the nature of a duty. This determines the internal structure of his relations, in the following manner: Legally and actually, office holding is not considered a source to be exploited for rents or emoluments, as was normally the case during the Middle Ages and frequently up to the threshold of recent times. Nor is office holding considered a usual exchange of services for equivalents, as is the case with free labor contracts. Entrance into an office, including one in the private economy, is considered an acceptance of a specific obligation of faithful management in return for a secure existence. It is decisive for the specific nature of modern loyalty to an office that, in the pure type, it does not establish a relationship to a *person,* like the vassal's or disciple's faith in feudal or in patrimonial relations of authority. Modern loyalty is devoted to impersonal and functional purposes. Behind the functional purposes, of course, 'ideas of culture-values' usually stand. These are *ersatz* for the earthly or supra-mundane personal master: ideas such as 'state,' 'church,' 'community,' 'party,' or 'enterprise' are thought of as being realized in a community; they provide an ideological halo for the master.

The political official—at least in the fully developed modern state—is not considered the personal servant of a ruler. Today, the bishop, the priest, and the preacher are in fact no longer, as in early Christian times, holders of purely personal charisma. The supra-mundane and sacred values which they offer are given to everybody who seems to be worthy of them and who asks for them. In former times, such leaders acted upon the personal command of their master; in principle, they were responsible only to him. Nowadays, in spite of the partial survival of the old theory, such religious leaders are officials in the service of a functional purpose, which in the present-day 'church' has become routinized and, in turn, ideologically hallowed.

II. The personal position of the official is patterned in the following way:

1. Whether he is in a private office or a public bureau, the modern official always strives and usually enjoys a distinct *social esteem* as compared with the governed. His social position is guaranteed by the prescriptive rules of rank order and, for the political official, by special definitions of the criminal code against 'insults of officials' and 'contempt' of state and church authorities.

   The actual social position of the official is normally highest where, as in old civilized countries, the following conditions prevail: a strong demand for administration by trained experts; a strong and stable social differentiation, where the official predominantly derives from socially and economically privileged strata because of the social distribution of power; or where the costliness of the required training and status conventions are binding upon him. The possession of educational certificates—to be discussed elsewhere—are usually linked with qualification for office. Naturally, such certificates or patents enhance the 'status element' in the social position of the official. For the rest this status factor in individual cases is explicitly and impassively acknowledged; for example, in the prescription that the acceptance or rejection of an aspirant to an official career depends upon the consent ('election') of the members of the official body. This is the case in the German army with the officer corps. Similar phenomena, which promote this guild-like closure of officialdom, are typically found in patrimonial and, particularly, in prebendal officialdoms of the past. The desire to resurrect such phenomena in changed forms is by no means infrequent among modern bureaucrats. For instance, they have played a role among the demands of the quite proletarian and expert officials (the *tretyj* element) during the Russian revolution.

   Usually the social esteem of the officials

as such is especially low where the demand for expert administration and the dominance of status conventions are weak. This is especially the case in the United States; it is often the case in new settlements by virtue of their wide fields for profitmaking and the great instability of their social stratification.

2. The pure type of bureaucratic official is *appointed* by a superior authority. An official elected by the governed is not a purely bureaucratic figure. Of course, the formal existence of an election does not by itself mean that no appointment hides behind the election—in the state, especially, appointment by party chiefs. Whether or not this is the case does not depend upon legal statutes but upon the way in which the party mechanism functions. Once firmly organized, the parties can turn a formally free election into the mere acclamation of a candidate designated by the party chief. As a rule, however, a formally free election is turned into a fight, conducted according to definite rules, for votes in favor of one of two designated candidates.

In all circumstances, the designation of officials by means of an election among the governed modifies the strictness of hierarchical subordination. In principle, an official who is so elected has an autonomous position opposite the superordinate official. The elected official does not derive his position 'from above' but 'from below,' or at least not from a superior authority of the official hierarchy but from powerful party men ('bosses'), who also determine his further career. The career of the elected official is not, or at least not primarily, dependent upon his chief in the administration. The official who is not elected but appointed by a chief normally functions more exactly, from a technical point of view, because, all other circumstances being equal, it is more likely that purely functional points of consideration and qualities will determine his selection and career. As laymen, the governed can become acquainted with the extent to which a candidate is expertly qualified for office only in terms of experience, and hence only after his service. Moreover, in every sort of selection of officials by election, parties quite naturally give decisive weight not to expert considerations but to the services a follower renders to the party boss. This holds for all kinds of procurement of officials by elections, for the designation of formally free, elected officials by party bosses when they determine the slate of candidates, or the free appointment by a chief who has himself been elected. The contrast, however, is relative: Substantially similar conditions hold where legitimate monarchs and their subordinates appoint officials, except that the influence of the followings are then less controllable.

Where the demand for administration by trained experts is considerable, and the party followings have to recognize an intellectually developed, educated, and freely moving 'public opinion,' the use of unqualified officials falls back upon the party in power at the next election. Naturally, this is more likely to happen when the officials are appointed by the chief. The demand for a trained administration now exists in the United States, but in the large cities, where immigrant votes are 'corraled,' there is, of course, no educated public opinion. Therefore, popular elections of the administrative chief and also of his subordinate officials usually endanger the expert qualification of the official as well as the precise functioning of the bureaucratic mechanism. It also weakens the dependence of the officials upon the hierarchy. This holds at least for the large administrative bodies that are difficult to supervise. The superior qualification and integrity of federal judges, appointed by the President, as over against elected judges in the United States is well known, although both types of officials have been selected primarily in terms of party considerations. The great changes in American metropolitan administrations demanded by reformers have proceeded essentially from elected mayors working with an apparatus of officials who were appointed by them. These reforms have thus come about in a 'Caesarist' fashion. Viewed technically, as an organized form of authority, the efficiency of 'Caesarism,' which often grows out of democracy, rests in general upon the position of the 'Caesar' as a free trustee of the masses (of the army or of the citizenry), who is unfettered by tradition. The 'Caesar' is thus the unrestrained master of a body of highly qualified military officers and officials whom he selects freely and personally without regard to tradition or to any other considerations. This 'rule of the personal genius,' however, stands in contradiction to the formally 'democratic' principle of a universally elected officialdom.

3. Normally, the position of the official is held for life, at least in public bureaucracies; and this is increasingly the case for all similar structures. As a factual rule, *tenure for life* is presupposed, even where the giving of notice or periodic reappointment occurs. In contrast to the worker in a private enterprise, the official normally holds tenure. Legal or actual life-tenure, however, is not recognized as the official's right to the possession of office, as was the case with many structures of authority in the past. Where legal guarantees against arbitrary dismissal or transfer are developed, they merely serve to guarantee a strictly objective discharge of specific office duties free from all personal considerations. In Germany, this is the case for all juridical and, increasingly, for all administrative officials.

Within the bureaucracy, therefore, the measure of 'independence,' legally guaranteed by tenure, is not always a source of increased status for the official whose position is thus secured. Indeed, often the reverse holds, especially in old cultures and communities that are highly differentiated. In such communities, the stricter the subordination under the arbitrary rule of the master, the more it guarantees the maintenance of the conventional seigneurial style of living for the official. Because of the very absence of these legal guarantees of tenure, the conventional esteem for the official may rise in the same way as, during the Middle Ages, the esteem of the nobility of office rose at the expense of esteem for the freemen, and as the king's judge surpassed that of the people's judge. In Germany, the military officer or the administrative official can be removed from office at any time, or at least far more readily than the 'independent judge,' who never pays with loss of his office for even the grossest offense against the 'code of honor' or against social conventions of the salon. For this very reason, if other things are equal, in the eyes of the master stratum the judge is considered less qualified for social intercourse than are officers and administrative officials, whose greater dependence on the master is a greater guarantee of their conformity with status conventions. Of course, the average official strives for a civil-service law, which would materially secure his old age and provide increased guarantees against his arbitrary removal from office. This striving, however, has its limits. A very strong development of the 'right to the office' naturally makes it more difficult to staff them with regard to technical efficiency, for such a development decreases the career-opportunities of ambitious candidates for office. This makes for the fact that officials, on the whole, do not feel their dependency upon those at the top. This lack of a feeling of dependency, however, rests primarily upon the inclination to depend upon one's equals rather than upon the socially inferior and governed strata. The present conservative movement among the Badenia clergy, occasioned by the anxiety of a presumably threatening separation of church and state, has been expressly determined by the desire not to be turned 'from a master into a servant of the parish.'

4. The official receives the regular *pecuniary* compensation of a normally fixed *salary* and the old age security provided by a pension. The salary is not measured like a wage in

terms of work done, but according to 'status,' that is, according to the kind of function (the 'rank') and, in addition, possibly, according to the length of service. The relatively great security of the official's income, as well as the rewards of social esteem, make the office a sought-after position, especially in countries which no longer provide opportunities for colonial profits. In such countries, this situation permits relatively low salaries for officials.

5. The official is set for a *'career'* within the hierarchical order of the public service. He moves from the lower, less important, and lower paid to the higher positions. The average official naturally desires a mechanical fixing of the conditions of promotion: if not of the offices, at least of the salary levels. He wants these conditions fixed in terms of 'seniority,' or possibly according to grades achieved in a developed system of expert examinations. Here and there, such examinations actually form a character *indelebilis* of the official and have lifelong effects on his career. To this is joined the desire to qualify the right to office and the increasing tendency toward status group closure and economic security. All of this makes for a tendency to consider the offices as 'prebends' of those who are qualified by educational certificates. The necessity of taking general personal and intellectual qualifications into consideration, irrespective of the often subaltern character of the educational certificate, has led to a condition in which the highest political offices, especially the positions of 'ministers,' are principally filled without reference to such certificates. . . . [pp. 202–204]

6. Technical Advantages of Bureaucratic Organization

The decisive reason for the advance of bureaucratic organization has always been its purely technical superiority over any other form of organization. The fully developed bureaucratic mechanism compares with other organizations exactly as does the machine with the nonmechanical modes of production.

Precision, speed, unambiguity, knowledge of the files, continuity, discretion, unity, strict subordination, reduction of friction and of material and personal costs—these are raised to the optimum point in the strictly bureaucratic administration, and especially in its monocratic form. As compared with all collegiate, honorific, and avocational forms of administration, trained bureaucracy is superior on all these points. And as far as complicated tasks are concerned, paid bureaucratic work is not only more precise but, in the last analysis, it is often cheaper than even formally unremunerated honorific service.

Honorific arrangements make administrative work an avocation and, for this reason alone, honorific service normally functions more slowly; being less bound to schemata and being more formless. Hence it is less precise and less unified than bureaucratic work because it is less dependent upon superiors and because the establishment and exploitation of the apparatus of subordinate officials and filing services are almost unavoidably less economical. Honorific service is less continuous than bureaucratic and frequently quite expensive. This is especially the case if one thinks not only of the money costs to the public treasury—costs which bureaucratic administration, in comparison with administration by notables, usually substantially increases—but also of the frequent economic losses of the governed caused by delays and lack of precision. The possibility of administration by notables normally and permanently exists only where official management can be satisfactorily discharged as an avocation. With the qualitative increase of tasks the administration has to face, administration by notables reaches its limits—today, even in England. Work organized by collegiate bodies causes friction and delay and requires compromises between colliding interests and views. The administration, therefore, runs less precisely and is more independent of superiors; hence, it is less unified and slower. All advances of the Prussian administrative organization have been and will in the future be advances of the bureaucratic, and especially of the monocratic, principle.

Today, it is primarily the capitalist market economy which demands that the official business of the administration be discharged precisely, unambiguously, continuously, and with as much speed as possible. Normally, the very large, modern capitalist enterprises are themselves unequalled models of strict bureaucratic organization. Business management throughout rests on increasing precision, steadiness, and, above all, the speed of operations. This, in turn, is determined by the peculiar nature of the modern means of communication, including, among other things, the news service of the press. The extraordinary increase in the speed by which public announcements, as well as economic and political facts, are transmitted exerts a steady and sharp pressure in the direction of speeding up the tempo of administrative reaction towards various situations. The optimum of such reaction time is normally attained only by a strictly bureaucratic organization.*

Bureaucratization offers above all the optimum possibility for carrying through the principle of specializing administrative functions according to purely objective considerations. Individual performances are allocated to functionaries who have specialized training and who by constant practice learn more and more. The 'objective' discharge of business primarily means a discharge of business according to *calculable rules* and 'without regard for persons.'

'Without regard for persons' is also the watchword of the 'market' and, in general, of all pursuits of naked economic interests. A consistent execution of bureaucratic domination means the leveling of status 'honor.' Hence, if the principle of the free-market is not at the same time restricted, it means the universal domination of the 'class situation.' That this consequence of bureaucratic domination has not set in everywhere, parallel to the extent of bureaucratization, is due to the differences among possible principles by which polities may meet their demands.

The second element mentioned, 'calculable rules,' also is of paramount importance for modern bureaucracy. The peculiarity of modern culture, and specifically of its technical and economic basis, demands this very 'calculability' of results. When fully developed, bureaucracy also stands, in a specific sense, under the principle of *sine ira ac studio*. Its specific nature, which is welcomed by capitalism, develops the more perfectly the more the bureaucracy is 'dehumanized,' the more completely it succeeds in eliminating from official business love, hatred, and all purely personal, irrational, and emotional elements which escape calculation. This is the specific nature of bureaucracy and it is appraised as its special virtue.

The more complicated and specialized modern culture becomes, the more its external supporting apparatus demands the personally detached and strictly 'objective' *expert,* in lieu of the master of older social structures, who was moved by personal sympathy and favor, by grace and gratitude. Bureaucracy offers the attitudes demanded by the external apparatus of modern culture in the most favorable combination. As a rule, only bureaucracy has established the foundation for the administration of a rational law conceptually systematized on the basis of such enactments as the latter Roman imperial period first created with a high degree of technical perfection. During the Middle Ages, this law was received along with the bureaucratization of legal administration, that is to say, with the displacement of the old trial procedure which was bound to tradition or to irrational presuppositions, by the rationally trained and specialized expert. . . . [pp. 214–216]

10. The Permanent Character of the Bureaucratic Machine

Once it is fully established, bureaucracy is among those social structures which are the hardest to destroy. Bureaucracy is *the* means of carrying 'community action' over into rationally ordered

---

*Here we cannot discuss in detail how the bureaucratic apparatus may, and actually does, produce definite obstacles to the discharge of business in a manner suitable for the single case.

'societal action.' Therefore, as an instrument for 'societalizing' relations of power, bureaucracy has been and is a power instrument of the first order—for the one who controls the bureaucratic apparatus.

Under otherwise equal conditions, a 'societal action,' which is methodically ordered and led, is superior to every resistance of 'mass' or even of 'communal action.' And where the bureaucratization of administration has been completely carried through, a form of power relation is established that is practically unshatterable.

The individual bureaucrat cannot squirm out of the apparatus in which he is harnessed. In contrast to the honorific or avocational 'notable,' the professional bureaucrat is chained to his activity by his entire material and ideal existence. In the great majority of cases, he is only a single cog in an ever-moving mechanism which prescribes to him an essentially fixed route of march. The official is entrusted with specialized tasks and normally the mechanism cannot be put into motion or arrested by him, but only from the very top. The individual bureaucrat is thus forged to the community of all the functionaries who are integrated into the mechanism. They have a common interest in seeing that the mechanism continues its functions and that the societally exercised authority carries on.

The ruled, for their part, cannot dispense with or replace the bureaucratic apparatus of authority once it exists. For this bureaucracy rests upon expert training, a functional specialization of work, and an attitude set for habitual and virtuoso-like mastery of single yet methodically integrated functions. If the official stops working, or if his work is forcefully interrupted, chaos results, and it is difficult to improvise replacements from among the governed who are fit to master such chaos. This holds for public administration as well as for private economic management. More and more the material fate of the masses depends upon the steady and correct functioning of the increasingly bureaucratic organizations of private capitalism. The idea of eliminating these organizations becomes more and more utopian.

The discipline of officialdom refers to the attitude-set of the official for precise obedience within his *habitual* activity, in public as well as in private organizations. This discipline increasingly becomes the basis of all order, however great the practical importance of administration on the basis of the filed documents may be. The naive idea of Bakuninism of destroying the basis of 'acquired rights' and 'domination' by destroying public documents overlooks the settled orientation of *man* for keeping to the habitual rules and regulations that continue to exist independently of the documents. Every reorganization of beaten or dissolved troops, as well as the restoration of administrative orders destroyed by revolt, panic, or other catastrophes, is realized by appealing to the trained orientation of obedient compliance to such orders. Such compliance has been conditioned into the officials, on the one hand, and, on the other hand, into the governed. If such an appeal is successful it brings, as it were, the disturbed mechanism into gear again.

The objective indispensability of the once-existing apparatus, with its peculiar, 'impersonal' character, means that the mechanism—in contrast to feudal orders based upon personal piety—is easily made to work for anybody who knows how to gain control over it. A rationally ordered system of officials continues to function smoothly after the enemy has occupied the area; he merely needs to change the top officials. This body of officials continues to operate because it is to the vital interest of everyone concerned, including above all the enemy.

During the course of his long years in power, Bismarck brought his ministerial colleagues into unconditional bureaucratic dependence by eliminating all independent statesmen. Upon his retirement, he saw to his surprise that they continued to manage their offices unconcerned and undismayed, as if he had not been the master mind and creator of these creatures, but rather as if some single figure had been exchanged for some other figure in the bureaucratic machine. With all the changes of masters in France since the time of the First Empire, the power machine has remained essentially the same. Such a machine makes 'revolution,' in the sense of the forceful creation of entirely new formations of authority, technically more and more impossible, especially when the apparatus controls the modern means of communication (telegraph, et cetera) and also by virtue of its internal rationalized structure. In classic fashion, France has demonstrated how this process has substituted *coups d'état* for 'revolutions': all successful transformations in France have amounted to *coups d'état*.

11. Economic and Social Consequences of Bureaucracy

It is clear that the bureaucratic organization of a social structure, and especially of a political one, can and regularly does have far-reaching economic consequences. But what sort of consequences? Of course in any individual case it depends upon the distribution of economic and social power, and especially upon the sphere that is occupied by the emerging bureaucratic mechanism. The consequences of bureaucracy depend therefore upon the direction which the powers using the apparatus give to it. And very frequently a crypto-plutocratic distribution of power has been the result.

In England, but especially in the United States, party donors regularly stand behind the bureaucratic party organizations. They have financed these parties and have been able to influence them to a large extent. The breweries in England, the so-called 'heavy industry,' and in Germany the Hansa League with their voting funds are well enough known as political donors to parties. In modern times bureaucratization and social leveling within political, and particularly within state organizations in connection with the destruction of feudal and local privileges, have very frequently benefited the interests of capitalism. Often bureaucratization has been carried out in direct alliance with capitalist interests, for example, the great historical alliance of the power of the absolute prince with capitalist interests. In general, a legal leveling and destruction of firmly established local structures ruled by notables has usually made for a wider range of capitalist activity. Yet one may expect as an effect of bureaucratization, a policy that meets the petty bourgeois interest in a secured traditional 'subsistence,' or even a state socialist policy that strangles opportunities for private profit. This has occurred in several cases of historical and far-reaching importance, specifically during antiquity; it is undoubtedly to be expected as a future development. Perhaps it will occur in Germany.

The very different effects of political organizations which were, at least in principle, quite similar—in Egypt under the Pharaohs and in Hellenic and Roman times—show the very different economic significances of bureaucratization which are possible according to the direction of other factors. The mere fact of bureaucratic organization does not unambiguously tell us about the concrete direction of its economic effects, which are always in some manner present. At least it does not tell us as much as can be told about its relatively leveling effect socially. In this respect, one has to remember that bureaucracy as such is a precision instrument which can put itself at the disposal of quite varied—purely political as well as purely economic, or any other sort—of interests in domination. Therefore, the measure of its parallelism with democratization must not be exaggerated, however typical it may be. Under certain conditions, strata of feudal lords have also put bureaucracy into their service. There is also the possibility—and often it has become a fact, for instance, in the Roman principate and in some forms of absolutist state structures—that a bureaucratization of administration is deliberately connected with the formation of *estates*, or is entangled with them by the force of the existing groupings of social power. The express reservation of offices for certain status groups is very frequent, and actual reservations are even more frequent. The democratization of society in its totality, and in the *modern* sense of the term, whether actual or perhaps merely formal, is an especially favorable basis of bureaucratization, but by no means the only possible one. After all, bureaucracy strives merely to level those powers that stand in its way and in those areas that, in the individual case, it seeks to occupy. We must remember this fact—which we have encountered several times and which we shall have to discuss repeatedly: that 'democracy' as such is opposed to the 'rule' of bureaucracy, in spite and perhaps because of its unavoidable yet unintended promotion of bureaucratization. Under certain conditions, democracy creates obvious ruptures and blockages to bureaucratic organization. Hence, in every individual historical case, one must observe in what special direction bureaucratization has developed.

12. The Power Position of Bureaucracy

Everywhere the modern state is undergoing bureaucratization. But whether the *power* of bureaucracy within the polity is universally increasing must here remain an open question.

The fact that bureaucratic organization is technically the most highly developed means of power in the hands of the man who controls it does not determine the weight that bureaucracy as such is capable of having in a particular social structure. The ever-increasing 'indispensability' of the officialdom, swollen to millions, is no more decisive for this question than is the view of some representatives of the proletarian movement that the economic indispensability of the proletarians is decisive for the measure of their social and political power position. If 'indispensability' were decisive, then where slave labor prevailed and where freemen usually abhor work as a dishonor, the 'indispensable' slaves ought to have held the positions of power, for they were at least as indispensable as officials and proletarians are today. Whether the power of bureaucracy as such increases cannot be decided *a priori* from such reasons. The drawing in of economic interest groups or other non-official experts, or the drawing in of non-expert lay representatives, the establishment of local, inter-local, or central parliamentary or other representative bodies, or of occupational associations—these *seem* to run directly against the bureaucratic tendency. How far this appearance is the truth must be discussed in another chapter rather than in this purely formal and typological discussion. In general, only the following can be said here:

Under normal conditions, the power position of a fully developed bureaucracy is always overtowering. The 'political master' finds himself in the position of the 'dilettante' who stands opposite the 'expert,' facing the trained official who stands within the management of administration. This holds whether the 'master' whom the bureaucracy serves is a 'people,' equipped with the weapons of 'legislative initiative,' the 'referendum,' and the right to remove officials, or a parliament, elected on a more aristocratic or more 'democratic' basis and equipped with the right to vote a lack of confidence, or with the actual authority to vote it. It holds whether the master is an aristocratic, collegiate body, legally or actually based on self-recruitment, or whether he is a popularly elected president, a hereditary and 'absolute' or a 'constitutional' monarch. . . . [pp. 228–233]

⬜ CASE STUDY 2

Introduction

At first glance, the following story may seem out of place—or odd—to follow such a highly abstract and theoretical essay by Max Weber. It is a personal story told by a father, George Lardner, who recounts the details of the shooting death of his 21-year-old daughter Kristin on May 30, 1992. She had been raised in Washington, D.C. and was living in Boston, studying in a fine arts program, jointly sponsored by the Museum of Fine

Arts and Tufts University. For two and a half months she had been dating 22-year-old Michael Cartier, a local nightclub bouncer, but had broken up with him on April 16. That night he became violent, beating her up a few blocks from her apartment. Increasingly he became obsessed by her rejection of him.

What follows is a sorry tale of Kristin's attempts to rely on the bureaucratic system and the subsequent breakdown of that system to protect her from a brutal "stalker." Although it is about the worst nightmares of women—and their parents and friends—the study dispassionately probes the background of Cartier and the reasons why "the system" left him "on the street," which ultimately led to Kristin's death as well as Cartier's. In the process of recounting the events surrounding this tragedy, the author, perhaps unconsciously, underscores the importance of a well-functioning, effective bureaucracy, one containing many of the key elements outlined in the foregoing essay by Max Weber, in order to protect the lives and safety of all of us.

As you read this selection, try to reflect on the following:

What were the chief elements in the overall bureaucratic system that failed to protect Kristin?

What caused their breakdown?

How does Weber's conceptualization of bureaucracy help us to understand bureaucracy, its role in society and sources of failure—as well as strengths?

Does this story "square" with Weber's conception of bureaucracy and the vital role he believed it fulfilled in modern society?

Do Weber's generalizations fit or fail to fit the American experience as portrayed by this case? The basic design of bureaucracy? Its formal scope and powers? Its informal influence on our lives? Sources of problems of modern bureaucracy?

How Kristin Died

GEORGE LARDNER, JR.

The phone was ringing insistently, hurrying me back to my desk. My daughter Helen was on the line, sobbing so hard she could barely catch her breath. "Dad," she shouted. "Come home! Right away!"

I was stunned. I had never heard her like this before. "What's wrong?" I asked. "What happened?"

"It's—it's Kristin. She's been shot . . . and killed."

Kristin? My Kristin? Our Kristin? I'd talked to her the afternoon before. Her last words to me were, "I love you Dad." Suddenly I had trouble breathing myself.

It was 7:30 p.m. on Saturday, May 30. In Boston, where Kristin Lardner was an art student, police were cordoning off an apartment building a couple of blocks from the busy, sunlit sidewalk where she'd been killed 90 minutes earlier. She had been shot in the head and face by an ex-boyfriend who was under court order to stay away from her. When police burst into his apartment, they found him sprawled on his bed, dead from a final act of self-pity.

This was a crime that could and should have been prevented. I write about it as a sort of cautionary tale, in anger at a system of justice that failed to protect my daughter, a system that is addicted to looking the other way, especially at the evil done to women.

But first let me tell you about my daughter.

She was, at 21, the youngest of our five children, born in Washington, D.C., and educated in the city's public schools, where not much harm befell her unless you count her taste for rock music, lots of jewelry, and funky clothes from Value Village. She loved books, went trick-or-treating dressed as Greta Garbo, played one of the witches in "Macbeth" and had a grand time in tap-dancing class even in her sneakers. She made life sparkle.

When she was small, she always got up in time for Saturday morning cartoons at the Chevy Chase library, and she took cheerful care of a succession of cats, mice, gerbils, hamsters and guinea pigs. Her biggest fault may have been that she took too long in the shower—and you never knew what color her hair was going to be when she emerged. She was compassionate, and strong-minded too; when a boy from high school dropped his pants in front of her, Kristin knocked out one of his front teeth.

"She didn't back down from anything," said Amber Lynch, a close friend from Boston University. "You could tell that basically from her art, the way she dressed, the opinions she had. If you said something stupid, she'd tell you."

Midway through high school, Kristin began thinking of becoming an artist. She'd been taking art and photography classes each summer at the Corcoran School of Art and was encouraged when an art teacher at Wilson High decided two of her paintings were good enough to go on display at a little gallery there. She began studies at Boston University's art school and transferred after two years to a fine arts program run jointly by the School of the Museum of Fine Arts and Tufts University. She particularly liked to sculpt and make jewelry and, in the words of one faculty member, "showed great promise and was extremely talented."

In her apartment were scattered signs of that talent. Three wide-banded silver and brass rings, one filigreed with what looked like barbed wire. Some striking sculptures of bound figures. A Madonna, painstakingly gilded. A nude self-portrait in angry reds, oranges and yellows, showing a large leg bruise her ex-boyfriend had given her on their last date in April.

"It felt as though she was telling all her secrets to the world," she wrote of her art in an essay she left behind. "Why would anyone want to know them anyway? But making things was all she wanted to do. . . . She always had questions, but never any answers, just frustration and confusion, and a need to get out whatever lay inside of her, hoping to be meaningful."

Kristin wrote that essay last November for a course at Tufts taught by Ross Ellenhorn, who also happens to be a counselor at Emerge, an educational program for abusive men. He had once mentioned this to his students. He would hear from my daughter in April, after she met Michael Cartier.

By then, Kristin had been dating Cartier, a 22-year-old bouncer, for about two and a half months. She broke off with him on the early morning of April 16. On that night, a few blocks from her apartment, he beat her up.

They "became involved in an argument and he knocked her to the ground and started kicking her over and over," reads a Brookline, Mass., police report. "She remembers him saying, 'Get up or I'll kill you.' She staggered to her feet, a car stopped and two men assisted her home.

"Since that night," the report continues, "she has refused to see him, but he repeatedly calls her, sometimes 10 or 11 times a day. He has told her that if she reports him to the police, he might have to do six months in jail, but she better not be around when he gets out.

"She also stated the injuries she suffered were hematomas to her legs and recurring headaches from the kicks."

Kristin didn't call the police right away. But she did call Ellenhorn in hopes of getting Cartier into Emerge. "I made clear to her that Emerge isn't a panacea, that there was still a chance of him abusing her," Ellenhorn says. "I told her that he could kill her . . . because she was leaving him and that's when things get dangerous."

Cartier showed up at Emerge's offices in Cambridge, around April 28 by Ellenhorn's calculations. Ellenhorn, on duty that night, realized who Cartier was when he wrote down Kristin's name under victim on the intake form.

"I said, 'Are you on probation?' " Ellenhorn remembers. "He said yes. I said, 'I'm going to need the name of the probation officer.' He said, '[Expletive] this. No way.' "

With that, Cartier ripped up the contract he was required to sign, ripped up the intake form, put the tattered papers in his pocket and walked out.

"He knew," Ellenhorn says. "He knew what kind of connection would be made." Michael Cartier was, of course, on probation for attacking another woman.

Cartier preyed on women. Clearly disturbed, he once talked of killing his mother. When he was 5 or 6, he dismembered a pet rabbit. When he was 21, he tortured and killed a kitten. In a bizarre 1989 incident at an Andover restaurant, he injected a syringe of blood into a ketchup bottle. To his girlfriends, he could be appallingly brutal.

Rose Ryan could tell you that. When Kristin's murder was reported on TV—the newscaster described the killing as "another case of domestic violence"—she said to a friend, "That sounds like Mike." It was. Hearing the newscaster say his name, she recalls, "I almost dropped."

When Ryan met Cartier at a party in Boston in the late summer of 1990, she was an honors graduate of Lynn East High School, preparing to attend Suffolk University. She was 17, a lovely, courageous girl with brown hair and brown eyes like Kristin's.

"He was really my first boyfriend," she told me. "I was supposed to work that summer and save my money, but I got caught up with the scene in Boston and hanging out with all the kids. . . . At first, everything was fine."

Cartier was a familiar face on the Boston Common, thanks to his career as a freelance nightclub bouncer. He had scraped up enough money to share a Commonwealth Avenue apartment with a Museum School student named Kara Boettger. They dated a few times, then settled down into a sort of strained coexistence.

"He didn't like me very much," Boettger said. "He liked music loud. I'd tell him to turn it down."

Rose Ryan liked him better. She thought he was handsome—blue eyes, black hair, a tall and muscular frame—with a vulnerability that belied his strength. To make him happy, she quit work and postponed the college education it was going to pay for. "He had me thinking that he'd had a bad deal his whole life," she said, "that nobody loved him and I was the only one who could help him."

Cartier also knew how to behave when he was supposed to. Ryan said he made a good first impression on her parents. As with Kristin, it took just about two months before Cartier beat Ryan up. She got angry with him for "kidding around" and dumping her into a barrel on the Common. When she walked away, he punched her in the head; when she kept going, he punched her again.

"I'd never been hit by any man before and I was just shocked," she said. But what aggravated her the most, and still does, is that "every time something happened, it was in public, and nobody stopped to help."

Cartier ended the scene with "his usual thing," breaking into tears and telling her, "'Oh, why do I always hurt the people I love? What can I do? My mother didn't love me. I need your help.' "

Shortly after they started dating, Ryan spent a few days at the Cartier-Boetgger apartment. He presented her with a gray kitten, then left it alone all day without a litter box. The kitten did what it needed to do on Cartier's jacket.

"He threw the kitten in the shower and turned the hot water on and kept it there under the hot water," Ryan remembers in a dull monotone. "And he shaved all its hair off with a man's shaving razor."

The kitten spent most of its wretched life hiding under a bed. On the night of Oct. 4, 1990, Cartier began drinking with two friends and went on a rampage. He took a sledgehammer and smashed through his bedroom wall into a neighbor's apartment. And he killed the kitten, hurling it out a fourth-floor window.

"I'd left the apartment without telling them," Ryan said. "When I came back, the police were in the hallway. . . . They said, 'Get out. This guy's crazy.' They were taking him out in handcuffs."

Three months later, Cartier, already on probation, plea-bargained his way to probation again—pleading guilty to malicious destruction. Charges of burglary and cruelty to animals were dismissed; the court saw nothing wrong with putting him back on the street.

"I thought he was going to jail because he violated probation," Kara Boettger said. So did Cartier.

"[But after the January hearing] he told me . . . 'Oh yeah, nothing happened. They slapped my wrist.' "

When Michael Cartier was born in Newburyport, Mass., his mother was 17. Her husband, then 19, left them six months later; Gene Cartier has since re-married twice. Her son, Penny Cartier says, was a problem from the first.

"He'd take a bottle away from his [step]sister. He'd light matches behind a gas stove. He was born that way," Penny Cartier asserted. "When he was five or six, he had a rabbit. He ripped its legs out of its sockets."

"None of this," she added in loud tones, "had anything to do with what he did to Kristin. . . . Michael's childhood had nothing to do with anything."

Life with mother, in any case, ended at age 7, when she sent him to the New England Home for Little Wanderers, a state-supported residential treatment center for troubled children. Staff there remember him—although Penny Cartier denies this—as a child abused at an early age. "That's the worst childhood I've ever seen," agrees Rich DeAngelis, one of Cartier's probation officers. "This didn't just happen in the last couple of years."

Cartier stayed at the New England Home until he was 12. In October 1982, he was put in the Harbor School in Amesbury, a treatment center for disturbed teenagers. He stayed there for almost four years and was turned over to his father, a facilities maintenance mechanic in Lawrence.

Michael Cartier was bitter about his mother. "I just know he hated her," Kara Boettger said. "He said he wanted to get a tattoo, I think maybe on his arm, of her hanging from a tree with animals ripping at her body."

Penny Cartier didn't seem surprised when I told her this. In fact, she added, after he turned 18, "he asked my daughter if she wanted him to kill me."

Cartier entered Lawrence High School but dropped out after a couple of years. "He was just getting frustrated. He couldn't keep up," said his father. By his second semester, he was facing the first of nearly 20 criminal charges that he piled up in courthouses from Lawrence to Brighton over a four-year period.

Along the way, he enjoyed brief notoriety as a self-avowed skinhead, sauntering into the newsroom of the Lawrence Eagle-Tribune with his bald friends in June 1989 to complain of the bad press and "neo-Nazi" labels skinheads usually got. "The state supported me all my life, with free doctors and dentists and everything," Cartier told columnist Kathie Neff. "My parents never had anything to do with that because they got rid of me. This is like my way of saying thanks [to them]."

Neff said Cartier cut an especially striking figure, walking on crutches and wearing a patch on one eye. He had just survived a serious car accident that produced what seems to have been a magic purse for him. He told friends he had a big insurance settlement coming and would get periodic advances on it from his lawyer. Gene Cartier said his son got a final payment late last year of $17,000 and "went through $14,000" of it before he murdered Kristin.

The high-ceilinged main courtroom in Brighton has a huge, wide-barred cell built into a wall. On busy days, it is a page from Dickens, crowded with yelling, cursing prisoners waiting for their cases to be called.

Cartier turned up in the cage April 29, 1991, finally arrested for violating probation. Ten days earlier, when Rose Ryan was coming home from a friend's house on the "T," Boston's trolley train and subway system, Cartier followed her—and accosted her at the Government Center station with a pair of scissors. She ducked the scissors and Cartier punched her in the mouth.

Even before that, Ryan and her older sister Tina had become alarmed. After a party in December, Cartier got annoyed with Rose for not wanting to eat pizza he'd just bought. She began walking back to the party when he back-handed her in the face so hard she fell down. "And I'm lying on the ground, screaming, and then he finally stopped kicking me after I don't know how long, and then he said, 'You better get up or I'll kill you.' "

The same words he would use with Kristin. And how many other young women?

Rose Ryan said Cartier threatened to kill her several times after they broke up in December and, in a chance encounter in March, told her he had a gun. The Ryan sisters called his probation officer in Brighton, Tom Casey. He told Rose to get a restraining order and, on March 28, he obtained a warrant for Cartier's arrest. It took a month for police to pick him up even though Cartier had, in between, attacked

Rose in the subway and been arraigned on charges for that assault in Boston Municipal Court.

"Probation warrants have to be served by the police, who don't take them seriously enough," said another probation officer. "Probationers know . . . they can skip court appearances with impunity."

When Cartier turned up in Brighton, "he was very quiet. Sullen and withdrawn," Casey said. "It was obvious he had problems, deeper than I could ever get to." Yet a court psychiatrist, Dr. Mike Annunziata, filed a report stating that Cartier had "no acute mental disorder, no suicidal or homicidal ideas, plans or intents." The April 29, 1991, report noted that Cartier was being treated by the Tri-City Mental Health and Retardation Center in Malden and was taking 300 milligrams of lithium a day to control depression.

Cartier, the report said, had also spent four days in January 1991 at the Massachusetts Mental Health Center in Boston. He was brought there on a "Section 12," a law providing for emergency restraint of dangerous persons, because of "suicidal ideation" and an overdose of some sort. On April 2, 1991, he was admitted to the Center on another "Section 12," this time for talking about killing Rose Ryan with a gun "within two weeks." He denied making the threats and was released the next day.

Tom Casey wanted to get him off the streets this time, and a like-minded visiting magistrate ordered Cartier held on bail for a full hearing in Brighton later in the week. When the Ryan sisters arrived in court, they found themselves five feet away from Cartier in the cell. "Soon as he saw me," Tina Ryan said, "he said, 'I know who you are, I'm going to kill you too,' all these filthy words, calling me everything he could. . . ."

After listening to what the Ryans had to say, the judge sent Cartier to jail on Deer Island for three months for violating probation. The next month, he was given a year for the subway attack, but was committed for only six months.

That didn't stop the harassment. Cartier began making collect calls to Ryan from prison and he enlisted other inmates to write obscene letters. The district attorney's office advised the Ryans to keep a record of the calls so they could be used against Cartier later.

Despite all that, Cartier was released early, on Nov. 5, 1991. "'He's been a very good prisoner and we're overcrowded,' " the Ryans say they were told.

Authorities in Essex County didn't want to see him out on the streets even if officials in Boston didn't care. As soon as he was released from Deer Island, Cartier was picked up for violating his probation on the ketchup-bottle incident and sentenced to 59 days in the Essex County jail. But a six-month suspended sentence that was hanging over him for a 1988 burglary—which would have meant at least three months in jail—was wiped off the books.

"That's amazing," said another probation officer who looked at the record. "They dropped the more serious charges."

Cartier was released after serving 49 of the 59 days.

Ryan had already been taking precautions. She carried Mace in her pocketbook, put a baseball bat in her car and laid out a bunch of knives next to her bed each night before going to sleep. "I always thought that he would come back and try to get me," she said.

Kristin loved to go out with friends until all hours of the morning, but she didn't have many steady boyfriends. Most men, she said more than once, "are dogs" because of the way they treated girls she knew.

She was always ready for adventure, hopping on the back of brother Charles's motorcycle for rides; curling up with Circe, a pet ball-python she kept in her room; and flying down for a few weeks almost every August to Jekyll Island, Ga., to be with her family, a tradition started when she was less than a week old. Last year she caught a small shark from the drawbridge over the Jekyll River.

"I think she'd give anything a go," said Jason Corkin, the young man she dated the longest, before he returned last year to his native New Zealand. "When she set her mind to something, she wouldn't give it up for anything."

She could also become easily depressed, especially about what she was going to do after graduation. As she once wrote, her favorite pastime was "morbid self-reflection." Despite that, laughter came easily and she was always ready for a conversation about art, religion, philosophy, music. "I don't really remember any time we were together that we didn't have a good time," said Bekky Elstad, a close friend from Boston University.

Left in her bedroom at her death was a turntable with Stravinsky's "Rites of Spring" on it and a tape player with a punk tune by Suicidal Tendencies. Her books, paperbacks mostly, included Alice Walker's "The Color Purple" and Margaret Atwood's "The Handmaid's Tale," along with favorites by Sinclair Lewis, Dickens and E.B. White and a book about upper- and middle-caste women in Hindu families in Calcutta.

Her essays for school, lucid and well-written, showed a great deal of thought about art, religion and the relationship between men and women. She saw her art as an expression of parts of her hidden deep inside, waiting to be pulled out, but still to be guarded closely: "Art could be such a selfish thing. Everything she made, she made for herself and not one bit of it could she bear to be parted with. Whether she loved it, despised it or was painfully ashamed of it . . . she couldn't stand the thought of these little parts of her being taken away and put into someone else's possession."

Buddhism appealed to her, and once she wrote this: "Pain only comes when you try to hang on to what is impermanent. So all life need not be suffering. You can enjoy life if you do not expect anything from it."

She met Cartier last Jan. 30 at a Boston nightclub called Axis, having gone there with Lauren Mace, Kristin's roommate and best friend, and Lauren's boyfriend. At Axis, Kristin recognized Cartier as someone she'd seen at Bunratty's, a hard-rock club where Cartier had been a bouncer. Cartier was easily recognizable; he had a large tattoo of a castle on his neck.

What did she see in him? It's a question her parents keep asking themselves. But some things are fairly obvious. He reminded her of Jason, her friend from New Zealand. He could be charming. "People felt a great deal of empathy for him," said Octavia Ossola, director of the child care center at the home where Cartier grew up, "because it was reasonably easy to want things to be better for him." At the Harbor School, said executive director Art DiMauro, "he was quite endearing. The staff felt warmly about Michael."

So, at first, did Kristin. "She called me up, really excited and happy," said Christian Dupre, a friend since childhood. "She said 'I met this good guy, he's really nice.' "

Kristin told her oldest sister, Helen, and her youngest brother, Charlie, too. But Helen paused when Kristin told her that Cartier was a bouncer at Bunratty's and had a tattoo.

"Well, ah, is he nice?" Helen asked.

"Well, he's nice to me," Kristin said.

Charlie, who had just entered college after a few years of blue-collar jobs, was not impressed. "Get rid of him," he advised his sister. "He's a zero."

Her friends say they got along well at first. He told Kristin he'd been in jail for hitting a girlfriend, but called it a bum rap. She did not know he'd attacked Rose Ryan with scissors, that he had a rap sheet three pages long.

Kristin, friends say, often made excuses for his behavior. But they soon started to argue. Cartier was irrationally jealous, accusing her of going out with men who stopped by just to talk. During one argument, apparently over her art, Cartier hit her, then did his "usual thing" and started crying.

Cartier, meanwhile, was still bothering Ryan. A warrant for violating probation had been issued out of Boston Municipal Court on Dec. 19, in part for trying to contact her by mail while he was in jail. But when he finally turned up in court, a few days before he met Kristin, he got kid-glove treatment. Rather than being sentenced to complete the one-year term he'd gotten for the scissors attack, he was ordered instead to attend a once-a-week class at the courthouse for six weeks called "Alternatives to Violence."

"It's not a therapy program, it's more educational," said John Tobin, chief probation officer at Boston Municipal Court. "It's for people who react to stress in violent ways, not just for batterers. Cartier . . . showed up each time. You don't send probationers away when they do what they're supposed to do."

What Tobin didn't mention was that Cartier had actually dropped out of his Alternatives to Violence course—and, incredibly, was allowed to sign up for it again. According to a chronology I obtained elsewhere, Cartier attended the first meeting of the group on Feb. 5 and skipped the class Feb. 12. His probation was revoked two days later. But instead of sending him back to jail, the court allowed him to start the course over, beginning April 1.

Cartier's probation officer, Diane Barrett Moeller, a "certified batterer specialist" who helps run the program, declined to talk to me, citing "legal limitations" that she did not spell out. Her boss, Tobin, said she was "a ferocious probation officer."

"We tend to be a punitive department," Tobin asserted. "We are not a bunch of social rehabilitators."

However that may be, it is a department that seems to operate in a vacuum. Cartier's record of psychiatric problems, his admissions to the Boston mental health center in January and April 1991 and his reliance on a drug to control manic-depression should have disqualified him from the court-run violence program.

"If we had information that he had a prior history of mental illness, or that he was treated in a clinic or that he had been hospitalized, then what we probably would have done is recommend that a full-scale psychological evaluation be done for him," Tobin told the Boston Herald last June following Kristin's murder. "We didn't know about it."

Probation officer Tom Casey in Brighton knew. All Tobin's office had to do was pick up the phone to find out what a menace Cartier was. Meanwhile, in Salem, where she had moved to work with her sister at a family-run business, Rose Ryan remained fearful. But she had a new boyfriend, Sean Casey, 23, and, as Rose puts it, "I think he intimidated Mike because he had more tattoos. Mike knew Sean from before."

Around March 1, Sean went to Boston to tell Cartier to leave Rose alone. As they were talking, Kristin walked by. Sean didn't know who she was, but recognized her later, from newspaper photos.

Cartier nodded at Kristin as she passed. "He said, 'I don't need Rose any more,' " Casey recalled. " 'I have my own girlfriend.' "

Cartier was a frequent visitor at the six-room flat Kristin shared with Lauren Mace and another BU student, Matt Newton, but he didn't have much to say to them or the other students who were always stopping by. He told Kristin they "intimidated" him because they were college-educated.

As the weeks wore on, they started to argue. When he hit her the first time, probably in early March, Kristin told friends about it, but not Lauren. She was probably too embarrassed. She had always been outspoken in her disdain for men who hit women.

"He hit her once. She freaked out on that . . . ," Bekky Elstad said. "She wanted him to get counseling. . . . He told her he was sorry. He was all broken up. She wanted to believe him."

Kristin came home to Washington in mid-March, outwardly bright and cheerful. She was more enthusiastic than ever about her art. She was "really getting it together," she said. She had yet to tell her parents that she had a boyfriend, much less a boyfriend who hit her.

When she got back to Boston, Cartier tried to make up with her. He gave her a kitten. "It was really cute—black with a little white triangle on its nose," Amber Lynch said. "It was teeny. It just wobbled around."

It didn't last long. Over Kristin's protests, Cartier put the kitten on top of a door jamb. It fell off, landing on its head. She had to have it destroyed.

Devastated, Kristin called home in tears and told her parents, for the first time, about her new boyfriend. Part of her conversation with her mother was picked up by a malfunctioning answering machine.

Rosemary: What does Mike do?
Kristin: Well, he does the same thing Jason did actually. He works at Bunratty's.
Rosemary: He does what?
Kristin: He works at Bunratty's.
Rosemary: Oh. Is he an artist also?
Kristin: No.
Rosemary: Well, that's what I was asking. What does he—? Is he a student?
Kristin: No. He just—he works. He's a bouncer.

"Oh," Rosemary said, asking after a long pause why she was going out with a boy with no education. Kristin told her that she wanted to have a boyfriend "just like everyone else does."

When I came home, Rosemary said, "Call your daughter." When I did, Kristin began crying again as she told me about the kitten. She was also upset because she had given Cartier a piece of jewelry she wanted to use for her annual evaluation at the Museum School. He told her he'd lost it.

Gently, perhaps too gently, I said I didn't think she should be wasting her time going out with a boy who did such stupid things. We talked about school and classes for a few minutes more and said goodnight.

She went out with him for the last time on April

16, the day after one of his Alternatives to Violence classes. He pushed her down onto the sidewalk in front of a fast-food place, cutting her hand. She told him several times to "go home and leave me alone," but he kept following her to a side street in Allston.

"Kristin said something like, 'Get away from me, I never want to see you again,'" Bekky Elstad remembers. But when Kristin tried to run, he caught up with her, threw her down and kicked her repeatedly in the head and legs. She was crying hysterically when she got home with the help of a passing motorist. She refused to see him again.

But Cartier kept trying to get her on the phone. He warned her not to go to the police and, for a while, she didn't. She felt sorry for him. She even agreed to take a once-a-week phone call from him the day he went to his Alternatives to Violence class.

He was rated somewhat passive at the meetings, but he got through the course on May 6 without more truancy. The next day, he walked into Gay's Flowers and Gifts on Commonwealth Avenue and bought a dozen red roses for Kristin. He brought in a card to be delivered with them.

Leslie North, a dark-haired, puffy-faced woman who had known Cartier for years, had helped him fill it out in advance. "He always called me when he had a fight with his girlfriends," she said. "He said that he was trying to change, that he needed help, that he wanted to be a better person. He said, 'I'm trying to get back with her.'"

Flower shop proprietor Alan Najarian made the delivery to Kristin's flat. "One of her roommates took them," Najarian remembers. "He was kind of reluctant. . . . I think he must have known who they were from."

Police think Cartier may have gotten his gun the day of the murder, but Leslie North remembers his showing it to her "shortly after [he and Kristin] broke up," probably in early May.

Why did he get the gun? "He said, 'Ah, just to have one,'" North says. "I asked him, 'What do you need a gun for?' He said, 'You never know.' I didn't realize you're not supposed to get a gun if you've been in jail. I didn't tell anyone he had it."

"He told me he paid $750 for it," she continues. "I showed him just a little bit of safety . . . how to hold it when you shoot. . . . It looked kind of old to me."

The gun found in Cartier's apartment after he killed Kristin and himself was 61 years old, a Colt .38

Super, serial number 13645, one of about a 100 million handguns loose in the United States. It was shipped brand new on Jan. 12, 1932, to a hardware store in Knoxville, Tenn., where all traces of it disappeared.

North remembered something else she says Cartier told her after he got the gun. "He goes, 'If I kill Kristin, are you going to tell anyone?'

"I said, 'Of course, I'm going to tell.' I didn't take him seriously. . . . He said that once or twice to me."

On May 7, the same day Cartier sent flowers to Kristin, he told her that he was going to cheat her out of the $1,000 Nordic Flex machine she'd let him charge to her Discover card. When she told him over the phone that she expected him to return the device, he laughed and said, "I guess you're out the $1,000."

Kristin was furious. She promptly called Cartier's probation officer, Diane Barrett Moeller, and gave her an earful: the exercise machine, the beating.

Kristin's call for help was another of the probation office's secrets. Tobin said nothing about it to the Boston press in the days after Kristin's murder, when it grew clear that there was something desperately wrong with the criminal justice system. Tobin told me only after I found out about it from Kristin's friends.

"Your daughter was concerned," Tobin said. "She put a lot of emphasis on the weight machine. Mrs. Moeller said, 'Get your priorities straight. You should not be worrying about the weight machine. You should be worrying about your safety. . . . Get to Brookline court, seek an assault complaint, a larceny complaint, whatever it takes . . . and get a restraining order.'"

According to Tobin, Kristin wouldn't give her name even though Moeller asked for it twice. "We can't revoke someone's probation on an anonymous phone call," he said. Kristin, he added, "did say she didn't want this man arrested and put behind bars."

Tobin also claimed that his office could have taken no action because Kristin was "not the woman in the case we were supervising," which is like saying that probationers in Boston Municipal Court should only take care not to rob the same bank twice.

The next day, Friday, May 8, instead of moving to revoke Cartier's probation, Moeller called Cartier and, in effect, told him what was up. Tobin recalled the conversation. "She told him to get the exercise machine back to her. She told him she didn't want to hear about it anymore. And she ordered a full-scale psychiatric evaluation of him. She also ordered him to report to her every week until the evaluation is completed."

Cartier did all that while planning Kristin's murder.

When Cartier called Kristin again, she told him that if he didn't return the exercise machine, she was going to take court action. "He called back 10 minutes later from a pay phone," remembers Brian Fazekas, Lauren's boyfriend. "He said, 'Okay, okay, I'll return the stupid machine.' "

Kristin was skeptical about that. And she was worried about more violence. The warnings of her friends, her brother Charlie, her teacher Ross Ellenhorn and now Cartier's probation officer rang in her ears. Her art reflected her anguish. She had painted her own self-portrait, showing some of the ugly bruises Cartier had left. Hanging sculptures showed a male, arms flexed and fists clenched. The female hung defensively, arms protecting her head.

By Monday, May 11, she had made up her mind. She was going to rely on the system. She decided to ask the courts for help. She talked about it afterwards with her big sister, Helen, a lawyer and her lifelong best friend. Kristin told her, sparingly, about the beating and, angrily, about the exercise machine. Helen kept the news to herself, as Kristin requested. "She said she found out what a loser he was. She said, 'He's even been taking drugs behind my back,' " Helen recalls. He was snorting heroin, confirms Leslie North—it helped him stay calm, she remembers him saying.

Late in the day, Kristin went to the Brookline police station, Lauren Mace and Brian Fazekas beside her.

"The courts were closed by the time we got there. We waited outside," Lauren said. "An officer showed her [Cartier's] arrest record. When she came out, she said, 'You won't believe the size of this guy's police record. He's killed cats. He's beat up ex-girlfriends. Breaking and enterings.' The officer just sort of flashed the length of it at her and said, 'Look at what you're dealing with.' "

Brookline police sergeant Robert G. Simmons

found Kristin "very intelligent, very articulate"—and scared. Simmons asked if she wanted to press charges, and she replied that she wanted to think about that. Simmons, afraid she might not come back, made out an "application for complaint" himself and got a judge on night duty to approve issuance of a one-day emergency restraining order over the phone. The next day, Kristin had to appear before Brookline District Judge Lawrence Shubow to ask for a temporary order—one that would last a week.

Other paperwork that Simmons sent over to the courthouse, right next door to the police station, called for a complaint charging Cartier with assault and battery, larceny, intimidation of a witness and violation of the domestic abuse law. It was signed by Lt. George Finnegan, the police liaison officer on duty at the courthouse that day, and turned over to clerk-magistrate John Connors for issuance of a summons.

The summons was never issued. Inexcusably, the application for it was still sitting on a desk in the clerk's office the day Kristin was killed, almost three weeks later.

Other officials I spoke with were amazed by the lapse. Connors shrugged it off. "We don't have the help," he said. "It was waiting to be typed."

Shubow was unaware of the criminal charges hanging over Cartier's head at the May 12 hearing. And Shubow didn't bother to ask about his criminal record. Restraining orders in Massachusetts, as in other states, have been treated for years by most judges as distasteful "civil matters." Until Kristin was killed, any thug in the Commonwealth accused under the domestic abuse law of beating up his wife or girlfriend or ex-wife or ex-girlfriend could walk into court without much fear that his criminal record would catch up with him. Shubow later told The Boston Globe, "If there is one lesson I learned from this case, it was to ask myself whether this is a case where I should review his record. In a case that has an immediate level of danger, I could press for a warrant and immediate arrest."

Instead, Shubow treated Docket No. 92-RO-060 as a routine matter. He issued a temporary restraining order telling Cartier to stay away from Kristin's school, her apartment and her place of work for a week, until another hearing could be held by another judge on a permanent order, good for a year.

"The system failed her completely," Shubow told me after Kristin's death. "There is no such thing as a routine case. I don't live that, but I believe that. All bureaucrats should be reminded of that."

Downtown, in Boston Municipal Court, chief probation officer Tobin said that "if we had found out about the restraining order, we would have moved immediately." But Tobin's office made no effort to find out. Cartier's probation officer knew that the anonymous female caller lived in Brookline; a call to officials there would have made clear that Cartier had once again violated probation by beating up an ex-girlfriend. No such call was made.

Apparently, the probation officer didn't ask Cartier for the details either. According to a state official who asked not to be identified, Diane Moeller met with Cartier on May 14, just eight days after he completed her Alternatives to Violence course and three days after Kristin obtained her first restraining order. Moeller did nothing to get him off the streets.

"She was concerned about getting additional assistance for this guy," the state official said of the May 14 meeting. "No charges were filed."

In Brookline, Lt. Finnegan said he sensed something was wrong. He walked up to Kristin outside the courthouse on May 12. "I had this gut feeling," he said. "I asked her, 'Are you really afraid of him?' She said, 'Yeah.' I asked her if he had a gun. She said, 'He may.' "

Finnegan told her to call the police if she saw Cartier hanging around.

The phone rang at the Brookline Police Station shortly after midnight on May 19; Kristin's request for a permanent restraining order was coming up for a hearing that morning. Now, in plain violation of the May 12 order, Cartier had called around midnight, got Kristin on the line and asked her not to go back to court. She called the cops.

Sgt. Simmons, on duty that night as shift commander, advised Kristin to file a complaint and sent officer Kevin Mealy to talk to her; Mealy arrived at her apartment at 1:10 a.m. "Ms. Lardner said that Mr. Cartier attempted to persuade her not to file for an extension of the order," Mealy wrote in his report, which he filed as soon as he got back to the station house. "A criminal complaint application has been made out against Mr. Cartier for violating the existing restraining order."

Sgt. Simmons says, "I told Kevin, 'They've got a hearing in the morning.' The documents went over there. But who reads them?"

Kristin arrived at the courthouse around 11:30 a.m. May 19, accompanied by Lauren Mace and Amber Lynch.

"He [Cartier] was out in front of the courthouse when we got there," Lynch said. "We all just walked in quickly. We waited a long time. He kept walking in and out of the courtroom. I think he was staring at her."

There was no one in the courtroom from the Norfolk County D.A.'s office to advise Kristin. Brookline probation officials didn't talk to her either. They had no idea Cartier was on probation for beating up another woman.

Neither did District Judge Paul McGill, a visiting magistrate from Roxbury. Like Shubow, he didn't check Cartier's criminal record. Unlike Shubow, it didn't trouble him. To him, it was a routine hearing. Kristin was looking for protection. She was processed like a slice of cheese.

"She thought he was going to be arrested," Lauren said. Brian Fazekas said, "It was her understanding that as soon as he got the permanent restraining order, he was going to be surrendered" for violating probation.

"What he [Cartier] did on the 19th was a crime," David Lowy, legal adviser to Gov. William Weld and a former prosecutor, said of the midnight call. "He should have been placed under arrest right then and there."

The hearing lasted five minutes. It would have been shorter except for a typical bit of arrogance from Cartier, trying to stay in control in the face of his third restraining order in 18 months. He agreed not to contact Kristin for a year and to stay away from her apartment and school. But he said he had a problem staying away from Marty's Liquors, where Kristin had just started working as a cashier. "I happen to live right around the corner from there," Cartier complained, according to a tape of the hearing.

The judge told him to patronize some other liquor store, but not before more argument from Cartier about how he would have to "walk further down the street" and about how close it was to Bunratty's, only half a block away. McGill ended the hearing by ordering Cartier to avoid any contact with Kristin, to stay at least 200 yards away from her and not to talk to her if he had to come closer when entering his home or the nightclub.

And with that, Cartier walked out scot-free. Yet, Massachusetts law, enacted in 1990, provides for mandatory arrest of anyone a law enforcement officer has probable cause to believe violated a temporary or permanent restraining order. In addition, a state law making "stalking" a crime, especially in violation of a restraining order, had been signed by Gov. Weld just the day before, May 18, effective immediately.

McGill later said that if he'd known Cartier had violated his restraining order by calling Kristin that morning, he would have turned the hearing into a criminal session.

The application for a complaint charging Cartier with violating the order was moldering in clerk John Connors's offices. Like the earlier complaint accusing him of assault and battery, it was still there the day Kristin was killed.

"Kristin could have said something [in court], I suppose," Lauren said. "But she just figured that after that, he would be out of her life. She said, 'Let's go home.' She felt very relieved that she had this restraining order."

Kristin, who now had 11 days to live, talked enthusiastically about going to Europe after graduation, only a year away. After that she was hoping to go to graduate school. She had lost interest in boys, wanting to concentrate on her art.

"I spoke to her the night before [she was killed]," Chris Dupre said. "She was like the most optimistic and happiest she'd been in months. She knew what she wanted to do with herself, with her art."

She even had a new kitten, named Stubby because its tail was broken in two places. She was working part-time in the liquor store and hoping for more hours as summer approached. But she liked to stay home and paint or just hang out with friends now that classes were over.

Cartier was still skulking about, even after issuance of the permanent restraining order. One afternoon, Kristin stepped out of the liquor store to take a break. She saw Cartier staring at her from the doorway of Bunratty's.

On the afternoon of May 28, she and Robert Hyde, a friend who had just graduated from BU, decided to get something to eat after playing Scrabble (Kristin won) and chess (Robert won) at Kristin's flat. The two hopped on the back of his Yamaha and were off. First stop was the Bay Bank branch on Commonwealth Avenue, two doors from Marty's Liquors. As they turned a corner, Kristin saw Cartier looking in Marty's window. "Did you see that?" she asked Hyde moments later as they got off the bike. "Mike was peeking in the window. What a weirdo!"

Hyde didn't think that Cartier saw them, but later that night, after taking Kristin home, he went over to Bunratty's to play pinball. Cartier was there, and he began an awkward conversation to find out where Hyde lived.

"I thought it was kind of weird, but I didn't think too much of it," Hyde said. He shuddered about it after the shooting.

Cartier had always been disturbingly jealous—and unpredictable. "He'd get under pressure, he'd start breathing heavy and start talking all wild," a longtime friend, Timothy McKernan, told the Lawrence Eagle-Tribune.

He couldn't handle rejection either. Cartier "told his friends that she broke up with him because she wanted to see other people," Bekky Elstad said. "That's not true. But that's why he killed her, I think. If he couldn't have her, no one else was going to."

If Kristin was bothered by the stalking incident that Thursday, she seemed to put it out of her mind. The usual stream of friends moved through the flat all day. She called me that afternoon in an upbeat mood. We talked about summer school, her Museum School evaluation and a half dozen other things, including the next month's check from home. I assured her it was in the mail. She had a big smile in her voice. All I knew about Cartier was that she had gotten rid of the creep. When I made some grumpy reference to boyfriends in general, she laughed and said, "That's because you're my dad."

Cartier called his father that day, too.

Gene Cartier knew about Kristin and about the restraining order. "I asked him what happened," the older Cartier said. "He said, 'Well, me and my girlfriend had a fight.' I figured they argued. . . . He loved animals, he loved children. He wouldn't hurt a fly."

A man with a persistent drinking problem, Gene

Cartier at times seemed to confuse Kristin with other girlfriends his son had, but his son's last call about her stuck firmly in his mind. "He said, 'She's busting my balls again,' " Cartier recalled. "I think she was seeing another guy—in front of Michael—to get him jealous. . . . He was obsessed with her."

Kristin went to bed that night with a smile. It had been Lauren's last day at Marty's and some of the students who worked there stopped by the flat. "We were having a really, really good time," Lauren Mace said. "I remember, I said, 'Good night, Kristin.' I gave her a hug. The next morning, I saw her taking her bike down the street, on the way to work. I did not see her again."

Saturday, May 30, was a beautiful spring day in Boston, a light breeze rustling the trees on Winchester Street below the flat. Kristin was looking forward to a full day's work; Lauren was supposed to meet her at 6, when she was done at Marty's. Lauren had just graduated from BU; they were going to buy a keg for a big going-away party at the flat on Sunday.

One of the managers at the liquor store, David Bergman, was having lunch across the street at the Inbound Pizza when Kristin walked in. He waved her over to his table. She had a slice of Sicilian pizza and then, as he remembers, two more. "We talked for half an hour," Bergman said. "She was going to travel to Europe with her friend, Lauren. She had all these plans laid on."

After lunch, the day turned sour. Leslie North walked into Marty's with another girl. So, clerks say, did a man in his thirties with rotting teeth and thinning hair—North's boyfriend. He got in Kristin's checkout line and started cursing at her.

Not long after North and her friend left Marty's, J.D. Crump, the manager at Bunratty's, walked in for a sandwich from the deli counter. He'd known Kristin since she had dated Jason. "She said she was having a tough day," he told the Globe. "The customers were being mean. I told her it would get better."

When Crump spoke with Kristin on May 30, it was about 4:30. Cartier, meanwhile, was at a noisy show at the Rathskellar on Kenmore Square. Friends told the Lawrence Eagle-Tribune that he was acting strangely, greeting people with long hugs instead of the usual punch in the arm or a handshake.

"He wasn't the hugging type," Timothy McKernan told the Eagle-Tribune. "I think he knew what he was going to do." Cartier left suddenly, running out the door.

Kristin was scheduled to work until 6, but at 5 p.m., she was told, to her chagrin, to leave early, losing an hour's pay. "We had other cashiers coming in," the manager explained. Instead of hanging around to wait for Lauren, Kristin decided to go to Bekky Elstad's apartment and return at 6. It was a decision that seems to have cost her her life.

Lauren had come by around 5:40 p.m., and left when told Kristin had already gone. Kristin was still at Bekky's, keeping her eye on the clock and by now recounting how this "disgusting . . . slimy person" had been cursing at her at the cash register.

"She was laughing about how gross he was and then his being with these two girls—friends of Michael's—who were so gross," Bekky Elstad said. "She seemed pretty much in a good mood."

It was getting close to 6. By now, Cartier was back in the neighborhood, looking for a crowbar. He first asked for one at the Reading Room, a smoke shop about a block away, "maybe 20 minutes before it happened," said the proprietor. "I asked him why he wanted a crowbar. He said he had to go help somebody." Then he went over to Bunratty's, in a fruitless search for the same thing.

At one minute to 6, Kristin was heading down Commonwealth Avenue toward Marty's. Cartier, approaching from the other direction, stopped at a Store 24 convenience shop on the other side of Harvard Avenue. J.D. Crump was there, buying a pack of cigarettes. According to the police report: "Crump stated that while in Store 24 . . . he saw Michael and asked him [whether] he was going to work that night. Mike said that he was but had [to] shoot someone first. Crump stated that he did not take him seriously and walked away from him."

The shots rang out seconds later. Mike Dillon, a clerk at Marty's who clocked out at 6, had just stepped onto the sidewalk when he heard the first shattering noise.

"It was very loud," he said. "I looked up immediately. I saw Kristin fall."

Dressed all in black, she dropped instantly to the

pavement outside the Soap-A-Rama, a combination laundromat, tanning salon and video rental store four doors from Marty's.

"She was lying on her right side, curled up in kind of a fetal position," Mike Dillon said. "I kind of froze dead in my tracks."

Cartier must have seen her and hid in a doorway or alley until she passed by him. Witnesses said he came at her from behind and shot into the rear of her head from a distance of 15 or 20 feet. Then he ran into a nearby alley.

Al Silva, a restaurant worker, started to walk towards Kristin to see if he could help when Cartier darted back out of the alley, rushed past Silva, and leaned down over her.

"He shot her twice more in the left side of the head," Mike Dillon said. "Then I saw him run down the alley again. . . . I was still in shock. I didn't know what to do. I took one of her hands for a second or so, I don't know why. Then I ran back to call the police, but I saw a woman in the flower shop. She was already on the phone."

Chris Toher, the proprietor at Soap-A-Rama, heard the first shot from the back of his store and hurried up to the doorway. "I saw him fire the final shots," Toher said. "It happened so fast she never had a chance. She was completely unconscious at the point he ran up to her. Her eyes were shut."

A brave young woman was dead.

The killer fled down the alley, which took him to Glenville Avenue where he lived in a red brick apartment building. Back on Commonwealth Avenue, police and an ambulance arrived within minutes. But the ambulance was no longer necessary.

Police questioned Crump at the Soap-A-Rama and learned where Cartier lived. Brooke Mezo, a clerk from Marty's who witnessed the interrogation, heard Crump say "that Michael had spoken to him in the past couple of weeks and said he couldn't live without her, that he was going to kill her. And he talked about where to get a gun."

That made at least two people who knew Cartier had or wanted a gun and was talking about killing Kristin. How many others should have known she was in grave danger?

Police quickly sealed off the area around Cartier's apartment. "He had apparently made statements to several people that he hated policemen and had no reservations about shooting a cop," homicide detective Billy Dwyer said in his report. "He stated that he would never go to prison again."

A police operations team entered Cartier's apartment at 8:30 p.m. He was dead, lying on his bed with the gun he used to kill Kristin in his right hand. He had put it to his head and fired once. Police recovered the spent bullet from the bedroom wall. They found three other shell casings in the area where he murdered Kristin.

Later that night, Leslie North walked into Bunratty's, looking for Cartier. "I said, 'He shot Kristin,'" said J.D. Crump. "She didn't look surprised. I said, 'Then he went and shot himself.' At that point, she lost it. She started screaming, 'What a waste! What a waste! He's dead!'"

Crump later said, "I've had to live the past couple of weeks feeling I could have stopped him. I should have called his probation officer."

It's doubtful that would have done any good. The system is so mindless that when the dead Cartier failed to show up in Boston Municipal Court as scheduled on June 19, a warrant was issued for his arrest.

It is still outstanding.

Chapter 2 Review Questions

1. What are the formal elements of Weber's model of bureaucracy? Based on your reading of the case or your own experiences with public bureaucracies, did Weber fail to mention any attributes of bureaucracy in his description?
2. What were her reasons for relying on public bureaucracy for protection? Why did the system fail to protect her? Are there comparisons with the previous case, "The Blast in Centralia No. 5," in response to this failure?

3. Does this case in your view support or contradict Weber's arguments about the monolithic power position of bureaucracy in society? About the nature of bureaucratic rationality? Its hierarchy? Specialization? Narrow latitude of bureaucratic rule enforcement? High degree of efficiency?

4. After reading the foregoing case study, where would you modify Weber's model to account more accurately for the pattern and the characteristics of America's bureaucracy?

5. According to the case, what are the sources of bureaucratic failure? What do you recommend to remedy the problems outlined in this case?

6. Think about the case and what it says about the value of bureaucracy in modern society. Why are bureaucracies important? And yet so disliked? In your view, can anything be done about the fundamental public hostility toward bureaucracy? And strengthen their effectiveness in serving the public?

Key Terms

ideal-types	objective experts
traditional authority	bureaucratic rules
charismatic authority	monied economy
legal-rational authority	bureaucratic power
bureaucratic hierarchy	bureaucratic secrecy
tenure in office	

Suggestions for Further Reading

For a thoughtful understanding of Weber's background, his intellectual development, and continuing influence, read the introduction of H. H. Gerth and C. Wright Mills, eds., *From Max Weber: Essays in Sociology* (New York: Oxford University Press, 1946); Reinhard Bendix, *Max Weber: An Intellectual Portrait* (New York: Doubleday, 1960); and Marianne Weber, *Max Weber: A Biography* (New York: John Wiley, 1975). For a short but insightful piece, see Alfred Diamant, "The Bureaucratic Model: Max Weber Rejected, Rediscovered, and Reformed," in *Papers in Comparative Administration,* edited by Ferrel Heady and Sybil L. Stokes (Ann Arbor, Mich.: The University of Michigan Press, 1962).

The current literature on bureaucracy is vast but uneven and should be read selectively. Some of the better introductions include Graham Alli-

son, *Essence of Decision: Explaining the Cuban Missile Crisis* (Boston: Little, Brown, 1971); Peter M. Blau and Marshall W. Meyer, *Bureaucracy in Modern Society,* Second Edition (New York: Random House, 1971); Francis E. Rourke, *Bureaucracy, Politics and Public Policy,* Third Edition (Boston: Little, Brown, 1984); Peter Woll, *American Bureaucracy,* Second Edition (New York: W. W. Norton, 1977); Kenneth J. Meier, *Politics and the Bureaucracy: Policy Making in the Fourth Branch of Government,* Second Edition (North Scituate, Mass.: Duxbury Press, 1987); Douglas Yates, *Bureaucratic Democracy: The Search for Democracy and Efficiency in American Government* (Cambridge, Mass.: Harvard University Press, 1982); Harold Seidman and Robert Gilmour, *Politics, Position, and Power,* Fourth Edition (New York: Oxford

University Press, 1986); Gary C. Bryner, *Bureaucratic Discretion* (New York: Pergamon Press, 1987); Richard J. Stillman II, *The American Bureaucracy,* Second Edition (Chicago: Nelson-Hall, 1995); James Q. Wilson, *Bureaucracy: What Government Agencies Do and Why They Do It* (New York: Basic Books, 1989); and Maureen Hogan Casamayou, *Bureaucracy in Crisis* (Boulder, Colo.: Westview Press, 1993). Francis E. Rourke's *Bureaucratic Power in National Politics,* Fourth Edition (Boston: Little, Brown, 1986), is a balanced, thorough collection of various excerpts from seminal writings on this subject as well as Ali Farazmand, ed., *Handbook of Bureaucracy* (New York: Marcel Dekker, 1994); and Larry B. Hill, ed., *The State of Public Bureaucracy* (New York: M. E. Sharpe, 1992).

For three excellent historic treatments of the rise of bureaucratic institutions, see the two volumes of E. N. Gladden, *A History of Public Administration* (London: Frank Cass, 1972); Ernest Barker, *The Development of Public Services in Western Europe, 1660–1930* (New York: Oxford University Press, 1944); and Frederick C. Mosher, *Democracy and the Public Service,* Second Edition (New York: Oxford University Press, 1982). Leonard D. White's four-volume history of American public administration up to 1900 (cited in the previous chapter's "Suggestions for Further Reading") is certainly valuable reading on this topic. Martin Albrow, *Bureaucracy* (New York: Praeger, 1970); Stephen Skowronek, *Building a New American State: The Expansion of National Administrative Capacities, 1877–1920* (New York: Cambridge University Press, 1982); Don K. Price, *America's Unwritten Constitution* (Baton Rouge, La.: Louisiana University Press, 1983); Martin J. Schiesl, *The Politics of Efficiency* (Berkeley, Calif.: University of California Press, 1977); Guy Benveniste, *The Politics of Expertise,* Second Edition (San Francisco: Boyd & Fraser, 1977); Thomas K. McCraw, *Prophets of Regulation* (Cambridge, Mass.: Harvard University Press, 1984); Frederick C. Mosher, *A Tale of Two Agencies* (Baton Rouge, La.: Louisiana Uni-

versity Press, 1984); Theda Skocpol, *Protecting Soldiers and Mothers* (Cambridge, Mass.: Harvard University Press, 1992); and Mathew Crenson, *The Federal Machine* (Baltimore: Johns Hopkins University Press, 1975) offer unique and highly original conceptual and historical perspectives, as well as James Q. Wilson's essay, "The Rise of the Bureaucratic State," in *The Public Interest* (Fall 1975).

Serious students of bureaucracy should examine primary materials—executive orders, legislative acts, and official reports. Many key materials are contained in Frederick C. Mosher, ed., *Basic Documents of American Public Administration, 1776–1950* (New York: Holmes and Meier, 1976), and Richard J. Stillman II, ed., *Basic Documents of American Public Administration Since 1950* (New York: Holmes and Meier, 1982). For the best recent defense of bureaucracy, see Charles T. Goodsell, *The Case for Bureaucracy,* Third Edition (Chatham, N.J.: Chatham House, 1993). Three recent articles dealing with the "image problem" of bureaucracy are Larry G. Hill, "Who Governs the American Administrative State? A Bureaucratic Centered Image of Governance," *Journal of Public Administration Research and Theory,* 1 (April 1991), pp. 261–294; Barry Bozeman, "A Theory of Government Red Tape," *Journal of Public Administration Research and Theory,* 3 (April 1993), pp. 273–303, and Francis E. Rourke, "American Bureaucracy in a Changing Political Setting," *Journal of Public Administration and Theory,* 1 (April 1991), pp. 111–129.

Two books that depict contemporary views of this topic are Gerald Gavey, *Facing the Bureaucracy* (San Francisco: Jossey-Bass, 1993); and B. Dan Wood and Richard W. Waterman, *Bureaucratic Dynamics* (Boulder, Colo.: Westview Press, 1994).

Works that attempt to view bureaucracy from a comparative perspective are Joel D. Aberbach, Robert D. Putnam, and Bert Rockman, *Bureaucrats and Politicians in Western Democracies* (Cambridge, Mass.: Harvard University Press,

1981); Metin Heper, ed., *The State and Public Bureaucracy* (New York: Greenwood, 1987); B. Guy Peters, *The Politics of Bureaucracy,* Fourth Edition (White Plains, N.Y.: Longman, 1995); and Ali Farazmand, ed., *Handbook of Comparative and Development Public Administration* (New York: Marcel Dekker, 1991).

For two excellent books devoted to the British experience, see Peter Hennessy, *Whitehall* (New York: Free Press, 1989); and Rosamund M. Thomas, *The British Philosophy of Administration* (Cambridge, England: Center for Business and Public Sector Ethics, 1989).

CHAPTER 3

The General Environment:
The Concept of Ecology

A *n ecological approach to public administration builds, then, quite literally*
from the ground up. . . .

John M. Gaus

Introduction

Ecology entered the lexicon of social science and public administration literature
long before it became popular in the media and on college campuses in the 1970s as
a word synonymous with protecting the natural beauty of the landscape. Originally,
the term was derived from the ancient Greek word *oikos,* meaning "living place," and
was used extensively by nineteenth-century Darwinian botanists and zoologists to describe how organisms live and adapt to their environments. Sociologists during the
1920s borrowed the ideas of plant and animal ecology and applied the concept to
human life; they emphasized the *interdependence* of human life within an increasingly
complex organic system and the tendency of living systems to move toward an *equilibrium,* or stabilization of life forms in relation to the surrounding environment.

Ecology was introduced into the public administration vocabulary primarily
through the writings of the late Harvard Professor John M. Gaus (1894–1969), one
of the early pioneers of public administration; he elaborated on ecology in a series of
famous lectures at the University of Alabama in 1945, later published as *Reflections
on Public Administration.*

In this work, as well as in his other writings, Gaus was particularly adept at weav-
ing the patterns and ideas of public administration into the total fabric of the issues
and events of modern American society. Better than most observers, he showed how
public administration, its development, and its activities were influenced by its setting, or its ecology. In his words, ecology "deals with all interrelationships of living
organisms and their environment." Thus, "an ecological approach to public administration builds . . . quite literally from the ground up; from the elements of a place—
soils, climate, location, for example—to the people who live there—their numbers and

ages and knowledge, and the ways of physical and social technology by which from the place and in relationships with one another, they get their living." For Gaus, administrative systems were inextricably intertwined with the fabric of society. In particular, he delineated several important elements that he found useful "for explaining the ebb and flow of the functions of government: people, place, physical technology, social technology, wishes and ideas, catastrophe, and personality." He addressed himself to the importance of these ecological factors in the following selection abridged from his *Reflections on Public Administration.*

Gaus began teaching political science shortly after World War I (prior to Harvard, he taught at the University of Wisconsin) with an early interest in public administration. He interspersed teaching with numerous state and national administrative assignments, and he brought these practical experiences to his classes. Throughout his career, Gaus was fascinated by the interplay of forces between public administration and the larger society.

Gaus shared much in common with Frederick Jackson Turner, an early twentieth-century American historian who poured over maps, soil samples, statistical data of regions, and voting records in his empirical study of the growth of the American nation. Similarly, Gaus asked students of public administration to observe the environment of administration so as to understand how the characteristics of its ecology influence the development of administrative institutions. For Gaus, the term *ecology* was relevant not only to cloistered scholars of administration at work on universal theories of the administrative process, but also to on-the-line practitioners of administration. A conscious awareness of ecological factors permits administrators to respond more wisely to the demands and challenges of the external environment of their organizations. Thus, in the hands of the practitioner, ecology can become a diagnostic tool; it can help in visualizing the major elements in the administrative processes and provide a yardstick for measuring their impact on an organization. However, Gaus was aware that prediction would not be simple: "The task of predicting the consequences of contemporary action, of providing the requisite adjustment, is immensely difficult with the individual or in family life. The difficulty increases with the size and complexity of the unit and expansion and range of variables."

Gaus's concern with ecology of administration was prompted by a special concern with "change." He was a member of the generation rocked by the hardships of a catastrophic economic depression in the 1930s, and he saw the American landscape rapidly being transformed in myriad ways. As he observed, "Change which we have found to be so characteristic of American life, change that has disrupted neighborhoods, that has destroyed cultural stabilities, that has reflected the sweep across the continent, the restless migration to city and back to farm, from one job to another, has brought widely hailed merits. Its merits have been so spectacular, indeed, that we speak of it as progress. . . . Its costs are also becoming clearer, registered in the great dramatic collapses of the depression, more subtly in the defeat, disintegration and frustration of individuals. . . ." Gaus looked to public administration "to find some new source of content, of opportunity for the individual to assert some influence on the situation in which he finds himself." In one essay, "American Society and Public Administration," he stated: "My thesis is that through public instruments some new institutional bases which will enable the individual to find development and satisfaction can be created and some sense of purpose may flower again."[1]

Gaus was both pessimistic and optimistic about the condition of human society. His pessimism welled up when he saw change destroying the patterns of existence familiar to his generation, breaking down the stabilizing institutional arrangements, and confronting individuals with serious economic and personal hardships. Yet Gaus perceived a bright hope in applied social science: through an ecological approach to public administration he believed that new and renewed institutional patterns could be devised for individuals living in an age of change. Ecology in public administration became for Gaus a vital instrument for comprehending, directing, and modulating the forceful shocks of change in contemporary life. In the more than 40 years that have passed since Gaus's studies of ecology were published, younger scholars in the field, such as Fred Riggs, have been active in the wider application of the ecological approach, especially in the newer areas of developmental and comparative public administration.

As you read this selection, keep the following questions in mind:

Why does Gaus argue that knowledge of the general environment is so critical for administrators?

If you were to revise this essay for today's readers, what other environmental factors that affect modern public administration might you add to Gaus's list? (You might include, for example, the generation gap or ethnic or media factors.)

In what ways can administrators recognize changes in the general environment?

What might be the price paid for the failure of organizations to respond swiftly and correctly to external environmental change?

As you read Gaus's essay, reflect on its relevance to Case Study 1, "The Blast in Centralia No. 5." How did ecological factors influence the outcome of that case?

The Ecology of Public Administration

JOHN M. GAUS

The study of public administration must include its ecology. "Ecology," states the Webster Dictionary,

[1]John Gaus, "American Society and Public Administration," in John M. Gaus, Leonard D. White, and Marshall E. Dimock, *The Frontiers of Public Administration* (Chicago: University of Chicago Press, 1936).

Abridged from *Reflections on Public Administration* by John M. Gaus, pp. 6–19. Copyright 1947 by The University of Alabama Press. Reprinted by permission of the Estate of Janette Gaus.

"is the mutual relations, collectively, between organisms and their environment." J. W. Bews points out that "the word itself is derived from the Greek *oikos,* a house or home, the same root word as occurs in economy and economics. Economics is a subject with which ecology has much in common, but ecology is much wider. It deals with all the interrelationships of living organisms and their environment."[1] Some social scientists have been returning to the use of the term, chiefly employed by the biologist and botanist, especially under the stimulus of studies of anthropologists, sociologists, and pioneers who defy easy classification, such as the late Sir Patrick Geddes in Britain. In the lecture of Frankfurter's already quoted, the linkage between physical area, population, transport and government is concretely indicated. More recently, Charles A. Beard formulated some axioms of government in which environmental change is linked with resulting public administration. "I present," he stated, "for what it is worth, and may prove to be worth, the following bill of axioms or aphorisms on public administration, as fitting this important occasion.

1. The continuous and fairly efficient discharge of certain functions by government, central and local, is a necessary condition for the existence of any great society.
2. As a society becomes more complicated, as its division of labor ramifies more widely, as its commerce extends, as technology takes the place of handicrafts and local self-sufficiency, the functions of government increase in number and in their vital relationships to the fortunes of society and individuals.
3. Any government in such a complicated society, consequently any such society itself, is strong in proportion to its capacity to administer the functions that are brought into being.
4. Legislation respecting these functions, difficult as it is, is relatively easy as compared with the enforcement of legislation, that is, the effective discharge of these functions in their most minute ramifications and for the public welfare.
5. When a form of government, such as ours, provides for legal changes, by the process of discussion and open decision, to fit social changes, the effective and wise administration becomes the central prerequisite for the perdurance of government and society—to use a metaphor, becomes a foundation of government as a going concern.
6. Unless the members of an administrative system are drawn from various classes and regions, unless careers are open in it to talents, unless the way is prepared by an appropriate scheme of general education, unless public officials are subjected to internal and external criticism of a constructive nature, then the public personnel will become a bureaucracy dangerous to society and to popular government.
7. Unless, as David Lilienthal has recently pointed out in an address on the Tennessee Valley Authority, an administrative system is so constructed and operated as to keep alive local and individual responsibilities, it is likely to destroy the basic well-springs of activity, hope, and enthusiasm necessary to popular government and to the following of a democratic civilization."[2]

An ecological approach to public administration builds, then, quite literally from the ground up; from the elements of a place—soils, climate, location, for example—to the people who live there—their numbers and ages and knowledge, and the ways of physical and social technology by which from the place and in relationships with one another, they get their living. It is within this setting that their instruments and practices of public housekeeping should be studied so that they may better understand what they are doing, and appraise reasonably how they are doing it. Such an approach is of particular interest to us as students seeking to cooperate in our studies; for it invites—indeed is dependent upon—careful observation by many people in different environments of the roots of government functions, civic attitudes, and operating problems.

With no claim to originality, therefore, and indeed with every emphasis on the collaborative nature of the task, I put before you a list of the factors which I have found useful as explaining the ebb and flow of the functions of government. They are: people, place, physical technology, social technology, wishes and ideas, catastrophe, and personality. I have over many years built up a kind of flexible textbook in a collection of clippings, articles and books illustrative of each, as any one can do for himself. Such illustrations of the "raw material of politics" and hence administration are in themselves the raw material of a science of administration, of that part of the science which describes and interprets why particular activities are undertaken through government and the problems of policy, organization and management generally that result from such origins.[3]

By illustrating concretely the relation of these environmental factors, a cooperative testing of the theory will be facilitated. The changes in the distribution of the people of a governmental unit by time, age and place throw light on the origins of public policy and administration. At our first census, we were a people 80 per cent of whom lived on farms; at our last census, one hundred and fifty years later, 80 per cent of us did not live on farms. Over a third are now living in a relatively few metropolitan areas; but the growth of these areas is not in the core or mother city; it is in the surrounding suburbs, separate political entities, frequently also separate economic-status and cultural entities, yet sharing with the mother city, which is often absolutely declining in population, the public housekeeping problems of a metropolitan organism for which no—or no adequate—political organization exists. Our population is increasingly one with a larger proportion distributed among the older age classes. These raw facts—too little known and appreciated by citizens, which should be at once placed before them in discussing many of our public questions—in themselves explain much about our functions of government. Coupled with factors of place and technology, they clarify many an issue that is usually expressed in sterile conflicts. For example, the old people in the more frequent large family on a farm of a century ago, where more goods and services were provided on the farm, had a function still to perform and a more meaningful place in the lives of younger generations of the family. In a more pecuniary economy, separated from the family-subsistence economy, ignored in the allocation of the work and rewards of an industrial society, the demand for pensions became irresistible.

The movement of people (by characteristic age and income groups) from the mother city to suburbs (as guided by factors of time-space and cost in the journey to work, the dispersal of shopping centers, the search of industry for land space for straight-line production facilitated by paved roads, trucks and distribution of power by wires, and other technological changes, and changes in what we wish for in residential environment) produces its repercussion in the values of land and buildings, in the tax basis for public services already existent in older areas and demanded in the new, in the differential requirements and capacities-to-pay of people for housing (including the site and neighborhood equipment) and in the adjustment of transport and utility requirements for the ever-changing metropolitan organism.

Thus the factors of people and place are inextricably interwoven. And not merely in crowded urban centers. I have watched the same process of change in sparsely settled areas of farm and forest, and its potent effect on government.

Where there are extensive cut-over areas in the Lake States, where the older farm lands of New England or New York are no longer profitable to agriculture and reforestation is too recent to yield timber crops, in the Great Plains where lands best suited to grazing and with limited rainfall have been subjected to the plough, in the cut-over and eroded lands of the Southern Piedmont, or in the anthracite region of Pennsylvania, physical conditions—the exhaustion of the resource which originally brought settlement—have produced a chain of institutional consequences. Land values and tax payments decline, tax delinquent land reverts to county or state, public schools, roads and other services can no longer be locally financed. Immediate relief through state financial aids or state administered services in turn are inadequate when widespread catastrophic economic depression undermines state revenues. Efforts aimed at restoring a source of production, such as encouragement of cropping timber through favoring taxation or the building up of public forests adequate for permanent wood-using industries, or the restoration of soil, will require a long period of time for efficacy, and equally require an atmosphere in which political leadership, the careful integration of national, state, local, and individual and corporate policies, and skilled technical personnel can be established and supported steadily. Such an atmosphere, however, is not likely to be present among the frustrate population of such areas, or the better-provided populations of other areas called upon to tax themselves for local units of government in areas which they have never seen or whose problems they do not understand. Thus changes in place, or the use of the resources and products of a place, are coercive in their effect upon public administration.[4]

My own generation has had a great lesson in the importance of change in physical technology in witnessing the adoption of the automobile and the role it has come to play. It may be noted that its widespread use was made possible by the development of paved highways provided necessarily as a public service. Highway expansion and design have been affected by the coercion of political forces created by the physical invention. Groups of automobile users, manufacturers, hotel proprietors, road builders, road machinery and materials suppliers, persons seeking jobs in highway construction and administration and many others, have contended with those using horses, carriage and harness makers and persons opposed to the increased taxation that paved roads would require. The original causes—a combination of physical inventions such as the internal combustion engine and the vulcanization of rubber—get obscured in the ultimate disputes over taxation, jurisdiction, requirement of liability insurance and examination for drivers' licenses, or over the merits or defects of systems of traffic control or the financing of overhead crossings or express highways. The citizen blames "bureaucrats" and "politicians" because the basic ecological causes have not been clarified for him. This process of public function adoption may also be reversed by other changes—as we see, for example, in the abandonment of many publicly financed and constructed canals, when new technologies of transport rendered them obsolete.

Changes in physical technology, however

slowly their institutional influences may spread, are more obvious even to the point of being dramatic, to the citizen. But he sometimes forgets the importance of the invention of social institutions or devices, and their continuing influences which coerce us. Thus the pooling and application of the savings of many through the invention of the corporation has set new forces to ripple through the social order, disarranging human relationships and creating new possibilities of large scale enterprise financially capable of utilizing extensive equipment and personnel and creating new relationships between buyer and seller, employer and employee—from which coercions for a new balance of forces, through consumer, labor and investor standards, have resulted.

You will have noted how interrelated all of these factors are in their operation. Perhaps the subtlest one is that for which I have difficulty in finding a satisfactory term. I have used the words "wishes and ideas." What you don't know, it is said, won't hurt you. I wonder whether this is true. If you do know that some new drug, or method of treatment of disease, will prevent the illness or perhaps death of those dear to you, you will have a new imperative for action, even if that action requires a public program. If you know or think you know that a combination of legislative and administrative measures will safeguard your bank deposit or insurance from destruction, that idea will have a coercive effect upon your political action. If you think that public officials are corrupt, that a tariff act or a regulation of a trade is a "racket," that too will influence the political decisions of your time. If you value material well-being, and if that desire takes so definite a form as a house and yard and garden, there are inevitable consequences in standards of public services that will facilitate the realization of your desire. Down that long road one will find the public insurance of mortgages to achieve lower interest rates and longer-term financing and zoning ordinances.

The originators of ideas and of social as well as physical invention are persons. We students of public administration will do well to study the elements in the influences which Bentham, the

Webbs, the city planner Burnham, the health officer Biggs, the pioneers in the New York Bureau of Municipal Research and its Training School for Public Service have wielded. Relevant preparation, longevity, personal or institutional resources for research, sympathetic disciples, frequently some catastrophic situation in which prevailing attitudes were sufficiently blasted to permit the new ideas to be applied, channels of publication and of communication generally, as well as inner qualities of industry and integrity all, or nearly all in some combination, will be found. We each will have touched some one of this kind, perhaps, in our own community; if not a pioneer in original invention, an enlightened civic interpreter, agitator, or organizer. Thus the late Governor Alfred E. Smith had a genius for relating his sense of people's needs, his experience in party and legislative processes and his position as Governor to a political and administrative program in which the special knowledge of many persons was most effectively used in the service of the State of New York.

Catastrophe, especially when leadership and knowledge are prepared with long-time programs into which the immediate hurried relief action can be fitted, has its place in the ecology of administration. It not only is destructive, so that relief and repair are required on a scale so large that collective action is necessary, but it also disrupts, jostles or challenges views and attitudes, and affords to the inner self as well as to others a respectable and face-saving reason for changing one's views as to policy. The atomic bomb gave to many, perhaps, a determining reason for a change of attitude toward international organization. But I incline to the view that the effects of catastrophe on our thinking are relatively short-lived, and confined to relatively smaller institutional changes, and that older forces flood back with great strength to cancel most of the first reaction. A frightened and frustrated society is not one in which really significant changes will take root, unless careful preparation and wise administration of the relief period are available. The night club fire in Boston in recent years in which so many service men from various parts of

the country were killed is a tragic example of one role of catastrophe. In the lurid glare of that fire, weaknesses in building codes and the administration of them were revealed. So many vested interests of materials, construction and crafts center in building codes that they are difficult to keep in tune with invention and changing social needs. The fact that many in the fire were from remote places, and were men in the armed services, gave unusually wide reporting of the tragedy for some days, especially as many victims lingered on in hospitals. One result of the shock of the catastrophe was therefore action in cities throughout the world to inspect their places of public amusement and survey their fire-prevention legislation and administration. On a vaster scale, the catastrophe of economic world depression led to a varied array of responses through collective action in which there was much similarity despite regional and ideological differences among the various states of the world, since there were also like ecological factors, common to modern power industry and the price system. World wars illustrate the extent to which a large area of collective action is necessarily adopted under modern conditions of total war— and equally illustrate the tremendous pull of older customary views at the close, when the pressure to remove the controls rises, and individuals in office are held responsible for the frustrations once borne as a patriotic offering. Wise and fortunate indeed is that community that has so analyzed its problems and needs, and has so prepared to make use of catastrophe should it come by plans for carrying out programs of improvements, that the aftermath of tragedy finds its victims as well cared for as humanly possible and in addition some tangible new advance in the equipment and life of the community. I have seen some communities which, because they had equipped themselves with personnel capable of fresh thinking, had obtained from depression work-relief programs recreation facilities that were their first amenities.

Such an approach as this to our study of public administration is difficult, in that it makes demands upon our powers to observe, upon a sensitive awareness of changes and maladjustment and upon our willingness to face the political—that is, the public-housekeeping—basis of administration. These factors—you may improve upon my selection—in various combinations lie behind a public agency. In their combination will be found the reasons for its existence, and the reasons for attack upon it as well. Only in so far as we can find some essentially public core in the combination can we hope to have an agency free from spoils or abuse of power. The process of growth and formulation of a public policy out of these environmental materials links environment and administration. We may be too responsive to change, or we may fail to achieve our best selves by ignoring what we might do to advantage ourselves by collective action, if we perform this task of politics badly.

"When I pay taxes," wrote Justice Holmes to his friend Sir Frederick Pollock, "I buy civilization." It is no easy task of the citizen in this complicated world to get fair value in what he buys. That task is one of discovery of the causes of problems, of the communication of possible remedies, of the organizing of citizens, of the formulation of law. It is the task, in short, of politics. The task will be more fruitfully performed if the citizen, and his agents in public offices, understand the ecology of government.

Notes

1. J. W. Bews, *Human Ecology* (London: Oxford University Press, 1935), p. 1.
2. From "Administration, A Foundation of Government," by Charles A. Beard, in *American Political Science Review,* XXXIV, No. 2 (April, 1940), p. 232. Reprinted by permission of the American Political Science Association.
3. The methods as well as the substantive interpretations of Frederick Jackson Turner should be familiar to students of public administration so far as the printed page permits. It was a rich experience to be present as he worked over maps and statistical data of a county, state or region, putting geology, soils, land values, origins of residents, and voting records together for light on the resulting social action.
4. A reverse picture is the sudden demand on the use of ores in the Adirondack region during the world war because of changes in the conditions of ocean shipment. In one remote village a public housing project, to take care of the expanded work force, was a consequence, again, of the catastrophe of war.

▭ CASE STUDY 3

Introduction

The concept *ecology of administration* can be well illustrated by most case studies on public administration, for it would be a rare public administrator who was *not* influenced by at least a few of the major ecological factors that John Gaus outlined in the preceding essay. The theme of ecology runs throughout administrative activities, serving to shape and reshape the course and direction of public policy. The following case study, "Dumping $2.6 Million on Bakersfield," is a good example of how ecological factors can affect public administration and what can happen to administrators who fail to take these external factors into account before initiating a public program.

Michael Aron, a California-based journalist, writes an interesting account of the planning and implementation of a federal program sponsored by the U.S. Department of Health, Education, and Welfare (HEW) to build health clinics for migratory farm workers near the small central California town of Bakersfield. Formulated with good intentions, the program sounded ideal in the initial planning stage, but it nearly failed because inadequate attention was paid to the surrounding social ecology of administration. Aron ably details the ensuing intense struggle between various local forces for control of the health program—the black community, Mexican-American groups, local politicians, and established medical groups. HEW's Washington office and its regional San Francisco office soon became caught in the middle of a conflict that they neither wanted, nor had anticipated.

When reading this selection, keep the following questions in mind:

If you had been the administrator at HEW responsible for the planning of this migratory health program, how would you have assessed the local administrative ecology and better adapted your program to suit its characteristics?

Who were the interest groups, and what were their individual points of view?

In what ways did HEW's own actions in implementing the program intensify the conflict among the major interest groups? In particular, what environmental factors did they fail to recognize in designing and implementing this program?

What were the various viewpoints of the Bakersfield situation *within* HEW? How did these conflicting forces, in turn, influence the course of development of HEW's program?

Do Gaus's ideas on the ecology of administration need adjusting to conform more closely to the current demands and problems confronting modern public administrators, such as those outlined in the case study? If so, specifically in what ways?

Dumping $2.6 Million on Bakersfield (Or How *Not* to Build a Migratory Farm Workers' Clinic)

MICHAEL ARON

Like the coming of the railroad, the arrival of big federal money in a small, out-of-the-way California town causes a certain amount of uproar, especially when it is dumped in a bundle by an agency that has to get rid of it quick. In this case, the money comes from the Department of Health, Education, and Welfare, for one of its 131 migrant health programs, and the town that has to fight over the grant is Bakersfield.

From "Dumping $2.6 Million on Bakersfield (Or How *Not* to Build a Migratory Farm Workers' Clinic)" by Michael Aron, *The Washington Monthly* (October 1972), pp. 23–32. Reprinted by permission of The Washington Monthly Company.

But it could just as well have been one of the other 130 migrant health programs, or any federal effort where the bureaucrat is mandated both to spend money fast and also to insure that local people control their own destinies. Controlling your own destiny, in these days of decentralization and revenue sharing, really means that the locals can help decide how to divvy up federal money among themselves. Bakersfield is a consequence of the whole idea of community participation in federal projects, but in this instance, the town only began participating after the money was pumped in—for very obvious reasons and with some very disruptive results.

Our story begins in Washington, D.C., in March, 1970, with the passage by Congress of the Migrant Health Act. Senator Walter Mondale's Migratory Labor subcommittee drafted the legislation, authorizing an $11-million appropriation for migrant programs in fiscal 1970, and it was Mondale, personally, who pressed for insertion of an amendment providing that "persons broadly representative of all elements of the population to be served [be] given an opportunity to participate in the implementation of such programs."

Since this was the time the Nixon Administration was striving to decentralize the "vast" federal bureaucracy, it fell to the regional offices of HEW to implement the legislation. Region IX, headquartered in San Francisco, and responsible for seven Western states (it has since lost Oregon and Washington), proposed four areas with heavy migrant "homebase" populations as possible locations for health projects. Three were in rural California counties, the fourth in the state of Washington. One was Bakersfield, Kern County, California.

HEW's plan was to find a chicano community group in each area to become its delegate agency for day-to-day administration of a project, in the same way that local anti-poverty groups became delegate agencies of the Office of Economic Opportunity. But there was a time problem: the legislation had been passed relatively late in the fiscal year, giving HEW only a few months in which to spend the money or else forfeit it back to Treasury. Compounding the problem was the fact that Bakersfield seemed to have no chicano community groups—20,000 chicanos, but no groups.

With the end of the fiscal year only six weeks away, anxious rural health officials turned their attention to a black group, the Kern County Liberation Movement (KCLM). Born six months earlier in the waning hours of a poor people's workshop and designated a consumers' auxiliary of the local anti-poverty agency, KCLM was little more than a collection of low-income citizens. As its first official act, KCLM had applied to HEW for a $70,000 planning grant to assay the health needs of Bakersfield's black ghetto; that application was still in the pipeline when regional HEW asked KCLM if it would accept $2.6 million to immediately establish a health center.

KCLM responded enthusiastically: certainly they would accept a grant—who wouldn't? In late May,

1970, an official from the Rural Health Office of the Community Health Service of the Health Services and Mental Health Administration (HSMHA) of the Public Health Service of the regional office of HEW flew to Bakersfield to help KCLM prepare a formal application. All this was done very quietly, without fanfare. Final contracts were signed in June, three weeks before the end of the fiscal year.

It wasn't until July that Kern County's health establishment got wind of the news—and when they did, all hell broke loose. The entire roster of local health agencies—the county medical society, the dental society, Kern General Hospital, the county health department, the board of supervisors, the state health department, the California Medical Association; and the congressionally mandated regional planning bodies, Comprehensive Health Planning and Regional Medical Programs—vented their spleen because none had been consulted prior to the awarding of the grant. The medical society had a special reason for bitterness: it had been operating its own federally-funded migrant clinic for years in two old trailers outside of town, and HEW was cutting the budget on that program at the same time it was handing $2.6 million to a bunch of poor people with no experience whatsoever in the administration or delivery of health care.

Creative Fumbling

For five days the flap over the award commanded headlines in the *Bakersfield Californian* (in sky-blue ink, no less); the paper also editorialized against the grant ("More Fumbling and Bumbling") and even ran a two-part feature on the medical society's "wonderful clinic." Bakersfield's two Republican state assemblymen called press conferences to denounce the award. Congressman Robert Mathias sent an angry telegram to HEW Secretary Elliot Richardson questioning how the department could possibly sanction such behavior on the part of its regional office. "Is this what the Administration means by 'creative federalism'?" Mathias asked. For the next three weeks the Bakersfield health establishment would virtually convulse in an effort to get the grant canceled.

On July 14, Dr. James Cavanaugh, deputy assistant secretary for health, announced a "full review" of the conditions surrounding the awarding of the grant, intimating that the contract would be canceled "if irregularities are detected."

On July 15, Cavanaugh flew from Washington to the regional office in San Francisco. In what is reported to have been a rather stormy session, Cavanaugh and regional officials rewrote the guidelines on community health grants so as to insure consultation with all appropriate state and local agencies. In Washington, meanwhile, Mathias' staff had done some checking and discovered that the Kern County Liberation Movement was not registered with OEO as an official delegate arm of the local anti-poverty agency. Mathias called Cavanaugh to ask if this were sufficiently "irregular" to warrant cancellation of the contract. When Cavanaugh said he didn't think so, Mathias asked if the contract could possibly be renegotiated under the new guidelines just promulgated. Cavanaugh said he doubted it. A Mathias press release the next day called HEW's action "inexcusable" and fixed the blame on "middle-level bureaucrats [who] ignored the letter of the law" (a reference to their failure to consult the congressionally mandated regional planning bodies).

While Mathias was busy reverse pork-barreling in Washington, physicians and politicians in Bakersfield were writing letters to anyone they could think of who might be able to reverse the decision. Let me quote from some of these letters:

Kern General Hospital Administrator Dr. Owen Hatley, to Dr. Vernon Wilson, an HEW official in Rockville, Maryland:

When an independent, unbiased consulting firm, experienced in developing health delivery systems, presents a program for Kern County, then and only then will I support any sponsoring agency in any of these endeavors. Reputable, experienced consulting firms are available, in contrast to falsefront organizations [KCLM] created to obtain desired answers to fuzzy-minded hypotheses conjured up by some social planners.

Congressman Barry Goldwater, Jr. (representing a neighboring district) to Secretary Richardson:

This group [KCLM] has absolutely no experience that would even remotely qualify them for a grant of this magnitude. . . . I request that you immediately investigate this matter and withdraw the grant.

State Assemblyman William Ketchum to HEW Undersecretary John Veneman, his former colleague in the California legislature:

I object to the "cart before the horse" manner in which this has been handled and request that you immediately stop funding . . . [HEW's] "better to spend now than undertake planning" philosophy is a classic symptom of the whole OEO syndrome.

On July 27, KCLM held a press conference to refute the "numerous unfounded charges leveled against us in recent days." Considering the group's relative inexperience, it was an artful performance. One moment they were militant: "The low income community of Kern County wants to see a migrant health center that will meet their needs and they want to see it not after a two- or three-year planning study. Frankly we are *tired* of being studied. We want direct medical services now." The next moment, conciliatory: "Naturally we welcome the cooperation and support of any agencies interested in meeting the common goal of comprehensive health care for the entire community."

In San Francisco, meanwhile, regional HEW was kept busy trying to explain its actions to HEW officials in Washington. An assistant regional director recalls: "Washington was not terribly happy with us, and that's the understatement of the year. Of course, we knew what we were doing all along. We were going to get funding into that area no matter who it upset, and not by the traditional route of currying favor with conservative county medical societies. To get things done, you go do them and fight the political battles after—especially in this Administration. We like to think of ourselves as 'bureaucratic guerrillas' fighting for what we believe in."

By July 29, it was compromise time. Cavanaugh and Mathias flew to Bakersfield together to announce that HEW was suspending project funds for 90 days pending a "restructuring" of the KCLM board of directors. The suspension, Cavanaugh told a press conference, would be lifted only when the board, then made up entirely of "consumers," added professional health-care "providers" to its membership.

Cavanaugh's, too, was an artful performance (which may help explain why he is now on the White House staff). He seemed genuinely pained by "this unfortunate misunderstanding." He urged the Bakersfield health establishment to play an "activist" role on the consumer-provider board, and assured his good friends that "this sort of thing will not happen again." Privately, he told Mathias that HEW would consider canceling the grant if KCLM should fail in any way to execute its provisions. And when the man from HEW left town that night, KCLM was still the beneficiary of the potential $2.6 million.

Although project funds were technically suspended, regional HEW began sending "emergency" funds to KCLM to keep it on its feet. The grant had called for expenditures of $391,000 in the first year—$248,000 for staff salaries and the rest for clinic facilities and supplies. (And when they tell you they're putting X million dollars into programs for poor people, remember: professionals, clericals, and private businesses get the money; the poor get services.) Before any of this money could be spent, however, it would be necessary to hire a project director, preferably one who could court the favor of the health establishment and orchestrate a restructuring of the board.

Regional HEW proposed that a young dental school graduate from San Francisco become interim project director until a permanent director could be found. KCLM agreed, and Robert Isman, D.D.S., assumed his duties in August.

Through the fall months Isman worked hard to win the cooperation of local health agencies, but two things were working against him: his longish hair and what they call in Bakersfield "ultraliberal leanings." City officials, whose own budgets only added up to something like $12 million, simply could not understand why HEW would select such a character to supervise a $2.6-million project. He had no experience, either dental or administrative. He showed up for meetings with bankers and lawyers wearing cut-off jeans and thongs. To this day, people talk about Isman as if his eight months in Bakersfield had been profitably spent dealing hashish on the side.

It took much persuasion and several trips to Bakersfield by regional HEW officials, but in November the KCLM board was restructured to include 10 professional health providers representing various agencies in the county, including the medical society, which put its migrant clinic director on the board but instructed him not to vote. (The argument is sometimes advanced that the medical society joined only to sabotage the project, because free health care for the poor takes money out of the pockets of local physicians and the county hospital; but there's too much conspiracy theory there, or at least not enough money involved to make it credible.)

That the consumers still outnumbered the providers 25 to 10 irked some people, however. Mathias' local aide called the restructuring "a token effort to appease the community." Assemblyman Stacey branded it "a sham and a fraud" and joined the ranks of the countless politicians who at one time or another have accused HEW of "strong-arm tactics."

With the board restructured, everyone expected funding to resume, but HEW suddenly attached new conditions to the lifting of the suspension. KCLM either had to demonstrate broad-based community support, or hire a permanent project director.

In the meantime, forces were still at work trying to get the grant canceled. In December, the medical society applied to HEW for $325,645, ostensibly to expand its existing clinic program, in effect proposing itself as an alternative to KCLM. In Washington, Mathias continued to warn HEW that the project was "doomed to failure" unless local agencies were brought into the fold and given more say in board policy. Quietly, Mathias also asked the Government Accounting Office for a full investigation of the activities of the local anti-poverty umbrella agency, the Kern County Economic Opportunities Corporation.

Three months went by with no progress made toward filling the project director's job and mounting hostility towards Isman from the establishment. Then in April, 1971, HEW decided to step in and temporarily take over the project itself. Vincent Garza, a Mexican-American public health officer stationed at headquarters, was dispatched to replace Isman as interim project director for 90 days. To complement this action, regional HEW abruptly canceled the dental component of the project, thus insuring Isman's complete removal from the scene. Both sides in Bakersfield welcomed the two moves—the health establishment because Garza was a professional like themselves; KCLM because it meant immediate resumption of funding.

From this point on, the struggle ceases to be one pitting organized medicine and its friends against poor people. As you will see, it evolves into a struggle pitting poor people of one race against poor people of another. There are no Machiavellian plots here, no designs by the establishment to divide and conquer. That's just the way it happens.

Dude Ranch Junket

Most of the farm workers of Kern County are Mexican-Americans; maybe 20 per cent are Mexican nationals who came north to follow the softfruit season (legally or illegally) and managed to linger longer.

For years, these people have lived in shacks and camps or slept unsheltered on the banks of irrigation canals. Their general health is not good. They get skin diseases from working in fields sprayed with pesticides; they suffer high incidences of venereal disease, eye defects, heart trouble, and nervous disorders; obesity, hypertension, and diabetes are so prevalent that local health authorities believe these conditions to be hereditary in Mexicans; 90 percent of the children have serious dental problems. "They're learning that an unhealthy body produces nothing," one official said, adding as an afterthought, "They've certainly learned it the hard way." It used to be that when someone got sick, he worked it off or waited it out—unless he got real sick, in which case his family piled him into a car and drove the 20 miles to Kern General Hospital where they would wait for hours in the emergency room hoping that the next intake nurse spoke Spanish. Of course, there was also the medical society's migrant clinic in trailers in Lamont, but it operated only during "the season" (May to September; the actual season is eight to 10 months), and then only three nights a week from 6 p.m. to 10 p.m. At regional HEW the clinic is still referred to as a "band-aid station."

The first thing on Garza's agenda when he arrived in Bakersfield was to find a suitable location for a health center. For several days he, an architect, and Mathias' local aide drove around the Lamont-Arvin-Weedpatch area looking for a site—and immediately a conflict arose. KCLM thought they ought to be looking in the Lakeview district, where blacks live. Garza explained that these were *migrant* funds and that it had been HEW's intention all along to put a health center someplace where the campesinos would have easy access to it. But this had not been

KCLM's understanding at all; they had been led to believe, they said, that the center would be located in a black neighborhood and that campesinos from all over the county would be encouraged to use it and think of it as their own.

KCLM felt suddenly betrayed. After fighting off the encroachments of the health establishment for almost a year, they now learned that HEW wanted to put the health center in a part of the county where less than one percent of the population is black. A bitter pill; several KCLM board members chose to resign rather than swallow it.

To sweeten it, perhaps, Garza organized a weekend outing for KCLM board members at a ranch-retreat 80 miles north of Bakersfield and invited the HEW regional director to come along and to bring some of his staff. A good time was presumably had by all, and the regional director soothed ruffled feathers by promising that no matter what happened in the future, KCLM's efforts would not go unrewarded; but folks in Bakersfield took a different view of the outing. Garza returned to Bakersfield on a Monday morning to find himself being blasted on the front page of the *Californian* for his $2,500 dude ranch junket financed by "the taxpayers." (The story was written by the son of the county health superintendent, which says something about small cities.) Three weeks later, Garza left Bakersfield and the Public Health Service and went to Yale on a fellowship.

Garza was replaced in July, 1971, by Charles Pineda, a Mexican-American native of Kern County, the son of a fruit picker and holder of a master's degree in social work. Pineda continued the search for a clinic site and also began to think about recruiting a medical staff.

Hmm . . . Federal Funding

In September, 15 months after the awarding of the grant, a makeshift clinic was finally opened in Lamont. Pineda had found a young doctor from Los Angeles to become clinic physician ($25,000), had lured an aging South American from a hospital in the Bronx to become medical director ($27,500), and the three of them had talked the medical society into renting its trailers to KCLM until a permanent location could be found ($1,600, which has never been paid). As soon as the medical society clinic shut down for the "winter," KCLM occupied the trailers and began treating its first farmworker patients. Pineda, meanwhile, found an old grocery store in Weedpatch, leased it, and gradually moved the project into it over the next three months.

The clinic in Weedpatch is a shock when you first see it. Somehow the term "migrant health center" leads you to expect a depressing storefront, partitioned in half, and dimly lit, with maybe a purple curtain separating the waiting room from the examining room, and a wizened old doctor inside waiting to grab you in his palsied, age-blotched hands. You walk into the clinic in Weedpatch, however, and your first thought is "hmmm . . . federal funding." The clinic is partitioned all right, but partitioned into a large reception room, two intake offices, five examining rooms, a treatment room, a laboratory, a records library, staff offices, and a lounge. The staff numbers about 25. The equipment is brand new, ultra-modern, and *clean*. When you open your mouth to say "aaahh . . ." in this clinic, you're opening it to an electronic implement coming out of a wall console.

To the campesinos and their families, the clinic is a godsend. It heals them, soothes them, educates them, trains them, employs a few of them—all free of charge, for the time being. HEW wants the clinic to become self-sufficient, so patient billings will begin in the near future; but treatment will still be "free" (sort of) for the 90 percent who belong to the union's "Robert F. Kennedy Farm Workers' Medical Plan" (for which a small premium is deducted from their paychecks). At last count, the clinic had given treatment to 6,000 patients from 1,200 families, and thanks to the imperatives of bureaucracy, each one now has a detailed record of his medical history, probably for the first time in his life. Ask the campesinos whom they thank for all this, and you get a surprising—no, not surprising—answer. Senator Kennedy, of course. The young one.

Chicanos in the Wings

But don't get the idea that just because the clinic opened, the infighting ceased. On the contrary, now there was something tangible to fight over.

An interesting bit of correspondence circulated around Bakersfield at this time, copies of an exchange between HEW Secretary Richardson and Senators Walter Mondale and Adlai Stevenson III, past and present chairmen of the Migratory Labor subcommittee. Richardson's letter to the subcommittee requested "clarification of congressional intent" regarding the consumer-participation amendment to the Migrant Health Act. Mondale wrote back: "I was shocked to learn that there is still substantial doubt as to your Department's implementation of an amendment which became effective in March of 1970." Stevenson wrote: "I am extremely concerned that Migratory Health Program relations and guidelines provide the basis for 'meaningful' farm-worker participation, rather than a degree of 'tokenism.' This, of course, requires a policy-making function for the farm-worker participants rather than merely an advisory role."

It was regional HEW that flooded Bakersfield with copies of the exchange. And for a reason. KCLM was still the delegate agency administering the project, but it no longer could be said to represent the true "consumers." Now that the clinic had opened in Weedpatch, the consumers were campesinos. It was *they* who should be doing the community-participating.

This was fine with project director Pineda, a chicano whose father was still out in the fields; it was fine, as well, with the clinic staff, half of whom were Mexican, and others who had to have been sympathetic to the plight of farm workers in the first place in order to have accepted a job in a town as Godforsaken as Weedpatch. KCLM, on the other hand, was naturally upset: first, they had "lost" the clinic itself; now they were faced with possible loss of control over it and forfeiture of their status as a bona fide government delegate agency.

Acting on their own authority, but with behind-the-scenes encouragement from regional HEW, Pineda and several clinic staff members appointed five reasonably intelligent, but non-English-speaking, campesinos to a "campesino board," a kind of shadow cabinet that would wait in the wings ready to take over at the earliest signal from HEW. That they were non-English-speaking meant that they had to rely on people like Pineda to tell them what was going on. This was in October.

On December 14, KCLM voted to fire Pineda. The official reasons are not worth going into—basically they questioned Pineda's competence. The actual reason was that Pineda had been attempting to serve two masters at once, KCLM and the campesinos, and his allegiance to the former seemed to be flagging. Informed of the dismissal, regional HEW immediately ordered him reinstated, saying that KCLM no longer had legal authority to make such a decision (because it no longer represented "consumers").

At its next regular meeting, on December 22, KCLM voted to change its name to the Kern County Health Committee (KCHC). This is not insignificant. It represents a conscious grab at respectability and tacitly acknowledges its new position in the battle configuration. How can you call yourself a liberation movement when you're fighting to preserve a vested interest?

Culturally Unfit

Two things of consequence happened in January. First, elections for a new campesino board were held in Lamont-Arvin-Weedpatch; four of the five men who had been appointed by Pineda in October won election to the board. (The fifth would have won, too, had he chosen to run.) The board then incorporated itself as Clinica De Los Campesinos, Inc. (CDLC). Second, the clinic's South American medical director failed his state medical board examination, meaning he was without a license to practice in California.

In February, the roof caves in.

On February 14, 24 hours before KCHC was supposed to transfer authority to CDLC, the KCHC board notifies Pineda of his dismissal in a memo listing eight specific grievances, one claiming he hired the South American medical director without consulting the board and another charging him with "loading" the clinic staff with Mexican-Americans.

On February 15: KCHC, citing election "irregularities," rejects the legitimacy of the CDLC board and refuses to transfer control of the project.

On February 16: 200 chicano demonstrators mass in front of the clinic, Pineda and two clinic staff members among them, carrying picket signs and threatening to "shut it down" (in Spanish). The black chairman of KCHC wades into the angry mob and fires the two staff members on the spot. Half of the demonstrators move down the highway to the

KCHC administrative office in Lamont. The demonstrations last until midnight without serious incident.

February 17: The clinic has been splattered with paint during the night. There are bullet holes in the plate glass window. KCHC's black chairman appoints himself "acting project director." Regional HEW officials fly down from San Francisco in the hope of restoring order; they put the KCHC chairman on notice that his assumption of the project directorship constitutes a flagrant conflict of interest. Two-thirds of the clinic staff send individual letters to HEW declaring their allegiance to CDLC.

February 18: A provider member of the KCHC board calls the executive secretary of the medical society at midnight and, on behalf of KCHC, pleads for help. The executive secretary calls his 30-year-old assistant, Riley McWilliams, at 2:30 a.m. and orders him to report to KCHC the next day to become interim project director.

February 23: Telegram to KCHC from regional HEW states: actions of KCHC in direct contradiction to agreements; therefore, project funds would be suspended indefinitely and funding to KCHC would terminate on April 15, 1972.

February 24: Local aide sends confidential memo to Mathias in Washington warning of black-brown racial conflict that could engulf the county; says black community promises reprisals if any harm comes to KCHC chairman; surmises that United Farm Workers are involved in demonstrations.

February 26: CDLC writes to Secretary Richardson—letter begins, "Honorable Sire"; informs that Riley McWilliams made project director without HEW approval; ends with veiled threat to close clinic down as "last resort."

February 28: Medical society applies to HEW for $155,891 grant to expand its own clinic; application states, "basic to this proposal is removal of the existing clinic."

February 29: KCHC chairman reports alleged threats to his person.

March 10: CDLC submits application to HEW to take over administration of project; application actually written by four clinic staff members.

March 17: Twelve clinic staff draft joint letter to HEW threatening to resign if CDLC not made delegate agency; claim Riley McWilliams culturally unfit to be project director.

Bent in the Fields

April 15, the date HEW said it would terminate the project funding to KCHC, came and went, with no word from San Francisco. Three weeks later, the regional director sent letters to KCHC and CDLC proposing a joint luncheon meeting on May 10 at the posh (for Bakersfield) Casa Royale motel. He also sent a letter to the medical society announcing an award of $67,000 to continue their clinic-on-wheels, providing they move it to Buttonwillow, in the southwest part of the county. (Buttonwillow's one physician raised a stink, but that is another story.)

The regional director, the black project officer, and the chicano Public Health Service officer from Los Angeles arrived in Bakersfield the morning of the 10th. At noon they joined the KCHC board for lunch. The CDLC board had been invited to come at 1 p.m., but the hour passed 2 p.m. and the five campesinos had yet to show. Someone suggested that they might have gotten lost, since surely they had never been to the Casa Royale before. Someone else was delegated to go look for them. He found them in their customary positions for that hour, bent over in the fields in 95-degree heat. They said they had not been notified of the meeting. There was reason to think that one of their advisors on the clinic staff had intercepted the letter for reasons she believed to be in their best interests. The meeting proceeded without them. A radical Lutheran minister acted as their unofficial spokesman.

When it was over, an elaborate compromise had been drawn up: 1) the CDLC board would be absorbed into the KCHC board; 2) four providers mutually agreed upon by KCHC and CDLC would join the five campesinos, together to constitute a separate board-within-a-board; 3) the mini-board would serve in a "policy-recommending" capacity and receive the benefit of "whatever training and experience is available"; 4) on or before January 1, 1973, KCHC would transfer administrative control of the project to CDLC, retaining for itself only the role of fiscal intermediary. A fifth provision went unstated, but was well understood nonetheless: in return for its great efforts and considerable sacrifice, KCHC would become HEW's "umbrella agency" for all future projects in the county.

HEW and KCHC signed the compromise that afternoon. In the evening the five campesinos met with their supporters in the basement of the Lutheran Church in Lamont. Heated debate lasted past midnight, but the campesinos finally decided to sign the compromise. "It was not a victory, it was not a defeat," said CDLC chairman, Natividad Arreolo, weary perhaps in the knowledge that he was due out in the fields again at 4 a.m.

If Weedpatch Had Movies

That should be the end of the story. You know it's not. In the months since, there have been controversial hirings and firings, protest resignations, accusations of petty theft, and at least one false rumor of a sexual nature deliberately planted to discredit a potential project director. Dr. Garcia, the South American medical director, took his state boards again in June, and the delay in reporting his grade leads to speculation that it is being deliberately held up in channels for political reasons. As of September 1, the young medical society executive was still project director, a fact from which few but the medical society derive any comfort, and yet he is there.

The question remains as to whether KCHC will cede its little fiefdom to the campesinos by January 1, as agreed. HEW says it is committed to seeing the campesinos take over on schedule, and it is hard to imagine what KCHC could possibly gain by holding out. One also can't help but wonder whether the campesinos really are capable of running the project.

The real problem with this project, and, one suspects, with others as well, has been the ease with which political considerations were able to obscure the stated objective, namely, comprehensive health care for farm workers—combined with the fact that HEW would seem to have subordinated the stated objective to an unstated, or at least secondary one, namely, Mexican-American community organization. Thus, it took 15 months of sparring and jockeying before a single patient was seen. And once opened, the clinic had to shorten its hours anytime HEW felt it necessary to suspend funds in order to reprimand this faction or that. The community of 20,000 is still without a dentist because of an essentially political decision.

The medical society seems to think that because doctors can save lives on a surgical table, their expertise necessarily embraces all facets of medicine, including how it should be delivered to people whom the doctors barely understand, can't talk to, and don't especially like—and the medical society fights to preserve the integrity of that idea. The poor people, black and brown, want better medical care than they are accustomed to receiving, but they also want power and respectability and anything else that might foster the illusion that they are swimming into the mainstream, and if a government health project is the only game in town, they'll jump at the chance to play it, and they'll play it as fiercely and seriously as they imagine it to be played elsewhere, and so what if the brothers and sisters have to wait a little longer for something they have never had anyway. And the whites on the clinic staff and the others lurking in the background all the time probably wouldn't be so eager to stir up the waters if only Weedpatch had a movie theater.

The government, through all this, has been like a ship captain steering the project towards shores the crew can't see yet. For the crowd in San Francisco, the project has been, and continues to be, "an interesting social experiment" (an assistant regional director's words), originally conceived to meet a singular need, but taking on added dimensions as it unfolds. Can blacks and browns work together? Are illiterate campesinos capable of self-administration? What adjustments can we make to keep the community from blowing apart? "I would say we've basically been more interested in using the clinic as an instrument of long-range social change than in meeting the short-run health needs of the target community," one HEW official admitted, fully aware that this is the kind of statement bureaucrats get roasted for every day.

To date $400,000 has been spent on the project, a mere fraction of the $13 billion HEW spends every year on health programs. One shudders at the thought of KCLMs and medical societies and campesino-equivalents plotting and maneuvering against each other and intramurally in every community where federal grants have been won; and yet, that is probably what happens, and is happening, all over the country at this moment.

"Kern County?" a project officer asked rhetorically. "Oh, it's not so bad there. These things are usually much worse in urban areas."

Chapter 3 Review Questions

1. What were the chief elements in the administrative ecology that HEW planners failed to take into account prior to developing the migratory farm workers' health clinic in Bakersfield? If you had been in charge of the project at HEW Regional Headquarters in San Francisco, what would you have done to ensure that the project began properly?

2. What was the role of the local press, politicians, and special interest groups in affecting the outcome of this federally supported program? Can you generalize about the impact of such special interest groups on national programs?

3. Can you distinguish between the institutional factors (such as the budgetary process) and the personnel leadership factors (such as the various persons assigned by HEW to administer the program at the local level) that prevented effective long-term comprehensive planning for this local public program? What reforms would you recommend to enhance better program planning in the future?

4. Compare Case Study 1, "The Blast in Centralia No. 5," with this case. How did the geographical distances in both cases influence the administrative decisions that were made? Can you generalize about the difficulties of effective administrative actions as the *distances* between the administrator and the "administered" expand?

5. Why were there various points of view about the purposes of this program *within*

HEW? What were these competing viewpoints? Can you generalize about the difficulties of effective administrative actions as the *levels of bureaucracy* between the administrative and the "administered" expand?

6. After reviewing this case study, how would you modify Gaus's ideas about the nature of modern administrative ecology? In your view, for instance, does he adequately cover the problems of ethnic differences? Class differences? Media influence? Leadership factors? Fragmented government oversight?

Key Terms

administrative ecology
physical technology
social technology

general environment
wishes and ideas
catastrophe

Suggestions for Further Reading

Gaus spent much of his life thinking about the ecology of public administration; therefore you would do well to begin by reading the entire book from which the reading in this chapter was reprinted, *Reflections on Public Administration* (University, Ala.: University of Alabama Press, 1947). In recent years comparative administrative scholars are perhaps the ablest group carrying on Gaus's investigations in this area; see Fred Riggs, *The Ecology of Administration* (New York: Asia Publishing House, 1967), as well as Ferrel Heady, *Public Administration: A Comparative Perspective,* Fifth Edition (New York: Marcel Dekker, 1996).

Biographies and autobiographies offer some of the finest observations on the interplay between social forces and public administration, and the most outstanding ones are Louis Brownlow, *A Passion for Anonymity* (Chicago: University of Chicago Press, 1958); Robert Caro, *The Power Broker: Robert Moses and the Fall of New York City* (New York: Random House, 1974); Leroy F. Harlow, *Without Fear or Favor: Odyssey of a City Manager* (Provo, Utah: Brigham Young University Press, 1977); Thomas K. McCraw, *Prophets of Regulation* (Cambridge, Mass.: Harvard University Press, 1984); David Stockman, *The Triumph of Politics: The Inside Story of the Reagan Revolution* (New

York: Harper & Row, 1986); Deborah Shapley, *Promise and Power: The Life and Times of Robert McNamara* (Boston: Little, Brown, 1993); as well as several biographies in Jameson W. Doig and Erwin C. Hargrove, eds., *Leadership and Innovation* (Baltimore: Johns Hopkins University Press, 1987). There are several classic social science studies of this subject, including Philip Selznick, *TVA and the Grass Roots: A Study of the Sociology of Formal Organization* (Berkeley: University of California Press, 1949); Herbert Kaufman, *The Forest Ranger—A Study in Administrative Behavior* (Baltimore: Johns Hopkins University Press, 1960); Arthur Maass, *The Army Engineers and the Nation's Rivers* (Cambridge, Mass.: Harvard University Press, 1951); Milton D. Morris, *Immigration: The Beleaguered Bureaucracy* (Washington, D.C.: Brookings Institute, 1985); and Paul Light, *Artful Work: The Politics of Social Security Reform* (New York: Random House, 1985). For an excellent set of current cases at the local level, read James H. Svárá and associates, *Facilitative Leadership in Local Government* (San Francisco: Jossey-Bass, 1994).

You should not overlook the rich case studies available through the Inter-University Case Program (P.O. Box 229, Syracuse, N.Y. 13210) as well as the John F. Kennedy School of Government

Case Program (Kennedy School of Government, Case Program, Harvard University, 79 JFK Street, Cambridge, Mass. 02138), most of which explore and highlight various dimensions of administrative ecology. The first ICP case book, Harold Stein, ed., *Public Administration and Policy Development: A Casebook* (New York: Harcourt Brace Jovanovich, 1952), contains an especially good introduction by Stein focusing on this topic.

Two short but useful pieces that should be read as well are Herbert G. Wilcox, "The Culture Trait of Hierarchy in Middle Class Children," *Public Administration Review* (March/April 1968), pp. 222–232, and F. E. Emery and E. L. Trist, "The Causal Texture of Organizational Environments," *Human Relations,* 18 (February 1965), pp. 21–32.

Certainly *must* reading for comprehending the whole cultural-social milieu within which American public administration operates remains the two volumes of Alexis de Tocqueville, *Democracy in America* (New York: Vintage, 1945), or for that matter, several of the other historical treatments of the American Experience: James Bryce, *The American Commonwealth,* 2 volumes (New York: Macmillan, 1888); Richard Hofstadter, *The American Political Tradition* (New York: Vintage Book,

1948); Michael Kammen, *People of Paradox* (New York: Vintage Books, 1972); Henry Steele Commanger, *The Empire of Reason* (New York: Doubleday, 1977); and Samuel P. Huntington, *American Politics; The Promise of Disharmony* (Cambridge, Mass.: Harvard University Press, 1981). For contemporary trends in the American social, economic, political, and fiscal landscape, read Aaron Wildavsky, "Ubiquitous Anomie: Public Service in an Era of Ideological Dissensus, *Public Administration Review* (July/August 1988), pp. 753–755; Harlan Cleveland, "Theses of a New Reformation: The Social Fallout of Science 300 Years After Newton," *Public Administration Review* (May/June 1988), pp. 681–686; Robert N. Bellah et al., *Habits of the Heart: Individualism and Commitment in American Life* (New York: Harper & Row, 1985); and E. J. Dionne, Jr., *Why Americans Hate Politics* (New York: Simon and Schuster, 1991).

For the best contemporary summary of the academic literature on this topic, read chapter 2, "The Environment of Public Organizations," in Hal Rainey, *Understanding and Managing Public Organizations* (San Francisco: Jossey-Bass, 1991).

CHAPTER 4

The Political Environment: The Concept of Administrative Power

The lifeblood of administration is power.

Norton E. Long

Introduction

While John Gaus stressed the broad evolutionary perspective of administrative ecology, Norton E. Long (1910–1994), a distinguished American political scientist and former New Deal civil servant, zeroes in on the immediate environment of public administration, namely, that of administrative power. In his classic essay, "Power and Administration," Long argues that administrative institutions—public agencies, departments, bureaus, and field offices—are engaged in a continual battle for political survival. In this fierce administrative contest bureaucrats contend for limited power resources from clientele and constituent groups, the legislative and executive branches, and the general public to sustain their organizations. As he writes, "The lifeblood of administration is power. Its attainment, maintenance, increase, and losses are subjects the practitioner and student can ill afford to neglect." And yet, "it is the most overlooked in theory and the most dangerous to overlook in practice."

For Long, the concept of power cannot be bottled in a jar and kept safely tucked away for future use; nor can its nature be revealed by simply examining the U.S. Constitution, the legislative mandates, or the formal hierarchy of an organizational chart. It is, rather, an ephemeral substance that is part of the disorderly, fragmented, decentralized landscape of American public administration—a landscape reminiscent more of tenth-century warring medieval fiefs than of twentieth-century modern government. Power in this chaotic terrain is everywhere, flowing "in from the sides of an organization, as it were; it also flows up the organization to the center from the constituent parts."

This fluid situation arises partly, in Long's view, from the failure of the American party system to protect administrators from political pressures and to provide adequate direction and support for government bureaus and agencies. The American party system "fails to develop a consensus on a leadership and a program that makes possible administration on the basis of acceptable decisional premises." Left to their own devices and discretion, public agencies are forced to enter the "business of building, maintaining and increasing their political support."

Administrators seek to build strong public relations and mobilize political support by developing a "wide range of activities designed to secure enough 'customer' acceptance to survive and, if fortunate, develop a consensus adequate to program formulation and execution." If public servants are to succeed, they must understand the political environment in which they operate and the political resources at their disposal. On this point, Long has direct relevance to some of the central political problems faced by administrators in Case Study 1, "The Blast in Centralia No. 5," and in Case Study 3, "Dumping $2.6 Million on Bakersfield."

How can Long's disorderly array of narrow interests weld itself together to develop an overall scheme of the national purpose? Rational schemes of coordination always run counter to "the self-centered demands of primary groups for funds and personnel." Again Long visualizes the power factor as significant in any reorganization plan for government. Improved coordination through any governmental reorganization plan will "require a political power at least as great as that which tamed the earlier feudalism." "Attempts to solve administrative reorganization in isolation from the structure of power and purpose in the polity are bound to prove illusory" and have "the academic air of South American Constitution-making."

In his perceptive essay, Long raises another important issue, namely, that because the decentralized nature of the American political system puts administrators in the midst of numerous competing interest groups, they are plagued with the continual problem, "To whom is one loyal—unit, section, branch, division, bureau, department, administration, government, country, people, world history, or what?" A precise consensus on what should be done and who should be obeyed rarely exists and will not so long as the American system fails to establish organized, disciplined political parties or so long as presidents are unable to find firm and continuing majorities in Congress for their legislative programs. Unlike the Parliamentary system, according to Long, each agency in the American executive branch must fend for itself in the political arena, grasping for its own share of political resources to sustain its programs. Therefore, Long advises American administrators to read Machiavelli, La Rochefoucauld, Duc de Saint Simon, or Madison on the reality of power rather than the classic texts on public administration that often only stress the formal components of public organizations.

The following excerpt from Long's essay, "Power and Administration," is based on his perceptive understanding, his training in classical political philosophy, as well as his practical administrative experiences while working at the local, state, and national levels during the Depression, World War II, and the postwar period, particularly his experience at the National Housing Administration in New York City and the Office of Price Administration in Washington. Long's perspectives on power were also significantly shaped by the "new realism" of such insightful students of governmental administration during the 1930s and 1940s as E. Pendleton Herring, Paul Appleby, and Herbert Simon who, like Long, were sober realists about the nature and substance of administrative power. For some traditionalists, Long may seem uncomfortably iconoclastic and politically cynical in his thinking, offering few simple answers to the questions he poses. Nevertheless, his essay raises several perplexing problems that are still critical in public administration today.

As you read this selection, keep the following questions in mind:

How does Long define administrative power? Why is it important? Are there any differences between political power and administrative power? How is administrative power attained and maintained?

What are the appropriate "ends" or "purposes" of the contest for power in administration?

Will the administrative struggle necessarily, if left unchecked, produce a coordinated, effective, and responsible public policy?

How can better planning and rationality be incorporated into the administrative system?

How does Long's approach differ from Weber's or Gaus's approach?

Power and Administration

NORTON E. LONG

There is no more forlorn spectacle in the administrative world than an agency and a program possessed of statutory life, armed with executive orders, sustained in the courts, yet stricken with paralysis and deprived of power. An object of contempt to its enemies and of despair to its friends.

The lifeblood of administration is power. Its attainment, maintenance, increase, dissipation, and loss are subjects the practitioner and student can ill afford to neglect. Loss of realism and failure are almost certain consequences. This is not to deny that important parts of public administration are so deeply entrenched in the habits of the community, so firmly supported by the public, or so clearly necessary as to be able to take their power base for

granted and concentrate on the purely professional side of their problems. But even these islands of the blessed are not immune from the plague of politics. . . . To stay healthy one needs to recognize that health is a fruit, not a birthright. Power is only one of the considerations that must be weighed in administration, but of all it is the most overlooked in theory and the most dangerous to overlook in practice.

The power resources of an administrator or an agency are not disclosed by a legal search of titles and court decisions or by examining appropriations or budgetary allotments. Legal authority and a treasury balance are necessary but politically insufficient bases of administration. Administrative rationality requires a critical evaluation of the whole range of complex and shifting forces on whose support, acquiescence, or temporary impotence the power to act depends.

Analysis of the sources from which power is

derived and the limitations they impose is as much a dictate of prudent administration as sound budgetary procedure. The bankruptcy that comes from an unbalanced power budget has consequences far more disastrous than the necessity of seeking a deficiency appropriation. The budgeting of power is a basic subject matter of a realistic science of administration.

It may be urged that for all but the top hierarchy of the administrative structure the question of power is irrelevant. Legislative authority and administrative orders suffice. Power adequate to the function to be performed flows down the chain of command. Neither statute nor executive order, however, confers more than legal authority to act. Whether Congress or President can impart the substance of power as well as the form depends upon the line-up of forces in the particular case. A price control law wrung from a reluctant Congress by an amorphous and unstable combination of consumer and labor groups is formally the same as a law enacting a support price program for agriculture backed by the disciplined organizations of farmers and their Congressmen. The differences for the scope and effectiveness of administration are obvious. The presidency, like Congress, responds to and translates the pressures that play upon it. The real mandate contained in an executive order varies with the political strength of the group demand embodied in it, and in the context of other group demands.

Both Congress and President do focus the general political energies of the community and so are considerably more than mere means for transmitting organized pressures. Yet power is not concentrated by the structure of government or politics into the hands of a leadership with a capacity to budget it among a diverse set of administrative activities. A picture of the presidency as a reservoir of authority from which the lower echelons of administration draw life and vigor is an idealized distortion of reality.

A similar criticism applies to any like claim for an agency head in his agency. Only in varying degrees can the powers of subordinate officials be explained as resulting from the chain of command. Rarely is such an explanation a satisfactory account of the sources of power.

To deny that power is derived exclusively from superiors in the hierarchy is to assert that subordinates stand in a feudal relation in which to a degree they fend for themselves and acquire support peculiarly their own. A structure of interests friendly or hostile, vague and general or compact and well-defined, encloses each significant center of administrative discretion. This structure is an important determinant of the scope of possible action. As a source of power and authority it is a competitor of the formal hierarchy.

Not only does political power flow in from the sides of an organization, as it were; it also flows up the organization to the center from the constituent parts. When the staff of the Office of War Mobilization and Reconversion advised a hard-pressed agency to go out and get itself some popular support so that the President could afford to support it, their action reflected the realities of power rather than political cynicism.

It is clear that the American system of politics does not generate enough power at any focal point of leadership to provide the conditions for an even partially successful divorce of politics from administration. Subordinates cannot depend on the formal chain of command to deliver enough political power to permit them to do their jobs. Accordingly they must supplement the resources available through the hierarchy with those they can muster on their own, or accept the consequences in frustration—a course itself not without danger. Administrative rationality demands that objectives be determined and sights set in conformity with a realistic appraisal of power position and potential. . . .

The theory of administration has neglected the problem of the sources and adequacy of power, in all probability because of a distaste for the disorderliness of American political life and a belief that this disorderliness is transitory. An idealized picture of the British parliamentary system as a Platonic form to be realized or approximated has exerted a baneful fascination in the field. The majority party with a mandate at the polls and a firmly seated leadership in the cabinets seems to solve adequately the problem of the supply of power necessary to permit administration to concentrate on the fulfillment of accepted objectives. It is a commonplace that the American party system provides neither a mandate for a platform nor a mandate for a leadership.

Accordingly, the election over, its political meaning must be explored by the diverse leaders in the executive and legislative branches. Since the parties have failed to discuss issues, mobilize majorities in their terms, and create a working political consensus on measures to be carried out, the task is left for others—most prominently the agencies concerned. Legislation passed and powers granted are frequently politically premature. Thus the Council of Economic Advisors was given legislative birth before political acceptance of its functions existed. The agencies to which tasks are assigned must devote themselves to the creation of an adequate consensus to permit administration. The mandate that the parties do not supply must be attained through public relations and the mobilization of group support. Pendleton Herring and others have shown just how vital this support is for agency action.

The theory that agencies should confine themselves to communicating policy suggestions to executive and legislature, and refrain from appealing to their clientele and the public, neglects the failure of the parties to provide either a clear-cut decision as to what they should do or an adequately mobilized political support for a course of action. The bureaucracy under the American political system has a large share of responsibility for the public promotion of policy and even more in organizing the political basis for its survival and growth. It is generally recognized that the agencies have a special competence in the technical aspects of their fields which of necessity gives them a rightful policy initiative. In addition, they have or develop a shrewd understanding of the politically feasible in the group structure within which they work. Above all, in the eyes of their supporters and their enemies they represent the institutionalized embodiment of policy, an enduring organization actually or potentially capable of mobilizing power behind policy. The survival interests and creative drives of administrative organizations combine with clientele pressures to compel such mobilization. The party system provides no enduring institutional representation for group interest at all comparable to that of the bureaus of the Department of Agriculture. Even the subject matter committees of Congress function in the shadow of agency permanency.

The bureaucracy is recognized by all interested groups as a major channel of representation to such an extent that Congress rightly feels the competition of a rival. The weakness in party structure both permits and makes necessary the present dimensions of the political activities of the administrative branch—permits because it fails to protect administration from pressures and fails to provide adequate direction and support, makes necessary because it fails to develop a consensus on a leadership and a program that makes possible administration on the basis of accepted decisional premises.

Agencies and bureaus more or less perforce are in the business of building, maintaining, and increasing their political support. They lead and in large part are led by the diverse groups whose influence sustains them. Frequently they lead and are themselves led in conflicting directions. This is not due to a dull-witted incapacity to see the contradictions in their behavior but is an almost inevitable result of the contradictory nature of their support.

Herbert Simon has shown that administrative rationality depends on the establishment of uniform value premises in the decisional centers of organization. Unfortunately, the value premises of those forming vital elements of political support are often far from uniform. These elements are in Barnard's and Simon's sense "customers" of the organization and therefore parts of the organization whose wishes are clothed with a very real authority.

A major and most time-consuming aspect of administration consists of the wide range of activities designed to secure enough "customer" acceptance to survive and, if fortunate, develop a consensus adequate to program formulation and execution.

To varying degrees, dependent on the breadth of acceptance of their programs, officials at every level of significant discretion must make their estimates of the situation, take stock of their resources, and plan accordingly. A keen appreciation of the real components of their organization is the beginning of wisdom. These components will be found to stretch far beyond the government payroll. Within the government they will encompass Congress, Congressmen, committees, courts, other agencies, presidential advisors, and the President. The Aristotelian analysis of constitutions is equally applicable and equally necessary to an understanding of administrative organization.

The broad alliance of conflicting groups that makes up presidential majorities scarcely coheres about any definite pattern of objectives, nor has it by the alchemy of the party system had its collective power concentrated in an accepted leadership with a personal mandate. The conciliation and maintenance of this support is a necessary condition of the attainment and retention of office involving, as Madison so well saw, "the spirit of party and faction in the necessary and ordinary operations of government." The President must in large part be, if not all things to all men, at least many things to many men. As a consequence, the contradictions in his power base invade administration. The often criticized apparent cross-purposes of the Roosevelt regime cannot be put down to inept administration until the political facts are weighed. Were these apparently self-defeating measures reasonably related to the general maintenance of the composite majority of the administration? The first objective—ultimate patriotism apart—of the administrator is the attainment and retention of the power on which his tenure of office depends. This is the necessary pre-condition for the accomplishment of all other objectives.

The same ambiguities that arouse the scorn of the naive in the electoral campaigns of the parties are equally inevitable in administration and for the same reasons. Victory at the polls does not yield either a clear-cut grant of power or a unified majority support for a coherent program. The task of the presidency lies in feeling out the alternatives of policy which are consistent with the retention and increase of the group support on which the administration rests. The lack of a budgetary theory (so frequently deplored) is not due to any incapacity to apply rational analysis to the comparative contribution of the various activities of government to a determinate hierarchy of purposes. It more probably stems from a fastidious distaste for the frank recognition of the budget as a politically expedient allocation of resources. Appraisal in terms of their political contribution to the administration provides almost a sole common denominator between the Forest Service and the Bureau of Engraving.

Integration of the administrative structure through an overall purpose in terms of which tasks and priorities can be established is an emergency phenomenon. Its realization, only partial at best, has been limited to war and the extremity of depression. Even in wartime the Farm Bureau Federation, the American Federation of Labor, the Congress of Industrial Organizations, the National Association of Manufacturers, the Chamber of Commerce, and a host of lesser interests resisted coordination of themselves and the agencies concerned with their interests. A presidency temporarily empowered by intense mass popular support acting in behalf of a generally accepted and simplified purpose can, with great difficulty, bribe, cajole, and coerce a real measure of joint action. . . . Only in crises are the powers of the executive nearly adequate to impose a common plan of action on the executive branch, let alone the economy.

In ordinary times the manifold pressures of our pluralistic society work themselves out in accordance with the balance of forces prevailing in Congress and the agencies. Only to a limited degree is the process subject to responsible direction or review by President or party leadership. . . .

The difficulty of coordinating government agencies lies not only in the fact that bureaucratic organizations are institutions having survival interests which may conflict with their rational adaptation to overall purpose, but even more in their having roots in society. Coordination of the varied activities of a modern government almost of necessity involves a substantial degree of coordination of the economy. Coordination of government agencies involves far more than changing the behavior and offices of officials in Washington and the field. It involves the publics that are implicated in their normal functioning. To coordinate fiscal policy, agricultural policy, labor policy, foreign policy, and military policy, to name a few major areas, moves beyond the range of government charts and the habitat of the bureaucrats to the marketplace and to where the people live and work. This suggests that the reason why government reorganization is so difficult is that far more than government in the formal sense is invovled in reorganization. One could overlook this in the limited government of the nineteenth century but the multi-billion dollar government of the mid-twentieth permits no facile dichotomy between government and economy. Economy and efficiency are the two objectives a laissez faire society can prescribe in peacetime as over-all government objectives. Their inadequacy either as motivation or standards has long been obvious. A planned economy clearly requires a planned government. But, if one can afford an unplanned economy, apart from gross extravagance, there seems no compelling and therefore, perhaps, no sufficiently powerful reason for a planned government.

Basic to the problem of administrative rationality is that of organizational identification and point of view. To whom is one loyal—unit, section, branch, division, bureau, department, administration, government, country, people, world history, or what? Administrative analysis frequently assumes that organizational identification should occur in such a way as to merge primary organization loyalty in a larger synthesis.

The good of the part is to give way to the reasoned good of the whole. This is most frequently illustrated in the rationalizations used to counter self-centered demands of primary groups for funds and personnel. Actually the competition between governmental power centers, rather than the rationalizations, is the effective instrument of coordination.

Where there is a clear common product on whose successful production the subgroups depend for the attainment of their own satisfaction, it is possible to demonstrate to almost all participants the desirability of cooperation. The shoe factory produces shoes, or else, for all concerned. But the government as a whole and many of its component parts have no such identifiable common product on which all depend. Like the proverbial Heinz, there are fifty-seven or more varieties unified, if at all, by a common political profit and loss account.

Administration is faced by somewhat the same dilemma as economics. There are propositions about the behavior pattern conducive to full employment—welfare economics. On the other hand, there are propositions about the economics of the individual firm—the counsel of the business schools. It is possible to show with considerable persuasiveness that sound considerations for the individual firm may lead to a depression if generally adopted, a result desired by none of the participants. However, no single firm can afford by itself to adopt the course of collective wisdom; in the absence of a common power capable of enforcing decisions premised on the supremacy of the collective interest, *sauve qui peut* is common sense.

The position of administrative organizations is not unlike the position of particular firms. Just as the decisions of the firms could be coordinated by the imposition of a planned economy so could those of the component parts of the government. But just as it is possible to operate a formally unplanned economy by the loose coordination of the market, in the same fashion it is possible to operate a government by the loose coordination of the play of political forces through its institutions.

The unseen hand of Adam Smith may be little in evidence in either case. One need not believe in a doctrine of social or administrative harmony to believe that formal centralized planning—while perhaps desirable and in some cases necessary—is not a must. The complicated logistics of supplying the city of New York runs smoothly down the grooves of millions of well adapted habits projected from a distant past. It seems naive on the one hand to believe in the possibility of a vast, intricate, and delicate economy operating with a minimum of formal overall direction, and on the other to doubt that a relatively simple mechanism such as the government can be controlled largely by the same play of forces. . . .

It is highly appropriate to consider how administrators should behave to meet the test of efficiency in a planned polity; but in the absence of such a polity and while, if we like, struggling to get it, a realistic science of administration will teach administrative behavior appropriate to the existing political system.

A close examination of the presidential system may well bring one to conclude that administrative rationality in it is a different matter from that applicable to the British ideal. The American presidency is an office that has significant monarchical characteristics despite its limited term and elective nature. The literature on court and palace has many an insight applicable to the White House. Access to the President, reigning favorites, even the court jester, are topics that show the continuity of institutions. The maxims of La Rochefoucauld and the memoirs of the Duc de Saint Simon have a refreshing realism for the operator on the Potomac.

The problem of rival factions in the President's family is as old as the famous struggle between Jefferson and Hamilton. . . . Experience seems to show that this personal and factional struggle for the President's favor is a vital part of the process of representation. The vanity, personal ambition, or patriotism of the contestants soon clothes itself in the generalities of principle and the clique aligns itself with groups beyond the capital. Subordinate rivalry is tolerated if not encouraged by so many able executives that it can scarcely be attributed to administrative ineptitude. The wrangling tests opinion, uncovers information that would otherwise never rise to the top, and provides effective opportunity for decision rather than mere ratification of prearranged plans. Like most judges, the executive needs to hear argument for his own instruction. The alternatives presented by subordinates in large part determine the freedom and the creative opportunity of their superiors. The danger of becoming a Merovingian is a powerful incentive to the maintenance of fluidity in the structure of power.

The fixed character of presidential tenure makes it necessary that subordinates be politically expendable. The President's men must be willing to accept the blame for failures not their own. Machiavelli's teaching on how princes must keep the faith bears rereading. Collective responsibility is incompatible with a fixed term of office. As it tests the currents of public opinion, the situation on the Hill, and the varying strength of the organized pressures, the White House alters and adapts the complexion of the administration. Loyalties to programs or to groups and personal pride and interest frequently conflict with whole-souled devotion to the presidency. In fact, since such devotion is not made mandatory by custom, institutions, or the facts of power, the problem is perpetually perplexing to those who must choose.

The balance of power between executive and legislature is constantly subject to the shifts of public and group support. The latent tendency of the American Congress is to follow the age-old parliamentary precedents and to try to reduce the President to the role of constitutional monarch. Against this threat and to secure his own initiative, the President's resources are primarily demagogic, with the weaknesses and strengths that dependence on mass popular appeal implies. The unanswered question of American government—"who is boss?"—constantly plagues administration.

CASE STUDY 4

Introduction

In the foregoing essay, Norton Long discusses how critically important it is for public administrators at all levels of government to understand the dynamics and realities of administrative power—its sources, influence, and impacts on their programs and
themselves, as well as the methods for enhancing and maintaining their power bases.
He argues that "power" is the most frequently overlooked or ignored aspect of public
administration. Recall his opening lines: "There is no more forlorn spectacle in the administrative world than an agency and a program possessed of statutory life, armed with
executive orders, sustained in the courts, yet stricken with paralysis and deprived of
power." Long's realism about the central importance and nature of administrative power
for practicing public administrators is underscored poignantly throughout his writings.

   Yet Long's essay was written almost a half century ago, and so is today's problem of
relating politics and administration the same? Or, as some suggest, is it indeed the reverse of what Long's essay outlines? Rather than neglecting "power," do contemporary
public administrators suffer from "too much political involvement" or too much "micromanagement" by their political superiors that prevents them from fulfilling their responsibilities effectively—or at all?

   The following case, "The Last Flight of Space Shuttle Challenger," by Michael T.
Charles, a professor at Illinois State University, describes the events leading up to the worst
disaster ever experienced by America's space program. It caused the deaths of the seven-
member crew of the *Challenger* on January 28, 1986, which included a teacher, Christa
McAuliffe. The flight of the *Challenger* began at 11:38 a.m. and ended 73 seconds later.
Before a worldwide television audience of an estimated eighty million people, the *Challenger* exploded in a fireball of hydrogen and oxygen propellents, destroying the rocket
and the space shuttle and killing all of the crew members. The immediate cause of the
accident, in the words of the Presidential Commission on the Space Shuttle Accident (the
Rogers Report): "The Commission concluded that the cause of the accident was the failure of the pressure seal in the aft field joint of the solid rocket motor. The failure was due
to a faulty design unacceptably sensitive to a number of factors. These factors were the
effects of temperature, physical dimensions, the character of the materials, the effects of
reusability processing and the reaction of the joint to dynamic loading." In plain language,
a small washer-like seal in the rocket, called an O-ring, failed to function correctly in
the extreme cold weather and was the immediate cause of the accident.

   Or was the O-ring responsible for the *Challenger* disaster?

   Professor Charles probes the causes behind the disaster and according to him, rather
than focusing on the technical flaw of the O-ring that caused the accident, or what he
calls, "the technical fix," he argues that it is far more important "to develop an appreciation of the human side of the management and its influence on the Shuttle Disaster" In
elaborating on the details of this terrible event, what the author reveals at the end is how
the enormous external political pressures placed upon NASA led to a chain of flawed
decisions to launch the shuttle. Top NASA officials and managers at Morton Thiokol, the
prime contractor responsible for building the *Challenger's* rocket booster, agreed to the
launch in order to maintain congressional funding as well as "the can-do" PR image of
NASA. They ignored or suppressed the repeated warnings of professional engineers who

were close to the O-ring problem. As Charles concludes, "engineers not having management responsibilities viewed the data regarding the O-ring performance at cold temperatures quite differently than did management personnel."

As you read this case, you might reflect on several issues:

Where did the political pressure come from for launching the *Challenger,* according to Charles?

Why were the views of the engineers who were close to the O-ring problem not fully considered or ignored entirely?

Do you agree with the author that the "appreciation of the human side of management" is more important than focusing on "the technical fix"?

Does this case support or contradict, in your view, Long's central thesis of the neglect of power and politics by public administrators?

The Last Flight of Space Shuttle Challenger

MICHAEL T. CHARLES

Public Affairs Officer: Coming up on the 90-second point in our countdown. Ninety seconds and counting. The 51-L Mission ready to go. . . .

T minus 10, 9, 8, 7, 6, we have main engine start, 4, 3, 2, 1. And liftoff. Liftoff of the 25th space shuttle mission and it has cleared the tower. . . .

Mission Control: Challenger, go with throttle up.

Franics R. Scobee, Challenger Commander: Roger, go with throttle up.

Public Affairs Officer: One minute 15 seconds, velocity 2,900 feet per second, altitude 9 nautical miles, down range distance 7 nautical miles. [Long pause.]

Flight controllers here looking very carefully at the situation. [Pause.]

Obviously a major malfunction. We have no

downlink [communications from Challenger]. [Long pause.]

We have a report from the flight dynamics officer that the vehicle has exploded.[1]

After being postponed four times and delayed several hours, Space Shuttle Challenger, Mission 51-L, lifted off from pad 39B at Kennedy Space Center, Merritt Island, Florida. The lift-off was on Tuesday January 28, 1986, at approximately 11:38 Eastern Standard Time (EST). This was to be the tenth mission of the Challenger Orbiter and the 25th mission of the Space Transportation System (STS) program. The flight appeared normal until Mission Control lost its signal from the Shuttle, 73 seconds into the flight. A bright flash was observed almost immediately after the last radio signal from the Challenger was received by Mission Control. The massive explosion resulted in the total destruction of the Orbiter and its external fuel tank (see Figure 4.1). The left and right Solid Rocket Boosters were blown clear by the initial explosion, but were destroyed some 30 seconds later by the Air Force range safety officer, as the boosters began to fly aimlessly toward populated areas.

Source: Michael T. Charles, "The Last Flight of Space Shuttle Challenger," in Uriel Rosenthal, Michael T. Charles, Paul T. Hart, *Coping with Crises: The Management of Disaster, Riots and Terrorism* . Courtesy of Charles C. Thomas, Publisher, Springfield, Illinois.

This was the worst disaster ever experienced in the United States space program, with all seven crew members lost, including the "First Teacher in Space," Christa McAuliffe.[2] In financial terms it would cost in excess of $2 billion to replace the lost STS. The disaster was a heart wrenching experience for a nation and a shock for the world. The catastrophe shook America's trust in the National Aeronautics and Space Administration (NASA), and it was the beginning of a long and difficult investigation designed to determine the cause of the disaster.

In the end the Presidential Commission on the Space Shuttle Challenger Accident concluded that the disaster was caused by:

In the view of the findings, the Commission concluded that the cause of the Challenger accident was the failure of the pressure seal in the aft field joint of the right Solid Rocket Motor. The failure was due to a faulty design unacceptably sensitive to a number of factors. These factors were the effects of temperature, physical dimensions, the character of materials, the effects of reusability, processing, and the reaction of the joint to dynamic loading.[3]

While it was extremely important for the Presidential Commission to discover and reveal the technical fault that caused the Challenger disaster, serendipitously, the Commission found that a faulty decision-making process was to blame for the launch of flight 51-L and the ultimate catastrophe. In fact, the Commission referred to the tragedy as "An Accident Rooted in History." It is to this end, i.e., elucidating the historical errors in decision making, that the author focuses attention in this case. Interestingly, there is strong evidence that many an "accident" is rooted in "management" history. . . .

Intriguingly, the decision making and judgmental errors made in the launch of STS 51-L appear to have been easily avoidable; however:

Although it is flattering to believe that we would have known all along what we could only know in hindsight, that belief hardly affords us a fair appraisal of the extent to which surprises and failures are inevitable. It is both unfair and self-defeating to castigate decision makers who have erred in fallible systems, rather than admitting to that fallibility and doing something to improve the system.[4]

Consequently, the reader must put him/herself into the environment of the shuttle program at the time decisions were made, and under the conditions in which they were decided. It is far less difficult to discern the errors made and to develop seemingly simplistic organizational remedies to overcome shortfalls in the system, than it is to truly understand the subtle side of human nature; the interaction between co-workers; the interpretations afforded policy documents by various individuals; non-verbal communication; the impact of statements made by important corporate executives and government officials on organizational members; and individual judgmental discretion, in a real life setting. However, to develop an appreciation of the human side of management and its influence on the Shuttle disaster, a chronology of events, dating as far back as the early seventies when Thiokol was awarded the contract by NASA to design and build the Solid Rocket Motor Boosters, must be understood.

The purpose of this case study, therefore, is: First, to demonstrate the organizational failings that resulted in the Challenger catastrophe. These failings included such phenomena as an environment of pressured decision making, lucrative contracts, Congressional funding, and bureau-political infighting within NASA and among NASA, the military, and other governmental agencies competing for space dollars. The second function is to provide an analysis of the organizational failings. This analysis will present several reasons, from a social-psychological perspective, on how an agency such as NASA, with its excellent reputation for management, technology, and safety, could produce such a catastrophic event. The particular significance of this case is the fact that "well managed," complex, and tightly coupled industries, i.e., organizations where ". . . different parts of the system can be quite dependent on one another . . .",[5] will have normal or system accidents. Simply stated, "The odd term normal accident is meant to signal that, given the system characteristics, multiple and unexpected interactions of failures are inevitable."[6]

The Challenger Crisis

Background: The Public and Private Sectors

The National Aeronautics and Space Administration is that governmental agency responsible for the development and management of the Space Shuttle Program. However, NASA has awarded several private firms contracts to develop and design the STS, and to assist in the launch process. Those private corporations included such major contractors as: (1) Rockwell International Corporation's Space Transportation Systems Division. They were responsible for the design and development of the Shuttle Orbiter. (2) Martin Marietta Denver Aerospace secured the contract from NASA for the development and fabrication of the Shuttle's external tank. (3) The Morton Thiokol Corporation won the contract to build the Solid Rocket Boosters, which are used to help launch the Shuttle. It was the right Solid Rocket Booster on STS 51-L that failed, causing the destruction of the vehicle. And, (4) Rocketdyne, a division of Rockwell, was chosen to design the main engines for the Orbiter.

Managing STS

Managerial responsibility for the shuttle program was divided by NASA into three field areas. Management of the Orbiter was the responsibility of the Johnson Space Center in Houston, Texas. Marshall Space Flight Center Huntsville, Alabama, assumed managerial responsibility for the Solid Rocket Boosters, the Orbiter's main engines, and the External Tank. Finally, the job of assembling the Shuttle components,

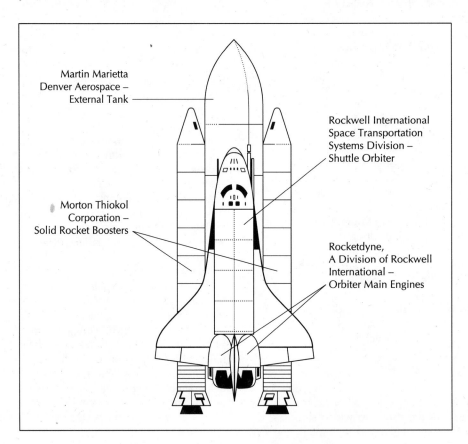

Figure 4.1 NASA Private Contractors Responsible for Shuttle Development

testing them, and conducting launches was the job of Kennedy Space Center, Merritt Island Florida.

NASA built a total of five space shuttles for their use. The first Orbiter built was the Enterprise, which while a full size vehicle, and used in early Shuttle testing, was constructed without engines and other systems needed for space flight. The vehicle was used to test aerodynamic and flight control characteristics of the Shuttle in atmospheric flight. The remaining Shuttles capable of space flight included: Columbia, Challenger, Discovery, and Atlantis. It was with these four reusable shuttles that the ambitious, if not unrealistic, 1986 and 1987 flight schedule of 17 missions each year, and the 24 scheduled missions in 1988, were to be accomplished.

After the first four test flights of the Space Transportation System were completed by Columbia in June of 1982, NASA declared the STS program "Operational," and then proceeded with the now "Routine" task of space flight. This philosophy and resulting attitude together created an atmosphere conducive to overconfidence, carelessness, and inattention to detail among many NASA officials and contractor personnel. A condition that played an important role in the decision to fly the STS 51-L on that cold morning in January.

The Decision-Making Process: Pre-Launch Meetings

Meeting One

After three postponements in the launch of STS 51-L, which was originally scheduled for lift-off in July 1985, and a scrubbed mission because of high winds at Kennedy Space Center on January 27, 1986, the Challenger was rescheduled for launch on January 28, 1986. During the short meeting following the Mission Management team's decision to scrub the January 27 lift-off, no mention of the Solid Rocket Boosters, or the earlier O-ring erosion found on previous shuttle flights launched in cold weather was made, even though temperatures were expected to drop into the low twenties overnight.

Meeting Two

The second meeting of the Mission Management Team on January 27 began at approximately 14:00

EST. Discussion at this meeting concentrated on the effect the expected cold weather would have on such things as eye wash and shower water, water drains, the fire suppression system, and the overpressure water trays. At this meeting it was decided that the Orbiter heaters should be activated, but again there was no mention of the Solid Rocket Booster O-rings.

Meeting Three

It was not until approximately 14:30 EST that Robert Ebeling (see Figure 4.2) (Manager, Ignition System and Final Assembly, Solid Rocket Motor Project, at Thiokol's Wasatch, Utah plant) after hearing about the cold weather forecast, convened a meeting of several engineers at the Wasatch facility. At the close of that meeting sufficient concerns regarding the low temperature forecasted for Kennedy Space Center were voiced that Mr. Ebeling phoned Allan McDonald (Director, Solid Rocket Motor Project, Morton Thiokol) who was staying at the home of a Morton Thiokol colleague near Kennedy Space Center while preparing for the upcoming launch. During this phone conversation Mr. Ebeling expressed his and the other engineers' misgivings regarding the performance of the O-rings in the Solid Rocket Booster field joints at cold temperatures. This conversation resulted in Mr. McDonald contacting the Kennedy Space Center launch operations center to collect temperature data for Mr. Ebeling to review.

Meeting Four

The fourth meeting was conducted via teleconference and began at 17:45 EST. This meeting included project managers from the Marshall Space Flight Center as well as numerous people from Kennedy Space Center and the Thiokol-Wasatch facility. At this meeting Thiokol representatives voiced their concerns about the performance of the Solid Rocket Booster O-rings at cold temperatures, and they presented what O-ring failure data related to temperature they were able to collect and organize prior to the hastily called meeting. In reviewing the Commission transcripts on this meeting, it appears that Thiokol recommended that the launch should be delayed until noon or later when the temperature was higher. However, some members of the teleconference such as Mr. Stanley R. Reinartz

(Manager, Shuttle Projects Office, Marshall Space Flight Center) testified before the Commission that, "I did not perceive it that way. I perceived that they were raising some questions and issues which required looking into by all the right parties, but I did not perceive it as a recommendation delay."[7]

Despite the conflicting opinions regarding Thiokol's position at this meeting, participants of the conference agreed to hold yet another teleconference. Additional Thiokol and NASA representatives were to be contacted for the follow-up meeting, so that a complete and thorough discussion of the O-ring problem could be held. In addition, it was also recommended by Dr. Judson A. Lovingood (Deputy Manager, Shuttle Projects Office, Marshall Space Flight Center) that, "I said that I thought we ought to have an inter-center meeting involving Dr. Lucas [Director, Marshall Space Flight Center] and Mr. Kingsbury [Director, Science and Engineering, Marshall Space Flight Center] and then plan to go on up to level II and level I."[8] In fact, at the close of the teleconference Dr. Lovingood telephoned Stanley Reinartz and told him that he should alert Mr. Arnold D. Aldrich (Manager, National Space Transportation Systems Program Office-level II, Johnson Space Center) to the possibility that levels II and I needed to consider the O-ring problem. However, Mr. Reinartz did not contact Mr. Aldrich, nor did he effectively relay, although he was in contact with Mr. Lucas and Mr. Kingsbury prior to the fifth meeting, the grave concerns some members of the teleconference had regarding the launch, or the invitation for them to join in the scheduled 20:15 EST teleconference.

Meeting Five

The penultimate meeting preceding the Challenger accident began at approximately 20:45 EST. Prior to the meeting several charts were telefaxed from Thiokol-Wasatch to both Kennedy Space Center and Marshall Space Flight Center. The charts included information regarding: (1) A history of O-ring blow-by and erosion in the Solid Rocket Booster joints of previous flights; and (2) the results of subscale testing and static tests on the O-rings.

Mr. Roger Boisjoly (Senior Scientist and member Seal Task Force, Thiokol-Wasatch) presented most of the data Thiokol personnel had quickly assembled for the teleconference. He was also the most vocal opponent of a January 28 launch, which would

---

Stanley R. Reinartz, Manager, Shuttle Projects Office, Marshall Space Flight Center

Judson A. Lovingood, Deputy Manager, Shuttle Projects Office, Marshall Space Flight Center

Dr. Lucus, Director, Marshall Space Flight Center

Mr. Kingsbury, Director, Science and Engineering, Marshall Space Flight Center

Arnold D. Aldrich, Manager, National Space Transportation Systems Program Office, Johnson Space Center

Roger Boisjoly, Senior Scientist and Member Seal Task Force, Thiokol-Wasatch

Robert K. Lund, Vice President, Engineering, Thiokol-Wasatch

George B. Hardy, Deputy Director, Science and Engineering, Marshall Space Flight Center

Lawrence B. Mulloy, Manager, Solid Rocket Booster Projects Office, Marshall Space Flight Center

Joe Kilminster, Vice President, Space Booster Programs, Thiokol-Wasatch

Allen J. McDonald, Director, Solid Rocket Motor Project, Thiokol-Wasatch

Jerald Mason, Senior Vice President, Thiokol-Wasatch

Calvin Wiggins, Vice President and General Manager, Space Division, Thiokol-Wasatch

Cecil Houston, Marshall Space Flight Center, Resident Manager at Kennedy Space Center

Dr. Rocco Petrone, President, Rockwell Space Transportation Systems Division, Downey, California

Robert Glaysher, assistant to Dr. Petrone at Kennedy Space Center

Martin Cloffoletti, assistant to Dr. Petrone at Kennedy Space Center

Figure 4.2 NASA, Thiokol, and Rockwell personnel responsible for the safety and development of STS.

---

occur outside the data base that Thiokol had at the present time. The three major reasons presented by

Mr. Boisjoly supporting a no-launch decision were as follows.

First, If there was erosion of the primary O-ring seal there would be a high probability that the secondary O-ring seal would be incapable of seating properly.

Originally the Solid Rocket Boosters were designed with two O-ring seals, the primary and secondary seals. This was done because if hot gases and flame were to blow-by and erode the primary seal because of its inability to seat quickly enough, the secondary seal would seat and contain the hot gasses and flames until the boosters burned out and were jettisoned from the vehicle. Redundancy, i.e., having two pieces of equipment designed to perform a similar function, was incorporated in the Solid Rocket Booster joints, because failure of a joint would result in the loss of human life and the vehicle. Consequently, the Solid Rocket Booster joints were originally classified on the Critical Items List, November 24, 1980, as Criticality 1R. This meant that NASA believed the secondary O-ring would seal in the event that the primary O-ring failed. More will be said of the O-ring criticality issue at a later point.

Second, bench tests of the O-rings indicated that during the initial phase of launch, from 0–170 milliseconds after the boosters were fired, there was capability for the primary O-ring to seal. However, Mr. Boisjoly based this conclusion on what he referred to before the Commission as, ". . . normal circumstances, normal being within the data base we had."[9]

Given the weather forecast for the morning of January 28 (low 20s Fahrenheit), the launch would not be conducted under "normal circumstances." The lowest temperature that the shuttle had been launched previously was 53 degrees Fahrenheit. The thrust of Mr. Boisjoly's argument, therefore, was that there would be a change in the O-ring timing function. The time it takes for the O-ring to expand and seal the Solid Rocket Booster joint might be slowed because of a decrease in resiliency due to cold temperature. If the cold temperature were to slow the O-ring resiliency to the extent that it took more than 170 milliseconds to seat, the possibility of joint failure was increased considerably. The analogy used by Mr. Boisjoly before the Commission to explain this phenomenon was, ". . . it would be likened to trying to shove a brick into a crack versus a sponge."[10]

Third, it was also pointed out by Mr. Boisjoly that there had been evidence of blow-by found in the Solid Rocket Motor joints on previous shuttle flights. Of particular importance to Mr. Boisjoly's contention that cold weather slowed O-ring resiliency was flight 51-C, Orbiter Discovery, which flew in January of 1985. Shuttle 51-C lifted-off from Kennedy Space Center with an O-ring temperature of 53 degrees Fahrenheit. In a post flight check of the field joints both Solid Rocket Boosters were found to have black grease between the O-rings, which meant that the integrity of the joint had been breached. This blow-by condition was considered quite serious by Thiokol. And, in the opinion of Mr. Boisjoly, and other engineers at Thiokol, it was sufficient evidence that cold temperatures affected O-ring resiliency and thus indicated the need to delay the Challenger launch.

During the discussion, however, it was pointed out that flight 61-A, another Orbiter Challenger mission, was launched in October of 1985 with an O-ring temperature of 75 degrees Fahrenheit, and that this flight had soot blow-by as well. The counter argument obviously being made was that the temperature of the O-rings was not an important factor. In addition, Mr. Boisjoly was asked to support his claim of slowed O-ring resiliency in quantitative terms. Mr. Boisjoly was unable to provide analytical data beyond that which he had already presented because, although he and Mr. Arnold Aldrich had tried to obtain this data since October of 1985, they had not as yet received it. Mr. Boisjoly did, however, point out to the members of the teleconference that by far the worst blow-by to occur in the Shuttle's history was on flight 51-C, and that this was an indication that temperature was a factor of O-ring resilience.

Other Thiokol-Wasatch personnel presented additional charts and their concerns regarding the effect of cold temperature on the O-rings. The final recommendation by Thiokol at this time was presented by Mr. Robert K. Lund (Vice President, Engineering, Thiokol-Wasatch). The recommendation was that STS 51-L should not be launched until the O-ring temperature reached 53 degrees Fahrenheit. This was the lowest temperature of any previous flight.

Shortly following Thiokol's no-fly recommendation, Mr. George B. Hardy (Deputy Director, Science and Engineering, Marshall Space Flight Center) was asked by Mr. Stanley R. Reinartz to comment on the Thiokol recommendation. Mr. Hardy stated that he was "appalled" by Thiokol's recommendation, but that he would not go against the contractor's no-launch recommendation. In addition, while Commission transcripts were unclear as to exactly what Mr. Lawrence B. Mulloy (Manager, Solid Rocket Booster Projects Office, Marshall Space Flight Center) said, it is clear that he did indicate that there were currently no-launch commitment criteria for temperature, and that Thiokol was trying to set new launch commitment criteria on the eve of the launch. Mr. Mulloy reportedly concluded by saying, "My God, Thiokol, when do you want me to launch, next April?"[11]

Mr. Mulloy and Mr. Hardy, two NASA administrators, were of the opinion that based on the Thiokol data presented, they had an effective simplex seal on STS 51-C, Orbiter Discovery, as was indicated in the 1982 Critical Items List. They were, therefore, not convinced that the cold weather would result in a slowed O-ring, blow-by, or ultimate disaster of the Challenger.

The Thiokol-Wasatch Caucus. Shortly after Mr. Mulloy's and Mr. Hardy's striking comments, Mr. Joe Kilminster (Vice President, Space Booster Programs, Thiokol-Wasatch) asked for a five-minute recess from the teleconference so that Wasatch personnel could caucus and discuss the concerns presented and review the data once again. However, before leaving the net to caucus, Mr. Allen J. McDonald (Director, Solid Rocket Motor Project, Thiokol, at Kennedy Space Center) who was representing Thiokol at Kennedy Space Center at the time, asked Mr. Kilminster to consider that the secondary O-ring would be ". . . in the proper position to seal if blow-by of the primary O-ring occurred."[12] Interestingly, while many members of the teleconference perceived Mr. McDonald's comment as a supporting statement for a launch go ahead, Mr. McDonald did not intend to communicate that message. In fact, even Mr. Roger Boisjoly was momentarily confused by McDonald's comment. Mr. McDonald merely wanted Thiokol-Wasatch to review this issue. In fact, Mr. McDonald was totally opposed to a launch at such cold temperatures.

The caucus began with Mr. Jerald Mason (Senior Vice President, Wasatch Operations) ". . . saying that a management decision was required."[13] During the caucus the Thiokol engineers and management people continued to discuss the issues presented during the teleconference. However, one additional piece of data was brought to the attention of the group. It was pointed out that in an earlier test, engineers had cut an O-ring 125 thousandths of an inch, and it still seated properly. This had no effect on either Mr. Boisjoly, or Mr. Arnold R. Thompson (Supervisor, Rocket Motor Cases). They both continued to argue vigorously against the launch because of the cold temperature. In addition, while Mr. Boisjoly and Mr. Thompson were the most vocal participants of the caucus opposing the launch of 51-L, not one engineer in a non-management position made any positive statement supporting a launch. In fact, Mr. Boisjoly stopped arguing only ". . . when it was apparent that I couldn't get anybody to listen."[14]

After some discussion Mr. Jerald Mason said, ". . . we have to make a management decision."[15] Mr. Mason then asked Mr. Robert Lund ". . . to take off his engineering hat and put on his management hat."[16] At that point a final "management" review was conducted among executives at Thiokol-Wasatch. Those managers involved in the management discussion included, in addition to Mr. Mason and Mr. Lund, Mr. Joe Kilminster and Mr. Calvin Wiggins (Vice President and General Manager, Space Division, Thiokol-Wasatch).

The Teleconference Continues. The final management decision was presented to all members of the teleconference by Mr. Kilminster when the meeting resumed at approximately 23:00 EST. Mr. Kilminster recommended that the STS 51-L launch proceed on January 28, 1986. This new recommendation was supported by Thiokol management in the following manner: (1) the temperature data was not conclusive in predicting primary O-ring blow-by; (2) the demonstrated sealing threshold of the O-ring was 0.038, which was three times greater than the erosion experienced on STS 51-C; and (3) if the primary seal fails to seat the secondary seal will.

The teleconference ended with Mr. Stanley R. Reinartz asking for any final comments from anyone on the net. No concerns were voiced at this time; even though none of the engineers at Thiokol-

Wasatch supported the launch decision. Mr. Kilminster was then asked by Mr. Mulloy to send a copy of his flight readiness rational and recommendation, via telefax, to Marshall Space Flight Center and to Kennedy Space Flight Center.

At this point in the meeting Mr. Allen McDonald informed NASA officials at Kennedy Space Center that ". . . I felt that I was the one who was going to have to sign it [the Thiokol flight readiness recommendation], because I was at the Cape; and I said I wouldn't sign it. I couldn't; it would have to come from the plant."[17]

McDonald's Doubts. Once the conference had ended, Mr. McDonald and NASA officials waited for the flight recommendation telefax from Thiokol-Wasatch. While waiting, Mr. McDonald presented his final concerns to NASA officials at Kennedy Space Center. Mr. McDonald pointed out that although he himself did not believe that the shuttle motor and all its elements had been qualified at 40 degrees Fahrenheit; although many NASA and Thiokol people did, he could not understand how either NASA or Thiokol could accept a launch recommendation when the predicted temperature was as low as 26 degrees Fahrenheit.

Mr. McDonald went so far as to say, "I told them I sure wouldn't want to be the person that had to stand in front of a board of inquiry to explain why we launched this outside of the qualification of the solid rocket motor or any shuttle system."[18] Mr. McDonald went on to present three reasons why the launch should be canceled: (1) the concern for cold O-rings; (2) the booster recovery ships were in a survival mode, with seas as high as 30 feet and winds of 50 knots and gusts of 70 knots. Recovery ships were heading for shore. Under those conditions it would be highly unlikely that the Solid Rocket Booster parachutes or the thrustums would be recovered; and (3) the formation of ice on the launch pad.

When Mr. McDonald left the room to retrieve the telefax from Wasatch, Mr. Mulloy and Mr. Reinartz telephoned Mr. Arnold D. Aldrich and relayed Mr. McDonald's concerns about icing on the launch pad and high seas at the Solid Rocket Booster recovery sight. Mr. Aldrich did not feel that the launch should be scrubbed because of high seas. The loss of parachutes and thrustums was acceptable, and it was felt that the Solid Rocket Boosters would

not be put in undue jeopardy. At the end of this conversation everyone left Kennedy Space Center for the evening.

Final Phase: Indecision at Rockwell

During the late night of January 27, and the early morning of January 28, the ice problem at Kennedy Space Center was causing concern for NASA and Rockwell representatives. Due to the imminent launch of 51-L it was decided that water should be left running through the water pipes to prevent their freezing. This caused considerable ice accumulation to form below the 240 foot level of the Shuttle's fixed service structure. The ice accumulation was discovered at approximately 02:00 on January 28, and was assessed periodically throughout the morning. A Mission Management Team meeting was called for 09:00 at Kennedy Space Center, and Rockwell was to provide its assessment of the ice condition relative to the safety of the launch.

Prior to the Mission Management Team meeting Dr. Rocco Petrone (President, Rockwell Space Transportation Systems Division, Downey, California facility) informed his two assistants, Mr. Robert Glaysher and Mr. Martin Cioffoletti, who were on site at Kennedy Space Center for the launch that:

> . . . we could not recommend launching from here [Downey, California], from what we see. We think the tiles would be endangered, and we had a very short conversation. We had a meeting to go through [the Mission Management Team Meeting], and I said let's make sure that NASA understands that Rockwell feels it is not safe to launch. . . .[19]

At the 09:00 meeting both Mr. Glaysher and Mr. Cioffoletti indicated Rockwell's position, or did they? Mr. Glaysher testified before the Commission that they informed the Mission Management Team that Rockwell could not say it was 100% safe to fly under the ice conditions. Perhaps Mr. Glaysher best described how the Rockwell no-fly decision was communicated. "[M]y exact quote—and it comes in two parts. The first one was, Rockwell could not 100 percent assure that it is safe to fly which I quickly changed to Rockwell cannot assure that it is safe to fly . . ."[20]

Unfortunately, this non-committal communication from Rockwell representatives was not perceived by NASA officials to be a no-launch recommendation. Horrace Lambarth (Director, Shuttle Engineering, NASA) reported to Commission investigators at Kennedy Space Center that the language used by Rockwell, "we can't give you 100 percent assurance," did not mean to him that the shuttle should not fly the morning of January 28.

Finally, it was quite clear from Commission testimony that crucial information did not reach important decision makers. Had top decision makers known that none of the Thiokol-Wasatch engineers supported the launch of 51-L, it is unlikely that the launch would have taken place.

The Challenger Disaster: Analysis

A variety of organizational phenomena impacting the decision-making process of the Challenger flight have been presented above; however, attempting to understand how these errors, blunders, and mistakes could occur in an organization as highly regarded for its management and professionalism as NASA, is extremely important. It is only through understanding of these phenomena that efforts to improve the decision-making process can occur.

The following analysis provides a review of the decision-making process: First, the political context of the space shuttle project is outlined; second, it is shown how the politics of space travel affected NASA management; and third, with this background it is possible to understand the operational decision-making process concerning the O-ring problem. Without reviewing the political and managerial context in which the shuttle program existed, it is impossible to develop a true understanding of the disaster scenario. A major failing of the Presidential Commission was their focus on what Kouzmin and Jarman call the "technical fix,"[21] e.g., emphasizing only the O-ring problem and the flawed operational decision-making process in the narrowest sense. An attempt is made here to move beyond the limits of "technocratic thinking" to a more comprehensive, contingent understanding of the organizational and political factors influencing decision making in high technological environments. . . .

I. NASA: Politics, Contracts, and Business Interests

The original selection of a contractor to design and build the boosters for the STS system was a political battle in which the winner would receive a lucrative cost-plus-fee contract. Thiokol won the contract from NASA with the help of the chairman of the Senate Aeronautics and Space Science Committee, Democratic Senator Frank Moss, and the NASA administrator Dr. James Fletcher, both of whom were part of the Utah political hierarchy.[22] Thiokol's victory was not, however, won without difficulty and protests from other unsuccessful bidders.[23] These protests, combined with lobbying efforts in Congress, resulted in Congressional pressure being placed on NASA to again open the bidding process for the production of solid rocket boosters. This decision put Thiokol, for the first time in thirteen years, in the position of losing a one-billion-dollar contract. Thiokol had been in serious negotiations with NASA for this contract through January of 1986. In fact a teleconference was scheduled for January 28, after the Challenger lift-off, between Thiokol representatives and NASA to discuss this very contract. The impact of this factor on Thiokol managers during Meeting Five when Mr. Stanley Reinartz stated that he was "appalled" by Thiokol's recommendation, or the equally disquieting comment of Mr. Lawrence B. Mulloy, "My God, Thiokol, when do you want me to launch, next April?" may never be fully known. However, immediately following these comments, Mr. Joe Kilminster (who was well aware of the contract negotiations between Thiokol and NASA) immediately requested an off net caucus for Thiokol. This caucus, which culminated in a "management decision," reversed Thiokol's earlier recommendation to NASA officials, and was contrary to the collective opinion of those engineers attending the caucus. Upon rejoining the teleconference thirty minutes later, Thiokol management recommended launch and provided "engineering" criteria to substantiate their decision.[24]

The High Politics of NASA. Equally difficult to discern is the impact of political infighting between Congress, NASA, Commerce, Transportation, and the military regarding the funding of the NASA space program. The Pentagon, which even at present has a budget three times NASA's budget for space projects, pushed hard for Congressional leaders to support military projects at the expense of the NASA budget.[25] If NASA could not (and can not) demonstrate that the shuttle program was in fact "Operational," and that they could meet an aggressive and pressure ladened launch schedule, NASA funding could, and most probably would, be diverted to the military so that they might increase their rocket fleet to place satellites in space.

NASA was aware of the importance of public and Congressional support for the continued flow of massive funding into NASA. Their selection of Utah Republican Jake Garn, who was chair of the Senate committee overseeing NASA's budget, to ride the shuttle in April 1985, was done for more than altruistic reasons. Equally, the teacher in space program was a public relations effort that not only demonstrated the President's support of education, but it put NASA in the limelight, and it furthered the image that shuttle flight was as safe and common as airline travel. In fact, the President was expected to mention the Challenger mission and the teacher in space program during his State of the Union address on January 28. While there is conflicting evidence regarding the impact of these factors on NASA officials,[26] it is difficult to believe that these real or perceived threats to the financial security of the space program did not affect the position of NASA officials, albeit we may never know to what extent, on the evening of January 27, during Meeting Five.

While it is uncertain to what degree each of these system pressures individually or collectively influenced decisions at Thiokol or NASA, or in what way these same pressures dominated the casual response of Thiokol management to the O-ring problem, they were a part of the decision process. Perhaps Otto Lerbinger provides a partial answer when he states, "People make convenient assumptions because they want to move on. They note risks involved, but forget their assumptions and forget the risks they originally recognized. . . ."[27]

II. Managing NASA: Victims of Success

It is not surprising that a Commission composed almost solely of individuals with scientific and engineering backgrounds serendipitously stumbled on the flawed managerial process at NASA. Equally predictable is the fact that although the Commission was able to describe some of the flaws in the formal organization, they were unable to explain how these

flaws came about from a social scientific viewpoint. In addition, the Commission was misleading when they gave the impression in their recommendations that changes in the formal structure of the agency would resolve the problems at NASA. The "formal" structure was not "the" problem. The major problem was the informal or shadow organization that had developed. The Commission only scratched the surface regarding the problems at NASA leading up to the Challenger disaster. Consider, as Romzek and Dubnick suggest, that there has been a shift in NASA from a system of professional accountability, which emphasizes ". . . deference to expertise within the agency,"[28] to a management system incorporating bureaucratic accountability, which emphasizes ". . . an organized and legitimate relationship between a superior and a subordinate in which the need to follow 'orders' is unquestioned; and close supervision or a surrogate system of standard operating procedures or clearly stated rules and regulations"[29] exists. For example, there is no better evidence of the autocratic management style and leadership tone at Marshall Space Flight Center than that presented in a letter simply signed "Apocalypse." The now famous Apocalypse letter was sent to Marshall's Inspector General two months after the Challenger disaster. Within this letter Apocalypse graphically condemns Marshall Director William Lucas,

It has been apparent for some time that the Flight Readiness Review process developed by Lucas and other senior NASA managers simply was not doing the job. It was not determining flight readiness. Rather, it established a political situation within NASA in which no center could come to a review and say that it was "not ready." To do so would invite the question "If you are not ready, then why are you not doing your job? It is your job to be ready." At each Flight Readiness Review, every center and every contractor are asked to vote on readiness. It is a "no win" situation. For someone to get up and say that they are not ready is an indictment that they are not doing their job. As a consequence, each center gets up and basically "snows" Headquarters with highly technical rationales that no one but the immediate experts involved can completely judge. Lucas made it known that, under no circumstances, is the Marshall Center to be the cause for delaying a launch. . . . [30]

In addition, Romzek and Dubnick suggest that superimposed on the bureaucratic model is the political accountability system, which requires the administrator to be responsive to various constituencies of his agency, be they Congress, the President, tax payers, or patrons of their service. Perhaps Michael Brody best represents the results of the dual bureaucratic-political accountability system proposed by Romzek and Dubnick:

> The agency's leaders have been preoccupied with raising money for NASA from Congress. To win over the politicians, they have set goals for the shuttle program totally out of sync with the resources at their command. Organizational components that were supposed to work closely together—the Marshall, Kennedy, and Johnson space centers—have behaved like quasi-independent baronies, uncommunicative with one another and with the top. Watching the agency's fortunes decline, employees have tended to act like cowed bureaucrats. The result: an organization in which the flow of vital information up and down was as flawed as the now notorious O-rings. . . . [31]

Certainly, government agencies have to be responsive to the needs and demands of their constituents in democratic countries, but while NASA's ". . . emphasis on political and bureaucratic accountability was a relevant response to changing institutional expectations in NASA's environment, . . . they were inappropriate for the technical tasks at hand."[32] Consequently, both the formal and informal structure of NASA began taking on an organizational ambiance that supported compliance to administrative needs, which were a response to both internal and external pressures. This environment produced directive agents[33] within the administrative ranks that imposed formal and informal constraints on the discovery and free flow of information that would "slow" the progress of space flight. Within this atmosphere it was possible for administrators to wittingly or unwittingly avoid or rationalize away scientific data that suggested needed time consuming and/or expensive design changes. While NASA maintained the external image of a highly efficient and safety conscious agency, over time they slowly became increasingly closed due to overconfidence and susceptibility to external and subsequently internal pressures.

III. The O-Ring Problem Revisited: Managerial Influence

The O-ring problem did not first come to light during the January 27 meeting. There had been blow-by and erosion on seven previous shuttle missions; in fact, concern for the integrity of the Solid Rocket Booster joints was severe enough that a special task force had been instituted by Thiokol at the request of NASA, to study the O-ring problem.

The O-rings were designed under the assumption that hot gasses would not come into contact with the seals. However, early tests and flight experience demonstrated that the O-rings not only could and did come into contact with hot gasses, but they were damaged as a result. The NASA and Thiokol response to these design flaws was to minimize the problem in briefings and to begin defining, however poorly, acceptable erosion depth. Considering the fact that it was known that a failure in the Solid Rocket Joints would result in catastrophe, a fact supported by the criticality 1R and later criticality 1 designation assigned to the O-rings on the Critical Items List, it seems folly that design changes were not instituted immediately.[34]

There are several reasons available to explain the NASA response to the O-rings. First, since the O-rings were similar to the O-rings used in the Titan design, which was the most successful rocket produced by NASA, it appears that there was an overconfidence in the similar O-ring design used in STS. Interestingly, however, there were five major design differences between the Booster joint design of the Titan and Challenger joints. These differences were conveniently overlooked by both Thiokol and NASA personnel;[35] consequently, by ignoring the differences between the two designs they were able to support the desired belief that the joints were safe. Second, one of the major considerations used by NASA in selecting Thiokol to produce the O-ring was the low budget they were able to submit. NASA had been quite concerned about maintaining and increasing Congressional funding for some years. NASA needed to produce success stories to impress

Congress and thus encourage funding. NASA did not want delays or large budget deficits caused by redesign. Third, over the years NASA had become famous for its gung ho, we-can-do-anything attitude. While this attitude had served them well in making the United States number one in the space race, it also encouraged unnecessary risk taking and over-confidence, especially in recent years.

Certainly, the fact that there had already been 24 successful shuttle missions, and that the O-rings had always held in the past, influenced their decision to fly. It must be remembered that NASA was in an "operational" mode. As far as most members of the teleconference were concerned, as well as others, there was no O-ring problem. The O-ring was well within the erosion parameters established. It must be remembered, however, that these parameters were established after it was discovered that the O-rings were experiencing erosion for which they were not designed to tolerate. Perhaps Dr. Richard Feynman; Presidential Commission member, and physicist; best summarized this attitude:

> a kind of Russian roulette. . . . [The Shuttle] flies [with O-ring erosion] and nothing happens. Then it is suggested, therefore, that the risk is no longer so high for the next flights. We can lower our standards a little bit because we got away with it last time. . . . You got away with it, but it shouldn't be done over and over again like that.[36]

NASA and ultimately its contractors had left the traditionally conservative design, development, and testing stage behind. The result was that they began to rationalize away, they failed to communicate, they improperly analyzed data, and generally became somewhat sloppy in their work and overconfident of their successes due to their past shuttle flights. . . .

Notes

1. "From the Beginning to the End," *The New York Times,* January 29, 1986, p. A 1.
2. The only other astronauts to lose their lives were Virgil I. Grissom, Edward H. White, and Roger B. Chaffee. They perished on January 27, 1967, when their Apollo spacecraft caught fire on the launch pad. See "Doubts and Changes After Past Disasters," *The New York Times* January 29, 1986, p. A 10.
3. *Report of the Presidential Commission on the Space Shuttle Challenger Accident,* Washington, D.C.: Government Printing Office, 1986, vol. I, p. 72. The facts concerning the Challenger disaster can be found in the five volume series prepared by the Presidential Commission. The overall summary of the Commissions findings can be found in volume one; consequently, references are provided only when direct quotations were incorporated into the text, or when other sources were used.
4. B. Fischhoff, S. Lichtenstein, P. Derby, L. Stephen, and R. Keeney, *Acceptable Risk* (New York: Cambridge University Press, 1981), p. 42.
5. C. Perrow: *Normal Accidents* (New York: Basic Books, 1984), p. 8.
6. Ibid., p. 5.
7. *Report of the Presidential Commission on the Space Shuttle Challenger Accident,* vol. I, p. 87.
8. Ibid.
9. Ibid., p. 88.
10. Ibid., p. 89.
11. Ibid., p. 96.
12. Ibid., p. 99.
13. M. McConnell, *Challenger: A Major Malfunction* (Garden City, New York: Doubleday, 1987), p. 199.
14. Ibid.
15. *Report of the Presidential Commission on the Space Shuttle Challenger Accident,* vol. I, p. 93.
16. Ibid.
17. *Report of the Presidential Commission on the Space Shuttle Challenger Accident,* Washington, D.C.: Government Printing Office, 1986, vol. IV, p. 725.
18. Ibid., p. 726.
19. *Report of the Presidential Commission on the Space Shuttle Challenger Accident,* vol. I, pp. 114–115.
20. Ibid.
21. Alan Jarman and Alexander Kouzmin, "Decision Pathways From Crisis: A Contingency-Theory Simulation Heuristic for the Challenger

Shuttle Disaster (1983–88)." Paper presented at the International Conference of the European Group of Public Administration, Leuven, Belgium. September 7–10, 1988 (mimeographed).

22. McConnell, p. 7.
23. Ibid., pp. 44–61.
24. *Report of the Presidential Commission on the Space Shuttle Challenger Accident,* vol. I, p. 104.
25. M. Beck and M. Hager, "Why Are We Up There?" *Newsweek* (October 10, 1988), pp. 36–38.
26. T.E. Bell and K. Esch, "The Fatal Flaw in Flight 51L" *IEEE Spectrum* (February, 1987).
27. Ibid., p. 50.
28. B.S. Romzek and M.J. Dubnick, "Accountability in the Public Sector: Lessons from the Challenger Tragedy," *Public Administration Review* (47), 1987, p. 229.
29. Ibid., p. 228. Cited from A. Gouldner, *Patterns of Industrial Bureaucracy* (New York: The Free Press, 1954), pp. 159–162.
30. McConnell, p. 109.
31. M. Brody, "NASA's Challenge: Ending Isola-

tion at the Top," *Fortune* (May 12, 1986), p. 26.
32. Romzek and Dubnick, p. 235. See also W.H. Starbuck and F.J. Milliken, "Challenger: Fine-Tuning the Odds Until Something Breaks," *Journal of Management Studies* (25:4) (July, 1988), pp. 319–340.
33. I.L. Janis and L. Mann, *Decision Making: A Psychological Analysis of Conflict, Choice, and Commitment* (New York: The Free Press, 1977), p. 256.
34. For safety reasons shuttle components were assigned criticality categories. The categories included: criticality 1—loss of life or vehicle if the component failed; criticality 2—loss of mission if the component failed; criticality 3—all others; criticality 1R—redundant components, the failure of both could cause loss of life or vehicle; criticality 2R—redundant components, the failure of both could cause loss of mission.
35. Bell and Esch, p. 42.
36. *Report of the Presidential Commission on the Space Shuttle Challenger Accident,* vol. I, p. 148. See also Starbuck and Milliken, pp. 321–322.

Chapter 4 Review Questions

1. On the basis of your reading of the Long essay and the case study, how would you define the term *administrative power*? Can it be measured? If so, how?

2. Based on the case study, how did the political environment influence the decision to launch the space shuttle *Challenger*? Particularly who was involved and who was not?

3. What were the sources of these political pressures? Their points of view?

4. In your view, who was most responsible or irresponsible for the decision to launch the shuttle? How can one determine "responsible" or "irresponsible" use of administrative power? *And* ensure its "responsible" use?

5. Can you list the reasons why "the political dimensions" are repeatedly overlooked or ignored? Was this true in this case study? Or in case No.1?

6. On the basis of Long's essay and your analysis of the case study, can you generalize about the most significant problems facing public administrators today in relating politics and administration? Does the Wilson essay in Chapter 1 offer any advice on this problem?

Key Terms

interest groups
organizational fragmentation
administrative rationality
balance of power

coordination of government
sources of conflict
sources of cohesion
maintaining political support

Suggestions for Further Reading

The classic works on interest groups and their influence on the governmental process are Arthur F. Bentley, *The Process of Government* (Cambridge, Mass.: Harvard University Press, 1908); E. Pendleton Herring, *Public Administration and the Public Interest* (New York: Russell and Russell, 1936); and David Truman, *The Governmental Process* (New York: Alfred A. Knopf, 1951). The influence of politics on public administration and the general power politics within administrative processes were especially emphasized and popularized by the "new postwar realism" of authors such as Paul H. Appleby, *Big Democracy* (New York: Alfred A. Knopf, 1945) and *Policy and Administration* (University, Ala.: University of Alabama Press, 1949); Robert A. Dahl and Charles E. Lindblom, *Politics, Economics, and Welfare* (New York: Harper and Brothers, 1953); and Herbert Simon et al., *Public Administration* (New York: Alfred A. Knopf, 1950). Of course, Long's numerous essays did much to explore as well as contribute to this topic and they are available in a single volume, *The Polity* (Chicago: Rand McNally and Co., 1962).

The last three decades have witnessed an enormous outpouring of books and articles on this subject. Some of the best that illuminate our understanding of the complex interplay between administration and politics have been more narrowly focused book-length cases of policy dilemmas such as A. Lee Fritchler, *Smoking and Politics,* Second Edition (Englewood Cliffs, N.J.: Prentice-Hall, 1975); Daniel P. Moynihan, *The Politics of a Guaranteed Income* (New York: Random House, 1973); Jeffrey L. Pressman and Aaron Wildavsky,

Implementation, Second Edition (Berkeley: University of California Press, 1979); Stephen K. Bailey and Edith K. Mosher, *ESEA: The Office of Education Administers a Law* (Syracuse: Syracuse University Press, 1968); Charles Perrow and Maurio F. Guillén, *The AIDS Disaster: The Failure of Organizations in New York and the Nation* (New Haven, Conn: Yale University Press, 1990); and Martha Derthick, *Agency under Stress: The Social Security Administration in American Government* (Washington, D.C.: The Brookings Institution, 1990). There are many, many more such cases, particularly those available through the Inter-University Case Program (P.O. Box 229, Syracuse, N.Y. 13210), and the John F. Kennedy School of Government Case Program, Kennedy School of Government, Harvard University, 79 JFK Street, Cambridge, Mass. 02138. For three books about administrative power based on some careful case studies, read Gary C. Bryner, *Bureaucratic Discretion* (New York: Pergamon Press, 1987); Irene S. Rubin, *Shrinking the Federal Government* (New York: Longman, 1985); and James P. Pfiffner, *The Strategic Presidency* (Chicago: The Dorsey Press, 1988).

Perhaps some of the very best contemporary analyses of the aspects of power influencing administrative actions are found in Harold Seidman and Robert Gilmour *Politics, Position, and Power,* Fourth Edition (New York: Oxford University Press, 1986); Francis E. Rourke, *Bureaucracy, Politics and Public Policy,* Third Edition (Boston: Little, Brown, 1984); as well as Rourke's excellent edited collection entitled *Bureaucratic Power in*

National Policy Making, Fourth Edition (Boston: Little, Brown, 1986). Particularly good treatments of congressional oversight of administrative agencies are found in Joel D. Aberbach, *Keeping a Watchful Eye: The Politics of Congressional Oversight* (Washington, D.C.: The Brookings Institution, 1990); Morris P. Fiorina, *Congress: Keystone of the Washington Establishment* Second Edition (New Haven: Yale University Press, 1989); and Christopher H. Foreman, Jr., *Signals from the Hill* (New Haven: Yale University Press, 1988). The rise of the power of "think tanks" in shaping policy agendas is well described by David M. Ricci, *The Transformation of American Politics: The New Washington and the Rise of Think Tanks* (New Haven: Yale University Press, 1993).

You should not overlook biographies and autobiographies as offering worthwhile insights, particularly Joseph A. Califano, Jr., *Governing America* (New York: Simon and Schuster, 1981); William Manchester, *American Caesar: Douglas MacArthur, 1880–1964* (Boston: Little, Brown, 1978); Norman Polmar and Thomas B. Allen, *Rickover: A Biography* (New York: Simon and Schuster, 1982); Robert Caro, *The Power Broker,* cited in Chapter 3; David Stockman, *The Triumph of Politics,* cited in Chapter 3; Deborah Shapley, *Promise and Power,* cited in Chapter 3; and Jameson W. Doig and Erwin C. Hargrove, *Leadership and Innovation,* cited in Chapter 3. For more current "overviews" of national political power, see Hedrick Smith, *The Power Game: How Washington Works* (New York: Random House, 1988); Bradley H. Patterson, Jr., *Rings of Power: The White House Staff and Its Expanding Role in Government* (New York: Basic Books, 1988); A. Lee Fritschler and Bernard H. Ross, *How Washington Works, The Executive Guide to Government* (Cambridge, Mass.: Ballinger, 1987) and at the local level, both Robert J. Waste, *Ecology of City Policy Making* (New York: Oxford University Press, 1989); and James H. Svara, *Official Leadership in the City: Patterns of Conflict and Cooperation* (New York: Oxford University Press, 1990). For a general review of academic literature pertaining to this topic, see Chapter 3, "The Impact of Political Power and Public Policy," in Hal Rainey, *Understanding and Managing Public Organizations* (San Francisco: Jossey-Bass, 1991).

CHAPTER 5

Intergovernmental Relations (IGR): The Concept of IGR as Interdependence, Complexity and Bargaining

The problems and tensions in the modern (intergovernmental) system are not primarily the product of ill will or ignorance, nor can they be traced to one level of government. Rather, the American intergovernmental system was founded on ambivalent principles and built to establish arenas for conflict and controversy.

Laurence J. O'Toole, Jr.

READING 5

Introduction

In some countries, the subject of intergovernmental relations (IGR) is not a frequent topic of conversation. Unitary forms of government, found in communist societies, Third World or developing nations, and even modernized traditional Western state regimes, allow for little or no semiautonomous local units of government. Within these unitary models, power flows from the top downward, and no competition with national sovereignty is tolerated from governmental subunits. Local autonomy is simply unknown.

By contrast, the central framing idea of the U.S. government was federalism. The federal structure, as designed by the U.S. Constitution, distributes authority among the various levels of federal, state, and local government. In part, federalism was a pragmatic requirement in 1787. The founders were faced with the difficult necessity of winning state support for ratification, and thus adopting a unitary form that would abolish or severely restrict state authority was clearly out of the question. However, ideological considerations were also important in opting for federalism. The founders had vivid memories of the dangers from top-down unitary government of George III's monarchy as well as the loose, extreme decentralization of the Articles of Confederation (in reality the U.S.'s first constitution). Neither had produced satisfactory government and so the founders chose a mixture of both, the novel federal format. Though it is and remains the central framing idea in the U.S. Constitution, the Constitution on the specifics of this subject, as in many others, was imprecise and unclear. The details of the wheres and whys of how the various functions of government would be parcelled out among the levels and units are not addressed in the U.S. Constitution beyond the items listed in Article I, Section 8.

In the United States, public administrators, thus, work within an unusual, complex framework in which authority over agency and program activities is frequently shared by various levels, jurisdictions, and units of government. Because of this "scattering" of authority, administrative problems arise, leading in turn to the important study of IGR, which involves comprehending the complexities of the federal system based on mutual interdependence, shared functions, and intertwined influence. Morton Grodzins once aptly showed the confusion for public administrators who operate under this system. In the case of a county health officer, called "a sanitarian" in a rural county:

> The sanitarian is appointed by the state under merit standards established by the federal government. His base salary comes jointly from state and federal funds, the county provides him with an office and office amenities and pays a portion of his expenses, and the largest city in the county also contributes to his salary and office by virtue of his appointment as a city plumbing inspector. It is impossible from moment to moment to tell under which governmental hat the sanitarian operates. His work of inspecting the purity of food is carried out under federal standards; but he is enforcing state laws when inspecting commodities that have not been in interstate commerce; and somewhat perversely, he also acts under state authority when inspecting milk coming into the county from producing areas across the state border. He is a federal officer when impounding impure drugs shipped from a neighboring state; a federal-state officer when distributing typhoid immunization serum; a state officer when enforcing standards of industrial hygiene; a state-local officer when inspecting the city's water supply; and (to complete the circle) a local officer when insisting that the city butchers adopt more hygienic methods of handling their garbage. But he cannot and does not think of himself as acting in these separate capacities. All business in the county that concerns public health and sanitation he considers his business. Paid largely from federal funds, he does not find it strange to attend meetings of the city council to give expert advice on matters ranging from rotten apples to rabies control. He is even deputized as a member of both the city and county police forces.[1]

Morton Grodzins's example of the county health officer may be extreme, but it is not uncommon to find public administrators wearing several "governmental hats." Federalism confounds and confuses public administrators' roles and responsibilities to an extreme degree in the United States. Who's the boss? The federal government? State? Locals? Or . . . ? For many administrators, the answer, as that of the county health officer cited by Grozdins, is the ambiguous: "It all depends."

Laurence J. O'Toole, Jr., a professor of political science at the University of Georgia and author of numerous works on intergovernmental relations, federalism, and pub-

---

[1]Morton Grodzins, "The Federal System," in The American Assembly, *Goals for Americans* (N.J.: Prentice-Hall, Inc., 1960), p. 265.

lic administration, explores the current dimensions of IGR. This essay served as an introduction to his own edited volume on the subject and provides readers with a unique broad-brush 200-year overview of the topic. In particular, O'Toole's study begins by carefully differentiating "federalism" from "intergovernmental relations" and demonstrates how these concepts are rooted in the framework of the U.S. Constitution. The author shows how the idea of "dual federalism" of the 19th century evolved into more complex interrelationships in the 20th century. The essay outlines the diverse factors that have resulted in fundamentally changed IGR dynamics and how particularly in recent decades various presidents have advanced different reforms to cope with the apparent dilemmas and issues of the intergovernmental system. O'Toole's thesis is: Despite the subsequent repeated reform initiatives by presidents, the modern pattern of IGR since the 1960s has been marked by three persisting characteristics: interdependence, complexity, and bargaining.

As you read O'Toole's insightful article, you might reflect on:

What does O'Toole mean by those three terms, "interdependence," "complexity," and "bargaining"?

How did this IGR pattern emerge and why does it persist today, according to O'Toole?

What does this concept of IGR mean for practicing public administrators and how should they train themselves to deal with these problems (think about the prior case study, "Dumping $2.6 Million on Bakersfield," in order to help you draw some conclusions)?

What were the various reform agendas proposed by presidents to improve and strengthen IGR, and why is it so difficult to change this intergovernmental system?

How does "federalism" differ from "IGR," according to O'Toole?

American Intergovernmental Relations: An Overview

LAURENCE J. O'TOOLE, JR.

Who (if anyone) should assist America's big cities with the financial responsibility for handling a spate of ills from homelessness to Acquired Immune Deficiency Syndrome (AIDS) to attracting business investment? Should state governments be able to force localities to initiate new activities without providing the cash to cover expenses? Should the nation adopt a common and upgraded school curriculum in an effort to improve education and also economic competitiveness with other nations? Or should local districts across the wide variety of states comprising the country be permitted, even encouraged, to innovate on their own?

Should the federal government be heavily involved in the enforcement of such important policies as ensuring citizens' civil rights, encouraging equal employment opportunity, and assisting with affirmative action? Alternatively, should Washington have *any* role in the operations of local police and fire departments?

How should the people handle problems that confront one region of the United States but surpass that locale's ability to cope? When a huge oil spill devastates parts of the precious Alaskan wilderness, who should take action, and how? When a reform of national tax law creates unintendedly negative effects on the finances of the states, what should be done? When acid rain from industrial air pollution contributes to the deterioration of natural resources a thousand miles away, whose problem and responsibility should it be? All these and many more are topics of intergovernmental relations.

Intergovernmental relations is the subject of how our many and varied American governments deal with each other; and what their relative roles, responsibilities, and levels of influence are and should be. The subject is no flash-in-the-pan concern; it has generated long-standing interest, indeed constant and pervasive controversy, throughout American political and administrative history.

In fact, the establishment of the United States was itself a sort of experiment in intergovernmental relations, since an effort to create a federal system like this one had never before been attempted. Nearly every major matter of domestic policy debated and decided throughout the nation's more than two hundred years has been imbued with important intergovernmental aspects. Intergovernmental issues have contributed to such significant events in American history as the Civil War, the establishment of the social-welfare state during the New Deal era, the attack on poverty in the 1960s, and the attempt to shift responsibilities to the states during the Reagan years.

But the subject is more than a collection of isolated issues. Indeed, it would be difficult to make

systematic sense of policy disputes like those mentioned above without first understanding the intergovernmental system per se—its historical development as well as its current structure. To prepare for an exploration of current issues and disputes and to provide a context for the [case] that follow, this chapter offers a brief overview of the intergovernmental system in the United States, emphasizing the federal government's role in the system's development.

Federalism, as the term is understood today, means a system of authority constitutionally apportioned between central and regional governments.[1] In the American system, the central, or national, government is often called the federal government; the regional governments are the states. The federal-state relationship is interdependent: neither can abolish the other and each must deal with the other. *Intergovernmental relations* is the more comprehensive term, including the full range of federal-state-local relations.

In the 1990s there are approximately 83,000 American governments—one national, 50 state, and the rest local. The latter consist of several distinct types. *Counties,* numbering some 3,000 units, are general-purpose governments originally created throughout most of the country to administer state services at the local level. Today, counties are genuine local governments providing an array of services to their citizens, and many—especially the larger, more urban ones—are increasingly involved in complex intergovernmental arrangements with other local jurisdictions, states, and the national government. *Municipalities,* numbering about 19,000, are local governments established to serve people within an area of concentrated population. The nation's largest cities and small villages alike are municipalities, although the types of powers they have and the services they offer may vary considerably. Municipalities are created to serve explicitly the interests of the local community. Through much of American history, municipalities have had extensive and often highly conflicting relationships with their "parent" states—relationships sometimes made all the more challenging from the point of view of the municipalities since they are not granted constitutionally independent status by the states, as are the states in the U.S. framework. Since the New Deal era in the 1930s and the rapid expansion of the intergovernmental system in the 1960s, municipalities—especially large cities—have dealt with Washington, as well, on many matters. And as federal cutbacks to these governments took hold beginning in the 1980s, municipalities have often developed defensive and somewhat conflictual relations with both state and national authorities—as they have also sought to develop additional revenue sources and less one-sided dependence on the other levels.

Additional local governments include:

- *townships* (approximately 17,000), which are usually subdivisions of rural counties and are relatively unimportant except in some parts of New England and the mid-Atlantic states;
- *school districts* (15,000), which are separate governments established in many parts of the country to direct public school systems; and
- *special districts* (numbering 29,532 in a recent count), which are limited-purpose governments set up to handle one or perhaps a few public functions over a specially designated area.[2]

Special districts are currently responsible for managing public housing; building and maintaining bridges, tunnels, and roads; supplying water and sewerage services to residents; assessing and regulating air quality; and caring for the district's mass transportation needs. The creation of many of these districts over the years has been directly or indirectly encouraged by other governments—such as the states and Washington—which sought "coordinated" local action on one or another policy problem.

If given a chance to view their handiwork today, it is likely that the founders of this nation would find much to surprise them in the operations of American politics and government, especially in the intergovernmental workings. Yet intergovernmental developments over the past two centuries have been affected greatly by some fundamental choices consciously made by those early Americans.

The Founding and the Framework

The framers of the U.S. Constitution sought a way to combine the several states into a structure that would minimize "instability, injustice, and confusion," in the words of James Madison.[3] The founders were familiar with the arguments of earlier political thinkers who claimed that government protection of individual rights would have to be small-scale and cover a geographically limited jurisdiction. Yet their own experience suggested problems with such an arrangement. Under the Articles of Confederation, enacted after the Revolution, the thirteen American states had agreed on a formal arrangement that is now called a *confederation*.[4] The states were loosely joined for certain purposes, but their association fell far short of a real nation. The states retained almost all power, and the "united states" under the Articles found it virtually impossible to act with dispatch on matters of importance.

To solve this problem, the "federalists" of that period proposed to organize a nation able to act in a unified and central fashion for certain purposes. They argued that large republics, not small ones, were more likely to be able to prevent internal tyranny. They also suggested, however, that the states themselves retain independent governments with correspondingly independent jurisdictions. As a matter of fact, state autonomy was a political necessity at the time if widespread support of a new constitutional order were to be elicited. In the absence of any such historical arrangement, the new experiment in intergovernmental relations would have to develop out of the American experience.

The founders' construction of the new system virtually ensured continuing controversy about the respective roles of the national and state governments by creating sufficient ambiguity to leave many of the most important questions unresolved. As a result, later years were to see major changes in American intergovernmental relations under the influence of various political, economic, and social forces, while the basic framework remained constant.[5]

What does that framework actually stipulate? The Constitution seems to divide responsibilities between the two levels of government according to subject. Certain functions (for example, interstate commerce and national defense) are assigned to the national authorities, while many others (such as selection of presidential electors) are left to the states. Furthermore, the Tenth Amendment in the Bill of Rights asserts that "the powers not delegated to the United States by the Constitution, nor prohibited by it to the States, are reserved to the States respectively, or to the people." The states appear to have been given an advantage.

Yet the explanation cannot end here, for the same Constitution provides conflicting cues, authorizing the national Congress to "provide for the . . . general Welfare" and to "make all Laws which shall be necessary and proper" for executing this and the other powers given to the legislature. What constitutes the "general welfare" and which laws are necessary and proper are inherently political questions. Thus, it should be no surprise that the answers adopted by different people and at different times have not been consistent. The founders established a framework in which American governments would have separate but not completely independent spheres. The different levels would find it both useful and necessary to engage in conflict and cooperation; neither would be willing or able to ignore the other.

The Idea of Dual Federalism

Even in the earliest decades of the nation's existence, this tension was evident between the idea of *dual federalism* (that is, each of the two levels of government operating within its separate sphere without relying on the other for assistance or authorization) on the one hand and ambiguous overlap on the other.

The notion of dual federalism influenced the decisions of the Supreme Court at least until the early decades of the twentieth century. Furthermore, during the 1800s various presidents sometimes vetoed legislation that would have created a federal presence in policy fields such as public works construction on the grounds that the Constitution simply did not permit such national involvement in arenas reserved for the states.[6] In 1854, for example, President Franklin Pierce vetoed legislation that would have authorized federal land grants to be used for state institutions for the insane. In a number of fields, like education and social policy, dual federalism was the predominant view of federal-state intergovernmental relations.

Conflict and Cooperation in Earlier Times

Yet neither sphere was completely independent, even in the early years. Throughout the nineteenth century, the national government and the states often disagreed about the limits of their own authority. The Civil War is perhaps the prime example, but conflict occurred on other matters as well, such as policy on labor, social welfare, and economic regulation. Through the necessity of resolving jurisdictional disputes, therefore, the federal and state governments found it necessary to recognize their interdependence.

Conflict was not the only stimulus, however, for interaction. As various policy problems captured the attention of the nation's officials and citizenry, federal and state governments were sometimes able to piece together intergovernmental mechanisms to address immediate concerns. For instance, if some early national and state leaders viewed direct federal aid for internal improvements (for example, road and canal construction) as a violation of constitutional restrictions on intergovernmental arrangements, the governments *were* able to agree to cooperate in the formation of *joint stock companies,* part public and part private entities created to surmount the restrictions on direct participation by the national government. (Governments and private businesses could buy stock in a company and appoint members to its board of directors, thus indirectly supporting and influencing its operations.)[7]

Another mechanism for cooperation during the previous century, before the dramatically increased intergovernmental interdependence of recent years, was the *land grant.* Through this device, the federal government would offer some of its land (it owned plenty) to the states for specified purposes. The recipient government would be obliged to abide by certain federal requirements, but direct involvement by the national government was minimal. Land grants were intended to help achieve goals in the fields of education (thus the origins of today's nationwide set of land-grant colleges and universities), economic development, and (on a very limited scale) social welfare.

Other forms of intergovernmental cooperation, such as technical assistance from federal to state governments and informal exchanges and loans of expert personnel during peak or crisis periods, were relatively common occurrences even during the nation's first century. Nevertheless, it was not until the twentieth century that the dual federal perspective declined appreciably in significance and American intergovernmental relations developed into a system with sustained high levels of *interdependence* and consequent *complexity.* Several political, economic, and social events and trends fueled these developments.

Developments in the Early Twentieth Century

From early in the present century until recent years, federal involvement, especially financial involvement, in intergovernmental relations escalated. The Progressive era at the turn of the century brought an expanded role for government in general, as re-

formers argued that the society and the economy could not tolerate laissez-faire. The concentration of power in large corporations, the reluctance of some state governments to enact regulatory and other social welfare legislation (although other states were leaders in enacting farsighted and sometimes tough policy on such subjects), and the dawning recognition that the nation's natural resources were limited and would have to be conserved encouraged an expanded domestic policy role for Washington. This shift was also encouraged in many cases by the newly developing and professionalizing state bureaucracies, which saw in federal involvement opportunities for upgrading and for expanded funding; and by some interest groups that had been pushing at the state level for public attention to one problem or another. (Then, as now, organized interests—whether concerned with expanded highway construction or social services—have recognized that it is usually easier and more effective to deal with one central government on such matters than with scores of divergent ones throughout the states.)

The growing national will to attempt action in new arenas was followed by the central government's acquiring the practical wherewithal for action. The resources needed were money and clear authority; by the 1920s both had been generated.

Federal Financial Aid

In 1913 the U.S. Constitution was amended to permit the enactment of a federal income tax. Previously the national government had provided some limited financial support to the states, but the intergovernmental fiscal ties were few and far between. Until very recently, however, the passage of the Sixteenth Amendment enabled the national government to raise revenue more easily than the subnational ones. The income tax, which was "elastic" (that is, its receipts increased faster than the economy during periods of growth), has been a more politically palatable revenue source than other sources typically emphasized by the states and local governments.

This situation has changed in recent years. First,

the income tax increased its bite in individuals' paychecks during the period of rapid inflation in the 1970s, resulting in a decline in its popularity and the enactment of an indexing provision to control the effects of inflation. Second, federal legislative changes during the 1980s reduced the progressiveness of the tax, that is, the extent to which it draws revenue from the affluent. And other federal taxes, especially social security, have begun to assume a larger burden. Third, most states and even some local governments enacted income taxes of their own, with formulas tied in complicated ways to various provisions of the federal tax code. The development of intergovernmental finances in recent decades therefore documents one way in which the system has been linked via complexity. Thus, with the income tax the federal government created a source of money that could be tapped repeatedly to fill needs that had not yet received the states' wholehearted attention.

The obvious mechanism of intergovernmental cooperation in many such cases was the *grant-in-aid.* By 1920 there were eleven grants-in-aid operating in the United States. Land grants and other varieties of intergovernmental assistance were never again to outstrip cash grants in importance. Because of the significance of grants-in-aid and their sustained use in the early twentieth century, it would be useful to explain at this point some of the basic implications of this kind of federal program.

A grant-in-aid is a transfer of funds from one government to another for some specified purpose. Typically the recipient government is asked by the donor to abide by certain terms as conditions of the assistance.[8] These usually include a requirement that the recipient unit match the donor's financial contribution with one of its own, as well as a series of "strings," or stipulations, as to how the funds will be utilized, how the program will be managed, and how the recipient government will report to the donor.

Starting on a small scale early in this century, and then expanding rapidly during certain periods—especially the New Deal and Great Society eras—grants-in-aid from the federal government to the states and eventually local governments be-

came extremely important features of the intergovernmental system in the United States. States too have provided financial support to their local governments. (In 1988 total state aid amounted to $149 billion. This total includes some federal aid passed to the local units through the states.)[9] But federal aid, because of its size, relative newness, and capacity to produce large-scale alterations in the intergovernmental system, may be considered an especially significant feature of America's fiscal federalism (see Table 1).

Validation of Grants-in-Aid

As the national government began to exercise influence through the use of grants-in-aid in the early 1900s, some observers wondered if the grant mechanism was an unconstitutional federal intrusion into the affairs of the states. Armed with the doctrine of dual federalism, critics of federal grants argued that Washington's offers were actually coercive inducements and violated the notion of separate spheres for these two levels of government. In a pair of landmark decisions in 1923 the Supreme Court paved the way for major expansions in the grant system—and for tremendously increased interdependence and complexity among levels of government—in succeeding years. The Court asserted that grants were voluntary arrangements and the federal government was therefore not violating the constitutionally established separation of functions in the federal system.[10] As the years elapsed, the grant framework became a dominant feature of the American intergovernmental network; it tied thousands of governments intricately together, whatever the direction preferred or perturbations experienced from any point in the system.

Basic Types of Assistance

Grants have offered the opportunity for substantially expanded federal influence over state and local governments, and a number of important political and administrative consequences flow from this fact. Yet it is essential to recognize that while grants create chances for national involvement,

Table 1   Federal Aid to State and Local Governments, Selected Years

Year	Amount (Billions)[a]	Amount in Constant 1982 Dollars (Billions)	Number of Grants
1902	$.028		5
1912	—		7
1913	.039		
1920	—		11
1922	.242		—
1932	.593		12
1934	2.4		—
1937	—		26
1940	2.1		—
1946	—		28
1952	3.1		38
1960	7.0	24.7	132
1964	10.1	33.6	—
1967	15.2	46.0	379
1975	49.8	87.1	442
1978	77.9	109.7	—
1981	94.8	100.7	539
1982	88.2	88.2	441
1984	97.6	90.2	405
1987	108.4	90.6	435
1990	133.8 (est.)	98.2	—
1992	149.4 (est.)	100.1	—

[a]1961 dollars through 1952; otherwise, current dollars.
SOURCE: U.S. Advisory Commission on Intergovernmental Relations, *The Federal Role in the Federal System: The Dynamics of Growth—A Crisis of Confidence and Competence* (Washington, D.C.: ACIR, July 1980), 120–121; and *Revenues and Expenditures,* vol. 2 of *Significant Features of Fiscal Federalism, 1990* (Washington, D.C.: ACIR, August 1990), 42.

they do not vitiate the pluralism of the intergovernmental system—at least not necessarily. Grants have developed as the prime instruments used to promote bargaining and jockeying for advantage among governments; they have frequently stimulated both cooperation and conflict among such governments. It should therefore surprise no one that the system of intergovernmental aid employed in this country has elicited ambivalent evaluations from participants and citizens alike.

Grants come in many shapes and sizes. The donor government may structure the purpose quite narrowly, offering aid for the construction of certain kinds of highways within a state. Such *categorical grants* were typical in the early part of this century. The donor may also design an intergovernmental program for a variety of purposes within a broad field such as education, community development, or social services. This type of aid,

called a *block grant,* gained some prominence in more recent decades. In the early 1970s a new form of aid, *revenue sharing,* was created to enable one government to offer financial aid to another with virtually no restrictions as to its use.[11]

When enacted, all of these types of intergovernmental assistance required some rules and regulations regarding the method of distributing the aid. How is a unit selected to receive assistance and how much is it entitled to? Some grants, including all federal block grants, specify a precise formula in the legislation creating the program. Such *formula grants* include quantifiable elements, such as size of population, amount of tax effort, proportion of population unemployed or below poverty level, density of housing, or rate of infant mortality. The specified formula is a rule that tells potential recipient governments precisely how they can calculate the quantity of aid to which they are entitled under the provisions of the law, so long as the recipient qualifies for such assistance under the other stipulations of the program. Usually, the elements in a formula are chosen to reflect characteristics related to the purpose of the aid (number of school-age children for an education grant, age and/or density of residential housing for housing assistance). Some factors in the formula are also likely to have political significance since there is no such thing as a "neutral" formula—all formulas reward some states or localities more than others, depending on their relative standing given the formula specified.

However, another method of distributing aid is possible. *Project grants* allocate funding on a competitive basis, and potential recipients have no advance knowledge about the size of the grant. Instead, the authorizing legislation typically indicates the sorts of jurisdictions that are eligible to apply for aid and the criteria that will be employed to judge the merit of a government's application. Whether or not a government then receives funding depends on how strong a case it can make in its own behalf. Bureaucrats in the federal departments that supply aid determine the relative worthiness of different proposals and different jurisdictions, often by means of a detailed decision-making and evaluation system.

Why bother to make these distinctions among types of aid? The answer is that different types of grants have tended to produce different types of relationships between and among the participating governments. Much of the intergovernmental system during this century can be rendered intelligible by analyzing the consequences of different types of aid, the subject of much of the remainder of this chapter.

The Legacy of the New Deal

Most of the grant-in-aid programs developed by the national government in the early decades of the 1900s were relatively limited. They assisted primarily in fields that commanded strong political support, such as agriculture and road construction.

Federal assistance, and thus national influence, was directed almost entirely toward the states rather than local governments. During this period, and until the 1960s, the system of intergovernmental aid was dominated by categorical formula grants. For the first part of the century, these were accompanied by relatively few strings, required considerable matching on the part of the recipients, and were rare enough that they did not seem to impose much of an administrative or political burden on the states.

With the New Deal in the 1930s the federal government under the leadership of President Franklin D. Roosevelt tackled the challenging economic and social problems of the Depression era. Although it would have been technically possible to establish new national-level programs to cope with the difficulties of the period, the more politically palatable method of the grant-in-aid was repeatedly used instead. Thus, while the national government's role expanded, the states and local governments retained significant leverage. Within a two-year period, categorical grants were established in such a variety of fields—free school lunches, aid to dependent children, emergency work relief, and so on—that they became the foundation for the social-welfare state in America. The first real forms of assistance to some of the nation's local governments, the cities, were initiated during this period as well. For the states and some of their local governments, then, national authorities were no longer distant or sporadically communicating entities. Instead, in many areas of domestic policy, two or three levels of government were tied together in intricate patterns of intergovernmental relations—much like a "marble cake," rather than a "layer cake" of dual federalism.[12]

Thus, the New Deal period witnessed a permanent increase in the density and importance of intergovernmental relationships in the United States, and during the next couple of decades—even during the administration of Republican president Dwight D. Eisenhower—the number of federal programs and quantity of federal aid continued to grow. Eisenhower himself was uncomfortable with the apparently prominent role of the national government in domestic policy matters, and he established the Commission on Intergovernmental Relations with the explicit charge to identify areas of federal involvement that could feasibly be "returned" to the states. But even the very modest suggestions of this commission went unimplemented. During the 1950s it seemed, as it often has since then, that the idea of separating functions by level of government was supported in the abstract, but was exceedingly difficult to execute. Concerted efforts to reduce the levels of interdependence and complexity in the intergovernmental system have, until very recently, been singularly unsuccessful. During the Reagan years, as discussed below, the federal government simplified the grant system in certain ways. Yet even these were not without costs (. . . intergovernmental regulations can provide policy benefits), and they introduced complicating changes as well, such as increased intergovernmental mandating in place of the grant mechanism in some policy spheres.

The difficulty experienced by American governments when they try to reduce their reliance on one another is not surprising. Since the New Deal citizens and public officials have tried to harness the national government's tremendous resources in order to attack pressing problems and redress inequities. They have at the same time attempted to retain diversity and innovation through vital state and local governments wherever possible. Shifting to some form of dual federalism, with a much less intense pattern of relationships and dependencies, could affect federal commitments in a multitude of important policy areas, like environmental protection, civil rights, income security, and education. Furthermore, such a change might entail radical shifts in the nation's tax system. And even the most carefully considered plans would have to face bewildering dilemmas about how to reduce intergovernmental interdependence without inflicting serious inequities on some states and localities.

These days, when, as in the 1950s, one hears proposals to limit the federal role in the intergovernmental system and simplify the pattern of American governments, such caveats are useful to keep in mind. While many of the states are as-

suming newly resurgent roles in the policy settings of the 1990s, Washington is certain to play a crucial part for the foreseeable future. It may even be asserted that creating a radically simplified intergovernmental arrangement by moving the national government out of a direct role in many important policy arenas is not a practical or responsible option. Why, then, the clamorous call for reform? Why have so many policymakers and intergovernmental experts complained about the "overloaded" pattern?[13] Later in this [essay], the considerable validity of a number of the criticisms will become clear. Focusing on the major developments affecting the intergovernmental system since the 1960s will be useful in understanding this controversy.

Creative Federalism and Its Implications

With Lyndon Johnson's presidency and the election of a heavily Democratic and activist Congress in 1964, a several-year period of tremendously expanded intergovernmental activities and initiatives began. Johnson proposed a "creative federalism" that would signify multiple new national commitments to assist states, localities, and private individuals and organizations in their efforts to solve many of the domestic difficulties afflicting American society. These efforts of the Johnson era were directed primarily at problems of racial discrimination, poverty, and urban and rural development. The president and the Congress responded not just with rhetoric but with hundreds of intergovernmental programs.

Indeed, the number of federal programs of grant-in-aid tripled from the beginning of the 1960s to 1975 (Table 1). Almost all of the new programs from Washington were categorical grants, and—unlike earlier times—most of them were project grants. By the late 1960s most of the grants available were project grants, although many of these were relatively small and in toto constituted a minority of the aid dollars. In addition, the amount of support aimed directly at local governments rose sharply. Many localities (especially the nation's older, larger, more fiscally strapped cities) came to consider the federal government more of an ally than their own state governments and became increasingly reliant on federal largesse. The results of these and other massive changes in the intergovernmental system enacted in such a compressed period were, as might be expected, mixed.

Intergovernmental Activism

In many respects the consequences of this major increase in intergovernmental activity were impressive. Although hampered by fiscal constraints, especially as the war in Southeast Asia drained its resources, the nation made measurable progress on a number of troubling problems.[14] The dramatic increase in federal support was especially welcome to many state and local governments, which had difficulty obtaining the resources to fund programs demanded by their citizenry; also, the emphasis on a variety of project grants meant that potential recipients could find appropriately targeted programs.

The explosion in the grants system had the further effect of encouraging or mandating the professionalization of personnel and the use of up-to-date financial procedures in the administrative agencies handling the programs in the recipient units. Intergovernmental programs became increasingly influenced by functional specialists at all levels of government. The requirements attached to many of the new grants also forced states and localities to devote renewed attention to public problems they may have overlooked in the past.

Another trend fueled by creative federalism was the growth of interest groups in the nation's capital, especially intergovernmental groups. Those concerned with specific intergovernmental programs, whether on environmental pollution or juvenile delinquency, increasingly looked to Washington as they tried to influence legislation and the implementation of regulations, to monitor the actions of the federal agency involved, and to maintain contact with other interested parties. The

tremendous expansion of the grants system in the 1960s was both a result of and a stimulus for a burgeoning number of interest groups operating at the national level in intergovernmental politics. These changes, too, contributed to the growing complexity of intergovernmental policy making.

These sorts of interest groups were not the only ones to achieve a heightened national presence. As the grants process became ever more important and the system increasingly more complex, officials of state and local governments found it crucial to acquire information about the process in Washington and the decisions being made. Furthermore, state and local officials began to realize that their own interests might deserve representation in the policy process at the national level. Accordingly, several groups of state or local general-purpose officials organized for the first time, moved their operations to Washington, or upgraded their staff and expanded their activities. These groups, including entities like the National Governors' Association, the Council of State Governments, the National Association of Counties, and the U.S. Conference of Mayors, refer to themselves as public interest groups, or *PIGs*. By the 1960s they became increasingly recognized as leaders in the representation of state and local interests in national policy making. In addition to the governments that began to locate offices and representatives in Washington, other more functionally specialized groups of state and local officials, such as highway officials, budget officers, and social workers, have organized into national groups and participate in the policy process. Nowadays, and even in the midst of the financial constraints of the 1990s, any discussion of an intergovernmental issue in Congress or an administrative agency is likely to elicit concern, participation, lobbying, and debate involving many such organizations.

Thus, the Johnson era encouraged several salutary developments in intergovernmental relations and further elaborated other interesting trends. Yet, as might be expected when such massive changes are effected, difficulties and tensions also arose.

Emergent Frustrations and Tensions

The almost limitless choices made available to state and local officials because of the tremendous increase in intergovernmental programs also meant that the potential recipients could afford to shop around among programs and federal agencies to bargain for the most favorable deal. As a result of the interagency competition for clients, federal policy in a program would sometimes be loosely enforced. Recipients were more and more able to evade federal intent while absorbing federal dollars.

Conversely, the system, which now had huge numbers of partially overlapping (and often project-duplicating) grants, created vexing difficulties for officials at state and local levels. With several related programs available to assist a city in such tasks as rebuilding its sewers, a great deal of time, effort, and information went into deciding which program(s) to pursue. Grants established ostensibly for the same purpose might be housed in different federal agencies, require entirely different application and approval processes, stipulate very different matching requirements, and be implemented with conflicting schedules. Furthermore, as potential recipients of project grants scrambled to complete detailed applications for scores of grant requests on short notice, the winners were not necessarily the most competent or the most needy jurisdictions. Instead, the one who packaged proposals in the most salable fashion (exercising what has come to be called "grantsmanship"), was often rewarded.

The systemic changes generated another set of tensions for state and local governments. With the multitude of programs, many of which were now funded by grants constructed with high matching ratios (that is, Washington would pay for most of the total expenses incurred under the program), state and local governments were finding it increasingly difficult either to abstain from commitments to federal aid or to make such commitments wholeheartedly. When a donor government offers a grant, this lowers the cost of the good or service provided for the potential recipient and thus renders it more attractive. However, when the number of individually appealing programs multiplies greatly, the consequence can be significant distortion in the recipient's own budget choices. Instead of spending its locally generated revenue on the public services judged most important by its own officials and citizens, a city can be encouraged to utilize a substantial portion as matching funds for programs that are, in essence, national priorities. The expansion of the aid system in the 1960s prompted complaints on this score from uneasy mayors, governors, and others who were concerned about their apparently declining ability to maintain some independence.

Such general-purpose officials had other concerns as well. Many of them believed the expanded system of categorical grants was composed of unduly narrow programs that were not easily adaptable to the needs in their own jurisdictions. Furthermore, the pattern, taken as a whole, had become so complex that it was all but impenetrable to generalists. These officials had a difficult time even discovering just how much aid was being received from federal sources. And many of the important, detailed decisions that are made as part of an intergovernmental grant bargain—for instance, determining the eligibility of clients for programs or establishing goals—were made far from the presence of the general-purpose officials. Increasingly important in the intergovernmental policy process was a great number of specialists across governmental levels—especially in administrative agencies charged with executing the program, legislative committees with responsibility for the substantive area, and pressure groups with a strong interest in the program. Intergovernmental experts, particularly those concerned about the decreasing ability of general officials to oversee and direct activities across this maze, dubbed these policy networks *vertical functional autocracies.*

In these chains of influence, it became increasingly difficult for anyone, even major officials like governors or mayors or presidents, to decipher just *who* was causing *what* to happen intergovernmentally. When responsibility is so diffused, the mechanisms of democratic government cannot readily ensure that policy reflects the will of the people or their representatives. In other words, another possible cost of such an arrangement is a decline in political responsiveness.

In short, then, the era of creative federalism brought energy and inventiveness to intergovernmental questions; but the massive changes in the system meant a significant escalation in costs and frustrations as well. It should not be surprising, therefore, that interdependence and complexity emerged as major political features during the quarter century following the Johnson era. Despite manifold differences in emphasis, approach, and impact, intergovernmental actors during the most recent period have grappled with a structure exhibiting common characteristics and daunting demands. The following pages first characterize the modern intergovernmental pattern in general terms and then explore important events and efforts during several recent national administrations.

The Modern Pattern: Interdependence, Complexity, and Intergovernmental Bargaining

In the pattern that emerged from the explosive growth of creative federalism, it became difficult for actors in the system to make rational decisions to benefit the individuals or activities for which they held responsibility. It was also difficult to design any coherent change in the system itself. These problems stemmed directly from the dominant characteristics of the intergovernmental system: its interdependence and related complexity.

It would be helpful to define these two concepts more precisely here. *Interdependence* means that power is shared among branches and layers of government, even within policy sectors. Instead of one level consistently controlling decisions about policy, nearly any change requires mutual accommodation among several levels of government. No one is in control of the system itself, and unanticipated consequences are a fact of life. *Complexity*

accompanies such interdependence. Complexity means that the intergovernmental network is large and differentiated; no one participant can possibly possess enough information about its components and dynamics consistently to make rational decisions on its own or to operate in isolation from the rest.

Especially since the era of creative federalism, but also as a consequence of the framework established by the founders, many participants in the intergovernmental system have plenty of opportunities to exercise influence—particularly to delay or frustrate action to which they are opposed. It is much more difficult, however, to generate and systematically execute *positive* action in a straightforwardly rational manner.

An important result of the system's grounding in interdependence and complexity (one that became obvious in the 1960s and endures in altered form to the present day) is that the typical style of decision making in the American intergovernmental system is one of bargaining under conditions of partial conflict among the participants. The actors in the system, including the various governments involved, have different interests to serve and objectives to seek; yet they cannot succeed by acting unilaterally. They may join together into one or more loose coalitions aimed at achieving some intergovernmental objective.[15] But they must perforce negotiate as a nearly ceaseless activity if they are to have any chance of defending themselves or achieving even some of their goals.

Of course, bargaining under conditions of partial conflict is a very abstract notion and encompasses many different types of situations. The bargaining between governments in a project-grant structure differs in predictable and important ways from the bargaining activity likely with a formula grant: the former setting typically provides more influence to bureaucratic actors associated with the donor government, those who write the rules and evaluate the competitive applications from potential recipients. The fact of bargaining and its pervasiveness throughout the system, however, is important to keep in mind. Bargaining is typical even during the 1990s, a time when grant programs will not grow at nearly the pace of earlier periods and when other, ostensibly more controlling, or unilateral, or regulatory ties have become prominent between the federal and other governments. . . . [R]ecent years have brought national judicial decisions that challenge the constitutional and fiscal bases of state autonomy; and unfunded mandates (rather than grants) have become increasingly utilized as a mechanism of coordination across governments. Yet these shifts do not unambiguously signify a new centralization. In some ways, . . . the states are now able to initiate more action, or to resist more, than in the previous period. And federal officials may have fewer levers to enforce their own efforts at intergovernmental influence when the grant mechanism is absent from, or less prominent in, the bargaining arena. It may be concluded, therefore, that the shifts of the past decade or more have altered the *types* of bargaining and the issues subject to negotiation. The fact of bargaining nevertheless remains crucial to an understanding of American intergovernmental dynamics.

Some of the tensions inherent in such an interdependent and complex system became visible in the 1960s and have escalated since. Red tape, which is the continuation of intergovernmental negotiation and conflict by other means, is one manifestation. The federal government has usually viewed the requirements it imposes on its grants as essential to ensure a program's integrity. Yet recipient units claim that the burdens have become excessive. (Localities also blame the states in part for their red-tape burden.) Federally created intergovernmental mandates have escalated sharply since 1975 and have become the bête noire of state and local officials.

Two general points emerge. First, the problems and tensions in the modern system are not primarily the product of ill will or ignorance, nor can they be traced primarily to one level of government. Rather, the American intergovernmental system was founded on ambivalent principles and built to establish arenas for conflict and controversy. A second and related point is that changing the particular pattern of intergovernmental relationships or reforming certain aspects of the system—for

example, through the enactment of spending and policy shifts such as Ronald Reagan sought during the 1980s—would have important consequences but could hardly resolve the value conflicts of a complex and interdependent system. At this point, accordingly, we should examine some of the developments in the American intergovernmental system since the period of creative federalism. Many of these are made comprehensible by an awareness of the difficulties just surveyed, and many, in turn, presage some of the topics of current interest and controversy.

Nixon's New Federalism

A number of the difficulties outlined above were obvious by the close of the Johnson administration. Richard Nixon reacted to the tensions in the changing system by proposing reforms ostensibly aimed at increasing the influence of general-purpose (especially elected) officials at all levels, shifting power away from Washington and toward federal field offices and state and local governments, reducing the control exercised by functional specialists, and trimming intergovernmental red tape. (This direction was maintained, though with somewhat diminished effort and effectiveness, by his successor, Gerald Ford.) Nixon's efforts were undoubtedly fueled by a desire to shift policy away from the social activism of the Johnson years.

Of what, exactly, did Nixon's "new federalism" consist? He proposed a series of initiatives: revenue sharing, block grants, and administrative proposals.

1. Revenue sharing. One of Nixon's most ambitious suggestions was the establishment of a program of revenue sharing from the federal level to state and local governments. Revenue sharing (also called "general revenue sharing") had acquired a certain currency for several reasons: it seemed to meet the demands of state and local governments for more discretion, it was attractive to the most financially hard-pressed jurisdictions, it could shift some influence to the general-purpose elected officials and away from the functional specialists in state and local governments, and (for those, like Nixon, who were looking for politically acceptable mechanisms of reducing categorical support) it might permit the simultaneous trimming of more narrowly targeted programs. In 1972 the State and Local Fiscal Assistance Act was passed with the support of much of the Democratic leadership in Congress and of the major PIGs of state and local officials. This law established a revenue-sharing program of approximately $6 billion per year for five years. All state governments and all general-purpose local governments were eligible for aid, which was to be allocated on the basis of complicated formulas. The program was extended, with modifications, in 1976, and again in 1980. In 1984 revenue sharing was reenacted for localities alone, as the federal budget tightened. And in 1986, following several efforts, the program was ended because Congress found itself facing an increasingly severe national deficit. During its tenure, revenue sharing helped many governments—too many, thought some observers, who believed that aid should be targeted more carefully to needy jurisdictions. But even at its peak of support and funding, it constituted only a small fraction of total federal assistance for the larger recipient governments.

2. Block grants. Another major proposal that would have a significant effect on the intergovernmental system did not originate with Nixon, although the idea is most closely identified with him. Block grants began during the Johnson administration, as intergovernmental analysts searched for mechanisms to alleviate some of the problems discussed above. Before the Nixon era, two block grants (one in health care, one in law enforcement) were created. Each was formed by combining a series of closely related categorical grants into a broader, formula-based package. Nixon then suggested a set of enactments in six policy sectors. These stimulated considerably more antagonism than did the general revenue-sharing proposal. De-

fenders of the categoricals, including members of the vertical functional autocracies, resisted; their concerns would have no statutory protection once a block grant was put into place. Although the general-purpose officials at the state and local levels were favorably inclined toward the *idea* of block grants, they were skeptical of some of the Nixon proposals, which would have reduced the overall level of intergovernmental funding. Ultimately, only three additional block grants emerged from this period: in employment, social services, and community development. Yet some of these programs have had a major impact on intergovernmental affairs, and they have been followed by additional block grants enacted during the Reagan years.

3. Administrative initiatives. Nixon encouraged the implementation of administrative reforms by supporting a series of efforts to alter the grant application and review process. By both legislation and executive order, potential recipient governments were allowed to expedite their applications by combining several related requests. In certain cities chief executives were granted increased control over some categorical funds. Also, a number of donor agencies reduced their decision-making time. The emphasis on block grants was designed in part to relieve administrative burdens. However, some of the alterations were just palliatives. The strength of the political forces responsible for the development of categorical programs has meant that block grants established with few restrictions tend over time to acquire more.

Despite all these changes, the intergovernmental system was not radically altered. For one thing, the more traditional categorical grant was by no means disused. Indeed, such programs and the amount of aid going to support them increased even through the Nixon years. In 1975 the intergovernmental apparatus was larger than it had been during the Johnson years (Table 1). For another, the return to formula-based grants eased certain difficulties (year-to-year funding uncertainties for recipients) but exacerbated others (such as interregional and interjurisdictional tensions because a formula would establish a set of clear winners and losers in legislation). Also, administrative and regulatory difficulties in the system proved to be more tenacious than many had anticipated.

In short, at the end of the Nixon-Ford period the intergovernmental system was larger than ever. Impressively complex and interdependent, it continued to face criticism from nearly everyone.

The Carter Period

President Jimmy Carter was not the activist in intergovernmental matters that Nixon was—or, for that matter, that his successor was. But, as a former governor familiar with the concerns of general political executives and of state and local units, Carter worked at developing communication links with the PIGs and with state and local governments, tried to advance some of the administrative reforms from the Nixon-Ford years, and paid special attention to economic problems facing the cities. He pushed passage, for example, of the Urban Development Action Grant (UDAG) program during a severe economic recession in the late 1970s. UDAG is representative of the way grant politics has developed in the modern era: Democrats have tended to emphasize urban constituencies (part of their standard coalition) as recipients of national support, while Republicans have sought shifts toward state assistance, partly as a way to channel aid to counties and thus to their suburban constituencies.

Yet Carter proposed no overall plan for reform of the system, nor did he recommend any major changes in the pattern of intergovernmental aid. Two developments in the late 1970s exacerbated some of the difficulties faced by policymakers and managers. First, a combination of sour economic conditions, federal budget difficulties, and Carter's fundamentally conservative fiscal instincts placed stringent limits on any efforts to increase federal aid. Federal spending increases slowed and in 1978 reversed direction. Yet the tensions that had come

to mark the modern period of intergovernmental relations were, if anything, increased; for federal aid was being limited at a time when many units of government had come to depend on it. Second, during this period of strained resources, the federal government, especially Congress, did not easily loosen its hold on other units of government; instead, Washington sought to accomplish its intergovernmental goals via direct requirements, frequently including some that were mandated across many different programs. Although Carter typically sought deregulation, he did consent to the addition of significant new requirements in a number of programs.

Reagan's Attempted Revolution, and Its Aftermath

The first part of Ronald Reagan's term in office saw perhaps the most systematic, if not the most sustained, effort to remake the American intergovernmental system since the New Deal. Like Carter, Reagan had served as a governor and understood some of the consequences of complexity and interdependence for many participants in the intergovernmental network. However, unlike Carter, he believed that the United States had been created as a system in which national powers and jurisdiction were severely limited, and in which the states had the strongest, most vital governments, with the broadest jurisdiction over domestic matters.

Furthermore, Reagan supported tax reductions for wealthier Americans as part of his "supply side" approach to fiscal questions. Popular resistance to higher taxes coupled with a Reagan-encouraged buildup in military expenditures in the 1980s meant that budget constraints became especially tight for domestic programs. Given the popularity of the most expensive federal entitlement programs, intergovernmental aid became vulnerable to significant cuts. Meanwhile, pressures by citizens and interest groups to address a whole set of policy issues at state and local levels did not abate. The stage was set for higher levels of fiscal tension and conflict in the intergovernmental system.

As a major part of his program early in the first term, Reagan offered several ideas for a massive restructuring of the intergovernmental system. In brief, Reagan's proposals, for which he adopted Nixon's term, the "new federalism," were as follows:

1. An additional series of block grants. In his first year in office, Reagan proposed that more than one hundred categoricals be combined into a handful of broadly based block grants with very few regulations. Congress complied with several of these initiatives.

2. A dramatic simplification of the system of intergovernmental aid. Program responsibilities were to be shifted to single levels of government and away from the "marble cake" intergovernmental configurations. Despite Reagan's backing, the plan attracted only spotty support among the PIGs and virtually none among the program advocates in the nation's vertical functional autocracies. Congress made no real move to approve the plan, and Reagan's attention was diverted from this contentious issue.

3. A devolution of responsibilities for many policies from the national level to the states. Reagan suggested that scores of intergovernmental programs involving federal participation, including most of the remaining expensive ones, be turned over to the states in their entirety and that an appropriate quantity of revenue be shifted to the states as well. No action was taken on this proposal. Yet several years after Reagan had left office, some of the intent behind this idea was nevertheless being fulfilled. One reason was a choice in Washington simply not to enforce or even to monitor the states regarding certain programs. Another had to do with the looming budget problems at the national level and the refusal of presidents Reagan and then Bush to advocate

federal tax increases. By the early 1990s new policy initiatives that might involve substantial new expenditures from Washington had thus become nearly impossible under these constraints. Meanwhile many states, which were being pressed by interest groups and the citizenry to address daunting public problems like health care, infrastructure financing, education, and economic development, had become centers of more policy activism than had been seen in years outside of the nation's capital.

4. Administrative simplification. The president worked to trim red tape and lighten the putative burden of federal mandates. In this regard, Reagan scored his "successes," as did his predecessors. Yet many complained about the abdication of federal responsibility for important national goals, and others felt the reforms did not go nearly far enough. Several years after Reagan's departure from the White House, the evidence accumulated that mandates from Washington have increased overall.

Reagan's efforts to restructure the intergovernmental system were challenged not only by proponents of increased national authority and advocates of strong categorical initiatives, but also by many who have traditionally sought more influence for the state and local governments. While the nation's governors and mayors were often delighted with the idea of reducing the red tape and mandate requirements, they could hardly have been expected to rejoice in other features of the Reagan program. The fact that Reagan accompanied his suggestions with significant budget reductions in many of the most important programs meant that he was giving these officials more discretion while reducing the size of the pie. (The cutbacks in federal aid under Reagan were far more severe than those experienced under Carter; see Table 1.) Also, the president's proposals to trade responsibilities and devolve many programs created quite a stir. Urban leaders were concerned that the federal assistance they had been receiving would end if funding decisions were moved to state capitals. And many states and localities were convinced that, ultimately, they would be the financial and political losers once governmental responsibilities were sorted out. By the second half of Reagan's first term, the most ambitious proposals had been set aside in favor of further grouping of categorical programs into block grants. Even these suggestions encountered hostility or indifference in Congress. The conflict between executive and legislative branches vis-à-vis intergovernmental assistance revealed another dimension of the politics of grants. Congress and the presidency, controlled by different parties, pursued divergent strategies to assist somewhat different constituencies. Thus the theme of divided government *within* the national structure—a prominent topic in recent political discussions—has had practical consequences in the intergovernmental system *across* levels of government as well.

Furthermore, in the latter portion of the Reagan era additional signals from the federal government suggested to states and localities that any effort toward independent action on their part might need to be tempered by an emerging set of new conditions emanating from the center. In a set of important decisions by the Supreme Court regarding the scope of state authority, especially in the now-famous *Garcia* case of 1985, federal judicial authorities determined that the main protector of the states' status as vital decision-making entities in the system would have to be the clout of states in the political institutions of the national government itself, rather than constitutional safeguards like the Tenth Amendment, enforceable by the Court.[16] States, in short, would have to look out for themselves, politically speaking, by lobbying in Washington against possible national intrusions into their domain. Thus in the 1990s, even as the federal judiciary developed a reputation for stricter constitutional construction, it seemed to pose the potential of eroding some of the formal underpinnings of the established intergovernmental order.

Nevertheless, the impact of the Reagan administration's efforts, though complicated, was far from incidental. The signs of change in the intergovernmental network of the 1990s are multiple. States have picked up some of the policy initiatives that heretofore had largely been controlled by Washington, although some observers are concerned that states will use their energies to benefit the most privileged interests. Local governments have scrambled to replace national funding for some of their programs with state aid and via alternative sources. The PIGs, which in earlier decades had organized into nationally important forces with the onset of large-scale federal assistance, struggled to define new roles of comparable influence in the emerging era of budgetary constraint. Limited now in its ability to stimulate complex shifts in policy via generously funded new grant programs, the federal government nevertheless seeks day-to-day influence through the channels of the hundreds of existing ones, persisting in attempts to control intergovernmental action through the instrument of mandates. All these participants clearly do not want to relinquish their influence in the interdependent, complex, and now fiscally strained system. How will this intricate interplay of political forces unfold is an important but presently unanswerable question. There are now many signs of renewed state governmental strength and creativity. But there are also numerous threats to the jurisdiction and to continued competence of many of these same units. Unproductive interstate competition for economic development thus remains a real prospect. Big cities are, in some cases, in even more desperate circumstances than ever. At the same time, however, mayors and city managers have succeeded in developing innovative financing arrangements, regional cooperative ventures, and partnerships with the private sector to address staggering social problems. Washington meanwhile continues to exert great, even intrusive, influence as national financing for new intergovernmental challenges recedes. The upshot is a set of challenges and crosscutting pressures.

The dizzying transformations of the 1980s, then, have resulted in an intergovernmental arrangement that differs in key respects from the one in place at the dawn of the Reagan period. And yet any vision of radical simplification, of a dual federalism that could meet the challenges of the country's twenty-first-century needs and aspirations, can be seen as chimerical. Indeed, the efforts of the Bush administration on intergovernmental matters have been devoted largely to maintaining the shape of the pattern inherited from the Reagan years rather than either asserting a new direction or, somehow, implementing the thoroughgoing ideas suggested in the "new American revolution" proposed by Reagan at the outset of his term in office. Despite the major developments of the last several years, the most fundamental aspects of American intergovernmental relations, including the strengths, weaknesses, frustrations, and dilemmas of the pattern, have remained prominent.

There is no denying that the form of the system has changed considerably since the nation's founding. Political, economic, and social forces have stimulated major changes in the overall scope of governmental activity, in the mix of values that intergovernmental arrangements are meant to serve, in the relative influence of the different governments, and in their degree of reliance on one another. Far from preserving a simple, stratified pattern, the choices made centuries ago created opportunities for dramatic shifts toward new forms of interdependence and complexity in the intergovernmental network.

Notes

1. Thus the term *federal* has two meanings in contemporary usage. One refers to a system of governance that employs a constitutional partitioning of authority between central and regional units. The other is as a synonym for the national government. Both notions are employed in this [essay]. . . .

2. U.S. Bureau of the Census, *1987 Census of Governments,* vol. 1, no. 1, *Governmental Organization* (Washington, D.C.: U.S. Government Printing Office, 1988), v.

3. Federalist No. 10, *The Federalist Papers,* ed. Clinton Rossiter (New York: New American Library, 1961), 77.

4. At the time, the term *federation* had a meaning close to that of *confederation* today. . . .

5. The concepts of federalism (in the first sense mentioned in n. 1) and intergovernmental relations are linked but not identical. The former refers to certain aspects of the dealings between national and regional governments, while the latter is meant to encompass relations among all governments within a nation. Intergovernmental relations are considerably affected but not completely determined by federalism. This examines federalism but focuses broadly on intergovernmental relations. Nevertheless, interstate and interlocal relations receive relatively less attention because of space limitations.

6. One example is Madison's veto of a bill to authorize construction of roads and canals in the states. See Daniel J. Elazar, *The American Partnership: Intergovernmental Co-operation in the Nineteenth Century* (Chicago: University of Chicago Press, 1962), 15.

7. Ibid.

8. The terms *recipient* and *donor* are borrowed from Jeffrey L. Pressman, *Federal Programs and City Politics* (Berkeley and Los Angeles: University of California Press, 1975).

9. U.S. Advisory Commission on Intergovernmental Relations, *Significant Features of Fiscal Federalism, 1990, Vol. 2, Revenues and Expenditures* (Washington, D.C.: ACIR, August 1990), 48.

10. The cases were *Massachusetts* v. *Mellon* and *Frothingham* v. *Mellon* 262 U.S. 447 (1923).

11. As explained later in this [reading], this experiment proved temporary. Federal financial constraints during the Carter and Reagan administrations persuaded Congress to follow presidential recommendations; the program was ended for state and then local governments, respectively.

12. See Morton Grodzins's classic essay.

13. For example, David B. Walker, *Toward a Functioning Federalism* (Cambridge,

Mass.: Winthrop, 1981); and see Deil S. Wright, *Understanding Intergovernmental Relations,* 3d ed. (Pacific Grove, Calif.: Brooks/Cole, 1988), 94.

14. See Norman Furniss and Timothy Tilton, *The Case for the Welfare State: From Social Security to Social Equality* (Bloomington: Indiana University Press, 1977); and John E. Schwarz, *America's Hidden Success: A Reassessment of Twenty Years of Public Policy* (New York: Norton, 1988).

15. Thomas Anton, *American Federalism and Public Policy: How the System Works* (Philadelphia: Temple University Press, 1989).

16. *Garcia* v. *San Antonio Metropolitan Transit Authority,* 469 U.S. 552 (1985).

☐ CASE STUDY 5

Introduction

In the foregoing essay, Professor O'Toole clearly and concisely presents an overview of the development of American intergovernmental relations as an important aspect of American government. He stresses that the contemporary nature of IGR particularly entails three characteristics: interdependency, complexity and bargaining among officials. How do these major features of IGR influence the practice of modern public administration? Shape the work of local government officials? Affect the outcomes of what they do?

The following case, "Wichita Confronts Contamination," by Susan Rosegrant of Harvard's John F. Kennedy School of Government, illustrates well several of the themes discussed in O'Toole's essay. In the summer of 1990, the Kansas Department of Health and Environment (KDHE), acting on behalf of the federal Environmental Protection Agency (EPA), reported that Wichita, Kansas, was sitting on a vast underground polluted lake of various commercial and industrial chemicals. It was located beneath the central downtown business district, called the Gilbert-Mosley site, and the hazardous chemicals were known to cause cancer and other health problems. The report said the contamination was spreading about a foot a day, and it was feared that serious community health problems and water quality deterioration would result if this underground pollution went unchecked. Besides the very vocal public outcry for government to "do something about the problem," the report also triggered an immediate reaction from the banking community which stopped making loans to downtown residential and commercial owners in the Gilbert-Mosley area, thereby causing serious economic repercussions. What should the city do to protect its environment and economy—indeed the very health of its citizens?

In the following case, the city manager, Chris Cherches, who is faced with the responsibility of drafting a plan of action to deal with this crisis, must work with various intergovernmental bodies such as the KDHE and EPA to frame options and devise a strategy to clean up the affected site. In the process, Cherches achieves a workable plan, but one that very much develops within—and depends on—an IGR framework, as described in the O'Toole essay.

As you read this case, try to think about:

How did IGR entities help to identify the problem, then frame the options for the city manager, and finally help him create a workable plan of action for the affected site?

Why were the environmental problems—*and* the IGR problems—so complex in this case?

Can you identify the negotiations among the various IGR actors in this story that occurred. Why were these negotiations so critical to dealing with Wichita's contamination?

In general what does this case tell us about the importance of IGR to the work of public administrators in the 1990s? And the IGR features of interdependency, complexity, and political bargaining?

Wichita Confronts Contamination

SUSAN ROSEGRANT

In the summer of 1990, the central business district of Wichita, Kansas, faced familiar problems of urban decline, along with the prospect of revitalization. The downturn in the regional oil and gas industry had exacerbated the nationwide real estate slump, leaving downtown Wichita stagnant. At the same time, local business leaders were pursuing a common formula for renewal: a project relying on substantial public improvements to leverage new private investment, a $375 million undertaking in all.

In downtown Wichita, however, a special problem was brewing. Hazardous chemicals known to cause cancer and other health problems had been detected in some private and industrial wells in Wichita's core area. Banks were growing more careful about requiring site inspections, and even soil and water sam-

This case was written by Susan Rosegrant for Professor Alan Altshuler, director of the Taubman Center for State and Local Government at the John F. Kennedy School of Government, for use at the Program on Innovation in State and Local Government "CEO Symposium," September 24–26, 1992. Funding provided by the Ford Foundation. (1292)

Source: Case Program, John F. Kennedy School of Government, Harvard University, Parts A & B C16-92-1157.0 & C16-92-1158.0

pling, before they would grant loans. And in June, local manufacturer Coleman Co., Inc., the venerable maker of camp stoves and other outdoor equipment, approached the city's legal department for advice about a contamination problem it had first discovered during routine tests in the fall of 1988.

In late August, the calm was shattered as the pieces of bad news suddenly fit together to form a frightening whole. The Kansas Department of Health and Environment (KDHE), acting on behalf of the Environmental Protection Agency (EPA), reported that Wichita was sitting on an underground lake polluted by a variety of commercial and industrial chemicals. The area of contamination—dubbed the Gilbert and Mosley site after a street intersection near its center—was extensive, covering a plot about four miles long and one-and-one-half miles wide. Moreover, the polluted aquifer lay squarely beneath the city's central business district. The 8,000 parcels affected had an assessed value of about $86 million. Major banks, hotels, industrial headquarters, and homes all lay in the six-square-mile area. The worst pollution, consisting of high concentrations of trichloroethene, a chemical degreaser used to clean metal parts before painting, was found at Coleman's headquarters at the north end of the site.

Although KDHE had completed a preliminary

study on Gilbert-Mosley the previous November, the August 1990 Listing Site Investigation was the first comprehensive contamination report that City Manager Chris Cherches had seen. According to his office's quick estimates, to clean the aquifer could cost as much as $20 million and take as long as 20 years. KDHE offered just two options in its report recommendations: either the companies responsible for the contamination could band together to clean up the area, or the state would rank the site for National Priority Listing, the first step toward activating Superfund.[1]

Contamination Fallout

The Wichita community did not view Gilbert-Mosley as a serious health risk. Although the contamination was moving south at the rate of about a foot a day, the polluted aquifer lay 15 feet below the surface and was not used for drinking water. "Kansas is not that concerned about water quality," explained William Cather, chair of the Sierra Club's small Kansas chapter. "We are concerned about water quantity."

But the potential economic impact of the contamination had the community up in arms. KDHE's report identified 508 area businesses as Potentially Responsible Parties (PRPs) under Superfund law. If Gilbert-Mosley became a Superfund site, all of these businesses would be potentially liable for cleanup costs regardless of whether they had contributed to the contamination. In the days following release of the Listing Site Investigation, KDHE received a barrage of phone calls from business owners anxious to understand the implications of their PRP status.

Even more threatening, however, was the response of the financial community. Just a few months earlier, in *US vs. Fleet Factors Corp.*, the US 11th Circuit Court in Atlanta had ruled that a lender may incur Superfund liability "by participating in financial management to a degree indicating a capacity to influence the corporation's treatment of hazardous wastes."[2]

Simply put, the ruling opened lenders to Superfund liability. Not only that, because of their relatively "deep pockets," financial institutions made ideal targets for Superfund cleanup cost recovery.

In the wake of the dramatic report, Wichita bankers took abrupt action, halting virtually all lending activity in Gilbert-Mosley, the heart of the city. "I don't think you could have hit a banker over the head with a two-by-four and gotten him to make a loan then," declared J.V. Lentell, chairman of the Kansas State Bank and Trust Co. "We already knew property values were plummeting in the downtown area. Downtown was drying up. It was the last thing we needed."

The banks' redlining had an immediate impact on both commercial and residential property owners. David C. Burk, for example, an architect turned developer, had formed an investment company to develop restaurant, retail, apartment, and office space in a few blocks of abandoned brick warehouses near Coleman's headquarters. Although he had drilled 20 test holes without finding contamination before launching his ill-timed venture, all three buildings he had contracts on, as well as those he had options to buy, fell within the contaminated zone. "As soon as Gilbert-Mosley came in, we lost our investors," he reported grimly. Residents were similarly affected, as they found it suddenly impossible to sell their homes. "There were hundreds of tragedies wrapped up here," declared Mayor Bob Knight. "I started getting calls from sons and daughters, trying to make provisions for a parent who was left alone and aged, who were unable to liquidate property."

As city government struggled in the days following the report's release to understand and respond to the crisis, it became clear that the twin threats of uncertain liability and the bank-imposed real estate freeze posed a substantial hazard to the city's tax base. Properties in the area had generated more than $12 million of the $203 million in local property taxes the previous year, but already, the county appraiser's office was receiving requests for reduced valuations. If all Gilbert-Mosley properties lost substantial value, or were frozen for months, or even years, not only would the redevelopment plan die,

---

[1]Congress created Superfund, the Comprehensive Environmental Response, Compensation and Liability Act of 1980 (CERCLA), to give EPA the resources to clean up hazardous waste sites nationwide. Six years later, Congress passed the Superfund Amendments and Reauthorization Act of 1986 in an attempt to improve what critics had characterized as a sluggish and ineffective program.

[2]David R. Tripp, "Wichita Strikes Back at the Blob," *Toxics Law Reporter*, June 25, 1991.

but the entire core area would be threatened. "When the groundwater problem came along," recalled city attorney Thomas R. Powell, "it looked like it was going to be the death knell."

The City Weighs Its Options

City Manager Cherches, who faced the immediate responsibility for drafting a plan, enlisted a cadre of staffers to study KDHE's two recommended options. In evaluating the possibilities, Cherches stressed that two priorities remained uppermost: to begin cleaning up the aquifer as soon as possible, and to preserve property values. The only way to do that: convince the banks to resume lending in the area.

1) *Let Companies Responsible for Contamination Clean Up the Site*

The first impulse on the part of some of Cherches's staff was to encourage Coleman and other polluters to take charge of the Gilbert-Mosley site. "In the very early stages, it was viewed as a business problem," recalled Mark Glaser, special assistant to the manager for management research. "The businesses contributed to the contamination. The businesses are basically responsible for cleaning up the contamination." Added city attorney Powell, "Our hope was that somehow Coleman would solve the problem."

But history argued strongly against this choice. Gilbert-Mosley was not the city's first experience with contaminated sites. Three years earlier, groundwater contamination had been discovered at a smaller site about two miles north of Gilbert-Mosley, known as 29th and Mead. There, also, the banks had stopped lending, and the county appraiser had lowered property values 40 percent. A group of about 100 potentially responsible parties at the site, including both the city and Coleman, had formed a PRP group to strike an agreement on how to pay for the initial EPA-required Remedial Investigation and Feasibility Study (RI/FS), which would identify sources and types of contamination along with remediation methods. But group negotiations had become divisive, then stalled, and the state had already placed the site on the National Priorities List (NPL). If the group fared no better in determining ultimate cleanup liability, it would face full im-

plementation of Superfund and many years of real estate paralysis.

Given this experience, it seemed highly unlikely that the more than 500 PRPs at Gilbert-Mosley would be able to reach a timely agreement on liability. In addition, it was questionable whether Coleman would cooperate. Although the company had been a lead party at 29th and Mead, it had not pushed for a speedy resolution. Moreover, while Coleman acknowledged that it had found some pollution at its Gilbert-Mosley site, it was already discounting its responsibility for the overall contamination. Remarked city attorney Powell, "When they said they were going to pay for what they were responsible for, I didn't know if we would ever *agree* on what they were responsible for." If a PRP group at Gilbert-Mosley fared no better than the one at 29th and Mead, there would be no quick cleanup in sight, and no incentive for banks to resume lending until the threat of contamination had been removed.

2) *Rank the Site for Possible Superfund Status*

As unproductive as forming a PRP group might appear, Cherches and his staff soon concluded that KDHE's second option—to allow the site to be ranked for Superfund—was far less appealing.

If EPA became directly involved, Cherches learned, the cost of cleaning up Gilbert-Mosley would increase dramatically. The agency typically hired an oversight contractor, for example, to watch over the work of the regular contractor—a step that automatically added up to 40 percent to the cleanup bill. In addition, possible polluters faced the prospect of paying for the administrative oversight of EPA itself; the Superfund law called on EPA staffers to charge their time to the private firms. Moreover, EPA was allowed to overcharge as a means of replenishing its cleanup fund and punishing noncomplying businesses.

The threat of prolonged multi-party litigation was an even bigger deterrent to reliance on Superfund. Because any business in a contaminated area could be held responsible for cleanup costs, regardless of its contribution, lawyers played a major part in any Superfund resolution, as polluters sought to spread the blame, and faultless property owners struggled to avoid liability. In fact, Superfund law spread potential liability to such a broad number of parties, many of whom were wholly innocent, that any hope of quick resolution became mired in stalling tactics and litigation. This legal wrangling, along with third party lawsuits against polluters seeking damages due to contamination-related declines in property values, had given rise to Superfund's nickname as "The Lawyers' Full Employment Act of 1980." One city that Cherches talked to reported that its $30 million cleanup had sparked an estimated $700 million in civil law suits. A study commissioned by the American Insurance Association estimated that cleaning up 1,800 Superfund sites would generate $8 billion in legal fees.[3]

Finally, both litigation, and the oversight and administrative steps that EPA requires, add years to a typical Superfund cleanup. Of the average 10 years taken to clean up a site, seven are spent on study and assessment, legal proceedings, and crafting a remedy before the actual cleanup begins.[4] Judging from this track record, if Gilbert-Mosley became a Superfund site, it would be years before cleanup could even start.

According to Mayor Knight, who consulted a number of other mayors about Gilbert-Mosley, cities with major contamination problems faced a bleak prognosis. "I couldn't find any successful models," he recalled. "The only thing we found was failure: division, frustration, assigning blame, financial ruin, and, ultimately, the very worst thing that can happen to people who love cities, decline."

Special Assistant Glaser also placed successive phone calls in a desperate bid to find a new alternative:

What we kept hearing was, "I can't tell you what to do, but do something. Don't let it go Superfund. Once it goes Superfund, you're in trouble." We knew we had to do something, but nobody knew what that something would be.

A Third Option

Cherches rejected both of KDHE's options, and made up his mind fast. Within a week of the Listing

Site Investigation's release, he decided to risk a major leap from existing precedents. Although no one had accused Wichita of being a polluter, and although the city had not even been listed as a PRP, Cherches proposed that the city take full responsibility for the Gilbert-Mosley cleanup. In doing so, Wichita would attempt to sidestep the time and resources normally spent on Superfund-related litigation, and to create some mechanism to get banks to start lending in the contaminated area again.

The most obvious and immediate barrier to a city-led cleanup was finding an acceptable way to finance it. Cherches was determined that Coleman and other contributors would pay as much as possible for the contamination they had caused. But the city could not count on recouping all cleanup costs from responsible polluters. Some likely contributors were no longer in business, for example, and others lacked the resources to support their share of the cleanup. Moreover, in order to sell the idea to the state and EPA, the city would have to prove it had the funds available to support what could be a 20-year project without relying on uncertain corporate contributions.

Cherches's staff prepared a list of financing alternatives, and the most powerful argument against each, as follows:

- *Establish a special assessment district:* All property owners in the area would be charged an assessment to cover the cost of cleanup. Likely to create an uproar over the inequity of making a large group, comprised mostly of innocent property owners, pay for the pollution of a few.
- *Issue bonds:* Taxes would be raised throughout the city to help pay off the bonds. Could cause a property tax revolt, and would require a change in state statute to allow bonds to be used for ongoing maintenance of the cleanup program.
- *Create a tax increment finance district:* Would dedicate an increment of Gilbert-Mosley property taxes—bolstered by the cleanup—to pay for the program. An untried use of this concept, and, like the bond option, would require a change in state legislation.

[3]Marc K. Landy and Mary Hague, "Private Interests and Superfund," *The Public Interest*, No. 108, Summer 1992.

[4]E. Donald Elliott, "Superfund: EPA Success, National Debacle?" *Natural Resources & Environment*, Vol. 6, No. 3, Winter 1992.

- *County pay entire cost, with state assistance:* Based on rationale that the economic health of Wichita is important to the entire county. Would face certain opposition from the county, which believed polluters should pay the tab. The county might seek state reimbursement.
- *Impose a statewide tax:* Would spread the burden to the broadest number of constituents. Certain to provoke strong opposition from a rural state uninterested in solving Wichita's industrial problems.

In addition to the backing of the Wichita City Council, most of these plans would require the approval of the Sedgwick County Council, as well as the Wichita School Board, since their tax bases would be affected.

Even with a financing mechanism in place, though, a city-led plan would face a number of additional obstacles. Politically, the concept probably wouldn't fly unless Coleman and other contributors could be held at least partially accountable. "Some of the very early public response was, 'Why would the city get involved and commit our tax dollars?'" recalled Glaser. "We were thinking of signing on the dotted line to say we would be responsible for $20 million. Politically and fiscally, that doesn't wash. It's not even reasonable." Unfortunately, if the city wanted to take charge, it would have to make a commitment long before it knew the likelihood of getting major contributors other than Coleman to pay.

Cherches would also have to convince EPA, which had a reputation for being bureaucratic and inflexible, that the city had the resources and the commitment to take on such an unusual arrangement. There was no record of any city ever having stepped in to accept liability for a contamination problem it had not caused.

In addition, unless Wichita could come up with a way to revive lending in the contaminated district, it wouldn't make any difference who was responsible for the cleanup. The central business district could not afford to wait 20 years for life to return to normal.

Finally, a survey of the obstacles made it clear that the ultimate success of the plan would depend on a complex collaboration between multiple, and sometimes opposed, constituencies, including the city manager's office, the city council, the county

commission, the school board, lenders, Coleman, KDHE, the state legislature, the governor, and EPA.

KDHE had already warned the city that it would have to report to EPA in January about progress at the Gilbert-Mosley site. Unless a cleanup plan had taken shape, the state would recommend that EPA take over. If Wichita was unable to solve any one of the obstacles it faced, it would have to confront the inevitability of Superfund, with all that could imply for the devastation of the city's core.

Developing the Plan

Wichita City Manager Chris Cherches moved fast to begin consolidating support for a city-led cleanup of the Gilbert-Mosley site. In order to present the plan to the various constituencies that would have to approve it, the city first had to decide how to pay for it. After weighing alternatives, Cherches concluded that creating a tax increment finance (TIF) district would be the most equitable and politically palatable way to raise funds. The city's approach, however, was a novel twist on the traditional TIF concept. Typically, a TIF district is set up in an area slated for redevelopment. After city-backed improvements are in place, the difference between the old, depressed property assessments and the new, higher values that have resulted from the improvements creates an increment that is then used to pay for the revitalization effort.

Wichita, by contrast, proposed what could be called a tax "decrement" plan: as a result of the contamination, the city would devalue all the property in the Gilbert-Mosley area—for example, by the 40 percent that property had dropped at the 29th and Mead contamination site—and then would immediately raise values back to their pre-contamination level, under the argument that the city plan would restore lost value. The difference would create the increment to be set aside each year to finance the cleanup. Although the city could find no examples of TIF being used to support environmental remediation, Glaser felt it was an ideal use of the concept. "This seemed like it really fit what the full intent of TIF was designed to do," he declared.

The city's initial talks with the Kansas Department of Health and Environment (KDHE) about assuming responsibility for Gilbert-Mosley had been encouraging. With the TIF proposal in place, KDHE became openly enthusiastic. Cherches began nego-tiating a plan for the state to oversee Wichita's cleanup in EPA's stead, thereby avoiding the agency's usual high oversight costs. After presenting the proposed plan to the public, and winning the unanimous approval of the city council, he next approached the local financial community.

Lenders, Cherches soon discovered, made eager allies. After all, they risked not only losing the value of their Gilbert-Mosley investments, but of being held liable for the actual cleanup. They also understood the importance to Wichita's economy—and to their own businesses—of returning real estate activity in the contaminated area to normal. But bankers would not resume lending until they had some sort of legal protection from cleanup liability in place.

The concept that the city and the lenders devised to satisfy this need was deceptively simple. Innocent property owners, including residents, businesses, and banks, could apply to the city for a document called the Certificate and Release for Environmental Conditions. If granted, the document would release the holder from any cleanup liability. With such a release in hand, properties could again be bought and sold without the specter of potential Superfund liability. But while the banking community overall embraced the plan, it would not implement it until the city had received EPA's assurance that it would not take over the site, negotiated firm agreements with KDHE and Coleman, and pushed through the changes in state law necessary to allow tax increment financing to be used for a long-term project.

Final Negotiations

Getting EPA's backing was easier than the city had expected. Cherches proposed that Wichita would follow all the usual EPA steps and requirements in cleaning up Gilbert-Mosley, but with KDHE acting as the primary oversight agency. Throughout the process, the city would report regularly to EPA on its progress. Although the city had expected some opposition, EPA actually had a great deal to gain and very little to lose: If the city succeeded, the agency could declare a victory with minimal expense or effort on its part. Conversely, if the plan failed, there was nothing to keep EPA from stepping in and implementing Superfund.

After just one meeting in late November, Morris Kay, director of EPA's four-state Region VII, agreed in principle to support both the city-led plan and the state's offer to oversee the process. Although there was no written agreement guaranteeing that EPA would not intervene, Kay assured the city that as long as it was operating according to agency requirements, it would not intercede.

With EPA's support secure, the city still faced a major legislative challenge. A Kansas state law designed to ensure fiscal responsibility, the Cash Basis and Budget law, would not let local government commit operating revenues beyond one year. Wichita needed an exception to that law, and an amendment to TIF law, in order to be able to commit funds raised from a TIF district to a long-term environmental cleanup. Without the changes, the city would be unable to contract with KDHE to take on and finance what could be a 20-year effort.

Getting legislative approval of the TIF bill promised to be a struggle. The Cash Basis law was, in Cherches's words, a "sacred cow" that the legislature was loathe to touch. In addition, the traditional antagonism that existed between urban Wichita and the largely rural legislature was certain to complicate the bill's chances for passage. The city had to dispel the impression that its plan might be geared in Coleman's favor, a difficult task with the company's liability agreement still in negotiation. Moreover, because Kansas's part-time legislature met only from January through April, the city had a limited window of opportunity to prove the merits of its plan.

Wichita's credibility wasn't helped in March when both the county assessor and the state property valuation director declared unworkable the city's original proposal to establish a tax increment by first lowering and then raising assessed property values. In its place, three Sedgwick County legislators responsible for reviewing the TIF bill worked with the city to craft a new amendment that allowed municipalities in the state that met narrowly defined requirements to earmark 20 percent of a specially created TIF district's base year property taxes, on an annual basis, for environmental cleanups. If the bill passed, Wichita would be able to reserve up to 20 percent of the first year's Gilbert-Mosley property tax revenues to use for groundwater cleanup each year, for the next 20 years.

On March 26, Wichita signed a consent decree with KDHE, spelling out the city's responsibilities, what KDHE's oversight obligations would be, and how the Certificate and Release program would work. But the major obstacle to legislative approval, the Coleman agreement, was not resolved until April 23, slightly more than a week before the legislature adjourned. The agreement divided the contaminated site into three zones: Coleman agreed to pay all cleanup costs for the area where it was the main polluter; it would split costs with the city in a second area where it was a contributor to contamination; and the city would be responsible for cleanup and cost recovery in the final area, where most of the pollution came from other sources. In addition, the camping equipment manufacturer agreed to pay $1 million for the initial Remedial Investigation/Feasibility Study required by EPA.

Although Special Assistant Glaser had expected the Coleman negotiations to be perhaps the biggest barrier to settlement, the manufacturer actually had good cause to settle. The agreement allowed Coleman to convey a responsible civic and environmental image, an important consideration for a maker of outdoor equipment. In addition, if Gilbert-Mosley had become a Superfund site, Coleman would have faced substantially higher costs, and would have been left vulnerable to almost endless third-party lawsuits. In fact, Coleman had already been sued by property owners seeking damages due to contamination-related declines in property values. "I feel we got a pretty good deal from Coleman," said city attorney Thomas Powell. "They needed it as badly as we did."

One week after the Coleman agreement was signed, the Kansas legislature approved the TIF bill, and Cherches began meeting again with the financial community the next day. On May 14, several major local banks signed an agreement not to refuse to lend on the security of real properties within Gilbert-Mosley if the owner had obtained a Certificate and Release for Environmental Conditions. With the start of the Certificate and Release program on August 2, there was no longer a reason for contamination, alone, to block real estate transactions in the Gilbert-Mosley site.

Epilogue

In August 1992, one year after the Certificate and Release program began, life had begun to return to normal in the Gilbert-Mosley area:

- The city of Wichita had granted more than 800 Certificate and Release forms. Some property owners just outside of the contaminated area had petitioned for inclusion, hoping to receive certificates that would remove all stigma of potential liability from their properties.
- Bank IV, one of Wichita's major lenders, had closed 11 loans in Gilbert-Mosley for a total of $6.4 million.
- Developer David Burk, who received the first Certificate and Release from the city, had wooed back investors to his redevelopment project, and had opened four restaurants and two retail stores in the contaminated area.
- The three plaintiffs in the first court case against Coleman received only $86,000, about one-fifth of what they had requested, after the jury ruled that as a result of the city-led cleanup plan, pollution-caused damage to downtown property values was temporary, not permanent. Thomas Powell, who had left his position as city attorney to enter private practice, appeared as an expert witness on Coleman's behalf to describe how the city plan had restored property values.
- Camp, Dresser & McKee, Inc., the environmental consultant hired by the city, was about to release the results of the Remedial Investigation/Feasibility Study, a site analysis that typically takes as long as five years to complete under Superfund.
- The business community had begun pushing forward on more modest plans for redevelopment. "The contamination is not even something that is widely discussed anymore," declared Mayor Bob Knight, "yet it could have been a total calamity for the city."

Gilbert-Mosley was still a depressed area, as it had been before the contamination was discovered. But with the city's plan in place, Knight once again had hope that the core downtown area might be rejuvenated. "If people are sufficiently committed to resolving complicated challenges, they can do extraordinary things," he declared. "I believe this is a moment in this community's history when we did something extraordinary."

Chapter 5 Review Questions

1. Why are federalism and intergovernmental relations so critical to effective program performance in the public sector today? What is the difference between federalism and IGR? What were the founding fathers' rationale for establishing U.S. government in this federal manner?
2. What has been the recent practice of intergovernmental relations in the United States according to Laurence J. O'Toole, Jr.? When and why did this IGR pattern emerge?
3. In what ways did the Wichita case study illustrate some of the characteristics and dilemmas of modern intergovernmental relations?
4. Who were the key IGR actors in this case, and how did they "calculate" to secure their own interests? Do you think that they successfully handled and resolved the complex issue? In particular, why was Cherches role so critical?
5. What does the case study say about the role and importance of experts involved in IGR? Who were the experts in this case and how did they derive their professional standards? Is there a problem that their specialized expertise may not always be applied in the public interest? What safeguards are available to ensure that these experts will be guided by the broad public interest?
6. What does the case study say about the significance of political bargaining and coalition-building in IGR and its role in influencing outcomes? Can these political dimensions of IGR be pointed out in Case Study 3, "Dumping $2.6 Million on Bakersfield"?

Key Terms

federalism	grants-in-aid	The New Federalism
PIGs	Sixteenth Amendment	Tenth Amendment
intergovernmental relations	ACIR	policy sectors
state discretion	project grants	creative federalism
dual federalism	marble-cake federalism	unfunded mandates
Garcia Decision	land grants	vertical functional autocrats
categorical grants	general revenue sharing	interdependence
formulas grant	formula grants	complexity
block grants	performance standards	intergovernmental bargaining
intergovernmental network	crosscutting requirements	

Suggestions for Further Reading

Some of the best up-to-date sources of information on the changing world of intergovernmental relations can be found in the frequent authoritative studies published by the Advisory Commission on Intergovernmental Relations, as well as in the ACIR journal, *Intergovernmental Perspective,* which can be obtained free of charge by writing to the ACIR, Washington, D.C. In addition, the new monthly journal *Governing* is well worth reading on IGR issues. The *National Journal* also contains excellent IGR coverage. Timothy Conlan, *New Federalism: Intergovernmental Reform from Nixon to Reagan* (Washington, D.C.: Brookings, 1988) offers one of the best accounts of IGR during the past three decades and for a fine analysis of the development of American federalism, read Samuel H. Beer, *To Make a Nation: The Rediscovery of American Federalism* (Cambridge, Mass.: Harvard University Press, 1993). For current overviews, read Deil S. Wright, "Federalism, Intergovernmental Relations and Intergovernmental Management: Historical Reflections and Conceptual Comparisons," *Public Administration Review* (March/April 1990), pp. 168–178; Martha Derthick, "American Federalism: Madison's Middle Ground," *Public Administration Review* 47 (January/February 1987), pp. 66–74; Alice M. Rivlin, "A New Vision of American Federalism," *Public Administration Review,* 52 (July/August 1992), pp. 315–320; James E. Kee and John Shannon, "The Crisis and Anticrisis Dynamic," *Public Administration Review,* 52 (July/August 1992), pp. 321–329; and David R. Berman, "Relating to Other Governments," in Charldean Newell, ed., *The Effective Local Government Manager,* Second Edition. (Washington, D.C.: ICMA, 1993), pp. 167–198.

There are also a number of excellent books available, including Deil S. Wright, *Understanding Intergovernmental Relations,* Fourth Edition (Monterey, Calif.: Brooks/Cole Publishing, 1995); Paul E. Peterson, *What Price Federalism?* (Washington, D.C.: The Brookings Institution, 1995); Robert Stoker, *Reluctant Partners* (Pittsburgh, Pa: Pittsburgh University Press, 1991); Neal Peirce et al., *Citistates* (Washington, D.C.: Seven Locks Press, 1993); Alice M. Rivlin, *Reviving the American Dream* (Washington, D.C.: The Brookings Institution, 1992); David Rusk, *Cities without Suburbs* (Baltimore: The Johns Hopkins Press, 1993); Thomas J. Anton, *American Federalism and Public Policy: How the System Works* (Philadelphia: Temple University Press, 1989); and Robert W.

Gage and Myrna P. Mandell, eds., *Strategies for Managing Intergovernmental Policies and Networks* (Westport, Conn.: Greenwood Press, 1990).

The several more scholarly and focused studies of IGR that should be examined as well include James D. Carroll and Richard W. Campbell, eds., *Intergovernmental Administration* (Syracuse, N.Y.: Maxwell School, 1976); Martha Derthick, *The Influence of Federal Grants: Public Assistance in Massachusetts* (Cambridge, Mass.: Harvard University Press, 1970); Jeffrey L. Pressman, *Federal Programs and City Politics: The Dynamics of the Aid Process in Oakland* (Berkeley: University of California Press, 1975); Vincent Ostrom, *The Meaning of American Federalism: Constituting a Self-Governing Society* (San Francisco: ICS Press, 1991); and Paul E. Peterson et al., *When Federalism Works* (Washington, D.C.: The Brookings Institution, 1987). Serious students of IGR also should read the Kesnbaum Commission Report (June 1955), which contains information still helpful for understanding modern IGR, as well as other basic documents on IGR contained in Richard J. Stillman, *Basic Documents of American Public Administration Since 1950* (New York: Holmes and Meier, 1982). Laurence J. O'Toole, Jr., ed., *American Intergovernmental Relations,* Second Edition (Washington, D.C.: Congressional Quarterly, 1993); Lewis G. Bender and James A. Stever, *Administering the New Federalism* (Boulder, Colo.: Westview Press, 1986); as well as Deil S. Wright and Harvey L. White, eds., *Federalism and Intergovernmental Relations* (Washington, D.C.: American Society for Public Administration, 1984) offer outstanding collections of current and classic IGR essays. For several recent survey essays on federalism by distinguished scholars in this field, see the entire issue of *The Annals of the American Academy of Political and Social Science* (May 1990), edited by John Kincaid, and entitled "American Federalism: The Third Century." Where we are with the research in this field today is summarized by Vincent L. Marando and Patricia S. Florestano, "Intergovernmental Management: The State of the Discipline," in Naomi B. Lynn and Aaron Wildavsky, eds., *Public Administration: The State of the Discipline* (Chatham, N.J.: Chatham House, 1990).

CHAPTER 6

Internal Dynamics: The Concept of the Informal Group

F or all of us the feeling of security and certainty derives always from assured membership of a group. If this is lost, no monetary gain, no job guarantee, can be sufficient compensation. Where groups change ceaselessly as jobs and mechanical processes change, the individual inevitably experiences a sense of void, of emptiness. . . .

Elton Mayo

READING 6

Introduction

Public administration was never the primary concern of Elton Mayo and Fritz Roethlisberger. Most of their research efforts centered around the study of business enterprises at the Harvard Business School, yet their impact on general administrative thought has been significant principally because from their investigations developed the *human relations* or *industrial sociological school* in organization theory. This school of thought emphasizes understanding and improving the dynamics of the internal human group within complex organizations; it was both a product of and a reaction to the scientific-management movement of the early part of this century. Frederick W. Taylor, an early founder of scientific management, had stressed that from the rational study of industrial organizations, "principles" of efficient, economical management could be derived.

Similarly, Elton Mayo, Fritz Roethlisberger, and a team of researchers from the Harvard Business School set out in 1927 at Western Electric's Hawthorne Electric Plant in Cicero, Illinois, near Chicago, to measure scientifically the effect of changes in the external environment on workers' output; they studied such matters as more or less lighting, shorter or longer lunch breaks, and increased or decreased hours in the work week. Their goal at first, like the goal of scientific management, was to discover the most efficient way to motivate workers. The Hawthorne Plant manufactured phones and telecommunications equipment for American Telephone and Telegraph (AT&T), employing at the time more than 40,000 workers. The company encouraged the Mayo-Roethlisberger experiments as part of its generally considered progressive management practices (progressive at least for that era).

While following the same methods as Taylor's scientific-management research, the Mayo-Roethlisberger team paradoxically arrived at different conclusions and insights from those of Taylor and his followers. The results of five years of intense study at the Hawthorne Plant revealed that the *primary work group* (that is, the relationships between workers and their supervisors and among workers themselves), had as much if not more impact on productivity as the formal physical surroundings and economic benefits derived from the job. For many, the Hawthorne experiment came "as the great illumination," or as Roethlisberger more modestly described it, "the systematic exploitation of the simple and obvious." It underscored a fundamental truth, obscured for some time by scientific-management theories, namely, that the employees of an organization constituted its basis, and that upon their attitudes, behavior, and morale within their primary groups ultimately depended industrial effectiveness and productivity. As Roethlisberger wrote:

> It is my simple thesis that a human problem requires a human solution. First, we have to learn to recognize a human problem when we see one; and second, upon recognizing it, we have to learn to deal with it as such and not as if it were something else.[1]

The Hawthorne investigators shifted the focus of management studies from simply the external elements of organizations to its internal and nonrational aspects. By interviewing techniques and by close observations of the dynamics of primary groups, that is, interrelations between workers, the investigators sought to understand the social codes and norms of behavior of informal work groups that were rarely displayed on the formal organization chart. "They studied the important social functions these groups perform for their members, the histories of these informal work groups, how they spontaneously appear, how they tend to perpetuate themselves, multiply, and disappear, how they are in constant jeopardy from technical change, and hence how they tend to resist innovation." In essence, like Freud and Jung in clinical psychology, they attempted to rationalize the irrational nature of human beings in the organizational context and find cures for the psychotic disorders of industrial institutions.

The Hawthorne experimenters also challenged the prevailing scientific management view of the individual employee, that is, that the greatest motivating factor for the worker was his or her paycheck. Rather, Roethlisberger argued, "Most of us want the satisfaction that comes from being accepted and recognized as people of worth by our friends and work associates. Money is only a small part of this social recognition. . . . We want the feeling of security that comes not so much from the amount of money we have in the bank as from being an accepted member of a group. A man whose job is without social function is like a man without a country; the activity to which he has to give the major portion of his life is robbed of all human meaning and significance."

After the termination of the Hawthorne Plant experiments, Mayo's writings led to broad speculations about administration and the problems of human society. In these

---

[1] Fritz J. Roethlisberger, *Management and Morale* (Cambridge, Mass.: Harvard University Press, 1941), p. 7.

later works, *The Human Problems of an Industrial Civilization* (1933), *The Social Problems of an Industrial Civilization* (1945), and *The Political Problems of Industrial Civilization* (1947), his central thesis emphasized that social skills have lagged behind technical skills. While the techniques of specialists, including engineers, chemists, and doctors, were important, it was by the leadership of administrators, in particular businesspeople, that human cooperation could be advanced and the problems of organization in society solved. In the deepest sense, Mayo became a social reformer who believed that improving the quality of administrative talent could help to build a better world. In his view, the administrator "becomes the guardian or preserver of the morale through the function of maintaining a condition of equilibrium, which will preserve the social values existing in the cooperative system."

To better understand the following selection by Mayo, it is helpful to know something about his background, which helped to shape the decidedly unique perspective of his writing. Mayo, the senior partner in the Hawthorne research effort, lived from 1880 to 1949 (his assistant, Roethlisberger, lived from 1898 to 1974). Born in Adelaide, Australia, Mayo was the second child in a large, impoverished family of seven. His life was unsettled—while growing up his family moved often, and in trying to find an occupation for himself, he drifted from one job to another. He went from business to publishing, to teaching, and then to medicine, but it was World War I that affected his life the most (as it did the lives of so many of his generation). While working as an interviewer of returning war veterans suffering from shell shock, Mayo learned firsthand about human suffering, dislocation, and tragedy.

Increasingly, thereafter, Mayo was drawn to the study of psychology—particularly the clinical writings of Janet and Freud, as well as the work of social systems theorists like Pareto and Henderson. It was Mayo's unique gift to be able to synthesize the ideas of clinical psychology and develop a grand systems theory into a way that would offer understanding and help for the problems of the worker in the industrial workplace. How were people to deal with and adapt to the traumatic upheavals caused by war, technology, and industrialization in the twentieth century? How could the suffering caused by these massive changes in the human condition be alleviated and possibly cured? How could human life for individuals and groups be improved? Mayo wrestled with these and other major philosophical and social issues for most of his life.

Grants from the Rockefeller and Carnegie Foundations brought Mayo to America in the 1920s, first to the University of Pennsylvania and then later to Harvard University to head the team of researchers at the Hawthorne Plant. There, with his probing mind and inspired personality, along with his emphasis on using rigorous, firsthand field investigations as a way to understand what really was happening inside American industrial life, he was able to give leadership to the overall direction of the Hawthorne experiments. The lasting fame of these experiments in social science and management literature is due in large measure to Mayo. He introduced the modern *team research* concept and indeed inspired other large-scale research efforts such as W. Lloyd Warner's *Yankee City*.

The following selection offers valuable insight into Mayo's views—his unique intuitiveness, his passionate concern for the betterment of human beings, his conviction that close, careful empirical-clinical analysis will yield "the facts" about human problems, and that this analysis can, in turn, lead to resolutions of these problems.

Fundamental to all his beliefs is the idea that if only the informal nature of human organizations is recognized and properly dealt with (rather than the scientific, technological, and economic processes), then it is indeed possible to build a better world. This fundamental, reformist conviction spawned much of the human relations literature of post–World War II management thought by writers such as Maslow, Likert, McGregor, Herzberg, and many others who owe a debt to Mayo's writings and the Hawthorne experiments.

Mayo, however, was not without critics: labor unions attacked him for being anti-union, which he denied, and methodologists criticized his work for being unscientific and methodologically unsound, but he never admitted to being a statistician. Some suggest Mayo's values were too "pro-productivity," and not "pro-society" or "pro-human development," to which he would no doubt reply, "I was simply researching industrial productivity, not other factors." And some critics argue that Mayo's emphasis on small, blue-collar unskilled labor groups is outdated in an era of white-collar, educated professionals; but here again, Mayo might respond that he indeed studied a group that was representative of his own era. Furthermore, others would contend that he stressed cooperation and solidarity of the primary work group so much that he failed to appreciate the values of conflict and competition in assuring freedom of workers and progress for the overall organization. Mayo might respond to these criticisms by saying, "I merely reported on what our investigations uncovered at the time."

Most curiously, despite all his work at the Hawthorne Plant, not one of his recommendations was put into practice by the plant's management. Of what importance, then, were Mayo's work and the Hawthorne experiments? Perhaps Mayo's real genius was that he emphatically restated an old truth: human needs, values, and concerns of the basic informal group play a primary role in successful management practices.

As you read this selection, keep the following questions in mind:

Do the informal groups identified by Mayo's experiments in an industrial setting exist in public sector agencies? If so, do they operate in the same way in government as they do in business?

What do you think the similarities, as well as differences, are in the operation of an informal group in the public versus private settings?

Are Mayo's suggestions for dealing with the problems of securing the cooperation of individuals and human groups compatible with the goals and practices of public organizations? Where might there be problems in applying his ideas and techniques?

Referring back to Case Study No. 1, "The Blast in Centralia No. 5," or Case Study No. 3, "Dumping $2.6 Million on Bakersfield," identify the primary groups in these cases. Do Mayo's theories and prescriptions apply to these cases?

Compare Weber's and Mayo's views on the human condition. How do the two theorists compare in their conclusions and prescriptions for solving the bureaucratic problems of modern society? For instance, does Mayo emphasize material motives less than Weber does?

Hawthorne and the Western Electric Company

ELTON MAYO

I shall make no attempt to describe at length that which has been already and fully described. The interested public is well acquainted with *Management and the Worker,* the official account of the whole range of experiments, by my colleagues F. J. Roethlisberger of Harvard University and William J. Dickson of the Western Electric Company. The same public has not yet discovered *The Industrial Worker,*[1] by another colleague, T. North Whitehead. This is unfortunate, for the beginning of an answer to many problems significant for administration in the next decade is recorded in its pages. I refer to the problems involved in the making and adaptive re-making of working teams, the importance of which for collaboration in postwar years is still too little realized. Assuming that readers who wish to do so can consult these books, I have confined my remarks here to some comments upon the general development of the series of experiments.

A highly competent group of Western Electric engineers refused to accept defeat when experiments to demonstrate the effect of illumination on work seemed to lead nowhere. The conditions of scientific experiment had apparently been fulfilled—experimental room, control room; changes introduced one at a time; all other conditions held steady. And the results were perplexing: Roethlisberger gives two instances—lighting improved in the experimental room, production went up; but it rose also in the control room. The opposite of this: lighting diminished from 10 to 3 foot-candles in the experimental room and production again went up; simultaneously in the control room, with illumination constant, production also rose.[2] Many other experiments, and all inconclusive; yet it had

From Elton Mayo, *The Social Problems of an Industrial Civilization.* Boston: Division of Research, Harvard Business School, 1945. Reprinted by permission of Harvard Business School Press.

seemed so easy to determine the effect of illumination on work.

In matters of mechanics or chemistry the modern engineer knows how to set about the improvement of process or the redress of error. But the determination of optimum working conditions for the human being is left largely to dogma and tradition, guess, or quasi-philosophical argument. In modern large-scale industry the three persistent problems of management are:

1. The application of science and technical skill to some material good or product.
2. The systematic ordering of operations.
3. The organization of teamwork—that is, of sustained cooperation.

The last must take account of the need for continual reorganization of teamwork as operating conditions are changed in an *adaptive* society.

The first of these holds enormous prestige and interest and is the subject of continuous experiment. The second is well developed in practice. The third, by comparison with the other two, is almost wholly neglected. Yet it remains true that if these three are out of balance, the organization as a whole will not be successful. The first two operate to make an industry *effective,* in Chester Barnard's phrase,[3] the third, to make it *efficient.* For the larger and more complex the institution, the more dependent is it upon the wholehearted cooperation of every member of the group.

This was not altogether the attitude of Mr. G. A. Pennock and his colleagues when they set up the experimental "test room." But the illumination fiasco had made them alert to the need that very careful records should be kept of everything that happened in the room in addition to the obvious engineering and industrial devices.[4] Their observations therefore included not only records of industrial and engineering changes but also records of physiological or medical changes, and, in a sense, of social and anthropological. This last took the form of a "log" that gave as full an account as possible of the actual events of every day, a record that proved most useful to Whitehead when he was remeasuring the recording tapes and recalculating the changes in productive output. He was able to relate eccentricities of the output curve to the actual situation at a given time—that is to say, to the events of a specific day or week.

First Phase—The Test Room

The facts are by now well know. Briefly restated, the test room began its inquiry by, first, attempting to secure the active collaboration of the workers. This took some time but was gradually successful, especially after the retirement of the original first and second workers and after the new worker at the second bench had assumed informal leadership of the group. From this point on, the evidence presented by Whitehead or Roethlisberger and Dickson seems to show that the individual workers became a team, wholeheartedly committed to the project. Second, the conditions of work were changed one at a time: rest periods of different numbers and length, shorter working day, shorter working week, food with soup or coffee in the morning break. And the results seemed satisfactory: slowly at first, but later with increasing certainty, the output record (used as an index of well-being) mounted. Simultaneously the workers claimed that they felt less fatigued, felt that they were not making any special effort. Whether these claims were accurate or no, they at least indicated increased contentment with the general situation in the test room by comparison with the department outside. At every point in the program, the workers had been consulted with respect to proposed changes; they had arrived at the point of free expression of ideas and feelings to management. And it had been arranged thus that the twelfth experimental change should be a return to the original

conditions of work—no rest periods, no midmorning lunch, no shortened day or week. It had also been arranged that, after 12 weeks of this, the group should return to the conditions of Period 7, a 15-minute midmorning break with lunch and a 10-minute midafternoon rest. The story is now well known: in Period 12 the daily and weekly output rose to a point higher than at any other time (the hourly rate adjusted itself downward by a small fraction), and in the whole 12 weeks "there was no downward trend." In the following period, the return to the conditions of work as in the seventh experimental change, the output curve soared to even greater heights: this thirteenth period lasted for 31 weeks.

These periods, 12 and 13, made it evident that increments of production could not be related point for point to the experimental changes introduced. Some major change was taking place that was chiefly responsible for the index of improved conditions—the steadily increasing output. Period 12—but for minor qualifications, such as "personal time out"—ignored the nominal return to original conditions of work and the output curve continued its upward passage. Put in other words, there was no actual return to original conditions. This served to bring another fact to the attention of the observers. Periods 7, 10, and 13 had nominally the same working conditions, as above described—15-minute rest and lunch in midmorning, 10-minute rest in the afternoon. But the average weekly output for each worker was:

Period 7—2,500 units

Period 10—2,800 units

Period 13—3,000 units

Periods 3 and 12 resembled each other also in that both required a full day's work without rest periods. But here also the difference of average weekly output for each worker was:

Period 3—less than 2,500 units

Period 12—more than 2,900 units

Here then was a situation comparable perhaps with the illumination experiment, certainly suggestive of the Philadelphia experience where improved conditions for one team of mule spinners were reflected in improved morale not only in the experimental team but in the two other teams who had received no such benefit.

This interesting, and indeed amusing, result has been so often discussed that I need make no mystery of it now. I have often heard my colleague Roethlisberger declare that the major experimental change was introduced when those in charge sought to hold the situation humanly steady (in the interest of critical changes to be introduced) by getting the cooperation of the workers. What actually happened was that six individuals became a team and the team gave itself wholeheartedly and spontaneously to cooperation in the experiment. The consequence was that they felt themselves to be participating freely and without afterthought, and were happy in the knowledge that they were working without coercion from above or limitation from below. They were themselves astonished at the consequence, for they felt that they were working under less pressure than ever before: and in this, their feelings and performance echoed that of the mule spinners.

Here then are two topics which deserve the closest attention of all those engaged in administrative work—the organization of working teams and the free participation of such teams in the task and purpose of the organization as it directly affects them in their daily round.

Second Phase—The Interview Program

But such conclusions were not possible at the time: the major change, the question as to the exact difference between conditions of work in the test room and in the plant departments, remained something of a mystery. Officers of the company determined to "take another look" at departments outside the test room—this, with the idea that something quite important was there to be observed, something to which the experiment should have made them alert. So the interview program was introduced.

It was speedily discovered that the question-and-answer type of interview was useless in the situation. Workers wished to talk, and to talk freely under the seal of professional confidence (which was never abused) to someone who seemed representative of the company or who seemed, by his very attitude, to carry authority. The experience itself was unusual; there are few people in this world who have had the experience of finding someone intelligent, attentive, and eager to listen without interruption to all that he or she has to say. But to arrive at this point it became necessary to train interviewers how to listen, how to avoid interruption or the giving of advice, how generally to avoid anything that might put an end to free expression in an individual instance. Some approximate rules to guide the interviewer in his work were therefore set down. These were, more or less, as follows:[5]

1. Give your whole attention to the person interviewed, and make it evident that you are doing so.
2. Listen—don't talk.
3. Never argue; never give advice.
4. Listen to:
   (a) What he wants to say.
   (b) What he does not want to say.
   (c) What he cannot say without help.
5. As you listen, plot out tentatively and for subsequent correction the pattern (personal) that is being set before you. To test this, from time to time summarize what has been said and present for comment (e.g., "Is this what you are telling me?"). Always do this with the greatest caution, that is, clarify but do not add or twist.
6. Remember that everything said must be considered a personal confidence and not divulged to anyone. (This does not prevent discussion of a situation between professional colleagues. Nor does it prevent some form of public report when due precaution has been taken.)

It must not be thought that this type of interviewing is easily learned. It is true that some persons, men and women alike, have a natural flair for the work, but, even with them, there tends to be an early period of discouragement, a feeling of futility, through which the experience and coaching of a senior interviewer must carry them. The important rules in the interview (important, that is, for the development of high skill) are two. First, Rule 4 that indicates the need to help the individual interviewed to articulate expression of an idea or attitude that he has not before expressed; and, second, Rule 5 which indicates the need from time to time to summarize what has been said and to present it for comment. Once equipped to do this effectively, interviewers develop very considerable skill. But, let me say again, this skill is not easily acquired. It demands of the interviewer a real capacity to follow the contours of another person's thinking, to understand the meaning for him of what he says.

I do not believe that any member of the research group or its associates had anticipated the immediate response that would be forthcoming to the introduction of such an interview program. Such comments as "This is the best thing the Company has ever done," or "The Company should have done this long ago," were frequently heard. It was as if workers had been awaiting an opportunity for expressing freely and without afterthought their feelings on a great variety of modern situations, not by any means limited to the various departments of the plant. To find an intelligent person who was not only eager to listen but also anxious to help to express ideas and feelings but dimly understood—this, for many thousand persons, was an experience without precedent in the modern world.

In a former statement I named two questions that inevitably presented themselves to the interviewing group in these early stages of the study:

1. Is some experience which might be described as an experience of personal futility a common incident of industrial organization for work?

2. Does life in a modern industrial city, in some unrealized way, predispose workers to obsessive response?[6]

And I said that these two questions "in some form" continued to preoccupy those in charge of the research until the conclusion of the study.[7]

After twelve years of further study (not yet concluded), there are certain developments that demand attention. For example, I had not fully realized in 1932, when the above was written, how profoundly the social structure of civilization has been shaken by scientific, engineering, and industrial development. This radical change—the passage from an established to an adaptive social order—has brought into being a host of new and unanticipated problems for management and for the individual worker. The management problem appears at its acutest in the work of the supervisor. No longer does the supervisor work with a team of persons that he has known for many years or perhaps a lifetime; he is leader of a group of individuals that forms and disappears almost as he watches it. Now it is difficult, if not impossible, to relate oneself to a working group one by one; it is relatively easy to do so if they are already a fully constituted team. A communication from the supervisor, for example, in the latter instance has to be made to one person only with the appropriate instructions; the individual will pass it on and work it out with the team. In the former instance, it has to be repeated to every individual and may often be misunderstood.

But for the individual worker the problem is really much more serious. He has suffered a profound loss of security and certainty in his actual living and in the background of his thinking. For all of us the feeling of security and certainty derives always from assured membership of a group. If this is lost, no monetary gain, no job guarantee, can be sufficient compensation. Where groups change ceaselessly as jobs and mechanical processes change, the individual inevitably experiences a sense of void, of emptiness, where his fathers knew the joy of comradeship and security. And in such a situation, his anxieties—many, no doubt, irrational or ill-founded—increase and he becomes more difficult both to fellow workers and to supervisor. The extreme of this is perhaps rarely encountered as yet, but increasingly we move in this direction as the tempo of industrial change is speeded by scientific and technical discovery.

In the first chapter of this book I have claimed that scientific method has a dual approach—represented in medicine by the clinic and the laboratory. In the clinic one studies the whole situation with two ends in view: first, to develop intimate knowledge of and skill in handling the facts, and, second, on the basis of such a skill to separate those aspects of the situation that skill has shown to be closely related for detailed laboratory study. When a study based upon laboratory method fails, or partially fails, because some essential factor has been unknowingly and arbitrarily excluded, the investigator, if he is wise, returns to clinical study of the entire situation to get some hint as to the nature of the excluded determinant. The members of the research division at Hawthorne, after the twelfth experimental period in the test room, were faced by just such a situation and knew it. The so-called interview program represented for them a return from the laboratory to clinical study. And, as in all clinical study, there was no immediate and welcome revelation of a single discarded determinant: there was rather a slow progress from one observation to another, all of them important—but only gradually building up into a single complex finding. This slow development has been elsewhere described, in *Management and the Worker;* one can however attempt a succinct résumé of the various observations, more or less as they occurred.

Officers of the company had prepared a short statement, a few sentences, to be repeated to the individual interviewed before the conversation began. This statement was designed to assure the worker that nothing he said would be repeated to his supervisors or to any company official outside the interviewing group. In many instances, the worker waved this aside and began to talk freely and at once. What doubts there were seemed to be resident in the interviewers rather than in those interviewed. Many workers, I cannot say the majority for we have no statistics, seemed to have

something "on their minds," in ordinary phrase, about which they wished to talk freely to a competent listener. And these topics were by no means confined to matters affecting the company. This was, I think, the first observation that emerged from the mass of interviews reported daily. The research group began to talk about the need for *"emotional release"* and the great advantage that accrued to the individual when he had "talked off" his problem. The topics varied greatly. One worker two years before had been sharply reprimanded by his supervisor for not working as usual: in interview he wished to explain that on the night preceding the day of the incident his wife and child had both died, apparently unexpectedly. At the time he was unable to explain; afterwards he had no opportunity to do so. He told the story dramatically and in great detail; there was no doubt whatever that telling it thus benefited him greatly. But this story naturally was exceptional; more often a worker would speak of his family and domestic situation, of his church, of his relations with other members of the working group—quite usually the topic of which he spoke presented itself to him as a problem difficult for him to resolve. This led to the next successive illumination for the inquiry. It became manifest that, whatever the problem, it was partly, and sometimes wholly, determined by the attitude of the individual worker. And this defect or distortion of attitude was consequent on his past experience or his present situation, or, more usually, on both at once. One woman worker, for example, discovered for herself during an interview that her dislike of a certain supervisor was based upon a fancied resemblance to a detested stepfather. Small wonder that the same supervisor had warned the interviewer that she was "difficult to handle." But the discovery by the worker that her dislike was wholly irrational eased the situation considerably.[8] This type of case led the interviewing group to study carefully each worker's *personal situation* and attitude. These two phrases "emotional release" and "personal situation" became convenient titles for the first phases of observation and seemed to resume for the interviewers the effective work that they were doing.

It was at this point that a change began to show itself in the study and in the conception of the study.

The original interviewers, in these days, after sixteen years of industrial experience, are emphatic on the point that the first cases singled out for report were special cases—individuals—and not representative either of the working group or of the interviews generally. It is estimated that such cases did not number more than an approximate two percent of the twenty thousand persons originally interviewed. Probably this error of emphasis was inevitable and for two reasons: first, the dramatic changes that occur in such instances seemed good evidence of the efficacy of the method, and, second, this type of interviewing had to be insisted upon as *necessary to the training of a skilled interviewer.* This last still holds good; a skilled interviewer must have passed through the stage of careful and observant listening to what an individual says and to all that he says. This stage of an interviewing program closely resembles the therapeutic method and its triumphs are apt to be therapeutic. And I do not believe that the study would have been equipped to advance further if it had failed to observe the great benefit of emotional release and the extent to which every individual's problems are conditioned by his personal history and situation. Indeed, even when one has advanced beyond the merely psychotherapeutic study of individuals to study of industrial groups, one has to beware of distortions similar in kind to those named; one has to know how to deal with such problems. The first phase of the interview program cannot therefore be discarded; it still retains its original importance. But industrial studies must nevertheless move beyond the individual in need of therapy. And this is the more true when the change from established routines to adaptive changes of routine seems generally to carry a consequence of loss of security for many persons.

A change of attitude in the research group came gradually. The close study of individuals continued, but in combination with an equally close study of groups. An early incident did much to set the new pattern for inquiry. One of the earliest questions proposed before the original test room experiment began was a question as to the fatigue involved in this or that type of work. Later a foreman of high reputation, no doubt with this in mind, came to the research group, now for the most part engaged in interviewing, and asserted that the workers in his department worked hard all day at their machines and must be considerably fatigued by the evening; he wanted an inquiry. Now the interviewers had discovered that this working group claimed a habit of doing most of their work in the morning period and "taking things easy" during the afternoon. The foreman obviously realized nothing of this, and it was therefore fortunate that the two possibilities could be directly tested. The officer in charge of the research made a quiet arrangement with the engineers to measure during a period the amount of electric current used by the group to operate its machines; this quantity indicated the overall amount of work being done. The results of this test wholly supported the statements made by the workers in interview; far more current was used in the morning period than during the afternoon. And the attention of the research group was, by this and other incidents, thus redirected to a fact already known to them, namely, that the working group as a whole actually determined the output of individual workers by reference to a standard, predetermined but never clearly stated, that represented the group conception of a fair day's work. This standard was rarely, if ever, in accord with the standards of the efficiency engineers.

The final experiment, reported under the title of the Bank Wiring Observation Room, was set up to extend and confirm these observations.[9] Simultaneously it was realized that these facts did not in any way imply low working morale as suggested by such phrases as "restriction of output." On the contrary, the failure of free communication between management and workers in modern large-scale industry leads inevitably to the exercise of caution by the working group until such time as it knows clearly the range and meaning of changes imposed from above. The enthusiasm of the efficiency engineer for the organization of operations is excellent; his attempt to resume problems of cooperation under this heading is not. At the moment, he attempts to solve the many human difficulties involved in wholehearted cooperation by organizing the organization of organization without any reference whatever to workers themselves. his procedure inevitably blocks communication and defeats his own admirable purpose.[10]

This observation, important as it is, was not however the leading point for the interviewers. The existence and influence of the group—those in active daily relationship with one another—became the important fact. The industrial interviewer must learn to distinguish and specify, as he listens to what a worker says, references to "personal" or group situations. More often than not, the special case, the individual who talks himself out of a gross distortion, is a solitary—one who has not "made the team." The usual interview, on the other hand, though not by any means free from distortion, is speaking as much for the working group as for the person. The influence of the communication in the interview, therefore, is not limited to the individual but extends to the group.

Two workers in a large industry were recently offered "upgrading"; to accept would mean leaving their group and taking a job in another department: they refused. Then representatives of the union put some pressure on them, claiming that, if they continued to refuse, the union organizers "might just as well give up" their efforts. With reluctance the workers reversed their decision and accepted the upgrading. Both girls at once needed the attention of an interviewer: they had liked the former group in which they had earned informal membership. Both felt adjustment to a new group and a novel situation as involving effort and private discontent. From both much was learned of the intimate organization and common practices of their groups, and their adjustments to their new groups were eased, thereby effectively helping reconstitute the teamwork in those groups.

In another recent interview a worker of eighteen protested to an interviewer that her mother was continually urging her to ask Mr. X, her supervisor, for a "raise." She had refused, but her loyalty to her mother and the pressure the latter exerted were affecting her work and her relations at work. She talked her situation out with an interviewer, and it became clear that to her a "raise" would mean departure from her daily companions and associates. Although not immediately relevant, it is interesting to note that, after explaining the situation at length to the interviewer, she was able to present her case dispassionately to her mother—without exaggeration or protest. The mother immediately understood and abandoned pressure for advancement, and the worker returned to effective work. This last instance illustrates one way in which the interview clears lines of communication of emotional blockage—within as without the plant. But this is not my immediate topic; my point is rather that the age-old human desire for persistence of human association will seriously complicate the development of an adaptive society if we cannot devise systematic methods of easing individuals from one group of associates into another.

But such an observation was not possible in the earliest inquiry. The important fact brought to the attention of the research division was that the ordinary conception of management-worker relation as existing between company officials, on the one hand, and an unspecified number of individuals, on the other, is utterly mistaken. Management, in any continuously successful plant, is not related to single workers but always to working groups. In every department that continues to operate, the workers have—whether aware of it or not—formed themselves into a group with appropriate customs, duties, routines, even rituals; and management succeeds (or fails) in proportion as it is accepted without reservation by the group as authority and leader. This, for example, occurred in the relay assembly test room at Hawthorne. Management, by consultation with the workers, by clear explanation of the proposed experiments and the reasons for them, by accepting the workers' verdict in special instances, unwittingly scored a success in two most important human matters—the workers became a self-governing team, and a team that cooperated wholeheartedly with management. The test room was responsible for many important findings—rest periods, hours of work, food, and the like: but the most important finding of all was unquestionably in the general area of teamwork and cooperation.

It was at this time that the research division published, for private circulation within the company, a monograph entitled "Complaints and Grievances." Careful description of many varied situations within the interviewers' experience showed that an articulate complaint only rarely, if ever, gave any logical clue to the grievance in which it had origin; this applied at least as strongly to groups as to individuals. Whereas economists and industry generally *tend to concentrate upon the complaint and upon logical inferences from its articulate statement* as an appropriate procedure, the interviewing group had learned almost to ignore, except as symptom, the—sometimes noisy—manifestation of discomfort and to study the situation anew to gain knowledge of its source. Diagnosis rather than argument became the proper method of procedure.

It is possible to quote an illustration from a recently published book, *China Enters the Machine Age*.[11] When industries had to be moved, during this war, from Shanghai and the Chinese coast to Kunming in the interior of China, the actual operation of an industry still depended for the most part on skilled workers who were refugees from Shanghai and elsewhere. These skilled workers knew their importance to the work and gained considerable prestige from it; nevertheless discontent was rife among them. Evidence of this was manifested by the continual, deliberate breaking of crockery in the company mess hall and complaints about the quality of the food provided. Yet this food was much better than could have been obtained outside the plant—especially at the prices charged. And in interview the individual workers admitted freely that the food was good and could not rightly be made the subject of complaint. But the relationship between the skilled workers as a group and the *Chih Yuan*—the executive and supervisory officers—was exceedingly unsatisfactory.

Many of these officers—the *Chih Yuan*—have been trained in the United States—enough at least to set a pattern for the whole group. Now in America we have learned in actual practice to accept the rabble hypothesis with reservations. But the logical Chinese student of engineering or economics, knowing nothing of these practical reservations, returns to his own country convinced that the workman who is not wholly responsive to the "financial incentive" is a troublemaker and a nuisance. And the Chinese worker lives up to this conviction by breaking plates.[12] Acceptance of the complaint about the food and collective bargaining of a logical type conducted at that level would surely have been useless.

Yet this is what industry, not only in China, does every day, with the high sanction of State authority and the alleged aid of lawyers and economists. In their behavior and their statements, economists indicate that they accept the rabble hypothesis and its dismal corollary of financial incentive as the only effective human motive. They substitute a logical hypothesis of small practical value for the actual facts.

The insight gained by the interviewing group, on the other hand, cannot be described as substituting irrational for rational motive, emotion for logic. On the contrary, it implies a need for competent study of complaints and the grievances that provoke them, a need for knowledge of the actual facts rather than acceptance of an outdated theory. It is amusing that certain industrialists, rigidly disciplined in economic theory, attempt to shrug off the Hawthorne studies as "theoretic." Actually the shoe is on the other foot; Hawthorne has restudied the facts without prejudice, whereas the critics have unquestioningly accepted that theory of man which had its vogue in the nineteenth century and has already outlived its usefulness.

The Hawthorne interview program has moved far since its beginning in 1929. Originally designed to study the comfort of workers in their work as a mass of individuals, it has come to clear specification of the relation of working groups to management as one of the fundamental problems of large-scale industry. It was indeed this study that first enabled us to assert that the third major preoccupation of management must be that of organizing teamwork, that is to say, of developing and sustaining cooperation.

In summary, certain entirely practical discoveries must be enumerated.

First, the early discovery that the interview aids the individual to get rid of useless emotional complications and to state his problem clearly. He is thus enabled to give himself good advice—a procedure far more effective than advice accepted from another. I have already given instances of this in discussing "emotional release" and the influence on individual attitude of personal history and personal situation.

Second, the interview has demonstrated its capacity to aid the individual to associate more easily, more satisfactorily, with other persons—fellow workers or supervisors—with whom he is in daily contact.

Third, the interview not only helps the individual to collaborate better with his own group of workers, it also develops his desire and capacity to work better with management. In this it resembles somewhat the action of the Philadelphia colonel.[13] Someone, the interviewer, representing (for the worker) the plant organization outside his own group, has aided him to work better with his own group. This is the beginning of the necessary double loyalty—to his own group and to the larger organization. It remains only for management to make wise use of this beginning.

Fourth, beyond all this, interviewing possesses immense importance for the training of administrators in the difficult future that faces this continent and the world. It has been said that the interviewer has no authority and takes no action. Action can only be taken by the proper authority and through the formally constituted line of authority. The interviewer, however, contributes much to the facilitation of communication both up and down that line. He does this, first, by clearing away emotional distortion and exaggeration; second, his work manifestly aids to exact and objective statement the grievance that lies beyond the various complaints.

Work of this kind is immensely effective in the development of maturity of attitude and judgment in the intelligent and sensitive young men and women who give time to it. The subordination of oneself, of one's opinions and ideas, of the very human desire to give gratuitous advice, the subordination of all these to an intelligent effort to help another express ideas and feelings that he cannot easily express is, in itself, a most desirable education. As a preparation for the exercise of administrative responsibility, it is better than anything offered in a present university curriculum. It is no doubt necessary to train young men and women to present their knowledge and ideas with lucidity. But, if they are to be administrators, it is far more necessary to train them to listen carefully to what others say. Only he who knows how to help other persons to adequate expression can develop the many qualities demanded by a real maturity of judgment.

Finally, there remains the claim made above that the interview has proved to be the source of information of great objective value to management. The three persistent problems of modern large-scale industry have been stated as:

1. The application of science and technical skill to a material product.
2. The systematization of operations.
3. The organization of sustained cooperation.

When a representative of management claims that interview results are merely personal or subjective—and there are many who still echo this claim—he is actually telling us that he has himself been trained to give all his attention to the first and second problems, technical skill and the systematic ordering of operations; he does not realize that he has also been trained to ignore the third problem completely. For such persons, information on a problem, the existence of which they do not realize, is no information. It is no doubt in consequence of this ignorance or induced blindness that strikes or other difficulties so frequently occur in unexpected places. The interview method is the only method extant[14] that can contribute reasonably accurate information, or indeed any information, as to the extent of the actual cooperation between workers—teamwork—that obtains in a given department, and beyond this, the extent to which this cooperation includes management policy or is wary of it. The Hawthorne inquiry at least specified these most important industrial issues and made some tentative steps toward the development of a method of diagnosis and treatment in particular cases.

Notes

1. Cambridge, Harvard University Press, 1938, 2 vols.
2. *Management and Morale,* pp. 9–10.
3. Op. cit., p. 56.
4. For a full account of the experimental setup, see F. J. Roethlisberger and William J. Dickson, *Management and the Worker,* and T. North Whitehead, *The Industrial Worker,* Vol. 1.
5. For a full discussion of this type of interview, see F. J. Roethlisberger and William J. Dickson, op. cit., Chap. XIII. For a more complete summary and perhaps less technical discussion, see George C. Homans, *Fatigue of Workers* (New York, Reinhold Publishing Corporation, 1941).
6. Elton Mayo, *The Human Problems of an Industrial Civilization* (New York, The Macmillan Company, 1933; reprinted by Division of Research, Harvard Business School, 1946), p. 114.
7. Ibid.
8. F. J. Roethlisberger and William J. Dickson, op. cit., pp. 307–310.
9. F. J. Roethlisberger and William J. Dickson, op. cit., Part IV, pp. 379 ff.
10. For further evidence on this point, see Stanley B. Mathewson, *Restriction of Output among Unorganized Workers,* and also Elton Mayo, *The Human Problems of an Industrial Civilization,* pp. 119–121.
11. Shih Kuo-heng (Cambridge, Harvard University Press, 1944).
12. Ibid., Chap. VIII, pp. 111–127; also Chap. X, pp. 151–153.
13. Chap. III, supra.
14. We realize that there are at present in industry many individuals possessed of high skill in the actual handling of human situations. This skill usually derives from their own experience, is intuitive, and is not easily communicable.

☐ CASE STUDY 6

Introduction

The concept of the informal group provides us with several critical insights into modern organizational life and the need for administrators to be realistic about what can and cannot be achieved, given the sentiments, feelings, values, and outlooks of men and women in any particular work setting. Clearly, as Mayo's essay points out, being realistic about the nature and workings of the human group is paramount in any successful administrative undertaking. Human groups present managers with both potentialities and pitfalls for effective internal operations. Whatever happens to organizations, these human groups must be considered.

The following case study by Curtis Copeland illustrates the importance of considering the human element before making any managerial innovations in the public sector. In this case, a city manager in a medium-sized Texas community hired a personnel director to establish a new city personnel department. With speed and efficiency the new director set out to develop a number of new personnel procedures where none had existed before and to make changes he considered necessary improvements for a modern community of its size, such as grievance procedures, performance-based selection procedures, and merit raises tied to annual bonuses.

Although these reforms had been developed by a well-regarded, outside consulting firm, they were proposed without prior employee consultation or involvement. The city employees became upset by the proposals because they were the ones directly affected by these new reforms. A controversy thus ensued involving not only the employees, but the city council and larger community as well, with important lessons for the practice of public administration.

As you read this selection, keep the following questions in mind:

Specifically, what promoted the complaints by the employee groups relative to the newly proposed personnel changes? How were these complaints voiced?

How, in turn, did the personnel director and city manager respond to the complaints?

If you had been either the city manager or personnel director, would you have initiated such reforms in a different manner? As the city manager, how would you have handled the problems caused by the reforms?

Does the foregoing reading by Mayo contain useful ideas for securing worker cooperation with management in achieving organizational goals?

On the basis of your reading of this case study, can you generalize about the importance of informal groups in the public management processes?

Personnel Changes in City Government*

CURTIS COPELAND

Jim Drummond, the city manager of Groveton, Texas, was a worried man. He had held his job for nearly two years, and during that time he and other city administrators had made a number of changes that were of benefit to the city, particularly in the field of personnel management. Those successes, however, were offset by the sometimes adverse reactions of the people affected by the changes. After a series of pitched battles, Drummond was being pressured by the city council to dismiss the current

personnel director, Dan Remmens. Drummond and Remmens had gone through a great deal together, but the dismissal of the personnel director could be the only way to please the council. In order to understand Drummond's dilemma, the reader must be given some background as to the setting and how the current situation developed.

The Setting

The city of Groveton is a typical Texas community of about 60,000 tucked away in the pine woods of the northeastern part of the state. Like many cities its size in the region, it is basically white and middle-class in nature, but it has a poorer black population that has grown rapidly in the past twenty years. The main highway running through the town serves as a

*Note: The names of persons and local jurisdictions used in this case are entirely fictitious.

Prepared under an IPA federal grant through the Office of Personnel Management and administered at the University of Pittsburgh.

Neither the author nor the University of Pittsburgh maintain any rights to this case as it was prepared with federal funding.

man-made boundary line for this racial and eco-nomic division, with the eastern portion of the city populated by the more well-to-do white families and the somewhat smaller western section occupied by blacks and other low-income groups. Most of the whites living in the western part of Groveton are older citizens, unable or unwilling to leave the homes in which their children were raised. They en-dure the steadily worsening conditions of their neighborhoods, hoping that their houses will last as long as they do.

Most of the city's working population is employed in one of several industries and wood products is the largest of these, due to the community's proximity to the abundant resources of the East Texas forests. About one-third of the working men in Groveton are employed in the wood-related industry, the compa-nies ranging in size from the numerous small family operations to the giant Nortex plant located just out-side the city limits. The other industries in the town may be classified under the general heading of "manufacturing," producing products as varied as Caterpiller tractors and office equipment. Most of these companies are nonunion, largely as a result of a "right-to-work" provision in the state constitution and the relatively high wages paid to the workers in these businesses.

The city grew rapidly when many of these in-dustries arrived in Groveton in the late 1950s and early 1960s, but that growth slowed considerably in the next ten to fifteen years. Growth in the black community more than kept up that pace, however. By 1980, their rate of increase was twice that of the city as a whole. Attracted by the employment op-portunities in the local industries, black families continued to migrate to Groveton from smaller com-munities in the area in the hope of finding a better life. Most of those that did find work, however, were employed in unskilled positions in most companies. By 1980, approximately 25 percent of the city's res-idents were black and another 5 percent were his-panic.

Groveton's Political Structure and Administration

The city of Groveton is governed and administered under a council-manager form of government. Five council members are selected in nonpartisan elec-tions for staggered two-year terms of office. After each election, the council meets privately and se-lects one of its own to serve as mayor for the up-coming year. The decision is formalized in the first official council session after the election. The mayor's duties are largely ceremonial, although he is usually the council opinion leader in major deci-sions.

Prior to 1967, the city had a strong-mayor coun-cil form of government. Council members were se-lected in partisan elections using the place system, with each portion of the city selecting its own coun-cil member to represent its interests and the mayor was elected at large. In reaction to excesses of pa-tronage and nonfeasance during the late 1950s and the first half of the 1960s by some members of the council, the citizens of Groveton approved a vastly revised city charter. Many reforms popular during the era were adopted, including the present form of government and the at-large election system. Under the current form of government, the city manager is selected by majority vote of the city council and may be dismissed or reprimanded by that body at any time. The city manager, in turn, is the chief ex-ecutive officer of the city, in charge of all city de-partments and personnel. He has the authority to hire and fire city personnel and to select department heads. According to newspaper articles published at the time of the reforms, the changes represented an attempt to "bring sound business and management principles to the city's administration."

Actually, however, the city's mode of adminis-tration changed relatively little during those years of transition. The city secretary, Jim Taylor, resigned to become the new city manager and continued to per-form many of the tasks he had carried out during his seven years at his previous post. (The city secretary is a position required by state law in all Texas cities to perform most of the recordkeeping and official functions in the community. In smaller cities, this job is tantamount to being city manager.) The five city departments (water, streets, sanitation, police, and fire) virtually ran themselves, so all Taylor had to do was perform some minimal coordinative activities and oversee the city finance officer's job.

Taylor had no formal education in public man-agement, although he did attend a few training ses-sions sponsored by the local regional planning commission over the years. He remained, however, unaware and uninterested in most aspects of mod-ern management, and he publicly scorned the new techniques. He often jokingly remarked that "most of the things they teach in those courses either don't work or you can't pronounce them." Nevertheless, the city ran smoothly during his administration and there were few complaints from the council, the employees, or the city as a whole.

Personnel Administration in Groveton

The city of Groveton employed nearly 500 people in 1980, but this was only slightly more than were working for the municipal government ten years earlier. Although personnel duties for nonuniformed employees were, according to the new city charter, legally the providence of the city manager, Taylor had delegated that responsibility in large part to the line managers of the major city departments early in his administration. As was the case under the mayor-council form of government, the line managers in Groveton's municipal departments were each responsible for recruitment, selection and control of the employees within their departments. Although each manager administered a general intelligence test, a major part of the selection process involved an oral interview and a background check. If the applicant had no record or prior arrests and seemed capable of getting along reasonably well with other employees, he or she would probably be hired.

The selection of uniformed personnel, those in the fire and police departments, is governed by a state civil service law. Under the provisions of the law, each city of 10,000 or greater is required to have a civil service commission selected by the city council. The commission is primarily charged with the responsibility of insuring the unbiased selection of fire and police officers and to act as an appeals board to which those officers may complain about unfair treatment. In Groveton, commission members have traditionally been respected businessmen and civic leaders. Over the years, however, the fire and police chiefs (like the managers in the other departments) assumed primary responsibility for recruitment and selection. Most of the time the commission's duties were confined to certification of the top three candidates for open positions (as required by state law) and hearing an occasional appeal from a disgruntled officer.

Since the line managers and the civil service commission performed most of the personnel-related duties, City Manager Taylor did little in the way of actual personnel management. In fact, Taylor liked to refer to his personnel department as the "bottom-right drawers of the big filing cabinet." It was there that a clerk in his office kept records of all employees in separate folders, with such information as the date of their selection, current salary, job title, absences, and supervisor reprimands. Taylor believed the essence of a sound personnel system was the maintenance of accurate records so every employment-related action that occurred in the city was duly recorded. Groveton's personnel system, like other city operations, ran without any major problems and the city council rarely if ever became involved in its operations.

City Manager Changes Lead to a New Personnel System

After thirteen years as city manager, Taylor announced his retirement as chief executive officer to "make way for a younger man." The city council reluctantly accepted his resignation and, after a two-month search, decided to hire Mr. Thomas ("Jim") Drummond as the new chief administrator. Drummond had been working as the assistant city manager in San Benedict in West Texas, and was a graduate of a state university not far from Groveton. He was anxious to take the job, not only because he would be moving back to the area in which he had gone to school, but also because he had a strong desire to use the management skills he had acquired as a result of his education and experience in San Benedict. Drummond recognized the political dimensions of his job, however, having seen the city manager in San Benedict fired because he disagreed with the will of the city council. But he was equally convinced that sound management practices could be applied in even the most foreboding of environments.

Drummond spent his first month or so in Groveton "learning the ropes." He held meetings with the department heads both separately and as a group to explain his philosophy of management and to hear their suggestions. As a result of these discussions and his own observations, the city's need for an autonomous personnel department became more and more apparent. He realized that if any semblance of coordinated management were to evolve in Groveton, some means of centralized staffing and control would be needed. The city manager decided to discuss the development of a personnel department at the next council work session.

As was mentioned earlier, the council was composed of five city businessmen. Two members of the council were essentially "followers"—that is, they usually voiced their opinions only when asked and even then said very little. The leaders were the Mayor, Earnest Wilson, and Councilmen Calvin Johnson and Albert Hunt. Wilson owned several small businesses in the city and had served on the council for eight years. Johnson owned a real estate agency and Hunt was an industrial engineer at the Nortex lumber plant. All three men were fiscal conservatives in most matters, and all three were long-term residents of Groveton.

Drummond gave an opening statement at the meeting during which he expressed his belief that the city needed a personnel department, outlined the approximate cost of the change to the city, and waited for the council's reaction. After a somewhat awkward silence, Mayor Wilson's comments clearly indicated he did not share Drummond's enthusiasm for management change.

Mayor Wilson: Jim, you know we want you to run this city in a more business-like fashion, and that we respect your ideas and opinions. But I don't think that Groveton really needs a full-fledged personnel department. After all, we have gotten along pretty well without one in the past. And besides, it's not as if this is Dallas or Houston or anything. We've got a small operation here and don't have any immediate plans to put on any new people.

Councilman Hunt: I agree, Earnest. Jim Taylor kept this city on an even keel for more years than I would like to remember. He kept good records on each and every employee. He even sent Christmas cards out to each employee every year. And birthday cards too! Now that was coordination! We've never had any real crisis among city employees so I don't see the need for a change right now.

Drummond: But gentlemen, we may be leading up to a "crisis" if something isn't done ahead of time. Look, I realize that Jim Taylor did a good job for the city these past thirteen years or so. And I know you all liked and respected what he did for the city. But

personnel management has changed a lot in that time, too. It is no longer good enough to "keep good records." This city, like all others, must keep up with the times.

Wilson: OK, Jim. We all realize that, but I just don't think we are ready to do something drastic like create a new city department. Why don't we do this. Why don't you get that young assistant of yours to do a study to determine if we need a personnel department, and we will take it up again at next month's work session. Alright?

Drummond: But we don't *need* a study, Mayor. It is perfectly obvious. Look at Jacksborough (a city about the size of Groveton some seventy-five miles away). They have had a personnel department since they adopted the city manager form of government in 1965.

Better yet, look at the major companies in this town. Most of them wouldn't think of operating without a personnel section. And neither should we. If I am to run this city in a more business-like manner, we have to start taking lessons from them.

All you have to do is give me the authority to spend about $30,000 of the money we have left over from the sanitation budget for a director and one staff position. I will make the necessary changes in the administrative regulations, delegating personnel authority to the director, and we can get started. It is as simple as that.

Hunt: You know, Earnest, he has a point. Out at Nortex we've got three people working full time in a personnel department and we don't have but about 400 employees all together in the plant.

Wilson: All right, Jim, you've made your point. But where will this personnel department of yours be housed? You yourself have said that office conditions are cramped in City Hall already. Won't this be another problem we will have to deal with?

Johnson: We could always put them in the basement of the Annex, Earnest. It's not being used for anything but storage right now. We could probably manage it, at least for a while.

After some further discussion, the council finally agreed to fund the new personnel department for a two year period. Formal approval was granted at the next scheduled council meeting the following week. As he drove home from the meeting that evening, however, Drummond could not shake the impression that had he wanted to build a new bridge or road, spend more money on street repair, or even buy a new garbage truck with the sanitation money he would have met with little if any council resistance. These would have been "monuments" to their political eras—physical proof of the good they had done for the city. "Invisible" management changes were different, however. They were of little or no political benefit, and might even backfire.

Drummond realized that this "bricks and mortar orientation" was not unique to the Groveton City Council, for he had seen it in San Benedict as well. The political leaders did not seem to understand that focusing solely upon visible changes was not only an inefficient use of the city's resources, but that it also ignored Groveton's largest resource and expenditures—its personnel. Nearly 75 percent of the annual budget was allocated for personnel costs. Every department and every operation within city government was dependent upon those who would carry out those tasks. Therefore, he concluded, the most important changes are those which determine the quality and effectiveness of those people carrying out the city's business, even though they are "invisible" at times. It was now up to Drummond to prove that philosophy correct.

City Manager Drummond began the search for a personnel director the following morning, and within a few weeks he selected Dan Remmens for the job. Because the personnel director answered directly to the city manager, council approval for Remmen's hire (beyond the allocation of funds) was not required. Remmens had known Drummond at the university they attended some years before, and he had been employed as a personnel specialist within the City of Dallas' personnel division for two years. Like Drummond, Remmens was tired of just being a "cog in a big machine" and longed for the greater responsibility and freedom of action that comes with being an administrator in a small city, even though it meant a slight reduction in pay. Both men were convinced that they would make a good working team.

In order for the new personnel director to properly exercise his authority, many of the personnel-related duties performed by the line managers in the departments were transferred to the newly created personnel office. As was mentioned earlier, these managers had exercised virtually complete control over the hiring and promotion processes in their departments during the period Taylor was city manager. The forthcoming diminution in their authority did little to engender support for the new city manager or the personnel director.

Drummond was aware of this reaction, and he had even expected it to happen. Shortly after the decision to hire Remmens was announced, the city manager called a meeting of the department heads and the new personnel director to explain the new procedures and to hear their comments. After a brief exchange of pleasantries, the city manager got down to the matter that was on everyone's mind.

Drummond: Gentlemen, I realize that you have had to perform many of the personnel functions in this city in the past. You have had people coming directly to you for jobs and you have had to handle all the paperwork pretty much on your own. At the same time, you have had the freedom to select the people you think are best for your departments and this city. What we plan to do in the future will make your jobs easier, but not cut into your authority or the operations of your departments.

From now on, all applications for jobs will be handled by the personnel department, headed by Mr. Dan Remmens. Mr. Remmens will administer examinations where needed and screen out all the "undesirables" before they get to your departments. He will then refer some number of applicants to your department for the interview and final decision. Therefore, you will still have the final word as to who will work for you and how the jobs should be done. All we are trying to do in this area is centralize the operations a bit and take some of the paperwork off your backs.

At this point, let me introduce Dan Remmens.

Remmens: Thank you, Jim. First of all, let me say that I am pleased to be in Groveton, and I am sure that we can work together effectively for the good of the city. I concur with what the city manager just said. I am not going to take over your jobs, just make them easier. As I see it, I will just be coordinating personnel duties a little more and making the operations more uniform. You will no longer have to keep track of job applicants or give tests. We can work out some reasonable relationship concerning job referrals, qualifications, and so on. In short, I'd like to think that I can help you manage your departments better. We can discuss the details of all of this at your convenience. I'm looking forward to working with you.

Drummond: Any questions?

Jack Collier (Sanitation Supervisor): Yeah. I've got a question. When can you start? If my job is going to get easier, I'm ready for you right now!

The brief meeting broke up amiably and Drummond was convinced that it had been a success. The supervisors' suspicions seem to have dissipated considerably when it became clear what the personnel director's (and their) responsibility would be and that they would still be able to make the decisions concerning selections and discipline of employees in their departments.

The New Personnel Director Takes Over

The following Monday, Remmens officially entered his new job with the City of Groveton. As the city manager had explained the job to him in the interview, it was largely a matter of "interpretation" of applicable city ordinances and state laws. Although he had the authority to write administrative procedure for city personnel, he could not add job titles, hire and fire employees in other departments, or change the ordinances passed by the city council. Before taking any action, however, Remmens felt he should familiarize himself with the city's current personnel "department"—the bottom drawers of the filing cabinets where former City Manager Taylor kept the personnel records.

The contents of that file revealed that the city lacked even the most rudimentary of personnel systems, and as a result the operations of the city as a whole suffered. Almost no data on employee characteristics or performance were maintained. Although job descriptions were noted, they were all over fifteen years old and were clearly out of date since the nature of the jobs in the city had changed a great deal during that period. The selection process, as mentioned earlier, consisted of a general aptitude test given to all applicants, a background check, and an interview. Also, no established grievance system other than complaints to the employee's immediate supervisor existed in the city. Finally, employees were given "merit raises" (bonuses) based upon their annual salaries once per year despite declines in production in virtually every department. Supervisors blamed the performance problems on the "poor quality of new employees," of which there were many. The city's turnover rate for all positions approached 85 percent.

Appalled by what the "filing-cabinet personnel department" revealed, Remmens met with the city manager to discuss the ramifications and how to deal with them. The two men decided that two immediate actions were called for before any other changes could be made. First, a basic social survey of all employees should be conducted, gathering data on personnel characteristics and the nature of their employment. With these data, the manager and the personnel director believed that they could more clearly see what sort of employees the city had and what jobs they actually performed. Secondly, all city jobs should be analyzed for up-to-date job descriptions and to set job qualifications and performance standards. Although the first of these two actions could be conducted in-house, both Drummond and Remmens recognized that the second required outside assistance.

Social Survey

Department supervisors were called in and the issue of the social survey was discussed at length. Although all parties agreed that such information would be valuable, the line managers were not quite sure what the city manager and the personnel director had up their sleeves. Their main concern was not the collection process itself or what would be discovered, but to what ends that information would be used once collected. Their suspicions were kept largely to themselves, however, and the social survey was conducted without any major problem.

The data indicated that the city was in even worse shape than either Drummond or Remmens had imagined. Only forty-seven of Groveton's nearly 500 employees were black, and only two were hispanic. All but three of these minority employees were working in either the streets or sanitation departments. No blacks had worked in the police department prior to

1973 and none had ever been employed in the fire department or had been a supervisor in the other departments. Women were similarly underrepresented, particularly in the fire and police departments. In sum, the city of Groveton was ripe for an EEO lawsuit. It was a classic case of "adverse impact" as defined in the Federal Uniform Selection Guidelines.

The fire and police chiefs told the personnel director that they had tried to get "qualified" minorities on their respective forces, but without much success. It seemed that a high percentage of the black and hispanic candidates either failed the aptitude tests given or were screened out by the interviews. Female applicants were often ruled out by the city's height and weight requirements.

Job Analysis

In order for the job analysis to be conducted properly, both Drummond and Remmens realized it would have to be conducted by qualified professionals. That, of course, meant an expense that would have to be authorized and paid for by the city council. Realizing the councilmen's reluctance to spend city tax dollars on "invisible" changes, the two men sought external help to finance the analysis and to convince the council of its utility.

Remmens had worked with several Intergovernmental Personnel Act (IPA) grants while employed by the City of Dallas, and wrote to the regional office there for information on their availability. With that information and the assistance of the local council of governments, the personnel director was able to obtain the commitment of Federal officials in Dallas to fund one-fourth of the expense of a consultant to conduct the job analysis. Both Remmens and Drummond realized that the more difficult portion of the process was just beginning—to convince the council to allow the expenditure of the city's portion of the study's cost.

The two men, accompanied by a representative from the council of governments, approached the council at the next work session. They explained why the job analysis and position classification were needed and made it clear that much of the city's expense would be absorbed through the provision of in-house services. Although initially skeptical, the enticement of Federal funds for what turned out to be a minimal investment proved to be too attractive to pass up. The city's portion of the expense was

agreed to at the next council meeting with a surprising lack of resistance, and the grant application received Federal approval shortly thereafter.

Remmens and his assistant did most of the administrative duties involved in the analysis themselves, and the entire process was completed within a short while. The results provided the personnel director with information he needed concerning the tasks that comprise each city job, the skills needed to perform those tasks, and provided the basis upon which subsequent changes could be made. However, exactly what those changes should be and how they should be administered were in no way clarified. Based upon the information from the survey and the job analysis, Drummond and Remmens finally decided that three changes should be made as soon as possible:

1. codification of employee grievance procedures;
2. begin using valid performance-based selection procedures where possible; and
3. begin a real "merit pay" system by tying annual bonuses to performance evaluations.

Grievance Procedure Codification

The two men decided that the codification of grievance procedures should be accomplished first, since it required no council action, no expenditure of city funds, and involved only nonuniformed personnel. (Fire and police grievance procedures were codified in the state civil service law.) It was also a change that many municipal employees apparently wanted to take place. Several city workers had approached both Drummond and Remmens about problems they were experiencing with their work assignments. These were particularly aggravating since most of the complaints could have been resolved at a much lower level of supervision.

In addition, many superior employees had reportedly resigned in the past because their complaints never went beyond their supervisors. According to several current employees, City Manager Taylor refused to become involved in these disputes, telling dissatisfied employees to "work it out with your boss." Since many of the complaints concerned their supervisors, the employees either learned to accept the situation or left the organization. Grievances which *were* settled often took over a year to complete, and often resulted in grossly unequal treatment.

The appeals process adopted by executive order was relatively simple and straightforward, copying in form if not in substance the grievance procedure of the nearby city of Jacksborough. Four levels of appeal were delineated, the first of which remained the employee's immediate supervisor (provided that the supervisor was not the subject of the complaint). The next two levels were the department manager and the director of personnel. If the grievance was still not settled, it could then be submitted to the city's Civil Service Commission in accordance with its appeal procedures. The entire process was to be completed within ninety days.

The change in appeals procedures was announced to city employees through notices posted in the departments and information sheets inserted in their pay envelopes. Within a few weeks the new process was running even more smoothly than had been expected. An initial flurry of complaints, stimulated in part by the new procedures, was handled to the satisfaction of most parties, and only a few reached the personnel director. Although Drummond and Remmens were pleased with their progress, they realized the other two innovations were going to be even more difficult, for they posed both real and imagined threats to various segments of the workforce.

Performance Selection

Drummond and Remmens were particularly anxious to get the new selection methods started, as the city could not afford an expensive lawsuit brought about by the currently used aptitude tests, interviews, and background checks. Since many of the entry-level positions in the city were of the unskilled or semiskilled variety, the use of aptitude tests for these positions was especially questionable. Remmens was enthusiastic about the prospect of change in this area, and discussed the possibilities with City Manager Drummond.

Remmens: Jim, I think we have a chance to really make this city a showplace in the area of selection and staffing. We could not only avoid the EEO prob-lems, but could set an example for other cities in the area or even the whole state. Groveton could become a model in the field with the changes we can make.

Drummond: Hold on, Dan. What sort of changes do you have in mind? After all, we do have the council to consider. You *do* remember the council, don't you? They haven't exactly been overjoyed with the prospect of spending money, you know.

Remmens: These changes won't cost much at all. All it will take is a strong desire on our part to make it work. I think we can set up a modified assessment center here and get rid of those intelligence tests that seem to be our biggest problem. Have you ever seen the system they have in Dallas?

Drummond: No, I haven't seen it but I've heard it is pretty complicated.

Remmens: Not really. All it involves is the use of the job descriptions in a performance format. For example, if a man's job involved garbage collections, he should be able to lift a can of garbage, dump it in the truck, and follow instructions. A back-hoe operator should essentially have to demonstrate that he knows how to operate a back-hoe. The same principle could be applied to the selection of managers and in promotional decisions. We can give them an in-basket test of the type of things they need to be able to do on the job and select the ones that are the highest scorers.

Drummond: If we are really going to touch all the bases on this thing, won't we have to validate the tests or something?

Remmens: Sure. Before we can start using them we have to show they are related to jobs. That is why we need to begin now. According to this EEOC guidebook, the first step should be the publication of our affirmative action program, of which this will be a major part.

Drummond: OK, then, let's get started. But be sure to follow those guidelines to the letter. I want to be able to explain the city's actions to the council and others as part of the federal mandate. There are a lot of people that may take offense to this sort of thing. Hopefully, we can explain it to the council *after* it is in place and running smoothly.

After the meeting, Remmens drafted an affirmative action statement based upon the suggestions in the EEOC manual and those he had seen elsewhere. It was a relatively simple document citing the city's poor record of minority hiring in the past and proposing goals for the future. The statement was printed in the local newspaper as part of a larger article on city hall happenings, along with Remmens' predictions that new professionally developed methods of selection would soon be utilized in Groveton. That process of constructing and validating the exams had not gone very far, however, when it ran into some major obstacles.

About two weeks after the plans were announced, a committee of black citizens confronted the city council at their formal evening meeting and publicly blasted the city for its hiring record. Citing figures they had received from the newspaper and elsewhere, they demanded a speedy end to the pattern of black exclusion from the city's fire and police departments. Unless changes were made immediately, they argued, preparations would be made to seek redress in the courts and at the ballot box. Municipal elections were scheduled to be held in about three months.

Several spokesmen for the fire and police employees also expressed their concern about municipal hiring policies, albeit more privately and in a different direction. They were concerned that the new "performance" tests would be catered to the needs of the black community to too great an extent. As a result, they feared that fire and police trainees selected would be of a lesser quality than required to perform the jobs properly. Plans to select virtually every job through performance tests were met with equal derision. One supervisor in the streets department was quoted as saying, "I'll be damned if I am going to let some guy off the street 'try out' on one of our $40,000 pieces of equipment. No way!"

Although the development of the resentment in each area is a story in itself, one thing had become quite clear. Instead of setting the stage for positive action, the publication of the plan generated a great deal of unexpected controversy and sparked an anger within the community that lay just below the surface. Mayor Wilson and Councilmen Johnson and Hunt held a hurried meeting with Drummond and Remmens shortly after the stormy council session with the black leaders. That meeting proved to be equally tumultuous.

Wilson: Dan and Jim, I will admit right off that I don't know as much about personnel management or city management as you do. But I *do* know this community. That "affirmative action plan" of yours has been anything but "affirmative" here. The public is upset, the employees are upset, and frankly I am too.

Drummond: I can understand and appreciate your concern, Mayor, but this situation has been brewing for some time. Maybe we had better just proceed with our plan and let the black community and the employees know exactly what is going on. After all, we are not doing anything so different here than is going on all over the United States. And validating these performance tests takes time to do it right.

Johnson: Unfortunately this is *not* "all over the United States." This is Groveton, Texas. Do you think the people here understand or care that we are doing this "for their own good" or that "validations take time?" They want action now or else. And if they don't get action, they will take some of their own.

Remmens: But we *are* taking action, the kind that this city needs. And if they don't understand it, well then that is just something we will have to explain better in the future. Perhaps if we had done that in the beginning—I mean years ago—we wouldn't have the problems we have today.

Wilson: Gentlemen, we could continue placing the blame for this from now until next week. However, I think we had better get on with the solution to this and right away. It is not something that we can allow to go on indefinately.

Dan, can't you just get a validated test used somewhere else and be done with it?

Remmens: Written tests can be purchased for some jobs like firemen and policemen, but they need to be locally validated before being used on a widescale basis.

Wilson: Since most of this flack is coming from the fire and police departments, I suggest that you buy and start using a fire and police exam, announce that it has been validated elsewhere and that it will be valid here too, and that should solve the problem. I would also suggest that it be done *immediately.* You can go ahead with your performance tests in some of the other jobs, but you'd better get this fire and police thing settled *now.*

Although the personnel director and city manager disagreed with the mayor's plan at first, it became clear that the council was adamant. The meeting adjourned with Remmens and Drummond agreeing to make the necessary changes. Generally validated written tests were again the primary selection devices used in the police and fire departments. The black leaders were cautiously pleased with the results, but promised to watch for the tests' effects on black applicants.

In the other departments, the changes were also more modest than expected, due to the negative reactions the proposed changes had generated. Still, the most obvious deficiencies in the earlier system were corrected. Laborers no longer had to pass intelligence tests for work on sanitation trucks or road crews. The changes instituted were painful for some and more limited than hoped for, but they had occurred.

Merit Pay

About six months after the performance-based examination process was announced, Personnel Director Remmens decided to go forward with the merit pay innovation. As mentioned earlier, the city had had a "merit pay" concept in operation for some time, but made no effort to tie the awards to performance appraisals. In fact, the only performance evaluations attempted were simple "unsatisfactory-satisfactory" employee ratings done by department supervisors, in which virtually all workers were judged to be in the "satisfactory" (i.e., meritorious) category. In some instances, employees were rated "satisfactory," given merit bonuses, and two months later were recommended for suspension or termination.

The new merit bonuses were to be based upon the position descriptions and qualification requirements derived as a result of the earlier job analysis. After developing an evaluation form, Remmens told department and first-line supervisors how to use the new procedures and provided other information about the program. They were also told that, unlike under the earlier system, only 50 percent of the employees in each department would be eligible for merit increases in order to make the awards more competitive. The bonuses would be financed from a percentage of each department's total salary package.

Word of this change in procedure spread rapidly. By the time the plan was made official, virtually every municipal employee knew what was in the offing. Although some city workers were glad to see the advent of a true merit system, the predominate emotion was one of profound mistrust and suspicion. Both supervisors and lower-level employees felt threatened by the change. Supervisors were concerned that they were going to jeopardize the trust and friendship they enjoyed with their employees if they had to exclude one half of them from receiving what had become an annual pay supplement. They were also wary of the time and energy required by the new process and how this would affect their everyday supervision. The employees, on the other hand, were not convinced that the new evaluation system was workable or that they would be treated fairly by a process that had been developed without their involvement.

Despite these misgivings, plans were made to put the proposal into effect throughout the city at the start of the new fiscal year. Both City Manager Drummond and Personnel Director Remmens were aware of the grumblings among city employees, but they took no overt action to respond to them other than by counseling individual employees. Remmens was convinced that these problems would be short-lived and that the merit pay plan would be successful by the end of the first year. Such resistance to change was to be expected, he said, but by sticking with the original plan, the complaints would slowly dissipate. Shortly before the official kick-off date for the new performance evaluations, however, Remmens' predictions again proved somewhat less than accurate.

A meeting of city employees was held one evening in which representatives of each city department were selected to talk to Drummond and Remmens about the new pay plan. Before that meeting, Drummond and Remmens met for lunch to discuss the matter at length and present a united front. The two men discussed the complaints they had heard previously and then each gave his impression of what should be done. There, the first real split between them surfaced.

Drummond: Dan, I think we should go slow with this new merit pay plan. After all, starting this sort of thing in Groveton would be like moving from the ice age into the space age. You've got to consider where we are coming from. People need time to adjust to something like this.

Remmens: Are you saying we shouldn't have real merit pay in this city? Is that annual gratuity for hanging on another year what we really want?

Drummond: Of course not. But we probably shouldn't spring it on them all at once, either. Look, I'm as anxious to get this town into the 1980s as much as you are. But this kind of thing can cause all kinds of problems. People feel threatened, and when they do they naturally try to protect their turf. We have got to figure out some way to make it less threatening to them while still making progress. That may mean we will have to take a more subtle tack than we had planned.

Remmens: You have something in mind, I hope?

Drummond: Well, not exactly.
Maybe we could do it on a small scale first. You know, kind of try it out on one group and then gradually expand it to all employees.

Remmens: And which division do you think will step forward to be first? They are *not* exactly falling over each other to be evaluated, you know.
Look, Jim, things like this are too important to do half-heartedly. If we evaluate one group and not another, then you are *really* going to hear the complaints of unfair treatment. What we need to do is go into this meeting firm in our resolve that what we are doing is right.

The two men failed to agree on a concerted strategy, and left for the meeting without resolving the issue.
That afternoon, representatives from all five divisions sat across the table from the city manager and the personnel director. Remmens again explained the rationale behind the plan, and the employees voiced no strong objections. After a somewhat restrained discussions from all parties, Harold Leavitt, an employee in the streets department, clearly expressed what most city employees were feeling.

Leavitt: Look, Mr. Drummond. We don't have any quarrel with being paid for how hard we work. I'm sure that most of the people working for the city feel like they deserve their bonuses and would get them under any fair system. The problem is that we don't think it is a fair system. You've got studies by someone who has never patched a street or driven a truck telling you what it is we do and what is important in

the streets department. The same thing is true in all the other departments. I'm sure we could do as good a job as he did or even better.(Nods and mumblings of agreement from the other employees present.)

Remmens: Mr. Leavitt, the study upon which the evaluation forms were designed was done by one of the finest consulting firms in the country. They have done similar job analyses and position descriptions in Dallas, Oklahoma City, St. Louis, and lots of other places.

Leavitt: Frankly, I don't care *where* they have done their work before coming here. If you think they are so good at setting these performance standards, why don't you use the ones they developed for *your* job first?
I just don't think that we should be at the mercy of someone who doesn't really know what we do. It's got a lot of people plenty upset. Some of the people are even starting to talk about getting a union started. Now you don't want that and neither do most of us. But something's got to give.

Drummond: Harold, let me pick up on something you said a minute ago. You said you thought you could do as good a job as the consulting firm did. Well, would you like a chance to try?

Leavitt and Remmens (simultaneously): What?

Drummond: I said, if you think you could do a better job in setting up the evaluations, why don't you give it a shot? You could use the forms that were developed for your jobs as a starting place and work from there. I'm sure we could start the evaluations a little late so we could get your comments. What do you say?

Leavitt: Well, I'll have to talk it over with the others but I think that sounds reasonable.

Drummond: Good. We'll talk more about it next week, then. Meanwhile, you get back with your people and I'll talk to the supervisors. Together, I think we can still get the program started.

After the meeting, Personnel Director Remmens was livid. He strongly objected to, what he termed, "caving in" to the demands of the employees.

Remmens: I can't believe that you are going to let

them set their own performance standards. Do you realize what that means? First of all, they will probably come in here with standards that will be so ludicrous that we won't be able to use them. Then we will be worse off than we are now. Also, they now have the impression that they can get whatever they want just by coming in here and making demands. They don't need a union; they've got one already.

Drummond: Dan, I know you are upset, but I don't think you realize the nature of the situation we have here. Performance evaluation is an issue that can bring all those people together like no other. And if you think we have trouble from the employees or the council now, just wait until this city gets a union. Then the council will blame you for causing it and will not give you any money for *any* of your ideas.

Remmens: Since you are making the decisions, I guess that means you are right. I guess this also means that you plan to run the personnel department from your office from now on, then?

Drummond: If I have to.

At that, the two men parted company and did not speak to each other for the remainder of the week. Drummond negotiated with the line supervisors and arranged a meeting with employee representatives for the following Friday. Remmens continued to operate his department and to perform his regular duties, but refused to alter his position that the job analysis derived performance standards be accepted without change. Any "tampering" with those standards he considered an abrogation of management rights.

Drummond had one more discussion with the employees on this matter, but he could not ethically or legally go forward with the development of the performance standards without Remmens' involve-

ment. He felt bad about the situation, but decided to allow things to cool off a little more before taking any action.

Mayor Wilson and the other members of the city council heard about the problems the new performance evaluations were causing a short while after the meeting. Although they were unaware of the specifics, the council also knew about the split between the city manager and the personnel director over which standards should be used in the performance appraisals. The one thing they wished to avoid was the establishment of a union in Groveton, and this question of standards was clearly pushing them in that direction. There had even been talk of a petition circulating that would establish a bargaining unit in the city. As a result, two council members—Hunt and Johnson—met privately with City Manager Drummond to discuss the matter. They urged him to dismiss Remmens for insubordination and get on with the process. This, they felt, would cut short any unionization effort and end the major part of the problem.

This, then, was the situation Drummond faced at the beginning of this review. He and Remmens had gone through much together, but it could be that his dismissal would be the only way to appease the council. If Remmens were fired, any subsequent personnel director would, based on past experience, probably be reticent to undertake any such sweeping reforms. That was probably what the councilmen had in mind. Who could have foreseen that such a simple thing as a performance-based bonus system would cause such complex problems?

Drummond scheduled another meeting with the employee representatives to iron out the details of their agreement. Before that meeting, he decided to resolve once and for all the problems between Remmens and himself. He sent a memo to the personnel director asking him to stop by as soon as possible.

Chapter 6 Review Questions

1. What is your definition of an informal group in organizations?
2. How are informal groups formed and how do they influence the activities of public organizations?
3. Do informal groups emerge and have an impact on *public* organizations in the same ways as they do upon *business* organizations?

4. If you had been City Manager Drummond or Personnel Director Remmens, would you have initiated such personnel changes any differently? If so, how?

5. Can you see any evidence of the influence of informal groups in organizations with which you are familiar? If so, how did these groups emerge and in what ways do they affect the policies and activities of those organizations?

6. Based on your personal observations of the workings of informal groups, would you modify the Mayo-Roethlisberger concept in any way? For example, could you add more specifics about how to identify informal groups? Measure their strength? Identify sources of influence in organizations? Reasons for weakness? Methods for achieving the support of management? Ways of communication? Means of motivation?

Key Terms

informal group
"great illumination"
social structure

Hawthorne experiments
interview program
scientific-technological change

Suggestions for Further Reading

The best book about the Hawthorne experiments is Fritz Roethlisberger and W.J. Dickson, *Management and the Worker* (Cambridge, Mass.: Harvard University Press, 1939). For a less complicated view, see Fritz Roethlisberger, *Management and Morale* (Cambridge, Mass.: Harvard University Press, 1941). Elton Mayo's broad philosophic interpretations are contained in his "trilogy": *The Human Problems of an Industrial Organization* (New York: Macmillan Co., 1933); *The Social Problems of an Industrial Civilization* (Boston: Graduate School of Business Administration, Harvard University, 1945); and *The Political Problems of an Industrial Civilization* (same publisher, 1947). For an excellent retrospective on Hawthorne, refer to "An Interview with Fritz Roethlisberger," *Organizational Dynamics,* 1 (Autumn 1972), pp. 31–45; "Hawthorne Revisited: The Legend and the Legacy," *Organizational Dynamics,* 4 (Winter 1975), pp. 66–80; and Alfred A. Bolton, ed, "Special Issue: Relay Assembly Testroom Participants Remember: Hawthorne a Half Century Later," *International Journal of Public Administration,* 17, 2 (1994), entire issue.

Two excellent and now classic interpretations of Hawthorne are George Homans, *The Human Group* (New York: Harcourt, Brace, 1950) and Henry Landsberger, *Hawthorne Revisited* (Ithaca, N.Y.: Cornell University Press, 1958). By contrast, to taste a small sampling of the scholarly arguments over Hawthorne, read Alex Carey, "The Hawthorne Studies: A Radical Criticism," *American Sociological Review,* 32 (June 1967), pp. 403–416; and for a review of small group theory applied to public administration, see Robert T. Golembiewski, "The Small Group and Public Administration," *Public Administration Review,* 19 (Summer 1959), pp. 149–156. For some interesting new perspectives on the psychological dimensions of public management, see Richard L. Schott, "The Psychological Development of Adults: Implications for Public Administration," *Public Administration Review,* 46 (November/December 1986), pp. 657–667; and Larry Hirshhorn, *The Workplace Within: Psychodynamics of Organizational Life* (Cambridge, Mass.: MIT Press, 1991). The legacy of Hawthorne can be found in numerous examples of the prolific postwar authors associated with the Human Relations School of Management, Chris Argyris, Warren Bennis, Frederick Herzberg, Daniel Katz, Robert Kahn, Rensis Likert, Douglas McGregor, Leonard Sayles, William Whyte, and many, many others who owe a tremendous debt to Hawthorne. In turn, their "spinoffs" and "impacts" on public administration have been profound and numerous but largely uncharted by scholars in the field, though for a useful compilation of many of their writings, refer to Frank J. Thompson, ed., *Classics of Public Personnel Policy,* Second Edition (Monterey, Calif.: Brooks/Cole, 1991); Jay Shafritz et al., eds., *Classics of Public Administration,* Second Edition, (Chicago: Dorsey Press, 1987); Thomas H. Patten, *Classics of Personnel Management* (Chicago: Moore Publishing Co., 1979); and Louis E. Boone and Donald D. Bowen, eds., *The Great Writings in Management and Organizational Behavior* (Tulsa, Okla.: The Petroleum Publishing Co., 1980). For a current overview of this topic, read Charles Perrow, *Complex Organizations: A Critical Essay,* Second Edition (Glenview, Ill.: Scott, Foresman, 1979), as well as Larry M. Lane and James El Wolf, *The Human Resource Crisis in the Public Sector: Rebuilding the Capacity to Govern* (New York: Quorum Books, 1991). For a similar point of view, read the Volcker Commission Report, entitled, "The Report of the National Commission on the Public Service," *Leadership for America: Rebuilding the Public Service* (Lexington, Mass.: Lexington Books, 1990). Interestingly, it is perhaps the success of Japanese business in the 1980s that has brought renewed attention on the informal group as the basis for effective management by Americans, as reflected in such popular texts as William Ouchi, *Theory Z: How American Business Can Meet the Japanese Challenge* (New York: Avon Books, 1982). Note the heavy influence of Hawthorne thinking in this and other such writings about the Japanese success story.

CHAPTER 7

Key Decision Makers Inside Public Administration: The Concept of Competing Bureaucratic Subsystems

O ur public bureaucracy is composed of identifiable clusters of individuals who work and act in influential ways inside bureaucracy. Each of these subsystems shapes the broad outcomes of bureaucracy.

Richard J. Stillman II

Introduction

Nearly 5 million people work for the federal government, and another roughly 15 million are employed by state and local governments in the United States. They may be highway engineers who maintain or build our roads; police who patrol neighborhoods; public school teachers who educate children; or forest rangers who run the national park system. America's public service is composed of many types of people who perform the vital and varied activities of modern government.

How can we generalize about these public servants? Their characteristics? The roles they play inside bureaucracy? The work they perform? Their influence on the policies and activities of public agencies? Why do *they* so significantly shape "the outcomes" of modern bureaucracy?

In the following selection by the author of this text, drawn from his book *The American Bureaucracy,* he gives us something of "an X-Ray" picture of the inside of modern public bureaucracy. He argues that government is not made up of simply *one* monolithic body of employees but rather distinctive clusters of five varieties of personnel: political appointees, professional careerists, civil servant generalists, unionized workers, and contract employees. The author outlines the attributes of each group, which he labels "bureaucratic subsystems," the roles they play within public agencies, their origins and evolution, sources of recruitment, motivation(s), ladders for promotions, impacts on public policies, and issues or problems confronting each of these bureaucratic subsystems. The writer contends that the types of subsystems that make up the inside of any agency decisively influence the content of its work, direction of its policies, and decisions it makes—or fails to make. "The balance or imbalance of these groups," concludes Stillman, "within any agency is fundamental to its character, policies, and performance."

Rarely does just *one* subsystem comprise any public organization, but rather several of these bureaucratic subsystems are normally found within most modern public bureaucracies. Which one is in charge and how they work out their relationships becomes critical to understanding what happens in public administration. As Stillman writes: "Most bureaucracies in the public sector are, however, dominated not by any one subsystem but by several; indeed, all these subsystems normally are found within their structures. Hence, policy outcomes frequently result from their jockeying for position, influence, and power over public bureaucratic actions. Conflicts between subsystems are common. Sometimes the competion for power and control over the policy-making apparatus can be quite severe and intense."

As you read this selection, you might keep in mind:

Why does the author conclude that contemporary public bureaucracy is *not* composed of only *one* variety of public officials but rather five types? How does this argument compare or contrast with that of Weber in Chapter 2?

According to the author, how did each distinctive subsystem begin, evolve, grow within government, and develop unique value-orientations?

In what ways does each one contribute to influencing decisively the public policy process as well as the implementation of public policy?

How does the size, composition, and relationships of groups in bureaucracy influence its work and "impacts" on society as a whole?

Inside Public Bureaucracy

RICHARD J. STILLMAN II

Once a young aide to President William Howard Taft kept repeating the phrase "machinery of government" while briefing the president. Taft, so the story goes, became exasperated and turned to a friend and whispered, "My God, the man actually *believes* government is a machine!"

Taft had it right. United States government, especially its bureaucracy, is not an automated as-

sembly line, devoid of human beings, lifeless and machinelike. Quite to the contrary, our public bureaucracy is composed of identifiable clusters of individuals who work and act in influential ways inside the bureaucracy. Each of these subsystems shapes the broad outcomes of bureaucratic institutions. Each competes for power and influence over its particular bureaucracy. These human subsystems perform different tasks in government. Through diverse strategies they aim to achieve different goals with different stakes or outcomes for bureaucracy. Each serves vitally important functions within bureaucracy and significantly determines in various ways what bureaucracy does or does not do and how well it performs these functions. The size and influence of each of these human subgroups vary considerably from agency to agency and locale to locale. Yet many public organizations contain several of these subsystems. Some public operations have all five subsystems, which jockey with one another for influence and status.

The boundary between each of the subsystems is not always clear. They tend to overlap with considerable gray areas between them. Subsystems in different agencies do not always exhibit the same exact dimensions, proportions, or precisely similar characteristics. Nor are all five groups necessarily found in every agency. Sometimes only one or two are represented. In other words, these subsystems are fairly open, fluid, and adaptive to differing organizational contexts and situations. They are also fundamentally *human and political, not machinelike in behavior*. Subsystems do have certain important similarities and differences in their roles, values, missions, power, status, functions, activities, and influence within public organizations. This chapter will examine the special characteristics of each subsystem within organizations and particularly how they affect the outputs of every agency from the inside. Brief descriptions of these five subsystems follow.

Political appointees are those individuals who serve without tenure and whose appointments are based often, though not always, upon political ties or party loyalties.

Professional careerists are various groups of personnel with specialized expertise in specific fields. Positions occupied by these groups are usually based on advanced professional training. This subsystem offers lifetime careers and stresses "rank-in-person" rather than "rank-in-job."

The *general civil service* operates under "merit concepts." Characteristics of this subsystem are tenure, rank in-position, and "classified" hierarchies of positions based upon the amount of tasks and responsibilities.

Unionized workers are blue collar and, increasingly, white collar workers whose employment is based upon negotiated contracts between union representatives and management within the jurisdictions they serve.

Contractual employees are untenured workers whose employment with government is directly or indirectly governed by various contractual agreements negotiated with individuals, private firms, nonprofit organizations, and universities for rendering specific services for a limited or specified time. They are not governed by civil service rules nor do they work under union contracts.

The Political Appointee Subsystem: The Birds of Passage

Most political appointees fill the top-level policy-making posts within federal, state, and local bureaucracies. These men and women serve in government without tenure, holding office at the pleasure of the chief elected official, who hires them, promotes them, or dismisses them. At the federal level, political appointees make up a fairly small group, with only 5,823 out of approximately 3 million federal civilian workers. Federal political appointees are divided into three categories: (1) PASs, or presidential appointments with the consent of the Senate (663); PAs, or presidential appointments not requiring Senate confirmation (1405); and agency appointments, those made by the agency chief (1725). The number of PAS has remained fairly stable over the past two decades (roughly 660), but the number of noncareer SES and schedule C political appointees has grown significantly. The number and categories of political appointees vary considerably in state and local jurisdictions. In some regions where there is no civil service system—particularly rural county governments or the machine-run cities—virtually all government jobs are handed out on the basis of party loyalty or political patronage. Today, however, most cities and states follow the federal pattern in reserving only top-level policy jobs for political appointees, who serve at the pleasure of a governor or mayor. Particularly in "reformed" or "clean" city and state governments, these posts are few and limited to only the very top levels. Colorado, for example, has only two dozen political appointees out of 5,000 manager-level posts. However, in Massachusetts all of the managers' positions in the state, some 3,500 jobs down to the supervisor's level, are considered "policy-making" positions and are available for the governor's appointees. Thus the "range" is quite wide, depending on the influence of "reformism" found within the local/regional politics.

Within federal bureaucracies, in particular, appointees' lack of tenure limits the length of their employment. The average federal political appointee serves only twenty-two months in office. Hugh Heclo has rightly observed that they are "birds of passage"[1] who recognize from the start that they will not be around for very long. The most they can look forward to is a four-year term, and if a president is reelected (and they are lucky) they *might* be reappointed for longer periods—though that is rare. Transience is their only common trademark. Most, therefore, set their sights and adapt their behavior for the short range by recognizing that if they are to accomplish *anything* in their jobs, they must move quickly. Short-term horizons, limited goals, and quick results tend to characterize their actions. This tendency among political appointees also probably characterizes state and local appointees within jurisdictions where there is a competitive party system. But elsewhere, if the top jobs have little or no turnover, political appointees can look forward to longer tenure in office, thus shifting their time horizons to somewhat longer perspectives.

Generally, though, appointees' job uncertainty means that they have to have another position, outside of government, to fall back on in case they fall out of favor or out of office (a good possibility given the hazards of these untenured posts today). Hence, many political appointees at the federal level are drawn from law firms or are on leave from big businesses, government, or universities. The pool from which they are drawn is thus quite small and tends to be, but is not always, confined to upperclass individuals who can afford a short time away from their regular lines of work. This qualification also tends to drastically limit the social characteristics of political appointees to white, urban, middle-aged males with advanced Ivy League educations and ambitions for high-status careers.[2] While President Jimmy Carter attempted to recruit greater numbers of women and minorities into these posts, the bulk of political appointees even in his administration in the late 1970s, and of Ronald Reagan's in the 1980s, was largely drawn from this very small pool. However, in the 1990s President Bill Clinton drew his top appointees from a wider cross section of Americans. Historically, as law firms, businesses, and universities tended to become more representative, so too the "pool" of political appointees has tended to become more diverse and varied. Political appointees at the state and local levels, particularly as one moves closer to the grass roots, represent much more diversity in talent, training, income, and background. Generally, there is greater heterogeneity and better representation of social groups at lower governmental jurisdictions, though there is by no means a wide popular representation even there.[3]

While there are several prominent examples of political appointees whose faces reappear in government, usually at higher levels of bureaucracy when their party assumes office (George Shultz, James Baker, and Caspar Weinberger crop up repeatedly in Republican administrations, and William Perry and Warren Christopher in Democratic ones), most political appointees have limited backgrounds in government. Very few serve repeated spells in government; few work for more than one administration. Few survive election turnovers in the executive branch. Many simply do not want to stay more than a few years in office, nor can they, because of pressing outside professional or business commitments. Yet most are *drawn from and return to related fields of endeavor*. Western ranchers, businesspersons, and lawyers have tended to occupy the top slots at the Department of the Interior because of their prolonged involvement with western public lands; just as defense contractors, former military officers, and business executives have long been recruited to top political slots at DoD. And most return to these jobs afterwards. Thus different bureaucracies tend to draw their political appointees from different occupational-economic sectors of society as well as from different regions primarily because of these appointees' prior experience with the tasks and activities of the agency. An appropriate "track record" in the policy concerns of the agency, and the correct party identification, and especially policy positions that are in accord with the chief executive's, are important qualifications for such appointments.

Their specific policy roles in bureaucracy can be conceived of as loose-jointed, concentric rings that emanate outward from the office of the elected chief executive—a president, governor, or mayor. The most powerful appointees are those who occupy leadership roles within the major Cabinet-rank departments, sometimes referred to at the federal level as the inner Cabinet. The inner Cabinet is composed of the secretaries of Defense, State, and of the Office of Management and Budget, as well as senior noncareer or career ambassadors to major governments, such as Europe or China. These individuals are responsible for the operations of the largest public agencies (like DoD) and subsequently have powerful policy agenda-setting functions (like OMB). Similarly, inner Cabinets, made up of those closest to the governor or mayor and exercising major policy-organizational tasks, are found at state and local levels as well, though their titles differ. Inner Cabinet members at the federal level are often at the White House with the president or are representing their agencies before Congress. They are responsible for setting—and defending—the major policy priorities of the president and the agency they represent. They also exert the overall leadership within their particular organization, appoint numerous political personnel within the organization, and represent it before the media and special interest groups. Their most important function within government is to translate the campaign platforms and promises of the elected officials into administrative actions of major policy-administrative importance to the chief executive—the president, governor, or mayor. In short, they serve as linchpins between election-night rhetoric and actual institutional performance.

The next ring, or the outer Cabinet, is composed of men and women who see the president (or governor or mayor) less frequently but nevertheless hold Cabinet rank (also normally requiring Senate or legislative confirmation). They are frequently charged with running a major public agency such as the Department of Housing and Urban Development or the Department of Corrections at the state level. They are a rung below the inner Cabinet in *informal* power and status only, for their legal titles and prerogatives are normally much the same as those of their counterparts in the inner Cabinet. Indeed, they may have many of the same responsibilities, such as directing a large department, providing its leadership, setting its policy agenda, defending it before Congress, and so on.

The third level is generally termed the sub-Cabinet. It is composed of deputy secretaries, assistant secretaries, and administrative heads of major non-Cabinet agencies and bureaus. These individuals also occupy important policy-making posts, and sometimes highly sensitive and critical ones, such as that of deputy attorney general in the Department of Justice, who is normally responsible for the daily management of the department's activities, or of the assistant secretary for International Security Affairs in the Department of Defense who is charged with shaping broad strategic policies within DoD. These men and women are generally more specialized in particular fields of expertise than the inner or outer Cabinet members. While they may have had a variety of experiences and backgrounds in government, business, law, or the professions, their training and work experiences tend to be more appropriate to the positions that they occupy. They have also usually had considerable experience handling political issues related to these offices and are expected to take positions on these issues in accordance with the president's overall priorities.

Given the increasing proliferation of special interest groups that watch closely these sub-Cabinet appointments and their pronouncements, key sub-Cabinet officials, at least during the last few years, are often drawn from the ranks of special interest groups and return to these after government service. Democrats tend to draw their appointees from left-leaning policy groups, while Republicans draw theirs from think tanks, legislative staffs, and policy-advocate groups on the right-wing.

Yet some scholars, such as Thomas P. Murphy, Donald E. Nuechterlein, and Ronald Stupak, have argued that the influence of this group of appointees over the policy-making process has declined in recent years, because of its increase in number.[4] Though as a collective group, their prominence and power has on the whole increased in recent years; a modified Gresham's law operates here; that is, increasing numbers of political appointees at this sub-Cabinet level drive down their individual influence over policy decisions. Put simply: a call from an assistant secretary does not mean what it once did.

The fourth group of appointees encompasses a wide variety of advisors to the secretary and directors of agencies and bureaus. Like the previous level of appointees, this level has expanded enormously in the past two decades as secretaries brought in their own people to help run their departments. At the federal level these assorted political appointees do not require Senate confirmation, so for the most part their ranks have grown without legislative oversight and control. Few, however, are active politicians or were closely involved with the election campaign of the chief executive. Most are more directly identified with the professional or policy issues of the agencies where they work. Many have had personal ties or friendships with their immediate supervisors. They are generally reputed to be experts in the field of law, business, or education and may have actually been

drawn from the ranks of the civil service. Some have known or worked with each other before or fought the opposition party together over the very sets of policy issues they are now actively administering and formulating.

Compared with appointees at other levels, these men and women are the most expert and specialized, and they are often more willing to push forward the interests of their particular agencies and resist political intrusions from others. And yet as Frederick Mosher has observed of these appointees: "Some are eminent figures in their fields, often principal representatives and defenders of the services which they superintend. Yet their stance differs from that of the members of the permanent services below them. They *can* be replaced or their situations can be made so uncomfortable as to induce them to resign or at least alter their behavior."[5] Their lack of tenure is the heavy stick that ensures their ultimate responsiveness to higher circles of appointees.

Finally, there is an increasingly large group of individuals in public bureaucracy today who occupy a limbo-land between quasipolitical and nonpolitical territory. Their position at the federal level has been institutionalizd through the creation of the Senior Executive Service (SES) in the 1978 Civil Service Reform Act.

SES developed a new category of upper-level administrators that is formed from supergrade officials in grades GS-16, 17, and 18 and in Executive Ranks IV and V, in which position assignments and pay are determined by political decision makers and yet are also protected by the civil service rules (career officials in SES have the option of retreating to GS-15 grades). The rationale for creating SES came mainly from argument that improved management in government could result from greater mobility of its top executives. Drawn from senior career ranks, it was argued that like in business, the president and top executives should be able to shift senior managers from one post to another more easily than the hide-bound civil service rules allowed prior to 1978. Further, as in the case of business, bonus incentives were provided for rewarding outstanding performances in SES.

On the other hand, unsatisfactory performances could cause removal or replacement in SES. By law, the bulk of these individuals must be drawn from the ranks of the civil service, since only 10 percent of SES members (or 703 of the current 8,130 SES employees) can be political appointees. About 40 percent of SES positions are designated as "career reserved" because of their sensitive positions. The number of SES positions has grown since 1980 but so has the number of noncareer or political-appointee positions.

While the jury is still out on whether or not the introduction of SES has proven successful, it remains a *potentially* important tool for improving federal management and control.

On the state level, twelve states have created SES systems. Four did so prior to the 1978 CSRA: California (1963), Minnesota (1969), Wisconsin (1973), and Oregon (1977). After the creation of the federal level SES, several states adopted their own SES systems shortly afterwards: Connecticut (1979), Florida (1980), Iowa (1980), Michigan (1980), Washington (1980), and Pennsylvania (1981). Both Tennessee and New Jersey passed their SES legislation in 1986, and Massachusetts gave the governor statutory authority to set up a senior career management system, which has not yet been implemented. While the state-level SES systems, like the federal-level one, offer *potentially* enhanced career mobility, managerial control, and leadership flexibility, as Sherwood and Breyer suggest in their evaluation of state-level SES systems: "Little in the twenty-four-year history of executive personnel systems in the states suggests that they have come to occupy a highly significant role in the processes of governance."[6]

Why the disappointing performance of state-level SES systems? According to Deborah D. Roberts, "State SES systems contain too many lofty and contradictory goals that cannot all be satisfied. These contradictions revolve around incentives, membership quandaries, and diversity among the important players." Due to such challenging contradictions, according to Professor Roberts, existing state SES systems "are undergoing painful retrenchment and redirection, and few states appear willing to adopt new SES initiatives."[7]

To sum up the influence of the political appointee subsystem: First, these individuals occupy the highest, most prominent posts within public organizations. Thus, they serve as linchpins between campaign promises and bureaucratic performance. However, they are characterized overall as a highly diverse, fragmented, and transitory group with little cohesiveness.

Second, their influence within bureaucracy depends upon the policy positions they hold, the length of their government service, their connections with top elected officials, their own personalities, their support from outside groups, the immediate tasks at hand, and whether these lend themselves to imminent solutions. Generally, as one moves up the hierarchy of political officials to the inner Cabinet, these individuals have the most generalized backgrounds, and must deal with the broadest, most critical policy issues. They also exercise the widest, most influential policy roles inside public bureaucracy, if their tenure is long enough and their external support adequate to the performance of the tasks at hand. Here at the top the political winds blow the fiercest; the "turf battles" are the most intense, and the stakes are the highest.

Third, as one moves down the hierarchy of these political officials toward those of quasi-political status, greater degrees of specialization are found as well as more identification with the programmatic goals, tasks, and issues within the agencies they serve. They are less generalist in outlook and more concerned with pushing narrower policy agendas, which often means they are less interested in and responsive to their own chief's reelection priorities.

Fourth, sharp turf fights over policy issues therefore ensue frequently between these various levels of political appointees, largely because of the different perspectives built into their hierarchical roles. Here is where pitched policy battles frequently occur and are resolved. In the pecking order of appointees, those at or near the top push agendas that are broader and more responsive to the chief executive's agenda, while those lower down tend to be more programmatic and responsive to the priorities and issues of the particular agencies in which they work.

Fifth, while the subsystem of political appointees is highly fragmented, these tend to cluster into networks in which those near the top have close personal ties, even long friendships, with the chief elected official (though not necessarily with each other, nor are they necessarily active in his political campaigns). Those on the lower rungs tend to be experts in particular fields and to have personal networks that run downward into the agency and outward into various external support groups associated with an agency's mission.

Sixth, what draws all appointees together and keeps them loyal and responsible, at least to some degree, to the elected official's policy agenda (and makes them a distinct bureaucratic subsystem) is the fact that they can be removed or transferred at any time by a president, governor, or mayor. Fear of losing a job can be a powerful incentive to stay in line with the top-level agenda, or at least to refrain from stating opposing views in public.

However, in this constantly shifting world of personnel and goals, as Norton Long pointed out, determining to whom one is loyal and what one should accomplish become difficult if not impossible tasks. This level in bureaucracy is an ambiguous world in which appearances frequently count more than on-the-job practices. Participants thus spend enormous amounts of time posturing and posing in order to appear to do the correct things for the right people and taking readings and soundings to find information about their own status and about the intentions of others. The closed door, an invitation to the right party, the frequency of meetings with the superior, and the seating arrangement at the conference table often signal more than the untrained eye can perceive or the written document explain. Hard-driving, ambitious men and women, even with considerable experience and exposure, become quickly frustrated and disillusioned with the confusion and pretense inherent in this subsystem, as autobiographies of recent incumbents testify. Policy activity at this level

of bureaucracy is very much like the greased pole competition at the old-fashioned county fair, where few, if any, climb to the top and reach the prize. The way up is slippery, uncertain, and treacherous, often crowded with many other frenzied competitors. There are no sure rules for success. And the prize, once reached, is often temporary, of little value, and hardly worth all that fierce competition and furiously expended energy. Many leave disillusioned and despairing about what they have done or failed to do. Good luck rather than personal skills often decides outcomes.

Seventh, political appointees, despite the highly ambiguous world in which they operate, ultimately are central to the governing processes at all levels of government. They are critical, individually and collectively, in the words of presidential scholar James P. Pfiffner, to assist chief executives in "hitting the ground running." But high job demands, family stress, extensive security checks, comparatively low pay (by contrast to other similarly responsible private-sector jobs), and detailed public and press scrutiny all combine to deter many from seeking such lines of work and to delay appointments. Indeed, President Clinton was slower than his recent predecessors in getting his own policy team in place, leading to criticism of Clinton's capacity to govern effectively.

The Professional Careerist Subsystem: Permanent Clusters of Powerful Experts

Professor Samuel H. Beer has said that U.S. society is governed by "technocratic politics" in which specialists with in-depth training and experience in different fields of government have assumed the duty of charting the course of various public organizations. As Beer argues:

I would remark how rarely additions to the public agenda have been initiated by the demands of voters or the advocacy of pressure groups or the platforms of political parties. On the contrary, in the fields of health, housing, urban renewal, transportation, welfare, education, poverty and energy, it has been in very great measure, people in government service or closely associated with it acting on the basis of their specialties and technical knowledge who first perceived the problem, conceived the program, initially urged it on the President and Congress, went on to help lobby it through to enactment and then saw to its administration.[8]

Some scholars, including Zbigniew Brzezinski, have called the phenomenon "the technetronic age"; Don Price calls it "the scientific estate"; for Daniel Bell it is "the post-industrial age"; for Guy Benveniste, "the politics of expertise."[9] But whatever term is used to describe the role of experts within government, the professional strata, a subsystem below that of political appointees, is now recognized by many scholars as a significant influence over the activities of modern public organizations. As Frederick C. Mosher has perceptively written, "For better or worse—or better and worse—much of government is now in the hands of professionals (including scientists). The choice of these professionals, the determination of their skills and the content of their work are now principally determined not by the general government agencies, but by their own professional elites, professional organizations and the institutions and facilities of higher education. It is unlikely the trend toward professionalization in or outside government will be reversed or even slowed."[10]

Professionalization in government influenced not only the domestic agenda, as Beer suggests, but also how we viewed our broad global responsibilities in the post–World War II era. According to Robert D. Kaplan:

The global responsibilities thrust upon the United States after World War II led to the creation of area experts in government, academia, and think tanks. Their effect on policy and public opinion has been to splinter and compartmentalize what used to be geographic wholes. The academic and policy-making nomenklatura

invented a new world based not on real borders so much as on the borders of their knowledge or lack thereof. As someone who has written extensively about Turkey and the Balkans, as well as the Middle East, I have seen how these areas constitute two entirely different subcultures of Washington society and workdom, with little or no cross-fertilization between the two.[11]

The development of professional control over the inner dynamics of U.S. bureaucracy came slowly and in piecemeal fashion, mostly in the twentieth century. Some agencies, such as DoJ, have since their inception been dominated by lawyers, but professionally trained lawyers with LL.B. degrees, steeped in learning, responsive to the American Bar Association's policy concerns. Specialists in highly diverse elements of the law did not appear at DoJ in any sizable numbers until the New Deal in the 1930s. Military officers held the top army posts from the time the War Department was established in 1789, but even throughout most of the nineteenth century officers were poorly trained and politically motivated amateurs with little or no technical competency (except for those trained as engineers at West Point).

The modern generalist-professional cadre of officers did not appear until after 1900, established largely through the reforms of secretary of war Elihu Root, who created the Army General Staff, a unified personnel system, as well as a series of advanced professional educational institutions for military officers. The Rogers Act of 1924 instituted what we now know as the professional foreign service, but the dominance of quality foreign service professionals such as George Kennan and Charles Bohlen throughout key State Department slots did not emerge until after World War II.

Likewise, the professional control of state and local agencies in many regions began at roughly the turn of the century with the formation of small, fledgling professional associations such as the International Association of Chiefs of Police (1893), the International Association of Fire Chiefs (1893), the American Society of Municipal Engineers (1894), the Municipal Finance Officers Association

(1906), the National Recreation Association (1906), the National Association of Public School Business Officials (1910), the National Organization for Public Health Nursing (1912), and the City Managers' Association (1914).

As Robert Wiebe observes of the process of grassroots professionalization in America:

Social workers . . . acted first to dissociate themselves from philanthropy and establish themselves as a distinct field within the new social sciences. Beginning with local leagues in Boston and New York, they had formed the National Federation of Settlements by 1911 and soon after captured the old National Conference of Charities and Corrections, renaming it the National Conference of Social Work. Also early in the century, they moved from ad hoc classes of special training to complete professional schools within such universities as Chicago and Harvard.[12]

The Federal government also had an important hand in stimulating professionalism at the state and local levels. For example, again in the area of social work, Martha Derthick writes:

Congress in 1939 gave the Social Security Board authority to set personnel standards, perhaps because it was sympathetic to some degree of professionalism in the performance of public administration (on the assumption that it would lead to "efficiency") if not in the performance of social work. Even before this was done, the Board was demanding—on the basis of its authority to require efficient administration—that state plans include minimum standards for education, training, and experience (for local social workers).[13]

In many respects, at the local level and to a great extent at the federal level as well, professionalism was a means of battling "corruption as well as inefficiency," as Jeremy F. Plant and David S. Arnold point out: "Professionalism had to pervade the entire fabric of modern government," at least in the eyes of reformers who sought better government.[14] But, for the most part, until after World War II these professional groups were weak and ineffective voluntary associations exercising little control over the inner dynamics of local public bureaucracy. The postwar era, however, brought into grass-roots and higher-level government an influx of university-educated specialists with wide assortments of technical competence. The postwar era also brought about a new respect for and demand for these specialists to deal with a myriad of technical tasks from constructing highways, educating children, cleaning air and water, and administering complex regulatory machinery—often spawned by the professionals themselves—for certifying and controlling the application of skills inside and outside government. Today professional public official associations are extensive and varied, exercising hidden yet pervasive influence over government policy through certification, training, setting ethical standards, and playing policy advocacy roles within their specialized fields.

Professionals in government today, however, by no means make up a monolithic group or a homogeneous mass of experts; indeed, they differ considerably from one another. Directly under political appointees, *professional elites* comprise the core group of experts. These are the senior and most prestigious and respected members of the profession. They give not only internal direction to the profession but also to the entire agency by controlling the important positions and advancement to those positions and by setting recruitment and entrance requirements as well as overall personnel policies and priorities for the organization. Rising to these posts is achieved only through long-term career investment in the field, attendance at the "right" schools for basic and advanced training in the field, and advancement through progressive levels of responsibility and prominence in areas closely identified with the central concerns of the agency. Pilots in the air force, line officers in the navy, doctors in the U.S. Public Health Service, foresters in the U.S. Forest Service, senior staff lawyers at DoJ, and top-ranking educators in local school systems or in state departments of education tend to fill the elite slots within their respective agencies.

"Status" at times becomes an obsession with professionals. Knowing where one is or is not or how to advance "in the pecking order" of influence is important to most professionals. The registered nurse is considered an elite within that cluster of professionals. And not only is certification as an RN increasingly important to a nurse's elite status today, further certification within a very narrow specialized field within which she or he works, such as emergency room, orthopedic care, or surgery room practice, is also desirable. The continuous specialization of those who are already specialists within government is staggering.

The elites, in turn, within these various strata of professional clusters, provide the leadership as well as set the work standards, the qualifications for entrance and advancement, and the overall values for the profession. Much of the critical tensions and conflicts between clusters of professional elites are over policy questions and control of turf—between doctors and nurses in hospitals or between air force, army, navy, and marine corps top-ranking officers within DoD. Much of this conflict is hidden from public view. Rarely does it become public, because it can most often be settled between the competing parties or by political superiors. But at times internal dissent can become so strained that work production slows and the mission of the unit becomes jeopardized.

Line professionals, who fall just below the level of the senior elites, actually carry out the day-to-day functions of the public agency. Whereas a few dozen three- and four-star generals compose the army's top professional elite, more than 200,000 army officers from second lieutenants to generals direct much of the real work of the army in a wide variety of combat and noncombat jobs. Some, given their West Point training and combat duties in the infantry, armor, or artillery (combat sections that are considered "ideal" rungs in the ladder to the level of the elite) may become part of the professional elite; others in the line may have neither the interest nor the proper backgrounds to attain those high level assignments. The line officers are essentially the "doing" and "implementing" functionaries of bureaucracy and are most directly associated with the central missions of an agency.

Staff professionals in public agencies include a wide assortment of specialists and technical assistants who have unique and specialized expertise that may not be directly connected with the central tasks of the agency but are nonetheless critical to carrying out its assigned functions. Today almost every public bureaucracy employs a wide array of these individuals. They assume the critical advisory roles within an agency and in some government offices also frequently assume large and powerful policy roles, even though they are not directly in either the line or the elite ranks. In every federal department, the legal counsels, for example, not only can command high salaries, large staffs, exemptions from civil service hiring rules, and the ear of the top brass in the agency, but also frequently exercise enormous yet quiet influence over central policies of an agency through knowledge and expertise in the law (and often this advice is quite conservative in nature—more "don'ts" than "dos"). The top political and professional cadre yield to such legal policy advice on technical matters because no one else can supply this knowledge (or if the advice is purchased at high cost from outside law firms). One only need attend a city council or county board of supervisors' meeting to watch the frequency with which elected members turn to legal counsel for assistance or to view federal organization charts to discover the strategic positions legal counsels occupy in most departments.

Administrative professionals comprise an assortment of budget officials; program officers; planning personnel; and finance, purchasing, auditing, and supply officials found in every public organization (the G-1 through G-5 jobs in the U.S. military). These men and women are critical to the activities of the agency because they essentially serve as "the directing brain" of the organization ("the directing brain" is Elihu Root's name for this group in his 1902 proposal for the creation of a general staff in the U.S. Army, which was a pattern copied by other public agencies and business corporations). In larger organizations some of these slots are temporarily held by line professionals, but many are filled by permanent careerists from emerging professional groups, such as budgeting, personnel, and purchasing specialists. While these individuals do not as yet rank as full-fledged professionals, they are increasingly taking on all the trappings of professionals, having their own associations, journals, "ideal career tracks," and educational requirements. Some even command higher salaries and status than their professional superiors. Municipal budget officers, for example, today are sometimes paid higher salaries than their bosses, city managers, or chief administrative officers, because of their critical budget and finance expertise in municipal decision-making processes.

In the uncertain environment within which agencies must operate, staff professionals must be adaptive and inventive in coping with the changing needs of their agencies. Much of their work is simply "fire-fighting" in order to maintain their structure amid turbulence, but much also is directed at thinking about the future of the organization, even if this planning is only incrementally achieved through short-term budgets, ad hoc personnel recruitment and selection, and partial programmatic design or redesign.

Finally, *paraprofessionals* make up another group increasingly seen within public agencies. These people receive substantially lower remunerative rewards for their work, although many units of government simply could not perform their assigned tasks without them. Many of these "paras" aspire to becoming full-fledged professionals in the field and use the experience as apprenticeship training. Others see this line of work as a rewarding lifetime career and seek no higher positions. From the standpoint of government, however, these workers are taking on increasing responsibility in various offices because of the rising costs of hiring fully qualified professionals. In other words, using paras is an effective governmental strategy for keeping down rapidly escalating personnel costs. In many cases paras perform the work as well as, if not better than, their highly

paid counterparts. In this respect, their primary roles inside public organizations may well be an important economic function.

On the whole, what can be said about the influence of all the professional subsystems upon the activities and outputs of public bureaucratic institutions?

First and foremost, they are essential to the performance of the central missions of virtually every public agency. They define its mission, decide how it should be accomplished and who should accomplish it, as well as when it should be accomplished and where.

Second, by comparison with top-level political appointees, professionals by and large have longevity within agencies, thus giving them an enormous edge in the policy-making processes.

Third, professionals are not a single, unified group. They are part of a well-established pecking order, from elites down to "paras," that is based on education, skills, seniority, levels of responsibility, and general competence and experience. Elites occupy the highest level of policy-making roles; line professionals shape actions mainly through implementation practices; staff professionals fill advisory roles; administrative professionals prepare and plan tasks; and paraprofessionals carry out lower-level and lower-cost work.

Fourth, continuing political strength and popular support of professionals ultimately rest upon their recognized expertise and competence as well as on their ability to exercise these skills in a regular, uniform manner in the public interest. The widespread popularity of city-manager government rests fundamentally on its ability to apply systematic expertise to urban issues at the local level. Since expertise is professionals' stock in trade and is a source of authority and of legitimacy within government, a great deal of their efforts are directed at higher education and improving professionals' reputation for competence and application of knowledge. Professionals look to institutions of higher learning to sustain and enrich their knowledge base through training programs that give the professionals their credentials, and nurture the fundamental ethos and values of the profession. If political appointees draw support from their elected chiefs, professionals in government conversely derive their legitimacy from expertise acquired through higher education. The content and perspectives of these sources of learning influence the long-term priorities and fundamental value of professions. Hence, professions pay enormous attention to the shaping of professional education programs, examinations, accreditation, and licensing processes that help to determine the nature and content of professional work, as well as the knowledge and skill it requires.

Fifth, professionals influence policies not only by contributing a substantial share of the public work force and its top leadership cadre but also by moving upward and outward beyond the contours of their roles within agencies. As noted in the discussion of political appointees, they frequently assume temporary assignments at this level. Similarly, the influence of professionals is moving increasingly outward into legislative staff assignments or related nonprofit or business firms that directly and indirectly influence the course of bureaucratic policies.

Finally, the most serious tensions and conflicts within public organizations are generally hidden from view, since they arise mainly from policy disputes *between* clusters of key professionals and not as much from disputes between professional elites and political superiors. Many top political appointees today look highly professional, indeed *are drawn* from professional cadres, thus the tensions between political appointees and careerists are not as sharp and long-term compared to those *between* professional groups. Fights between the army, navy, and air force over defense appropriations and priorities are a permanent part of the Washington landscape, but it is within these professional service battles that defense policies for DoD develop. Likewise, the typical controversies that occur at the grass roots between police and firefighters over annual budget appropriations, length of work day, and salary increases figure equally prominently in determining the directions of local public safety policies.

The General Civil Service Subsystem: Ladders of Bureaucratic Specialists, Generalists, and Workers

While bits and pieces of the "ideal professional model" are being incorporated gradually into the general civil service, the bulk of government personnel are members of civil service and do not share in the professional model. Civil service is founded on the merit system, whereby positions are assigned on the basis of open, competitive examinations (written and/or oral) and candidates are evaluated and ranked in relationship to particular task requirements of a specific job. Generally, selection is made from among the top three scorers. Unlike the professional subsystem, civil service has no progressive job planning or control by elites but has, rather, a laissez-faire approach in which each individual seeks out and designs his or her own path within the system. Advanced training may or may not be essential. Rank is inherent in the job, not the person. Meeting the specific task requirements of the job is what counts most in landing a slot in civil service. Status, in turn, is derived from the specific job. A GS-9 civil servant, for instance, is a GS-9 because he or she holds that slot. If the employee leaves it, he or she is no longer a GS-9, unlike an air force colonel, who is a colonel wherever he or she serves. In the professional subsystem, conversely, rank inheres in the person, not the job.

The civil service subsystem was grafted onto U.S. bureaucracy somewhat haphazardly almost a century after the creation of the Republic. Even today its "fit" into government seems somewhat awkward and unsure. For the most part, this uncertainty about its place in U.S. public bureaucracy is caused by, as many scholars have noted, the growth of the general civil service out of a reaction to the excesses of the nineteenth-century spoils system, in which employment in public service was based largely, though not entirely, upon party loyalty and political patronage. In other words, it was built on a negative moral reaction to what was perceived as "evil" rather than on a positive and deliberate design.

The story of its growth is long and complex. To sum it up, in the late 1860s and throughout the 1870s a small band of reformers waged aggressive moral and political campaigns on behalf of civil service reform and against incompetence, graft, favoritism, and partisanship within the public service. Merit, they argued, should be the basis of appointment. Substantially modeled on the English civil service system, which had been in operation for nearly a half-century and was adapted to special pragmatic U.S. needs and concerns, the Civil Service Act (Pendleton Act) was enacted in 1883 mainly as a national reaction to the shooting of President James Garfield by a political supporter who had been refused a small patronage post.[15]

Pendleton became the classic model for "good personnel practices" throughout the nation. Extended gradually through executive order to cover increasing percentages of federal workers, it was also copied almost word for word by numerous states and localities. Localities borrowed from it their basic structural arrangements and concepts of merit processes, such as notions of a nonpartisan commission appointed by the chief executive to oversee the system, requirements of open, competitive examinations, probationary period prior to tenure, strict provision against political interference within civil service activities, classification of positions, and equal pay for equal work.

On the state level, New York passed a civil service law the same year as the federal government, and Massachusetts passed one the following year. Much of the civil service movement came in fits and starts. Some states, like Texas, never adopted a civil service system, and others like Virginia, recently abandoned the system entirely. Municipalities likewise moved to developed civil service systems, and most large cities by 1940 had some kind of merit system in place. Counties, though, have remained more backward; relatively few have merit systems in place.

The impetus for adoption of state/local merit systems came from essentially three forces. One was local and state reform groups that saw "merit"

as a method of improving economy and efficiency in government and ridding government of corrupt political machines; another was the federal government, which played a major role in the adoption of grassroots civil service systems. The Social Security Act of 1935 and its 1940 amendments required state and local government employees administering health, welfare, and employment programs funded by the federal government to be covered by merit systems. The Intergovernmental Personnel Act (IPA) of 1970 further spurred local merit system development through its various programs to upgrade public personnel systems and employee skills. Finally, Supreme Court decisions played a major role, especially in limiting patronage systems. In such cases as *Elrod v. Burns* (1976) and *Branti v. Finkel* (1980), the Court struck down patronage practices involving the firing of nonpolicy-making, nonconfidential employees.

The federal civil service work force has stayed fairly constant in size over the past forty years, but the local and state work force has grown, nearly tripling during the same period. In fact, the federal share of the public work force fell from 27.7 percent of the total in 1961 to 16.2 percent in 1992. Also, the distribution of the federal work force shows certain regional biases; a higher percentage (32 percent) is located in the South, compared to 17 percent of the total civilian work force.

Today, 91 percent of the federal civilian work force, or approximately 3 million workers, are covered under civil service personnel rules. While several structural and procedural adaptations over time have been added, such as the Civil Service Reform Act of 1978, its essential concepts of "merit," "open, competitive examinations," and "equal pay for equal work" remain intact. Patricia W. Ingraham and David H. Rosenbloom summed up the current status of "merit" on the federal level: "While there continues to be strong support for the fundamental principles of merit, dissatisfaction with and confusion about the current system is high." They cited the complexity of regulations, the lack of training and trust of agency personnel dealing with civil service provisions, the absence of a clear definition of "merit" or of guidance for achieving a quality work force as critical problems.[16]

Even though a considerable diversity in civil service laws is found across the United States, in those areas of the public service covered by its practices scholars have discovered several common characteristics: First, the U.S. civil servant is largely representative of the general population. Repeated studies have indicated that civil service members—unlike political appointees or upper-level professionals—are broadly reflective of the American people's education, income, social status, age, and geographic backgrounds. Though these representational attributes appear in the aggregate—that is, when the entire public service is viewed statistically—they tend to break down in the various particular units or levels of government. Women are predominant in the bottom ranks as well as in certain fields such as nursing and teaching but are small minorities in police, fire, or other traditionally male occupational roles. Blacks and other minorities have made impressive gains in recent years in all areas of the public service, but the upper ranks still tend to be heavily representative of white males.

Members of the general civil service subsystem generally lack the cohesiveness and unity found among professionals. When asked what she or he does, the typical bureaucrat will say, "I work at the Office of Education" or "I'm with the County Sheriff's Department." Few are likely to see themselves in broader terms and to say, "I'm a bureaucrat" or "I work for the civil service." Whether because of the pejorative connotations attached to government work or the more personal attachment to a particular assigned task, most bureaucrats lack common ties with government as a whole or with the broad *public orientation* of their work. This phenomenon no doubt exists in the private sector as well, where few business people see themselves as dedicated to the free market, but rather perceive themselves as real estate agents, autobody repairmen, or retail sales clerks. Most are like civil servants, who identify with the agency or skill at which they work or with the people with whom

they work. The grand design of the organization or the broad purposes of their occupation generally elude their interests or understanding.

This lack of common ties to the broad aspects and purposes of government may in large part be caused by the general lack of mobility within the civil service. In theory, the civil service subsystem provides for open, competitive exams that permit advancement into every level or part of government (though restricted to particular federal, state, or local jurisdictions). In practice, however, most civil servants spend their working lives within one agency. Eugene B. MacGregor, Jr., who studied the mobility of civil servants at the GS-14 level and above, discovered an average of seventeen to twenty-five years of service in the same agency or department.[17] Civil servants' depth of policy understanding, long-term views of issues, and particular expertise in an agency is therefore unmatched by comparison with those of transitory political appointees, who last in a post a mere twenty-two months at the federal level. Their longevity in an agency, expertise, sheer numbers, and longer time perspectives also make civil servants the core of modern bureaucracy.

So far, this discussion has pointed up several salient features of the civil service subsystem—its representational attributes as a whole, yet its uniquely unrepresentative elements in agencies or levels within the hierarchy: its lack of cohesiveness; its absence of mobility; its emphasis on rank inherent in the job; its diversity of jobs; the long-term career perspectives of its members; and its function as "the reservoir" of government expertise. Given these attributes, it is especially difficult to generalize about its influence on "bureaucratic outputs." As one veteran of government service says, "Civil servants don't really have mutual bonds or ties. There's nothing in particular in common except that these are people who know all the angles about how government works."[18]

Such seasoned cynicism, however, may obscure some of this subsystem's fundamental influences on bureaucratic activities. For one thing, as has already been emphasized, civil servants generally take the longer view of issues, problems, events, and actions, at least by comparison with political appointees (though they share this attribute with professional careerists). Their tenured positions make them somewhat more immune to the need for "quick fixes" or "instant results," compared with their politically driven bosses, who often see no further than the next election. For the most part, permanent bureaucrats realize that much that passes for "instant success" is ephemeral and that any real achievements in government come only in the long haul, after much struggle and persistence. Their view of what constitutes real, enduring change is therefore fundamentally different from the view of political appointees and leads to a much more realistic, conservative approach based upon recognition of the worth of incrementalism; namely that small steps taken over a long period of time will lead to permanent, solid achievements. This strategy of gradualism can be the source of exasperation and deep conflicts between civil servants and endless successions of political appointees, who normally want government to accomplish this or that task immediately, even yesterday. In particular, appointees in recent administrations who are fired up to make speedy changes and who have had little exposure to the realities of government find this philosophy of incrementalism frustrating. It quickly becomes the butt of their jokes about those "damn bureaucrats." These negative references symbolize the radically different time zones within which each subsystem operates. Their different "internal clocks" influence the basically different approaches to handling issues.

Also unlike political appointees, civil servants are restrained by the Hatch Act, and various "little Hatch Acts" that operate on state and local levels, from going public with their political opinions or policy views. Occasionally it may happen that dissent leaks out in the press, but active campaigning is expressly forbidden by law. Hence, civil servants generally must be discreet and work behind the scenes in dealing with the development, formulation, and implementation of policy questions. They realize that a head-on frontal assault on policy issues will only get them into needless politi-

cal controversy. Experience over the years has taught them that those sorts of political firestorms are to be avoided at all costs; they waste time and energy and lead to few tangible results. As a result, on the whole they favor quiet discretion in handling problems.

This cautious attitude comes not merely from pragmatism in effecting programmatic change but also from fear about long-term personal survival. In a world of endlessly shifting political appointees, the civil servant, at least in the top ranks, knows quite well that job security depends on his or her not being too closely allied with any one political party, else he or she become "politically tainted" and shunned by the next group taking office. The desire to stay neutral from the political appointee subsystem and to work quietly from the inside, at least for most top-level civil servants, springs from a very fundamental interest in long-term survival.

Unlike the professional careerist, on the other hand, the general civil servant operates *without* the control of a professional elite and without an extensive mutual support network of peers with status in the subsystem. In the civil service subsystem, every employee charts his or her own way through the bureaucracy. The hazards are many and the minefields often hard to locate. Thus much of their time is spent networking outward and downward into the bureaucracy, building personal bridges and personal friendships inside and outside agencies in order to develop the myriad horizontal and vertical contacts that are necessary for gaining information, accurately assessing the landscape, and making alliances in this hazardous, uncertain, and lonely bureaucratic world.

These clusters of civil servants influence public policies through the social networks they have established over long periods, running in strange and uncharted pathways that run through an agency and outside into other unlikely agencies and even beyond government where information is swapped informally and ideas are traded within social contexts. When presidents complain about government leaking like a sieve, this is why. The informal group, as Elton Mayo and the Hawthorne researchers discovered long ago, operates with a similar potency in government and in business settings, though it is well hidden in the civil service.

What challenges are facing the civil service subsystem as a whole? Three significant task force reports have appeared in recent years examining civil service performance and making numerous recommendations for reform: *Civil Service 2000,*[19] a 1988 study prepared by the Hudson Institute on the federal public service; also at the federal level, *Leadership for America,*[20] a 1989 privately sponsored review, called "The Volcker Commission" in honor of its chair, former Federal Reserve chairman Paul A. Volcker; and at the state and local levels, *Hard Truths/Tough Choices,*[21] a 1993 "Winter Commission" report, named for its chair, former Governor William F. Winter. These studies drew upon some of the most talented expertise from a wide cross section of business, nonprofit, and government to analyze many of the present problems facing America's public service. Collectively, they offered numerous suggestions for improvement. While these reports are too complicated to be summarized in any concise way, overall they found no simple solutions for reforming civil service subsystems, but each one stressed important issues needing attention:

1. *Poor public image:* The Volcker Commission placed the first priority on dealing with the poor public image of the federal civil service. The report repeatedly cited data and examples of the low esteem that Americans had for public service. These negative perceptions led, in the Commission's thinking, to a general distrust of government and to its broader incapacity to function effectively and recruit capable candidates to serve in government. The Commission surveyed, for example, 403 of the "best and brightest" college graduates who accepted employment and found only 16 percent chose positions in government (and half of those who selected public employment were graduates of public administration programs). Big businesses, small businesses, and academic institutions were preferred by a wide margin, leading to the conclusion that "the public service cannot compete for top graduates." Thus, this report laid stress upon targeting the recruitment of a better pool of candidates.

2. *Competence crisis:* Similarly, the Hudson Institute study's key findings and recommendations centered upon the "competency crisis" facing the federal public service. *Civil Service 2000* argued that there was a rising need for "a highly educated-skilled work force," yet attacting these workers in the 1990s "will become much more difficult." Recruitment is a problem, especially in high-wage locales such as New York City and in those top civil service grades, above GS-9 in which "the gap between top federal personnel civil service salaries and comparable private salaries was an average of 24 percent.

3. *Removing barriers to a high performance work force:* On the state and local levels, the Winter Commission Report, by contrast, focused on the problems of "the highly fragmented local structures that impeded executive leadership and performance of the grassroots civil service systems." At the outset of the Winter Report, the priority was seen to:
Give leaders the authority to act. Put them in charge of lean, responsive agencies. Hire and nurture knowledgeable, motivated employees and give them the freedom to innovate in accomplishing the agencies' missions. Engage citizens in the business of government, while at the same time encouraging them to be partners in problem-solving.

The report emphasized that achieving such reforms will "hardly be painless or easy. Reforms may require constitutional amendments, new legislations, changes in rules and regulations, and restructuring many agencies and departments. Accomplishment of many of the changes may require political leaders and civic groups to mount aggressive campaigns."

The Unionized Subsystem: Cadres of Workers Inside Bureaucracy

Most texts on government or bureaucracy ignore an important policy-making subsystem of public agencies that over the past three decades has grown rapidly into one of the most potent forces determining the internal directions and external outputs of bureaucracy: namely, unionized public service workers. As David Stanley observes, "A whole new ball game has started since unions in the public sector have begun to operate"[22] Like the aforementioned subsystems, unionization has increasingly gained its own share of power and a role in shaping the inner dynamics of public bureaucracy—that is, its rules, regulations, operating procedures, and structural relationships. Unions also exercise external controls over bureaucratic performance and influence upon society—that is, its productivity, enforcement practices, political relationships, and policy agendas.

The formal institutional structure of public sector collective bargaining is essentially derived from the private sector, and Joel Douglas writes: "The present Public Service Labor Relations (PSLR) . . . legislative and legal framework is based on an adversarial relationship rooted in the National Labor Relations Act (NLRA) and is structured on private sector principles. These include narrow unit determination requirements, bargaining agent election procedures, exclusive union representation, a series of unfair labor and employment practices, and a decentralized bargaining structure. Reliance on the private sector model was successful in developing the (PSLR) legal framework in which employees, subject to restrictions, most notably the anti-strike ban, negotiate with government the terms and conditions of employment. Although the private and public sectors contain many similarities, distinct difference is noted in the public sector, since the government is both employer and regulator at the bargaining table. Other differences include the private sector's reliance on market forces, distributive bargaining and the use of strikes and lockouts."[23]

Much like the professional careerist and civil service subsystems, the union subsystem was not a planned innovation. It just grew inside government, evolving particularly rapidly since the 1960s. As Frederick C. Mosher remarked, "The founders of the civil service did not bargain on collective bargaining."[24] If the Pendleton Act was the landmark piece of legislation creating the civil service, the explosion of union involvement within bureaucracy did not begin in earnest until John F. Kennedy signed Executive Orders 10987 and 10988 in 1962. These two orders for the first time gave unions the right to bargain collectively with federal management representatives on a limited range of items. They stimulated similar measures in numerous states and localities throughout the 1960s and 1970s. And while the unionization movement in government has slowed perceptibly during the 1980s because of cutbacks and the weakening of unions generally, the collective bargaining processes now in place are based largely upon legislation of the 1960s and 1970s and are accepted institutional practices within many jurisdictions throughout the United States.

Though the phenomenon of significant union influence over the activities of public bureaucracy is relatively new, some deep pockets of union activity date from the turn of the century. Indeed, in 1912 the Lloyd-La Follette Act gave federal workers the right to unionize, and for a number of years several large unions represented most of the U.S. postal employees as well as employees in certain fields of civilian defense and in several government corporations such as the Tennessee Valley Authority. States and localities with large urban and industrial populations, which had traditionally strong private sector unions, also saw unionization in limited areas of their public bureaucracies, such as in New York, Michigan, and California. Yet these public service unions were, for the most part, economically weak, poorly organized, and had few legal rights to bargain collectively with representatives from the agency's management.

Why did the 1960s usher in a new era of union influence inside government? The historical reasons are still not clear. Certainly the election of

John F. Kennedy in 1960 was a critical factor. Throughout Kennedy's campaign he pledged union recognition and collective bargaining at the federal level. Shortly after his election, he appointed a task force headed by Arthur Goldberg to make recommendations on how to handle union-management relations within government. In turn, this task force study led to the two executive orders just cited. But other factors were also at work behind the scenes. Statistics show that private sector unionization reached it high point in 1955 with one-fourth of the national work force belonging to unions. This percentage of national union membership has been declining gradually ever since (now standing at 14.2 percent). With the "drying up," so to speak, of the private sector, major union leaders as early as the 1950s recognized that the public service was the last major untapped pool of nonunionized workers, and so they pressed their demands on Kennedy and subsequent administrations for the extension of union rights and prerogatives within this governmental sector. The American Federation of State, County and Municipal Employees (AFSCME) and other groups were instrumental in lobbying state legislatures for the right to organize and bargain collectively with state and local jurisdictions on behalf of public workers. Virtually all states permit some form of collective bargaining, yet today six states prohibit collective bargaining and public employees joining unions, and forbid recognition of unions in government.

Much of the union intrusion into the ranks of bureaucracy resulted from a more tolerant, even perhaps permissive, public attitude toward unions in government. By the 1960s unions were no longer considered entirely "evil" and antithetical to the public interest. No doubt, very real economic forces were at work as well. The promises of higher paychecks, shorter work weeks, and better working conditions lured many government workers, principally blue collar employees but increasing numbers of white collar employees as well, into public service unions. Certainly the postal strike of 1970 and the New York City transit strike of 1966—two early key disputes—stimulated union membership. Finally, union growth was fostered

by legislation such as the Civil Service Reform Act of 1978, which formalized union-management collective bargaining procedures by federal statute. Likewise, on the local level, in New York State, representatives of the Civil Service Employees Association had been meeting with management representatives since the early 1900s, but the Taylor Law was established by statute's formal collective bargaining arrangement for state and union representatives in 1967. In a few states, such as Massachusetts, union membership became a requirement for attaining a public job. In order for workers to have a job and a voice that would represent them at the bargaining table and involve them in the determination of their agency's activities, they joined public employee unions.

Whatever the causes of growth—and there are undoubtedly many—in contrast to the private sector, a sporadic but continuous climb in union strength has been apparent within public organizations. Today 35.9 percent of all federal civilian employees belong to unions (not including the 600,000 postal workers, 90 percent of whom are unionized); 34.3 percent of state and local workers are union members. Levels of unionization, however, range significantly from agency to agency and locale to locale. Thus, in practice the political clout of union members inside bureaucracy varies considerably. The postal service, made up largely of blue collar workers, is almost entirely unionized, whereas the employees of the Federal Reserve Board and the State Department are mainly white collar professionals, largely (though not altogether) untouched by unions. Urban industrial states and large metropolitan communities are heavily unionized, and public unions play major policy-making roles within their various public bureaucracies. On the other hand, rural, poorer, and less-industrialized regions contain fewer union members, who therefore have less policy involvement in their regions of the public sector. Some functional areas, such as education, transportation, and refuse collection, show a much higher level of union activity than other fields.

Today there are three prominent and powerful public service unions (and numerous lesser ones) that speak for many, though certainly not all, public employees: the American Federation of State, County and Municipal Employees, the American Federation of Government Employees (AFGE), and the American Federation of Teachers (AFT). The National Education Association is technically *not* a union but rather a professional association of primary and secondary schoolteachers, yet it looks and acts like a union, often aggressively by representing its rank and file in collective bargaining negotiations in various school districts across the country. NEA became especially active within the Democratic party, substantially assisting President Jimmy Carter's election in 1976 and his bid for re-election in 1980. AFSCME, AFT, and AFGE have grown rapidly in power and prominence within the AFL-CIO labor council over the last decades, extending their activism well beyond traditional union concerns into national political circles of the Democratic party by aiding the party financially as well as through considerable campaign manpower. Public service unions are active at the state and local levels as well, particularly where there are large concentrations of public workers (such as in state or county capitals) and strong Democratic party organizations.

However, the actual conduct of negotiations between unions and management within government—the principal source of union inputs into bureaucracy—remains a highly decentralized process, with local representatives of public employee unions conducting agency-by-agency or local jurisdiction-by-jurisdiction negotiated agreements. In other words, while the public employee unions have grown into the "big three" (or four, depending on how one counts NEA), no one person or group speaks for "the entire management side" of government. Separate bargains must be made with roughly 80,000 governmental jurisdictions in the United States and with many more "suborganizational" units within these separate governments that recognize the union right of negotiation. Not only is the process decentralized, but who actually speaks for the employers or management is also a highly complex and unsettled issue in many areas. Some governments use the civil service as

spokescommission for management (Office of Personnel Management at the federal level); others have teams of top-level executives from *both* legislature and bureaucracy that speak for management. Highly diverse institutional arrangements for representation and the conducting of the actual negotiations are found across the United States, largely because the process still remains somewhat new, experimental, and undeveloped.

Equally unsettled is the scope of the bargaining that is allowed. In most jurisdictions, wages and hours—the two principal bargaining concerns in private industry—are legislatively determined and beyond the scope of public sector negotiations. These negotiations, therefore, mostly center on working conditions, grievance procedures, and other less major subjects. But even here, working conditions, grievance procedures, and "fringes" are often precisely prescribed by legislation, leaving little room for negotiations, even over these seemingly mundane matters. Further, laws on the books often stack the deck in management's favor. For example, according to the 1978 Civil Service Reform Act (CSR), management officials are authorized "to determine the mission, budget, organization, number of employees, and internal security practices of an agency . . . to hire, assign, direct, lay off and retain employees . . . or to suspend, remove, reduce in grade or pay, or take other disciplinary action."[25] In short, the CSR's tilt clearly favors management prerogatives over union rights, although through court decisions and legislative amendments unions have chipped away at these restrictions.

Another important condition of the union subsystem in government is that the actual means for enforcing their views at the bargaining table remain drastically restricted because of the ban on strikes by public employees at every level of government. The basic weapon used by private sector unions to enforce their demands in negotiations is illegal at the federal and many state and local settings. Though thirteen states allow some or all public employees the right to strike. As Theodore Kheel writes, "The strike enables employees through their representatives to participate in the decisions setting wages, hours and working conditions. In the absence of the right to strike, an alternative system of determination is required when negotiating parties reach an impasse."[26] However, no such technique has yet been found for breaking public sector impasses. In reality, however, whether or not public employees are legally permitted to strike, strikes do occur in the public sector; sometimes they are called "the blue flu" or "sick-outs," or they are actual walk-outs. Public unions know very well how to play the inside political game. During negotiations they regularly make "end runs" around management to outside supporters, such as sympathetic legislators on city councils, in state assemblies, or in Congress. These potent friends of public unions frequently enable them to cut deals and achieve their priorities through the back door, thus undercutting management's position or dividing it so badly that its official bargaining position crumbles.

How then can the union subsystem's influence over policy outputs in bureaucracy be summarized vis-à-vis the other previously mentioned bureaucratic subsystems?

The first and perhaps the most significant aspect of union involvement with what happens inside U.S. bureaucracy is its variety. Some unions strive for nothing less than complete control from top to bottom of public bureaucracy. They want the options to select a public agency's top-ranking political cadre; to determine its internal structural arrangements, procedures, and rules as well as its methods of promotion, hiring, and firing; to specify its relations with other external groups; and most of all to call the shots as to what the agency will or will not do for the public. In general, those agencies are characterized by weak political executive oversight, an absence of a controlling professional elite, a strongly unionized rank and file, a degree of institutional autonomy, and traditions of union assertiveness, such as in the federal postal system and in large "weak-mayor" cities such as New York and San Francisco, where public service unions exert powerful long-term influence. At the other extreme, public sector unions are dormant or ineffective in right-to-work states, where public sector unions are outlawed entirely, and in agencies in the tight grip of professionals (strong city manager communities or the military) or under strong, united antiunion political executive leadership. Most situations in which unions operate, though, are at neither extreme, and so unions end up jockeying with other internal bureaucratic subsystems—political appointees, professionals, and civil servants—for varying degrees of autonomy and control over bureaucratic policies and outputs.

Second, the growth and intrusion of unions within bureaucracy have added new levels of complexities and complications to an already complex bureaucratic world. Whether such complexification of government has slowed down its institutional outputs or made it more productive is unclear and unmeasured, but it is apparent in many instances that new personnel and attendant rules and procedures have been added to administer this new subsystem and that relationships between labor and management have therefore become more formal and legalistic.

Third, in cases where the union subsystem has matured fully within public bureaucracies but has not become the dominant subsystem, it has brought with it new bipartisanship management practices. Collective bargaining forces management to sit down at regular intervals with union representatives to discuss grievances, working conditions, and other matters of concern to both parties.

Fourth, in many cases public service unions have won positive reforms that have long been advocated by public administration specialists to enhance, on the whole, the cause of "good government," such as better wages, working conditions, training programs and staffing levels, and organizational reforms promoting institutional productivity.

Finally, the real loser with the advent of public service unions into the internal dynamics of bureaucratic policy making has probably been the underlying philosophy and practices of the century-old civil service subsystem. Concepts such as merit selection, open competitive exams, nonpartisan civil service boards, and "color blind" promotions based upon individual competence have yielded in many areas to union concerns about seniority, "closed shop" union membership, and neutral third-party mediation of disputes by those outside civil service. Indeed, in many instances the old neutral civil service commission has been replaced by highly partisan and political oversight agencies such as the Office of Personnel Management at the federal level. This is not to argue that the civil service subsystem will soon fade into a distant memory and its controlling procedures, rules, and personnel become history. To the contrary, it is alive and well today in many bureaucratic institutions, but it certainly has changed, or given ground to the influx of unionization over the last three decades inside the public service. In several cases as well, due to the fiscal constraints of recent years, we have witnessed considerable union cooperation with civil service managers for the self-interest of each party.[27]

Contract Employment: The Newest, Fastest-Growing Bureaucratic Subsystem

At the federal, state, and local levels, public agencies up to roughly 1950 did most, if not all, of the tasks assigned to them in-house, using their own personnel and resources and the facilities allocated by legislatures and political executives. Hence much of the theory of bureaucracy, as well as the managerial approaches to public enterprise put forward by public administration experts and scholars, were based upon assumptions, increasingly erroneous, that bureaucracies controlled their own operations, did their assigned work inside, with neat, clear lines of managerial control running from top political executives down to the workers who actually carried out the agency's assigned missions.

The reality of internal bureaucratic life today, however, is far different. In the 1990s the federal budget tells another story about how government agencies actually function. Roughly 14 percent of the national budget goes for its own internal personnel services and benefits (excluding pensions). This means that only slightly more than one-eighth of the total federal budget is spent on directing activities that the government performs itself, such as law enforcement, food and drug regulation, forestry service, air traffic control, and so on. However, the category of "other contractual services" indicates the roughly 16 percent of the total annual operating budget is spent for sundry activities performed by others who are contracted to render services from *outside* the federal bureaucracy.

In other words, close to 60 percent of the total obligation for goods and services produced by the federal government is contracted out (excluding funds for grants-in-aid to states and localities, direct transfer payments to individuals, debt servicing, and so on). The percentages run much higher for some agencies, such as NASA and the Department of Energy, which have traditionally contracted out most of their work. The development of most major weapons systems is contracted out to private businesses, as is the construction of large capital projects such as dams, roads, bridges, and sewer systems. Three-fourths of research and development funding at the federal level is contracted out to universities, think tanks, consultants, and private industry.

At the state and local levels there are no comparable figures on the levels of contracting-out by governmental bureaucracy, though they probably mirror the federal pattern, with some communities going to extremes, such as Lakewood, California (originators of the Lakewood Plan), which contracts out all its municipal functions, including police protection. City Hall consists of little more than a city manager and a secretary, who principally act as contract-managers for the city council. While most localities do not go to that extreme degree of contracting for municipal services, most do draw upon private vendors and business enterprises in many ways for the construction of capital projects as well as for a variety of ongoing services, such as data collection, medical facilities, computer services, refuse disposal, as well as for accounting, auditing, and payroll functions. Today, most government agencies house varying mixes of full-time employees and temporary or long-term contract employees working side by side. The regular public employees and contractual employees are often difficult to differentiate from one another.

The story of the rise of contract labor inside bureaucracy is a complicated one. Early in the history of the U.S. government, mail delivery and canal projects were contracted out. However, until 1950 the use and application of contractual arrangements were drastically limited in most public agencies. All this changed, with the hot and cold war demands of the postwar era, when government increasingly needed highly skilled scientific and engineering talent from universities, private enterprises, and consulting firms to conceptualize, build, and implement numerous weapons programs. The Rand Corporation and the National Science Foundation were created by the federal government as outside sources for accomplishing in-house missions of DoD.

The growth of contracting-out for government services since then has been unprecedented in size, scope, and intensity. Government has been driven into contracting willy-nilly in so many fields because it has been asked to perform greater numbers of tasks of ever-greater complexity within shorter time frames, tasks for which it has neither the expertise nor the capacity to acquire it on a short-term basis. At the state and local levels, contractual employment accelerated in the 1970s, 1980s, and 1990s as a device for accomplishing programmatic goals while avoiding rising costs of hiring permanent civil servants (today a permanent civil servant costs government roughly twice the worker's *actual* salary, largely because of "hidden fringes" such as retirement programs and health and other benefit packages). Contracting-out is also a method of doing complex work in which states and localities have little expertise. But it has broad implications.

Some effects on public agencies and their outputs are fairly obvious. First, the growth of the contractual subsystem makes it increasingly hard to tell where government bureaucracy begins and ends. Is the permanent public agency that relies on the expertise of a single outside contractor *really* independent of that outside private enterprise? Or is the private contractor who relies on a public bureaucracy for all or most of his annual income *really* private, and not merely an extension of a public bureaucracy? Increasingly, the worlds separating government agencies and private sector businesses, universities, and consulting firms are dissolving into an area where boundaries overlap or are unclear and difficult to define.

What is clear, however, is that these "outside" groups perform much of the bureaucratic work of government. If their personnel were counted as government employees, the size of government bureaucracy would probably be twice as large as it is. Contracting-out, then, enables politicians to gain services for their constituents *and then* claim that they have "kept the lid on government personnel costs." Such a claim is clearly untrue and leads to further confusion—and deception—about the realities of the size and true nature of government.

Second, some sectors of government have clearly become "captives" of their contractors. The purveyors of many large DoD weapons systems, such as Hughes, Boeing, Rockwell, and McDonald Douglas, not only design and develop these multibillion dollar, multiyear systems but by proposing new weapons systems are also actively involved in establishing DoD and individual service priorities, budget requirements, personnel needs, and even the broad global strategic priorities of U.S. defense policy. And once the weapons are sold, these firms become the sole-source suppliers virtually dictating the costs—often overrun by huge amounts—to the contracting agency. Top executives move back and forth with ease between these firms and top policy-making posts within DoD. Harold Brown (DoD secretary under President Carter), William C. Foster (Brown's research and development specialist), Caspar Weinberger (a former DoD secretary under President Reagan), and John Lehmann (Weinberger's former secretary of the navy), and William J. Perry (President Clinton's secretary of defense) are all products of the contract world surrounding DoD. This is not meant to suggest that these individuals or others who serve "in-and-out" at high DoD policy-making levels have acted unethically or dishonestly; it simply means that their backgrounds and skills are utilized in *both* government and business at various managerial and staff levels and that they therefore significantly influence policies and administration in *both* sectors.

Another effect of the increasing rise and reliance upon the contractual subsystem within public bureaucracy is that there is less and less use for traditional bureaucratic techniques, such as standard in-house top-down rules, for direction and control of personnel and resources. More emphasis is now placed upon contract negotiations, formal agreements, legal sanctions, economic rewards and penalties for inducing compliance by contractors, and auditing and management information systems for "tracking" completion dates. All these procedures are essential for quality control and to make the contractors and subcontractors perform their services according to schedule. Bureaucrats at all levels increasingly are becoming contract managers as opposed to fulfilling their traditional line management roles.

Also, as suggested before, with the growing numbers of public personnel "off the books" because of their nontenured status, the traditional sorts of personnel work rules, personnel oversight controls, and procedures governing employee behavior have diminished in importance. Thus the problems of imposing public accountability on contract workers grow as the numbers of contract agents and subcontractors grow. Proper policy performance and implementation in regard to legality, honesty, competence, correctness of action, and effective completion of projects become increasingly difficult to ensure as the number of private businesses, universities, and others who perform the work of public agencies increases. Recent leaks of highly sensitive national security information by Hughes employees and the massive fraud cases of General Electric subcontractors working on vari-

ous navy projects illustrate these enormous problems of public accountability and oversight. Indeed, *should* bureaucracy impose its public standards of accountability on such "private" groups and citizens? The difficult and uncharted ethical dimensions of the problems loom large. Finally, as the pressures of the contractual subsystem force new commitments and expenditures of funds years ahead of time, contractual arrangements become legally and politically "untouchable." As many scholars and budget experts now observe, not only is the federal budget out of control but also no one even knows how much is really being spent annually, largely because of the pressures of the growing contractual subsystem. Many contractors simply operate independently of the budget process—off the books and out of sight—developing independent accounting, auditing, and budgeting systems along with separate personnel rules, regulations, and procedures that are well beyond public scrutiny and oversight mechanisms.

Notes

1. Hugh Heclo, *A Government of Strangers* (Washington, DC: Brookings Institution, 1977), p. 103.
2. These characteristics of political appointees have been true for some time. See David T. Stanley, Dean E. Mann, and Jameson W. Doig, *Men Who Govern* (Washington, DC: Brookings Institution, 1967).
3. For data on the backgrounds of city managers that tend to show a high degree of heterogeneity, read Richard J. Stillman II, "Local Public Management in Transition," *The Municipal Year Book 1982* (Washington, DC: International City Management Assoc., 1982), pp. 161–73.
4. Thomas P. Murphy, Donald E. Nuechterlein, and Ronald Stupak, *Inside Bureaucracy: The View from the Assistant Secretary's Desk* (Boulder: Westview Press, 1978).
5. Frederick C. Mosher, *Democracy and the*

Public Service, 2d ed. (NY: Oxford University Press, 1982), p. 183.

6. Frank P. Sherwood and L. J. Breyer, "Executive Personnel Systems in States," *Public Administration Review* 47 (Sept./Oct. 1987):410f.

7. Deborah D. Roberts, "The Governor as Leader: Strengthening Public Service Through Executive Leadership," in Frank J. Thompson (ed.), *Revitalizing State and Local Public Service: Strengthening Performance, Accountability, and Citizen Confidence* (San Francisco, CA: Jossey-Bass, 1993), pp. 51–52.

8. See Samuel H. Beer's presidential address before the American Political Science Association, "Federalism, Nationalism and Democracy in America," *American Political Science Review,* 72(1) (March 1978).

9. Zbigniew Brzezinski, *Between Two Ages: America's Role in the Technetronic Era* (New York: Viking, 1970); Don Price, *The Scientific Estate* (Cambridge: Harvard University Press, 1965); Daniel Bell, "Notes on the Post-Industrial Society," *Public Interest,* 6 (Winter 1967): 24–35; and Guy Benveniste, *The Politics of Expertise,* 2d ed. (San Francisco: Jossey-Bass, 1983).

10. Mosher, *Democracy,* p. 142.

11. Robert D. Kaplan, "There Is No 'Middle East,' " *New York Times Magazine,* Feb. 20, 1994, pp. 42–43.

12. Robert Wiebe, *The Search for Order: 1877–1920* (New York: Hill and Wang, 1967), pp. 120–21.

13. Martha Derthick, *The Influence of Federal Grants: Public Assistance in Massachusetts* (Cambridge, MA: Harvard University Press, 1970), p. 159.

14. David S. Arnold and Jeremy F. Plant, *Public Official Associations and State and Local Government: A Bridge across One Hundred Years* (Fairfax, VA: George Mason University Press, 1994), p. 59.

15. The best account of the development of civil service remains Paul P. Van Riper's *History of the United States Civil Service* (Evanston, Ill.: Row Peterson, 1958).

16. Patricia W. Ingraham and Donald F. Kettl, *Agenda for Excellence: Public Service in America* (Chatham, New York: Chatham House, 1993).

17. Eugene B. MacGregor, "Politics and Career Mobility of Civil Servants," *American Political Science Review,* 68 (1974): 24.

18. As cited in Heclo, *Government,* p. 142.

19. The Hudson Institute, *Civil Service 2000* (Washington, DC: U.S. Office of Personnel Management, 1988).

20. Paul A. Volcker, chair, *Leadership for America: Rebuilding the Public Service* (Lexington, MA: Lexington Books, 1990).

21. William A. Winter, chair, *Hard Truths, Tough Choices: Agenda for State and Local Reform,* Winter Commission Report, (San Francisco: Jossey Bass 1993).

22. David T. Stanley, *Managing Local Government under Union Pressure* (Washington, DC: Brookings Institution, 1972), p. 136.

23. Joel M. Douglas, "Public Sector Collective Bargaining in the 1900s," in Frederick S. Lane (ed.), *Current Issues in Public Administration,* 5th ed. (New York: St. Martin's Press, 1994), p. 261.

24. Frederick C. Mosher, *Democracy and the Public Service* (New York: Oxford University Press, 1968), p. 178.

25. PL 95-45, October 13, 1978, Section 7106.

26. As quoted in Harry H. Wellington and Ralph K. Winter, Jr., *The Union and the Cities* (Washington, DC: Brookings Institution, 1971), p. 30.

27. As Joel M. Douglas concludes, "Bilateralism has replaced unilateralism in the decision-making processes." In Douglas, "Public Sector Collective Bargaining in the 1990s," *op. cit.,* pp. 271–72.

☐ CASE STUDY 7

Introduction

Among the five critical personnel subsystems outlined in the foregoing essay, that of the professional careerist is one of the most influential, for the various reasons outlined by the author. Though they do not operate in a vacuum as a group or as individuals, they do interact with and are surrounded by other personnel subsystems that decisively determine the extent of their influence, the sorts of issues they handle, and what they achieve—or fail to achieve—in their work.

In the following case, "Twisting in the Wind? Ambassador Glaspie and the Persian Gulf Crisis," by Jillian Dickert at Harvard's Kennedy School of Government, we can see firsthand the interplay among various sorts of personnel in the shaping of a professional's line of work—in this case a career diplomat's interaction with her political superiors. April C. Glaspie served as the American ambassador to Iraq prior to the outbreak of the Gulf War in August 1990. She had been a professional diplomat for twenty-five years, specializing in Middle Eastern affairs, and worked her way up through the ranks to become the "finest Arabist in the State Department," which ironically was a field that from the beginning she had been discouraged to enter. As a "pro's pro," so to speak, she therefore had earned her position as the first woman ever appointed to any Middle Eastern nation ambassadorship by the United States *and* to Iraq, which at the time was considered the most difficult assignment in the region. Since 1980 Iraq had been engaged in a long, bloody war with Iran, and when Glaspie took up her post in the last days of the Reagan administration, the White House had wanted her to pursue the creation of better ties with Iraq in order to improve the "balance of power" and political stability in the area. They wanted "her to maintain a careful balancing act simultaneously encouraging and restraining Saddam Hussein, but Glaspie hoped to strengthen the volatile Iraqi leader's ties to the U.S."

This policy she actively pursued with all the skill and talent of her experienced professional diplomacy. Yet things worked out very differently from what was planned: that is, a growing distance between both nations, strained diplomatic relations, and the eventual war that broke out between Iraq and the United States. The following case not only recounts how Glaspie tried vigorously to implement what she had been instructed by her superiors should be the American policy toward Iraq—that ultimately failed—but outlines the firestorm of controversy that surrounded her in the aftermath. Both the press and politicians loudly criticized her attempts to follow a policy of moderation toward Saddam Hussein after he invaded Kuwait on August 2, 1990. The case therefore provides a good account of what happens to "a woman-in-the-middle" of a failed policy with which she became closely identified and from which her political superiors at the State Department quickly wanted to distance themselves. On a deeper level the case exemplifies how public professionals today do not operate in isolation and how they are very much dependent upon others—in this case upon political appointees providing the instructions *and* support.

As you read this case, you might think about:

How did Glaspie "earn her way" up through the ranks to this sensitive assignment? Why did she become so highly regarded by her peers?

What was her assigned mission as ambassador to Iraq? Do you judge her work as successful in fulfilling that mission?

Who were the political appointees in this case from whom she received her instructions, and why didn't they defend her openly after August 1990?

Can you generalize about what this case says concerning the role of professionals in government and their relationships with their superiors?

Twisting in the Wind? Ambassador Glaspie and the Persian Gulf Crisis

JILLIAN P. DICKERT

In September 1990, as events moved with seeming inevitability toward a Persian Gulf war, a debate broke out in the press that could have been called "who lost Kuwait"; had there been American policies that had somehow given the "green light" to Iraq's lightning-fast invasion of its small, oil-rich neighbor to the south? At the center of the controversy was April Glaspie, a heretofore obscure career diplomat serving as ambassador to Iraq. Precipitated by Iraq's release of a transcript of a conversation between Iraqi President Saddam Hussein and Glaspie, the debate focused on the question of whether—as the transcript seemed to indicate—she had led Saddam Hussein to believe the U.S. would not intervene in the event of an invasion. Glaspie, some argued, had grievously misread the intentions of Iraq's ruthless leader and failed to respond strongly to his intimations that he would invade Kuwait; others contended that the ambassador had, rightly or wrongly, merely articulated a position formulated by the White House and was now being made the scapegoat for a failed administration policy.

Conspicuously silent throughout much of the debate was Glaspie herself. She had been, as political observers noted with great interest, deskbound in Washington in the weeks following the invasion and,

This case was written by Jillian Dickert under the supervision of Phil Heymann for use in the Senior Managers in Government Program at the John F. Kennedy School of Government, Harvard University. (0891) Copyright © 1991 by the President and Fellows of Harvard College. Reprinted with permission of the Kennedy School of Government Case Program, Harvard University.

[1]*New York Times,* March 21, 1991, p. A15.

[2]*New York Times,* September 12, 1990, p. A19.

as the brewing controversy about her talk with Saddam Hussein intensified, unavailable to the press for comment or rebuttal. Now, with the U.S. contemplating the profound implications of military action against Iraq, the demand to understand what had brought the nation to the point of war grew louder. With increasing insistence, Glaspie was being called upon to explain publicly what she had said to Saddam Hussein, and why she had said it.

Background: A Career in Foreign Service

Over the course of 25 years in the Foreign Service, April Catherine Glaspie's career had been marked by a steady rise through the ranks of desk officers to the pinnacle of her field. Canadian-born but raised in California, she had graduated Phi Beta Kappa in history and government from Mills College and gone on to earn a master's degree in advanced international studies at Johns Hopkins University. From her widowed mother's British family, who had served with the British army in Palestine, Glaspie had "cultivated a love for the Arab world,"[1] but she had had to battle the Foreign Service bureaucracy to study Arabic at a time when women were not encouraged to make their careers in that arena. Described by some as a workaholic with a stubborn streak, Glaspie had persisted and was considered by some of her colleagues to be "the finest Arabist in the State Department."[2]

Glaspie went on to serve in Amman, Kuwait, Stockholm, Beirut, Cairo, London, and New York. She got her first career break, Sidney Blumenthal reports in *The New Republic,* when she was serving "in a lowly position" in the U.S. Embassy in Cairo. During a visit by then-Secretary of State Henry Kissinger, she "proved herself invaluable by discovering an Egyptian laundry that would instantly wash and iron his shirts." From that point, adds Blumenthal, "[h]er promotions were steady as she proved her expertise in other areas as well."[3] From 1981–83, she directed the Language Institute at the U.S. Embassy in Tunisia, moving from there to the post of deputy chief of mission at the embassy in Damascus, Syria. In 1985, she assumed the directorship of the State Department's Office of Jordan, Lebanon and Syrian Affairs, where she helped initiate a diplomatic shuttle between Damascus and Beirut, in an effort to bring some stability to that troubled region. During this period, then-Secretary of State George Shultz praised Glaspie as "a genuine hero" for her work in securing the freedom of 104 Americans held hostage by terrorists aboard a TWA plane.

As she progressed in her career, Glaspie gained a reputation as a hard-driving worker "married" to her job. She was "so intense," according to one report, that "she would weed the garden of her Georgetown townhouse at night by flashlight, so intrepid that she often drove the eight-hour trip from Baghdad to Kuwait to buy groceries, leaving her chauffeur behind."[4] Colleagues variously characterized her as "warm, blunt, funny, brilliant, stubborn and unyielding."[5] This latter trait, detractors claimed, prevented her from "backing off fixed positions"; supporters, on the other hand, called it "an overwhelming confidence that comes from knowing her brief better than most anyone else."[6]

In the summer of 1988, Glaspie's upward climb through the Foreign Service ranks culminated in her appointment as ambassador to Iraq—making her the first woman ambassador to a Middle Eastern nation. Along with the precedent, she would be assuming a challenging and prestigious position that put her at the center of one of the most sensitive areas of U.S. foreign policy. That August, Glaspie, taking with

her—as was her habit in each overseas assignment— her mother and her King Charles spaniel, set off for her new post in Baghdad.

U.S. Policy Toward Iraq

As ambassador, April Glaspie inherited a policy toward Iraq that could be described as ambiguous but hopeful. In the aftermath of the Islamic revolution in Iran—made searingly memorable in the U.S. by the public humiliation of American Embassy workers taken hostage in Teheran—the U.S. had begun to tilt favorably toward Iraq and its problematic leader, Saddam Hussein. While Hussein, whose Ba'athist party had ruled Iraq since the late 1960s, was seen by many as a brutal and dictatorial president, he also represented the only credible regional counterbalance to Iran, which had openly avowed its intention of spreading its fiery (and anti-American) brand of fundamentalism throughout the Middle East. Therefore, when Saddam Hussein invaded Iran in 1980, setting off a bloody eight-year conflict, the Reagan administration ultimately chose to support Iraq, if only indirectly. In 1982, after Iranian successes in the battlefield, the White House removed Iraq from the State Department's list of countries supporting terrorism—a move that lifted many trade restrictions between the U.S. and Iraq. Over the next eight years, despite evidence that it did in fact at times harbor terrorists, Iraq remained off the list and continued to benefit from U.S. loans and credits. In 1984, ending a breach that dated back to 1967, the White House restored diplomatic relations with Iraq.

The path to improved ties with Iraq was not always smooth, however—usually as a result of Saddam Hussein's propensity for acquiring worrisome weapons capabilities. In 1981, Israel, suspecting a covert nuclear weapons development effort, destroyed an Iraqi nuclear reactor, putting the U.S. in an awkward diplomatic situation both with Iraq and with one of its closest allies. Then, in 1984, evidence was turned up indicating that Iraq was using chemical weapons in its war with Iran; in response, the Reagan administration announced curbs on the export of certain chemicals to Iraq, citing their "dual use" capabilities. This move—as with later revelations of the "arms-for-hostages" deal with Iran and

---

[3]Sidney Blumenthal, "April's Bluff," *The New Republic,* 205:6 (August 5, 1991) p. 9.

[4]*New York Times,* September 12, 1990, p. A19.

[5]Roger Simon, "Did Non-meeting of Minds Result in War?" *Los Angeles Times,* July 21, 1991, p. E2.

[6]*New York Times,* March 21, 1991, p. A15.

the apparently (but not clearly) accidental Iraqi missile attack that killed 37 Americans aboard the USS *Stark* frigate in 1987—led to strains in U.S.-Iraq relations, but the White House remained hopeful about what it viewed as a moderating trend in Saddam Hussein's actions. Trade with Iraq was booming—it had grown sevenfold between 1983 and 1989—and administration officials generally regarded Saddam Hussein as "a man you could do business with."[7] This optimism was considerably bolstered in July 1988, when the Iraqi president unexpectedly declared a ceasefire in the war with Iran. Earlier that year, he had buoyed the administration by endorsing PLO leader Yasir Arafat's proposal to recognize Israel as a step toward regional peace.

It was following this upbeat turn of events that April Glaspie took up her post in Baghdad, in the waning days of the Reagan administration. The White House's ambiguous policy would require her to maintain a careful balancing act of simultaneously encouraging and restraining Saddam Hussein, but Glaspie hoped to strengthen the volatile Iraqi leader's ties to the U.S. As it turned out, her tenure as ambassador would be marked by strain and a growing distance between the two nations.

April in Baghdad

Glaspie's first crisis on the job came within a month of her arrival in Baghdad. In August 1988, reports began filtering out that Iraqi troops had been using poison mustard gas on rebellious Kurds, killing tens of thousands and creating a flood of refugees. As outrage over Saddam Hussein's brutal methods of crushing the Kurdish revolt built up in the U.S. and abroad, Glaspie received one of her first major assignments as U.S. ambassador: to lodge a formal protest with the Iraqi Foreign Ministry regarding the use of chemical weapons. Her official protest met only with silence from the Iraqi government. In the U.S., however, there was a response, as Congress pondered bipartisan legislation—introduced by

Senators Claiborne Pell (D-R.I.) and Jesse Helms (R-N.C.)—that would require sanctions against Iraq for its treatment of the Kurds. Under the weight of the Reagan administration's opposition, the bill died in the final hours of the 100th Congress, but the idea of sanctions surfaced frequently, as some congressional critics took aim at the White House's policy of accommodation with Saddam Hussein.

Meanwhile, Glaspie pursued her objectives of improving Iraq's relationship with the U.S. Believing Saddam Hussein was "out of touch" with the West, she directed her staff to find creative ways of educating him and senior officials in his government, particularly about American values and policies, the press, and the intricacies of American constitutional structures. In addition, hoping to break through the wall she felt Hussein had built around the Iraqi people, Glaspie organized an intercultural exchange program through the U.S. Embassy.[8] Glaspie also continued to encourage the warming trend in U.S.-Iraq commercial relations. In a brochure welcoming visitors to an international business fair held in Baghdad in 1989, she wrote: "We are pleased to announce that a record number of companies are participating, representing a wide range of America's most advanced technologies and demonstrating America's confidence in Iraq's bright future. The American Embassy places the highest priority on promoting commerce and friendship between our two nations." As if to put an official seal on such sentiments, on January 17, 1990, President Bush signed a presidential order declaring that expanded trade with Iraq, guaranteed by the Export-Import Bank, was in the national interests of the U.S.[9] Within a month, however, the friendly tone of U.S.-Iraq relations had begun to sour, and Glaspie's dream of an improved rapport with Saddam Hussein to dim.

Friction

Despite U.S. claims of a moderating trend in Iraq, disquieting signs of activities in less positive directions continued to trouble U.S.-Iraqi diplomatic relations. In late January, Amnesty International reported that Iraqi troops had attacked dozens of Shiite villages and killed many citizens, apparently

[7]Ted Gup, "A Man You Could Do Business With," *Time*, 137:10 (March 11, 1991), p. 59.

[8]House Foreign Affairs Subcommittee on Europe and the Middle East Hearing, March 21, 1991.

[9]Don Oberdorfer, "Was War Inevitable?" *Washington Post Magazine*, March 17, 1991, p. 20.

in an attempt to capture army deserters. A couple of weeks later, another human rights group, Middle East Watch, issued a report in which it described Iraq as "a well-organized police state" that "ruthlessly suppresses even small gestures of dissent." Soon thereafter, the State Department added its own voice to the criticism in its human rights report, which it was required to submit annually to Congress. The section on Iraq, written by Glaspie's staff in Baghdad, termed that nation's human rights record "abysmal."

Amid this flurry of reports on Iraq's human rights abuses, the Voice of America weighed in with a stinging editorial. Broadcast overseas on February 15, the editorial, entitled "No More Secret Police," strongly criticized secret police abuses in Iraq and seven other countries. The "rulers of these countries," it declared, "hold power by force and fear, not by consent of the governed. The tide of history is against such rulers. We believe the 1990s should belong not to the dictators and secret police, but to the people."

Saddam Hussein did not respond directly to the Voice of America piece, but in an address shortly after the editorial was aired, he spoke out bitterly against the U.S. and its ally, Israel. At a February 24 "Summit of Arab Cooperation" in Amman, Jordan, Hussein asserted that there was a "real possibility" that in the next five years Israel would embark on "new stupidities" as a result of encouragement from the U.S. now that it was in "a superior position in international politics"—a reference to the decline of Soviet power. He also called for the U.S. fleet, which had operated in the Persian Gulf since 1949, to return to the states now that the Iran-Iraq war had ended.

A few days after that, on February 27, in a cable not made public until some months later, Glaspie informed Washington that Iraqi leaders had "read the [Voice of America] editorial as U.S. Government sanctioned mudslinging with the intent to incite revolution." The next day, Glaspie added that "the Soviet Embassy is also busy here ensuring that news of the editorial has been spread throughout Baghdad." On instructions from the State Department, Glaspie then wrote a letter to Iraqi Foreign Minister Tariq Aziz declaring that "it is absolutely not U.S. policy to question the legitimacy of the Iraqi government nor to interfere in any way with the domestic concerns of the Iraqi people and government." "My government," she added, "regrets that the wording of the editorial left it open to incorrect interpretation." Glaspie reminded Aziz that "as Assistant Secretary [of State

for Near Eastern and South Asian Affairs John] Kelly told his Excellency the President [Saddam Hussein] on February 12, President Bush wants good relations with Iraq, relations built on confidence and trust."

Glaspie's assurances appeared to do little to appease the Iraqi president, who continued to view Israeli, and American, motives with suspicion. More troubling events followed. On March 15, an Iranian-born British journalist was hanged on charges of spying for Israel. Then, on April 1, amid reports of Iraqi Scud missile launchers being constructed within striking range of Israel and an attempt (foiled by British customs officials) to smuggle nuclear triggering devices into Iraq, Saddam Hussein spoke out again in even stronger language. He announced that Iraq had developed binary chemical weapons—previously possessed only by the U.S. and the Soviet Union—and cautioned Israel against launching another attack against Iraqi facilities. If the U.S. and Great Britain were trying to give Israel a pretext for striking at Iraq, he warned, "by God, we will let the fire eat up half of Israel. . . ."

Despite his threatening language, the White House, like Glaspie, held firmly to the view that Saddam Hussein could be brought around to a more reasonable view of U.S. interests. This message was conveyed by Senate Minority Leader Robert Dole (R-Kan.) who, along with four other U.S. senators, paid a visit to the Iraqi president in Mosul on April 12, 1990, in an effort to cool down U.S.-Iraq tensions. According to an Iraqi transcript of their meeting, Saddam Hussein charged that the U.S. and Europe were waging an "all-out campaign against Iraq" to provide political cover for Israel's plan to attack his country, and criticized the U.S. for supplying Israel with defensive Patriot missiles. In turn, Dole delivered to the Iraqi president a letter from Bush warning him that Iraq's advanced weapons programs [might] "provoke dangerous tensions throughout the Middle East"; but at the same time the senator spoke in more conciliatory terms, assuring Saddam Hussein that the president had told him personally "that he wants better relations, and the U.S. government wants better relations with Iraq."[10]

---

[10]According to *New York Times* columnist William Safire, Dole also—inaccurately it turned out—told the Iraqi leader that the offending Voice of America editorialist had been fired. Safire was highly critical of the senator's behavior with Saddam Hussein, at one point labeling them "obsequious" in manner.

Assistant Secretary of State John Kelly repeated this view before the House Foreign Affairs Subcommittee on Europe and the Middle East on April 26. "Our policy toward Iraq," he testified, "has been to develop gradually a mutual beneficial relationship in order to strengthen positive trends in Iraq's foreign and domestic policies." Kelly also reasserted administration opposition to imposing sanctions on Iraq and other countries that used chemical weapons—a measure that was once again before Congress for consideration—arguing that "[w]e believe it is important to give the government of Iraq an opportunity to reverse this deterioration in relations."[11]

The hopeful administration outlook met with strong skepticism from some quarters of Congress and the press. During Kelly's testimony, Rep. Thomas Lantos (D-Calif.) told the assistant secretary that he detected an "Alice in Wonderland quality" in Kelly's vision. "You sort of expressed a hope," said Lantos, "which boggles my mind, that somehow this will change and Iraq under Saddam Hussein will turn in the direction of being a responsible and civilized and peace-loving and constructive member of the international community. And I find this, to put it mildly, a non sequitur." Glaspie as well came in for criticism for her naive view of Saddam Hussein. Writing in the *Washington Post* on May 3, columnist Jack Anderson reported that the "latest secret cable traffic from the U.S. Embassy in Baghdad concedes that Hussein has been something of a thug in the past, but that he is well on the road to becoming a 'kinder, gentler' thug today." Anderson continued:

> On the surface, Hussein is trying to look like a new man. He has been courting the United States for more than a year. April Glaspie, the U.S. Ambassador to Iraq, has been surprised at the enthusiasm with which the reclusive Hussein has tried to cement relations with Washington.

Despite this skepticism, and a continuing stream of belligerent comments from Saddam Hussein, the administration, preoccupied with the dramatic

changes in Eastern Europe, did not change its basic approach to the Iraqi leader. It was not until the summer of 1990—when Saddam Hussein acted on his threats to Kuwait—that it would become painfully clear that Glaspie's objectives as U.S. ambassador to Iraq would never be realized.

War Clouds

Iraq and Kuwait had had a history of ill will between them, chiefly due to longstanding border disputes, but the proximate cause of Iraq's threat to Kuwait in the summer of 1990 was the price of oil. Hard-pressed by loans that had financed its war with Iran, Iraq had been pushing its fellow OPEC members to raise the price of oil to $18 a barrel (it had dropped from $21/barrel the previous December to a recent low of $12). On July 17, in a televised "state of the union" address on Iraq's National Day, Saddam Hussein accused Kuwait (as well as the United Arab Emirates) of overproducing—an action he linked directly to U.S. influence. The oil overproduction, he charged, was part of a plan "inspired by America to undermine Arab interests and security. . . ." "If words fail to protect Iraqis," he warned, "something effective must be done. Cutting necks is better than cutting the means of living. Oh God, be witness that we have warned them."

To underline his message, the Iraqi president began moving his troops to the Kuwaiti border. Their presence was detected by U.S. intelligence as early as July 20; by July 25, some 100,000 Iraqi soldiers were reported massed and poised for action. What that action would be was a matter of some discussion in the U.S. That day, the CIA first predicted that Iraq would probably use force against Kuwait, but some government officials continued to believe it would seize only those border areas that were under dispute.

As coverage of the buildup began to dominate the news in the U.S., the administration adopted an ambiguous stance. Speaking to reporters on July 23, State Department Spokeswoman Margaret Tutwiler said that "Iraq and others know there is no place for coercion and intimidation in a civilized world." Asked about a U.S. commitment to defend Kuwait, Tutwiler responded that "we do not have any defense or security treaties or commitments to Kuwait," adding that "we also remain strongly committed to supporting the

---

[11]The Senate unanimously approved the sanctions legislation, after eliminating an amendment that would cut off U.S. aid to Iraq. Ultimately, Bush pocket-vetoed the measure, contending that sanctions would "severely constrain presidential authority in carrying out foreign policy."

individual and collective self-defense of our friends in the Gulf, with whom we have deep longstanding ties."

Several days later, Assistant Secretary of State John Kelly echoed those points in testimony before the House Foreign Affairs Subcommittee on Europe and the Middle East. The administration "would be extremely concerned" in the event that Iraq crossed into Kuwait's border, Kelly told Chairman Lee Hamilton (D-Ind.), but, he added, the U.S. had historically "taken no position on the border disputes in the area nor on matters pertaining to internal OPEC disputes." Like Tutwiler, he reminded the subcommittee that the US had "no defense treaty relationship with any Gulf country. We support the security and independence of friendly states in the region."

The administration also continued to resist efforts in Congress to take punitive action against Iraq, holding firm to the position that there were more persuasive ways of reining in Saddam Hussein. Nonetheless, on July 27, both chambers voted for economic sanctions. The Senate legislation, sponsored by Alfonse D'Amato (R-N.Y.)—who contended that the administration had been "mollycoddling Iraq for some time"—cut off new financial credits for Iraq until the president certified Iraq's compliance with international agreements on human rights and weapons nonproliferation, while the House measure proposed to suspend export guarantees. Both measures met with opposition from the State Department, which argued that they would "impair our ability to exercise a restraining influence on Iraqi actions" and "would not help us achieve U.S. goals with Iraq."

Nevertheless, behind the scenes, the Bush administration had been seeking some clear answers from Saddam Hussein regarding his intentions toward Kuwait. These efforts would call on April Glaspie to play a central role in the evolving crisis.

Meeting Saddam

Glaspie's first actions followed instructions she received from the State Department on July 18: she was to seek clarification of Saddam Hussein's statements in his National Day television address. Accordingly, she began making formal demands to the Iraqi Foreign Ministry to obtain such clarification, returning to the ministry every day for a week except

Friday, an Islamic holy day. She met with no response.

On July 24, Glaspie received new instructions from Washington that seemed certain to help her capture President Hussein's attention. She was to bring word to the highest available Iraqi official that, a day earlier, the U.S. had begun a joint military exercise with the United Arab Emirates (UAE) involving two U.S. refueling tankers and one U.S. cargo transport—it would be the first such exercise undertaken by both the U.S. and the UAE.[12] She was also instructed to bring a copy of Margaret Tutwiler's July 23 statement from the State Department. These steps got the desired results. When Iraq's Deputy Foreign Minister Nizar Hamdoon received these messages from Glaspie on July 25, he immediately brought them to Saddam Hussein's attention. Shortly afterward, Hamdoon contacted Glaspie and asked her to return to the ministry a second time. When she arrived, he took her by limousine to the presidential palace. With less than one hour's notice, there was no time for the State Department to forward new instructions for what would be Glaspie's first private meeting with the Iraqi leader.

The following day, the State Department issued a brief "official readout" on Glaspie's encounter with Saddam Hussein. "During the meeting," the statement read, "Hussein stated his desire for a peaceful resolution of the Gulf situation. He informed Glaspie of his plans for discussions with Kuwait. Glaspie reaffirmed United States commitment to peace and stability in the Gulf region, and urged that all sides seek to settle their disputes by peaceful means."

For the time being at least, that was the final word on Glaspie's meeting. On July 28, she received a cable calling her back to the U.S. for a high-level policy review. The cable from Washington also contained a "presidential message" to Hussein from President Bush. It read, "we believe that differences are best resolved by peaceful means and not by threats involving military force or conflict. My Administration continues to desire better relations with Iraq."

Glaspie immediately delivered Bush's message to Iraq's Foreign Minister Tariq Aziz. Two days later, assured that negotiations between Iraq and Kuwait were about to begin, Glaspie boarded a plane in Baghdad for the trip back to Washington. On August 1, Iraq walked out on the talks with Kuwait, claim-

---

[12]Subsequently, the UAE denied involvement in the exercise.

ing Kuwait was intransigent about cutting back on oil production. The following day, during an overnight stopover in London, Glaspie turned on the television in her hotel room and learned that Iraq had begun a full-scale invasion of Kuwait.

Where Is April Glaspie?

The next several weeks saw intense diplomatic and military activity, as Iraq announced its formal annexation of Kuwait and moved armored brigades toward the Saudi border, and the U.S. countered with a decision to send troops—its own and those of the nations it had hastily pulled together into an anti-Iraq coalition—to "draw a line in the sand." At the same time, members of the administration—chiefly CIA and White House officials—squabbled among themselves over who was responsible for the government's being unprepared for the Iraqi attack. Amid the flurry of activity and high-level diplomacy, some observers in Washington noticed that April Glaspie had not returned to her post in Baghdad. While the Soviet and British ambassadors—who, like Glaspie, had been out of Iraq at the time of the invasion—had resumed their duties in Baghdad, and Iraq's ambassador to the U.S. was permitted to remain at his post, Glaspie stayed on in Washington, well out of public view.

Queried by the press about Glaspie, administration officials responded ambiguously. The day after the invasion, White House spokesman Marlin Fitzwater told reporters that Glaspie had "gone home on leave"—i.e., vacation. Soon after that, State Department Deputy Spokesman Richard Boucher amended that to say that Glaspie was being consulted "when we thought that she could contribute her expertise and experience."[13] Still later, Boucher told reporters that she was "providing advice to the State Department's [Kuwait] Task Force concerning Iraq. For the foreseeable future, there are no plans for her to return to her post." Boucher also ascribed her absence from Iraq to the administration's desire not to "send the signal to Baghdad that it's business as usual."

On September 12, 1990, however, the *New York Times* offered a different explanation of Glaspie's

presence in Washington. In an article sympathetic to Glaspie, Elaine Sciolino wrote:

> Forty days after Iraqi tanks rolled across the Kuwaiti border, April C. Glaspie, the American Ambassador to Iraq, is stuck behind a desk at the State Department, playing only a minor role in the Administration management of the Persian Gulf crisis and longing to go back to Baghdad. Her only direct contact with Iraq is a daily phone call to her embassy staff.

The "word around the State Department," Sciolino continued, was that Glaspie "was too closely linked to the policy of cooperation with President Saddam Hussein that the Bush Administration pursued until the invasion, a policy that most officials would now like to forget." Sciolino wrote that administration officials were intimating that Glaspie had not been "tough enough in her dealings" with Saddam Hussein, that she should have been "more skeptical of Mr. Hussein's assurances that he would not invade Kuwait." It was "Ms. Glaspie's familiarity with the Arab world," Sciolino speculated, "that helped make her suspect in the eyes of some Administration officials, and her blunt style is often interpreted as abrasiveness by those who do not know her well."

The *Times* article also alluded to Glaspie's cables to Washington following the Voice of America editorial—cables which William Safire had obtained through the Freedom of Information Act and made public for the first time two days before. "Critics who say [Glaspie] was too soft on Iraq," Sciolino wrote, "point to her attempt at diplomatic damage control" after the Voice of America aired its editorial.

Glaspie also had her defenders, as the article made clear. Her supporters described Glaspie "as a tough, loyal diplomat who has never broken the rules . . . faithfully executing a difficult brief handed to her by the President and Secretary of State [James Baker]," Sciolino wrote. Glaspie had " 'inherited an effort of years' standing to try to help mold a more sensible Iraq and develop commercial and industrial relationships so that there would be a richer set of ties,' " argued Richard W. Murphy, assistant secretary of state for Near Eastern and South Asian affairs during most of the Reagan administration. "She didn't invent the policy."

[13]*New York Times*, September 12, 1990, p. A19.

Sciolino's article was noteworthy not just for the story it told. In it, April Glaspie broke her silence, granting the first—and only—interview she was to give in the weeks and months following the invasion. "Although [Glaspie] has always made herself available to journalists in her overseas assignments," Sciolino noted, "she has declined all requests to talk about American policy since her return, saying, 'Any ambassador away from post has to be kept able to go back.'" Glaspie did, however, use the interview as an opportunity to respond to criticism that she had failed to be sufficiently skeptical of Saddam Hussein's assurances. "Obviously," she told Sciolino, "I didn't think—and nobody else did—that the Iraqis were going to take all of Kuwait. Every Kuwaiti and Saudi, every analyst in the Western world was wrong, too. That does not excuse me. But people who now claim that all was clear were not heard from at the time."

Asked when she would return to Baghdad, Glaspie echoed earlier State Department responses. It was up to the president to decide, she replied. "We want to choose the right time. We certainly don't want my going back to be misconstrued as a signal of our irresolution, but a signal of our determination to continue on the course the President has set." But she responded wistfully when Sciolino asked if she wanted to go back. "'You're damned right I do,' she said. 'I talk every morning to the boys. They're so tired and I'm so proud of them. God, I wish I were there.'"

But while the page 19 *New York Times* story brought Glaspie to the sympathetic attention of some, it was Iraq that brought her into the limelight and put her name on the front pages of American newspapers.

What the Transcript Said

The occasion for Glaspie's notoriety was Iraq's release of a transcript of her July 25 meeting with Saddam Hussein. First partially quoted on an ABC-TV special on September 11—the same day Glaspie gave her interview to Elaine Sciolino—the story was soon picked up by the *Washington Post,* the *New York Times,* and newspapers across the country. On September 23 and again on September 30 (when it printed a corrected version), the *Times* published extensive excerpts from the transcript. According to the Iraqi transcript, the following occurred:

Hussein opened the meeting with a message to President Bush, repeating his frustration with Kuwait and the UAE for their "deliberate policy [of forcing] the price of oil down without good commercial reasons," and calling their actions "another war against Iraq." A copy of Tutwiler's July 23 statement on the table in front of him, Hussein commented on the United States' professed commitment to its friends in the Gulf. "But you know you are not the ones who protected your friends during the war with Iran," he said. "I assure you, had the Iranians overrun the region, the American troops would not have stopped them, except by the use of nuclear weapons. . . . Yours is a society which cannot accept 10,000 dead in one battle. . . . So what can it mean when America says it will now protect its friends? . . . The United States must . . . declare who it wants to have relations with and who its enemies are."

Hussein then said, "We know that the U.S. wants an easy flow of oil," but "if you use pressure, we will deploy pressure and force. We know that you can harm us. But we too can harm you." Hinting at possible terrorist actions, the Iraqi president said, "We cannot come all the way to the United States, but individual Arabs may reach you." He then suggested that Iraq would fight to salvage their pride, even if it meant death. "You can come to Iraq with aircraft and missiles, but do not push us to the point where we cease to care," he warned. "When we feel that you want to injure our pride and take away the Iraqis' chance of a high standard of living, then we will cease to care and death will be the choice for us. Then we would not care if you fired 100 missiles for each missile we fired. Because without pride life would have no value."

According to the Iraqi transcript, Glaspie's response was sympathetic. "I have a direct instruction from the President to seek better relations with Iraq," she told Hussein. "I admire your extraordinary efforts to rebuild your country. I know you need funds. We understand that and our opinion is that you should have the opportunity to rebuild your country. But we have no opinion on the Arab-Arab conflicts, like your border disagreement with Kuwait." Glaspie continued in this vein. "I was in the American Embassy in Kuwait in the late '60s. The instruction we had during this period was that we should express no opinion on this issue. . . . James Baker has directed our official spokesman to emphasize this instruction."

In the course of the conversation, Glaspie also alluded to the Voice of America editorial and to a Diane Sawyer interview with Saddam Hussein that had aired on June 28. In that program, Sawyer had described the Iraqi leader as "ruthless," "fierce," and "cold-blooded," referred to him as "the butcher of Baghdad" for his use of chemical weapons on the Kurds, and even asked Hussein if the report that he had personally killed one of his cabinet ministers was true. (He denied it.) Referring to the Sawyer program, Glaspie told Saddam Hussein, "[W]hat happened in that program was cheap and unjust. And this is a real picture of what happens in the American media—even to American politicians themselves. These are the methods the Western media employs. I am pleased that you add your voice to the diplomats who stand up to the media. Because your appearance in the media, even for five minutes, would help us to make the American people understand Iraq. This would increase mutual understanding. If the American president had control over the media, his job would be easier."

Glaspie directed the conversation to the Iraqi troops poised for action on the Kuwait border. "We can only see that you have deployed massive troops in the south," she began carefully. "Normally that would be none of our business. But when this happens in the context of what you said on your national day, then when we read the details in the two letters of the Foreign Minister, then when we see the point of view that the measures taken by the UAE and Kuwait is, in the final analysis, parallel to military aggression against Iraq, I received an instruction to ask you, in the spirit of friendship—not in the spirit of confrontation—regarding your intentions."

President Hussein responded with exasperation. "We want to find a just solution . . . but our patience is running out. We tried everything. . . . We regard this kind of war as a military action against us." At this point, the meeting was interrupted by a telephone call from Egyptian President Hosni Mubarak. About a half hour later, President Hussein returned and gave Ambassador Glaspie a rundown of their conversation. Hussein told Glaspie they had arranged for Kuwaiti and Iraqi delegations to meet in Saudi Arabia immediately, to be followed by deeper negotiations in Baghdad no later than July 30. Hussein said he told Mubarak that "regardless of

how many [troops] are there, and what they are doing, assure the Kuwaitis and give them our word that we are not going to do anything until we meet with them. When we meet and see there is hope, then nothing will happen. But if we are unable to find a solution, then it will be natural that Iraq will not accept death, even though wisdom is above everything else."

Glaspie congratulated Hussein and told him, "I am planning to go to the United States next Monday. I hope I will meet with President Bush in Washington next week. I thought to postpone my trip because of the difficulties we are facing. But now I will fly on Monday."[14]

The Eye of the Storm

The release of the Iraqi transcript—coming amid growing tensions and fears of war—created a storm of criticism in the press. At the center of it was April Glaspie, who was alternately cast as an appeaser or a scapegoat, or both.

"Glaspie met a menacing tirade from Saddam with respectful and sympathetic responses," wrote Jim Hoagland in the *Washington Post* on September 17. Characterizing the ambassador as "effusive in Saddam's presence," Hoagland asserted that Glaspie "quickly turn[ed] the other cheek when it [was] her turn to reply." While acknowledging that Glaspie was likely acting on instructions from Washington, he added, "Even admirers in Washington's Arabist establishment believe she erred in not seeking to change or dilute those instructions as Saddam's intentions unfolded."

Glaspie's remarks about the media came under attack in a number of articles. Calling her "placating" remarks about the media "unfortunate if heartfelt," J. Collins, writing in *Newsday* on September 30, declared, "That a U.S. official would voice such a regret, even in the name of diplomatic expediency and appeasement, and still keep her job, should be regarded as outrageous but seems to have hardly caused a ripple." Commenting in the *Washington Post* the same day, Kenneth Adelman, deputy

[14]Three days after her meeting with Saddam Hussein, Glaspie received a cable from Washington calling her back to the U.S. She postponed her departure for two days, to make sure the negotiations between Iraq and Kuwait would get underway.

permanent U.S. representative to the UN from 1981–83, characterized Glaspie's remarks as "a case of rampant clientitis, falling in love with the country that you are assigned to, and being an advisor to that country on how to deal with America, rather than a representative of America in that country."[15]

Other commentators, while critical of Glaspie, nonetheless pointed their fingers past her to the administration officials who, they argued, had been the architects of the policy of "appeasement." On September 17, William Safire wrote in the *New York Times* that Glaspie had been an "overly distraught diplomat" who had "pleaded for better relations, which further emboldened the dictator." But, he added, "her career is now being ruined, as the posterior-covering Mr. Kelly [assistant secretary of state] tries to make her a scapegoat for Baker's policy of appeasement."

While being more or less pilloried in the press, Glaspie did receive some support from the administration, which so far had not challenged the authenticity of the Iraqi transcript.[16] On September 13, Marlin Fitzwater defended Glaspie as "an outstanding professional who has represented her country well and correctly." She had, he continued, "done a fine job of reading the situation there. The fact is that Saddam lied to everyone in the world, including Mubarak and King Hussein [of Jordan], and Glaspie, and many others. And the whole world was misled." Fitzwater also told reporters that the ambassador's actions had "reflected United States policy . . . to nurture relations with Iraq."

About a week later, on NBC's "Meet the Press," Secretary of State Baker—who had come in for his share of criticism since the release of the transcript— offered a more muted defense of Glaspie. Referring to Glaspie's remark to Saddam Hussein about the U.S. having "no opinion on Arab-Arab conflicts," he explained: "That had to do with taking sides on a border dispute, not taking sides on the question of unprovoked aggression. There are border disputes going on all over the world, and we take positions on some and not on others." At the same time, however, Baker—who also claimed that it was "absolutely ludicrous" to suggest that the administration had given Iraq the "green light" to invade Kuwait— appeared to distance himself from Glaspie, implying that she had not been acting under his explicit instructions. "There are," he said, "probably 312,000 cables or so that go out under my name."

Surprisingly, it was Saddam Hussein himself who appeared most strongly to exonerate Glaspie of responsibility for mishandling their conversation. In October 29 interviews on CNN, Hussein responded to the suggestion that Glaspie could have used stronger language at their meeting—warning, for example, the interviewer suggested, "If you set one foot into Kuwait, we will be there with 200,000 troops and thousands of tanks." Hussein replied:

> I didn't say to her in that meeting that we were going into Kuwait for her to respond by saying that if we did . . . then the U.S. would be prepared to bring . . . 200,000 soldiers and tanks and so on. And let me ask here . . . will an ambassador of the U.S. be in a position to give an answer or respond in this manner? . . . For argument's sake, . . . even if I were to tell her that we were going to enter in Kuwait in the manner or in the conditions that were in fact described clearly in the statement in the communique which we issued on that day, do you expect that an ambassador of the U.S. will be in a position to give such a reply? Unless, of course, the U.S. was itself prepared and preparing for such a situation and had equipped the ambassador with such a reply to give.

The Quiet American

Meanwhile, Glaspie herself remained silent. She had not been seen or heard from since her Sep-

---

[15]Interestingly, Sen. Alan Simpson (R-Wyo.), who had accompanied Robert Dole on his April 12 visit to Saddam Hussein was reported to have made similar remarks on the press to the Iraqi leader. "I believe your problem lies with the Western media, and not with the U.S. government," he told Hussein. ". . . As long as you are isolated from the media, the press—and it is a haughty and pampered press—they all consider themselves political geniuses. That is, the journalists do. They are very cynical. What I advise is that you invite them to come here and see for themselves." Asked about those remarks later, an unrepentant Simpson responded, "You bet I said [that]," and added that he had "not a whit of regrets."

[16]Later reports, however, indicated that Assistant Secretary Kelly and others in the State Department had passed the word along that the transcript was "essentially accurate." (William Safire, "I'll Remember April," *New York Times*, p. A17).

tember 11 interview with Elaine Sciolino—under instructions from Baker, some speculated, not to speak out publicly. As war tensions continued to build, people wondered when, and if, they would hear her story.

It was not until late March of 1991—almost eight months after her July meeting with Saddam Hussein—that April Glaspie appeared before Congress to publicly defend her statements to the Iraqi president. No reporter was allowed to interview Glaspie during those months, although many tried. CBS even staged a stakeout at her Georgetown home, and a videotape of the stakeout was aired in February during Connie Chung's "Face to Face" interview with Secretary of State James Baker. While chasing her down the street with a microphone, Chung quizzed Glaspie about her July meeting with Hussein. "You're asking me to comment on a conversation which the State Department has explained to you we don't intend to discuss in

public," Glaspie replied.[17] The State Department's official position was that Glaspie was "too busy" to give interviews.

Although they declined to say so on the record, senior State Department officials continued to criticize Glaspie's conduct during her meeting with President Hussein as much too weak. Confident that she would ultimately be vindicated, however, Glaspie rejected the advice of friends and colleagues that she "play the game of Washington guerrilla warfare" by publicizing her side of the story. "It's a matter of service discipline," she told them. "I won't stoop to that."[18] Instead, Glaspie struggled to play a more active role in the crisis while Deputy Chief of Mission Joseph C. Wilson IV, an African specialist with no prior experience in the Middle East, conducted day-to-day diplomacy in Baghdad in her absence. According to the *New York Times,* Glaspie told colleagues of her longing to accompany Secretary of State James Baker to his January meeting with the Iraqi foreign minister, Tariq Aziz, on the eve of the allied attack on Iraq. But during her hour-long meeting with the secretary, Glaspie could not bring herself to ask, and he did not invite her.[19] Mostly, Glaspie attended mid-level interagency meetings and often worked nights and weekends on the State Department's emergency Kuwait task force.[20] By late January, Peter A. Burleigh—a career foreign service officer and personal friend—had already been named as her successor as ambassador to Baghdad.

[17]During the show, Chung asked Baker if, in Glaspie's conversation with Saddam Hussein, she was specifically conveying a policy he directed her to express. Baker replied, "No, . . . there were no formal security guarantees" for Kuwait. Chung then flashed a videotaped clip of Glaspie saying, "but I don't think either the secretary or the president has ever been in doubt about that policy" as she hurried to her car to escape from Chung's microphone.

[18]*New York Times,* March 21, 1991, p. A15.

[19]Ibid., p. A15.

[20]During Glaspie's Senate testimony, she revealed a trace of the desire to play a more central role when she stated that "it would have been fun if I had been with him [Secretary of State Baker]" on his recent diplomatic trip to the Middle East.

[21]The State Department had ignored previous requests from the committees for her testimony.

[22]Iraqi casualties were estimated at over 100,000.

[23]The Senate voted 52–47 approving a resolution authorizing the use of military force against Iraq. The House supported the use of force by a vote of 250–183. Republicans lined up solidly behind President Bush (by 42–2 votes in the Senate and by 164–3 in the House). Democrats voted against authorizing military action by large margins (by 45–10 in the Senate and by 179–86 in the House). One prominent and unexpected voice against the immediate use of military force was Senator Sam Nunn (R-Ga.), conservative chair of the Armed Services Committee. During January 1991 hearings on the Persian Gulf Crisis, Nunn said, "If we have a war, we are never going to know whether they [sanctions] would have worked, are we?"

[24]George Gedda, "Truth or Dare: The Glaspie Affair," *Foreign Service Journal,* 68:7 (July, 1991) p. 26.

Breaking the Silence

On March 20, 1991, with two formal requests for her testimony from two congressional committees,[21] the opportunity for Glaspie to defend herself finally arrived. By this time, President Bush had declared that the war in the gulf was over; Iraq had withdrawn from Kuwait, with relatively few American lives lost in the battle.[22] Congress had voted (albeit along partisan lines[23]) to authorize the president's use of 500,000 American troops to force Iraq's withdrawal. After the war, some Republicans had pilloried Democrats who voted against the resolution to use force. Many Democrats now felt it fair game to demand from Glaspie an explanation of how the administration had led the country into war in the first place.[24]

Senate Foreign Relations Committee Chair Claiborne Pell (D-R.I.) began the committee's "informal discussion"[25] not by critiquing Glaspie, but the policy she was charged with conveying. "Nobody can fault you for carrying out your instructions," Pell said. "Rather, I question the instructions." Continuing in this vein, Pell said he believed "that over many years we sent Saddam Hussein several wrong signals, and that our policy did encourage him in the belief we might not react strongly if the invasion occurred. It was the opposition of both administrations to congressional efforts to sanction Iraq for its illegal and immoral conduct that sent the real signal, in my view, to Saddam Hussein that his ambitions in the region were unlikely to be thwarted from the West."

In her testimony, however, Glaspie defended both her conduct and that of the administration regarding Hussein. Glaspie told the committee that during her July meeting with Hussein, she emphasized the United States' insistence that "all disputes with Iraq's neighbors be settled peacefully . . . not by threats, not by intimidation, and certainly not by aggression." Glaspie said she repeatedly "told him orally we would defend our vital interests, we would support our friends in the Gulf, we would defend their sovereignty and integrity." She explained to Hussein that the U.S. was "a superpower and intended to act like one." The statements, however, were omitted from the Iraqi account, Glaspie said. Hussein, in response to her firmness, "was conciliatory and normally he is not . . . He surrendered. He . . . told me that he told [Egyptian President] Mubarak, and he wanted me to inform President Bush, that he would not solve his problems by force, period." Their only mistake, Glaspie said, was that "we did not understand . . . that he would be impervious to logic and diplomacy. . . . Like every other government in the world, we foolishly did not believe he was stupid, that he did not believe our clear

and repeated warnings that we would support our vital interests."

Responding to the controversy surrounding her comment that "we have no opinion on Arab-Arab conflicts, like your border dispute with Kuwait," Glaspie explained that the other part of her sentence, "but we insist that you settle your disputes with Kuwait non-violently," was "maliciously" edited out of the Iraqi document. The context of her statement, Glaspie said, was as follows: "Hussein was hinting that we should bully the Kuwaitis into paying up, that this was an appropriate thing for the U.S. to do, that we should take the Iraqi position on their border dispute. My point was that it was not our business, it was Kuwait and Iraq's business to decide whether a border post should go one meter to the left or one meter to the right . . . but it was emphatically our business that they make this settlement in a non-violent way." Glaspie then assailed the Iraqi version of her meeting as "a fabrication." "It is disinformation," she claimed. "It is not a transcript. This is the kind of thing the Iraqi Government has done for years and not very subtly."

Senator Joseph Biden (D-Del.) asked Glaspie if her reporting cables from Baghdad to her superiors in Washington reflected this insistence on peaceful resolution. Glaspie said yes, but later expressed opposition to the release of her cables. "In my 25 years, I do not recall any government other than Saddam Hussein issuing a transcript of a confidential diplomatic exchange," Glaspie said. "If we are going to maintain confidence and our own confidentiality, no matter how great the temptation to expose the lies of the other side, I personally think it is wise not to begin issuing transcripts."

When asked about her comments to Hussein regarding his ABC-TV interview with Diane Sawyer, Glaspie explained that her remarks were made in regard to a videotape of the program shown on Iraqi television. The Iraqi video, Glaspie said, cut out all scenes where Hussein was unable to satisfactorily answer any of Sawyer's tough questions. Glaspie said she told Hussein that she thought "the editing of transcripts—not just transcripts, of video tapes—was cheap and unjust," as in the case of Sawyer's interview.[26]

Committee members wondered aloud why the State Department, given Glaspie's responses, had not permitted her to testify weeks earlier. Glaspie, in a seemingly practiced answer, responded:

[25]Because an unnamed committee member objected to holding a formal hearing with Glaspie that afternoon, Pell conducted "an informal but public discussion" instead. Senator Jesse Helms was absent from the discussion due to simultaneous Senate floor action on a bill for which he had offered an amendment.

[26]In her House testimony [the] following day, Glaspie said Diane Sawyer "did American journalism proud."

Our President has certainly been running our foreign policy. He's been briefing the press. He has been briefing all of you, I think, very routinely. His emphasis, of course, was on building a coalition and making sure then that the aims of the coalition were filled. As you yourself said, the emphasis should be on the job at hand, and now on what will come in the future, how we can do a better job in the future. Now we've won, the war is over, the troops are back, and I'm here on instructions to answer your questions. It simply seemed that it was not a time for retrospective. It was a time to build our coalition, to support our troops on the field. And now is the time, if you wish, for retrospectives. And, as I say, I'm here on instructions. [laughter] I was glad to come, but I was certainly on instructions.

Each successive response from Glaspie appeared to further disarm most committee members so that, by the end of the discussion, they were praising her performance.

Glaspie returned to Capitol Hill the following day to testify before the House Foreign Affairs Subcommittee on Europe and the Middle East. She was treated far less gently at this formal hearing. Subcommittee Chair Lee Hamilton (D-Ind.) complained that she and other officials sent mixed signals to Iraq prior to the invasion, leaving the impression that Hussein was free to act as he did. Referring to statements that the United States had no defense pact with Kuwait—statements which were repeated right up until the invasion by Ambassador Glaspie, Assistant Secretary of State for Near East and South Asian Affairs John Kelly, and State Department Spokeswoman Margaret Tutwiler—Hamilton said, "[T]his is not a record of unambiguous clarity with respect to American positions. It is a record that confused me, confused the subcommittee, confused much of the Washington press, and it is not unreasonable for me to think that it might have confused Saddam Hussein as well."

Glaspie responded with confidence. "Mr. Chairman, I'm glad to reassure you, Saddam Hussein had no question in his mind. I am quite convinced of that," she said. "I am absolutely sure that he knew—he knew that we would fight." But when asked if she specifically told Hussein that the United States was going to fight if he invaded Kuwait, Glaspie replied, "I did not need to say that. I have no doubt in my

mind that he knew we meant business . . . Saddam Hussein, who is a man who lives by the sword, believed we were going to do it by the sword."

Representative Tom Lantos (D-Calif.), who had previously ascribed an "Alice in Wonderland" quality to the administration's attitude toward Iraq, was astounded by Glaspie's statements:

I am appalled by the frighteningly flawed judgment you display even in retrospect. . . . You even now tell us that you were sure Hussein knew we would move militarily. Let me tell you, very few people knew that we would move militarily on this committee or in this country. And for you to say in retrospect that Saddam Hussein absolutely knew that we would move in a military way is simply absurd. I think you need to have a very high dose of humility in retrospect given the pattern of appalling judgments made by you and your associates.

Glaspie held her ground, arguing that Hussein told her "straight out indirectly" that he knew the United States would fight because "he railed against what he believed we were threatening. . . . A whole series of comments . . . made it perfectly clear that that is what he was (A), concerned about, and (B), had come to believe we were [intending]. . . . He felt secure in the belief that no Arab government would ever allow us to use their land for that purpose." But Glaspie backed away from her more assured approach. "I didn't say now I was absolutely confident," she said. "I said I believe that he probably had decided on that day or the day before for the first time that we would fight if we had to."

Rep. Stephen Solarz (D-N.Y.) grilled Glaspie regarding the Voice of America editorial entitled "No More Secret Police" broadcast in Iraq in February 1990. According to the Iraqi transcript of her meeting with Hussein, Glaspie told the Iraqi president she thought the VOA editorial was "sad." After reading parts of the editorial aloud to the committee, Solarz said, "I have to say for the life of me, I don't see a single word or sentence in here that is unfortunate. This is a statement of the most fundamental American values." Glaspie, who said she believed the editorial was written in a way that could have been misinterpreted as a U.S. attempt to incite revolution in Iraq, defended the written apology she gave to the Iraqi government. "I was trying to create some kind of influence for the United States of America in this very dangerous country so that we could influence it and moderate it, and the major impediment to what was their [the Iraqis'] belief that for twenty years we had been trying to subvert their regime," Glaspie explained. "This was a serious handicap in the job the president had given me to do."

"The sentence '[T]he 1990s should belong, not to the dictators and secret police, but to the people' expresses exactly the sentiments of the American people," Solarz countered. "I would like to believe it expresses the sentiments of the Administration. I think we should be and should have been utterly unapologetic about [the VOA editorial]. And if they were offended by it, the answer, I think, should have been 'Get rid of your secret police and let the people run the country.'"

Again, Glaspie was asked why the administration did not allow her to appear publicly prior to her congressional hearings. Dante Fascell (D-Fla.), head of the House Foreign Affairs Committee, said to Glaspie, "I'm not a suspicious person, but I do have a question as to why a career foreign service officer would be taken advantage of, in my mind, by being kept locked up in the halls of the State Department or someplace else for all these months, while all these questions were floating around in the air, bouncing only on her head, and nobody's else's. I don't think that's fair."

Glaspie admitted that Secretary of State Baker had made the decision not to allow her to appear publicly. "That's his job to run his department as he wishes to," she said. "If he wishes to be the spokesman for it, with one designated spokeswoman, then it seems to me, frankly, his business." Regarding the Iraqi transcript, Glaspie said "it was explained to me that a decision had been made that it would be unwise for the Department, of which obviously I am a member, to argue about it in public at that time. A point-by-point rebuttal would focus our national energies where we should not be focusing them . . . the time would come later."

"I find that explanation inherently implausible," Rep. Solarz argued, puzzled as to why the administration did not immediately discredit the Iraqi transcript as disinformation. "In fact, the Iraqi version of the discussion was compromising our capacity to muster support for the President's policy here at home. It contributed to the view that we were somehow or other responsible for what had happened by giving Saddam the impression that he could get away with what he did." Solarz challenged Glaspie's opposition to the release of her reporting cables, arguing that doing so "would hardly be unprecedented." "Professionally, I fundamentally disagree with your judgment," he said. "For one thing, this committee is frequently given access to cables involving discussions between ambassadors and foreign leaders, including heads of state. And secondly, to the extent that there is a legitimate concern about confidentiality, that could presumably be protected if the cables were provided on a classified basis."

A New Official Explanation

At a State Department briefing following Glaspie's congressional testimony, Deputy Spokesman Richard Boucher stated clearly, for the first time, that the Iraqi transcript was "heavily edited to the point of inaccuracy." One reporter questioned why, previously, there was "no vigorous effort [on the part of the State Department] to clear the record for the sake of the policy, the department, or the Ambassador." "I suppose people in public service have to take a certain amount of trashing for the good of the country or something, but . . . why didn't Mr. Baker, in one of his many television appearances, say something about the doctoring of what she had told Saddam Hussein?" the reporter asked. Boucher's reply was consistent with Glaspie's testimony. "We considered the Iraqi transcript to be a sideshow," he explained. "Our focus throughout the crisis remained the crisis and what we could do about it." The reporter did not buy that answer. "The sideshow was created because you weren't responding and defending her, not because you were. Had you responded and defended her, according to the way you're doing today, there never would have been a sideshow."

When asked why the White House refused to correct the record, Spokesman Marlin Fitzwater offered a more revealing answer. "Because we knew the truth and the facts of the matter and felt that it was best to hold that debate until we had conducted the war." When asked if the president had any hesitancy in offering Glaspie another post, Fitzwater replied, "we have no hesitancy. She's done very well . . . what April Glaspie told Saddam Hussein was exactly what she was supposed to have said, it represented U.S. policy, and she said exactly the right things." Would the president then like to see her appointed to another ambassadorship? "Well, we'll just have to wait and see," returned Fitzwater.

Later, it was announced that Glaspie would be spending the 1991–1992 academic year as a "diplomat in residence" at the University of California–San Diego.

Curious Cables

Within a week of Glaspie's congressional testimony, William Safire of the *New York Times* reported that Secretary of State James Baker had been hailed at the Gridiron Club dinner for releasing Glaspie "physically unharmed." Still, doubts about Glaspie's meeting with Hussein lingered. According to the *Times,* a senior official sympathetic to Baker said, "if you read her cable you would not say that the entire Iraqi transcript was phony baloney. Since her cable was not 250 degrees different from the Iraqi transcript, no one felt entirely comfortable in going out and saying it was all false." A few weeks later, Ralph Nader's advocacy group, Public Citizen, had filed suit against the State Department to secure the release of records concerning Glaspie's meeting with Hussein. Alan Morrison, director of the Public Citizen Litigation Group argued that "once the government chooses to discuss bits and pieces of the information it has concerning the Glaspie file, it can no longer legally hide the rest claiming it is exempt from the Freedom of Information laws."

On July 12, Glaspie's reporting cables were released to the Senate Foreign Relations Committee, which subsequently leaked them to the press. Excerpts from Glaspie's cables, still classified as secret, were printed in the *New York Times* the following day.

In a letter to Secretary of State Baker, Senator Claiborne Pell wrote that Glaspie's own cables raised doubts that she had warned Hussein several times during their conversation that the United States would defend its vital interests in the Gulf region. "No place does she report clearly delivering the kind of warning she described in her testimony" and in some instances, "her statement is contradicted by the reporting cable," Pell wrote. "I would ask that the de-

partment look into this situation and would also appreciate an explanation as to why no effort was made to correct the public record."

Glaspie's cables appeared quite similar in tone and in substance to the Iraqi transcript released in September of 1990. While her cables contained one sentence where she said she told Hussein "we can never excuse settlement of disputes by any but peaceful means," they generally suggested Glaspie took a conciliatory approach toward Hussein, emphasizing Bush's "desire for friendship" and better relations. The cables contained no direct account of Glaspie telling Hussein that "we would defend our vital interests." Instead, Glaspie seemed to believe that events were improving. "His [Hussein's] emphasis that he wants peaceful settlement is surely sincere," Glaspie wrote in her conclusion. "The Iraqis are sick of war." Glaspie added, "I believe we would now be well-advised to ease off on public criticism of Iraq until we see how the negotiations develop."

Contradicting her promise to Senator Biden, Glaspie's cable did not record her insistence on peaceful dispute resolution, which Glaspie claimed was cut from her sentence, "we have no opinion on Arab-Arab disputes, like your border disagreement with Kuwait." According to her cable, Glaspie followed up instead with "[T]he ambassador said that she served in Kuwait 20 years before; then, as now, we took no position on these Arab affairs." Also, in a direct contradiction to the explanation Glaspie gave regarding her remarks about the Diane Sawyer interview with Hussein, Glaspie wrote in her cable that she "had seen the Diane Sawyer show and thought it was cheap and unfair."

"April Glaspie deliberately misled Congress and the country," about her role in the Persian Gulf tragedy, said Senator Alan Cranston [D-Calif.], senior member of the Foreign Relations Committee. "A stern warning to Saddam Hussein about the likely American response to an Iraqi invasion of Kuwait could have prevented the invasion and all the death and destruction it caused. Ambassador Glaspie sought to convince us she issued such a warning. Her secret cable is evidence that she did not."

A senior State Department official tried to explain the discrepancy. "The traditional way of writing a diplomatic cable about an ambassador's meeting with a foreign leader is to emphasize what the leader told the ambassador rather than the other way around. That was what Ambassador Glaspie did, and that is why her cables stress what she was told by Saddam. Later, when questions arose about what kind of message she gave Saddam on behalf of the United States, she filled in the gaps in her testimony." In an interview with CNN, Brent Scowcroft, President Bush's national security advisor, also defended Glaspie. "I have great faith in Ambassador Glaspie and what she said," Scowcroft said. "You have to remember she was with Saddam Hussein by herself. She came back and jotted down what she recalls of what he said . . . I would defy a congressman to write down word for word what happened in a conversation an hour or two afterwards when there was no one else in the room."

Again, Glaspie's strongest defense came from the Iraqis. In an interview with *The New Yorker* published in June 1991, Iraqi Foreign Minister Tariq Aziz, who had been present at Glaspie's meeting with Hussein, said, "having been a Foreign Minister, I understand the work of an ambassador, and I believe Miss Glaspie's behavior was correct. She was summoned suddenly. We knew she was acting on available instructions. She spoke in vague diplomatic language, and we knew the position she was in. Her behavior was a classic diplomatic response, and we were not influenced by it."

Another Chance

In light of the release of her reporting cables, the Senate Foreign Relations Committee called upon Glaspie to testify a second time. The State Department requested that Acting Secretary of State Lawrence S. Eagleburger accompany her to the hearing. According to a committee staffer, the department's request was refused because there was a feeling within the committee that Eagleburger's presence might inhibit or otherwise influence Glaspie's testimony.

Update

It wasn't until late September, 1991, that the Senate Foreign Relations Committee settled its dispute with the State Department over when, how, and with whom April Glaspie would return to testify on Capitol Hill to explain what Democrats called "gross dis-

crepancies" between her March testimony and her secret cables to Washington before Iraq's invasion of Kuwait. The State Department—which had vehemently opposed another appearance by Glaspie—was finally forced to relent after the committee put the brakes on the confirmation of two top Foggy Bottom appointments until the department permitted Glaspie to testify.

Meanwhile, the press mysteriously dropped the story like a hot potato. Remarkably, when Glaspie finally reappeared before the Senate panel on November 21, 1991—this time in a closed session—not a single major news outlet covered the event. And Glaspie, who had assumed her yearlong position as diplomat-in-residence at the University of California at San Diego—continued to maintain a low profile, refusing all interview requests.

By 1992, however, the Glaspie story was superseded by the release of new information—internal memos, cablegrams, letters and interviews—demonstrating that Glaspie, in assuming a conciliatory approach toward Iraqi president Saddam Hussein up until the day he invaded Kuwait, had not acted alone. Months of congressional investigations had unearthed stacks of evidence suggesting that, in the years before the 1990 invasion, the Reagan and Bush administrations had channeled billions of dollars in U.S. farm aid and commercial exports to Iraq in an attempt to preserve a stable balance of power in the Persian Gulf—despite a series of warnings from government officials that the aid was being diverted to build Hussein's military machine, that Iraq was a credit risk, and that earlier assistance efforts to Iraq were plagued by "financial irregularities."[27]

Specifically, declassified materials showed that through 1990—in accordance with Bush's secret National Security Directive 26 (NSD-26), signed in October, 1989 (less than ten months before the invasion of Kuwait) to order closer ties with Baghdad—Bush, Secretary of State James Baker III and other White House officials urged the Commerce and Defense departments to approve sales to Iraq of sensitive U.S. technology that was eventually used in Hussein's weapons programs, including his efforts to develop nuclear capabilities. At that time, the Bush administration was aware of mounting evidence that suggested that Hussein was pushing ahead with the development of nuclear and biolog-

[27]*Los Angeles Times,* 2/23/92.

ical weapons, enhancing his chemical weapons, and working on his own long-range ballistic missiles.[28]

Documents also showed that nine months before the invasion, Bush approved $1 billion in aid for Iraq—$500 million of which Iraq had already spent by February 1990—in the form of loan guarantees for the purchase of U.S. farm commodities.[29] The federal loan program enabled Hussein to buy foodstuffs on credit and to spend his scarce reserves of hard currency on the massive arms buildup that eventually brought war to the Persian Gulf.[30] (Hussein spent $10 billion—40 percent of Iraq's oil revenues—in 1988 and 1989 on military equipment and personnel.)[31] However, of the $5 billion in economic aid provided to Iraq over an eight-year period from 1982–1990, American taxpayers were stuck with $2 billion in defaulted guaranteed loans.[32]

Glaspie's Role

Several of the newly declassified documents and cables implicated Ambassador Glaspie in the drive to assist Iraq both militarily and economically in order to bring Iraq towards "moderation." In November 1989, the U.S. Central Command for the Depart-

ment of Defense in Tampa said in a cable to Washington that "we concur with Ambassador Glaspie that implementation of low-level, non-lethal military assistance would greatly facilitate developing an improved military dialogue with and access to the senior military leadership and the government of Iraq."[33] In May, 1990—after the U.S. Department of Agriculture decided to suspend the second $500 million of the $1 billion loan guarantee program because, as one department official explained, "all the worst fears [about the program] were realized: fraud and mismanagement, kickbacks, diversion of funds for the military"—Glaspie sent urgent cables to Washington urging that the credit program be resumed. "From a foreign policy perspective," Glaspie wrote in a secret cable on May 18, 1990, cutting off the credits would have been a "decision difficult to justify" to the Iraqis. "My own thinking," Glaspie continued, "is that unless Agriculture has uncovered a legal hornets' nest, we will want to proceed with the second tranche of credits. It remains unclear why we would want to use food as a weapon:"[34]

> Turning down the CCC [Commodity Credit Corporation] credits would send the signal that the administration has decided to join those in Congress who had already reached the conclusion that the U.S. had no option but to pursue a policy of sanctions and containment. A sudden shift now will be read by the Iraqis as purely political—part of the U.S. conspiracy against Iraq.

Glaspie went on to urge that if a negative decision was to be made on the credits, it be withheld from the Iraqis for the time being.[35]

And as late as July 9, 1990—less than one month before Iraq invaded Kuwait—Glaspie assured Iraqi officials that the Bush administration was still trying to get the second $500 million in CCC credits released, according to another classified cable.[36]

Admitting Failure

"The selective disclosure out of context of classified documents has led, knowingly or otherwise, to distortions of the record, half-truths and outright falsehoods, all combined into spurious conspiracy theories and charges of a cover-up," bristled Deputy

[28]*New York Times*, 6/27/92. On November 6, 1989, a month after Bush's directive, a secret CIA document concluded that: "Baghdad has created complex procurement networks of holding companies in Western Europe to acquire technology for its chemical, biological, nuclear and ballistic missile programs." (Quoted in the *New York Times* on 7/19/92.)

[29]The second $500 tranche was to be delivered only if no further problems arose from the concurrent Banca Nazionale del Lavoro (BNL) investigation.

[30]*Los Angeles Times*, 2/23/92.

[31]*New York Times*, 6/27/92.

[32]*Los Angeles Times*, 2/23/92.

[33]The cable from Central Command, then headed by Army General H. Norman Schwarzkopf—later the director of the international military campaign that ousted Iraqi forces from Kuwait—listed 10 separate initiatives that should be pursued with Iraq. They ranged from supplying Army field manuals and English language textbooks to training Iraqi personnel in military medicine, mine countermeasures, aviation security and infrared countermeasures "for the [Iraqi] President's aircraft." (*Washington Post*, 8/4/92.)

[34]These excerpts from Glaspie's cable were read into the *Congressional Record* on 7/9/92.

[35]*Associated Press*, 6/7/92.

[36]*Los Angeles Times*, 2/23/92.

Secretary of State Lawrence S. Eagleburger at a May, 1992 hearing before the House Banking Committee. The Bush administration—after months of ignoring criticism of its pre-invasion support for Saddam Hussein—finally took the offensive, accusing Democratic lawmakers (led by Banking Committee chair Henry B. Gonzalez [D-Tex.]) of lying and distorting the record. Eagleburger argued that the administration had followed a "prudent" policy toward Iraq, and insisted that the CCC loan guarantee program had been properly executed.

But Committee Democrats would not let up on their criticism. Rep. Charles E. Schumer (D-NY) charged that "Saddam Hussein is President Bush's Frankenstein, a run-of-the-mill dictator the president fed with billions of U.S. taxpayer dollars and turned him into a monster. Created in the White House laboratory with a collection of government programs, banks and private companies, Saddam grew beyond the administration's control. It was the mother of all foreign policy blunders."

Even Eagleburger found it difficult to defend the policy. "It is clear that policy did not work," Eagleburger conceded. "I have said fifteen times today that it didn't work":

> . . . It is not the first foreign policy of the United States . . . that didn't work. We tried and we failed. . . . My point is—it is easy to defend a policy that works. It's not so easy when a policy didn't work. But the fact of the matter is—because we tried to work with Iraq and with Saddam Hussein does not mean we created a Frankenstein's monster. He was there, he was his own monster. We tried to contain him. We did not succeed.

In response to this new admission, Chairman Gonzalez cut to the point: "The documents speak for themselves," Gonzalez said. "In other words, the documents and the history are clear. And so is the lesson. The policy was wrong. It was pursued despite warning signs and despite Hussein's well-known brutality, and it failed. You admit it."

On June 4, 1992, President Bush also tried to defend his dealing with Iraq before the invasion of Kuwait: "We tried to work with him," Bush said of Saddam Hussein. "And it failed. That approach, holding out a hand, trying to get him to renounce terrorism, didn't work," he told a press conference at

the White House. "I know what we did," he added. "It wasn't anything illegal."

Despite Bush's assertion, some in Congress charged that his administration did more than simply misjudge Saddam Hussein. "Certain aspects of this affair bear the marks of a major scandal involving at best improper conduct, and at worst criminal activity, by U.S. government officials," charged Rep. Schumer, regarding irregularities in the CCC program. "We already know the President's biggest foreign policy success, the Persian Gulf War, was made necessary by his most enormous foreign policy failure, his tilt toward Iraq."

A Gag Order?

On June 23, 1992, the House Judiciary Committee held a hearing to determine if a special prosecutor was needed to investigate U.S. aid provided to Iraq before the Gulf War. To strengthen its case, the panel heard testimony and reviewed declassified documents suggesting that after the invasion of Kuwait, senior aides to Bush and Baker conspired to restrain the release of information about earlier U.S. aid to Iraq. "The administration didn't want criticism during the Iraq engagement," said Iain Baird, director of the Commerce Department's Office of Export Licensing, in an interview with the Commerce Department's Inspector General (IG)—according to one document containing the IG's notes of the interview. Under orders from the White House, high-ranking Commerce Department officials altered records to conceal military applications of U.S. exports that had been licensed by the administration. Baird told questioners from the IG's office that the State Department—notified of a congressional request for U.S. export license records—"said trucks classified as military vehicles should be reclassified as cargo trucks." Baird also told the IG that he "thought Commerce had been 'set up' as a conscious effort to distance Bush and Baker from Iraq."

Had Glaspie been "set up" as well—a victim of a similar gag order? Rep. Sam Gejdenson (D-Conn.) thinks so: "I think they hung April Glaspie out to dry for not being tough enough with Saddam Hussein."[37] Hume Horan, a former ambassador to Saudi

[37]ABC-News, "Nightline," 6/9/92.

Arabia and Sudan, agrees. "April's our Joan of Arc, top of the curve, a first-class Arabist. The media need a villain, so they've painted her as 'the appeaser.' But ambassadors look only as good or as bad as the policy they represent." Horan adds that "there is a Kleenex quality to ambassadors. We're policy instruments—not policy makers—there to take the blame, to be wiped away so the process can continue."[38]

Still, says a former colleague of Glaspie's who knows her well, "April has never been involved in any issue where she was not a policy driver. She was dynamic, aggressive, and supremely confident—she dominated issues. It was just not in her character to be a passive ambassador implementing a policy she did not fully agree with."[39]

The Court of Public Opinion

In a July 9, 1992 letter to Attorney General William Barr, House Judiciary Committee Democrats re-

[38]Robert D. Kaplan, "Tales From the Bazaar," *The Atlantic*, Vol. 270, No. 2, August 1992, pp. 44, 57.

[39]*Ibid.*, p. 57.

[40]*New York Times*, 8/11/92.

quested the appointment of an independent prosecutor to investigate U.S. aid to Iraq, suggesting that there may have been "activities by both current and former officials to illegally assist the regime of Saddam Hussein prior to the August 1990 invasion of Kuwait." Much to the Democrats' dismay, however, Barr declined on August 10 to grant the request. In a letter to the committee, Barr accused Democrats of playing politics in an election year: "We have found those allegations to be hollow. . . . As attorney general, I believe strongly that we cannot allow the criminal process to be used as a political weapon or for partisan purposes."

House Judiciary Chairman Jack Brooks (D-Tex.) responded to the decision with outrage: "It is stonewalling, plain and simple. . . . What is the administration trying to hide in the record of its assistance to Saddam Hussein?" Although Democrats vowed to continue to press the issue, Barr's decision appeared to be final; the law on appointing special prosecutors states that the Attorney General's decision "shall not be reviewable in any court." However, because the decision cannot be challenged in court, Congress was likely to intensify its own investigations. As Brooks put it: "The court of public opinion is open for business twenty four hours a day, and that court will not be satisfied with the subterfuge concocted today."[40]

Chapter 7 Review Questions

1. What are the five major subsystems in public agencies that decisively influence bureaucratic policy? Briefly describe the characteristics of each one.
2. Where are political appointees situated in the bureaucracy and what functions do these individuals serve in U.S. government? Who were the political appointees in the case and what were the roles they played? Especially in setting the policy agenda for Glaspie?
3. What are the essential differences between the professional careerist subsystem and the political appointee subsystem? What are the sources of each one's influence and authority?
4. Why was Glaspie considered a "professional elite" in the foreign service?
5. What were the causes of conflict between Glaspie and the foreign policy political leadership? Why did they fail to protect her after the start of the Gulf War?
6. What does the case say about the ethical dilemmas of modern public professionals and the sources of these issues? Do top government officials have to possess a "kleenex quality" or be considered expendable, as this case suggests?

Key Terms

political appointees	GS rating
sub-Cabinet officials	rank "in person" versus "in job"
professional careerists	Kennedy's Executive Orders
professional elites	10988 and 10987
SES	public service unions
"inner" versus "outer" Cabinet	contract employment
Pendleton Act	line versus staff professionals

Suggestions for Further Reading

A number of excellent books deal with the origins, growth, and operations of the various types of bureaucratic subsystems discussed in this chapter. The best account of the rise of the U.S. civil service remains Paul Van Riper's *History of the U.S. Civil Service* (1958). For a history of the European civil service, read Brian Chapman's *The Profession of Government* (1959). For accounts of professionalism in the civil service, read C. L. Gibb, *Hidden Hierarchies* (1966), Don Price, *Scientific Estate* (1965), and Frederick C. Mosher, *Democracy and the Public Service,* Second Edition. (1982). Studies advocating reforms in the civil service systems, such as the Volcker Commission Report, *Leadership for America* (1989), The Hudson Institute, *Civil Service 2000* (1988), and Frank J. Thompson (ed.), *Revitalizing State and Local Government: Strengthening Performance, Accountability, and Citizen Confidence* (1993), are some of the best guides to current civil service practices.

For a thoughtful look at the meaning of "merit" in relation to contemporary civil service, read Patricia W. Ingraham, *The Foundation of Merit* (1995). For an account of the interplay between political appointees, professionals, and civil servants, read Frank J. Thompson, *Personnel Policy in the City* (1975), Hugh Heclo, *A Government of Strangers* (1977), James P. Pfiffner, *The Strategic Presidency* (1988), and Robert F. Durant, *The Administrative Presidency Revisited* (1992). Three books dealing with political appointees include John W. Macy, Bruce Adams, and J. Jackson Wal-

ter, eds., *America's Unelected Government: Appointing the President's Team* (1983), G. Calvin MacKenzie, *The Politics of Presidential Appointments* (1981), and by the same author, *The In and Outers* (1987). Excellent reviews of the impact of the 1978 Civil Service Reform Act are found in Patricia W. Ingraham and Carolyn Ban, eds., *Legislating Bureaucratic Change* (1984), and Patricia W. Ingraham and David H. Rosenbloom (eds.), *The Promise and Paradox of Civil Service Reform* (1993). For the current operation of SES that was created by CSRA 1978, see OPM, *The Status of the Senior Executive Service* (1991), the Merit Protection Board, *The Senior Executive Service— Views of Former Federal Executives* (1989), Mark W. Huddleton and William A. Boyes, *The Higher Civil Services in the United States* (1995), and the thoughtful essay by Norton Long, "SES and the Public Interest," *Public Administration Review* (May/June 1981). For a helpful overview of the civil service today, review Patricia W. Ingraham et al. David H. Rosenbloom, *Agenda for Excellence* (1992) as well as Carolyn Ban and Norma Riccucci, *Public Personnel Management* (1991).

For useful perspectives on professional career systems, see Frederick C. Mosher and Richard J. Stillman II, eds., *Professions in Government* (1982). For more current aspects of professionalism, see James A. Smith, *The Idea Brokers* (1991), and David S. Arnold and Jeremy F. Plant, *Public Official Associations and State and Local Government: A Bridge Across One Hundred Years*

(1994), and for unions, A. Lawrence Chickering, ed., *Public Employee Unions* (1977), and David T. Stanley, *Managing Local Government under Union Pressure* (1972). For perhaps the best current studies of where we are today involving the problems of unions and the public service, read Joel M. Douglas's three essays: "Collective Bargaining and Public Sector Supervisors: A Trend Towards Exclusion?" *Public Administration Review* (Nov./Dec. 1987); "State Civil Service and Collective Bargaining Systems in Conflict," *Public Administration Review* (March/April, 1992); and "Public Sector Labor Relations in the 21st Century: New Approaches, New Strategies," in Carolyn C. Ban and N. Riccucci, eds., *Public Personnel Management* (1991).

Even though the contractual subsystem has emerged as a powerful and significant force within public bureaucracy today, few scholars have examined the subject in recent years. This is both surprising and regrettable, though Clarence H. Danhof's *Government Contracting* (1968), although somewhat dated, is still helpful for its history. Various recent books offer useful insights into portions of the contract subsystem: Harold Orlans, ed., *Nonprofit Organizations* (1980); Ruth Hoogland De Hoog, *Partners in Public Service* (1986); Daniel Jimenez, *A Study in Contracting Problems between Government Agencies and Non-Profit Organizations in California* (1981); Don Kettl, *Sharing Power* (1993); and Susan R. Bernstein, *Managing Contracted Services in a Nonprofit Agency* (1991).

One should not overlook several good agency studies that analyze aspects of this issue such as John T. Tierney, *The U.S. Postal Service* (1988), Donald F. Kettl, *Leadership at the Fed* (1986), and Paul C. Light, *Monitoring Government* (1993). Also helpful on this topic are a few first-hand "insider" views, including Alexander Haig, *Caveat* (1984), Joseph Califano, *Governing America* (1981), Elliot Richardson, *The Creative Balance* (1976), Ben W. Heineman and Curtis A. Hessler, *Memorandum for the President* (1980), Thomas P. Murphy, Donald E. Nuechterlein, and Ronald J. Stupak, *Inside the Bureaucracy* (1978), Deborah Shapely, *Promise and Power* (1993), as well as the several leadership profiles found in Jameson W. Doig and Erwin C. Hargrove, eds., *Leadership and Innovation* (1990) and Norma M. Riccucci, *Unsung Heroes* (1995).

PART TWO

The Multiple Functions of Public Administrators: Their Major Activities, Responsibilities, and Roles

Public administrators must fulfill many functions, often simultaneously. Part Two focuses on several of the important activities performed by public administrators—decision making, administrative communications, management, personnel motivation, budgeting, and implementation. The extent, scope, and capability with which administrators perform these functions vary widely from administrator to administrator, from job to job, and from locale to locale. However, it is safe to say these six functions are considered some of the most critical activities that public administrators must perform if they are to succeed—indeed survive—in their jobs.

As in Part One of this book, in Part Two, chapter by chapter, a single concept is discussed in a reading and its relevance is illustrated in a case study. Although the six major roles of administrators are individually discussed in the following chapters, it should be emphasized that the reality of the administrative processes frequently forces public administrators to assume all these responsibilities at the same time; this makes their work much more complex, less neatly compartmentalized or clear-cut than these individual chapters may suggest. The significant functional concepts discussed in Part Two include:

CHAPTER 8
Decision Making: *The Concept of Incremental Choice* How are decisions made in the public sector and why do public administrators frequently feel as if they are "flying by the seat of their pants"?

CHAPTER 9
Administrative Communications: *The Concept of Information Networks* How does the flow of communications inside organizations influence the way decisions are made and how well (or how poorly) administrators perform their work? And what can be done to improve administrative communications?

CHAPTER 10
Executive Management: *The Concept of the Uniqueness of Public Management* What is a successful management practice for public administrators to adopt? Why is public management often very different from business management?

CHAPTER 11
Public Personnel Motivation: *The Concept of Rational, Norm-Based, Affective Motives* Why is personnel motivation so significant to organizational performance and productivity? How can public administrators most effectively motivate their employees?

CHAPTER 12
Public Budgeting: *The Concept of Budgeting as Political Choice* What is the nature of the budgetary process in government? Why is a knowledge of budgeting so fundamental to administrative survival?

CHAPTER 13
Implementation: *The Concept of Optimal Conditions for Effectively Accomplishing Objectives* What is the best way for administrators to get their jobs done effectively, timely, efficiently, correctly, and responsibly? How can one best conceptualize this approach as a model?

CHAPTER 8

Decision Making: The Concept of Incremental Choice

A *wise policy-maker consequently expects that his policies will achieve only part of what he hopes and at the same time will produce unanticipated consequences he would have preferred to avoid. If he proceeds through a succession of incremental changes, he avoids serious lasting mistakes. . . .*

Charles E. Lindblom

Introduction

Few concepts are debated in administration more frequently than decision making—how decisions are made; whom they are made by; why they are decided on in the first place; and what impact they have once the choice is made. Gallons of ink have been spilled in academic journals debating whether decision making is an art or a science, how best to construct a decision-making model, or how to arrive at the most rational (or optimal) choice. One point emerges from these seemingly endless discussions: the process by which individuals and groups determine a correct course of action from various alternatives is one of the central functions of an administrator and thus deserves careful consideration by students of public administration.

What is the decision-making function? On one level, we all use decision making daily in confronting a myriad of personal choices, such as when to get up in the morning and what clothes to wear. On the larger and more complicated level of public administration, however, the decisional process involves vital community or societal choices—where to build a new school, when to negotiate an arms limitation treaty, or how to organize a new federal program for poverty relief. The process of choice runs the length and breadth of public administration and involves 4, 40, 400, or 4,000 steps, depending on the complexity and range of variables presented by the problem at hand.

Charles E. Lindblom (1917–   ), a Yale economist and long-time scholar of public policy issues, offers an important conceptual understanding of governmental decision making in his essay, "The Science of 'Muddling Through.' " Lindblom, unlike most economists, has seriously thought about the relationships between economics and politics for many years, an interest evident in his earliest writings with Robert A. Dahl in *Politics, Economics and Welfare* (1953), as well as in his more recent book,

Politics and Markets (1977). In an effort to realistically analyze the way governmental decisions are made, at the heart of Lindblom's brilliant studies is a model of decision making that he succinctly outlines in the following essay.

Based on earlier writings by Chester Barnard and Herbert Simon, Lindblom's central thesis is that there are two distinct varieties of decision making. One he calls the rational-comprehensive or root method, and the second, the successive limited comparisons or branch method. The first method is found in the classic texts on administration, and the latter is the "real" way decisions are arrived at in government. In the traditional *rational-comprehensive* or *root method* an administrator confronts a given objective, such as reducing poverty by a certain amount. The decision maker, in choosing the best policy to pursue, rationally ranks all the relevant values (or advantages) in attaining this objective, such as improving the health of the poor, reducing crime, improving property values, and eliminating illiteracy. He or she then formulates as many possible alternatives to achieve the stated objective—for example, a guaranteed income plan, direct government subsidies, higher welfare payments, or work-relief programs—and selects from among the options the *best* alternative that serves to maximize the ranked list of values. This approach to decision making is *rational,* because the alternatives and values are logically selected and weighed in relative importance. It is also *comprehensive,* for all the alternatives and values are taken into account by the policy maker.

What *actually* occurs in administrative decision making, argues Lindblom, is quite another process, namely, the *successive limited comparisons* or *branch method.* An objective is established—reducing poverty by a set amount, for example—but in public discussions this objective quickly becomes compromised. It may soon be mixed up with other goals such as educating minority students or providing work relief for the jobless. Administrators tend to overlook or avoid many of the social values that could be derived from their program, concentrating instead on those that they consider immediately relevant. In selecting the appropriate course of action, administrators outline not a broad range of possibilities, but only a few incremental steps that experience tells them are feasible. Furthermore, in practice, policy makers do not rationally select the optimal program that satisfies a clearly delineated list of values. To the contrary, under the successive limited comparisons method, contends Lindblom, public administrators pragmatically select from among the immediate choices at hand the most suitable compromise that satisfies the groups and individuals concerned with the program.

Lindblom sees the first approach, the root method, as wrongly assuming that administrators making decisions have unlimited amounts of time and resources available to them. "It assumes intellectual capacities and sources of information that simply do not exist and it is even more absurd as an approach to policy when the time and money that can be allocated to a policy problem is limited as is always the case." Second, the root method holds that there are always clear-cut values on which all interested parties agree. In fact, argues Lindblom, in a democratic society in which members of Congress, agencies, and interest groups are in continual disagreement over the relative importance of program objectives, policy makers cannot begin to rank explicitly the values derived from any program. There are simply too many groups with too many unknown values. The weight given to their relative importance depends ultimately on personal perspectives. "Even when an administrator resolves to follow his own values as a criterion for decisions, he will often not know how to rank them when they conflict with one another as they usually do." Third, the root method assumes that ends and means in policy choices are distinct, when in fact they are frequently intertwined. Selection of a goal to be accomplished often cannot easily be separated from the means by which it is achieved. For instance, the objective of slum clearance is intrinsically associated with the removal of residents from the neighborhood and the other methods used to achieve the goal, such as the clearing of buildings. Means and ends often become hopelessly confused in public policy choices. Finally, says Lindblom, the choice of a given course of action depends ultimately not on whether it maximizes the intended values (even if the values could be identified and ranked), but rather on whether it serves as a compromise acceptable to all parties concerned. "If agreement directly on policy as a test for the 'best' policy seems a poor substitute for testing the policy against its objectives, it ought to be remembered that objectives themselves have no ultimate validity other than they are agreed upon. . . . Agreement on policy thus becomes the only practicable test of the policy's correctness," argues Lindblom.

Lindblom's view of the reality of administrative decision making contains five characteristics. First, it is *incremental,* for small steps are always taken to achieve objectives, not broad leaps and bounds. Second, it is *noncomprehensive.* In other words, because policy makers' resources are always limited, they cannot take into consideration the full range of policy choices available to them at any given moment, nor can they possibly understand the full effects of their decisions or all of the values derived from any alternative they select. Third, the branch technique of decision making involves *successive comparisons* because policy is never made once and for all, but is made and remade endlessly by small chains of comparisons between narrow choices. Fourth, in practice, decision making *suffices* rather than maximizes from among the available options. "A wise policy maker completely expects that his policies will achieve only part of what he hopes and at the same time will produce unanticipated consequences he would have preferred to avoid." Finally, Lindblom's picture of governmental decision making rests on a *pluralist* conception of the public sector, in which many contending interest groups compete for influence over policy issues, continually forcing the administrator, as the person in the middle, to secure agreement among the competing parties. The political arts of compromise thus become a major part of decision-making methods.

There are two advantages of the branch method, asserts Lindblom. The first is that "if he proceeds through a succession of small incremental changes, the administrator therefore has the advantage of avoiding serious lasting mistakes" as well as permitting easy alterations should the wrong course be pursued. The second benefit of incrementalism is that it fits "hand and glove" with the American political system, which operates chiefly by means of gradual changes, rarely by dramatic shifts in public policies. "Non-incremental policy proposals are therefore typically not only politically irrelevant but also unpredictable in their policy consequences," writes Lindblom. The branch method allows for the art of compromise that American politics demands and produces the gradual changes that American tradition generally favors.

However, from the perspective of the "outside expert" or the academic problem solver, Lindblom points out, this approach seems "unscientific and unsystematic." Indeed, administrators may appear as if they were flying "by the seat of their pants," although in fact the outside theorists do not grasp that administrators are "often practicing a systematic method" of successive limited comparisons. Yet, as Lindblom says, ". . . sometimes decision makers are pursuing neither a theoretical approach nor successive comparisons nor any systematic method."

Lindblom's approach to governmental decision making, which for some may be too descriptive and not sufficiently prescriptive, debunks the classic view of how public choices are made, substituting an incremental model that is peculiarly a product and extension of economic theory of choice (subsequently, much of the language used in decisional theory—words like "optimizing" and "maximizing"—is derived from economics). Kenneth Arrow, Thomas Schelling, Herbert Simon, Edward Banfield, and Robert Dahl are among the major contemporary economists and political scientists who have pioneered the incremental view of decision making in the post–World War II era (refer to the numerous varieties of decision models outlined in the Suggestions for Further Reading at the end of this chapter). Lindblom has fully developed this idea into an elaborate working model in the following article, "The Science of 'Muddling Through.' "

As you read this selection, keep the following questions in mind:

Is Lindblom too pessimistic about the ability of administrators to make profound choices that will significantly alter or reshape their external environment?

What do you see as the benefits and disadvantages of the branch method and are there any remedies for its defects?

How does Lindblom's concept square with any of the previous case studies, such as Case Study 7?

Does Lindblom's "muddling through" idea primarily apply in normal governmental decisions involving simple issues? How about catastrophes such as in Case Study 1, "The Blast in Centralia No. 5"? What decisional methods might have averted the unfortunate choices made in that case?

Do you agree with Lindblom that "the branch method compared to other decisional models often looks far superior," particularly from the perspective of the practitioner?

The Science of "Muddling Through"

CHARLES E. LINDBLOM

Suppose an administrator is given responsibility for formulating policy with respect to inflation. He might start by trying to list all related values in

order of importance, e.g., full employment, reasonable business profit, protection of small savings, prevention of a stock market crash. Then all possible policy outcomes could be rated as more or less efficient in attaining a maximum of these values. This would of course require a prodigious inquiry into values held by members of society and an equally prodigious set of calculations on how much of each value is equal to how much of each other value. He could then proceed to outline all possible policy alternatives. In a third step, he would undertake systematic comparison of his multitude of alternatives to determine which attains the greatest amount of values.

In comparing policies, he would take advantage of any theory available that generalized about classes of policies. In considering inflation, for example, he would compare all policies in the light of the theory of prices. Since no alternatives are beyond his investigation, he would consider strict central control and the abolition of all prices and markets on the one hand and elimination of all public controls with reliance completely on the free market on the other, both in the light of whatever theoretical generalizations he could find on such hypothetical economies.

Finally, he would try to make the choice that would in fact maximize his values.

An alternative line of attack would be to set as his principal objective, either explicitly or without conscious thought, the relatively simple goal of keeping prices level. This objective might be compromised or complicated by only a few other goals, such as full employment. He would in fact disregard most other social values as beyond his present interest, and he would for the moment not even attempt to rank the few values that he regarded as immediately relevant. Were he pressed, he would quickly admit that he was ignoring many related values and many possible important consequences of his policies.

As a second step, he would outline those relatively few policy alternatives that occurred to him. He would then compare them. In comparing his limited number of alternatives, most of them familiar from past controversies, he would not ordinarily find a body of theory precise enough to carry him through a comparison of their respective consequences. Instead he would rely heavily on the record of past experience with small policy steps to predict the consequences of similar steps extended into the future.

Moreover, he would find that the policy alternatives combined objectives or values in different ways. For example, one policy might offer price level stability at the cost of some risk of unemployment; another might offer less price stability but also less risk of unemployment. Hence, the next step in his approach—the final selection—would combine into one the choice among values and the choice among instruments for reaching values. It would not, as in the first method of policy-making, approximate a more mechanical process of choosing the means that best satisfied goals that were previously clarified and ranked. Because practitioners of the second approach expect to achieve their goals only partially, they would expect to repeat endlessly the sequence just described, as conditions and aspirations changed and as accuracy of prediction improved.

By Root or by Branch

For complex problems, the first of these two approaches is of course impossible. Although such an approach can be described, it cannot be practiced except for relatively simple problems and even then only in a somewhat modified form. It assumes intellectual capacities and sources of information that men simply do not possess, and it is even more absurd as an approach to policy when the time and money that can be allocated to a policy problem is limited, as is always the case. Of particular importance to public administrators is the fact that public agencies are in effect usually instructed not to practice the first method. That is to say, their prescribed functions and constraints—the politically or legally possible—restrict their attention to relatively few values and relatively few alternative policies among the countless alternatives that might be imagined. It is the second method that is practiced.

Curiously, however, the literatures of decision making, policy formulation, planning, and public administration formalize the first approach rather than the second, leaving public administrators who handle complex decisions in the position of practicing what few preach. For emphasis I run some risk of overstatement. True enough, the literature is well aware of limits on man's capacities and of the inevitability that policies will be approached in some such style as the second. But attempts to formalize rational policy formulation—to lay out explicitly the necessary steps in the process—usually describe the first approach and not the second.[1]

The common tendency to describe policy formulation even for complex problems as though it followed the first approach has been strengthened by the attention given to, and successes enjoyed by, operations research, statistical decision theory, and systems analysis. The hallmarks of these procedures, typical of the first approach, are clarity of objective, explicitness of evaluation, a high degree of comprehensiveness of overview, and, wherever possible, quantification of values for mathematical analysis. But these advanced procedures remain largely the appropriate techniques of relatively small-scale problem-solving where the total number of variables to be considered is small and value problems restricted. Charles Hitch, head of the Economics Division of RAND Corporation, one of the leading centers for application of these techniques, has written:

> I would make the empirical generalization from my experience at RAND and elsewhere that operations research is the art of suboptimizing, i.e., of solving some lower-level problems, and that difficulties increase and our special competence diminishes by an order of magnitude with every level of decision making we attempt to ascend. The sort of simple explicit model which operations researchers are so proficient in using can certainly reflect most of the significant factors influencing traffic control on the George Washington Bridge, but the proportion of the relevant reality which we can represent by any such model or models in studying, say, a major foreign-policy decision, appears to be almost trivial.[2]

Accordingly, I propose in this paper to clarify and formalize the second method, much neglected in the literature. This might be described as the method of *successive limited comparisons*. I will contrast it with the first approach, which might be called the rational-comprehensive method.[3] More impressionistically and briefly—and therefore generally used in this article—they could be characterized as the branch method and root method, the former continually building out from the current situation, step-to-step and by small degrees; the latter starting from fundamentals anew each time, building on the past only as experience is embodied in a theory, and always prepared to start completely from the ground up.

Let us put the characteristics of the two methods side by side in simplest terms.

Rational-Comprehensive (Root)

1a. Clarification of values or objectives distinct from and usually prerequisite to empirical analysis of alternative policies.

2a. Policy-formulation is therefore approached through means-end analysis: First the ends are isolated, then the means to achieve them are sought.

3a. The test of a "good" policy is that it can be shown to be the most appropriate means to desired ends.

4a. Analysis is comprehensive; every important relevant factor is taken into account.

5a. Theory is often heavily relied upon.

Successive Limited Comparisons (Branch)

1b. Selection of value goals and empirical analysis of the needed action are not distinct from one another but are closely intertwined.

2b. Since means and ends are not distinct,

means-end analysis is often inappropriate or limited.

3b. The test of a "good" policy is typically that various analysts find themselves directly agreeing on a policy (without their agreeing that it is the most appropriate means to an agreed objective).

4b. Analysis is drastically limited:

i) Important possible outcomes are neglected.

ii) Important alternative potential policies are neglected.

iii) Important affected values are neglected.

5b. A succession of comparisons greatly reduces or eliminates reliance on theory.

Assuming that the root method is familiar and understandable, we proceed directly to clarification of its alternative by contrast. In explaining the second, we shall be describing how most administrators do in fact approach complex questions, for the root method, the "best" way as a blueprint or model, is in fact not workable for complex policy questions, and administrators are forced to use the method of successive limited comparisons.

Intertwining Evaluation and Empirical Analysis (1b)

The quickest way to understand how values are handled in the method of successive limited comparisons is to see how the root method often breaks down in *its* handling of values or objectives. The idea that values should be clarified, and in advance of the examination of alternative policies, is appealing. But what happens when we attempt it for complex social problems? The first difficulty is that on many critical values or objectives, citizens disagree, congressmen disagree, and public administrators disagree. Even where a fairly specific objective is prescribed for the administrator, there remains considerable room for disagreement on sub-objectives. Consider, for example, the conflict with respect to locating public housing, described in Meyerson and Banfield's study of the Chicago Housing Authority[4]—disagreement which occurred despite the clear objective of providing a certain number of public housing units in the city. Similarly conflicting are objectives in highway location, traffic control, minimum wage administration, development of tourist facilities in national parks, or insect control.

Administrators cannot escape these conflicts by ascertaining the majority's preference, for preferences have not been registered on most issues; indeed, there often *are* no preferences in the absence of public discussion sufficient to bring an issue to the attention of the electorate. Furthermore, there is a question of whether intensity of feeling should be considered as well as the number of persons preferring each alternative. By the impossibility of doing otherwise, administrators often are reduced to deciding policy without clarifying objectives first.

Even when an administrator resolves to follow his own values as a criterion for decisions, he often will not know how to rank them when they conflict with one another, as they usually do. Suppose, for example, that an administrator must relocate tenants living in tenements scheduled for destruction. One objective is to empty the buildings fairly promptly, another is to find suitable accommodation for persons displaced, another is to avoid friction with residents in other areas in which a large influx would be unwelcome, another is to deal with all concerned through persuasion if possible, and so on.

How does one state even to himself the relative importance of these partially conflicting values? A simple ranking of them is not enough; one needs ideally to know how much of one value is worth sacrificing for some of another value. The answer is that typically the administrator chooses—and must choose—directly among policies in which these values are combined in different ways. He cannot first clarify his values and then choose among policies.

A more subtle third point underlies both the first two. Social objectives do not always have the same relative values. One objective may be highly prized in one circumstance, another in another circumstance. If, for example, an administrator values highly both the dispatch with which his agency can carry through its projects *and* good public relations, it matters little which of the two possibly conflicting values he favors in some abstract or general sense. Policy questions arise in forms which put to administrators such a question as: Given the degree to which we are or are not already achieving the values of dispatch and the values of good public relations, is it worth sacrificing a little speed for a happier clientele, or is it better to risk offending the clientele so that we can get on with our work? The answer to such a question varies with circumstances.

The value problem is, as the example shows, always a problem of adjustments at a margin. But there is no practicable way to state marginal objectives or values except in terms of particular policies. That one value is preferred to another in one decision situation does not mean that it will be preferred in another decision situation in which it can be had only at great sacrifice of another value. Attempts to rank or order values in general and abstract terms so that they do not shift from decision to decision end up by ignoring the relevant marginal preferences. The significance of this third point thus goes very far. Even if all administrators had at hand an agreed set of values, objectives, and constraints, and an agreed ranking of these values, objectives, and constraints, their marginal values in actual choice situations would be impossible to formulate.

Unable consequently to formulate the relevant values first and then choose among policies to achieve them, administrators must choose directly among alternative policies that offer different marginal combinations of values. Somewhat paradoxically, the only practicable way to disclose one's relevant marginal values even to oneself is to describe the policy one chooses to achieve them. Except roughly and vaguely, I know of no way to describe—or even to understand—what my relative evaluations are for, say, freedom and security, speed and accuracy in governmental decisions, or

low taxes and better schools than to describe my preferences among specific policy choices that might be made between the alternatives in each of the pairs.

In summary, two aspects of the process by which values are actually handled can be distinguished. The first is clear: evaluation and empirical analysis are intertwined; that is, one chooses among values and among policies at one and the same time. Put a little more elaborately, one simultaneously chooses a policy to attain certain objectives and chooses the objectives themselves. The second aspect is related but distinct: the administrator focuses his attention on marginal or incremental values. Whether he is aware of it or not, he does not find general formulations of objectives very helpful and in fact makes specific marginal or incremental comparisons. Two policies, X and Y, confront him. Both promise the same degree of attainment of objectives $a, b, c, d,$ and e. But X promises him somewhat more of f than does Y, while Y promises him somewhat more of g than does X. In choosing between them, he is in fact offered the alternative of a marginal or incremental amount of f at the expense of a marginal or incremental amount of g. The only values that are relevant to his choice are these increments by which the two policies differ; and, when he finally chooses between the two marginal values, he does so by making a choice between policies.[5]

As to whether the attempt to clarify objectives in advance of policy selection is more or less rational than the close intertwining of marginal evaluation and empirical analysis, the principal difference established is that for complex problems the first is impossible and irrelevant, and the second is both possible and relevant. The second is possible because the administrator need not try to analyze any values except the values by which alternative policies differ and need not be concerned with them except as they differ marginally. His need for information on values or objectives is drastically reduced as compared with the root method; and his capacity for grasping, comprehending, and relating values to one another is not strained beyond the breaking point.

Relations Between Means and Ends (2b)

Decision-making is ordinarily formalized as a means-ends relationship: means are conceived to be evaluated and chosen in the light of ends finally selected independently of and prior to the choice of means. This is the means-ends relationship of the root method. But it follows from all that has just been said that such a means-ends relationship is possible only to the extent that values are agreed upon, are reconcilable, and are stable at the margin. Typically, therefore, such a means-ends relationship is absent from the branch method, where means and ends are simultaneously chosen.

Yet any departure from the means-ends relationship of the root method will strike some readers as inconceivable. For it will appear to them that only in such a relationship is it possible to determine whether one policy choice is better or worse than another. How can an administrator know whether he has made a wise or foolish decision if he is without prior values or objectives by which to judge his decisions? The answer to this question calls up the third distinctive difference between root and branch methods: how to decide the best policy.

The Test of "Good" Policy (3b)

In the root method, a decision is "correct," "good," or "rational" if it can be shown to attain some specified objective, where the objective can be specified without simply describing the decision itself. Where objectives are defined only through the marginal or incremental approach to values described above, it is still sometimes possible to test whether a policy does in fact attain the desired objectives; but a precise statement of the objectives takes the form of a description of the policy chosen or some alternative to it. To show that a policy is mistaken one cannot offer an abstract argument that important objectives are not achieved; one must instead argue that another policy is more to be preferred.

So far, the departure from customary ways of looking at problem-solving is not troublesome, for many administrators will be quick to agree that the most effective discussion of the correctness of policy does take the form of comparison with other policies that might have been chosen. But what of the situation in which administrators cannot agree on values or objectives, either abstractly or in marginal terms? What then is the test of "good" policy? For the root method, there is no test. Agreement on objectives failing, there is no standard of "correctness." For the method of successive limited comparisons, the test is agreement on policy itself, which remains possible even when agreement on values is not.

It has been suggested that continuing agreement in Congress on the desirability of extending old age insurance stems from liberal desires to strengthen the welfare programs of the federal government and from conservative desires to reduce union demands for private pension plans. If so, this is an excellent demonstration of the ease with which individuals of different ideologies often can agree on concrete policy. Labor mediators report a similar phenomenon: the contestants cannot agree on criteria for settling their disputes but can agree on specific proposals. Similarly, when one administrator's objective turns out to be another's means, they often can agree on policy.

Agreement on policy thus becomes the only practicable test of the policy's correctness. And for one administrator to seek to win the other over to agreement on ends as well would accomplish nothing and create quite unnecessary controversy.

If agreement directly on policy as a test for "best" policy seems a poor substitute for testing the policy against its objectives, it ought to be remembered that objectives themselves have no ultimate validity other than they are agreed upon. Hence agreement is the test of "best" policy in both methods. But where the root method requires agreement on what elements in the decision constitute objectives and on which of these objectives should be sought, the branch method falls back on agreement wherever it can be found.

In an important sense, therefore, it is not irrational for an administrator to defend a policy as good without being able to specify what it is good for.

Non-Comprehensive Analysis (4b)

Ideally, rational-comprehensive analysis leaves out nothing important. But it is impossible to take everything important into consideration unless "important" is so narrowly defined that analysis is in fact quite limited. Limits on human intellectual capacities and on available information set definite limits to man's capacity to be comprehensive. In actual fact, therefore, no one can practice the rational-comprehensive method for really complex problems, and every administrator faced with a sufficiently complex problem must find ways drastically to simplify.

An administrator assisting in the formulation of agricultural economic policy cannot in the first place be competent on all possible policies. He cannot even comprehend one policy entirely. In planning a soil bank program, he cannot successfully anticipate the impact of higher or lower farm income on, say, urbanization—the possible consequent loosening of family ties, possible consequent eventual need for revisions in social security and further implications for tax problems arising out of new federal responsibilities for social security and municipal responsibilities for urban services. Nor, to follow another line of repercussions, can he work through the soil bank program's effects on prices for agricultural products in foreign markets and consequent implications for foreign relations, including those arising out of economic rivalry between the United States and the U.S.S.R.

In the method of successive limited comparisons, simplification is systematically achieved in two principal ways. First, it is achieved through limitation of policy comparisons to those policies that differ in relatively small degree from policies presently in effect. Such a limitation immediately reduces the number of alternatives to be investigated and also drastically simplifies the character of the investigation of each. For it is not necessary to undertake fundamental inquiry into an alternative and its consequences; it is necessary only to study those respects in which the proposed alternative and its consequences differ from the status quo. The empirical comparison of marginal differences among alternative policies that differ only marginally is, of course, a counterpart to the incremental or marginal comparison of values discussed above.[6]

Relevance as Well as Realism

It is a matter of common observation that in Western democracies public administrators and policy analysts in general do largely limit their analyses to incremental or marginal differences in policies that are chosen to differ only incrementally. They do not do so, however, solely because they desperately need some way to simplify their problems; they also do so in order to be relevant. Democracies change their policies almost entirely through incremental adjustments. Policy does not move in leaps and bounds.

The incremental character of political change in the United States has often been remarked. The two major political parties agree on fundamentals; they offer alternative policies to the voters only on relatively small points of difference. Both parties favor full employment, but they define it somewhat differently; both favor the development of water power resources, but in slightly different ways; and both favor unemployment compensation, but not the same level of benefits. Similarly, shifts of policy within a party take place largely through a series of relatively small changes, as can be seen in their only gradual acceptance of the idea of governmental responsibility for support of the unemployed, a change in party positions beginning in the early 30's and culminating in a sense in the Employment Act of 1946.

Party behavior is in turn rooted in public attitudes, and political theorists cannot conceive of democracy's surviving in the United States in the absence of fundamental agreement on potentially disruptive issues, with consequent limitation of policy debates to relatively small differences in policy.

Since the policies ignored by the administrator are politically impossible and so irrelevant, the simplification of analysis achieved by concentrating on policies that differ only incrementally is not a capricious kind of simplification. In addition, it can be argued that, given the limits on knowledge within which policy-makers are confined, simplifying by limiting the focus to small variations from present policy makes the most of available knowledge. Because policies being considered are like present and past policies, the administrator can obtain information and claim some insight. Nonincremental policy proposals are therefore typically not only politically irrelevant but also unpredictable in their consequences.

The second method of simplification of analysis is the practice of ignoring important possible consequences of possible policies, as well as the values attached to the neglected consequences. If this appears to disclose a shocking shortcoming of successive limited comparisons, it can be replied that, even if the exclusions are random, policies may nevertheless be more intelligently formulated than through futile attempts to achieve a comprehensiveness beyond human capacity. Actually, however, the exclusions, seeming arbitrary or random from one point of view, need be neither.

Achieving a Degree of Comprehensiveness

Suppose that each value neglected by one policy-making agency were a major concern of at least one other agency. In that case, a helpful division of labor would be achieved, and no agency need find its task beyond its capacities. The shortcomings of such a system would be that one agency might destroy a value either before another agency could be activated to safeguard it or in spite of another agency's efforts. But the possibility that important values may be lost is present in any form of organization, even where agencies attempt to comprehend in planning more than is humanly possible.

The virtue of such a hypothetical division of labor is that every important interest or value has its watchdog. And these watchdogs can protect the interests in their jurisdiction in two quite different ways: first, by redressing damages done by other agencies; and, second, by anticipating and heading off injury before it occurs.

In a society like that of the United States in which individuals are free to combine to pursue almost any possible common interest they might have and in which government agencies are sensitive to the pressures of these groups, the system described is approximated. Almost every interest has its watchdog. Without claiming that every interest has a sufficiently powerful watchdog, it can be argued that our system often can assure a more comprehensive regard for the values of the whole society than any attempt at intellectual comprehensiveness.

In the United States, for example, no part of government attempts a comprehensive overview of policy on income distribution. A policy nevertheless evolves, and one responding to a wide variety of interests. A process of mutual adjustment among farm groups, labor unions, municipalities and school boards, tax authorities, and government agencies with responsibilities in the fields of housing, health, highways, national parks, fire, and police accomplishes a distribution of income in which particular income problems neglected at one point in the decision processes become central at another point.

Mutual adjustment is more pervasive than the explicit forms it takes in negotiation between groups; it persists through the mutual impacts of groups upon each other even where they are not in communication. For all the imperfections and latent dangers in this ubiquitous process of mutual adjustment, it will often accomplish an adaptation of policies to a wider range of interests than could be done by one group centrally.

Note, too, how the incremental pattern of policy-making fits with the multiple pressure pattern. For when decisions are only incremental—closely related to known policies, it is easier for one group to anticipate the kind of moves another might make and easier too for it to make correction for injury already accomplished.[7]

Even partisanship and narrowness, to use pejorative terms, will sometimes be assets to rational decision-making, for they can doubly insure that what one agency neglects, another will not; they specialize personnel to distinct points of view. The claim is valid that effective rational coordination of the federal administration, if possible to achieve at all, would require an agreed set of values[8]—if "rational" is defined as the practice of the root method of decision-making. But a high degree of administrative coordination occurs as each agency adjusts its policies to the concerns of the other agencies in the process of fragmented decision-making I have just described.

For all the apparent shortcomings of the incremental approach to policy alternatives with its arbitrary exclusion coupled with fragmentation, when compared to the root method, the branch method often looks far superior. In the root method, the inevitable exclusion of factors is accidental, unsystematic, and not defensible by any argument so far developed, while in the branch method the exclusions are deliberate, systematic, and defensible. Ideally, of course, the root method does not exclude; in practice it must.

Nor does the branch method necessarily neglect long-run considerations and objectives. It is clear that important values must be omitted in considering policy, and sometimes the only way long-run objectives can be given adequate attention is through the neglect of short-run consideration. But the values omitted can be either long-run or short-run.

Succession of Comparisons (5b)

The final distinctive element in the branch method is that the comparisons, together with the policy choice, proceed in a chronological series. Policy is not made once and for all; it is made and remade endlessly. Policy-making is a process of successive approximation to some desired objectives in which what is desired itself continues to change under reconsideration.

Making policy is at best a very rough process.

Neither social scientists, nor politicians, nor public administrators yet know enough about the social world to avoid repeated error in predicting the consequences of policy moves. A wise policy-maker consequently expects that his policies will achieve only part of what he hopes and at the same time will produce unanticipated consequences he would have preferred to avoid. If he proceeds through a *succession* of incremental changes, he avoids serious lasting mistakes in several ways.

In the first place, past sequences of policy steps have given him knowledge about the probable consequences of further similar steps. Second, he need not attempt big jumps toward his goals that would require predictions beyond his or anyone else's knowledge, because he never expects his policy to be a final resolution of a problem. His decision is only one step, one that if successful can quickly be followed by another. Third, he is in effect able to test his previous predictions as he moves on to each further step. Lastly, he often can remedy a past error fairly quickly—more quickly than if policy proceeded through more distinct steps widely spaced in time.

Compare this comparative analysis of incremental changes with the aspiration to employ theory in the root method. Man cannot think without classifying, without subsuming one experience under a more general category of experiences. The attempt to push categorization as far as possible and to find general propositions which can be applied to specific situations is what I refer to with the word "theory." Where root analysis often leans heavily on theory in this sense, the branch method does not.

The assumption of root analysis is that theory is the most systematic and economical way to bring relevant knowledge to bear on a specific problem. Granting the assumption, an unhappy fact is that we do not have adequate theory to apply to problems in any policy area, although theory is more adequate in some areas—monetary policy, for example—than in others. Comparative analysis, as in the branch method, is sometimes a systematic alternative to theory.

Suppose an administrator must choose among a small group of policies that differ only incrementally from each other and from present policy. He might aspire to "understand" each of the alternatives—for example, to know all the consequences of each aspect of each policy. If so, he would indeed require theory. In fact, however, he would usually decide that, *for policy-making purposes,* he need know, as explained above, only the consequences of each of those aspects of the policies in which they differed from one another. For this much more modest aspiration, he requires no theory (although it might be helpful, if available), for he can proceed to isolate probable differences by examining the differences in consequences associated with past differences in policies, a feasible program because he can take his observations from a long sequence of incremental changes.

For example, without a more comprehensive social theory about juvenile delinquency than scholars have yet produced, one cannot possibly understand the ways in which a variety of public policies—say on education, housing, recreation, employment, race relations, and policing—might encourage or discourage delinquency. And one needs such an understanding if he undertakes the comprehensive overview of the problem prescribed in the models of the root method. If, however, one merely wants to mobilize knowledge sufficient to assist in a choice among a small group of similar policies—alternative policies on juvenile court procedures, for example—he can do so by comparative analysis of the results of similar past policy moves.

Theorists and Practitioners

This difference explains—in some cases at least—why the administrator often feels that the outside expert or academic problem-solver is sometimes not helpful and why they in turn often urge more theory on him. And it explains why an administrator often feels more confident when "flying by the seat of his pants" than when following the advice of theorists. Theorists often ask the administrator to go the long way round to the solution of his problems, in effect ask him to follow the best canons of the scientific method, when the administrator knows the best available theory will work less well than more modest incremental comparisons. Theorists do not realize that the administrator is often in fact practicing a systematic method. It would be foolish to push this explanation too far, for sometimes practical decision-makers are pursuing neither a theoretical approach nor successive comparisons, nor any other systematic method.

It may be worth emphasizing that theory is sometimes of extremely limited helpfulness in policy-making for at least two rather different reasons. It is greedy for facts; it can be constructed only through a great collection of observations. And it is typically insufficiently precise for application to a policy process that moves through small changes. In contrast, the comparative method both economizes on the need for facts and directs the analyst's attention to just those facts that are relevant to the fine choices faced by the decision-maker.

With respect to precision of theory, economic theory serves as an example. It predicts that an economy without money or prices would in certain specified ways misallocate resources, but this finding pertains to an alternative far removed from the kind of policies on which administrators need help. On the other hand, it is not precise enough to predict the consequences of policies restricting business mergers, and this is the kind of issue on which the administrators need help. Only in relatively restricted areas does economic theory achieve sufficient precision to go far in resolving policy questions; its helpfulness in policy-making is always so limited that it requires supplementation through comparative analysis.

Successive Comparison as a System

Successive limited comparison is, then, indeed a method or system; it is not a failure of method for which administrators ought to apologize. None the less, its imperfections, which have not been explored in this paper, are many. For example, the method is without a built-in safeguard for all relevant values, and it also may lead the decision-maker to overlook excellent policies for no other reason than that they are not suggested by the chain of successive policy steps leading up to the present. Hence, it ought to be said that under this method, as well as under some of the most sophisticated variants of the root method—operations research, for example—policies will continue to be as foolish as they are wise.

Why then bother to describe the method in all the above detail? Because it is in fact a common method of policy formulation, and is, for complex problems, the principal reliance of administrators as well as of other policy analysts.[9] And because it will be superior to any other decision-making method available for complex problems in many circumstances, certainly superior to a futile attempt at super-human comprehensiveness. The reaction of the public administrator to the exposition of method doubtless will be less a discovery of a new method than a better acquaintance with an old. But by becoming more conscious of their practice of this method, administrators might practice it with more skill and know when to extend or constrict its use. (That they sometimes practice it effectively and sometimes not may explain the extremes of opinion on "muddling through," which is both praised as a highly sophisticated form of problem-solving and denounced as no method at all. For I suspect that in so far as there is a system in what is known as "muddling through," this method is it.)

One of the noteworthy incidental consequences of clarification of the method is the light it throws on the suspicion an administrator sometimes entertains that a consultant or adviser is not speaking relevantly and responsibly when in fact by all ordinary objective evidence he is. The trouble lies in the fact that most of us approach policy problems within a framework given by our view of a chain of successive policy choices made up to the present. One's thinking about appropriate policies with respect, say, to urban traffic control is greatly influenced by one's knowledge of the incremental steps taken up to the present. An administrator enjoys an intimate knowledge of his past sequences that "outsiders" do not share, and his thinking and that of the "outsider" will consequently be different in ways that may puzzle both. Both may appear to be talking intelligently, yet each may find the other unsatisfactory. The relevance of the policy chain of succession is even more clear when an American tries to discuss, say, antitrust policy with a Swiss, for the chains of policy in the two countries are strikingly different and the two individuals consequently have organized their knowledge in quite different ways.

If this phenomenon is a barrier to communication, an understanding of it promises an enrichment of intellectual interaction in policy formulation. Once the source of difference is understood, it will sometimes be stimulating for an administrator to seek out a policy analyst whose recent experience is with a policy chain different from his own.

This raises again a question only briefly discussed above on the merits of like-mindedness among government administrators. While much of organization theory argues the virtues of common values and agreed organizational objectives, for complex problems in which the root method is inapplicable, agencies will want among their own personnel two types of diversification: administrators whose thinking is organized by reference to policy chains other than those familiar to most members of the organization and, even more commonly, administrators whose professional or personal values or interests create diversity of view (perhaps coming from different specialties, social classes, geographical areas) so that, even within a single agency, decision-making can be fragmented and parts of the agency can serve as watchdogs for other parts.

Notes

1. James G. March and Herbert A. Simon similarly characterized the literature. They also take some important steps, as have Simon's recent articles, to describe a less heroic

model of policy-making. See *Organizations* (John Wiley and Sons, 1958), p. 137.

2. "Operations Research and National Planning—A Dissent," 5 *Operations Research* 718 (October, 1957). Hitch's dissent is from particular points made in the article to which his paper is a reply; his claim that operations research is for low-level problems is widely accepted.

    For examples of the kind of problems to which operations research is applied, see C. W. Churchman, R. L. Ackoff and E. L. Arnoff, *Introduction to Operations Research* (John Wiley and Sons, 1957); and J. F. McCloskey and J. M. Coppinger (eds.), *Operations Research for Management,* Vol. II, (The Johns Hopkins Press, 1956).

3. I am assuming that administrators often make policy and advise in the making of policy and am treating decision-making and policy-making as synonymous for purposes of this paper.

4. Martin Meyerson and Edward C. Banfield, *Politics, Planning and the Public Interest* (The Free Press, 1955).

5. The line of argument is, of course, an extension of the theory of market choice, especially the theory of consumer choice, to public policy choices.

6. A more precise definition of incremental policies and a discussion of whether a change that appears "small" to one observer might be seen differently by another is to be found in my "Policy Analysis," 48 *American Economic Review* 298 (June, 1958).

7. The link between the practice of the method of successive limited comparisons and mutual adjustment of interests in a highly fragmented decision-making process adds a new facet to pluralist theories of government and administration.

8. Herbert Simon, Donald W. Smithburg, and Victor A. Thompson, *Public Administration* (Alfred A. Knopf, 1950), p. 434.

9. Elsewhere I have explored this same method of policy formulation as practiced by academic analysts of policy ("Policy Analysis," 48 *American Economic Review* 298 [June, 1958]). Although it has been here presented as a method for public administrators, it is no less necessary to analysts more removed from immediate policy questions, despite their tendencies to describe their own analytical efforts as though they were the rational-comprehensive method with an especially heavy use of theory. Similarly, this same method is inevitably resorted to in personal problem-solving, where means and ends are sometimes impossible to separate, where aspirations or objectives undergo constant development, and where drastic simplification of the complexity of the real world is urgent if problems are to be solved in the time that can be given to them. To an economist accustomed to dealing with the marginal or incremental concept in market processes, the central idea in the method is that both evaluation and empirical analysis are incremental. Accordingly I have referred to the method elsewhere as "the incremental method."

☐ CASE STUDY 8

Introduction

On August 2, 1990, Iraqi President Saddam Hussein invaded his neighbor, oil-rich Kuwait, to the surprise of the United States as well as the entire world. Three days later,

Sunday, August 5, U.S. President George Bush, speaking on the White House lawn about the Iraqi invasion, said, "This will not stand." Throughout the crisis, Bush was firm in his conviction that Iraq must completely withdraw from Kuwait. However, what remained in question, at least during the first few months of the ordeal, was the method for achieving that goal. Some favored a "wait and see" approach; others supported a "defer and defend" strategy; others, "economic containment"; and still others argued, "take the offensive!"

The following case study, "The Decision to Liberate Kuwait," an excerpt from *The Commanders* by Bob Woodward, assistant managing editor of the *Washington Post,* describes events from late September to early November 1990 when the decision was made by the United States to go on the offensive and liberate Kuwait. Woodward, of course, is best known as the investigative reporter who, along with Carl Bernstein, broke the Watergate story, which led to the resignation of President Richard Nixon in 1974 (recounted in their books, *The Final Days* and *All the President's Men*). Woodward also has written other well-known "Washington-insider" investigations of the CIA *(Veil: The Secret Wars of the CIA, 1981–87)* and the Supreme Court (*The Brethren,* co-authored with Scott Armstrong).

Woodward explains why he wrote *The Commanders* in the opening "Note to the Reader":

> I initially planned to focus on the military and civilian leadership of the Pentagon, headquarters for one of the world's largest enterprises, the modern American defense establishment. . . .
>
> My initial research emphasized the Pentagon under Bush. . . . The fast-approaching end of the Cold War suggested it could be a quiet time for the military, an opportunity for me to try to understand the Defense Department's subtle intricacies.
>
> The December 1989 Panama invasion and more importantly, the 1990 Gulf Crisis, changed all that. The military was not going to play a smaller role in the new world (order). . . . From the time of the Iraqi invasion of Kuwait in August 1990, I concentrated on the evolution of the Persian Gulf Crisis and the decision to go to war against Saddam Hussein.

As the author emphasizes, "It is above all a book about how the United States decides to fight its wars before shots are fired." In particular, "The Decision to Liberate Kuwait" looks closely at how various options facing top Washington policy makers were raised, addressed, and decided on during the Gulf Crisis. In the process of telling this story, Woodward focuses on the top-level participants in the White House, Pentagon, and State Department and offers an insightful narrative about how several key figures thought and acted during these fateful deliberations. He interviewed more than 400 people over 27 months, "some on a regular basis as events unfolded." Nearly all the interviews were done on "a deep background basis"; that is, the sources agreed to speak to Woodward only with the understanding that they would not be identified by name or title. He spoke to some "within the hour or day of events in which they played a role." His account, as he points out, is possibly "somewhere between newspaper journalism and history." This technique nonetheless remains controversial because of his failure to identify sources as well as for his being too close to events after they occurred.

This case tells us much about how decisions are made at the highest levels of government in the 1990s. Therefore, it is well worth reading in relationship to Charles Lindblom's foregoing essay. Think about these questions as you read:

How did each of the major "players" in this case study perceive of the alternatives in the Gulf Crisis by early Fall 1990? What were their motivations and individual assumptions concerning how to handle the Iraqi invasion? What were their preferred strategies and method(s) by which they "pushed forward" their own policy agendas?

Why did some options like "containment" and "strangulation" never receive open debate or wide-spread support? Were all options heard and fairly considered, in your opinion?

Who were the "major players" and why were some included and others left out of the discussions? How did the personalities of this group and their interactions influence the type of options raised, debated, and ultimately the way the final decision was reached? Why was "personal chemistry" so critical, according to Woodward?

What major fears were evident involving the policy options? By what means were these uncertainties dealt with? How did the press and instantaneous communications help *and* hinder decision making throughout this case?

Does the case support or contradict Lindblom's incremental model of decision making? Why, at the end of the reading, did General Colin L. Powell, Chairman of the Joint Chiefs of Staff, liken the decisional process to "high stakes poker"? Do you agree that the gambling metaphor is more apt than "incrementalism" to explain how choices were made in the Gulf Crisis?

Do you find this story supports the concept, described in Chapter 7, regarding the influence of various personnel groups in government? Who were they and how did they influence the outcome of the case?

What were the important policy differences exhibited here between the professionals and politicians? Which group was in charge? What were the sources of these differences? Do you judge such conflicts to be healthy or detrimental to the policy making processes?

The Decision to Liberate Kuwait

BOB WOODWARD

On September 21, the sixth week into the U.S. deployment, [Iraqi President] Saddam [Hussein's] Revolutionary Command Council issued a bellicose statement saying, "There is not a single chance for any retreat. . . . Let everybody understand that this battle is going to become the mother of all battles."

Reprinted by permission from *The Commanders* by Bob Woodward (New York: Simon & Schuster, 1991). © 1991 by Bob Woodward.

Satellite photos and other intelligence presented to President [George] Bush showed that Iraq was systematically dismantling Kuwait, looting the entire nation. Everything of value was being carried back to Iraq; the populace was being terrorized, starved, beaten, murdered. Kuwait would soon become a perpetual no-man's-land, Bush was told. He could see much of it with his own eyes.

U.S. intelligence claimed that Saddam had 430,000 troops in Kuwait and southern Iraq. His forces were digging in, moving into even more defensive positions. This made an offensive attack by Saddam into Saudi Arabia less likely. In order to attack, the Iraqis would have to dig out and move into the so-called killing zones—swatches of open desert miles wide—where the United States could obliterate troops and tanks with superior airpower and [General Norman] Schwarzkopf's own ground forces. Though the United States had less than half as many troops in the theater as Iraq, [Secretary of Defense Dick] Cheney and [Chairman of the Joint Chiefs of Staff Colin] Powell told Bush they now felt quite sure the U.S. and allied forces could defend Saudi Arabia.

Friday, September 28, was the Day of the Emir. Bush had the exiled emir of Kuwait, who was visiting the United States for the first time, into the Oval Office for a meeting. Scowcroft joined them for the hour-long meeting. Though the emir did not directly ask for military intervention to liberate his country, [Brent] Scowcroft [National Security Council Director] could see that that was his subliminal message. Bush then took the exiled leader to meet with the cabinet and later to have lunch with the cabinet members in the White House residence. That afternoon, Cheney and Powell met with the emir privately.

Afterwards Bush said that Kuwait was running out of time. It certainly wasn't going to be around as a country if they waited for sanctions to work. The emir himself, the stories of destruction supported by intelligence reports, left an indelible mark on the President, both Cheney and Powell could see. Bush was personally moved. Iraq will fail and Kuwait will endure, Bush said.

At the same time, Powell realized that Schwarzkopf in Saudi Arabia was growing increasingly uneasy. Schwarzkopf had chewed out [Lt. General Thomas W.] Kelly [Director of Operations for the Joint Chiefs of Staff] on the phone once when Powell had requested some information within 30 minutes. Kelly was not afraid, and had barked back that he was just conveying Powell's order: "I didn't give it to you, the Chairman did." But Schwarzkopf had just about everyone else intimidated. Schwarzkopf needed to be consoled not about the hard tasks that might lie ahead but about his uncertainty as to what Washington might order. He was increasingly nervous about the scale of the Iraqi buildup and was asking questions about U.S. objectives and force levels. Though his stated military

mission was still only the defense of Saudi Arabia, Schwarzkopf was aware of repeated presidential statements moving the mission close to the liberation of Kuwait.

At times brooding in his daily secure phone conversations to Powell in the Pentagon, Schwarzkopf was regularly looking for clues, or asking directly, about the next step. Were they going to hold to the defensive mission? Or were they going to build up the forces to do more?

"Norm, I'm working on it," Powell had been telling him.

In their regular 5 P.M. meetings, Cheney and Powell spent much time on these questions.

"You know," Powell told Cheney in early October, "we're going to have to get a decision." The President had to tell them whether to continue deploying forces, or to stop, well before the cut-off date of December 1, when they expected to have in place all the forces and supplies needed for the defensive mission. "When I put the last thing in the funnel, two weeks later it will come out in Saudi Arabia. We need to know when to stop putting things in the funnel." Powell reminded Cheney that he had not participated in a full policy review or a discussion of the options and their merits.

Cheney didn't give much of a response.

Powell started jotting down some notes. He felt that containment or strangulation was working. An extraordinary political-diplomatic coalition had been assembled, leaving Iraq without substantial allies—condemned, scorned and isolated as perhaps no country had been in modern history. Intelligence showed that economic sanctions were cutting off up to 95 percent of Saddam's imports and nearly all his exports. Saddam was practically sealed off in Iraq and Kuwait. The impact could not be measured in weeks, Powell felt. It might take months. There would come a point a month or six weeks before Saddam was down to the last pound of rice when the sanctions would trigger some kind of a response.

Paul Wolfowitz, the undersecretary for policy, told Powell that he felt strangulation was a defensible position as long as it meant applying sanctions indefinitely. Saddam had to know he was facing strangulation forever. To adopt a policy that said, or implied, that sanctions would be in effect for one year or 18 months would give the Iraqi leader a point when he could count on relief. He would have only to tell his people to hold out another so-many months. Wolfowitz said he thought it was a hard call; probably 55 percent of the merit was for one side, 45 percent for the other.

• • •

Powell went to Cheney to outline the case for containment. He had not reduced his arguments to a formal paper; there was no memo, no plan, nothing typed up. All he had were his handwritten notes. Until they were sure sanctions and strangulation had failed, it would be very difficult to go to war, Powell said. If there was a chance that sanctions might work, there might be an obligation to continue waiting—at least to a certain point. To do something premature when there was still a chance of accomplishing the political objectives with sanctions could be a serious mistake.

"I don't know," Cheney responded. "I don't think the President will buy it." Cheney thought that containment was insufficient, and did not see any really convincing evidence that the sanctions were going to guarantee success. The President was committed to policy success. Containment could leave Kuwait in Saddam's hands. That would constitute policy failure. It would be unacceptable to the President.

Powell wanted another dog in the fight. He was concerned that no one was laying out the alternatives to the President. Bush might not be hearing everything he needed to hear. A full slate of options should be presented. Several days later Powell went back to Cheney with an expanded presentation on containment.

"Uh—hmm," Cheney said, noncommittal. "It certainly is another way to look at it."

Powell next went to see [Secretary of State James A.] Baker to talk about containment. The Secretary of State was Powell's chief ally in the upper ranks of the administration. They thought alike on many issues. Both men preferred dealmaking to confrontation or conflict. And both worked the news media assiduously to get their points of view across and have them cast in the most favorable light. Baker was very unhappy about the talk of using or developing an offensive military option. He wanted diplomacy—meaning the State Department—to achieve the policy success. He informed Powell that he had some of his staff working on an analysis of the advantages of containment. This should force a discussion of containment within the Bush inner circle, Baker indicated, or at least it would get out publicly.

But no White House meetings or discussion followed. Powell felt that he'd sent the idea up the flagpole but no one had saluted or even commented. He could see, all too plainly, that the President was consistent and dug in, insisting that Kuwait be freed. Bush had not blinked, and frustrations were obviously mounting in the White House. After more than two months, neither the United Nations resolutions, nor diplomacy, nor economic sanctions, nor rhetoric appeared to be forcing Saddam's hand. Powell had too often seen presidential emotions drive policy; Reagan's personal concern for the American hostages in Lebanon had been behind the Iran-contra affair. Powell decided to go see Scowcroft in the White House.

Scowcroft indicated he was having a difficult time that Powell, as a former national security adviser, would understand. He was trying to manage and control an incredibly active President. Bush was out making statements, giving press conferences almost daily, up at dawn making calls, on the phone with one world leader after another, setting up meetings. Scowcroft found himself scrambling just to catch up. On a supposedly relaxing weekend Bush talked with or saw more people related to his job than most people did in a normal work week.

After listening sympathetically, Powell turned to the question of the next steps in the Gulf. He said he wondered about containment and strangulation, the advantages of economic sanctions.

Scowcroft knew Powell's attitude because Cheney had hinted at it. But now Powell was indirect. He did not come out and say, in so many words, this is my position.

"The President is more and more convinced that sanctions are not going to work," Scowcroft responded. He made it clear that he had a solid read on the President. Bush's determination was undisguised and he had virtually foreclosed any possibility that his views could be changed.

Powell could see that Scowcroft agreed with Bush, and was strongly reinforcing the President's inclinations. As national security adviser, it was his job. As the overseer of the administration's entire foreign policy, he had to mirror the President. But the security adviser also had a responsibility to make sure the range of alternatives was presented.

Scowcroft was substantially more willing to go to war than Powell. War was an instrument of foreign policy in Scowcroft's view. Powell did not disagree; he just saw that instrument much closer, less a disembodied abstraction than real men and women, faces—many of them kids' faces—that Powell looked into on his visits to the troops. In the West Wing of the White House where Scowcroft sat, the Pentagon seemed far away, and the forces even further away. Powell knew that. He had been there.

Powell told Scowcroft that if there was an alternative to war, he wanted to make sure it was fully considered. If there were any possible way to achieve the goals without the use of force, those prospects had to be explored.

Scowcroft became impatient. The President was doing everything imaginable, he said.

Powell left. He had become increasingly disenchanted with the National Security Council procedures and meetings. Scowcroft seemed unable, or unwilling, to coordinate and make sense of all the components of the Gulf policy—military, diplomatic, public affairs, economic, the United Nations. When the principals met, Bush liked to keep everyone around the table smiling—jokes, camaraderie, the conviviality of old friends. Positions and alternatives were not completely discussed. Interruptions were common. Clear decisions rarely emerged. Often Powell and Cheney returned from these gatherings and said to each other, now what did that mean? What are we supposed to do? Frequently, they had to wait to hear the answer later from Scowcroft or the television.

The operation needed a field marshal—someone of the highest rank who was the day-to-day manager, Powell felt. The President, given his other domestic and political responsibilities, couldn't be chief coordinator. It should be the national security adviser. Instead, Scowcroft had become the First Companion and all-purpose playmate to the President on golf, fishing and weekend outings. He was regularly failing in his larger duty to ensure that policy was carefully debated and formulated.

[White House Chief of Staff John] Sununu only added to the problem, exerting little or no control over the process as White House chief of staff.

As a result, the President was left painted into a corner by his own repeated declarations. His obvious emotional attachment to them was converting presidential remarks into hard policy. The goal now, more than ever, was the liberation of Kuwait at almost any cost.

• • •

"Why don't you come over with me and we'll see what the man thinks about your idea," Cheney said to Powell on Friday. Cheney had a private Oval Office meeting scheduled with the President. It was time reserved for the key cabinet members—"the big guys," as Powell privately referred to them. These included just Bush, a cabinet member and Sununu or Scowcroft. Normally, Powell was not included.

At the White House, Cheney and Powell went to the Oval Office to see Bush and Scowcroft. At this meeting Powell made his pitch for containment but pulled away from the brink of advocating it personally.

• • •

Powell's thoughts that containment had not been fully shot down by Bush were soon corrected. Within days, Scowcroft told Cheney that Bush wanted a briefing right away on what an offensive operation against Saddam's forces in Kuwait might look like. This planning was being done by Schwarzkopf and his staff in Saudi Arabia, so Powell passed the word to Schwarzkopf to send someone to Washington.

Over the Columbus Day weekend of October 6–8, Army Chief Carl Vuono flew to Saudi Arabia to see Schwarzkopf. They'd been friends since they were teen-aged cadets together at West Point in the 1950s. Schwarzkopf had been a class ahead, but Vuono had been promoted a little faster, so on three occasions during their careers Schwarzkopf had worked for Vuono. Vuono considered Schwarzkopf one of the most difficult, stubborn and talented men in the Army.

When they went off for a private talk, Vuono could see that Schwarzkopf was upset. The CINC, all 6 foot 3, 240 pounds of him, seemed about to explode out of his desert fatigues. He was precisely halfway through the 17 weeks he'd told the President he would need to put the defensive force in place. Now Washington was beginning to talk offense. Les Aspin had said publicly that the administration was "looking more favorably on an early war option." *The New York Times* had reported that the word around the Pentagon was that the offensive would begin on October 15. Worse, Powell had just told Schwarzkopf in a secure phone conversation that Bush wanted a briefing right away on what an offensive operation against Saddam's forces in Kuwait would look like.

Schwarzkopf was furious. They had to be kidding.

He was not ready to present such a plan. He had received no warning, and he didn't want to be pushed prematurely into offensive operations. Now he was afraid some son-of-a-bitch was going to wake up some morning and say, let's get the offense rolling. He had two more months' work to do on defense, and he had told the President in August it would take 8 to 12 months to be ready for offense. That meant next March, but now in October they wanted an offensive plan that they could carry out right away.

Powell had told him that everyone understood it would be a preliminary plan. He gave the Central Command about 48 hours to get someone to Washington with a briefing. Schwarzkopf couldn't leave Saudi Arabia so he would have to send a subordinate.

After listening to Schwarzkopf for four hours, Vuono felt as if he'd been through a psychotherapy session. He could see that his old friend felt very lonely and vulnerable. Vuono promised to do what he could.

On Wednesday morning, October 10, Powell received Schwarzkopf's chief of staff, Marine Major General Robert B. Johnston, at the Pentagon. In the afternoon, Cheney, Wolfowitz, Powell, the other chiefs [of the Army, Navy, Air Force, and Marine Corps] and Kelly went to the Tank. They were all in the most restricted group cleared for top-secret war plans. It was absolutely essential that word not leak out that the Pentagon was considering an offensive operation. It might be an invitation for Saddam to attack before the full defensive force was in place.

Johnston, a stiff, deferential, buttoned-down Marine with extensive briefing experience, began by reminding them that the Central Command had deployed its forces in accordance with the President's deter-and-defend mission. But if the President tells us to go on the offense tomorrow, he said, here's what we would do. Though we haven't had a lot of time to think this through, and we're not prepared to say in detail this is the right plan, this is our best shot at it.

The plan was broken into four phases, he explained. The first three were exclusively an air campaign, and the fourth was a ground attack.

Phase One would be an air attack on Iraqi command, control and communications, attempting to sever Saddam in Baghdad from his forces in Kuwait and southern Iraq. Simultaneously, airpower would destroy the Iraqi Air Force and air defense system. In addition, Phase One would include an air attack to destroy Iraqi chemical, biological and nuclear weapons facilities.

Phase Two would be a massive, continuous air bombardment of Iraqi supply and munitions bases, transportation facilities and roads, designed to cut off the Iraqi forces from their supplies.

Phase Three would be an air attack on the entrenched Iraqi ground forces of 430,000 men, and on the Republican Guard.

The phases would overlap somewhat. As early as a week after the beginning of the first air phase, the Phase Four ground assault would be launched on the Iraqi forces in Kuwait. One of Johnston's slides was a map with three large arrows showing the three attack points where coalition forces would hit the Iraqis. One arrow represented U.S. Marines in an amphibious assault from the Gulf; another was the U.S. Army on the ground attacking directly into Iraqi lines; and the third was an Egyptian ground division, also going straight into enemy forces, while protecting one of the U.S. flanks.

Cheney, Powell and several of the others asked question after question. Could they count on the Egyptians to protect the American ground troops? What about back-up forces if the Iraqis counterattacked?

Powell and Vuono wanted to know if it was possible to move the U.S. forces out to the west along the Iraqi border and then come up on the Iraqi Army from the side and behind. Could the U.S. forces be repositioned fast enough so the Iraqis would not know?

The initial terrain analysis showed that the Iraqi desert was too soft and wet for the support vehicles to carry the necessary supplies, Johnston said.

Kelly was sure that the straight-up-the-middle plan briefed by Johnston was not going to cut it and would not survive a serious review. Two of the main rules of war were "Never attack the enemy's strength" and "Go where they are not." The plan needed mobility.

Cheney felt pretty good about the three phases of the air campaign. The planning looked detailed and complete. Even after the Dugan firing, the Air Force was basically saying they would take care of it all. Cheney didn't believe it, but he could see airpower would have a tremendous advantage in the desert. In addition, the plans anticipated that targets missed on the first run would be hit again and again as necessary.

The Phase Four ground plan, however, looked inadequate to Cheney. The offensive U.S. Army and Marine units would be sent against a potentially larger defensive Iraqi force, depending on what remained of Saddam's troops after the bombing. Even to a civilian like himself, Cheney reflected, it looked unwise.

Cheney remarked that many of the U.S. forces like the 18th Airborne Corps were lightly armed and might have to fight heavily armored tanks. There were no reserve forces for back-up. He also questioned whether the U.S. ground forces could be kept supplied with food, fuel and munitions for a long period.

He noted that the ground plan called for the U.S. forces to make their assault straight into the Iraqi entrenchments and barricades, the Iraqi strength. Why go right up the middle? he asked.

Johnston deflected most of the questions. The plan was preliminary, he reminded them, and the questions reflected the caveats from Schwarzkopf that were listed in the last slide. By the time Johnston reached the last slide, however, the Phase Four plan was pretty much shredded. That slide said that Schwarzkopf felt an attack now on the Iraqi force twice the size of his, even with U.S. air, naval and technological superiority, was loaded with problems. "We do not have the capability on the ground to guarantee success," Johnston said. Schwarzkopf felt that he would need an additional Army Corps of three heavy armored divisions for a proper offensive option.

Cheney concluded that an attack with the U.S. forces now in place and based on this plan would be a risk of a high order.

Johnston said there was a window of opportunity of some six weeks, from about January 1 to February 15, when offensive action would be most desirable. After that, the weather and Muslim religious holidays would conspire to make combat more difficult. Heavy rains would begin in March and the temperatures could rise to 100 degrees or more. But they could work around the weather. It could not and should not determine their timetable, he said.

On March 17, the Muslims would start the observation of Ramadan, one month of fasting from sunrise to sunset, and in June would be the annual pilgrimage to Mecca, Johnston noted. The timing could present another complication for Arab states in the anti-Saddam coalition.

Cheney recognized that he had an obligation to present this brief to President Bush. The President needed to know exactly where Schwarzkopf was, the status of the deployment, and what might happen if offensive operations were ordered. The President, Scowcroft and Sununu at least had to be educated on the magnitude of the task. Cheney did not want to walk over to the White House one day, months down the road, to say, "Here's the plan, bang, go." The President had to comprehend the stakes, the costs and the risks, step by step.

By now Cheney had come to realize what an impact the Vietnam War had had on Bush. The President had internalized the lessons—send enough force to do the job and don't tie the hands of the commanders. In a September 12 speech in California, Cheney had said, "The President belongs to what I call the 'Don't screw around' school of military strategy."

Though this perhaps was inelegantly stated, Cheney was certain that the President didn't want to screw around. That meant a viable offensive option.

Schwarzkopf, in Saudi Arabia, was unhappy that he would not be there when the President was briefed on a subject of such paramount importance.

The next day, October 11, Johnston made the presentation to Bush at the White House. In the Situation Room, Johnston laid out the same plan. The meeting took nearly two hours. Bush was interrupted several times. He and Scowcroft had many questions on various subjects, such as minefields and weapon systems. When Johnston said Schwarzkopf would need a full corps of three additional heavy divisions to have the capability to attack on the ground, he was asked how long it would take to move that many divisions.

Two to three months to get them in place, Johnston said.

He hoped his briefing proved that the existing forces were inadequate for an offense.

Bush's reaction was similar to Cheney's, particularly on the Phase Four ground plan. The military was not ready for an offensive operation; they didn't have enough strength.

What would be enough? Bush asked.

Cheney promised the President a detailed answer soon.

• • •

On Wednesday, October 24, Cheney was summoned to the White House. The administration had finally reached a budget compromise with the Democrats after a bruising and politically damaging six months, particularly the last two. Now Bush had time to focus on some of the answers to the question he had left with Cheney—how much additional force? The President said he was leaning toward adding the forces necessary to carry out offensive operations to expel Iraqi troops from Kuwait. Nothing could be announced for two weeks, until after the November 6 elections, because any move would be assumed to be an attempt to influence the elections. Cheney said that he was waiting for Powell's report from Saudi Arabia, and they should wait.

It was apparent to Cheney that Bush would be happy with some public hint. Cheney was already scheduled the next day to go on the early morning shows of the three major networks and CNN. He felt that the White House's inept handling of its budget talks with Congress had cast a pall over the entire administration, and raised fundamental questions about whether Bush and the cabinet knew what they were doing. It had affected Bush's standing in the polls and the way people looked at Washington and government, even eroding confidence in the Gulf operation. Cheney also felt that it was best to prepare the public for the likely decision. He had consistently stated that there was no upper ceiling on the troop deployment and had repeatedly warned that the United States was in for the long haul.

Later that day Cheney joined Baker in giving a classified briefing to legislators in the secure room, S-407, in the Capitol. Neither dropped a hint that a reinforcement was being considered.

But in the television interviews the next morning, October 25, Cheney intentionally laid the seed. "We are not at the point yet where we want to stop adding forces," he said on ABC. On CBS he was asked if the Pentagon was getting ready to send another 100,000 troops. Cheney replied, "It's conceivable that we'll end up with that big of an increase."

He repeated this point on NBC, but added that this would not affect the relief of troops already there after six to eight months. "There clearly will be a rotation policy. . . . I would guess we'll end up around six months."

The big news of Cheney's statements reached Powell, who was on a stopover in Europe. "What is going on?" he asked an aide. When it sank in, he told

one person, "Goddammit, I'll never travel again. I haven't seen the President on this." There had been discussions but no decision as far as he knew. But there it was in clear language from Cheney, a man who chose his words carefully.

Bush, Scowcroft and Sununu were making decisions again without a full airing of views. Powell was tired of learning of major administration decisions after the fact. Sununu had been advising and urging the President to speak out strongly and to back up his words with a military threat. He or someone else apparently had won.

One thing that could be said for Bush: he had stated consistently that the Kuwait invasion would not stand. Powell, however, felt that the economic sanctions still loomed as the large unknown. When might they work? When would they be deemed to have failed? He was eager to get back to Washington.

In Saudi Arabia, Schwarzkopf also heard Cheney's remarks. Before his own surprise and distress could fully register, the Saudis were on the phone pounding him with questions: What is this? What's going on? Where were the consultations before making such a decision or announcement? Schwarzkopf tried to stumble through with some answers. He was fuming. Not only did he have to learn about something this important from the media, but he had to explain it to the Saudis without any guidance from Washington.

Schwarzkopf gave a long interview to *The Atlanta Journal and Constitution* that week. "Now we are starting to see evidence that the sanctions are pinching," Schwarzkopf said. "So why should we say, 'Okay, gave 'em two months, didn't work. Let's get on with it and kill a whole bunch of people?' That's crazy. That's crazy." He recounted how in Vietnam the United States, unopposed in the air, would pound the villages with bombs and then go in and find the North Vietnamese coming right out of their holes fighting like devils. Schwarzkopf also said, "War is a profanity because, let's face it, you've got two opposing sides trying to settle their differences by killing as many of each other as they can."

Wolfowitz, who visited the Central Commander around this time, felt that Schwarzkopf was making these statements partly for the benefit of his troops, to make it absolutely clear that if there was a war, it would be the civilians who would be taking them there.

Schwarzkopf told Wolfowitz that he had had

some discussions with Middle East experts who had convinced him that while war would be damaging to the United States in the region, a failure to go to war would be far more damaging. Schwarzkopf said he felt that a prolonged stalemate would be a victory for Saddam.

Powell arrived back in Washington, but Cheney was going off the next day to do some fishing in Wyoming with Baker. A White House meeting with the President was planned for early the following week to discuss the Gulf options.

• • •

Several times in October, Robert Teeter, Bush's chief pollster, talked with the President about the Gulf policy. Teeter said he thought the administration had too many messages flying around. There was a lack of focus. He suggested that Bush return to the fundamentals that he had stated in August. The two with the strongest appeal were fighting aggression and protecting the lives of Americans, including the more than 900 Americans being held hostage in Iraq and Kuwait. About 100 had been moved to Iraqi military and industrial installations to serve as "human shields" to deter an American attack.

Bush acknowledged the points, but nonetheless seemed confident. The President said that he felt he knew more than anyone about the region, and also about the diplomacy, the military, the economics and the oil. I have been dealing with these issues for 25 years, Bush said. One night he told Teeter it was important that he had served as United Nations ambassador, U.S. envoy to China, CIA director and Vice President. Those experiences allowed him to see all the pieces. Now he could put them together.

Bush described how, since taking office as President, he had been laying the groundwork, building relations with other heads of state. He'd had no specific purpose in mind, just a strategic sense that it was a good idea. Now his good working relationships with the Thatchers, Mubaraks, Fahds and Gorbachevs of the world could be put to use. There might be some rough times, some down times, Bush conceded, but he felt good. "This will be successful," he assured Teeter.

• • •

For months Scowcroft had been concerned that Baker was not a supporter of the Gulf policy. In the inner-circle discussions he seemed to oppose the large deployment of troops, favoring a diplomatic so-

lution almost to the exclusion of the military pressure. But Baker was coming around. Cheney was fishing with him over the weekend and they would have time to talk.

Baker felt the foundation for the Gulf policy was not solid enough. The plight of the emir of Kuwait, his people, aggression and oil were not selling to the American people. The polls showed that the greatest concern was over the American hostages in Iraq and Kuwait. Baker had argued that the focus of the Gulf policy should be shifted to the hostage issue. It was the one issue that would unite Americans and the international community because most nations, including the Soviets, had hostages held in Iraq. It was the one issue that might justify a war.

Scowcroft thought a new emphasis on the hostages would be changing horses in the middle of the stream, but he saw that public opinion polls were showing increasing doubts about the military deployment. Baker wanted to play the hostage card himself in a strong speech. Scowcroft was willing to go along. The national security adviser also realized that Baker saw the handwriting on the wall. The Bush presidency was likely to rise or fall on the outcome of the Gulf policy. Baker, Bush's friend of 35 years, his campaign manager and the senior cabinet officer, had no other choice than to become an aggressive supporter of the policy.

On Monday, October 29, Baker addressed the Los Angeles World Affairs Council. The more than 100 American human shields, he said, "are forced to sleep on vermin-ridden concrete floors. They are kept in the dark during the day and moved only at night. They have had their meals cut to two a day. And many are becoming sick as they endure a terrible ordeal. The very idea of Americans being used as human shields is simply unconscionable."

The Secretary of State added: "We will not rule out a possible use of force if Iraq continues to occupy Kuwait."

• • •

[On the afternoon of October 30], Bush met with Baker, Cheney, Scowcroft and Powell in the Situation Room.

"We are at a 'Y' in the road," Scowcroft began. The policy could continue to be deter-and-defend, or it could switch to developing the offensive option.

Powell was struck once again by the informality of the rolling discussion among these five men who had been friends for years. There was no real

The Persian Gulf War: Chronology

August 2, 1990	At around 02:00 hours Thursday morning (Gulf time) Iraqi troops invade Kuwait.
	The United Nations Security Council condemns the Iraqi invasion and calls for immediate withdrawal.
	U.S. freezes Iraqi and Kuwaiti assets. *Independence* and *Eisenhower* sail toward the Gulf.
August 3	Fresh Iraqi troops continue to arrive in Kuwait.
	U.S. House and Senate vote unanimously to impose trade sanctions and cut off credits to Iraq.
August 6	The U.N. Security Council votes to impose mandatory economic sanctions on Iraq.
	President Bush orders U.S. forces ("Operation Desert Shield") to Saudi Arabia and Gulf region.
August 8	Iraq announces the annexation of Kuwait, but U.N. Security Council declares the annexation of Kuwait "null and void."
August 12	Bush orders American naval units to block shipping in and out of Iraq.
August 18	Iraq declares the U.S.-led quarantine an "act of war."
September 24	U.N. Security Council imposes an air embargo on Iraq.
November 8	President Bush orders an additional 150,000 troops.
November 19	Iraq announces that it is sending 250,000 more troops to the "Basra and Kuwait provinces."
November 28	U.N. Security Council approves a U.S.-sponsored resolution authorizing member states to take military action if Iraq does not withdraw from Kuwait and release foreign hostages by January 15, 1991.
January 9, 1991	Foreign ministerial talks between U.S. and Iraq. After a six-hour session, U.S.-Iraqi talks end in Geneva without progress.
January 16	At about 18:30 hours (EDT) the U.S. and coalition air forces launch Operation Desert Storm attacking Iraqi forces in Iraq and Kuwait, bombing targets deep inside Iraq.
January 17–26	Iraq launches Scud missiles at Israel, sets several Kuwaiti oil installations on fire, and deliberately releases crude oil into the Persian Gulf.
February 12–20	Coalition forces launch an attack against Iraqi infantry, artillery and armor concentrations along the southern Kuwait border. U.S. ground forces mount a cross-border attack against an Iraqi troop encampment along the border.

February 22	President Bush and coalition give Iraq 24 hours to withdraw from Kuwait.
February 23–24	Ten minutes prior to the deadline, Iraq fires a Scud missile at Israel.
	Shortly after 20:00 hours EDT, the ground phase of Operation Desert Storm begins with coalition forces racing into Iraq and Kuwait along a 300-mile front. The 101st Airborne Division penetrates 50 miles into southern Iraq in a large-scale, helicopter-borne operation.
	Coalition forces reach the outskirts of Kuwait City before nightfall.
	An Iraqi radio broadcast announces the withdrawal of Iraqi troops from Kuwait.
February 26	U.S. marines enter Kuwait City and liberate it.
February 27	President Bush orders the conditional suspension of the coalition attack.
April 6	Iraq formally accepts the Security Council cease-fire resolution but calls it "unjust."

Sources:

Blair, Arthur H. *At War in the Gulf: A Chronology.* Texas: Texas A&M University Press, 1992.

Nye, Joseph S., Jr. and Roger K. Smith. *After the Storm: Lessons from the Gulf War.* Maryland: Aspen Institute for Humanistic Studies, 1992.

organization to the proceedings as they weighed the options. Ideas bounced back and forth as one thought or another occurred to one of them. Bush and Scowcroft seemed primed to go ahead with the development of the offensive option. Baker, less anxious and more cautious, was measured, inquiring about the attitudes in Congress and in the public, but he was no longer reluctant.

Listening, Cheney saw no willingness on Bush's part to accept anything less than the fulfillment of his stated objective, the liberation of Kuwait. The Secretary of Defense was not going to recommend any military action unless they were sure of success. He said that he had a growing conviction that they had to develop the offensive option. The international coalition was too fragile to hold out indefinitely—to outsiders it might look different, but they knew, from the inside, that the arrangements were delicate. Cheney felt it was quite likely that some outside event could absolutely shatter the coalition.

Powell saw that patience was not the order of the day. As in the past, he did not advocate containment. Powell had found the others previously tolerated his broad political advice, but now he sensed that he had less permission to speak up, having already made the case for containment to the President. Now

no one was soliciting Powell's overall political advice on this subject.

The meeting had been billed in advance as a chance for the Chairman to report on his discussions with Schwarzkopf.

"Okay, okay, okay," the President finally said, "let's hear what he has to say."

"Mr. President," Powell began, "we have accomplished the mission assigned." The defense of Saudi Arabia had been achieved earlier than expected. He described how Schwarzkopf had moved some of his forces around to accomplish this in light of the continuing Iraqi buildup.

"Now, if you, Mr. President, decide to build up—go for an offensive option—this is what we need." He then unveiled the Schwarzkopf request to double the force. A central feature was the VII Corps so Schwarzkopf would have the high-speed tanks to conduct flanking attacks on the Iraqis. In this way, they could avoid a frontal assault into Iraqi strength.

Scowcroft was amazed that Schwarzkopf wanted so much more. The request for three aircraft carriers in addition to the three he already had especially surprised Scowcroft. Several oohs and ahs were heard around the table, but not from Bush.

Powell said he supported Schwarzkopf's recommendations, if the President wanted an offensive option. He turned to the President. "If you give me more time, say three months, I'll move more troops. It's that important. You can take me to the Savings and Loan bailout account, and we'll all go broke together." Powell's message: it was going to be expensive.

As far as Powell was concerned, the only constraint was going to be the capacity of the transportation system.

Cheney said he supported Schwarzkopf and Powell without conditions. He went even further. It was not a question *if* the President wanted the offensive option; the President should want it and should go ahead and order it, Cheney said. He explained that this would guarantee success if they had to fight. He did not want to be in the position of making another request for more forces come January or February. Saddam was fully capable of responding with more of his own forces. Cheney did not want to be back here in the Situation Room saying then, "Mr. President, I know what we told you back in October, and

we put the additional force over there, but we still can't do it."

Finally, Bush said, "If that's what you need, we'll do it."

The President gave the final approval the next day.

• • •

Paul Wolfowitz, who as undersecretary for policy was one of few Pentagon civilians granted oversight of war plans, was worried that the administration had transitioned into the decision on the offensive option without a lot of clear thought. There was little or no process where alternatives and implications were written down so they could be systematically weighed and argued. Wolfowitz, a scholarly senior career government official and former ambassador, thought it would have been possible to decide to send additional troops and not say specifically whether they were replacements or an offensive reinforcement. The decision as to their ultimate purpose could be made later. But Wolfowitz didn't have time to get the idea considered.

Chapter 8 Review Questions

1. What are the key differences between the *root* and *branch* methods of decision making? Summarize the advantages and disadvantages of each method.
2. Does the case study, "The Decision to Liberate Kuwait," exemplify the root or branch method of decision making? Or, another approach? Explain your reasons for your selection by citing examples from the case.
3. How does the case point up the influence of professionals in the decisional process? Which professionals in this case influenced its outcome? In what ways did they impact on the decisional processes? Does the case support Stillman's concept of competing bureaucratic subsystems of personnel discussed in the previous chapter? If so, how? Or, does this case point up the *cooperation* that takes place among personnel subsystems in government?
4. Compare this case involving the Gulf Crisis with Case Study 4. Discuss the major differences in the way these two critical national decisions were reached. In particular, consider the number and kinds of people who became involved in the decisional processes, the care and manner by which the options for administrative action were presented and considered, the factors forcing the final decision, and the overall effectiveness of the decisional processes.
5. On the basis of your comparative appraisal of the two cases, can you generalize about how proper timing as well as the general historic time period play important roles in the way these or other public decisions are reached?

6. Also on the basis of your comparison of the two cases, why does who gets involved in the decisional process (or who is left out) play such a critical role in the quality and kind of decisions that are made in government?

Key Terms

incremental decision making
root method
branch method
clarification of objectives
intertwining ends and means
successive limited comparisons

rational comprehensive analysis
policy alternatives
maximization of values
empirical analysis
policy outcomes
ranking objectives

Suggestions for Further Reading

Making good, correct, and efficient decisions in the public interest has been a major concern of public administration literature since the early, "conscious" development of the field. In particular, the writings of Frederick Taylor and his followers about scientific management examined methods of rational decision making in organizations at the lower levels of industrial or business hierarchies. However, the post–World War II writings of Herbert Simon, especially his *Administrative Behavior: The Study of Decision Making Processes in Administrative Organization* (New York: Macmillan, 1947), shifted the focus of administrative thinking to *the decision* as the central focus of study and analysis. The enormous impact of this book (for which Simon won the Nobel Prize in 1978), as well as his other writings on public administration, make it worthy of careful attention by students of the field even today. For useful background information on Simon's life and work, read his autobiography, Herbert A. Simon, *Models of My Life* (New York: Basic Books, 1991). A recent thoughtful and extensive challenge to the Simonism approach can be found in Roger Penrose, *The Emperor's New Mind* (New York: Oxford University Press, 1989).

Other important writings on this topic include Charles E. Lindblom, *The Intelligence of Democ-*

racy: Decision Making Through Mutual Adjustment (New York: Free Press, 1965), and his book co-authored with David Braybooke, *A Strategy of Decision* (New York: Free Press, 1963). For criticisms of the Simon-Lindblom incrementalist approach see Yehezkel Dror, "Muddling Through—Science or Inertia?" *Public Administration Review,* 24 (September 1964), pp. 154–157, and Amitai Etzioni, "Mixed Scanning: A Third Approach to Decision Making," *Public Administration Review,* 27 (December 1967), pp. 385–392. The debate over incrementalism is hardly over, for an entire symposium in the *Public Administration Review,* 39 (November/December 1979) was devoted to its pros and cons. Pay particular attention to the articles by Charles E. Lindblom, "Still Muddling, Not Yet Through" (pp. 511–516); Camille Cates, "Beyond Muddling" (pp. 527–531); and Bruce Adams, "The Limitations of Muddling Through" (pp. 545–552); plus Amitai Eztioni, "Mixed Scanning Revisited," *Public Administration Review,* 46 (January/February 1986), pp. 8–14. By contrast, Aaron Wildavsky, "Toward a Radical Incrementalism," in Alfred DeGrazia, *Congress: The First Branch of Government* (Washington, D.C.: American Enterprise Institute, 1966) pushes the incremental concept about as far as possible; whereas Paul R. Schulman, "Nonincremental Policy Making: Notes

Toward an Alternative Paradigm," *American Political Science Review,* 69 (December 1975), presents possibly the most searching critique of the incremental model. James G. March, *A Primer on Decision-Making: How Decisions Happen* (New York: Free Press, 1994), offers a highly developed restatement of the incremental model in the 1990s. Also see Herbert A. Simon et al., *Economics, Bounded Rationality and the Cognitive Revolution* (Brookfield, Utah: E. Elgar Publishing Co., 1992).

Since the 1960s numerous decision models other than incrementalism have been proposed with various degrees of success. The most prominent include the *systems model* as represented in Fremont J. Lyden and Ernest G. Miller, eds., *Planning Programming-Budgeting: A Systems Approach to Management* (Chicago: Markham Publishing Co., 1968); *games theory* as outlined in Thomas C. Schelling, *The Strategy of Conflict* (Cambridge, Mass.: Harvard University Press, 1963); the *bureaucratic model* as represented in Graham T. Allison, *Essence of Decision: Explaining the Cuban Missile Crisis* (Boston: Little, Brown, 1971); *cost-benefit* as found in Edward M. Gramlich, *Benefit-Cost Analysis of Government Programs* (Englewood Cliffs, N.J.: Prentice-Hall, 1981); *personal judgment* approach of Harvey Sherman, *It All Depends* (University, Ala.: University of Alabama Press, 1966); the *policy analysis method* as discussed in William N. Dunn, *Public Policy Analysis: An Introduction* (Englewood Cliffs, N.J.: Prentice-Hall, 1981); and the *garbage can model,* Michael D. Cohen et al., "A Garbage Can Model of Organizational Choice," *Administrative Science Quarterly,* 17 (1972), pp. 1–25. These only scratch the surface of a vast, complex area of decision-making study. You would be well advised to read the current issues of such journals as *Public Administration Review, Administrative Science Quarterly, Journal of Policy Analysis and Management, Public Manage-*ment, or *Harvard Business Review* for up-to-date perspectives on decision-making methodology.

For two survey textbooks that outline a broad range of public sector quantitative decision techniques, see Michael J. White et al., *Managing Public Systems: Analytic Techniques for Public Administration* (No. Scituate, Mass.: Duxbury Press, 1981); and Richard D. Bingham and Marcus E. Ethridge, eds., *Reaching Decisions in Public Policy and Administration* (New York: Longman, 1982). For a scholarly review of various decision-making approaches and where we stand today regarding their application to government, read George W. Downs and Patrick D. Larkey, *The Search for Government Efficiency: From Hubris to Helplessness* (New York: Random House, 1986); James G. March, "Theories of Choice and Decision Making," *Society,* 20 (1982); Michael Murray, *Decisions: A Comparative Analysis* (New York: Longman, 1986); David Wilson, *Top Decisions* (San Francisco: Jossey-Bass, 1986); S. S. Nagel, "Introduction to Decision-Aiding Software in Public Administration," *International Journal of Public Administration,* 14 (1991), pp. 125–128; Douglas L. Kiel, "Non-Linear Dynamic Analysis: Assessing Systems Concepts in a Government Agency," *Public Administration Review,* 53 (March/April 1993), pp. 143–153; Linda Dennard, "Non-Darwinism and Simon's Bureaucratic Antihero," *Administration and Society,* 26 (February 1995), pp. 464–487; Young B. Choi, *Paradigms and Conventions* (Ann Arbor: University of Michigan Press, 1993); and for an excellent collection of applied cases involving local decision making, see James M. Banovetz, ed., *Managing Local Government: Cases in Decision Making* (Washington, D.C.: International City Management Assoc., 1990). The recently published book, Geoffrey Vickers, *The Art of Judgment* (London: Sage, 1995 and first printed in 1965) offers one of the best arguments for practical judgment as the key to effective decision making.

CHAPTER 9

Administrative Communications: The Concept of Information Networks

B lockages in the communications system constitute one of the most serious problems in public administration. They may occur in any one of the three steps in the communication process: initiation, transmission, or reception.

H. Simon, D. Smithburg, and V. Thompson

READING 9

Introduction

In arriving at even the most routine policy decisions, the typical public administrator is a prisoner of a seemingly endless communications network that defines the problem at hand and the possible alternatives. Administrators are normally pressed from many sides with informational and data sources flowing into their offices from their superiors, subordinates, other agencies, citizen groups, and the general public. Sometimes the information arrives through routine formal channels; at other times it wells up or trickles down to the administrator via unsolicited routes. Whatever the source, the public decision maker must selectively sort out this information, and, in turn, dispense a substantial quantity of information to people within and outside the organizational structure; this is done by memoranda, reports, conferences, phone conversations, and informal encounters that touch off a new chain of communications and decisions by others. Similar to a telephone switchboard, a policy maker's office acts as a nerve center where the lines of communications cross and are connected and where information is received, processed, stored, assembled, analyzed, and dispensed.

Our conceptual understanding of the importance and complexity of the communications links within public organizations and their critical role in administrative decisions depends to a large extent on the work of Herbert A. Simon (1916–). In collaboration with Donald Smithburg and Victor Thompson, Simon wrote the text *Public Administration* (1950); this work, drawing on Simon's earlier writing, *Administrative Behavior* (1947), for which Simon won the Nobel Prize for economics in 1978, offered one of the first integrated behavioral interpretations of public administration. By introducing ideas from sociology, psychology, and political science, Simon and his associates sought to discover "a realistic behavioral description of the process of administration," emphasizing its informal human dynamics.

At the root of public administration, according to Simon, Smithburg, and Thompson, were continual conflicts among contending groups that resulted from such internal pressures as empire-building tendencies, differing individual backgrounds, and varying group identifications, as well as such external pressures as competing interest groups, members of Congress, and other agency heads struggling for scarce resources and influence. Similar to Norton Long's conception of the political power contest surrounding administrative activities (discussed in Chapter 4), the authors envision administrators as people "in the middle of continual conflict" whose actions and activities demand a considerable effort directed toward conflict resolution and compromise. As they write, "public administrators, and particularly those responsible for directions of unitary organizations, are themselves initiators and transformers of policy, brokers, if you like, who seek to bring about agreement between the program goals of government agencies and the goals and values of groups that possess political power." In short, "the greatest distinction between public administration and other administration is . . . to be found in the political character of public administration."

Decisions within this political setting can never be wholly rational but rather, the authors contend, are of a "bounded rational" nature. Instead of insisting on an "optimal solution," the public policy maker must be satisfied with what is "good enough," or as Lindblom suggests more simply in Chapter 8, must "muddle through." The prime ends of a public administrator's efforts are decisions that are not "maximizing" but "sufficing," that have as their goals not efficiency but achieving agreement, compromise, and ultimately survival.

One of the major vehicles for achieving coordination and compromise, in the view of Simon, Smithburg, and Thompson, is the communications network, which they define as the "process whereby decisional premises are transmitted from one member of an organization to another." The communications network acts principally as an integrating device for bringing together frequently conflicting elements of an organization to secure cooperative group effort. Three steps are involved in the communications process: first, "someone must initiate the communication"; second, "the command must be transmitted from its source to its destination"; and third, "communications must make its impact on the recipient." The information travels in two ways: (1) the formal or planned channels such as memoranda, reports, and written communications; and (2) the unplanned or informal ways such as face-to-face contacts, conferences, or phone calls to friends. Simon, Smithburg, and Thompson place considerable emphasis on the informal lines of communications that many refer to as "the grapevine." "In most organizations, the greater part of the information that is used in decision-making is informally transmitted," they observe.

The central problems in communications are the blockages that occur: "Blockages in the communication system constitute one of the most serious problems in public administration. They may occur in any one of the three steps in the communications process: initiation, transmission, or reception. Those who have information may fail to tell those who need the information as a basis of action; those who should transmit the information may fail to do so; those who receive the information may be unwilling or unable to assimilate it."

Seven critical types of communications blockages in public organizations are enumerated by the authors, the first being, simply, *barriers of language.* Words are frequently misinterpreted or understood differently as messages pass from one individual to another within organizations. Second, *frames of reference* differ so that the perception of information varies among individuals. Personal "mental sets" thus often prevent accurate comprehension of the problem at hand. Third, *status distance* can block communications because as information moves upward or downward through the various hierarchical levels of an organization "a considerable filtering and distorting" occurs. Fourth, *geographical distance* impedes the communications process; a far-flung department with many field offices spread over the nation or the world has great difficulty in ensuring prompt and accurate information exchange among its component units. Fifth, *self-protection* of the individual who reports actions plays a role in the informational links. Often "information that will evoke a favorable reaction will be played up; the mistakes and the fumbles tend to be glossed over." Sometimes the deception is conscious and at other times unconscious, but this activity always serves to distort objective reality. Sixth, *the pressures of work* tend to leave important matters overlooked or unreported. Finally, the *censorship* inherent in many governmental activities such as foreign intelligence or military operations limits the accurate flow of information within many public agencies.

These characteristic psychological and institutional communication blockages, suggest Simon, Smithburg, and Thompson, raise the vital question of "where a particular decision can best be made." Selection of the appropriate place for decision making directly depends on how effectively and easily information can be transmitted from its source to a decisional center, and how effectively and easily the decision can be transmitted from the decision maker to the point where action will occur. For instance, a military hierarchy could grant to individual company commanders the authority for deciding on the use of tactical nuclear weapons. This action would reduce the "time costs" associated with communicating to higher headquarters in the event of possible enemy attack and thus would allow for extreme military flexibility at lower echelons, but "local option" in this case might very well increase other costs, such as the likelihood of a nuclear accident. On the other hand, if authority for using these weapons had to be cleared, say, by the president of the United States and by other major Allied powers, the risk of accident might very well be reduced, but the time costs of gaining consent to use these weapons from many sources might make a decision so cumbersome and lengthy that no opportunity for swift retaliatory response would exist. As Simon, Smithburg, and Thompson point out, "Ease or difficulty of communications may sometimes be a central consideration in determining how far down the administrative line the function of making a particular decision should be located." The authors thus view the communications process not only as determining the outcome of particular decisions but as a prime influence on the structure of decision making within organizations. Extreme decentralization may achieve flexibility and initiative at the local level but may exact costs in terms of uniformity and control of response; vice versa, extreme centralization may produce maximum oversight but may reduce organizational responsiveness. Ultimately, the costs associated with delegating such decisional authority within an organizational hierarchy are always relative and are determined by the values and objectives of the organization. In the following selection from Simon, Smithburg, and Thompson's *Public Administration,* many of the enduring and difficult dilemmas of communications within public organizations are outlined. As you read this selection, keep the following questions in mind:

Can you think of any additional blockages to administrative communications other than those outlined by the authors? For instance, reflect on any communications barriers that might have been apparent to you in the previous cases, such as "The Decision to Liberate Kuwait" or "The Last Flight of the Space Shuttle Challanger."

Is it possible to trace the *formal* network of communications in an organization? The *informal* network? What factors would create or determine a formal informational network? For example, what impact have computers had in recent years?

Can you draw from this essay generalizations concerning the communications process as a means for establishing executive authority and control over an organization? How does fragmentation of executive authority occur in public organizations and how can communications be used effectively "to cure" this problem (think about the first case, "The Blast in Centralia No. 5")?

Finally, consider the following essay in relation to Norton Long's concept of administrative power—do administrative communications influence the patterns of administrative power? How did communications influence the outcomes in the case study in Chapter 3, "Dumping $2.6 Million on Bakersfield"?

The Communication Process

HERBERT A. SIMON, DONALD W. SMITHBURG, AND VICTOR A. THOMPSON

The American disaster at Pearl Harbor is one of the dramatic examples in modern times of the possible consequences of failure of an organization communication system. Quite apart from the question of who or what was to "blame" for Pearl Harbor, a large part of the military damage inflicted by the Japanese undoubtedly could have been avoided if two serious breaks in the military communication system had not occurred. The first was the failure to secure proper top-level attention to the in-

tercepted "Winds" message that gave warning an attack was impending. The second was the failure to communicate to the military commander in Hawaii information accidentally obtained from the radar system by an enlisted man that unidentified planes were approaching Pearl Harbor.

Less dramatic, but of equal importance, is the role that communication plays in the day-to-day work of every organization. Without communication, not even the first steps can be taken toward human cooperation, and it is impossible to speak about organizational problems without speaking about communication, or at least taking it for granted.

This process, which is central to all organizational behavior, can be illustrated with the example of a policeman operating a patrol car. He is told to patrol in a particular patrol area; he is provided with a manual of regulations and approved procedures; when he reports for duty in the morning, he may receive specific instructions of things to watch for during the day. He may be given a list of license numbers of recently stolen automobiles and perhaps a description of a fugitive. As he patrols his beat, a call may come to him from the police radio informing him of a store burglary to investigate.

The patrolman, in turn, becomes a source of communications that influence other organization members. His report on the burglary investigation is turned over to the investigations division where it becomes the basis of further activity by a detective. Certain data from this report are recorded by a clerk and are later summarized for the weekly report that goes to the chief of police. Information contained in this weekly report may lead to a redistribution of patrol areas to equalize work loads. Meanwhile, other data from the report have gone into the pawnshop file where they are used by other detectives who systematically survey local pawnshops for stolen goods.

Communication and Organization Structure

By tracing these and other communications from source to destination, we discover a rich and complex network of channels through which orders and information flow. Viewing the communication process from a point in an organization where a decision is to be made, the process has a twofold aspect: communications must flow to the decision center to provide the basis for decision, and the decision must be communicated from the decision center in order to influence other members of the organization whose cooperation must be secured to carry out the decision.

The question of where in the organization a particular decision can best be made will depend in considerable part upon how effectively and easily information can be transmitted from its source to a decision center, and how effectively and easily the decision can be transmitted to the point where action will take place. The decision of a social worker in a public welfare agency in granting or refusing an application for assistance illustrates how these factors enter into the picture. The principal facts and values that have to be brought to bear on this decision are: (1) the economic and social facts of the applicant's situation; (2) accepted principles of casework; and (3) the eligibility regulations and casework policies of the agency. The first set of facts is obtained by interviewing the applicant, by correspondence, and by field investigation. The second set of considerations is derived from the education and training of the social worker and his supervisors. Policies governing the third set of considerations are largely established by the legislative body and the top administrative levels of the agency and communicated downward.

If the decision on the application is to be made by the social worker himself, these three sets of considerations must be communicated to him. The costs of communication here are the time cost of his own investigational activities, the costs of training him adequately in the accepted principles of casework, and the costs of indoctrinating him in agency policies by formal training, instructions, discussion with his supervisor, or otherwise. Once he has made the decision, it must be communicated to the applicant—a relatively simple step—and certain reports on his action must be transmitted to his superiors for supervisory and control purposes.

On the other hand, the decision on the application might be placed in the hands of the casework supervisor, rather than the social worker. This might shorten the communication chain required to bring agency policy to bear on the decision and the chain that reports on the action would have to travel. Further, if the social workers were relieved of this decision, they would probably not need to be as thoroughly trained in casework as if they made the decisions themselves—training efforts could be concentrated on the supervisors. However, in other respects new costs of communication would be incurred. It would be necessary to communicate from social worker to supervisor all the circumstances of the applicant's situation—a very voluminous reporting job and an almost impossible one if intangible impressions received by the social worker in the interview are to be communicated. Moreover, there would be an extra step in communicating the decision on the application to the applicant via the social worker.

Ease or difficulty of communication may sometimes be a central consideration in determining how far down the administrative line the function of making a particular decision should be located (or, as it is usually put, "how far authority should be delegated"). Delegation increases the difficulty of communicating organization policies that are decided at the top and reports from the decision center to the top that are required to determine compliance with policy. Delegation may also involve greater training costs by multiplying the number of persons who have to be competent to make a particular decision. Delegation usually reduces the difficulty of communicating to the decision center information about the particular situation in question, and usually reduces the difficulty of communicating the decision to the point where it is placed into operation. All these factors were illustrated in the previous example.

Steps in the Communication Process

In the study of communication processes it is convenient to distinguish three steps:

1. Someone must initiate the communication. If the communication is a monthly report, someone must be assigned the task of preparing the report. Many of the most important communications originate outside the organization, or in special "intelligence" units of the organization. Examples of the first would be a fire alarm, a phone call to the police department, or the filing of a patent application or a workman's compensation claim. Examples of the second would be the reports of military reconnaisance aircraft, an information report by an embassy to the State Department on developments

abroad, or a compilation of employment statistics by the U.S. Department of Labor.
2. The communication must be transmitted from its source to its destination.
3. The communication must make its impact upon the recipient. The communication has not really been "communicated" when it reaches the desk of the recipient, but only when it reaches his mind. There is a potential gap here 'twixt cup and lip. It will receive attention in later portions of this chapter.

We shall see that costs and difficulties of communication may be encountered at each of these three stages of the process. Before we proceed to a detailed analysis of these costs and difficulties, however, it is necessary to describe in somewhat greater detail the elements that go to make up an organization communication system.

Elements of the Communication System

Roughly, organizational communications fall in two categories: planned or "formal" communications and unplanned or "informal" communications. Every organization has some formal arrangements whereby knowledge can be transmitted to those who need it. But this formal transmission of information is supplemented by a great deal of communication that springs from the willingness, indeed, the eagerness, of employees to share information with one another even when such transmission is not formally authorized, and even when it is forbidden.

Formal Communication

The administrative manual of a large organization often specifies who may write officially to whom; who must report to whom and on what occasions; who shall see memoranda on particular subjects; who shall give out information on specified subjects. This attempt to plan and to channel communications can be seen in perhaps its most elaborate form in the armed services, where extremely intricate patterns of communication are incorporated into formal rules and where channels are rigidly enforced.

Where the work of an organization consists of processing applications or claims, the written procedures will usually specify in considerable detail just how the application is to be routed, what information is to be entered on it at each step, and what work is to be performed. Similarly, the form, content, and responsibility for preparation of accounting records is almost always formally determined.

Informal Communications

. . . The growth of an informal communication system . . . supplements the formal, prescribed system. For example, the unit chief who wants advance information as to whether it is going to be easy or difficult to secure a budget increase for the coming year may find that a friend who is assistant to the bureau chief can give him the desired information long before any formal bulletin flows down through the established channels.

Method of Informal Communication. The ways in which information is disseminated informally are many. Jones, Smith, and Goldberg who work in different sections lunch together. Each has connections with various parts of the organization, and they swap information. Mrs. Johnson belongs to the same lodge auxiliary as the wife of Mr. Alexander who is administrative assistant to the bureau chief. Mrs. Johnson gets some information which she transmits to her husband who, in turn, passes it on to his section.

But informal communication is not only the inevitable, if somewhat illicit, shop talk and gossip. It includes any kind of information outside the specified channels. Nor is it always easy to define what is meant by "channels"—normally these include communications along the lines of formal authority, or along lines that have been explicitly authorized by the formal hierarchy. In most organ-

izations, the greater part of the information that is used in decision-making is informally transmitted.

Barriers to Effective Communication

The amount of misunderstanding in the world caused by failure of people to communicate effectively with each other can hardly be exaggerated. Words are tenuous. The failure of human plans and aspirations are all too often bitterly recalled in terms like "if it could have been gotten across," or "if I had said it this way rather than that, he might have understood."

Blockages in the communication system constitute one of the most serious problems in public administration. They may occur in any one of three steps in the communications process: initiation, transmission, or reception. Those who have information may fail to tell those who need the information as a basis of action; those who should transmit the information may fail to do so; those who receive the information may be unwilling or unable to assimilate it.

The Barrier of Language

Among the barriers to effective communication one of the most serious is the use of language that is not understandable to the recipient. In a society as specialized as ours there are literally hundreds of different languages which cluster around the various specialties. Many words quite understandable to a physician are Greek to the layman. Many words quite understandable to the skilled machinist are incomprehensible to the doctor. The vocabulary shared by all Americans is meager indeed.

Not only is the shared vocabulary meager, but the words that are shared often mean different things to different people. Philosophers like Ogden and Richards and Carnap have shown how many traps in philosophy have at their base a faulty use of language. At a more popular level, students of semantics have also shown us that many so-called problems are really pseudoproblems which, when correctly formulated, disappear.

Within administration, the written communication is likely to be even more plagued by language difficulties than the oral communication. Most persons in face-to-face contacts try to speak in terms that will be understood by the listener—and if they do not, they will soon be aware of the fact. They can repeat the communication in different terms. They can explain what they "really mean." The author of a written communication has no such an opportunity to assess his audience or to gauge the degree to which his words are being understood.

Frame of Reference

Very often the communication process is impeded because those giving, transmitting, or receiving the communication have a "mental set" that prevents accurate perception of the problem. The stimuli that fall on a person's eyes and ears are screened, filtered, and modified by the nervous system before they even reach consciousness— and memory makes further selections of the things it will retain and the things it will forget. This selecting process is an important reason why our judgments of people are so often wrong. If we have a favorable impression of a man, we are likely to remember the good things about him that come to our attention and to forget, discount, or explain away the bad things. Only a series of several vivid, undesirable impressions is likely to change our initial estimate of him.

Status Distance

Communication between persons distant in scalar status most often takes place through a chain of intermediaries. When there is contact between individuals of different status, communication from the superior to the subordinate generally takes place more easily than communication from the subordinate to the superior. If communication were not difficult between persons of widely different status, organizations would not feel the need, as they so often do, to install suggestion boxes that

permit low-level employees to bring their ideas to the attention of top executives. And experience with formal suggestion systems shows that even this device is often inadequate to lower the barrier of status difference.

Status differences exert a considerable filtering and distorting influence upon communication— both upward and downward. Upward communication is hampered by the need of pleasing those in authority. Good news gets told. Bad news often does not. The story of Haround al Raschid, the caliph who put on beggar's clothes and went out among his people to hear what they really thought, is the story of the isolation of every high status executive. Most executives are very effectively insulated from the operating levels of the organization. For a number of reasons, pleasant matters are more apt to get communicated upwards than information about mistakes. Subordinates do not want to call attention to their mistakes, nor do they want the executive to think that they can't handle their own difficulties without turning to him. They want to tell him the things he would like to hear. Hence, things usually look rosier at the top than they really are. . . .

Geographical Distance

One of the most striking and far-reaching phenomena of our era has been the tremendous extension of the mechanical techniques of communication. Changes in the technology of communication have changed both the structure and the problems of administrative organizations. Probably more than any other single factor, the improvement of the means of communication has had a centralizing effect upon administration—centralizing in the sense that a field officer can now be supervised in much greater detail than was previously possible.

Far-flung organizations can now be within hour-to-hour communication with their headquarters. This has enabled central offices to keep a far tighter check rein upon the activities of their agents in the field. Ambassadors who formerly had broad discretion to act in their negotiations with other nations, now can and must constantly check their views with a central office. The operations of widely dispersed field offices can come under the constant scrutiny of central headquarters.

Even where geographical dispersion is not wide, such as in modern police and fire departments, the effect of instantaneous communication has changed the whole pattern of their operations. It has made possible a greater efficiency and greater specialization. The radio police car can be summoned rapidly to an area of trouble. The work of the fire department can be directed rapidly and efficiently.

Inadequacy of Techniques. But modern communication techniques have not completely overcome the problems of communicating at a distance, and, in addition, they have added new problems of their own. Communication by letter, wire, or telephone, although it may be rapid, is no effective substitute for the face-to-face interchange. As Latham has pointed out:

> Impediments to the free exchange of thought are difficult enough to overcome in the same city, building, or even room. They become even more difficult with the increase of distance between the central office and the field. In the same environment, geographical, social, and professional, the common milieu sometimes gives many clues to understanding which precise words could not have spelled out. This element is missing in communications at a distance.[1]

The difficulties of communication at a distance, even with modern means, are several. Oral communication by telephone, while the closest counterpart to face-to-face conference, is by no means a perfect substitute. It is costly, and mechanically imperfect over great distances, and the important overtones of oral communication that are ordinarily conveyed by facial expression and gesture are missing.

Written communication is an even less adequate substitute for the conference. Even in verbal con-

tent, a two-page single-spaced letter is the equivalent of only ten minutes' conversation. A division head, with offices adjacent to those of his bureau chief, might confer with his superior individually and in conference a half hour or an hour daily. To communicate the same material in writing would require an interchange of six to twelve single-spaced pages a day. Even then, the letter is much less likely to convey exact ideas than is a conversation, where misunderstanding can be detected and corrected immediately, questions raised, and so forth.

Insufficient Communication. Moreover, daily personal contact stimulates communication. A man may think to pass on to his superior or subordinate over a luncheon table a piece of information that it would not occur to him to put down in a letter. Where there is geographical separation, the person at each end of the communication line finds it difficult to visualize and keep constantly in mind the needs for information at the other end of the line. A constant complaint of field offices is that they learn from the daily newspapers or from clients things that should have been communicated to them from the central office.

Consider, for example, the problem of communicating a change in rent control regulations. Such a change will probably be publicly announced by the central office at a press conference and instantly transmitted in more or less complete form by newspaper wire services throughout the country. Washington representatives of real estate groups will also advise their local clients of the new regulation, often by telegraph or telephone. To prevent premature disclosure of the regulations, the central office may be reluctant to send them in advance to local field offices, with the result that these field offices may be bombarded by questions from tenants and landlords before they have had any detailed information on the new regulations from the central office. This pattern repeated itself again and again in wartime regulatory programs and was a continual source of friction between central and field offices.

Excessive Communication. Paradoxically, field offices often complain that they receive too many communications at the same time that they complain that they are insufficiently informed on new developments. The attempt of the central office to supervise closely the operations in the field often results in a steady flow of procedural regulations, instructions, bulletins, and whatnot to the field offices. If too much of this material is trivial, detailed, or unadapted to local problems—and the field office will often feel that it is—it may remain unread, undigested, and ineffective. This problem is not one of geographical separation alone, but applies generally to organization communications.

Self-protection of the Initiator

We have already pointed out that most persons find it difficult to tell about actions that they believe would put them in a bad light. It is much easier to secure reports about overtime than it is to get reports on the number of times the workers reported late or took extra time for lunch. Furthermore, the ordinary work code demanding loyalty to work groups also prevents the communication of information that would seem to reflect upon one's friends or upon the organization of which one is a part. In consequence, reports flowing upward in the organization, such as reports to Congress, the President, or the public, tend to be "sugar-coated." Information that will evoke a favorable reaction will be played up; the mistakes and the fumbles tend to be glossed over. Information going downward is equally suspect. A casual reading of any house organ will reveal how carefully the higher executives and their actions are "explained" to employees in a way that will show the wisdom of their decisions and their benevolence toward those who occupy the lower levels. In part, this deception is conscious. In part, it is unconscious. These upward and downward distortions make an actual and objective view of the organization difficult to obtain.

Pressure of Other Work

A person in an ordinary work situation is normally pressed for time. He must establish a system of priorities as to the various demands made upon him. In such circumstances he is likely to respond to the pressures of the immediate work situation while giving lower priority to the more abstract demands of communicating with others. Furthermore, the constant demand for information concerning the details of his work often meets with unspoken resentment because it seems to reflect upon his integrity. If he does not know why he is asked for specific types of information, he is likely to conjure up ideas that the "head office" will use the information against him or that the request has no purpose—that it is mere make-work.

Similarly, the central office is likely to take an authoritarian view of the communication process and resent the constant inquiries from those lower in the hierarchy or the field. It, too, is likely to slough off the job of communication and to regard it as less important than the task of setting policy. Thus, in many agencies the task of communication is thought of as something basically clerical—a mere stenographic transmittal of decisions. Communication is likely to be shunted into the background.

Deliberate Restrictions upon Communication

One problem of much government communication is to see that it reaches those who should have the information and yet to prevent it from reaching those who would use it in an undesirable way. There is always disagreement between those individuals who believe that the public should have information concerning every aspect of government policy and policy formulation—particularly those in the press whose business is the dissemination of information—and those in government service who would argue that the compromises which are essential in the formation of public policy would not be possible if every move had to be carried on in the relentless glare of publicity.

Whether or not to have publicity is not a new problem. The founding fathers determined that the only possible way in which agreement could be reached on a new constitution was to conduct the deliberations without continuous publicity. To prevent the publication of the deliberations they even went so far as to establish a guard for the aged, brilliant, but garrulous Benjamin Franklin to see that his disclosures in the neighborhood taverns would not jeopardize the goals of the convention.

Note

1. Earl Latham, *The Federal Field Service* (Chicago: Public Administration Service, 1947), pp. 8–9.

⬜ CASE STUDY 9

Introduction

For public administrators today, one of the most potent political actors influencing their work, both in terms of helping to set the agenda for what they do and then decisively shaping public opinion about how well or poorly they perform their roles, is the media. Radio, TV and newspaper coverage, its volume and content, help to create the issues public agencies address and then largely determine public perceptions of what they accomplish. In our modern media-drenched environment, for many government agencies, the visual and print media may well be the most important sources of political power "impacting" their programs and generating political support or opposition.

Few instances of media influence on public officials in recent years were more pronounced than what happened in the federal assault on the Branch Davidian Compound. On February 28, 1993, near Waco, Texas, four agents from the Treasury Department's Bureau of Alcohol, Tobacco, and Firearms (ATF) were killed, and more than twenty other agents were wounded when David Koresh and members of his religious cult, the Branch Davidian, ambushed a force of seventy-six ATF agents. The agents were attempting to execute a search and issue arrest warrants at the Branch Davidian Compound. Tipped off that the agents were coming, Koresh and more than one hundred followers waited inside the Compound and opened fire using assault weapons even before the agents reached the door. The gunfire continued until the Davidians agreed to a cease-fire, but the ensuing standoff lasted fifty-one days, ending on April 19, when the entire compound erupted in a fire that had been set by cult members after the Federal Bureau of Investigation (FBI) used tear gas to force the occupants to leave. The fire destroyed the compound, and more than seventy residents died, many from gunshot wounds apparently inflicted by their fellow cult members.

The Branch Davidian movement was started by a number of Seventh Day Adventists, who believed strongly in the biblical prophecies of the book of Revelation. David Koresh, then named Vernon Wayne Howell, took over the leadership of the cult in 1987. The members became extremely devoted to Koresh, and many believed that he was "The Lamb of God." ATF involvement with the cult began in June, 1992, when its Special Agent Davy Aguilera started an investigation of the Davidians on suspicion of their purchasing illegal firearms.

Over the course of events that led to ATF's raid on the cult, in retrospect, the agency made several mistakes, such as in the planning for the assault, in their flawed decision-making process that approved this raid and the ineffective oversight exhibited by Treasury officials. Media relationships were also a central problem with this ATF operation. In the official study of the Waco tragedy, *Report of the Department of the Treasury on*

ATF's Investigation of Vernon Wayne Howell, also known as David Koresh (issued September 1993), a central portion focuses on the story of ATF's media relations. The following excerpt not only explicitly shows generally the power of the media in shaping a public agency's activities, but specifically how communications—or its lack—with media representatives influenced the timing of ATF's actions against the Branch Davidians and even the entire outcome of ATF's operations.

As you read this piece, try to keep in mind several issues:

What was ATF's strategy in dealing with the media, and what were "the flaws" in its communications approach?

Why was the media a powerful agenda-setter in this case and what were their motivations? Who were the key media and ATF representatives in this case?

How did the print and visual media ultimately influence the outcome of the ATF raid on February 28?

If you had been ATF's special agent in charge of this operation, how would you have dealt with the media? Or, better communicated with the media and our agents?

ATF and the Media Prepare for the Raid on the Branch Davidian Compound

Even before ATF began its inquiry into firearms and explosives violations at the Branch Davidian Compound, a local newspaper, the *Waco Tribune-Herald,* had been investigating David Koresh and his followers. In spring 1992, Mark England, a *Tribune-Herald* reporter who had covered Koresh's 1988 trial for attempted murder, became intrigued by reports that Koresh proclaimed he was Jesus Christ and that there might be a mass suicide at the Branch Davidian Compound during Passover. With reporter Darlene McCormick, England gathered information and interviewed Koresh, former cult members, and the families of current cult members. By fall 1992, the reporters had information that children were being physically and sexually abused at the Compound. Having also learned that the Branch Davidians were using a buried school bus as a shooting range and that they were stockpiling large amounts of weapons and munitions, the reporters decided that law en-

forcement and social service agencies were not taking the situation seriously.

In October 1992, McCormick called Assistant U.S. Attorney Bill Johnston in Waco to ask what constitutes an illegal firearm. According to McCormick, Johnston informed her that the "Treasury guys" could tell her if any Branch Davidians had permits for automatic weapons. While Johnston did not give McCormick any specific information about the ATF investigation, she concluded that federal authorities were in fact investigating the Branch Davidians. After the call, Johnston notified ATF that the newspaper was working on a story.

By January 1993, England and McCormick had drafted a "Sinful Messiah" series of articles and submitted them to their editors. By early February, the galleys (used to detect and correct errors before a newspaper page is composed) went to Randall Preddy, the *Tribune-Herald*'s publisher, for his review. Because of its startling revelations of Branch Davidian lifestyles and its disclosure of dangerous weapons at the Compound, Preddy sent the galleys to his superiors at Cox Enterprises, the newspaper's

Source: *Report of the Department of the Treasury on the Bureau of Alcohol, Tobacco, and Firearms Investigation of Vernon Wayne Howell also known as David Koresh,* USGPO, Sept. 1993, pp. 67–107 and pp. 157–163.

parent company in Atlanta, for review. He also asked Cox's Vice President for Security, Charles Rochner, to assess the potential for violence against the *Tribune-Herald*'s plant and personnel and to recommend any necessary security procedures. Preddy and Rochner discussed the situation at the February Cox publishers meeting in Orlando, Florida, and Rochner agreed to visit Waco later in the month.

ATF Discussions About the *Tribune-Herald* Investigation and Contacting the Media

ATF first learned about media interest in the Compound when, in October 1992, Johnston told [Special Agent Davy] Aguilera that the *Tribune-Herald* was preparing a major story about Koresh. In December 1992, when Aguilera learned that Marc Breault, a former Branch Davidian, was supplying information to both law enforcement and the *Tribune-Herald,* Aguilera located Breault and asked him to stop dealing with the newspaper. That same month, Aguilera told his supervisor, Earl Dunagan, acting RAC [Resident Agent-in-Charge] of the Austin office, about the *Tribune-Herald*'s parallel investigation. Dunagan, in turn, suggested to ASAC [Asst. Special Agent-in-Charge Chuck] Sarabyn, his supervisor in Houston, that ATF try to convince the *Tribune-Herald* to delay the story until after the ATF operation took place. At a meeting to discuss the investigation on December 4, SAC [Special Agent-in-Charge Phillip] Chojnacki suggested meeting with the *Tribune-Herald* to request a delay in publication, but James Cavanaugh (then a Dallas ASAC and later Deputy Tactical Commander for the raid) opposed any such contact. By January 1993, however, an agreement was reached that a delay should be sought to ensure the safety of the undercover agents and the integrity of the investigation.

The February 1, 1993, Meeting with a *Tribune-Herald* Official

In mid-January, Barbara Elmore, the *Tribune-Herald*'s managing editor, contacted Assistant U.S. Attorney Johnston to assess the likelihood that the Branch Davidians would retaliate against the *Tribune-Herald*'s plant or personnel in the wake of the publication of the Koresh series. Johnston advised

her of ATF concerns about publication of the articles and suggested a meeting.

On February 1, Sarabyn and Dunagan met with Elmore at the U.S. Attorney's Office and, citing their ongoing investigation, asked her to delay publication of the Davidian series. Johnston introduced the parties but did not participate in the meeting. The agents offered to give *Tribune-Herald* reporters "front-row seats" during the execution of the contemplated law enforcement action if the newspaper delayed publication of its series until after the raid. Elmore said that her publisher would have to make that decision and mentioned her concerns about the security of the *Tribune-Herald*'s personnel and building. At the conclusion of the meeting, Dunagan told Elmore that ATF planned to execute the search warrant on February 22 and that he would inform her if the date changed. Elmore recalls only that ATF told her that it might take some type of action concerning the cult in two to four weeks.

About two weeks later, Dunagan, with Sarabyn's approval, told Elmore that the raid had been postponed to March 1. According to Elmore, she told Dunagan that the *Tribune-Herald* had made no decisions about publication, but alerted other *Tribune-Herald* personnel of the date change. Dunagan believed the paper was cooperating with ATF's request to hold the story because Elmore had not told him anything to the contrary. Editors at the *Tribune-Herald,* on the other hand, have indicated that they felt no obligation to respond to ATF one way or the other; indeed, they report having been surprised that ATF agents did not contact other members of *Tribune-Herald* management after Elmore had told ATF she could not make the decision to delay publication of the articles.

Continued Discussions Between ATF and the *Tribune-Herald*

After these initial contacts, Chojnacki assumed sole responsibility for ATF communications with the *Tribune-Herald.* On February 9, Rochner informed Chojnacki that he would act as the *Tribune-Herald*'s liaison with ATF and that he was conducting a threat assessment for the *Tribune-Herald* in connection with its "Sinful Messiah" series. *Tribune-Herald* staff members, however, have said that they did not regard Rochner as the paper's liaison with ATF, but only as a security consultant to the paper. Because Rochner planned to be in Waco the week of February

22, Chojnacki agreed to meet with him. In the meantime, Chojnacki invited Rochner to observe raid training at Fort Hood on the 25th, later changing the invitation to the 26th or 27th.

To prepare for the meeting with the *Tribune-Herald,* Chojnacki sought advice from Jack Killorin, Chief of ATF's Public Affairs Branch. ATF's media policy does not require that headquarters personnel be notified of media involvement at the operational stages of an ATF action. It does, however, require such approval for media "ride-alongs" (ATF Order 1200.2B, January 20, 1988). Noting Koresh's messiah complex and his paranoia, they agreed that taking the press along on a raid could create an inflammatory situation. Chojnacki said that he would offer *Tribune-Herald* key interviews and would recognize their hard work, but that he would not accept a demand that they be present at the raid or tell them the date or time of the raid. Killorin advised that ATF should not give the *Tribune-Herald* an exclusive story. He did not discuss this conversation with his supervisor, ATF Assistant Director of Congressional and Media Affairs James Pasco.

The *Tribune-Herald* Decision to Publish

By mid-February, reporters and editorial staff at the *Tribune-Herald* were eager to publish the "Sinful Messiah" series. Internal revisions and attorney libel review had been completed, and, at Rochner's direction, new security procedures were in place at the newspaper. Entrances to the building were locked, building passes were issued, and identifying decals had been removed from all *Tribune-Herald* vehicles. England and McCormick would leave Waco when the series appeared, and the homes of the *Tribune-Herald* executives would be protected. Only three hurdles remained before publication: Koresh was to be interviewed a final time so that his reaction could be included in the series; Rochner was to approve security procedures upon his arrival on February 24; and Chojnacki was scheduled to meet with *Tribune-Herald* editors on February 26. Preddy had told his staff that the series would not go forward until he had a face-to-face meeting with ATF officials.

On Friday, February 19, the *Tribune-Herald* editors took the first step toward publication and instructed England to interview Koresh. After contacting Koresh on Monday, February 22, for his reaction to the series, England left for Dallas on

Wednesday, February 24, pursuant to the security plan. McCormick was already out of the country on vacation. On Wednesday morning, Rochner arrived in Waco and at Preddy's request, rescheduled the meeting with Chojnacki for that afternoon. Preddy recalls that before the meeting, Rochner mentioned that Chojnacki had invited him to observe ATF training at Fort Hood.

The February 24 Meeting with the *Tribune-Herald*

On February 24, Chojnacki, Rochner, and Preddy met with editor Robert Lott, City Editor Brian Blansett, and Managing Editor Barbara Elmore. Lott recalls that, at the time, he was committed to publication, absent clear and convincing evidence that the publication would cause harm. It is not clear, however, whether Chojnacki understood that this was to be the newspaper's standard for holding publication.

Chojnacki opened the meeting by thanking the *Tribune-Herald* editors for delaying the series, but the editors immediately made it clear that they had not held the series in deference to ATF—they had not been ready to run it for other reasons. Noting that he was concerned with the safety of ATF personnel as well as the safety of *Tribune-Herald* employees and facilities, Chojnacki begged the editors to hold off publication until after ATF had conducted its operation. Koresh appeared to be relaxed, Chojnacki explained, but publication of the series would agitate him and disrupt ATF's planned operation.

Chojnacki did not, however, give the paper any sense of when ATF's operation would take place or what it would entail. He noted that he had not yet obtained warrants and was not sure he would be able to get any; if he were unable to obtain such judicial authorization, he explained, he would have to "go home." While he told the editors that he could not "afford" a siege, Chojnacki refused to answer questions as to "what he had in mind" and "if he had an undercover." The most he would say was that a law enforcement action would likely take place "fairly soon." Asked if ATF planned to act within the next 7 to 14 days, Chojnacki declined to answer.

Chojnacki then asked the *Tribune-Herald* editors if their series would run in one to seven days. He recalls having received an affirmative answer. He asked the editors to give him some advance notice of the publication. He concluded by asking: "So, does that mean that you are willing to run this story even though we are asking you to keep it quiet for a few more days so that we can do what we have to do?" According to Chojnacki, Lott replied "The important thing to us is the public's right to have information that they need to know, and that's our job. We're not concerned about where it falls in or falls out in terms of your law enforcement case." Chojnacki then left the meeting and, as he told the Review, he was "hot."

All participants left the 30-minute meeting with the impression that the *Tribune-Herald* had not agreed to delay publication, and ATF had not revealed any specifics about its impending action. Elmore remembers the tone of the meeting as formal, but not antagonistic. Rochner recalls that Chojnacki appeared to be businesslike and that the meeting ended with an understanding that Preddy and the editors would discuss his request and that Rochner would get back to him. Chojnacki's impression of the meeting was that it was tense and did not end cordially. He had not expected to meet with all the *Tribune-Herald* editors and he was upset with the outcome of the meeting.

ATF and the Media Prepare for the Raid February 24–27

After the meeting with Chojnacki, the *Tribune-Herald* editors agreed that they had heard nothing to persuade them to delay publication. According to those at the meeting, their chief concern was to inform the public about the Branch Davidians as soon as the security of the paper and its employees allowed. Preddy tentatively decided that the series would begin on Saturday, February 27. This day was chosen, according to *Tribune-Herald* management, to allow the newspaper to gauge Branch Davidian reaction during the two weekend days, when activity at the newspaper's office and plant was reduced. Preddy decided not to notify ATF of the decision to publish until after Rochner had answered all security questions.

Tribune-Herald officials have asserted that the March 1 ATF raid date was not a factor when they chose the publication date on Wednesday afternoon. Chojnacki's discussion of his difficulty securing warrants and his problems funding his operation made the March 1 date appear unlikely to the editors and publisher. In their view, his presentation was consistent with the *Tribune-Herald* editors' belief that local law enforcement had failed to take action for two years.

After the meeting on Wednesday, Tommy Witherspoon, the *Tribune-Herald* reporter who covered the courts, told City Editor Blansett that he had received a tip from a confidential informant that something "big" might happen at the Branch Davidian Compound between 9:00 and 10:00 a.m. next Monday, that the roads might be blocked, and that Witherspoon might want to be there when it happened. (The *Tribune-Herald* has told the Review that this confidential informant was not an ATF employee.) Without asking Witherspoon to verify the tip or making assignments, Blansett decided he would send a few reporters to the Compound area that Monday.

In the wake of his meeting with the newspaper, Chojnacki realized that it was unlikely that the newspaper would accommodate his request to delay its series. At the ATF command post, he and other ATF leaders concluded that the Koresh series would begin on Sunday, February 28, and Chojnacki told as much to the SRT [Strategic Response Team] leaders at Fort Hood. Chojnacki then asked Sarabyn whether it would be possible to move the raid date up two days to Saturday. Sarabyn said that such a change was impossible, but that the raid could be done a day earlier, on Sunday. Chojnacki set the raid for Sunday, alerted Hartnett and Conroy of the change in plans, and they concurred.

ATF Raid Preparations: February 24–26. Even as Chojnacki met with the *Tribune-Herald*, ATF's preparations were in full swing. On February 24, ATF's forward observers and SRTs began arriving at Fort Hood for three days of rigorous training. On Thursday, the first day of training, Sarabyn briefed the SRT leaders on the overall plan and set out each team's assignment. The team leaders then briefed their respective teams. In addition, Rodriguez told the assembled agents about the Compound. On Friday, the agents, coordinating with a Fort Bragg Army Special Forces unit, were able to use the Military Operations Urban Terrain (MOUT) site at Fort Hood, a mock setting for urban military exercises, and the firing ranges. . . .

Securing Search and Arrest Warrants. After Aguilera and Chojnacki briefed ATF officials, including Director Higgins and ADLE Hartnett, in Washington, D.C., on February 11 and 12, Chojnacki received approval to seek both an arrest warrant for Koresh and search warrants for the Compound and the Mag Bag. On February 25, Aguilera signed a sworn affidavit he had prepared with the assistance of Assistant U.S. Attorneys Bill Johnston and John Phinizy. On the same day, after reviewing the affidavit, Dennis Green, U.S. Magistrate-Judge for the U.S. District Court for the Western District of Texas, issued an arrest warrant for Koresh for violating federal firearms laws and a warrant to search both the Mag Bag and the Compound for evidence of that crime. Even though, to avoid disclosing the progress of the investigation, Aguilera had intentionally curtailed his contacts with firearms dealers who had sold weapons and components to Koresh, his affidavit's account of the documented flow of materials into the Compound gave some sense of the arsenal that Koresh had amassed in 1992. Listed in the affidavit were:

104 AR-15/M-16 upper-receiver groups with barrels

8,000 rounds of 9mm and .22-caliber ammunition

20 100-round-capacity drum magazines for AK-47 rifles

260 M-16/AR-15 magazines

30 M-14 magazines

2 M-16 E-2 kits

2 M-16 car kits

1 M-76 grenade launcher

200 M-31 practice rifle grenades

4 M-16 parts sets—Kits "A"

2 flare launchers

2 cases (approximately 50) inert practice grenades

40 to 50 pounds of black gunpowder

30 pounds of potassium nitrate

5 pounds of magnesium metal powder

1 pound of igniter cord

91 AR-15 receiver units

26 various calibers and brands of handguns and long guns

90 pounds of aluminum metal powder

30 to 40 cardboard tubes

Other Waco Media Learn About the Raid.
While ATF agents were training at Fort Hood, reports of the impending raid were beginning to circulate among the Waco media. On Thursday, February 25, *Tribune-Herald* reporter Witherspoon told his friend Dan Mullony, who was a cameraman for television station KWTX, that something was going to happen at the Branch Davidian Compound on Monday. Mullony, in turn, alerted KWTX reporter John McLemore about the impending raid. Mullony attempted to confirm the tip. Darlene Helmstetter, his friend who was a dispatcher for American Medical Transport (AMT) ambulance service, told him that three ambulances had been put on standby for Monday at the request of law enforcement. On Friday, ATF advised AMT that the operation had been moved up and that ambulances should be at the Bellmead Civic Center rather than the airport. On Friday afternoon, at a wreck site, an AMT paramedic also told Mullony that something "big" was going to happen on Monday.

The *Tribune-Herald* Notifies ATF of Its Decision to Publish on Saturday, and ATF Reacts.
On Friday, February 26, publisher Preddy gave his final approval for the series to be published the next day. At about 3:30 p.m., Rochner gave this information to Chojnacki, advising him that a copy would be available at the *Tribune-Herald* loading dock at 12:15 a.m. on Saturday. Rochner says that he told Chojnacki that he would try to talk again with the newspaper editors and publisher if ATF had strong objections to publication. Chojnacki does not recall this offer. At Chojnacki's request, Rochner and Preddy reviewed the first story, and Rochner assured Chojnacki that it did not mention ATF.

That evening, Chojnacki advised other ATF supervisors, now gathered at Fort Hood, that the story would run the next morning. As a precaution, Chojnacki and Sarabyn decided they would send Rodriguez into the Compound on Saturday to gauge the effect of the article on conditions in the Compound.[1] Saturday was the Branch Davidian Sabbath, which usually entailed an all-day service in which Koresh preached to his followers. According to the revised plan, Rodriguez would enter the Compound at about

---

[1]The original raid plan had not provided for this undercover visit, or for the one on the day of the raid.

8:00 a.m. before the service began and look for signs that the article had caused Koresh to be on the alert for action by law enforcement or had otherwise caused a change in Compound routine.

ATF Notifies the Treasury Department's Office of Enforcement About the Raid.

On Friday afternoon in Washington, ATF officials notified the Treasury Department's Office of Enforcement—which oversees ATF—of the impending raid. A one-page memorandum from ATF's liaison to that office went to Acting Deputy Assistant Secretary for Law Enforcement Michael D. Langan. The memo was later shared with John P. Simpson, who was acting as Assistant Secretary of the Treasury, and Ronald K. Noble, who had been designated to be the Assistant Secretary of the Treasury for Enforcement, but who, pending nomination and confirmation, was working as a part-time consultant to the office. After Langan, Stanley Morris, who had been detailed to the Office of Enforcement, Noble and others expressed grave reservations about the operation outlined in the memorandum, Simpson contacted ATF Director Higgins and, noting these concerns, directed that the operation not go forward. Higgins spoke with Associate Director Hartnett, who was able to obtain additional information from Chojnacki that appeared to answer the Office of Enforcement's concerns. Higgins was thus able to assure Simpson and Noble that the raid plan recognized the dangers posed by Koresh's weaponry, and to assure them that though children were present at the Compound, the raid could be executed safely. Higgins noted that an undercover agent would be sent into the Compound before the raid to ensure that there had been no change in routine; he also assured them that the raid would be aborted if things did not look right. After these assurances were given, Simpson said he would permit the raid to go forward. . . .

Saturday, February 27: Media Preparations.

On Saturday, February 27, the first installment of the "Sinful Messiah" series appeared in the *Tribune-Herald*. The article described child abuse at the Compound, saying that Koresh encouraged the whipping of children as young as eight months and alleged that Koresh had fathered children with 15 women, many underage, living at the Compound. The article traced the 50-year history of the Branch

Davidians and explained the importance of the Seven Seals from the *Book of Revelations* to Koresh and his followers. The newspaper also featured a sidebar entitled, "The Law Watches, But Has Done Little," and an editorial asking when the McLennan County sheriff and the district attorney would take action.[2]

The *Tribune-Herald* then shifted its focus away from its investigative series and prepared to cover the developing story of law enforcement activity at the Branch Davidian Compound. Tommy Witherspoon's confidential informant told Witherspoon on Saturday that the raid had been moved up 24 hours. As a result, early Saturday afternoon, Preddy, Lott, Blansett, and Rochner met and decided to send reporters to the Compound area on Sunday morning. Preddy encouraged them to consider the safety of the reporters, but left before specific plans for coverage were discussed. After the meeting, while returning to Waco from a drive to see the Branch Davidian Compound, Lott, Blansett, and Rochner saw a military helicopter headed toward the airport at Texas State Technical College (TSTC). Blansett, familiar with landing patterns at TSTC, believed that the helicopter was landing in an area not usually used by military aircraft. When the three drove to TSTC to investigate, they saw approximately 10 people, some in uniforms, greeting the helicopter pilot. Rochner thought that these individuals must be with ATF and that TSTC could be the staging area for the raid.

Blansett returned to his office about 4:30 p.m., developed story assignments, and directed reporters to meet at the *Tribune-Herald* office at 8:00 a.m. on Sunday. Because most reporters did not have Sunday assignments and he believed the updated tip about the raid to be reliable, Blansett assigned nine reporters to the story, triple the number he had contemplated on Wednesday. Blansett was interrupted by a call from Steve Schneider, one of Koresh's senior deputies. Schneider told Blansett that Koresh was upset by the first "Sinful Messiah" article and wanted an opportunity to tell the *Tribune-Herald* the "real story," the story of the Seven Seals and not, as Schneider put it, "seven days of lies." Promising to call Schneider back, Blansett called Mark England in

---

[2]On Monday, March 1, the day after the ATF raid was repulsed, the *Tribune-Herald* published the remaining five parts of its "Sinful Messiah" series.

Dallas and told him about the raid tip and Koresh's request for an interview. England left Dallas for Waco. Blansett next called Rochner, who suggested that England interview Koresh in a restaurant, so that Rochner and an off-duty police officer could be nearby. Rochner also asked if reporters wanted flak jackets for the raid, noting that he might be able to locate some. When England arrived in Waco, he told Blansett that he did not want to interview Koresh. Blansett never called Schneider back.

Rochner talked with Chojnacki twice that Saturday. First, he sought, unsuccessfully, to get Chojnacki's reaction to the story. That evening he also sought Chojnacki's counsel on Schneider's request that someone from the newspaper interview Koresh. They discussed sending reporters into the Compound on Saturday, which Chojnacki discouraged, explaining that he did not think it would be safe to enter the Compound.[3]

KWTX's preparations to cover the raid also moved forward. On Saturday morning, Mullony learned from Helmstetter, the AMT ambulance service dispatcher, that the ATF operation had been moved up a day. Helmstetter also told him that he should plan to be in town on Sunday. On Saturday afternoon, Mullony and Witherspoon acknowledged to each other that they knew the ATF operation was set to occur the next day. By Saturday evening, Mullony concluded that the raid would occur at about 9:00 a.m. Sunday based on standby times Helmstetter had given him. Helmstetter had also told Mullony that ATF had placed CareFlite, a Fort Worth helicopter medical transport service, on standby for Sunday. This fact led KWTX to believe the operation would be a major one.

That night, at the direction of KWTX News Director Rick Bradfield, Mullony asked Jim Peeler, another KWTX cameraman, and reporter McLemore to meet him and Bradfield early Sunday morning. Mullony was so concerned about what might happen the next day that he drafted his will. In contrast, McLemore, unconcerned, took his wife out to a local

club. According to one witness, in a conversation at the bar, McLemore said ATF was going to conduct a big raid the following day. McLemore admits that he alluded to a big event but denies saying anything about ATF.

Saturday, February 27: ATF Preparations. Saturday was a hectic day for ATF as raid preparations continued. At the morning briefing, Sarabyn discussed the first installment of the "Sinful Messiah" series. He pointed to Koresh's picture, noting that the article did not mention an ongoing investigation, and explained to the agents that Rodriguez would be sent in Saturday and Sunday to gauge Koresh's reaction to the series. . . .

Meanwhile, ancillary and support elements converged on Waco. Two marked ATF bomb-disposal trucks and National Guard support trucks, including a two-and-a-half ton military transport truck and a water truck, arrived at TSTC. After Fort Hood training, three National Guard helicopters also proceeded to TSTC. The Texas Department of Public Safety was prepared to set up roadblocks and the sheriff's department was prepared to provide other support functions. ATF reserved 153 rooms at three Waco hotels for the evening of the 28th. At 8:00 that evening Chojnacki and Sarabyn conducted a briefing at the Best Western Hotel for arrest and support teams, including National Guard members, explosives specialists, dog handlers, and laboratory technicians. Phillip Lewis, Support Coordinator, had arranged with local suppliers for such diverse items as the ambulance services, portable toilets, and the Bellmead Civic Center. On Saturday, he ordered doughnuts at a Waco grocery store, arranging to pick them up the next morning. He also arranged with the sheriff's department for coffee at the Bellmead Civic Center site the next morning.

Special Agent Sharon Wheeler, the ATF public information officer (PIO) assigned to the operation, prepared for the raid. Several weeks earlier, Chojnacki had asked that public information be handled by Killorin, but his request was denied because Pasco and Killorin determined that Killorin was needed in Washington on other matters. Wheeler was chosen because the Houston PIO was less experienced and New Orleans did not have a PIO.

Responding to direction from her SAC, Ted Royster, Wheeler contacted one Dallas television station

[3]Rochner recalls that he next proposed sending a reporter into the Compound on Sunday. According to Rochner, Chojnacki said, "Good luck, you will not be in our way if you go on Sunday." Rochner contends that this reinforced his view that no raid was planned for Sunday. Chojnacki does not recall making such a statement. In any event, the *Tribune-Herald* did not send reporters to the Compound on February 28 to interview Koresh; it sent reporters to cover a raid.

for a weekend contact number. Then, following her press plan, she called two other Dallas television stations to obtain similar telephone numbers. While she indicated to all the stations that ATF might have something going on during the weekend, she did not describe the action or provide its timing, location, or any other information specific to the raid. She did not contact Waco television stations or newspapers, out of a concern that the raid's security might be threatened.[4]

Rodriguez entered the Branch Davidian Compound at 8:00 a.m. Saturday to join Koresh's worship service. Koresh preached about the "Sinful Messiah" article and told his followers that "they" were coming for him. He cautioned that, when this happened, his followers should not get hysterical and should remember what he had told them to do; he did not specify at the time what those instructions were. Between noon and 5:00 p.m., Rodriguez met with Chojnacki at the TSTC command post. Chojnacki asked Rodriguez whether he had seen any guns or preparations to resist law enforcement. Rodriguez said he had not.

ATF Agents Assemble

On the morning of February 28, Cavanaugh and the forward observers watched the Compound from the undercover house for signs of unusual activity. They saw nothing out of the ordinary. A few men were walking about the grounds and some women were emptying waste buckets. The weather was overcast with traces of precipitation.

Meanwhile, at Fort Hood, the 76 agents assigned to the cattle trailers assembled at 5:00 a.m.[5] They traveled to the staging area, the Bellmead Civic Center, in an approximately 80-vehicle convoy with a cattle trailer at each end. Many of the vehicles bore the telltale signs of government vehicles—four-door, late-model, American-made vehicles with extra an-

tennas. All the vehicles had their headlights on. Agents report that, once underway, the convoy stretched at least a mile.

The convoy arrived at the Bellmead Civic Center between 7:30 and 8:00 a.m. The civic center is adjacent to a residential neighborhood and is visible from the nearby intersection of Interstate 84 and Loop 340, 9.4 miles from the Compound. An ATF agent wearing an ATF raid jacket and local police were in the street in front of the civic center directing the convoy into the parking lot. While waiting to be briefed, some of the agents went inside the center to have coffee and doughnuts; others milled about outside. A supervisor became concerned about the visibility of the agents, many of whom wore ATF insignia or were otherwise unmistakably law enforcement personnel. He ordered everyone to go inside and to remain in the civic center.

The Media Sets Out to Cover the Raid

Even as ATF agents were gathering to embark on the raid, local reporters were deploying to cover the operation. At 7:00 a.m. at KWTX, Jim Peeler, John McLemore, and Dan Mullony received maps of the area and reviewed assignments with the station's news director, Rick Bradfield. Bradfield anticipated a major law enforcement operation because he had learned from Mullony's AMT Ambulance Service informant, Darlene Helmstetter, that CareFlight, a Fort Worth–based trauma flight company, was involved. Bradfield told the Review that KWTX did not call ATF to confirm the raid because asking for information or permission is generally unproductive. (According to Bradfield, the policy of KWTX when covering law enforcement operations is to go to the news site, obey law enforcement orders, and respect private property.)

Peeler was sent to the intersection of Double E Ranch and Old Mexia roads where, according to Mullony, Peeler was to watch for and film raid helicopters. Peeler denies receiving any information concerning helicopters. Peeler thought his job was to film any prisoners brought out during the raid. Mullony and McLemore were sent to Farm Road 2491 (FR 2491) on the other side of the Compound's grounds. Bradfield, from the newsroom, communicated with his employees by cellular telephone. Radios were not used so that competitors could not overhear their conversation.

---

[4]Despite earlier accounts to the contrary, Wheeler did not divulge any information about the raid in these contacts. The reporters she contacted were not able to determine what law enforcement action she was referring to, based on their conversation. Indeed, none of the stations she contacted were at the Compound until well after the firefight began.

[5]With few exceptions, no definitive record exists of times for the events on February 28. Accordingly, except where otherwise noted, all times are approximations derived from witness recollections, logs, and other records.

Prior to the raid, nine *Tribune-Herald* reporters were assigned to the developing story. The morning of the raid, some of them gathered at the newspaper's office before departing for the Compound in four cars, three heading for the Compound and the fourth to TSTC to watch for helicopter activity. The newspaper, concerned about the enormous cache of weapons at the Compound and Koresh's potential for violence, had gone to extraordinary lengths to ensure the safety of its plant and personnel. In contrast, the reporters were not given any safety instructions about covering the raid, nor were they instructed about possible affects their presence or actions might have on the raid.

As the reporters drove to the Compound they mistakenly expected to encounter roadblocks. In law enforcement operations however, a roadblock is usually not established until the action begins. In this case, establishing a roadblock more than two hours before the raid was to begin likely would have compromised the secrecy of the operation.

At about 7:30, after driving up and down the Double E Ranch Road in front of the Compound twice, Mullony parked on FR 2491 about one mile north of its intersection with Double E Ranch Road. By 8:30, other *Tribune-Herald* vehicles were patrolling the two roads bordering the Compound. At 9:30, Mark England asked a DPS officer parked on the side of the road if he could go by what he believed to be a roadblock. The officer told England that he could pass but that the road would later be closed. In the hour before the raid, five media vehicles could be seen driving or parked on roads near the Compound. The agents in the undercover house reported the increased traffic to Cavanaugh. The Review has been unable to verify whether Cavanaugh forwarded the information to the command post.

But while other reporters were waiting for the raid to begin, KWTX cameraman Peeler became lost. At about 8:30, he used his cellular telephone to ask Bradfield and Mullony for directions. Despite getting directions, Peeler remained lost somewhere near the intersection of Old Mexia and Double E Ranch roads. There he encountered David Jones, a local letter carrier who was driving a yellow Buick with "U.S. Mail" painted on the door. Jones pulled up behind Peeler and asked him whether he was lost. Peeler, who was wearing a KWTX jacket, introduced himself as a cameraman with the station and asked for directions to "Rodenville," the name by which many Waco residents had referred to the Compound ever since it had been owned by the Roden family. Peeler did not know that Jones was one of Koresh's followers. Jones pointed to the Compound, which was in sight, and commented that he had read about the cult in the paper and thought they were weird. Peeler, deceived into believing that Jones was not affiliated with Koresh, warned Jones that some type of law enforcement action was about to take place at the Compound. He indicated that the action was likely to be a raid of some type and that there might be shooting.[6]

After the chance encounter with Peeler, Jones returned to his car and as he sped away toward the Compound, Peeler began to wonder whether Jones was affiliated with the cult. After this conversation, Peeler drove to a nearby store and called Bradfield, who told him to return to the intersection of Old Mexia and Double E Ranch roads, wait 30 minutes, and if nothing happened, go home. When Peeler returned to the intersection, DPS officers and ATF agents had set up a roadblock. Peeler was not allowed to pass, but he was told where he could set up his camera.

Peeler's encounter with Jones was witnessed by one of the ATF undercover agents who was taking the forward observers and their arrest support teams to a hay barn behind the Compound. The undercover agent was dressed in casual clothes; the forward observers wore ATF battle dress utilities. When the undercover agent saw the two vehicles parked together on the road, he recognized Jones's postal vehicle. Jones was talking to the occupant of the second car, whom the agent did not recognize but suspected was a reporter. The agent, fearing that Jones might spot the uniformed agents in his car, told them to crouch down. Jones did not appear to look

---

[6]There are conflicting reports about what Peeler actually told Jones. In a statement to the Texas Rangers, Koresh's attorneys stated that in one of their visits to the Compound during the standoff between the cult and the FBI, David Jones (now deceased) told them that Peeler warned him not to go near the Compound as there were going to be "60 to 70 TABC (Texas Alcohol Beverage Commission) guys in helicopters and a shoot-out would occur." Peeler has denied giving this much detail to Jones. However, he has admitted that on the morning of the 28th he believed that TABC was involved and had tuned his scanner to the TABC frequency. TABC was not involved in the action on the 28th and Peeler is the only witness interviewed by the Review who believed that TABC was involved. Peeler's admission lends credibility to the account provided by Koresh's attorneys.

in the agents' direction and the undercover agent was satisfied that his group had not been seen. He drove to the hay barn, deposited the forward observers and arrest support team, and returned to the undercover house where he told Cavanaugh what he had seen. Cavanaugh claims to have relayed the information to the command post although no one there recalls receiving it.

Rodriguez Enters the Compound

At 8:00 a.m., not long before Peeler had his conversation with David Jones, Rodriguez went to the Compound one final time for the most critical phase of his undercover assignment, assessing whether the *Herald-Tribune* articles had incited Koresh and his followers to take up arms or otherwise increase their security measures. Koresh greeted the undercover agent and invited him to join a "Bible study" session with two of his followers. There were no signs of unusual activity.

While Koresh and Rodriguez were engaged in this Bible session, David Jones arrived at the Compound, fresh from his encounter with Peeler. He told his father, Perry Jones, what had happened. Perry Jones devised a pretext to draw Koresh away from Rodriguez.[7] He called to Koresh that he had a phone call. When Koresh ignored the request, Jones added that it was long distance from England.

Early interpretations of Jones' reference to England speculated that Jones was referring to Mark England, the co-author of the *Tribune-Herald* series whom Koresh had been trying to contact. This interpretation led to speculation that Mark England alerted Koresh to the impending raid. However, Koresh's attorneys have said that Jones told them that he was referring to the country. In any event, contrary to early accounts, there is no evidence that Mark England placed a call to the Compound on the morning of February 28. Records provided by the *Tribune-Herald* of their telephone calls contain no record of a call to the Compound on the morning of February 28.

When Koresh left the room to take the fictitious

[7]Cult members released from the Compound after the raid have stated that prior to the 28th, Koresh had suspected that Rodriguez was an undercover agent. One cult member stated that despite his suspicions, Koresh continued to meet with Rodriguez believing that he could nonetheless successfully recruit him.

call, David Jones described his conversation with Peeler. Upon Koresh's return, Rodriguez could see that he was extremely agitated, and although he tried to resume the Bible session, he could not talk and had trouble holding his Bible. Rodriguez grabbed the Bible from Koresh and asked him what was wrong. Rodriguez recalls that Koresh said something about, "the Kingdom of God," and proclaimed, "neither the ATF nor the National Guard will ever get me. They got me once and they'll never get me again." Koresh then walked to the window and looked out, saying, "They're coming, Robert, the time has come." He turned, looked at Rodriguez and repeated, "They're coming Robert, they're coming."

Rodriguez was shocked. As Koresh repeatedly looked out the window and said, "They're coming," Rodriguez wondered whether the raid was beginning even though he was still in the Compound. Needing an excuse to leave, Rodriguez told Koresh he had to meet someone for breakfast but Koresh did not respond. Other male cult members entered the room, effectively if not intentionally coming between Rodriguez and the door. Fearing that if he did not leave he would be trapped in the Compound, Rodriguez contemplated jumping through the window. He repeated that he had to leave for a breakfast appointment. Koresh approached him, and in a manner Rodriguez believed highly uncharac- teristic, shook Rodriguez's hand and said, "Good luck, Robert." Rodriguez left the Compound, got into his truck and drove to the undercover house.

Rodriguez Reports

Agents in the undercover house recall that Rodriguez was visibly upset when he returned from the Compound. He complained that the windows of the undercover house were raised and that he could see a camera in one of them. Cavanaugh asked Rodriguez what had happened in the Compound. Rodriguez announced that Koresh was agitated and had said ATF and the National Guard were coming. Cavanaugh asked Rodriguez whether he had seen any guns, had heard anyone talking about guns, or had seen anyone hurrying around. Rodriguez responded in the negative to all three questions. Cavanaugh then told Rodriguez to report his observations to Sarabyn.

Initial accounts by the participants in and

witnesses to Rodriguez's conversations with Cavanaugh and Sarabyn differed significantly with respect to whether Rodriguez clearly communicated that Koresh knew the raid was imminent. Although there remains some variance with respect to Rodriguez's actual words, all key participants now agree that Rodriguez communicated, and they understood, that Koresh had said the ATF and National Guard were coming.

Now Sarabyn hurried out of the command post to the tarmac to confer with Royster and Chojnacki. The helicopters had already begun warming up. In order to hear over the noise of the rotors, the three supervisors moved to a fence bordering the tarmac, approximately 50 feet away. Although the noise still made conversation difficult, the three men huddled together so Sarabyn could pass on what he had learned. Sarabyn related that he had just spoken with Rodriguez who had said that Koresh knew ATF and the National Guard were coming but that, when Rodriguez had left, Koresh was reading the Bible and shaking. Sarabyn also stated, based on what Rodriguez had said, that Koresh was not ordering anyone in the Compound to do anything. Chojnacki asked Sarabyn whether Rodriguez had seen any guns. When Sarabyn responded that Rodriguez had not, Chojnacki asked Sarabyn what he thought should be done. Sarabyn expressed his belief that the raid could still be executed successfully if they hurried. Chojnacki responded, "Let's go." The conference lasted no more than three minutes. Sarabyn left immediately for the staging area.

Events began to reflect Sarabyn's perceived need for speed. News of Rodriguez's report spread rapidly among the ATF agents at the command post, creating an atmosphere of great urgency and commotion. Various agents were heard yelling that Koresh knew of the raid and that they needed to depart immediately. Royster hastened to the helicopters and told the agents there that Koresh knew of the raid and therefore it was beginning immediately. Royster then ran back to the command post, joined by Chojnacki who called the National Command Center and reported to Special Agent Jensen, responsible for the Center's communications, that the undercover agent was out of the Compound and that the raid was commencing. Chojnacki did not relate the substance of Rodriguez's report. Chojnacki then ran to and boarded his helicopter. A few minutes later, the helicopters departed. Shortly thereafter, Rodriguez ar-

rived at the command post only to find that Sarabyn, Chojnacki and Royster had departed. Witnesses recount that Rodriguez became distraught, repeatedly asking how the raid could have gone forward when he had told them that Koresh knew they were coming.

The Raid Goes Forward

Sarabyn arrived at the staging area at 9:10 a.m. Witnesses report that he was excited and obviously in a hurry. Agents in the parking lot when Sarabyn arrived recall that he ran to them and told them that they had to hurry, making statements such as, "Get ready to go, they know we are coming," and "They know ATF and the National Guard are coming. We're going to hit them now."

Within 15 minutes of Sarabyn's arrival at the staging area, the special response and the arrest teams boarded the trailers and left. According to agents in the trailers, although there was some lighthearted banter, the overall mood in the trailers was uncharacteristically somber. While some felt confident, others began to wonder why they were proceeding if Koresh knew they were on their way.

Sarabyn rode in the truck pulling the first cattle trailer. He maintained an open cellular phone contact with Cavanaugh throughout the trip to the Compound, keeping Cavanaugh posted as to the team's location and asking for reports on the level of activity at the Compound. Cavanaugh reported that he could not see any signs of activity in the Compound or on its grounds.

Activity in the Compound

According to some of the former cult members in the Compound at the time, preparations were being made in the Compound, although not detectable by Cavanaugh and the forward observers. Even as Rodriguez was departing, Perry Jones and the female members of the Compound had gathered in the chapel, thinking that they had been called for a church service. They had been waiting almost an hour when Koresh came in and ordered them back to their rooms. The older women and children went to the second floor and began to lie on the floor in the hallway, away from the outer walls of the Compound. Many of the cult members began to arm themselves, some with 9mm pistols, some with automatic and semiautomatic assault rifles, and others with both pistols and rifles. Some donned bullet-proof vests, others put on ammunition vests. Ammunition was distributed. The Compound members assumed stations at the windows, waiting for the ATF agents to arrive.

The Media Covers the Approach of the Raid Teams

According to *Tribune-Herald* cellular phone records, at 9:26 a.m., photojournalist Robert Sanchez called Blansett to advise him that several helicopters were leaving TSTC. Sanchez had earlier reported to his colleagues waiting near the Compound that he had seen agents at TSTC in camouflage fatigues loading duffle bags and gear into vehicles, and lining up to go. As Sanchez drove to the Compound he caught up to the two cattle trailers filled with uniformed agents. He relayed this information to his colleagues near the Compound. Agents in the second trailer reported that a vehicle was following them and two ATF agents in a chase car following the trailers stopped Sanchez. Sanchez again called his colleagues and advised them that he had been turned back and was unable to continue to the Compound.

Media personnel used radio and cellular telephones to communicate with one another and used scanners to monitor law enforcement frequencies during the hour before the raid. Several members of the press heard on scanners "no guns in the windows," and "it's a go" moments before ATF raid trucks entered the Compound's driveway.

Once Blansett relayed Sanchez's information, the reporters in the area moved closer to the Compound. *Tribune-Herald* reporters, Witherspoon, Aydelotte, and Masferrer drove to the house beside the undercover house to observe the raid from its front yard. Witherspoon knocked on the door to ask permission, but the agent safeguarding the residents inside declined to answer. As Witherspoon was knocking another agent approached. Believing the approaching agent to be a resident, Witherspoon said there was about to be a raid and asked whether he and his colleagues could observe it from the front yard. Without identifying himself, the agent ordered the reporters to leave the property. As the reporters were backing their car onto Double E Ranch Road, the trailers were turning into the Compound's driveway.

The reporters parked their car on the road in front of the house next to the undercover house. Aydelotte was retrieving his camera from the trunk of his car, when a second car containing two more *Tribune-Herald* reporters pulled alongside. Aydelotte managed to shoot several frames before gunfire began striking the car, forcing all five reporters into a ditch alongside the road.

Meanwhile, KWTX's Mullony and McLemore turned onto Double E Ranch Road and followed the ATF cattle trailers up the Compound's driveway. McLemore pulled up behind a parked bus. As the trailers continued the short distance to the front of the Compound, Mullony set up his tripod. Seconds later gunfire erupted from the Compound.

The Raid Team Arrives

As the cattle trailers entered the driveway there was no sign of activity inside or outside the Compound. The approaching agents realized the absence of activity was a bad omen. When one agent noted over the radio, "There's no one outside," a second agent responded, "That's not good."

The trucks stopped in front of the Compound's main building as planned. Agents with fire extinguishers for holding the Compound's dogs at bay were the first to exit the trailer. One agent opened the gate in the wall in front of the Compound, and another discharged a fire extinguisher at the dogs. Simultaneously, agents began exiting the second trailer. Koresh appeared at the front door and yelled, "What's going on?" The agents identified themselves, stated they had a warrant and yelled "freeze" and "get down." But Koresh slammed the door before the agents could reach it. Gunfire from inside the Compound burst through the door. The force of the gunfire was so great that the door bowed outward. The agent closest to the door was shot in the thumb before he could dive for cover into a pit near the door. Then gunfire erupted from virtually every window in the front of the Compound. The Dallas and Houston SRTs, which were approaching the front of the Compound and the pit area to the left, took the brunt of the initial barrage. Agents scrambled for cover. One of the first shots fired hit the engine block of the lead pickup truck. Consequently, neither the first, nor the second vehicle were able to leave.

In contrast to the extensive casualties inflicted

upon the agents during the ensuing action, there were few casualties among the cult members. Autopsies revealed that two cult members were killed by agents in the entry teams returning fire. Autopsies of two other cult fatalities reveal that they were shot at close range: Perry Jones was killed by a shot in his mouth, a manner of death consistent with suicide; Peter Hipsman was wounded but was later killed by a cult member who shot him at close range in the back of his skull—an apparent mercy killing, although the autopsy revealed that his initial wound would not have been fatal. Koresh was wounded both in the pelvic area and in his wrist.

Chapter 9 Review Questions

1. Why do public administrators have to be concerned with effective communications especially the media today? How does one find out about the lines of communications both inside and outside an organization and learn to deal with them effectively?

2. What methods of communications are illustrated in the case? Which were the most important in creating the dilemmas that ATF officials faced in obtaining and communicating critical information?

3. What types of communications blockages discussed in the Simon, Smithburg, and Thompson reading were illustrated in the case? What strategies did ATF devise for dealing with these blockages? In your estimation, what were the flaws with their approach?

4. What does the case study tell us about the interrelationships between the media and public agencies today? Why do they *both* need each other? Yet, why are their norms and values *not* the same—and can never be?

5. How do communications systems make or break an administrator's ability to control and direct the policies of his or her organization? As an administrator, what techniques would you utilize to ensure that the information you receive is accurate, timely, and *not* distorted by preconceived personal or institutional biases? And how would you deal with the media in an accurate, timely, and fair manner?

6. Can you generalize about the moral dilemmas created by the media for those who work for a public organization and strongly values truthfulness in performing his work? What potential risks does this sort of individual face within the organization given the possibility of not being able to communicate everything to the press? Can you identify your own ethical standards that would determine at what point you might withhold information from the media?

Key Terms

formal communications
informal communications
deliberate restrictions on
    communication
censorship

language barriers
status differences
geographic differences
frames of reference

Suggestions for Further Reading

The importance placed on communications processes in shaping governmental and organizational decisions was largely the result of several seminal works. These writings of the following key theorists should be studied with some care: Chester Barnard, *The Functions of the Executive* (Cambridge, Mass.: Harvard University Press, 1938); Herbert Simon, *Administrative Behavior: A Study of Decision-Making Processes in Administrative Organization* (New York: Macmillan, 1947); Karl W. Deutsch, *The Nerves of Government* (New York: Free Press, 1950); Norbert Weiner, *Cybernetics: Or Control and Communication in the Animal and the Machine* (New York: John Wiley & Sons, 1948). For a useful study of Herbert Simon and his contributions not only to this area but the entire field of public administration, see the whole issue *Public Administration Quarterly* (Fall 1988), especially the opening interview with Simon. One should also read Simon's autobiography, *Models of My Life* (New York: Basic Books, 1991). For an evaluation of Barnard's contributions, see the entire issue of Jack Rabin and Thomas Vocino, eds., "Special Issue: Papers in Honor of Chester I. Barnard," *International Journal of Public Administration,* 17 (1994) as well as William G. Scott, *Chester I Barnard and the Guardians of the Managerial State* (Lawrence, KS: University Press of Kansas, 1994). Harlan Cleveland, *The Knowledge Executive: Leadership in an Information Society* (New York: E. P. Dutton, 1985), presents a current, lively study of this topic from a leadership perspective. For a report on "the payoffs" from computerization, see Alana Northrop, Kenneth L. Kraemer, Debora Dunkle, and John Leslie King, "Payoffs from Computerization: Lessons Over Time," *Public Administration Review* (September/October 1990), pp. 505–514.

For more pragmatic works on the subject, review Herbert Kaufman in collaboration with Michael Couzens, *Administrative Feedback: Monitoring Subordinates' Behavior* (Washington,

D.C.: The Brookings Institution, 1973); Hindy Schachter, *Public Agency Communication* (Chicago: Nelson-Hall, 1983); Lyman W. Porter and Kathleen H. Roberts, "Communications in Organizations," in Marvin Dunette, ed., *Handbook of Industrial and Organizational Psychology* (Chicago: Rand McNally, 1976), pp. 1527–1551; Lyman W. Porter, "Communications: Structure and Process," in Harold L. Fromkin and John L. Sherwood, eds., *Integrating the Organization* (New York: Free Press, 1974), pp. 237–240; and George C. Edwards III, "Problems in Bureaucratic Communications," Herbert Kaufman, "Red Tape," and Francis E. Rourke, "Executive Secrecy," in Francis E. Rourke, ed., *Bureaucratic Power in National Policy Making,* Fourth Edition (Boston: Little, Brown, 1986). The best practical textbooks on this topic are David S. Arnold, Christine S. Becker, and Elizabeth K. Kellar, *Effective Communication: Getting the Message Across* (Washington, D.C.: International City Management Association, 1983); James L. Garnett, *Communicating for Results in Government: A Strategic Approach for Public Managers* (San Francisco, Calif.: Jossey-Bass, 1992); and P. V. Lewis, *Organizational Communications: The Essence of Effective Management,* Third Edition. (New York: Wiley, 1987).

For general handbooks that provide useful overviews of this topic, see C. C. Arnold and J. W. Bowers, eds., *Handbook of Rhetorical and Communication Theory* (Needham Heights, Mass.: Allyn & Bacon, 1984); C. R. Berger and S. H. Chafee, eds., *Handbook of Communication Science* (Newbury Park, Calif.: Sage, 1987); and James L. Garnett, ed., *Handbook of Administrative Communication* (New York: Marcel Dekker, 1994).

Certainly during the last two decades the computer revolution has rocked the field of administrative communications, as it will no doubt continue to do. For informative works on this topic, see Lee Spraull and Sara Kiesler, *Connections: New Ways of Working in Network Organizations*

(Cambridge, Mass: MIT Press, 1991); Kenneth L. Kraemer et al., *Managing Information Systems: Change and Control in Organizational Computing* (San Francisco, Calif.: Jossey-Bass, 1989); David F. Andersen and Sharon S. Dawes, *Government Information Management: A Primer and Casebook* (Englewood Cliffs, N.J.: Prentice Hall, 1991); John F. Sacco and John W. Ostrowski, *Microcomputers and Government Management: Design and Use of Applications* (Monterey, Calif.: Brooks/Cole, 1991).

The crisis of war can illuminate problems of administrative communications with unusual clarity. For some excellent examples, see Gordon W. Prange, *At Dawn We Slept: The Untold Story of Pearl Harbor* (New York: McGraw-Hill, 1981); E. B. Potter, *Battle for Leyte Gulf: Command and Communications* (Syracuse, N.Y.: Inter-University Case No. 126); John W. Spanier, *The Truman-MacArthur Controversy and the Korean War* (Cambridge, Mass.: Harvard University Press, 1959); Sam Adams, "Vietnam Cover-up: Playing War with Numbers," *Harper's Magazine* (May 1975); Deborah Shapley, *Promise and Power: The Life and Times of Robert McNamara* (Boston: Little, Brown, 1993); and from the Gulf War, in Bob Woodward, *The Commanders* (New York: Simon and Schuster, 1991).

The current studies on communications as related to the world of public administration tend to be highly specialized, focusing on such topics as "The Freedom of Information Act" and "Management Information Systems" as reflected in two recent *Public Administration Review* symposia: Barry Bozeman and Stuart Bretschneider, eds., "Public Management Information Systems," *Public Administration Review,* special issue, 46 (November 1986); and Lotte E. Feinberg and Harold C. Relyea, "Symposium: Toward a Government Information Policy—FOI at 20", *Public Administration Review,* 46 (November/December 1986). Also see several essays in James L. Perry, *Handbook of Public Administration* (San Francisco, Calif.: Jossey-Bass, 1989).

CHAPTER 10

Executive Management: The Concept of the Uniqueness of Public Management

The debate between the assimilators and the differentiators, like the dispute between proponents of convergence and divergence between the U.S. and the Soviet Union, reminds me of the old argument about whether the glass is half full or half empty. I conclude that public and private management are at least as different as they are similar, and that the differences are more important than the similarities.

Graham T. Allison, Jr.

READING 10

Introduction

Writings on public management are a comparatively new phenomena; in fact, they are peculiarly products of this century because large-scale formal organizations, both public and private, are modern in origin and existence. Humanity's dependence on massive organizations that span the continent and the globe is therefore recent; hence, the comprehensive, detailed analysis of these institutions is also new to scholarly interest. The flood of modern literature analyzing the nature, behavior, and ideal methods for constructing viable human institutions and internal personal relationships has been prompted in part by the need to establish and construct these organizations in ways that effectively cope with problems of the present age.

The central dilemma in studying modern organizations and their management lies in the proper theoretical perspective. As Dwight Waldo reminds us, studying organization is akin to the fable of the blind men and the elephant. "Each of the blind men . . . touched with his hands a different part of the elephant, and as a result there was among them a radical difference of opinion as to the nature of the beast."[1]

A principal cause of the considerable divergence of opinion about organizations thus stems from the specialized vantage points from which observers come to exam-

[1]Dwight Waldo, *Ideas and Issues in Public Administration* (New York: McGraw-Hill, 1953), p. 64.

ine human institutions. The economist has a different view than the philosopher, so also the insider versus the outsider and the worker versus the manager. These ideas are not right or wrong; rather, a number of approaches exist for reaching the truth about complex formal organizations. In studying organizations, material that is valid or useful to one individual may not seem so to another.

For one reason or another, very often *one* theoretical perspective in America tends to dominate our understanding of what constitutes good or appropriate public sector organizational practices, namely business perspectives. Not infrequently do we read about political candidates or their appointees promising, "I can make government more businesslike!" or citing as their reason for holding high public office "a successful track-record as a manager in private enterprise." Editorial writers, civic association speakers, and media pundits often echo these refrains in favor of applying entrepreneurial talent to public enterprises. Popular opinion generally supports the viewpoint that if only public administrators would simply manage their affairs like business, government—and maybe even the entire country—would run a lot better.

The tendency to identify good management in government with good business management is common even in serious public administration literature. Indeed, discussions of business management methods dominated much of the early development of the conscious study of public administration at the beginning of the twentieth century. Frederick W. Taylor and his business-oriented scientific management concepts served as the core of much of the field of public administration prior to World War II. The Brownlow Committee Report (1937), which some scholars believe was the highwater mark of the influence of public administration thinking on government, largely mirrored the business organization practices of the day. In many respects, this strong influence of business practices on government continues today through such imported private sector techniques as performance budgets, cost-benefit analysis, cost-accounting procedures, performance appraisals, management by objective, zero-based budgeting, and so on. Indeed, you only need to think about the names of major governmental processes and institutions to appreciate the enormous influence of what Waldo calls "our business civilization"—there are government corporations, city managers, efficiency ratings, the contracting out for services, chief administrative officers, and county executives.

Yet, despite the deep-rooted and continuing enthusiasm—on both the popular and the scholarly levels—to make government more business-like, the fundamental issue remains unanswered: Is government like business? Can the public sector, in fact, be run like the private sector? Indeed, it is a critical question for the field as a whole, for if public and private management are the same in scope, purpose, and process, why do we have the separate field of public administration and, therefore, public administrators? Why not simply teach and practice "administration" without distinguishing between "public" and "private"? This issue goes to the heart of the intellectual discipline and the professional practice of our field. In many ways, this issue has been a dilemma since the inception of public administration and is of continuing interest to many scholars and practitioners today.

Graham T. Allison, Jr. (1941–   ), formerly dean of the John F. Kennedy School of Government at Harvard University and author of several important books in the field such as *The Essence of Decision* (1971), reflected on this question before a major symposium on public management research agendas sponsored by the Office of Personnel Management. In the following essay, Allison summarizes his remarks on this subject. He takes off on a frequently quoted "law" from the late political scientist Wallace Sayre, which maintains that public and private management are fundamentally alike in all unimportant respects. Allison probes this law from several standpoints: first, by the *personal impressions* of managers who have seen both sides of the fence, for example, John Dunlop; second, by *scholarly surveys* of the literature comparing both public and private management practices and activities; and third, by an *operational perspective* of two actual administrators in action—Doug Costle at the EPA and Roy Chapin at American Motors.

By looking at this issue from a number of angles, Allison is able to draw these important conclusions: (1) while the need for increased governmental efficiency is real, "the notion that there is any significant body of private management practices and skills that can be transferred directly to public management . . . is wrong"; (2) while "performance in many public management positions can be improved substantially," an improvement will not come "from massive borrowing of specific private management skills and understandings"; (3) while it is possible to learn from experiences in public or private settings, "the effort to develop public management as a field of knowledge should start from the problems faced by practicing public managers." Worthy of careful attention, too, are the lists at the end of Allison's essay that outline the specific strategies he sees as necessary for the development of both the professional practice and the academic dimensions of public management.

As you read this selection, keep the following questions in mind:

What essential arguments does Allison put forward in favor of the uniqueness of public management? How does Allison arrive at his conclusions? Do you agree or disagree with Allison's argument and his reasoning?

What model for public management does Allison propose? What are its elements? How does he support its value?

What are the implications of his argument—namely, the uniqueness thesis—for teaching, practice, and scholarship in the field of public management?

Public and Private Management: Are They Fundamentally Alike in All Unimportant Respects?

GRAHAM T. ALLISON, JR.

My subtitle puts Wallace Sayre's oft quoted "law"

Reprinted by permission from pp. 27–38 of *Setting Public Management Research Agendas: Integrating the Sponsor, Producer and User*. Washington, D.C.: Office of Personnel Management. OPM Document 127–53–1. February 1980.

as a question. Sayre had spent some years in Ithaca helping plan Cornell's new School of Business and Public Administration. He left for Columbia with this aphorism: public and private management are fundamentally alike in all unimportant respects.

Sayre based his conclusion on years of personal observation of governments, a keen ear for what his colleagues at Cornell (and earlier at OPA) said about business, and a careful review of the literature and data comparing public and private management. Of the latter there was virtually none. Hence, Sayre's provocative "law" was actually an open invitation to research.

Unfortunately, in the 50 years since Sayre's pronouncement, the data base for systematic comparison of public and private management has improved little. Consequently . . . I, in effect, take up Sayre's invitation to *speculate* about similarities and differences among public and private management in ways that suggest significant opportunities for systematic investigation. . . .

Framing the Issue: What Is Public Management?

What is the meaning of the term "management" as it appears in Office of *Management* and Budget, or Office of Personnel *Management*? Is "management" different from, broader or narrower than "administration"? Should we distinguish between management, leadership, entrepreneurship, administration, policy making, and implementation?

Who are "public managers"? Mayors, governors, and presidents? City managers, secretaries, and commissioners? Bureau chiefs? Office directors? Legislators? Judges?

Recent studies of OPM and OMB shed some light on these questions. OPM's major study of the "Current Status of Public Management Research" completed in May 1978 by Selma Mushkin of Georgetown's Public Service Laboratory starts with this question. The Mushkin report notes the definition of "public management" employed by the Interagency Study Committee on Policy Management Assistance in its 1975 report to OMB. That study identified the following core elements:

1. *Policy Management* The identification of needs, analysis of options, selection of programs, and allocation of resources on a jurisdiction-wide basis.
2. *Resource Management* The establishment of basic administrative support systems, such as budgeting, financial management, procurement and supply, and personnel management.
3. *Program Management* The implementation of policy or daily operation of agencies carrying out policy along functional lines (education, law enforcement, etc.).[1]

The Mushkin report rejects this definition in favor of an "alternative list of public management elements." These elements are:

- Personnel Management (other than work force planning and collective bargaining and labor management relations)
- Work Force Planning
- Collective Bargaining and Labor Management Relations
- Productivity and Performance Measurement
- Organization/Reorganization
- Financial Management (including the management of intergovernmental relations)
- Evaluation Research, and Program and Management Audit.[2]

Such terminological tangles seriously hamper the development of public management as a field of knowledge. In our efforts to discuss public management curriculum at Harvard, I have been struck by how differently people use these terms, how strongly many individuals feel about some distinction they believe is marked by a difference between one word and another, and consequently, how large a barrier terminology is to convergent discussion. These verbal obstacles virtually prohibit conversation that is both brief and constructive among individuals who have not developed a common language or a mutual understanding of each other's use of terms. . . .

This terminological thicket reflects a more fundamental conceptual confusion. There exists no over-arching framework that orders the domain. In an effort to get a grip on the phenomena—the buzzing, blooming confusion of people in jobs performing tasks that produce results—both practitioners and observers have strained to find distinctions that facilitate their work. The attempts in the early decades of this century to draw a sharp line between "policy" and "administration," like more recent efforts to mark a similar divide between "policy making" and "implementation," reflect a common search for a simplification that allows one to put the value-laden issues of politics to one side (who gets what, when, and how), and focus on the more limited issue of how to perform tasks more efficiently.[3] But can anyone really deny that the "how" substantially affects the "who," the "what," and the "when"? The basic categories now prevalent in discussions of public management—strategy, personnel management, financial management, and control—are mostly derived from a business context in which executives manage hierarchies. The fit of these concepts to the problems that confront public managers is not clear.

Finally, there exists no ready data on what public managers do. Instead, the academic literature, such as it is, mostly consists of speculation tied to bits and pieces of evidence about the tail or the trunk or other manifestation of the proverbial elephant.[4] In contrast to the literally thousands of cases describing problems faced by private managers and their practice in solving these problems, case research from the perspective of a public manager is just beginning. . . .[5] But the paucity of data on the phenomena inhibits systematic empirical research on similarities and differences between public and private management, leaving the field to a mixture of reflection on personal experience and speculation.

For the purpose of this presentation, I will follow Webster and use the term management to mean the organization and direction of resources to achieve a desired result. I will focus on *general managers,* that is, individuals charged with managing a whole organization or multifunctional sub-unit. I will be interested in the general manager's full responsibilities, both *inside* his organization in integrating the diverse contributions of specialized sub-units of the organization to achieve results, and *outside* his organization in relating his organization and its product to external constituencies. I will begin with the simplifying assumption that managers of traditional government organizations are public managers, and managers of traditional private businesses, private managers. Lest the discussion fall victim to the fallacy of misplaced abstraction, I will take the Director of EPA and the Chief Executive Officer of American Motors as, respectively, public and private managers. Thus, our central question can be put concretely: in what ways are the jobs and responsibilities of Doug Costle as Director of EPA similar to and different from those of Roy Chapin as Chief Executive Officer of American Motors?

Similarities: How Are Public and Private Management Alike?

At one level of abstraction, it is possible to identify a set of general management functions. The most famous such list appeared in Gulick and Urwick's classic *Papers in the Science of Administration.*[6] Gulick summarized the work of the chief executive in the acronym POSDCORB. The letters stand for:

- Planning
- Organizing
- Staffing
- Directing
- Coordinating
- Reporting
- Budgeting

With various additions, amendments, and refinements, similar lists of general management functions can be found through the management literature from Barnard to Drucker.[7]

I shall resist here my natural academic instinct to join the intramural debate among proponents of various lists and distinctions. Instead, I simply

Table 10.1   Functions of General Management

Strategy

1.   **Establishing objectives and priorities** for the organization (on the basis of forecasts of the external environment and the organization's capacities).

2.   **Devising operational plans** to achieve these objectives.

Managing internal components

3.   **Organizing and staffing:** In organizing the manager establishes structure (units and positions with assigned authority and responsibilities) and procedures (for coordinating activity and taking action); in staffing he tries to fit the right persons in the key jobs.*

4.   **Directing personnel and the personnel management system:** The capacity of the organization is embodied primarily in its members and their skills and knowledge; the personnel management system recruits, selects, socializes, trains, rewards, punishes, and exits the organization's human capital, which constitutes the organization's capacity to act to achieve its goals and to respond to specific directions from management.

5.   **Controlling performance:** Various management information systems—including operating and capital budgets, accounts, reports and statistical systems, performance appraisals, and product evaluation—assist management in making decisions and in measuring progress towards objectives.

Managing external constituencies

6.   **Dealing with "external" units** of the organization subject to some common authority: Most general managers must deal with general managers of other units within the larger organization—above, laterally, and below—to achieve their unit's objectives.

7.   **Dealing with independent organizations:** Agencies from other branches or levels of government, interest groups, and private enterprises that can importantly affect the organization's ability to achieve its objectives.

8.   **Dealing with the press and public** whose action or approval or acquiescence is required.

---

*Organization and staffing are frequently separated in such lists, but because of the interaction between the two, they are combined here. See Graham Allison and Peter Szanton, *Remaking Foreign Policy* (Basic Books, 1976), p. 14.

offer one composite list (see Table 10.1) that attempts to incorporate the major functions that have been identified for general managers, whether public or private.

These common functions of management are not isolated and discrete, but rather integral components separated here for purposes of analysis. The character and relative significance of the various functions differ from one time to another in the history of any organization, and between one organization and another. But whether in a public or private setting, the challenge for the general manager is to integrate all these elements so as to achieve results.

Differences: How Are Public and Private Management Different?

While there is a level of generality at which management is management, whether public or pri-

vate, functions that bear identical labels take on rather different meaning in public and private settings. As Larry Lynn has pointed out, one powerful piece of evidence in the debate between those who emphasize "similarities" and those who underline "differences" is the nearly unanimous conclusion of individuals who have been general managers in both business and government. Consider the reflections of George Shultz (former Director of OMB, Secretary of Labor, Secretary of the Treasury; now President of Bechtel), Donald Rumsfeld (former congressman, Director of OEO, Director of the Cost of Living Council, White House Chief of Staff, and Secretary of Defense; now President of GD Searle and Company), Michael Blumenthal (former Chairman and Chief Executive Officer of Bendix, Secretary of the Treasury, and now Vice Chairman of Burrows), Roy Ash (former President of Litton Industries, Director of OMB; now President of Addressograph), Lyman Hamilton (former Budget Officer in BOB, High Commissioner of Okinawa, Division Chief in the World Bank and President of ITT), and George Romney (former President of American Motors, Governor of Michigan and Secretary of Housing and Urban Development).[8] All judge public management different from private management—and harder!

Three Orthogonal Lists of Differences

My review of these recollections, as well as the thoughts of academics, has identified three interesting, orthogonal lists that summarize the current state of the field: one by John Dunlop; one major *Public Administration Review* survey of the literature comparing public and private organizations by Hal Rainey, Robert Backoff and Charles Levine; and one by Richard E. Neustadt prepared for the National Academy of Public Administration's Panel on Presidential Management.

John T. Dunlop's "impressionistic comparison of government management and private business" yields the following contrasts.[9]

1. Time Perspective. Government managers tend to have relatively short time horizons dictated by political necessities and the political calendar, while private managers appear to take a longer time perspective oriented toward market developments, technological innovation and investment, and organization building.

2. Duration. The length of service of politically appointed top government managers is relatively short, averaging no more than 18 months recently for assistant secretaries, while private managers have a longer tenure both in the same position and in the same enterprise. A recognized element of private business management is the responsibility to train a successor or several possible candidates while the concept is largely alien to public management since fostering a successor is perceived to be dangerous.

3. Measurement of Performance. There is little if any agreement on the standards and measurement of performance to appraise a government manager, while various tests of performance—financial return, market share, performance measures for executive compensation—are well established in private business and often made explicit for a particular managerial position during a specific period ahead.

4. Personnel Constraints. In government there are two layers of managerial officials that are at times hostile to one another: the civil service (or now the executive system) and the political appointees. Unionization of government employees exists among relatively high-level personnel in the hierarchy and includes a number of supervisory personnel. Civil service, union contract provisions, and other regulations complicate the recruitment, hiring, transfer, and layoff or discharge of personnel to achieve managerial objectives or preferences. By comparison, private business managements have considerably greater latitude, even under collective bargaining, in the management of subordinates. They have much more authority to direct the employees of their organization. Government personnel policy and administration are more under the control of staff (including civil service staff outside an agency) compared to the private sector in which personnel are much more subject to line responsibility.

5. Equity and Efficiency. In governmental management great emphasis tends to be placed on providing equity among different constituencies, while in private business management relatively greater stress is placed upon efficiency and competitive performance.

6. Public Processes Versus Private Processes. Governmental management tends to be exposed to public scrutiny and to be more open, while private business management is more private and its processes more internal and less exposed to public review.

7. Role of Press and Media. Governmental management must contend regularly with the press and media; its decisions are often anticipated by the press. Private decisions are less often reported in the press, and the press has a much smaller impact on the substance and timing of decisions.

8. Persuasion and Direction. In government, managers often seek to mediate decisions in response to a wide variety of pressures and must often put together a coalition of inside and outside groups to survive. By contrast, private management proceeds much more by direction or the issuance of orders to subordinates by superior managers with little risk of contradiction. Governmental managers tend to regard themselves as responsive to many superiors while private managers look more to one higher authority.

9. Legislative and Judicial Impact. Governmental managers are often subject to close scrutiny by legislative oversight groups or even judicial orders in ways that are quite uncommon in private business management. Such scrutiny often materially constrains executive and administrative freedom to act.

10. Bottom Line. Governmental managers rarely have a clear bottom line, while that of a private business manager is profit, market performance, and survival.

The *Public Administration Review*'s major review article comparing public and private organizations, Rainey, Backoff and Levine, attempts to summarize the major points of consensus in the literature on similarities and differences among public and private organizations.[10]

Third, Richard E. Neustadt, in a fashion close to Dunlop's, notes six major differences between Presidents of the United States and Chief Executive Officers of major corporations.[11]

1. Time-Horizon. The private chief begins by looking forward a decade, or thereabouts, his likely span barring extraordinary troubles. The first-term President looks forward four years at most, with the fourth (and now even the third) year dominated

by campaigning for reelection. (What second-termers look toward we scarcely know, having seen but one such term completed in the past quarter century.)

2. Authority over the enterprise. Subject to concurrence from the Board of Directors which appointed and can fire him, the private executive sets organization goals, shifts structures, procedure, and personnel to suit, monitors results, reviews key operational decisions, deals with key outsiders, and brings along his Board. Save for the deep but narrow sphere of military movements, a President's authority in these respects is shared with well-placed members of Congress (or their staffs); case by case, they may have more explicit authority than he does (contrast authorizations and appropriations with the "take-care" clause). As for "bringing along the Board," neither the Congressmen with whom he shares power or the primary and general electorates which "hired" him have either a Board's duties or a broad view of the enterprise precisely matching his.

3. Career System. The model corporation is a true career system, something like the Forest Service after initial entry. In normal times the chief himself is chosen from within, or he is chosen from another firm in the same industry. He draws department heads et al. from among those with whom he's worked, or whom he knows in comparable companies. He and his principal associates will be familiar with each other's roles—indeed he probably has had a number of them—and also usually with one another's operating styles, personalities, idiosyncrasies. Contrast the President who rarely has had much experience "downtown," probably knows little of most roles there (much of what he knows will turn out wrong), and less of most associates whom he appoints there, willy nilly, to fill places by Inauguration Day. Nor are they likely to know one another well, coming as they do from "everywhere" and headed as most are toward oblivion.

4. Media Relations. The private executive represents his firm and speaks for it publicly in exceptional circumstances; he and his associates judge the exceptions. Those aside, he neither sees the press nor gives its members access to internal operations, least of all in his own office, save to make a point deliberately for public-relations purposes. The President, by contrast, is routinely on display, continuously dealing with the White House press and with the wider circle of political reporters, commentators, columnists. He needs them in his business, day by day, nothing exceptional about it, and they need him in theirs: the TV Network news programs lead off with him some nights each week. They and the President are as mutually dependent as he and Congressmen (or more so). Comparatively speaking, these relations overshadow most administrative ones much of the time for him.

5. Performance Measurement. The private executive expects to be judged, and in turn to judge subordinates, by profitability, however the firm measures it (a major strategic choice). In practice, his Board may use more subjective measures; so may he, but at risk to morale and good order. The relative virtue of profit, of "the bottom line" is its legitimacy, its general acceptance in the business world by all concerned. Never mind its technical utility in given cases, its apparent "objectivity," hence "fairness," has enormous social usefulness: a myth that all can live by. For a President there is no counterpart (except *in extremis* the "smoking gun" to justify impeachment). The general public seems to judge a President, at least in part, by what its members think is happening to them in their own lives; Congressmen, officials, interest groups appear to judge by what they guess, at given times, he can do for or to their causes. Members of the press interpret both of these and spread a simplified criterion affecting both, the legislative box-score, a standard of the press's own devising. The White House denigrates them all except when it does well.

6. Implementation The corporate chief, supposedly, does more than choose a strategy and set a course of policy; he also is supposed to oversee what happens after, how in fact intentions turn into results, or if they don't to take corrective action, monitoring through his information system, acting, and if need be, through his personnel system. A President, by contrast, while himself responsible for budgetary proposals, too, in many spheres of policy, appears ill-placed and ill-equipped to monitor what agencies of states, of cities, corporations, unions, foreign governments are up to or to change personnel in charge. Yet these are very often the executants of "his" programs. Apart from defense and diplomacy the federal government does two things in the main: it issues and applies regulations and it awards grants in aid. Where these are discretionary, choice usually is vested by statute in a Senate-confirmed official well outside the White House. Monitoring is his function, not the President's except at second-hand. And final action is the function of the subjects of the rules and funds; they mostly are not federal personnel at all. In defense, the arsenals and shipyards are gone; weaponry comes from the private sector. In foreign affairs it is the *other* governments whose actions we would influence. From implementors like these a President is far removed most of the time. He intervenes, if at all, on a crash basis, not through organizational incentives.

Underlying these lists' sharpest distinctions between public and private management is a fundamental *constitutional difference*. In business, the functions of general management are centralized in a single individual: the Chief Executive Officer. The goal is authority commensurate with responsibility. In contrast, in the U.S. government, the functions of general management are constitutionally spread among competing institutions: the executive, two houses of Congress, and the courts. The constitutional goal was "not to promote efficiency but to preclude the exercise of arbitrary power," as Justice Brandeis observed. Indeed, as *The Federalist Papers* make starkly clear, the aim was to create incentives to compete: "the great security against a gradual concentration of the several powers in the same branch, consists in giving those who administer each branch the constitutional means and personal motives to resist encroachment of the others. Ambition must be made to counteract ambition."[12] Thus, the general management functions concentrated in the CEO of a private business are, by constitutional design, spread in the public sector among a number of competing institutions and thus shared by a number of individuals whose ambitions are set against one another. For most areas of public policy today, these individuals include at the federal level the chief elected official, the chief appointed executive, the chief career official, and several congressional chieftains. Since most public services are actually delivered by state and local governments, with independent sources of authority, this means a further array of individuals at these levels.

An Operational Perspective: How Are the Jobs and Responsibilities of Doug Costle, Director of EPA, and Roy Chapin, CEO of American Motors, Similar and Different?

If organizations could be separated neatly into two homogeneous piles, one public and one private, the task of identifying similarities and differences between managers of these enterprises would be relatively easy. In fact, as Dunlop has pointed out, "the real world of management is composed of distributions, rather than single undifferentiated forms, and there is an increasing variety of hybrids." Thus for each major attribute of organizations, specific entities can be located on a spectrum. On most dimensions, organizations classified as "predominantly public" and those "predominantly private" overlap.[13] Private business organizations vary enormously among themselves in size, in management structure and philosophy, and in the constraints under which they operate. For example, forms of ownership and types of managerial control may be somewhat unrelated.

Compare a family-held enterprise, for instance, with a public utility and a decentralized conglomerate, a Bechtel with ATT and Textron. Similarly, there are vast differences in management of governmental organizations. Compare the Government Printing Office or TVA or the Police Department of a small town with the Department of Energy or the Department of Health and Human Services. These distributions and varieties should encourage penetrating comparisons within both business and governmental organizations, as well as contrasts and comparisons across these broad categories, a point to which we shall return in considering directions for research.

Absent a major research effort, it may nonetheless be worthwhile to examine the jobs and responsibilities of two specific managers, neither polar extremes, but one clearly public, the other private. For this purpose, and primarily because of the availability of cases that describe the problems and opportunities each confronted, consider Doug Costle, Administrator of EPA, and Roy Chapin, CEO of American Motors.[14]

Doug Costle, Administrator of EPA, January 1977

The mission of EPA is prescribed by laws creating the agency and authorizing its major programs. That mission is "to control and abate pollution in the areas of air, water, solid wastes, noise, radiation, and toxic substances. EPA's mandate is to mount an integrated, coordinated attack on environmental pollution in cooperation with state and local governments."[15]

EPA's organizational structure follows from its legislative mandates to control particular pollutants in specific environments: air and water, solid wastes, noise, radiation, pesticides and chemicals. As the new Administrator, Costle inherited the Ford Administration's proposed budget for EPA of $802 million for federal 1978 with a ceiling of 9,698 agency positions.

The setting into which Costle stepped is difficult to summarize briefly. As Costle characterized it:

- "Outside there is a confusion on the part of the public in terms of what this agency is all about: what it is doing, where it is going."
- "The most serious constraint on EPA is the inherent complexity in the state of our knowledge, which is constantly changing."
- "Too often, acting under extreme deadlines mandated by Congress, EPA has announced regulations, only to find out that they knew very little about the problem. The central problem is the inherent complexity of the job that the agency has been asked to do and the fact that what it is asked to do changes from day to day."
- "There are very difficult internal management issues not amenable to a quick solution: the skills mix problem within the agency; a research program with laboratory facilities scattered all over the country and cemented in place, largely by political alliances on the Hill that would frustrate efforts to pull together a coherent research program."
- "In terms of EPA's original mandate in the bulk pollutants we may be hitting the asymptotic part of the curve in terms of incremental clean-up costs. You have clearly conflicting national goals: energy and environment, for example."

Costle judged his six major tasks at the outset to be:

- assembling a top management team (six assistant administrators and some 25 office heads);
- addressing EPA's legislative agenda (EPA's basic legislative charter—the Clean Air Act and the Clean Water Act—were being rewritten as he took office; the pesticides program was up for reauthorization also in 1977);
- establishing EPA's role in the Carter Administration (aware that the Administration would face hard tradeoffs between the envi-

ronment and energy, energy regulations and the economy, EPA regulations of toxic substances and the regulations of FDA, CSPS, and OSHA, Costle identified the need to build relations with the other key players and to enhance EPA's standing);
- building ties to constituent groups (both because of their role in legislating the agency's mandate and in successful implementation of EPA's programs):
- making specific policy decisions (for example, whether to grant or deny a permit for the Seabrook Nuclear Generating Plant cooling system. Or how the Toxic Substance Control Act, enacted in October 1976, would be implemented; this act gave EPA new responsibilities for regulating the manufacture, distribution, and use of chemical substances so as to prevent unreasonable risks to health and the environment. Whether EPA would require chemical manufacturers to provide some minimum information on various substances, or require much stricter reporting requirements for the 1,000 chemical substances already known to be hazardous, or require companies to report all chemicals, and on what timetable, had to be decided and the regulations issued);
- rationalizing the internal organization of the agency (EPA's extreme decentralization to the regions and its limited technical expertise).

No easy job.

Roy Chapin and American Motors, January 1977

In January 1967, in an atmosphere of crisis, Roy Chapin was appointed Chairman and Chief Executive Officer of American Motors (and William Luneburg, President and Chief Operating Officer). In the four previous years, AMC unit sales had fallen 37 percent and market share from over six percent to under three percent. Dollar volume in 1967 was off 42 percent from the all-time high of

1963 and earnings showed a net loss of $76 million on sales of $656 million. Columnists began writing obituaries for AMC. *Newsweek* characterized AMC as "a flabby dispirited company, a product solid enough but styled with about as much flair as corrective shoes, and a public image that melted down to one unshakeable label: loser." Said Chapin: "We were driving with one foot on the accelerator and one foot on the brake. We didn't know where the hell we were."

Chapin announced to his stockholders at the outset that "we plan to direct ourselves most specifically to those areas of the market where we can be fully effective. We are not going to attempt to be all things to all people, but to concentrate on those areas of consumer needs we can meet better than anyone else." As he recalled: "There were problems early in 1967 which demanded immediate attention, and which accounted for much of our time for several months. Nevertheless, we began planning beyond them, establishing objectives, programs and timetables through 1972. Whatever happened in the short run, we had to prove ourselves in the marketplace in the long run."

Chapin's immediate problems were five:

- The company was virtually out of cash and an immediate supplemental bank loan of $20 million was essential.
- Car inventories—company owned and dealer owned—had reached unprecedented levels. The solution to this glut took five months and could be accomplished only by a series of plant shutdowns in January 1967.
- Sales of the Rambler American series had stagnated and inventories were accumulating; a dramatic merchandising move was concocted and implemented in February, dropping the price tag on the American to a position midway between the VW and competitive smaller U.S. compacts, by both cutting the price to dealers and trimming dealer discounts from 21 percent to 17 percent.

- Administrative and commercial expenses were judged too high and thus a vigorous cost reduction program was initiated that trimmed $15 million during the first year. Manufacturing and purchasing costs were also trimmed significantly to approach the most effective levels in the industry.
- The company's public image had deteriorated; the press was pessimistic and much of the financial community had written it off. To counteract this, numerous formal and informal meetings were held with bankers, investment firms, government officials, and the press.

As Chapin recalls "with the immediate fires put out, we could put in place the pieces of a corporate growth plan—a definition of a way of life in the auto industry for American Motors. We felt that our reason for being, which would enable us not just to survive but to grow, lay in bringing a different approach to the auto market—in picking our spots and then being innovative and aggressive." The new corporate growth plan included a dramatic change in the approach to the market to establish a "youthful image" for the company (by bringing out new sporty models like the Javelin and by entering the racing field), "changing the product line from one end to the other" by 1972, acquiring Kaiser Jeep (selling the company's non-transportation assets and concentrating on specialized transportation, including Jeep, a company that had lost money in each of the preceding five years, but that Chapin believed could be turned around by substantial cost reductions and economies of scale in manufacturing, purchasing, and administration).

Chapin succeeded: for the year ending September 30, 1971, AMC earned $10.2 million on sales of $1.2 billion.

Recalling the list of general management functions in Table 10.1, which similarities and differences appear salient and important?

Strategy

Both Chapin and Costle had to establish objectives and priorities and to devise operational plans. In business, "corporate strategy is the pattern of major objectives, purposes, or goals and essential policies and plans for achieving these goals, stated in such a way as to define what business the company is in or is to be in and the kind of company it is or is to be."[16] In reshaping the strategy of AMC and concentrating on particular segments of the transportation market, Chapin had to consult his Board and had to arrange financing. But the control was substantially his.

How much choice did Costle have at EPA as to the "business it is or is to be in" or the kind of agency "it is or is to be"? These major strategic choices emerged from the legislative process which mandated whether he should be in the business of controlling pesticides or toxic substances and if so on what timetable, and occasionally, even what level of particulate per million units he was required to control. The relative role of the President, other members of the Administration (including White House staff, Congressional relations, and other agency heads), the EPA Administrator, Congressional committee chairmen, and external groups in establishing the broad strategy of the agency constitutes an interesting question.

Managing Internal Components

For both Costle and Chapin, staffing was key. As Donald Rumsfeld has observed "the single, most important task of the chief executive is to select the right people. I've seen terrible organization charts in both government and business that were made to work well by good people. I've seen beautifully charted organizations that didn't work very well because they had the wrong people."[17]

The leeway of the two executives in organizing and staffing were considerably different, however. Chapin closed down plants, moved key managers, hired and fired, virtually at will. As Michael Blu-

menthal has written about Treasury, "if you wish to make substantive changes, policy changes, and the Department's employees don't like what you're doing, they have ways of frustrating you or stopping you that do not exist in private industry. The main method they have is Congress. If I say I want to shut down a particular unit or transfer the function of one area to another, there are ways of going to Congress and in fact using friends in the Congress to block the move. They can also use the press to try to stop you. If I at Bendix wished to transfer a division from Ann Arbor to Detroit because I figured out that we could save money that way, as long as I could do it decently and carefully, it's of no lasting interest to the press. The press can't stop me. They may write about it in the local paper, but that's about it."[18]

For Costle, the basic structure of the agency was set by law. The labs, their location, and most of their personnel were fixed. Though he could recruit his key subordinates, again restrictions like the conflict of interest law and the prospect of a Senate confirmation fight led him to drop his first choice for the Assistant Administrator for Research and Development, since he had worked for a major chemical company. While Costle could resort to changes in the process for developing policy or regulations in order to circumvent key office directors whose views he did not share, for example, Eric Stork, the Deputy Assistant Administrator in charge of Mobile Source Air Program, such maneuvers took considerable time, provoked extensive infighting, and delayed significantly the development of Costle's program.

In the direction of personnel and management of the personnel system, Chapin exercised considerable authority. While the United Auto Workers limited his authority over workers, at the management level he assigned people and reassigned responsibility consistent with his general plan. While others may have felt that his decisions to close down particular plants or to drop a particular product were mistaken, they complied. As George Schultz has observed: "One of the first lessons I learned in moving from government to business is that in business you must be very careful when you tell someone who is working for you to do something because the probability is high that he or she will do it."[19]

Costle faced a civil service system designed to prevent spoils as much as to promote productivity. The Civil Service Commission exercised much of the responsibility for the personnel function in his agency. Civil service rules severely restricted his discretion, took long periods to exhaust, and often required complex maneuvering in a specific case to achieve any results. Equal opportunity rules and their administration provided yet another network of procedural and substantive inhibitions. In retrospect, Costle found the civil service system a much larger constraint on his actions and demand on his time than he had anticipated.

In controlling performance, Chapin was able to use measures like profit and market share, to decompose those objectives to subobjectives for lower levels of the organization and to measure the performance of managers of particular models, areas, divisions. Cost accounting rules permitted him to compare plants within AMC and to compare AMC's purchases, production, and even administration with the best practice in the industry.

Managing External Constituencies

As Chief Executive Officer, Chapin had to deal only with the Board. For Costle, within the executive branch but beyond his agency lay many actors critical to the achievement of his agency's objectives: the President and the White House, Energy, Interior, the Council on Environmental Quality, OMB. Actions each could take, either independently or after a process of consultation in which they disagreed with him, could frustrate his agency's achievement of its assigned mission. Consequently, he spent considerable time building his agency's reputation and capital for interagency disputes.

Dealing with independent external organizations was a necessary and even larger part of Costle's job. Since his agency's mission, strategy,

authorizations, and appropriations emerged from the process of legislation, attention to Congressional committees, and Congressmen, and Congressmen's staff, and people who affect Congressmen and Congressional staffers rose to the top of Costle's agenda. In the first year, top level EPA officials appeared over 140 times before some 60 different committees and subcommittees.

Chapin's ability to achieve AMC's objectives could also be affected by independent external organizations: competitors, government (the Clean Air Act that was passed in 1970), consumer groups (recall Ralph Nader), and even suppliers of oil. More than most private managers, Chapin had to deal with the press in attempting to change the image of AMC. Such occasions were primarily at Chapin's initiative, and around events that Chapin's public affairs office orchestrated, for example, the announcement of a new racing car. Chapin also managed a marketing effort to persuade consumers that their tastes could best be satisfied by AMC products.

Costle's work was suffused by the press: in the daily working of the organization, in the perception by key publics of the agency and thus the agency's influence with relevant parties, and even in the setting of the agenda of issues to which the agency had to respond.

For Chapin, the bottom line was profit, market share, and the long-term competitive position of AMC. For Costle, what are the equivalent performance measures? Blumenthal answers by exaggerating the difference between appearance and reality: "At Bendix, it was the reality of the situation that in the end determined whether we succeeded or not. In the crudest sense, this meant the bottom line. You can dress up profits only for so long—if you're not successful, it's going to be clear. In government there is no bottom line, and that is why you can be successful if you appear to be successful—though, of course, appearance is not the only ingredient of success."[20] Rumsfeld says: "In business, you're pretty much judged by results. I don't think the American people judge government officials this way. . . . In government, too often you're measured by how much you seem to care, how hard you seem to try—things that do not necessarily improve the human condition. . . . It's a lot easier for a President to get into something and end up with a few days of good public reaction than it is to follow through, to pursue policies to a point where they have a beneficial effect on human lives."[21] As George Shultz says: "In government and politics, recognition and therefore incentives go to those who formulate policy and maneuver legislative compromise. By sharp contrast, the kudos and incentives in business go to the persons who can get something done. It is execution that counts. Who can get the plant built, who can bring home the sales contract, who can carry out the financing, and so on."[22]

This casual comparison of one public and one private manager suggests what could be done—if the issue of comparisons were pursued systematically, horizontally across organizations and at various levels within organizations. While much can be learned by examining the chief executive officers of organizations, still more promising should be comparisons among the much larger numbers of middle managers. If one compared, for example, a Regional Administrator of EPA and an AMC division chief, or two Comptrollers, or equivalent plant managers, some functions would appear more similar, and other differences would stand out. The major barrier to such comparisons is the lack of cases describing problems and practices of middle-level managers.[23] This should be a high priority in further research.

The differences noted in this comparison, for example, in the personnel area, have already changed with the Civil Service Reform Act of 1978 and the creation of the Senior Executive Service. Significant changes have also occurred in the automobile industry: under current circumstances, the CEO of Chrysler may seem much more like the Administrator of EPA. More precise comparison of different levels of management in both organizations, for example, accounting procedures used by Chapin to cut costs significantly as compared to equivalent procedures for judging the costs of EPA mandated pollution control devices, would be instructive.

Implications for Research on Public Management

The debate between the assimilators and the differentiators, like the dispute between proponents of convergence and divergence between the U.S. and the Soviet Union reminds me of the old argument about whether the glass is half full or half empty. I conclude that public and private management are at least as different as they are similar, and that the differences are more important than the similarities. From this review of the "state of the art," such as it is, I draw a number of lessons for research on public management. I will try to state them in a way that is both succinct and provocative:

- First, the demand for performance from government and efficiency in government is both real and right. The perception that government's performance lags private business performance is also correct. But the notion that there is any significant body of private management practices and skills that can be transferred directly to public management tasks in a way that produces significant improvements is wrong.
- Second, performance in many public management positions can be improved substantially, perhaps by an order of magnitude. That improvement will come not, however, from massive borrowing of specific private management skills and understandings. Instead, it will come, as it did in the history of private management, from an articulation of the general management function and a self-consciousness about the general public management point of view. The single lesson of private management most instructive to public management is the prospect of substantial improvement through recognition of and consciousness about the public management function.

Alfred Chandler's prize winning study, *The Visible Hand: The Managerial Revolution in American Business,*[24] describes the emergence of professional management in business. Through the 19th century most American businesses were run by individuals who performed management functions but had no self-consciousness about their management responsibilities. With the articulation of the general management perspective and the refinement of general management practices, by the 1920s, American businesses had become competitive in the management function. Individuals capable at management and self-conscious about their management tasks—setting objectives, establishing priorities, and driving the organization to results—entered firms and industries previously run by family entrepreneurs or ordinary employees and brought about dramatic increases in product. Business schools emerged to document better and worse practice, largely through the case method, to suggest improvements, and to refine specific management instruments. Important advances were made in technique. But the great leaps forward in productivity stemmed from the articulation of the general management point of view and the self-consciousness of managers about their function. (Analogously, at a lower level, the articulation of the salesman's role and task, together with the skills and values of salesmanship made it possible for individuals with moderate talents at sales to increase their level of sales tenfold.)

The routes by which people reach general management positions in government do not assure that they will have consciousness or competence in management. As a wise observer of government managers has written, "One of the difficult problems of schools of public affairs is to overcome the old-fashioned belief—still held by many otherwise sophisticated people—that the skills of management are simply the application of 'common sense' by any intelligent and broadly educated person to the management problems which are presented to him. It is demonstra-ble that many intelligent and broadly educated people who are generally credited with a good deal of 'common sense' make very poor managers. The skills of effective management require a good deal of uncommon sense and uncommon knowledge."[25] I believe that the most significant aspect of the Civil Service Reform Act of 1978 is the creation of the Senior Executive Service: the explicit identification of general managers in government. The challenge now is to assist people who occupy general management positions in actually becoming general managers.

- Third, careful review of private management rules of thumb that can be adapted to public management contexts will pay off. The 80-20 rule—80 percent of the benefits of most production processes come from the first 20 percent of effort—does have wide application, for example, in EPA efforts to reduce bulk pollutants.

- Fourth, Chandler documents the proposition that the categories and criteria for identifying costs, or calculating present value, or measuring the value added to intermediate products are not "natural." They are invented: creations of intelligence harnessed to operational tasks. While there are some particular accounting categories and rules, for example, for costing intermediate products, that may be directly transferable to public sector problems, the larger lesson is that dedicated attention to specific management functions can, as in the history of business, create for public sector managers accounting categories, and rules, and measures that cannot now be imagined.[26]

- Fifth, it is possible to learn from experience. What skills, attributes, and practices do competent managers exhibit and less successful managers lack? This is an empirical question that can be investigated in a straight-forward manner. As Yogi Berra noted: "You can observe a lot just by watching."

- Sixth, the effort to develop public management as a field of knowledge should start from problems faced by practicing public managers. The preferences of professors for theorizing reflects deep-seated incentives of the academy that can be overcome only by careful institutional design.

In the light of these lessons, I believe one strategy for the development of public management should include:

- *Developing a significant number of cases on public management problems and practices.* Cases should describe typical problems faced by public managers. Cases should attend not only to top-level managers but to middle and lower-level managers. The dearth of cases at this level makes this a high priority for development. Cases should examine both general functions of management and specific organizational tasks, for example, hiring and firing. Public management cases should concentrate on the job of the manager running his unit.
- *Analyzing cases to identify better and worse practice.* Scientists search for "critical experiments." Students of public management should seek to identify "critical experiences" that new public managers could live through vicariously and learn from. Because of the availability of information, academics tend to focus on failures. But teaching people what not to do is not necessarily the best way to help them learn to be *doers*. By analyzing relative successes, it will be possible to extract rules of thumb, crutches, and concepts, for example, Chase's "law": wherever the product of a public organization has not been monitored in a way that ties performance to reward, the introduction of an effective monitoring system will yield a 50 percent improvement in that product in the short run. GAO's handbooks on evaluation techniques and summaries suggest what can be done.
- *Promoting systematic comparative research:* management positions in a single agency over time; similar management positions among several public agencies; public management levels within a single agency; similar management functions, for example, budgeting or management information systems, among agencies; managers, across public and private organizations; and even cross-nationally. The data for this comparative research would be produced by the case development effort and would complement the large-scale development of cases on private management that is ongoing.
- *Linking to the training of public managers.* Intellectual development of the field of public management should be tightly linked to the training of public managers, including individuals already in positions of significant responsibility. Successful practice will appear in government, not in the university. University-based documentation of better and worse practice, and refinement of that practice, should start from problems of managers on the line. The intellectual effort required to develop the field of public management and the resources required to support this level of effort are most likely to be assembled if research and training are vitally linked. The new Senior Executive Service presents a major opportunity to do this.

The strategy outlined here is certainly not the only strategy for research in public management. Given the needs for effective public management, I believe that a *major* research effort should be mounted and that it should pursue a number of complementary strategies. Given where we start, I see no danger of overattention to, or over-investment in the effort required in the immediate future.

Any resemblance between my preferred strategy and that of at least one school of government is not purely coincidental.

Notes

1. Selma J. Mushkin, Frank H. Sandifer, and Sally Familton. *Current Status of Public*

Management: Research Conducted by or Supported by Federal Agencies (Public Services Laboratory, Georgetown University, 1978). p. 10.

2. *Ibid.,* p. 11.

3. Though frequently identified as the author who established the complete separation between "policy" and "administration," Woodrow Wilson has in fact been unjustly accused. "It is the object of administrative study to discover, first, what government can properly and successfully do, and, secondly, how it can do these proper things with the utmost possible efficiency . . ." (Wilson, "The Study of Public Administration," published as an essay in 1888 and reprinted in *Political Science Quarterly,* December 1941, p. 481.) For another statement of the same point, see Brooks Adams, *The Theory of Social Revolutions* (Macmillan, 1913), pp. 207–208.

4. See Dwight Waldo, "Organization Theory: Revisiting the Elephant," *PAR,* (November–December 1978). Reviewing the growing volume of books and articles on organization theory, Waldo notes that "growth in the volume of the literature is not to be equated with growth in knowledge."

5. See *Cases in Public Policy and Management,* Spring 1979 of the Intercollegiate Case Clearing House for a bibliography containing descriptions of 577 cases by 366 individuals from 79 institutions. Current casework builds on and expands earlier efforts of the Inter-University Case Program. See, for example, Harold Stein, ed., *Public Administration and Policy Development: A Case Book* (Harcourt, Brace, and World, 1952), and Edwin A. Bock and Alan K. Campbell, eds., *Case Studies in American Government* (Prentice-Hall, 1962).

6. Luther Gulick and Al Urwick, eds., *Papers in the Science of Public Administration* (Institute of Public Administration, 1937).

7. See, for example, Chester I. Barnard, *The Functions of the Executive* (Harvard University Press, 1938), and Peter F. Drucker, *Management: Tasks, Responsibilities, Practices* (Harper and Row, 1974). Barnard's recognition of human relations added an important dimension neglected in earlier lists.

8. See, for example, "A Businessman in a Political Jungle," *Fortune* (April 1964); "Candid Reflections of a Businessman in Washington," *Fortune* (January 29, 1979); "A Politician Turned Executive," *Fortune* (September 10, 1979); and "The Ambitions Interface," *Harvard Business Review* (November–December 1979) for the views of Romney, Blumenthal, Rumsfeld, and Shultz, respectively.

9. John T. Dunlop, "Public Management," draft of an unpublished paper and proposal, Summer 1979.

10. Hal G. Rainey, Robert W. Backoff, and Charles N. Levine, "Comparing Public and Private Organizations," *Public Administration Review* (March–April 1976).

11. From "American Presidents and Corporate Executives" by Richard E. Neustadt from a paper prepared for a meeting of the National Academy of Public Administration's Panel on Presidential Management, October 7–8, 1979. Reprinted by permission of the American Society for Public Administration, 1120 G Street, N.W., Suite 500, Washington, D.C. 20005.

12. *The Federalist Papers.* No. 51. The word "department" has been translated as "branch," which was its meaning in the original papers.

13. Failure to recognize the fact of distributions has led some observers to leap from one instance of similarity between public and private to general propositions about similarities between public and private institutions or management. See, for example, Michael Murray, "Comparing Public and Private Management: An Exploratory Essay," *Public Administration Review* (July–August 1975).

14. These examples are taken from Bruce Scott,

"American Motors Corporation" (Intercollegiate Case Clearing House #9-364-001); Charles B. Weigle with the collaboration of C. Roland Christensen, "American Motors Corporation II" (Intercollegiate Case Clearing House #6-372-350); Thomas R. Hitchner and Jacob Lew under the supervision of Philip B. Heymann and Stephen B. Hitchner, "Douglas Costle and the EPA (A)" (Kennedy School of Government Case #C94-78-216); and Jacob Lew and Stephen B. Hitchner, "Douglas Costle and the EPA (B)" (Kennedy School of Government Case #C96-78-217). For an earlier exploration of a similar comparison, see Joseph Bower, "Effective Public Management," *Harvard Business Review* (March–April 1977).

15. U.S. Government Manual, 1978/1979, 507.
16. Kenneth R. Andrews, *The Concept of Corporate Strategy* (Dow Jones-Irwin, 1971), p. 28.
17. "A Politician-Turned-Executive," *Fortune* (September 10, 1979), p. 92.
18. "Candid Reflections of a Businessman in Washington," *Fortune* (January 29, 1979), p. 39.
19. "The Abrasive Interface," *Harvard Business Review* (November–December 1979), p. 95.
20. *Fortune* (January 29, 1979), p. 36.
21. *Fortune* (September 10, 1979), p. 90.
22. *Harvard Business Review* (November–December 1979), p. 95.
23. The cases developed by Boston University's Public Management Program offer a promising start in this direction.
24. Alfred Chandler, *The Visible Hand: The Managerial Revolution in American Business,* Belknap Press of Harvard University Press, 1977.
25. Rufus Miles, "The Search for Identity of Graduate Schools of Public Affairs," *Public Administration Review* (November 1967).
26. Chandler, *op. cit.,* pp. 277–279.

☐ CASE STUDY 10

Introduction

One of the most explosive urban events of recent decades occurred in Philadelphia on May 13, 1985, when the Philadelphia police confronted the black activist cult MOVE. As the introduction to the following case, "The MOVE Disaster," recounts:

> After massive gunfire, deluges of water and explosive charges failed to dislodge the group from their fortified row house, police dropped plastic explosives from a helicopter onto a rooftop bunker. The bomb ignited an unexpected fire. Believing they could contain the fire, Police Commissioner Gregore Sambor and Fire Commissioner William Richmond decided to let the bunker burn. They miscalculated badly, and the fire raged out of control. Sweeping through three adjoining blocks, the inferno destroyed 61 homes and left 250 people homeless. Of the occupants of the MOVE house, one adult and one child fled through the flames into police custody. In the ashes were found the bodies of six adults and five children.

What caused this tragedy? Several investigative organizations and other observers attributed much of the blame to ineffective management by the city's mayor, W. Wilson

Goode. Ironically, Goode previously had been viewed as a highly successful mayor, not only by those within the city but throughout the nation. This single event severely damaged his reputation as "an effective manager, a rising star in national politics, and a symbol of hope for his city," according to the author, Jack H. Nagel, a professor of political science and public policy and management at the University of Pennsylvania.

In the following case, Nagel focuses on Goode's managerial behavior related to the MOVE decision and explores the causes of why a previously well-regarded public manager should exhibit such an uncharacteristic breakdown in his performance, bordering on what some viewed as irresponsible behavior. The author first explains the background of MOVE as a controversial activist group within Philadelphia and the two central paradoxes of Mayor Goode's behavior in response to MOVE's actions. Though what makes Nagel's case study especially remarkable and insightful is how the author then goes on to probe beneath the surface of Goode's managerial actions related to MOVE. Nagel analyzes three particular psychological problems that the mayor exhibited and relates these mental difficulties to current theories of the psychology of decision making. From this case, the author generalizes important lessons and implications for public management that relate directly and profoundly to the previous reading by Graham T. Allison, Jr.

As you review the following case, try to reflect on:

What managerial approach did Mayor Goode first attempt to use in response to MOVE's activities? What misconceptions did he have about MOVE? What were the sources of these misconceptions, in your view?

Do you agree with the author that these misconceptions were ultimately rooted in the mayor's "unresolved decisional conflicts that impeded responsible and rational handling of the problem"? What were these "three decisional conflicts" according to the author? How does Nagel support his argument by drawing on the theory of decision making developed by Irving Janis and Leon Mann? What are the assumptions of the Janis/Mann thesis?

Does this case ultimately support the "uniqueness thesis" of Graham T. Allison, Jr.? Or does Nagel's story suggest an entirely different understanding of the theory and practice of public management? And what are Nagel's implications for public management?

The MOVE Disaster

JACK H. NAGEL

On May 13, 1985, a confrontation between Philadel-

"The MOVE Disaster," (Originally titled "Psychological Obstacles to Administrative Responsibility: Lessons of the MOVE Disaster"), by Jack H. Nagel, *Journal of Policy Analysis and Management*, Vol. 10, No. 1, pp. 1–23. © 1991 by John Wiley & Sons, Inc. Reprinted by permission of John Wiley & Sons, Inc.

phia police and a cult called MOVE resulted in one of the most astounding debacles in the history of American municipal government. After massive gunfire, deluges of water, and explosive charges failed to dislodge the group from their fortified row house, police dropped plastic explosives from a helicopter onto a rooftop bunker. The bomb ignited an unexpected fire. Believing they could contain the fire, Police Commissioner Gregore Sambor and Fire Commissioner William Richmond decided to let the bunker burn. They miscalculated badly, and the fire raged out of control. Sweeping through three adjoining blocks, the inferno destroyed 61 homes and left 250 people homeless. Of the occupants of the MOVE house, one adult and one child fled through the flames into police custody. In the ashes were found the bodies of six adults and five children.

The MOVE tragedy severely damaged the reputation of Philadelphia Mayor W. Wilson Goode, who until then had been considered an effective manager, a rising star of national politics, and a symbol of hope for his city. In the aftermath of the disaster, a controversial grand jury decided not to bring criminal charges against the mayor and his chief aides, but condemned them for "morally reprehensible behavior" [Philadelphia Court of Common Pleas, 1988, p. 279]. The Philadelphia Special Investigation Commission (PSIC), appointed by the mayor himself, charged that "the Mayor abdicated his responsibilities as a leader," a condemnation shared by most informed observers.[1] With respect to the twelve values Charles Gilbert [1959] identifies with administrative responsibility, Goode and his key subordinates conspicuously failed to satisfy at least seven—responsiveness, consistency, stability, leadership, competence, efficacy, and prudence.

None of the many commentators ever satisfactorily explained why the previously impressive mayor was so irresponsible in this instance and in particular why his behavior contrasted so sharply with his reputation for hands-on management. Many observers subsequently avoided the incongruity by concluding that Goode had simply been "incompetent" all along. Whereas before MOVE he could do no wrong, after the disaster he seldom got credit for doing anything right. This paper will argue instead that, lamentable though it was, the mayor's performance exemplifies universal tendencies well understood by psychologists of decisionmaking. Analysis of the MOVE case therefore can suggest insights that may enable other administrators to recognize and control situations in which they too might otherwise succumb to irresponsible patterns of action and inaction.

The presentation that follows is organized into five sections: (a) a brief history of MOVE and its conflict with the City of Philadelphia; (b) a description of two central paradoxes in Mayor Goode's response to MOVE; (c) an explanation of both paradoxes using a standard theory about the psychology of decisionmaking; (d) a closer examination of three decisional conflicts that may explain why Goode had such difficulty dealing with this particular problem; and (e) reflections on lessons the MOVE disaster offers for the education of present and future public managers.

MOVE Versus Philadelphia

The origins of MOVE can be traced to the early 1970s in the Powelton Village section of West Philadelphia, near the campuses of Drexel University and the University of Pennsylvania.[2] In this tolerant community, a haven for political and cultural rebels, a charismatic black handyman named Vincent Leaphart developed an anarchistic, back-to-nature philosophy, the main tenets of which were reverence for all animal life, rejection of "the [American] Lifestyle," and absolute refusal to cooperate with "the System." Aided by a white graduate in social work from Penn named Donald Glassey, who transcribed Leaphart's thoughts and taught them in a course at the Community College of Philadelphia, Leaphart attracted a "family" that eventually numbered at least forty members, most but not all of whom were black. At first they called themselves the American Christian Movement for Life, but they later shortened the name to MOVE. Following the example of Leaphart, who now referred to himself as John Africa, all the core members adopted the surname Africa, in honor of the continent where they believed life began.

As they put John Africa's philosophy into practice, MOVE generated frequent tension with landlords and neighbors, who complained about members' grossly unsanitary practices and their harboring of dogs, cats, rats, roaches, and flies. Beyond these spillovers of their peculiar lifestyle, MOVE members courted friction with authorities by confronting "the System" in all its manifestations, from the Philadelphia Zoo to Jimmy Carter. Using bullhorns to demonstrate and disrupt meetings, they perfected a vituperative rhetoric, profane and filled with sexual and racial provocation. When brought to trial, as they were literally hundreds of times, MOVE members acted as their own attorneys and clogged the courts by noncooperative, contemptuous tactics.

During the 1970s, a virtual feud developed between MOVE and the Philadelphia police. The mayor of Philadelphia was then Frank Rizzo, a former police commissioner famous for tough law enforcement. The majority of whites revered Mayor Rizzo's large and aggressive police department as a bulwark against crime and disorder, but political dissidents, blacks, and journalists accused the police of frequent brutality and disregard for civil liberties. As Anderson and Hevenor [1987, p. 11] observe, "MOVE demonstrators were frequently arrested, often harassed, and nearly always regarded with unconcealed disgust and contempt by Philadelphia policemen. With their unwashed, garlic-reeking bodies, dreadlocks, and inpenetrable and obscene harangues, MOVE people were a constant affront to a police force that was (and is) largely white, ethnic . . . and Catholic."[3]

After a melee in March 1976, when MOVE accused the police of causing the death of a MOVE infant, John Africa apparently decided to turn to armed resistance. By this time, core members of MOVE occupied a house owned by Glassey on North 33rd Street. Using loudspeakers fixed in trees, they frequently harangued their neighbors. Responding to complaints, city officials attempted to investigate code violations but were refused admittance. In September 1975, the city began the protracted process of enforcing the code through the courts. A judgment mandating inspections was obtained in July 1976, whereupon MOVE constructed an eight-foot stockage around their compound. Heeding MOVE warnings that they would "cycle" (kill) their own children before submitting to inspections, the city refrained from enforcing the order. On May 20, 1977, mistakenly anticipating a city attempt to enter the premises, MOVE members brandished guns on the platform of their stockade. Shortly afterwards, Donald Glassey was arrested for filing false information when purchasing firearms. Turning informant to save himself, Glassey helped police seize MOVE guns and explosives at a location elsewhere in Philadelphia.

The stalemate in Powelton continued for nearly a year. On March 1, 1978, the city obtained court permission to blockade the MOVE headquarters for nonpayment of utility bills and refusal to admit inspectors. Police cordoned off a four-block area around the house and shut off gas and water. The siege appeared to have succeeded when intermediaries helped negotiate a settlement that was announced on May 3. MOVE surrendered weapons, allowed officials to inspect the Powelton property, and promised to vacate the house by August 1. In return, the city relaxed its blockade, freed eighteen jailed MOVE members on their own recognizance, and promised to drop all charges once MOVE departed from Powelton.

When August 1 came, MOVE refused to leave, because no one had found a site for relocation they would accept. On August 8, Police Commissioner Joseph O'Neill directed a carefully planned operation to drive the occupants from the house. Announcing each action in advance in order to protect MOVE women and children, whom they regarded as hostages, the police used a bulldozer, ram, and armored truck to breach the walls of the compound. A crane began demolishing the upper stories. Believing that all MOVE weapons had been confiscated in May, authorities were careless about concealing themselves. Suddenly, police saw a gun muzzle protruding from a basement window. After deluge guns flooded the basement, gunfire erupted, killing Officer James Ramp and wounding eight other policemen and firefighters. Following the exchange of shots, police poured in more water and smoke to flush out the occupants. As the MOVE members surrendered, officers beat and kicked Delbert Africa while news photographers recorded the action.

During the next five years, MOVE was visible to most Philadelphians only through a series of trials. In 1980, nine members were sentenced to lengthy prison terms for the murder of Officer Ramp; a tenth followed in 1982. In 1981, three police officers were tried for the beating of Delbert Africa and acquitted.[4] On May 13, 1981, Federal agents arrested John Africa and eight followers in Rochester, New York, where MOVE had owned houses since 1977. (At various times, MOVE also had enclaves in Richmond, Virginia, and Chester, Pennsylvania.) Defending himself and Alphonso Robbins Africa against bombmaking charges, John Africa won acquittal from a jury in Philadelphia in July 1981, after which he dropped out of sight.

As it turned out, the MOVE leader had not gone far. With a group of about a dozen adults and children, he was living in a house owned by his sister, Louise James, at 6221 Osage Avenue in the Cobbs Creek section on the western edge of Philadelphia, three miles from the site of the demolished house in Powelton.

Whereas the 33rd Street house had been a free-standing structure surrounded by a yard and located on a busy street, the new MOVE headquarters was a row house on a narrow, quiet residential street. These physical differences were to prove tactically important during the 1985 confrontation, but events in the two years preceding that catastrophe pivoted around social and political differences between the two neighborhoods. Nonconformist, racially mixed Powelton was a bastion of opposition to Mayor Rizzo. Its residents divided bitterly over whether the cultists or the police were the more distasteful presence in their midst. One can easily imagine Frank Rizzo enjoying some amusement at their discomfort.

In 1980, barred by the City Charter from serving three consecutive terms, Rizzo was succeeded as mayor by the more liberal former Congressman, William J. Green, Jr. Fulfilling a campaign promise to Philadelphia's increasingly powerful black voters, Green appointed W. Wilson Goode as Managing Director, the city's chief appointive official. Goode, a former civil-rights activist, had previously served as executive director of the nonprofit Philadelphia Council for Community Advancement—where he was credited with building more housing than all the city's housing agencies combined [Cohn, 1982, p. 27]—and as chair of the Pennsylvania Public Utilities Commission. As Managing Director, Goode was in charge of ten operating departments, including police and fire. Hard-working, accessible, and highly visible, he soon became hugely popular among blacks and many whites as well. When Green announced in late 1982 that he would not seek a second term, Goode resigned to campaign for the mayoralty. In May 1983, he defeated Frank Rizzo in the Democratic primary, winning the votes of 98% of blacks and 23% of whites. In the November general election, he would face two white opponents.

The Cobbs Creek neighborhood was typical of Wilson Goode's bedrock political base. Its residents, almost all black, were generally stable working- and middle-class families. Most owned their homes and took pride in keeping them pleasant and attractive. By the fall of 1983, MOVE had become an intolerable affliction to this peaceful community. The home of Lloyd and Lucretia Wilson next door was invaded by insects that had spread from 6221. When the Wilsons sought to fumigate, Conrad Africa went berserk. "The bugs are our brothers and sisters. If you

exterminate the bugs, you exterminate us," he berated Lloyd Wilson [PSIC, 1985, 10/9 AM, pp. 89–90]. In September 1983, following a dispute over a parking space, a MOVE male struck a neighbor named Butch Marshall to the ground, and three MOVE women bit Marshall on the face, back, and groin. After another assault in October, the neighbors circulated to city authorities a petition that complained about attacks, garbage, rats, a pigeon coop, animals, and MOVE's blocking of a common driveway behind the row.

As the neighbors "were reaching the breaking point," they met with State Representative Peter Truman.[5] Truman implored them not to do anything that would endanger the election of the city's first black mayor. If they would endure a few months longer, he assured them, Goode would solve their problem. Aided by the arrival of cold weather, which lessened health hazards and reduced outdoor interaction with MOVE, the neighbors waited. In November 1983, Goode won a resounding victory with 55% of the vote.

If Goode's triumph held promise of deliverance for the 6200 block, John Africa saw it as a different sort of opportunity, one that would produce intensified torment for the Osage neighbors. Obsessed with freeing his followers from prison, the MOVE leader believed that the mayor had the power to obtain their release and that the residents of Osage Avenue could persuade him to use that power. MOVE therefore embarked upon a campaign of what Goode later would call "psychological warfare" against their neighbors, holding the block "hostage" in order to obtain as ransom the release of their ten convicted comrades. MOVE launched their campaign on Christmas morning, 1983. Beginning near dawn and continuing for eight hours, their rooftop loudspeakers blared an obscene diatribe that denounced the neighbors, the mayor-elect, and the System, and demanded freedom for MOVE prisoners. Eight days later, Wilson Goode became mayor of Philadelphia.

Two Paradoxes

Mayor Goode's response to MOVE's challenge can be characterized by describing two patterns, both of which seem paradoxical. First, for sixteen months he avoided any significant action; but when he finally decided to enforce the law, the city mobilized against MOVE in less than a week and tried to execute a hastily prepared plan in the span of twenty-four hours. Second, although he was widely perceived to be an energetic, detail-oriented administrator, when he decided the city should act against MOVE, Goode had minimal personal involvement in both the planning and the execution of the attack.

Delay Followed by Haste

MOVE's war against the System, by way of their neighbors, continued through 1984 and the spring of 1985. In December 1983, they began fortifying their house by nailing boards across the windows; the ramshackle effect contrasted starkly with the neat white trim and porches of the other houses. In October 1984 they started a rooftop construction that eventually became a bunker made of railroad ties, logs, and steel plates. Similar materials were placed against the interior walls of the house and basement. In May 1984, a hooded MOVE member brandished a shotgun on the roof, and the cultists began the practice of running across the roofs of the row at night, waking frightened residents. Loudspeaker harangues were conducted daily for six to eight hours through the summer and fall of 1984. In these and other communications, MOVE members threatened the lives of President Reagan, Mayor Goode, judges, and any police officers who might try to enforce the law on Osage Avenue. A favorite tactic was to target a particular neighbor for a day, during which the unfortunate individual would be subjected to personal attacks filled with accusations of homosexuality, child molestation, promiscuity, or sexual inadequacy. As Bennie Swans of the Crisis Intervention Network later commented, "MOVE did not let up on those residents. They simply did not let up" [PSIC, 1985, 10/9 AM, p. 68].

Mayor Goode was aware of most of these developments. On March 9, 1984, Commissioner Sambor briefed him about the deteriorating situation on Osage Avenue. On May 28 and July 4, he met at their request with delegations of residents; they found the mayor knowledgeable about their plight and personally familiar with MOVE members, but unwilling to act. In June 1984, District Attorney Edward Rendell provided Goode with a memo outlining a legal strategy for disarming MOVE and abating

the nuisance on Osage Avenue. Goode also received several phone calls from block captain Clifford Bond. On August 9, Lloyd Wilson came to City Hall to complain of an assault he had suffered the day before at the hands of Frank James Africa, while police officers watched from the corner. Goode "whisked" Wilson off to a side office, where he had a lengthy but unproductive conversation with Managing Director Leo Brooks and Commissioner Sambor. Subsequently, Wilson and his family abandoned their home, driven out by vermin, noise, and fear from which their government would not protect them.

During this time, city policy barred operating departments (including Health, Water, Human Services, Streets, and Licenses and Inspections) from carrying out their responsibilities with respect to MOVE, which they were told was "a police matter." For their part, the police maintained surveillance of the 6200 block, but refrained from intervention. They even discouraged state parole officials from serving outstanding fugitive warrants against two residents of the house, Frank James Africa and Larry Howard [Philadelphia Court of Common Pleas, 1988, p. 26]. In response to the neighbors' entreaties, Goode took only two tangible actions: He extended the hours of nearby city recreation centers so residents' children could escape the loudspeakers, and he arranged psychological counseling to help the children cope with chronic tension.

Five of the MOVE Commission's findings describe and condemn this protracted phase of inaction:

3. Mayor Goode's policy toward MOVE was one of appeasement, non-confrontation, and avoidance.
4. The Managing Director and the city's department heads failed to take any effective action on their own and, in fact, ordered their subordinates to refrain from taking action to deal meaningfully with the problem on Osage Avenue. . . .
6. In the first several months of his administration, the mayor was presented with compelling evidence that his policy of appeasement, non-confrontation, and avoidance was doomed to fail.
7. In the summer of 1984, the mayor was told that the legal basis existed at that time to act

against certain MOVE members. Yet, the mayor held back, and continued to follow his policy of avoidance and non-confrontation.

8. From the fall of 1984 to the spring of 1985, the city's policy of appeasement conceded to the residents of 6221 Osage Ave. the continued right to exist above the law. [PSIC, 1986, pp. 11–13]

To this indictment should be added two more charges. First, by tolerating MOVE's abuses, the city government for two years abdicated its most basic responsibilities to the law-abiding residents of Osage Avenue. As Clifford Bond put it, "I was placed in a position of feeling not as a citizen" [PSIC, 1985, 10/9 AM, p. 4]. Second, by giving MOVE time to fortify their house, the policy of nonconfrontation made the task of dislodging the cult immensely more difficult when the mayor finally decided to act.

Sixteen months of delay abruptly gave way to fourteen days of hasty action in the spring of 1985. The shift in policy was precipitated by the neighbors. Unwilling to accept another summer of stench and harangues, they organized themselves as the United Residents of the 6200 Block of Osage Avenue and held a public protest meeting on April 25, during which several men announced they would respond to MOVE "in kind." At a May 1 press conference, the United Residents expressed their disgust with the city's inaction and requested intervention by Pennsylvania Governor Dick Thornburgh, a Republican. Coupled with new provocations by MOVE, these actions got the attention of the media, and editorialists demanded that the city meet its responsibilities.

On May 3, Mayor Goode convened a high-level meeting at which he asked District Attorney Edward Rendell to establish a legal basis for city action against the occupants of 6221. On May 5 Rendell's staff interviewed Osage residents in order to prepare warrants. At a second high-level meeting on May 7, Goode directed Commissioner Sambor to develop a plan that was to be carried out under the supervision of Managing Director Leo Brooks, a former Army major general.

Having anticipated action, Sambor had set up a planning group a week earlier. Remarkably low in rank for such a major operation, it consisted of three men who had served under Sambor in his previous post as commander of the Police Academy: Lieu-

tenant Frank Powell, head of the Bomb Disposal Unit; Sergeant Albert Revel, a pistol instructor; and Officer Michael Tursi, the Department's top sharpshooter.

On May 9, with Managing Director Brooks at his daughter's graduation in Virginia, Sambor briefed Goode on the plan the three officers had devised. He recommended that warrants be served on Sunday, May 12, which was Mother's Day. Out of concern for the holiday, Goode authorized Sambor to proceed on May 13. On May 11, a judge issued the warrants, and Sambor again briefed Goode. On the afternoon of May 12, police evacuated the neighborhood. Returning from Virginia that evening, Brooks heard on his car radio that the operation he was to head was underway. He arrived in Philadelphia in time to get a quick briefing from Sambor followed by a few hours' sleep.

At 5:35 a.m. on Monday, May 13, Sambor read an ultimatum to MOVE over a bullhorn, demanding that the four MOVE members named on the warrants surrender within fifteen minutes. MOVE used their own loudspeaker to reject the ultimatum in typical style, telling the police that their wives would be collecting insurance and sleeping with black men that night. When the fifteen minutes had expired, authorities directed water, tear gas, and smoke at the house and its roof. According to the police, MOVE responded with gunfire, and officers retaliated massively, firing many thousands of rounds in the next ninety minutes. The debacle was underway.

As the MOVE Commission and the grand jury pointed out, less hurried planning and execution might have prevented numerous errors and oversights. A full list would occupy many pages, so I shall mention just a few of the more egregious consequences of haste:

- Commissioner Sambor and his planners made little attempt to draw on the resources of other agencies, inside or outside the city government; consequently, they failed to consider alternative strategies and deprived themselves of expertise—such as the use of trained hostage negotiators—that might have resulted in better implementation of their plan.
- Goode, Sambor, and Brooks went ahead with the operation even though they knew that the mayor's directive to pick up the MOVE

children before the assault had not been implemented. (MOVE adults usually took the children on daily outings to nearby Cobbs Creek Park, and as late as May 12, two of the children were observed outside the house.) Thus they "clearly risked the lives" of six innocent children, five of whom subsequently died in the conflagration [PSIC, 1986, p. 16].

- The quick, secretive, informal planning process deprived the tacticians of crucial knowledge possessed by others in city government, including surveillance officers. As a result, to take just one example, they did not appreciate the extent of the interior fortifications that foiled their initial strategy of attempting to insert tear gas through the walls.

- Contingency plans were not developed; the final, fatal decision to drop the bomb was the result of ill-considered improvisation. After the primary plan failed, officials were apparently determined to occupy the house before dark. When Brooks informed Goode of the bomb proposal by telephone at 5 p.m., the mayor paused only thirty seconds before approving the idea.

- Insufficient attention was given to communication systems, resulting in slow, incompatible, or nonexistent communication channels between crucial actors—police and the occupants of the MOVE house, police and fire units, the mayor and managing director, and the managing director and police commissioner. Slow communications may have prevented Goode and Brooks from reversing in time Sambor's and Richmond's decision to let the bunker burn.

Arms-Length Action by a Hands-on Mayor

Until May 1985, both as Managing Director and as Mayor, Wilson Goode was perceived by the public as an incredibly hard-working, demanding, detail-oriented manager. Contemporary press descriptions give a vivid sense of his style: "He appears to be everywhere. . . . He annoys a lot of people because he continues to ask questions until he gets an answer that makes sense."[6] "He loves to come down hard on details" [Mallowe, 1980, p. 139]. "His zeal is

prodigious, his double-digit days are legend . . ." [Javers, 1983]. "Today, in Philadelphia, in the first year of Wilson Goode's first term of office, there is absolutely no doubt about *who* is in charge" [Mallowe, 1984, p. 168]. Indeed, one of the few criticisms of Goode in this happy period was that he delegated too little: "He seeks near-absolute control over his operating departments" [Cohn, p. 21]. "He has an aversion to delegating authority. He tries to do too much on his own" [Mallowe, 1984, p. 226].

Goode's view of himself corresponded to the public image: "I want to know what the problems are in this city. . . . I can't do that sitting on the 16th floor here, I really can't" [Cohn, 1982, pp. 13]. *"Someone has to be in charge. People through the government must know that the mayor is there giving directions . . ."* [Mallowe, 1984, p. 168]. "I'm a nuts-and-bolts person" [Mallowe, 1980, p. 139]. Perhaps his favorite term was "hands-on."

However, after he authorized an armed confrontation with MOVE, Goode was anything but hands-on. He held only two high-level meetings to plan the operation. The May 7 meeting focused on the legal basis for action, and the May 9 meeting lasted less than thirty minutes. On both occasions, Goode prevented detailed discussion of the police plan. The contrast in styles was pointed out to the MOVE Commission by District Attorney Rendell:

And I turned to the [Police] Commissioner and I said, "Are you going to use tear gas and water?" And he said yes and started to explain a little bit, and the Mayor said . . . , "Look, I will leave that up to you all. It's your plan and execute it." In other words, he cut off discussion. . . .

And I thought it was somewhat unusual. . . . I had known Wilson for the three years that he was Managing Director. I worked very closely with him . . . , and then while he was Mayor I had significant contact with him. Wilson's management style has always been one where he got involved in all—not in all of the details, but in certainly the significant details. And I thought that was . . . a little out of character. . . . [PSIC, 1985, 10/22 AM, pp. 71–72]

Rendell speculated that Goode wished to avoid leaks, that perhaps he "intended as soon as I walked out of the room to sit down and go over it blow by blow with the Police Commissioner" [PSIC, 1984, 10/22 AM, p. 95]. In fact, Sambor did brief Goode about the plan on May 11, but only because Brooks was out of town—at all other times, including May 13, Goode and Sambor strictly followed the chain of command, communicating with each other only through Brooks. Goode seems not to have been deeply engaged in the May 11 meeting, for he recalled it as occurring over the telephone, whereas Sambor testified in detail that he went to Goode's office. Goode's last briefing was by telephone on the evening of May 12, when Brooks called him to relay the discussion he had just had with the Police Commissioner.

On May 13 itself, Goode heeded the advice of his staff and Brooks by staying away not only from Osage Avenue, but also from Brooks' command post four blocks north at the Walnut Park Plaza, the tallest structure in the area. As the operation began, Goode followed developments together with four black elected officials whom he had invited to his home in Overbrook, about two miles from Osage Avenue. Later, in his office at City Hall, he was understandably preoccupied with MOVE. Although the mayor frequently conferred by phone with Brooks, Goode's distance from the scene and the clumsiness of his communication links prevented him from exercising effective control over the terrible events of that day.

In short, as the MOVE Commission concluded, "The mayor failed to perform his responsibility as the city's chief executive by not actively participating in the preparation, review and oversight of the plan" [PSIC, 1986, p. 16].

Irresponsibility and Decisional Conflict

In 1977, eight years before the MOVE disaster, the psychologists Irving Janis and Leon Mann published a treatise called *Decision Making*.[7] In it, they outlined a model based on psychological conflict that economically explains the two central paradoxes in Wilson Goode's actions, as well as many otherwise puzzling subsidiary aspects of his behavior during this tragic episode.

Janis and Mann premise their theory on the idea that decisionmaking is not merely a cool intellectual process but also involves "hot" emotional influences.

The need to make a decision is inherently stressful. Although moderate anxiety improves cognitive functioning, excessive stress can severely impair the quality of decision processes. The greatest stress occurs when all known options threaten to impose severe losses, especially if those losses are not merely "utilitarian" but include "highly ego-involving issues," such as severe social disapproval and/or self-disapproval [Janis and Mann, 1977, p. 46].

When a decision maker is faced with an emotionally consequential, no-win choice, how he or she copes with the problem depends crucially on two factors—hope and time. If the decision maker sees realistic hope of finding a solution superior to any of the risky options that are immediately apparent, then that person's efforts are likely to follow the desirable pattern Janis and Mann call *vigilance*, which is close kin to the familiar rational-comprehensive ideal. The vigilant decision maker canvasses a wide set of alternatives; considers the full range of goals and values involved; carefully weighs costs, risks, and benefits; intensively seeks and accurately assimilates new information; reexamines all alternatives before settling on a final choice; makes detailed provisions for implementing the chosen course; and devotes special attention to contingency plans [Janis and Mann, 1977, p. 11].

If, however, a decision maker loses hope of finding an acceptable option, he or she is likely to fall into either of two patterns of seriously defective search and appraisal. The first and more common syndrome, called *defensive avoidance,* typically occurs when there is no overwhelming pressure to change the existing policy even though its consequences are (like those of all other alternatives) highly unfavorable. The chief symptoms of defensive avoidance are procrastination, passing the buck and other ways of denying personal responsibility, and bolstering [Janis, 1989, p. 80]. "Bolstering" is a process of cognitive distortion in which one "spreads" or exaggerates the value of the chosen course compared to alternatives by avoiding exposure to disturbing information, selective attention and recall, wishful thinking, oversimplification, rationalization, and denial.

Defensive avoidance "satisfies a powerful emotional need—to avoid anticipatory fear, shame, and guilt" [Janis and Mann, 1977, p. 85]. Its emotional benefit is a state of "pseudocalm," resulting from the decision maker's suppression of troubling thoughts and avoidance of stimuli that might evoke the painful dilemma.

When external pressures impose a deadline or threaten an imminent disaster if the existing policy is maintained, the state of pseudocalm is shattered and the underlying conflict breaks through to the surface, arousing unbearable emotional stress. In such circumstances, the decision maker is likely to respond with the pattern of behavior Janis and Mann call *hypervigilance*.[8] Responding to "the strong desire to take action in order to alleviate emotional tension," the hypervigilant decision maker "superficially scans the most obvious alternatives open to him . . . , hastily choosing the first one that seems to hold the promise of escaping the worst danger" [Janis and Mann, 1977, pp. 47, 74]. Like defensive avoidance, hypervigilance involves severely defective search and appraisal:

> A person in this state experiences so much cognitive constriction and perseveration that his thought processes are disrupted. The person's immediate memory span is reduced and his thinking becomes more simplistic. . . . [T]he person in a state of hypervigilance fails to recognize all the alternatives open to him and fails to use whatever remaining time is available to evaluate adequately those alternatives of which he is aware. He is likely to search frantically for a solution, persevere in his thinking about a limited number of alternatives, and then latch onto a hastily contrived solution that seems to promise immediate relief, often at the cost of considerable postdecisional regret. [Janis and Mann, 1977, p. 51]

An explanation for the first paradox of Wilson Goode's behavior toward MOVE should now be obvious. His delay/haste pattern is a textbook example of defensive avoidance followed by hypervigilance. The two stages are not really paradoxical, because they resulted from the same underlying decisional conflict. As Janis and Mann [1977, p. 66] observe, a "person's defensive avoidance pattern might abruptly change to hypervigilance if he encounters a new, dramatic danger signal." The mobilization of the Osage neighbors signaled to Goode that a continued policy of nonconfrontation would be fraught with new, unacceptable dangers—a certainty of severe political embarrassment and a high probability

of unofficial violence against MOVE. The mayor was forced to act, and in his state of hypervigilance, he accepted the first option presented to him—the ill-fated proposal devised by Sambor's planners.

But why was the MOVE problem in particular so difficult for Wilson Goode to handle, when he had been able to deal effectively with many other issues in a distinguished career of public service? Janis and Mann [1977, p. 75] contend that both vigilant and defective patterns of problem solving are within the repertoire of every decision maker. Anyone, they believe, can fluctuate from one pattern to another depending not only on the objective circumstances of action, but also on the relation of those circumstances to personal values and affiliations, which determine whether actions and outcomes will be conducive to self-esteem and social approval for a particular individual. To explain the second paradox, it will therefore be necessary to look more closely at Wilson Goode, as well as at the finer details of his decision processes with respect to MOVE.

The Mayor's Decisional Conflicts

Goode's testimony to the MOVE Commission, coupled with other evidence about his personality and values, suggests that the drama on Osage Avenue aroused within the mayor severe conflicts that he was never able to resolve. Instead, he in effect fled from them, with the result that he virtually abdicated his responsibility as the city's chief administrator.[9] The mayor's conflicts may be summarized as three dilemmas: (1) MOVE's intransigence and irrationality appeared to necessitate the use of force that would almost surely end in bloodshed, but Goode saw himself as a peacemaker and a preserver of life; (2) to enforce the law against MOVE would require the mayor to depend on the Philadelphia Police Department, but the police might well be unreliable, among other reasons because his own relationship with them was uneasy and because many of them hated MOVE; (3) as a black committed to a policy of respecting civil rights, Goode felt dissonance about authorizing official coercion of a black group; but MOVE's bizarre behavior must also have aroused in him anger that he would have difficulty acknowledging, given his religious values and self-image as a controlled person.

Blood on the Hands of a Peacemaker

At first glance, Goode's desire to avoid action against MOVE appears readily understandable. In retrospect, everyone saw Osage Avenue as a no-win situation. If the city refrained from confronting MOVE, the cultists would make life intolerable for their neighbors. If the city attempted to enforce the laws, MOVE would respond violently, producing a high probability of death. District Attorney Rendell described the effect of this realization on the emotions of participants in the crucial meeting:

> I have attended a lot of meetings since I have been in public life, but I never ever had attended a meeting that had the impact on me that my meeting on Thursday, May 7, 1985 did, when in fact the plan of action was signed, sealed and delivered; when the arrest warrants and the search warrants were approved, signed by a judge; when we had picked a time and date to act; when we knew it was going to occur. There was almost a dread in that room so thick that you could have cut it with a knife. Because, understand, every one of us in that room knew that someone—there was an extraordinarily high likelihood that someone was going to die. [PSIC, 1985, 10/22 AM, p. 34]

Nevertheless, to some politicians the MOVE problem might have seemed a golden opportunity. Throughout history, leaders have won popularity by unleashing violence against unpopular enemies, foreign or domestic. By 1985, MOVE had alienated virtually everyone in Philadelphia. Confronting them would have cost Goode little if any support among his black political base, because the neighbors who were pleading for relief were not only black but also representative of his most reliable constituency. MOVE instead offered Goode an excellent chance to broaden his already impressive popularity, because forceful action against them in the name of law and order would have appealed most to those whites who were not yet part of his coalition.

Goode himself noted the political value of decisive leadership. Asked at the MOVE Commission hearings whether his staff's advice that he stay away from the scene of action was "substantive or political or both," he replied:

> I thought it was substantive. I don't think that it . . . had anything to do with politics. From my vantage point, both in foresight and hindsight, . . . it is far better for a Mayor to be perceived as being out there on the scene with hands-on than not to be and, therefore, from a political point of view I think I lose points. . . . [PSIC, 1985 10/15 PM, p. 94]

In fact, despite the debacle, polls in the aftermath of May 13 showed strong public support for Goode's decision to act against MOVE. His approval ratings did not drop precipitously until the fall of 1985, when information revealed by the hearings made him appear inept, irresponsible, and evasive [Wilentz, 1985; Stevens, 1985].

True, as 1978 and the aftermath of 1985 showed, the public would be distressed at death to innocent parties—police, firefighters, or MOVE children. Police officers and firefighters do, however, accept mortal risks as part of their jobs; and, forewarned by MOVE's treachery in 1978, they could more carefully protect themselves from gunshots.[10] As for the children, if Goode had insisted on implementation of his explicit order to pick them up before commencing the operation, they probably could have been saved. Thus the people most likely to die in a properly planned and executed operation were MOVE adults. Most Philadelphians perceived them as dangerous, deranged, and incorrigible; their deaths in resisting legitimate authorities would have been mourned by few and welcomed by many.

Although the conclusion of this cold political logic might not have troubled most citizens, it appears to have been unacceptable for Wilson Goode. Perhaps the most revealing moment of his testimony to the MOVE Commission came when he was asked to describe his emotions as his office television showed the fire raging out of control:

> I went through very deep emotions at that time. I cried because I knew at that point that lives would be lost, and I knew that homes would be destroyed and I knew that despite all of our good intentions, that we had . . . an absolute disaster.

And I can't explain to you or to anyone the kind of emotions that I went through, because everything about me is about preserving life and to know that any plan that I've had anything to do with would, in fact, bring about the cessation of life, was very tough. [PSIC, 1985, 10/15 PM, p. 95]

There are independent reasons for believing the sincerity of Goode's statement. Widely regarded as a deeply religious man, he has been a devoted and active member of the First Baptist Church of Paschall since 1955, serving during most of this time as a deacon and lay leader of the congregation. Well into adult life, he seriously considered entering the ministry. On his pastor's advice, he prayed for guidance. "I came away feeling strongly that I *was* called," he said later. "But it was a ministry of a different kind, a ministry of public service." An early profiler wrote, "His whole notion of public service is grounded in his faith, and he approaches his work at City Hall with almost an evangelical fervor" [Cohn, 1982, p. 13].

Indeed, most of Goode's career exhibits a marked inclination toward conciliation and peacemaking. As a community activist in the 1960s and early 1970s, "his low-key manner usually helped keep potentially explosive situations under control" [Cohn, p. 27]. As a politician, he first unified the previously divided black community, then established an effective alliance with white liberals in the Democratic primary, and finally in the 1983 general election, through a series of conciliatory gestures, won the support of Frank Rizzo. Consequently, he carried 27% of the white vote, and Philadelphia during the first year of his term rode a wave of elation, smugly comparing its newfound racial harmony to the bitter divisions in Chicago and other cities. As mayor, many of Goode's early string of triumphs depended on his ability to build consensus and placate opposition. The few criticisms of Goode during this period centered on claims that he was too willing to appease opponents and too reluctant to lead in the absence of consensus. His own view was more positive: "I've had a charmed life as mayor because I've learned the arts of compromise and negotiation" [Wilentz, 1985, p. 22].

A commitment to peacemaking is also consistent with the full pattern of Goode's dealings with MOVE.

The disastrously little time and attention he devoted to planning the use of force contrasts strikingly with his extensive involvement in efforts to understand MOVE and to negotiate a solution [Marimow, 1985]. When Managing Director, he met about fifteen times with John Africa's sisters, Louise James and Laverne Sims, both of whom had been involved with MOVE and were also the mothers of MOVE members. "I always had a comfortable relationship with them, when we have shared together, where they have talked with me and I have listened a lot" [PSIC, 1985, 10/15 AM, p. 29]. The open door continued after he became mayor. On July 31, 1984, when city officials were anticipating a confrontation with MOVE on the August 8 anniversary of the Powelton shootout, the two sisters requested a meeting and were given almost instant access. Goode told the MOVE Commission, "I literally jumped at that meeting because for the first time, I thought I had someone that I could talk to that could, in fact, avoid a conflict out there" [PSIC, 1985, 10/15 AM, p. 25]. (Note how the procrastination of defensive avoidance vanishes when hope appears.) As late as May 9, Goode sandwiched in his fateful meeting with Sambor between discussions with community activists, through whom he hoped to arrange a meeting with Gerald Ford Africa:

I then asked them to go back, to indicate to Gerald Ford Africa that I was willing to meet at any point that he decided, that he decided that he wanted to meet. I would come to his house. I would go to a neutral house. . . . I would personally negotiate with him any type of release from the house that they were talking about, any movement they wanted to make at that time. . . . After the optimism on Thursday, about noon, they got back to me the next day and said that there was a 360 degrees turn in the attitude of Gerald Ford Africa when they went back, and that he became profane towards them and said he would not meet with me under any circumstances ever for anything. And it was at this point that that hope which I had of bringing about some negotiation in fact fell through. [PSIC, 1985, 10/15 AM, pp. 62–64]

In directing his personal effort concerning MOVE toward negotiation, Goode was clearly playing to the area where he "felt familiar, resourceful, and competent" [Marimow, 1985]. But such skills had probably developed precisely because they were so consistent with Goode's religious motivation and self-image. In contrast, to be "on the scene with hands-on" in managing a police operation against MOVE would be to risk coming away with blood on his hands—blood that might be politically advantageous but personally intolerable.

Unleashing on Unreliable Force

Thus, when the Osage neighbors precipitated Goode's final stage of hypervigilance, he kept the police operation at arms length, shielding himself from personal responsibility for the onslaught to come by entrusting the planning and execution to the police, whom he described time and again in the hearings as "experts" and "professionals." Goode's seemingly blind trust in his police force prompted this sarcastic interrogation by Commissioner Neil J. Welch, who had once directed the Philadelphia office of the FBI:

Welch: Now, we got a Mayor that's been a Mayor for a year or two and before that he was the Managing Director, and certainly isn't the first time he's seen the Philadelphia Police Department and its personnel perform. . . . [W]hat was your judgment as to the professional capability, the dependability, the quality and integrity of the Philadelphia Police Department to execute, to draft a plan and to execute it successfully?

Goode: My judgement was that Greg Sambor had the ability within the parameters which I set forth, to go out and to develop a plan. . . . It was my judgment that . . . being the kind of trained professional person and manager he is, that he, in fact, could do that. . . . That when he finished that plan, he was to discuss that with Leo Brooks, who I felt with his 30 years in the armed services, as a Major General, could evaluate appropriately and properly that overall plan. . . . So I left that meeting with full confidence that Greg Sambor and Leo Brooks could, in fact, carry out the assignment given to them.

Welch: Mayor, you displayed great confidence in your Police Department and your Police Commissioner, as you have just outlined. This is the same department that has been or would have been under almost continuous federal investigation, had it not, for a period of some time?

Goode: That's correct. [PSIC, 1985, 10/15 PM, pp. 119–121]

Having had responsibility for the Police Department during most of the past five years, to admit the department's faults would clearly arouse dissonance for Goode; but it is inconceivable that he did not know, at some level, that his police were an unreliable instrument for this task. The Federal investigations to which Welch referred were not only for corruption, but for brutality and civil rights violations; and the mutual hatred between the police and MOVE was obvious, especially after the death of Officer Ramp and the beating of Delbert Africa in 1978.

In his initial attempt to solve the MOVE problem, Goode in fact sought to bypass the Philadelphia police. On May 30, 1984, just two days after his first meeting with a delegation from Osage Avenue, the mayor led ranking city officials to a session with U.S. Attorney Edward Dennis and representatives of the FBI and Secret Service. They rebuffed his argument that MOVE's threats against President Reagan and violations of their neighbors' rights constituted grounds for U.S. intervention. Although consistent with the buck-passing pattern typical of defensive avoidance, Goode's attempt to enlist Federal authorities can also be interpreted as a prudent effort to find an armed force more detached, disciplined, and reliable than his own police.

Worries about controlling the city police were also present, though not emphasized, in the days before the final confrontation. At the May 7 meeting, prompted by Councilman Lucien Blackwell's strong warning about officers who might seek vengeance for 1978, Goode instructed Sambor to "handpick" the men who would serve in the Osage Avenue confrontation. (Sambor later claimed not to have heard such an order and in any case did not implement it. One of the gas-insertion teams included two officers who had been accused of beating Delbert Africa [Anderson and Hevenor, 1987, p. 115].) Goode ultimately admitted to the MOVE Commission that he doubted police fire control so much that he feared their bullets might endanger his own life if he went to the scene:

Commissioner Audrey Bronson: I understand that

you felt that your life would have been at risk—by whom?

Goode: Well, I have received a lot of information that simply people said to me, and I will share this candid discussion with you, that I should be careful of, first of all, of people who were MOVE sympathizers in the neighborhood, that with shots going on out there that a shot could easily go awry and hit me, that I should be—I should be—beware of even the potential for police shots going awry on the scene and therefore, there have been, as I was told, instances of the fact that commanders in the Army have, in fact, been mistakenly shot and I should be aware of those kinds of things and the people who talked with me simply persuaded me that, in fact, it would be a risk for me to be in the area. [PSIC, 1985, 11/6 PM, p. 54]

Although not explicit about who were "the people who talked with me," Goode's statement to the Commission is consistent with reports that telephoners purporting to be police officers warned the mayor he might be shot by police if he came to Osage Avenue.

In short, part of Goode's reluctance to act against MOVE must have resulted from doubts, whether conscious or suppressed, that he could sufficiently control the use of force by the police. In the end he made no real attempt to manage the violence he had authorized. Perhaps, as many in Philadelphia believe, Goode rationally calculated that any such effort might fail and therefore deliberately distanced himself from a potential disaster in order to avoid legal or political responsibility. Such motives cannot be ruled out, but they do not adequately explain the string of cognitive distortions by which the mayor apparently avoided appreciating the reality of what his forces were doing. He told his breakfast guests that police were only firing over the roof of the MOVE house; he interpreted explosions he heard from his home as stun grenades; he thought that the "explosive device" would be placed on MOVE's roof rather than dropped from a helicopter; and he mistook "snow" on his television screen for water from firefighters' squirts [PSIC, 1985, 10/15 AM, pp. 74, 97; 10/15 PM, p. 111; 11/6 AM, p. 111; 10/15 PM, p. 31]. Avowing these beliefs—all unsupported by others' testimony—would hardly help against criminal charges, and they only added to Goode's political vulnerability by subjecting him to ridicule. Such a consistent pattern of misperception seems more suited to deceive on self than to deceive others, and better protection against self-condemnation than against the judgment of courts or voters. It therefore appears likely that deeper sources of ambivalence prevented the mayor from admitting to himself the full import of his decision to unleash official violence against MOVE.

Black Against Black: Identification and Anger

The foregoing analysis is not meant to portray Wilson Goode as a pacifist or as one whose values are entirely antithetical to those of the police. After completing ROTC at Morgan State University, he served in the U.S. Army from 1961 to 1963, rising to the rank of captain and commanding a unit of 223 military policemen. His military experience made a deep impression on Goode. He has said that he learned more about management in the army than he did earning a master's degree in governmental administration at the University of Pennsylvania.[11] As mayor, he has shown a marked penchant for appointing former military officers to high posts—including Leo Brooks, a major general in charge of the Philadelphia Defense Personnel Support Center before Goode persuaded him to become Managing Director, and Gregore Sambor, a veteran and an officer in the reserves.

To Goode, however, the military seems to represent not so much legitimate violence as it does an organization that develops personal discipline and rewards it, regardless of race—in marked contrast to most of American society in his formative years. Early profiles of Brooks suggest the virtues that Goode most admires:

[A mutual acquaintance described Brooks as] "made out of the same mold as Wilson." Goode and Brooks shared poor childhoods in the South, Army-officer training and strong religious underpinnings. Brooks' father is a Baptist minister . . . Brooks also is a black man who, like his new boss, has achieved success by making hard work his credo. [Cooke and Klibanoff, 1983]

At heart a traditionalist, Brooks believes in the old-fashioned virtues of hard work, self-discipline . . . and taking responsibility for one's own actions. To him, nothing exceeds the importance of family. [Klibanoff, 1984]

To a black man with Wilson Goode's values, MOVE must have aroused deep and intense conflicts.[12] On the one hand, as a former civil rights activist who had himself been twice picked up by police for allegedly creating disturbances [Cohn, 1982, p. 21], Goode must have had some lingering identification with MOVE. In 1978, much of the black and liberal communities had seen the MOVE problem as a racially motivated attack by the Rizzo administration on the rights of a predominantly black group. On one occasion, five thousand demonstrators marched around City Hall to protest the siege in Powelton; their chants linked MOVE with South African blacks as fellow victims of racial oppression. In 1984, U.S. Attorney Dennis, himself black, strongly warned city officials against violating MOVE's civil rights [PSIC, 1985, 10/22 PM, p. 127]. Goode invoked his own concern for minority rights in explaining his reluctance to act:

I think that if I was a different person, that perhaps I may have acted differently back in 1984. But I . . . do not feel that anyone who holds an office ought to use that office to infringe and violate other people's rights in order to achieve the overall good, and I guess I feel that way because I know that for so long in this country that laws were, in fact, used to deprive blacks and women and Hispanics and others who were different, and therefore, I do not want, as mayor of this city to say to a group: Because you are different, because you don't comply with all the laws, therefore, I have the right, as the mayor, to simply go full speed and trample on you and all your rights. . . . [PSIC, 1985, 10/15 PM, pp. 97–98]

On the other hand, MOVE represented the antithesis of every standard by which Wilson Goode lived. They dwelt in filth; he was always well groomed. They lived communally; he had raised a family. They spewed profanity; he attended church every Sunday. They survived casually; he worked fifteen-hour days. They rejected the system; he aspired to run a major corporation. As they spurned his efforts to negotiate a peaceful solution, as they vilified him and threatened his life, the bizarre cultists must have aroused increasing anger in Goode. The impulse to vent this anger must have been strong, but his religious belief in preserving life and his self-

image as a controlled person forbade yielding to it. "I've always felt that I have to be in control of me at all times," he once told an interviewer [Cohn, 1982, p. 27]; and another profiler got "the feeling that the emotion bottled up inside Wilson Goode is always close to eruption. You can see him almost counting to ten, thinking before he responds, calculating each sentence, crafting every phrase, then struggling mightily to reign in what might be rage" [Mallowe, 1984, p. 170].

For a time, the mayor hoped that MOVE itself would assume the moral burden of precipitating violence. After receiving Rendell's memo justifying urgent action in June 1984, Goode delayed until August 8, the anniversary of the Powelton shootout, because reports indicated that MOVE planned a major confrontation with "the System" on that date. At the mayor's direction, the police prepared a plan for capturing the MOVE house,[13] and three hundred officers were assembled near Osage Avenue. Goode's choice of language in describing this incident is revealing:

The August 8th 1984 plan was a reactive plan, was geared to go into effect only if certain types of aggressive behavior, aggressive steps were taken by MOVE members themselves. And therefore when they did not take any aggressive steps, nothing, in fact, was done at that time. [PSIC, 1985, 10/15 PM, p. 59]

The words "aggressive" and "aggression" recur frequently when Goode refers to the initiation of armed confrontation. It appears that he was willing in 1984 to do battle with MOVE, but only if MOVE were the aggressor, if MOVE bore the responsibility of having clearly initiated violence. To let deaths occur (or appear to occur) merely because of noise, stench, code violations, and unpaid utility bills was, to Goode, a morally unbalanced equation.[14]

On August 8, however, MOVE did nothing except take notes about the police preparations. After that day, Goode and other city officials entered a stage of full-blown defensive avoidance that lasted until May 1985. As the MOVE Commission observed about this period. "The policy of appeasement produced a rule of silence in City Hall, where information on the Osage Avenue situation was not disseminated and where city officials knowledgeable about the problems chose not to speak of them" [PSIC, 1986, p. 13]. Goode and his colleagues were thus able to entertain the wishful hope that the Osage Avenue problem "would disappear" by ignoring the readily available knowledge that MOVE members were vigorously and visibly fortifying their compound [PSIC, 1985, 10/15 PM, pp. 76–7]. Goode justified his policy of nonintervention on the grounds that no action should be taken "until such time as we worked out an overall plan that would be comprehensive in nature," but this argument was a rationalization for avoidance, as is shown by the fact that he did absolutely nothing to force the creation of such a plan [PSIC, 1985, 10/15 PM, pp. 75–80]. Indeed, the mayor had no contact with anyone concerning MOVE from August 9 until the end of April 1985 [PSIC, 10/15 AM, p. 40].

Goode's nine months of pseudocalm were then shattered by the United Residents' initiative, which revived what threatened to be an excruciating inner struggle. Rather than endure the tension during a protracted period of careful search and appraisal, the mayor sought to eliminate his conflict quickly by authorizing the police plan. Although he unleashed the violence of the police and perhaps in part vented his own anger through their vengeance, the use of force in this context was so dissonant with his self-image that he could not accept—psychologically at least as much as politically—the ownership that hands-on management would imply.

To shield himself from personal responsibility for violating crucial values, Wilson Goode thus abdicated his responsibility as an administrator. In so doing, he lost his best chance to control and minimize the inevitable violence. Because he was so reluctant to transgress his values, he permitted a series of events that in the end inflicted on them far greater damage than was necessary. The outcome has the irony of genuine tragedy. The preserver of life bore responsibility for eleven deaths; the builder of homes presided as sixty-one burned; the protector of rights permitted grotesquely excessive official violence.

Lessons for Present and Future Managers

Perhaps the only consolation we can take from so awful a disaster is the hope that its lessons will help

prevent future catastrophes. Thus the MOVE Commission concluded their report with no fewer than thirty-eight recommendations covering such matters as communication systems, assignment of authority and responsibility, policies for controlling weapons and explosives, strategic planning processes, interdepartmental coordinating groups, and so forth. Though the Commission's proposals may be sensible and worthwhile, from the perspective of the analysis offered in this paper, such advice misses the most fundamental lessons of the MOVE debacle.

Organizational systems, policies, and procedures are ultimately controlled and implemented by human beings. Effective communication will not occur when subordinates believe that their superiors cannot bear to hear the truth. Clear allocation of authority will be wasted on executives who, succumbing to painful quandaries, rationalize evasion of responsibility.

Programs for educating public managers should therefore devote much more attention to the psychology of decisionmaking, with a special focus on its prescriptive implications. For example, Janis [1989, ch. 10] concludes his recent book by suggesting twenty sets of leadership practices that might help policy makers avoid pitfalls that often result in defective decisionmaking. As he observes, most of these recommendations will be costly to leaders and their support staffs in time, effort, and stress. Adjusting curricula to sensitize present and future decision makers to psychological factors will also demand new investments by schools, teachers, and students.

Dramatic examples like the MOVE disaster can help motivate such efforts, but in teaching the case during the past several years, I have found that students adopt their own avoidance strategies. Like the general public, their natural reaction is to debate, as one student put it, "whether moral bankruptcy or simple incompetence best explains this disaster." Whichever verdict is chosen, the effect is to distance oneself from the officials who are blamed for the debacle. The observer in effect is saying, "*I* would never be so evil, or so uncaring, or so inattentive, or so blundering as to permit such a horror!"

Interpreting the MOVE case in terms of a general theory such as the Janis and Mann conflict model elevates it from an idiosyncratic failure to a universal warning. Students can then move beyond emotional condemnation of a few officials to a sobering recognition of their own vulnerability to similar errors.

The generality of the problem can be further emphasized by exploring parallel cases (though few will be so well documented as the MOVE incident). To take several recent examples, the delay/haste pattern appears to fit the British government's treatment of IRA strongholds in Belfast and Derry during the early 1970s, the Chinese government's response to the 1989 student demonstrations in Tienanmen Square, and the U.S. invasion of Panama to overthrow General Manuel Noriega.[15]

Once managers understand the dynamics of defensive avoidance and hypervigilance, what can they do to protect themselves? Because rationalization, denial, selective perception, and wishful thinking are so insidious, no one can be assured of immunity against defective decision processes. For this reason, Janis and Mann [1977, p. 396] recommend embedding preventive strategies in organizational standard operating procedures,[16] because "if the anti-defensive avoidance procedures are not institutionalized but are rather left to the discretion of the leader or the members, they will be more honored in the breach than in the observance."

Nevertheless, it is not unreasonable to hope that individual awareness will also help. Relying on face validity rather than any systematic evidence of effectiveness, I would suggest the following strategy to managers who wish to reduce their vulnerability.

First, learn to recognize the behavioral symptoms of defective decisionmaking. For defensive avoidance, these include procrastinating, buck-passing, and downplaying danger signals. Symptoms of hypervigilance include grabbing the first available alternative, neglecting contingency plans, and believing that action must be taken under extreme time pressure whether or not compelling deadlines exist. Wise managers will not only monitor themselves for these symptoms, but will also encourage trusted advisors to fight the battle for their minds by calling such tendencies to their attention.

Second, when these symptoms are observed, identify the central no-win dilemma or dilemmas.[17] Conflicts that impede effective decisionmaking are not always obvious and will vary from individual to individual. The desire to avoid responsibility and shield oneself from reality behind a screen of cognitive distortions becomes strongest when one's most central values are threatened, so the manager must heed the ancient injunction to "know thyself."

Third, learn to grasp problems firmly even when all options entail distasteful consequences for important values. The example of Wilson Goode shows that cherished virtues, if excessively protected, can be the source of tragic failure. Though vigilant problem solving and decisive management may induce stress, they are usually rewarded—if not with unequivocal triumph, then at least by controlled damage and the respect that strong leaders are accorded. In contrast, the inferno on Osage Avenue should burn into our memories the lesson that however bad available alternatives seem, potential outcomes can be far worse if avoidance and hasty action permit a tough situation to deteriorate into a nightmare.

References

Anderson, John, and Hilary Hevenor (1987), *Burning Down the House: MOVE and the Tragedy of Philadelphia* (New York: W.W. Norton and Co.).

Assefa, Hizkias, and Paul Wahrhaftig (1988), *Extremist Groups and Conflict Resolution: The MOVE Crisis in Philadelphia* (New York: Praeger).

Bowser, Charles W. (1989), *Let the Bunker Burn: The Final Battle with MOVE* (Philadelphia: Camino Books).

Boyette, Michael, with Randi Boyette (1989), *"Let It Burn!" The Philadelphia Tragedy* (Chicago: Contemporary Books).

Cohn, Roger (1982), "Wilson Goode Has Something to Prove," *Today Magazine, Philadelphia Inquirer* (July 25), pp. 10ff.

Cooke, Russell, and Hank Klibanoff (1983), "Work Is the Credo for New Managing Director," *Philadelphia Inquirer* (November 29), p. 12-A.

George, Alexander L. (1973), "The Case for Multiple Advocacy in Making Foreign Policy," *American Political Science Review* 66, pp. 751–785.

Gilbert, Charles E. (1959), "The Framework of Administrative Responsibility," *Journal of Politics* 21, pp. 373–407.

Goodman, Howard (1989), "Still Haunted by MOVE, Richmond Is Telling His Story," *Philadelphia Inquirer* (May 15), p. B-1.

Janis, Irving L. (1972), *Victims of Groupthink* (Boston: Houghton Mifflin).

Janis, Irving L. (1989), *Crucial Decisions: Leadership in Policymaking and Crisis Management* (New York: The Free Press).

Janis, Irving L., and Leon Mann (1977), *Decision*

Making: A Psychological Analysis of Conflict, Choice, and Commitment (New York: The Free Press).

Javers, Ron (1983), "On the Run: Lunch with Wilson Goode," *Philadelphia Magazine* 74 (April), p. 8.

Klibanoff, Hank (1984), "The General," *Philadelphia Inquirer* (May 21), p. 4-B.

Mallowe, Mike (1980), "And Now, the Goode News," *Philadelphia Magazine* 71 (August), pp. 128ff.

Mallowe, Mike (1984), "The No-Frills Mayor," *Philadelphia Magazine* 75 (December), pp. 168ff.

Marimow, William K. (1985), "Two Images of Goode: Activism vs. Delegation," *Philadelphia Inquirer* (October 23), p. 1-A.

Philadelphia Court of Common Pleas (1988), *Report of the County Investigating Grand Jury of May 15, 1986.*

Philadelphia Special Investigation Commission (1985), *Hearings.*

Philadelphia Special Investigation Commission (1986), *Findings, Conclusions, and Recommendations.*

Sharifi, Jahan (1990), Unpublished student paper, University of Pennsylvania.

Stevens, William K. (1985), "Mayor Goode's Once-Solid Path Turns Rocky in Philadelphia," *New York Times* (October 23).

Wilentz, Amy (1985), "Goode's Intentions," *Time* 125 (May 27), p. 22.

Notes

1. PSIC, 1986, Finding 22; see also Findings 3, 15, 17, and 24, which use comparable language. The PSIC is generally known as "the MOVE Commission."

2. This account draws on the following sources, in addition to the author's knowledge as a resident of West Philadelphia during the period described: PSIC [1986], which includes a chronology; Philadelphia Court of Common Pleas [1988], which includes a history of MOVE; Anderson and Hevenor [1987]; Assefa and Wahrhaftig [1988]; Bowser [1989]; and Boyette [1989]. Charles Bowser and Michael Boyette were, respectively, members of the MOVE Commission and the grand jury. The eighteen days of hearings the MOVE Commission conductd in October and November 1985 are my principal source [PSIC, 1985]. Transcripts are available in the Government Publications Department of the Philadelphia Free Library and the Urban Archives Center of Temple University. There is a volume for each day of hearings, with pages numbered separately within each volume for morning and afternoon sessions. I supplemented the transcripts by watching videotapes of key witnesses' testimony. (The hearings were televised live by WHYY-TV, the PBS station in Philadelphia.)

3. See also the testimony of Laverne Sims [PSIC, 1985, 10/10 AM, pp. 65–77].

4. District Attorney Edward Rendell later blamed the acquittal on the invective and curses that Delbert directed at the judge and jury [PSIC, 1985, 10/22 AM, pp. 119–120].

5. PSIC, 1985, 10/8 PM, p. 104. In Philadelphia there are 28 districts for the lower house of the state legislature compared with only 10 councilmanic districts; thus the state representative is often the elected official closest to the people of a neighborhood.

6. Cohn, 1982, p. 27. The second sentence is a quotation from Shirley Hamilton, Goode's chief of staff.

7. Janis is better known among students of politics, policy, and management for his earlier work on "groupthink" [Janis, 1972]. Elements of groupthink can be found in various official groups involved in the MOVE problem, but the full-blown syndrome does not appear, perhaps because the mayor's interpersonal style inhibited development of the requisite emotional cohesiveness. (Like other cults, MOVE itself exhibited a virulent form of groupthink.) Janis's work on organizational decisions has developed from the specific to the general. In *Decision Making,* he and Mann depict groupthink as a collective version of the broader phenomenon of defensive avoidance, which in turn is part of a "conflict model" based on psychological stress. In his latest book, *Crucial Decisions* [Janis, 1989], the conflict model becomes a component of a still more general "constraints model." The comprehensiveness of the constraints model is a virtue for some purposes, but I believe the

paradoxical features of the MOVE case are explained best by the conflict model. Thus my account relies more on *Decision Making* than on *Crucial Decisions*.

8. The choice of words is unfortunate, because the authors use "vigilance" for their ideal problem-solving process; thus, "hypervigilance" suggests too much of a good thing. The hypervigilant actor exhibits too much emotional arousal and too much haste, but no true vigilance.

9. Although based as much as possible on published materials, the analysis that follows is necessarily inferential and speculative.

10. On May 13, only one police officer was struck by a MOVE bullet, and a bulletproof vest saved him from serious harm. A policy of protecting firefighters from possible MOVE gunfire was one reason the fire spread so fast and so far. Having vowed that no firefighter would face gunfire, Fire Commissioner William Richmond deliberately chose to sacrifice property in order to save lives [Goodman, 1989].

11. In a conversation with the author in February 1981.

12. Much the same argument can probably be made for Leo Brooks, which may help explain why he too failed to fulfill his responsibility in the MOVE operation. Despite the advantages of similarity in promoting trust and comfortable personal relations, leaders take a great risk in depending excessively on key subordinates who are too much like themselves.

13. This plan, prepared by Sergeant Herbert Kirk of the Police Academy, was the forerunner of the strategy employed the following May [PSIC, 1985, 10/11 PM].

14. Because some of his radical and civil libertarian supporters, both black and white, might have had the same attitude, Goode's calculation can be seen as both political and moral. As Sharifi [1990] observes, successful political leaders often mirror the potential reactions of key constituencies in their own concerns.

15. I owe these and other suggested parallels to an anonymous reviewer [of this article].

16. An example already well known in the policymaking community is the system of multiple advocacy recommended by Alexander George [1973].

17. One device that might help raise conflicts to consciousness is the decisional balance sheet, a kind of expanded cost-benefit analysis that includes not only utilitarian gains and losses but also the approval and disapproval of reference groups and oneself [Janis and Mann, 1977, ch. 6]. Note that the purpose is to recognize consciously the role of emotional influences, not necessarily to eliminate them.

Chapter 10 Review Questions

1. Briefly, what arguments does Allison put forward to underscore the uniqueness of public management in comparison with business management? Do you agree with his reasoning? Why or why not?

2. Despite Allison's thesis, there is a repeated public demand—evidenced in the popular press and in political campaigns—that government *should* become more business-like. In your opinion, what are the sources and causes of this repeated public outcry?

3. From your own experiences, can you give an example to support or contradict Allison's "uniqueness thesis"? Does your example essentially suggest more similarities than differences between public and private management?

4. Does the case "The MOVE Disaster" ultimately support Allison's "uniqueness" thesis? Or, does the author of the case offer a different, more convincing model?

5. If you were charged with constructing a better management system that would prevent such problems as the MOVE disaster from recurring in the future, what would you recommend?

6. Does this case study support the argument that effective public management is perhaps the most important element in making good government a reality today? Explain why or why not. In your view, how does "management" differ from "leadership"? Is this an important distinction?

Key Terms

Sayre's "law"

common management functions

measurement of performance

personnel constraints on public managers

career systems

media relations

terminological tangles

time perspectives of managers

equity and efficiency values

managing internal components

managing external components

POSDCORB

implementation

operational plans

agency strategy

Suggestions for Further Reading

Much of the earliest literature on management in this century focused on the role of line managers in business, for example, Henri Fayol, *General and Industrial Management,* translated by Constance Storrs (London: Pitman, 1949); or Frederick W. Taylor, *Scientific Management* (New York: Harper & Row, 1911). Their emphasis on the values of efficiency, rationality, and clear lines of hierarchy was carried over into the public sector by such authors as Henry Bruere, W. F. Willoughby, Frederick Cleveland, Luther Gulick, and others, who pioneered the development of management techniques in the public sector prior to World War II. For a good collection of the works of these writers, see Frederick C. Mosher, *Basic Literature of American Public Administration, 1787–1950* (New York: Holmes and Meier, 1981). And for several excellent summary essays on the lives of key management theorists, read Brian R. Fry, *Mastering Public Administration* (Chatham, N.J.: Chatham House, 1989).

A book that should be read in its entirety is Chester I. Barnard, *The Functions of the Executive* (Cambridge, Mass.: Harvard University Press,

1938), because Barnard stands in marked contrast to the pre–World War II scientific management theorists and because he made an enormous impact on other postwar writers like Herbert Simon, writers who decisively reshaped our whole view of this field. William B. Wolf, *The Basic Barnard* (Ithaca, N.Y.: Institute of Labor Relations, Cornell University, 1974) offers the best available commentary on Barnard's life and work. A good summary of the work of another important figure, Henry Mintzberg, can be found in Henry Mintzberg, *Mintzberg on Management: Inside Our Strange World of Organizations* (New York: Free Press, 1989).

Postwar management thought is aptly described by Harold Koontz as "the management theory jungle," i.e., it is divided into multiple schools and perspectives. To sample some of these diverse points of view, read C. West Churchman, *The Systems Approach* (New York: Dell Publishing, 1968), or Bertram M. Gross, *The Managing of Organizations* (New York: Free Press, 1964), for the *systems approach;* read Harry Levinson, *The Exceptional Executive: A Psychological Conception* (Cambridge, Mass.: Harvard University Press, 1968), or Rensis Likert, *The Human Organization: Its Management and Value* (New York: McGraw-Hill, 1967), for the *human behavioral school;* refer to the several hundred cases available through the Harvard Business School that were instrumental in pioneering the methodology of the *case method;* for the *policy emphasis,* see Paul Appleby, *Policy and Administration* (University, Ala.: University of Alabama Press, 1949); and the *decision school* of management is well represented in books by Charles E. Lindblom and Herbert A. Simon, Donald W. Smithburg, and Victor A. Thompson (discussed in Chapters 8 and 9).

Where are we today in public management thought? Again, no consensus prevails as described in the excellent overview essay by Hal G. Rainey, "Public Management: Recent Developments and Current Prospects," in Naomi B. Lynn and Aaron Wildavsky, eds., *Public Administration: The State of the Discipline* (Chatham, N.J.: Chatham House, 1990). The older schools are still very influential. But unquestionably the economic pressures have brought about a new outpouring of ideas on efficiency and cutback management, which are reflected in the *practical efficiency-oriented writings* of Elizabeth Kellar, *Managing with Less* (Washington, D.C.: International City Management Association, 1979), and Mark W. Huddleston, *The Public Administration Workbook* (New York: Longman, 1987). The new world of the *knowledge manager* is vividly portrayed in Harlan Cleveland, *The Knowledge Executive* (New York: E. P. Dutton, 1985). A more specialized focus on peculiar management problems associated with various levels of government is found in Brian W. Rapp and Frank M. Patitucci, *Managing Local Government for Improved Performance: A Practical Approach* (Boulder, Colo.: Westview Press, 1977); Martha W. Weinberg, *Managing the State* (Cambridge, Mass.: M.I.T. Press, 1977); or, on the federal level, Laurence E. Lynn, Jr., *Managing the Public's Business* (New York: Basic Books, 1981); Barry Bozeman and Jeffrey D. Straussman, *Public Management Strategies: Guidelines for Managerial Effectiveness* (San Francisco: Jossey-Bass, 1990);

Steven Cohen, *The Effective Public Manager* (San Francisco: Jossey-Bass, 1988); and John Rehfuss, *The Job of the Public Manager* (Chicago: Dorsey Press, 1989). There are numerous books on management in specialized policy fields like defense, law enforcement, health care, and others. The *effective leadership trait* perspective is emphasized in such recent business-oriented books as Leonard Sayles, *Leadership* (New York: McGraw-Hill, 1979), and John P. Kotter, *The General Manager* (New York: Free Press, 1982) or public sector leadership, John W. Gardner, *On Leadership* (New York: Free Press, 1990); and Jameson W. Doig and Erwin C. Hargrove, eds., *Leadership and Innovation: Entrepreneurs in Government* (Baltimore: Johns Hopkins University Press, 1990). Humanistic management still remains a vital concern of *new public administration* writers, such as H. George Frederickson, *New Public Administration* (University, Ala.: University of Alabama Press, 1980), and Michael Harmon, *Action Theory for Public Administration* (New York: Longman, 1981). On the opposite side, quantitative, *efficiency-oriented* management is also apparent and popular, as found in Michael J. White et al., *Managing Public Systems: Analytic Techniques for Public Administration* (No. Scituate, Mass.: Duxbury Press, 1981). *Comparative approaches* also find favor, as in Joseph Bowers, *The Two Faces of Management* (Boston: Houghton Mifflin, 1983), and Donald F. Kettl, *Government by Proxy* (Washington, D.C.: Congressional Quarterly Press, 1988). *Specific management issue/problem* books also are frequently written, such as John J. DiIulio, Jr., *Governing Prisons: A Comparative Study of Corrections Management* (New York: Free Press, 1987); David S. Brown, *Management, Hidden Enemy—And What Can Be Done About It* (Mt. Airy, Md.: Lomond Publications, 1987); and Jeffrey S. Luke et al., *Managing Economic Development* (San Francisco: Jossey-Bass, 1988).

For two excellent textbooks that provide a realistic picture of the recent problems and prospects in public management, see Hal G. Rainey, *Understanding and Managing Public Organizations* (San Francisco: Jossey-Bass, 1991); and Charldean

Newell, ed., *The Effective Local Government Manager,* Second Edition. (Washington, D.C.: ICMA, 1993). For two useful readers on this topic, refer to J. Steven Ott et al., eds. *Public Management* (Chicago: Nelson-Hall, 1991); and Patricia W. Ingraham et al., eds. *New Paradigms for Government* (San Francisco: Jossey-Bass, 1994).

In the 1990s, public management practices have been dominated by the "reinventing government movement" and so the two critical works that are "must" reading on this topic are David Osborne and Ted Gaebler, *Reinventing Government* (Reading, Mass: Addison-Wesley, 1992); and Vice President Al Gore, *Creating a Government That Works*

Better and Costs Less (Washington, D.C.: USGPO, 1993). For a current critical appraisal of the application of reinventing ideas to federal government, see Donald F. Kettl and John J. DiIulio, Jr., eds. *Inside the Reinvention Machine* (Washington, D.C.: The Brookings Institution, 1995). Some of the best treatments in the 1990s of key public management issues by scholars include: Mark H. Moore, *Creating Public Value* (Cambridge: Harvard University Press, 1995); Paul C. Light, *Thickening Government* (Washington D.C.: The Brookings Institute, 1995); and Donald F. Kettl, *Sharing Power* (Washington D.C.: The Brookings Institue, 1993).

Public Personnel Motivation: The Concept of Rational, Norm-Based, Affective Motives

A variety of rational, norm-based, and affective motives appear to be primarily or exclusively associated with public service. This is not to say that all public employees are driven by these needs. Public service motivation is seldom identified with individual utility maximization. . . .

James L. Perry and
Lois Recascino Wise

READING 11

Introduction

The emphasis on contemporary research in personnel motivation has resulted in an impressive subfield of public administration that deals with the many ramifications of the individual in public organizations. Today, most scholars and practitioners of public administration are aware that the handling of personnel issues can be one critical key to the successful management of any public agency.

Chapter 6 explored how our important understanding of the role of the informal group within organizations began. Though concerned primarily with business organizations, Elton Mayo's discoveries in the field of human relations at Western Electric in the 1920s expanded the traditional theories of public administration by showing how critical an impact the human group had on the management process.

However, early researchers in the personnel field tended to accept the basic goals of increased efficiency in organizational activities and actually sought ways by which management could obtain greater productivity from workers. Initially, monotony, alienation, and worker fatigue frequently were problems focused on in personnel studies. These studies often recommended a restructuring of the formal or procedural aspects of the institution as the means of control.

The second-generation personnel specialists like Chris Argyris, Warren Bennis, Rensis Likert, and Douglas McGregor have continued to stress the significance of the problems of the individual in organizations, but frequently with less concern about organizational performance and more careful attention toward helping to achieve worker satisfaction and personal growth on the job. Such writers have de-emphasized traditional administrative goals such as efficiency and, instead, have shown a greater interest in support of individual values and a humanistic environment within organizations.

In the following essay, "The Motivational Bases of Public Service," James L. Perry and Lois Recascino Wise, who are currently professors at the School of Public and Environmental Affairs at Indiana University, offer a unique assessment of the current state of motivational research as it pertains to the public service. They begin by pointing up that the decline in confidence in American institutions has taken a heavy toll on the morale and motivation of those in the civil service. While many observers today call for a rebirth of dedication to the public service and a better motivated workforce, the assumption is that such improvements easily translate into a more effective, efficient, and economical public personnel. The authors argue, however, that evidence regarding what successfully motivates civil servants is limited. What we do know, say these writers, is that government is *not* like a business in which workers respond to "self-interest" and "economic incentives." Rather, as Perry and Wise show, the actual research on public service motivation tends to emphasize other key motivational factors. Their article reviews the different theories for public service motivation and identifies a three-fold typology of motives associated with government employment that include rational, norm-based, and affective motives. They further suggest the behavioral implications of their findings for the public service, but they conclude that past research still offers a limited understanding of the way to simulate individual behavior in public organizations. It is apparent that the need for further study of this important subject, both in terms of empirical research and theory development, is necessary, according to both authors.

As you review their thoughtful exploratory essay on the "state of the art" of this subject, you might consider the following questions:

How do these scholars define the term "public service motivation"?

Why do the authors argue that most of our understanding of personnel motivation derives from business administration and therefore has limited application to the public sector?

Do you agree with their fundamental conclusion that "public service motivation is seldom identified with individual utility"? Why or why not?

What do they mean by the terms "rational," "norm-based," and "affective"? How did they develop these concepts and the assumptions they make about role(s) in public service motivation?

How can the three-fold behavioral implications that they draw from their research apply to practicing public administrators for motivating their employees? Is it a valid conceptual framework, in your view, for covering all levels of public service—local, state, and federal?

The Motivational Bases of Public Service

JAMES L. PERRY AND LOIS RECASCINO WISE

The past two decades have brought enormous changes in the environment for public service. Beginning in the mid-1960s, public confidence in American institutions began a two-decade decline.[1] Nowhere is the decline in public trust more apparent than in government. At the start of this last decade of the twentieth century, only one in four Americans expressed confidence in government to "do what is right."

The decline in public trust has precipitated a "quiet crisis" in the federal civil service.[2] The recent report of the National Commission on the Public Service, more commonly referred to as the Volcker Commission after its chair, Paul Volcker, the former chairman of the Federal Reserve Board, recited a litany of shortcomings in the federal personnel system.[3] Although no comparable evidence is available on the status of state and local government civil service systems, they no doubt have suffered problems similar to those experienced at the federal level.

In the face of these long-term trends and their associated consequences, political leaders have begun to call for a rebirth of the public service ethic. The 1988 presidential race was the first in over a decade in which bureaucrat bashing was not one of the favorite pastimes of the candidates. President Bush has been joined in his call for a renewal of interest in public service by other prominent public servants, including former Secretary of State George Shultz and former Comptroller General Elmer B. Staats.[4]

Calls for a recommitment of Americans to values associated with government service, among them personal sacrifice and duty to the public interest, raise practical questions about the power of these values to stimulate and direct human behavior. At their core, calls for a renewal of public service motivation assume the importance of such motivations for an effective and efficient public service. Those who advocate using public service motivation as the primary steering mechanism for bureaucratic behavior perceive that it is essential for achieving high levels of performance.

At least two developments of recent years, one intellectual and one practical, call into question the strength of a public service ethic. One is the rise of the public choice movement, which is predicated on a model of human behavior that assumes that people are motivated primarily by self interest.[5] According to this view, because self interest is at the root of human behavior, incentives, organizations, and institutions must be designed to recognize and to take advantage of such motivations. A related development, this one arising within government, is the growing popularity of monetary incentive systems, especially at top organizational levels.[6] Extrinsic rewards controlled by one's supervisor are now seen as a major means for directing and reinforcing managerial and executive behavior. These related trends stand in opposition to the view that public service motives energize and direct the behavior of civil servants.

The present study seeks to clarify the nature of public service motivation and to identify and evaluate research related to its effects on public employee behavior. The article reviews existing literature about public service motivation to identify the phenomena more precisely. It then discusses the implications of public service motivation for behavior in public organizations. Needs for future research are discussed in conclusion.

Theories of Public Service Motivation

Public service is often used as a synonym for government service embracing all those who work in the public sector. But public service signifies much more than one's locus of employment. For example, Elmer Staats has written: " 'Public service' is a concept, an attitude, a sense of duty—yes, even a sense of public morality."[7] Staats' observation reflects both the breadth and depth of meaning that has been associated with the idea of public service.

Public service motivation may be understood as an individual's predisposition to respond to motives grounded primarily or uniquely in public institutions and organizations.[8] The term "motives" is used here to mean psychological deficiencies or needs that an individual feels some compulsion to eliminate. Following Knoke and Wright-Isak, this discussion recognizes that these motives may fall into three analytically distinct categories: rational, norm-based, and affective.[9] Rational motives involve actions grounded in individual utility maximization. Norm-based motives refer to actions generated by efforts to conform to norms. Affective motives refer to triggers of behavior that are grounded in emotional responses to various social contexts.

The motivational characteristics of public service have drawn the attention of scholars dating to the beginnings of the field of public administration. The concern that motives affect the quality and content of public outputs is equally long. The most prominent stream of research on public service motivation historically has focused on attitudes of citizens and various elites toward government employment. Most recognizable among these contributions is Leonard White's *The Prestige Value of Public Employment in Chicago* and Kilpatrick, Cummings, and Jennings', *The Image of the Federal Service.*[10] Although prestige is a factor that influences the attractiveness of public sector jobs, it does not set apart the motivational bases of public service from other sectors of employment. Early

incentive theorists identified prestige as an incentive derived from the size and growth of an organization.[11]

Despite obvious differences in extrinsic rewards, other research has looked comparatively at motivation levels of public and private managers and generally has found few differences in overall measures of motivation.[12] However, this research has not identified what other motives public employment serves to compensate for its limited appeal to traditional rational motives. Do specific motives exist that are associated with public service primarily or exclusively, and, if there are, what are they?

Rational

Little of the literature on public service motivation acknowledges that some of the motives unique to public service are rational in nature; motives are usually treated as wholly altruistic. A strong case can be made, however, that public service motivation is sometimes grounded in individual utility maximization.

In a recent article, Steven Kelman posed the question: "What are the distinctive advantages that might draw people to government?"[13] One of his answers was that public servants are drawn to government to participate in the formulation of good public policy. Although Kelman associates an individual's desire to participate in the formulation of good public policy with the norm of public spirit, it is likely to appeal to many civil servants in more rational terms. *Participation in the process of policy formulation* can be exciting, dramatic, and reinforcing of an individual's image of self importance. Rawls asserts that a greater realization of self emanates from "skillful and devoted exercises of social duties."[14] Someone drawn to the public sector to participate in policy making may therefore be satisfying personal needs while serving social interests.

Anthony Downs argued that some civil servants are motivated by *commitment to a public program because of personal identification* with the program.[15] He offered Billy Mitchell and the military use of aircraft as an example of such a motivational base, but other examples such as J. Edgar Hoover and Hyman Rickover come readily to mind. Rickover, for example, was so dedicated to the nuclearization of the U.S. Navy that, even in the face of opposition to his amassing influence and power, he remained at his post well beyond normal retirement age.

A related rational motive that for many individuals may not be served outside of government is *advocacy for a special interest*. Individuals may be drawn to government or pursue particular courses of action within government because of their belief that their choices will facilitate the interests of special groups. One of the arguments frequently found in the literature on representative bureaucracy is that a widely representative bureaucracy facilitates inclusion of a range of policy perspectives in a society.[16] Such an argument assumes that one motive prevalent in pluralistic societies is an individual's conscious or unconscious advocacy for special interests.

Norm-Based

Frederickson and Hart have argued that one of the primary reasons why American public administration has had difficulty coping in recent years is its excessive and uncritical reliance upon the values of business administration.[17] Careerism has displaced idealism as a guide for bureaucratic behavior, although there are some notable exceptions to this trend.

One of the most commonly identified normative foundations for public employment is *a desire to serve the public interest*.[18] Downs argues that the desire to serve the public interest is essentially altruistic even when the public interest is conceived as an individual's personal opinion. Others may disagree with Down's interpretation of public interest but still agree that the norm is integral to most conceptions of public service motivation.[19] The role of values such as nationalism and loyalty to country in shaping a career dedicated to public service is reflected in the life of Louis Brownlow. In recounting Brownlow's career on the one-

hundredth anniversary of his birth, Barry Karl described a man fully dedicated to the profession of serving the public and totally disinclined from making any personal gains from his work.[20] In *Private Lives of Public Servants,* Kenneth Lasson describes a physician who was similarly motivated. The physician, who joined the Food and Drug Administration to protect the public from inadequately tested drugs, provided the following reflection about his motivations: "I realize, intellectually, that I have accomplished far more in my years at Food and Drug than I could have in private practice. When I helped take 'MER/29' off the market I did more good than a lifetime of seeing individual patients."[21]

A desire to serve the public interest is only one value integral to the construct of public service motivation. Bruce Buchanan, citing Frederick Mosher's classic, *Democracy and the Public Service,* argues that the public service ethic involves a unique sense of *loyalty to duty and to the government as a whole*.[22] Buchanan speculates that this norm derives from the state's sovereign power and the role of public employees as nonelected trustees of portions of this power. Similarly, Heclo has argued that the extent to which public policies are responsive to citizens' preferences is significantly affected by the public bureaucracy.[23]

A related normative anchor for public administrators flows from the concept of *social equity*.[24] Social equity involves activities intended to enhance the well-being of minorities who lack political and economic resources. Frederickson argues that the obligations of public administrators are threefold: to provide services efficiently and economically while enhancing social equity. He suggests that the inclusion of social equity among the values served by public administrators helps to define the political nature of public administration roles.

Affective

As noted above, some public employees may be motivated by a commitment to a public program because of personal identification with a program. In many instances, however, *commitment to a program* may emanate *from a genuine conviction about its social importance.* The sources of commitment to a program may be difficult to distinguish in practice, but they are conceptually distinct. Luther Gulick captured the distinction in referring to what he termed "the nobility of the great objectives of the public service." He believed that motives derived from service to society would be more lasting than those based on the profit motive.[25]

Frederickson and Hart suggest that the central motive for civil servants should be the *patriotism of benevolence.* They define patriotism of benevolence as "an extensive love of all people within our political boundaries and the imperative that they must be protected in all of the basic rights granted to them by the enabling documents."[26] They go on to suggest that the patriotism of benevolence combines love of regime values and love of others. Although Frederickson and Hart argue that the patriotism of benevolence represents a particular moral position, it also may be understood to describe an emotional state. In fact, the type of moral "heroism" envisioned by Frederickson and Hart may be attainable only through an emotional response to humankind, which brings with it a willingness to sacrifice for others.

Of course, people are a mix of motives, exhibiting combinations of values over a lifetime and focusing on different motives at various points in their careers. Personal or environmental factors might account for changes in individual motives, but clearly an individual can switch among public service motives as well as away from these stimuli altogether. For example, Robert Caro's autobiography of Robert Moses traces his progression from the norm-based motives of a civil service reformer to the rational motives of a power broker. Describing the failure of Moses' attempts to reform the New York City civil service and the lesson that power makes dreams come true that he drew from it, Caro writes:

> The net result of all his work was nothing. There was no civil service standardization. . . . Convinced he was right, he had refused to soil the white suit of idealism with compromise. He had

really believed that if his system was right—scientific, logical, fair—and if it got a hearing, the system would be adopted. . . . But Moses had failed in his calculations to give certain factors due weight. He had not sufficiently taken into account greed. He had not sufficiently taken into account self-interest. And, most of all, he had not sufficiently taken into account the need for power.[27]

To summarize, a variety of rational, norm-based, and affective motives appear to be primarily or exclusively associated with public service. This is not to say that all public employees are driven by these needs. Public service motivation is seldom identified with individual utility maximization, but motives such as participation in the process of policy formulation, commitment to a public program because of personal identification with it, and advocacy for special or private interests are essentially rational in nature. Public service motivation is most commonly associated with particular normative orientations—a desire to serve the public interest, loyalty to duty and to the government as a whole, and social equity. The affective aspects of public service motivation have been relatively neglected and may be the least important component of the overall concept. However, motives such as patriotism of benevolence seem to be grounded in an individual's emotional state.

Behavioral Implications of Public Service Motivation

Of what significance is the public service motivation construct? Although theory has not been well developed, the literature on public administration has contended that what has historically been called the public service ethic and what is defined more formally in the present study as public service motivation has significant behavioral implications. The level and type of an individual's public service motivation and the motivational composition of a public organization's workforce have been posited to influence individual job choice, job performance, and organizational effectiveness. Some of the potential behavioral implications of public service motivation can be summarized in propositional form.

1. *The greater an individual's public service motivation, the more likely the individual will seek membership in a public organization.*

The general attraction-selection framework implied by this proposition has broad acceptance and has received substantial empirical support.[28] It presumes that organizations with certain properties attract and/or select employees with particular personal attributes. These personal attributes, in turn, influence how employees react to the organization. Thus, the proposition suggests that the greater the strengths of rational, norm-based, and affective public service motives are to an individual, the more likely the individual is to seek public organizations as environments in which to satisfy these needs.

Although evidence indicates that public organizations attract different types of individuals than do private organizations, only limited research attention has been given to issues surrounding the individual-organization match.[29] Available empirical research on the attraction-selection framework involving public organizations provides moderate support for a public service motivation-membership relationship. A comparative study of sectoral choice by Blank found that although clear correlations exist between wages and sectoral choice, sectoral choice involves more than wage comparisons.[30] Among Blank's conclusions was that highly educated and more experienced workers are far more likely to choose the public sector, offsetting lower wages with rewards arising from the characteristics of their jobs.

In two studies comparing graduate students about to enter or reenter the profit and nonprofit sectors of the economy, Rawls and his associates found that nonprofit entrants valued helpfulness (working for the welfare of others), cheerfulness, and forgiveness (willing to pardon others) more

Table 1　Public Service Motives

Rational

Participation in the process of policy formulation.
Commitment to a public program because of personal identification.
Advocacy for a special or private interest.

Norm-Based

A desire to serve the public interest.
Loyalty to duty and to the government as a whole.
Social equity.

Affective

Commitment to a program from a genuine conviction about its social importance.
Patriotism of benevolence.

---

highly than students bound for the private sector. Nonprofit entrants placed less value on a comfortable life and economic wealth.[31] These empirical findings are strongly supportive of the relationship in proposition one.

Further theoretical support for the proposition is provided by Albert Hirschman. In *Shifting Involvements,* Hirschman described a cycle of collective behavior that shifts over time between two ends of a public-private continuum.[32] The spectrum is associated with public affairs or civic involvement at one end and private interests at the other. Hirschman argues that shifts along the continuum are products of factors that both pull masses of people into public or private affairs, such as exceptional economic conditions, and, when preferences change, push individuals away from such activities.

The theory is applicable to decisions by individuals about whether to join and remain with public organizations. Hirschman argues that shifting involvements represent preference changes resulting from disappointments experienced in pursuing either public or private interests. It follows that if individuals are drawn to public organizations because of expectations they have about the rewards of public service but those expectations go unfulfilled, they are likely either to revise their preferences and objectives or to seek membership in organizations compatible with their interests. Thus, public service motivation should be understood as a dynamic attribute that changes over time and, therefore, may change an individual's willingness to join and to stay with a public organization.

Collectively perceived frustrations associated with public life or, conversely, with the perceived moral bankruptcy of private pursuits can produce a similar phenomenon on a larger scale. Dramatic shifts in the attractiveness of government service since the early 1960s could be attributed to the types of collective behavior posited by Hirschman's model.[33] More generally, the literature on "the image of public service"[34] often identifies the push and pull factors contributing to mass shifts in preferences for or frustrations with government service that influence recruitment and retention of members.

In their classic book, *Organizations,* March and Simon posit that organizations depend on individuals to make two broad sets of decisions on behalf of the organization: to participate and to perform. Proposition one posited a direct relationship between membership or the decision to participate and public service motivation. Although the evidence is less compelling, proposition two suggests a similar relationship between public service motivation and the decision to perform.

2. *In public organizations, public service motivation is positively related to individual performance.*

Systematic empirical evidence about the relationship between public service motivation and performance does not exist, but other research regarding the effects of motivational factors on individual performance can be drawn upon to support this proposition. The connection between job characteristics and work performance, which is based on the research of Turner and Lawrence, has been examined by a number of different researchers.[35] The expectation is that individuals will be motivated to perform well when they find their work meaningful and believe that they have responsibility for the outcomes of their assigned tasks. Among the job characteristics that contribute to performance motivation are autonomy, task

identity, and perceived task significance. It can be argued that these are the attributes that individuals with public service motives derive from public sector employment. For individuals with high levels of public service motivation, significant tasks include those that provide opportunities to address questions of social equity, to express loyalty to country, to advocate a valued special interest, or to pursue social programs.

Public service motivation is likely to be positively related to an individual's organizational commitment. Individuals who are highly committed are likely to be highly motivated to remain with their organizations and to perform. In addition, because committed employees are likely to engage in spontaneous, innovative behaviors on behalf of the organization, such employees are likely to facilitate an organization's adjustment to contingencies. In some instances, public service motivation, by inducing high levels of commitment, may produce negative outcomes. Individuals motivated by public service may carry their commitment beyond reasonable boundaries. Extreme commitment could lead to fanatical behavior, suspension of individual judgment, and the like, i.e., the syndrome that Schein termed "failures of socialization."[36]

3. *Public organizations that attract members with high levels of public service motivation are likely to be less dependent on utilitarian incentives to manage individual performance effectively.*

The question of what sort of motives serve as the principal motivational bases in public organizations is integrally related to the way incentive systems are structured. As a general rule, the incentives that organizations provide are likely to be most effective if they are contingent on the motives of individual members. Thus, organizations whose members are motivated primarily by rational choice are likely to find utilitarian incentives most effective. Organizations whose members are motivated by norm-based and affective considerations must rely more heavily on normative and affectual incentives.

Utilitarian incentives, if maintained at a satisfactory level, are not likely to be critical determinants of outputs where individuals identify with the tasks or mission of the organization. Thus, public organizations that attract employees with high levels of public service motivation will not have to construct incentive systems that are predominantly utilitarian to energize and direct member behavior. Where public service motivation is absent, individual utilitarian benefits may be the most effective incentives. In those instances in which organizational leadership incorrectly matches incentives to motives, the organization is unlikely to reach its maximum potential performance.

The great risk in the current trend of treating the public service like private enterprise is that it fails to acknowledge unique motives underlying public sector employment and the critical linkage between the way a bureaucracy operates in an administrative state and the advancement of social and democratic values. Current crises of ethics and accountability among politically appointed senior managers in government may be an outgrowth of the idea that management in the public sector is not unique.[37] At the same time, declines in the advancement of social goals may be linked to the emphasis on business management techniques in government. As others have demonstrated, these trends are not unique to the American scene.[38]

Rainey's comparative research on incentives provides empirical support for proposition III. Rainey compared the responses of middle managers in public agencies and private profit-making corporations on a series of scales measuring incentive structures, organizational goal clarity, and individual role characteristics.[39] He found that public managers perceived a weaker relationship between performance and extrinsic rewards. It would have been reasonable to expect differences on scales measuring organizational goal clarity and motivation, but Rainey found no differences. He speculated that different incentives in public organizations act as alternatives to the constrained extrinsic incentive structure and positively influence motivation and effort. In support of this interpretation, he found a comparatively stronger relationship between expected timeliness, quantity and quality of work, and sense of meaningful public service for public sector managers. In a study of public and private managers in Atlanta, Georgia, Baldwin replicated Rainey's results, finding no differences in levels of expressed motivation.[40]

Research Implications

This study suggests several areas where future research might be focused. An obvious priority is that more research needs to be conducted to explore and test the propositions above and to refine understanding of the behavioral implications of public service motivation. Within this context, an understanding of the way values and incentive structures shift over time is a critical ingredient for developing an understanding of cyclical swings in the popularity of public sector employment.

A second research need is the development of measurement methods that facilitate better understanding of how public service motivation contributes to organizational commitment and performance. A necessary component of efforts to advance understanding of the different aspects of public service motivation is a system for defining and measuring public service motives. The available literature does not provide operational indicators of these motives that can be used in research. Development of a psychometric instrument capable of measuring an individual's public service motivational structures along with a model that operationalizes the linkages between individual values, organizational environment and task structure, and outcome (such as commitment, performance, and job satisfaction) is a critical next step.

A third research priority has a greater applied emphasis: how can public service motives be instilled in potential recruits for government service? The problem of transferring to young people the motives of public service has been addressed by statespersons and researchers. Certainly, the image of the public service is a critical ingredient.[41] The public bureaucracy cannot serve as the 'whipping boy' for politicians and the public and still attract large numbers of excellent young people into its ranks. Some would argue that highly competitive rates of pay are a critical element for a prestigious public sector,[42] but high rates of pay may not attract individuals with high levels of public service motivation.

National initiatives may serve as a catalyst for activating public service motivation. A charismatic leader or collective action can effectively transmit a call for public service. Current discussion in the U.S. Congress has focused on legislation that would provide public service opportunities for young people. These programs are intended to develop normative and affective bases of public service motivation. One idea is to provide a public service experience as a component of high school education. Another approach is to make financial aid for college contingent on public service.

Socialization or inculcation of motives, as Chester I. Barnard labeled it, can also be achieved through managerial techniques both in the pre-entry and entry stages of organizational membership.[43] The identification of common motives and the development of nationalistic motives are the techniques upon which military recruitment and training are based. Similarly, recent college graduates were recruited into a leading edge computer development company by a combination of incentives presented during the job interview process. The chance to participate in an important project, to create a prototype, was a key incentive for young engineers, but they were also attracted by the description of autonomy in job structure and the idea that only the best engineers would be offered jobs.[44]

Conclusion

This review suggests that while a crisis in government service is widely recognized, understanding the motives of public servants and the way to stimulate public service motivation are, at best, at a preliminary stage. The popular notion that man-

agement in government is not different from private business or industry runs counter to the development and advancement of a theory of public service motivation. The field lacks a clear definition of the different motives that people experience as well as a theoretical context for linking these motives to motivational strategies and incentive structures. Further, a more sophisticated understanding of the effects of cyclical factors on the value of public service employment is fundamental to the development of a working model. Finally, the relationship between individual value structures and the conduct of government remains a critical concern for administrative states where democracy is largely implemented by the bureaucracy.

Notes

1. Seymour Martin Lipset and William Schneiders, *The Confidence Gap* (Baltimore, MD: The Johns Hopkins University Press, 1987).

2. Charles H. Levine with the assistance of Rosslyn S. Kleeman, "The Quiet Crisis of the Civil Service: The Federal Personnel System at the Crossroads," Occasional Paper No. 7 (Washington: National Academy of Public Administration, December 1986).

3. *Report of the National Commission on the Public Service* (Washington: National Commission on the Public Service, March 1989).

4. George Schultz, "Public Service in America" (Washington: United States Department of State, Bureau of Public Affairs, Office of Public Communication, January 1989); and Elmer B. Staats, "Public Service and the Public Interest," *Public Administration Review,* vol. 48 (March/April 1988), pp. 601–605.

5. One of the first and most prominent statements of the public choice perspective is William A. Niskanen, Jr., *Bureaucracy and Representative Government* (Chicago: Aldine-Atherton, 1971).

6. See, among others, Peter Smith Ring and James L. Perry, "Reforming the Upper Levels of the Bureaucracy: A Longitudinal Study of the Senior Executive Service," *Administration and Society,* vol. 15 (May 1983), pp. 119–144; James L. Perry, "Merit Pay in the Public Sector: The Case for a Failure of Theory," *Review of Public Personnel Administration,* vol. 7 (Fall 1986), pp. 57–69; James L. Perry, Beth Ann Petrakis, and Theodore K. Miller, "Federal Merit Pay, Round II: An Analysis of the Performance Management Recognition System," *Public Administration Review,* vol. 49 (January/February 1989), pp. 29–37.

7. Staats, "Public Service and the Public Interest," p. 601.

8. For an earlier call for research on public service motivation, see Hal G. Rainey, "Reward Preferences Among Public and Private Managers: In Search of the Service Ethic," *American Review of Public Administration,* vol. 16 (Winter 1982), pp. 288–302.

9. David Knoke and Christine Wright-Isak, "Individual Motives and Organizational Incentive Systems," *Research in the Sociology of Organizations,* vol. 1 (1982), pp. 209–254.

10. Leonard D. White, *The Prestige Value of Public Employment* (Chicago: University of Chicago Press, 1929); Franklin P. Kilpatrick, Milton C. Cummings, Jr., and M. Kent Jennings *The Image of the Federal Service* (Washington: The Brookings Institution, 1964).

11. Herbert A. Simon, *Administrative Behavior,* 2d ed. (New York: Free Press, 1957), p. 116.

12. See, for example, Hal G. Rainey, "Public Agencies and Private Firms: Incentive Structures, Goals, and Individual Roles," *Administration and Society,* vol. 15 (August 1983), pp. 207–242, and J. Norman Baldwin, "Are We Really Lazy," *Review of*

Public Personnel Administration, vol. 4 (Spring 1984), pp. 80–89.

13. Steven Kelman, " 'Public Choice' and Public Spirit," *The Public Interest,* no. 87 (Spring 1987), pp. 80–94.

14. John Rawls, *A Theory of Justice* (Cambridge, MA: Belknap Press, 1971).

15. Anthony Downs, *Inside Bureaucracy* (Boston: Little Brown, 1967).

16. Kenneth John Meier, "Representative Bureaucracy: An Empirical Analysis," *The American Political Science Review,* vol. 70 (June 1975), pp. 526–542.

17. H. George Frederickson and David K. Hart, "The Public Service and the Patriotism of Benevolence," *Public Administration Review,* vol. 45 (September/October 1985), pp. 547–553.

18. See, for example, Anthony Downs, *Inside Bureaucracy.*

19. Gary L. Wamsley, Charles T. Goodsell, John A. Rohr, Camilla M. Stivers, Orion F. White, and James F. Wolf, "The Public Administration and the Governance Process: Refocusing the American Dialogue," in Ralph Clark Chandler, ed., *A Centennial History of an American Administrative State* (New York: The Free Press, 1987), pp. 291–317.

20. Barry D. Karl, "Louis Brownlow," *Public Administration Review,* vol. 39 (November/December 1979), pp. 511–516.

21. Kenneth Lasson, *Private Lives of Public Servants* (Bloomington: Indiana University Press, 1978), pp. 81–133.

22. Bruce Buchanan II, "Red Tape and the Service Ethic: Some Unexpected Differences Between Public and Private Managers," *Administration and Society,* vol. 4 (February 1975), pp. 423–444, and Frederick C. Mosher, *Democracy and the Public Service* (New York: Oxford University Press, 1968).

23. Hugh Heclo, *A Government of Strangers: Executive Politics in Washington* (Washington: Brookings Institution, 1977).

24. H. George Frederickson, "Toward a New

Public Administration," *Toward a New Public Administration: The Minnowbrook Perspective* (Scranton, PA: Chandler Publishing, 1971), pp. 309–331.

25. Stephen K. Blumberg, "Seven Decades of Public Administration: A Tribute to Luther Gulick," *Public Administration Review,* vol. 41 (March/April 1981), pp. 245–248.

26. Frederickson and Hart, "The Public Service and the Patriotism of Benevolence," *supra.*

27. Robert A. Caro, *The Power Broker: Robert Moses and the Fall of New York* (New York: Knopf, 1974), p. 85.

28. Greg R. Oldham and J. Richard Hackman, "Relationships Between Organizational Structure and Employee Reactions: Comparing Alternative Frameworks," *Administrative Science Quarterly,* vol. 26 (March 1981), pp. 66–83.

29. See James L. Perry and Lyman W. Porter, "Factors Affecting the Context for Motivation in Public Organizations," *Academy of Management Review,* vol. 7 (January 1982), pp. 89–98.

30. Rebecca M. Blank, "An Analysis of Workers' Choice Between Employment in the Public and Private Sectors," *Industrial and Labor Relations Review,* vol. 38 (January 1985), pp. 211–224.

31. James R. Rawls, Robert A. Ullrich, and Oscar Tivis Nelson, Jr., "A Comparison of Managers Entering or Reentering the Profit and Nonprofit Sectors," *Academy of Management Journal,* vol. 18 (September 1975), pp. 616–623.

32. Albert O. Hirschman, *Shifting Involvements: Private Interest and Public Action* (Princeton, NJ: Princeton University Press, 1982).

33. *Idem.*

34. See, for example, Marc Holzer and Jack Rabin, "Public Service: Problems, Professionalism, and Policy Recommendations," *Public Productivity Review,* no. 43 (Fall 1987), pp. 3–12.

35. Arthur N. Turner and Paul R. Lawrence, *Industrial Jobs and the Worker* (Cambridge, MA: Harvard Graduate School of Business Administration, 1965); Clifford Hurston, "Job Reconstruction in Progress," *Management World,* vol. 17 (March/April 1988), p. 19; Y. Fried and G. R. Ferris, "The Validity of the Job Characteristics Model: A Review and Meta-analysis," *Personnel Psychology,* vol. 40 (Summer 1987), pp. 287–322.

36. Edgar H. Schein, "Organizational Socialization and the Profession of Management," *Industrial Management Review,* vol. 9 (Winter 1968), pp. 1–15.

37. See Candace Hetzner, "Lessons for America One Hundred Years After Pendleton," *Public Productivity Review,* no. 43 (Fall 1987), pp. 15–30, and Frederickson and Hart, "The Public Service and the Patriotism of Benevolence."

38. Patricia W. Ingraham and B. Guy Peters, "The Conundrum of Reform: A Comparative Analysis," *Review of Public Personnel Administration,* vol. 8 (Summer 1988), pp. 3–16.

39. Hal G. Rainey, "Public Agencies and Private Firms: Incentive Structures, Goals, and Individual Roles," *supra.*

40. J. Norman Baldwin, "Are We Really Lazy," *supra.*

41. Marc Holzer and Jack Rabin, "Public Service: Problems, Professionalism and Policy Recommendations," *Public Productivity Review,* no. 43 (Fall 1987), pp. 3–13.

42. Twentieth Century Fund, *The Government's Managers: Report of the Twentieth Century Fund Task Force on the Senior Executive Service* (New York: Priority Press, 1987).

43. Chester I. Barnard, *The Functions of the Executive* (Cambridge, MA: Harvard University Press, 1938), pp. 150–152.

44. Tracy Kidder, *The Soul of a New Machine* (New York: Avon Books, 1981).

CASE STUDY 11

Introduction

The Border Patrol is the federal agency within the Justice Department's Immigration and Naturalization Service charged with securing the borders of the United States from illegal immigration and other activities. Traditionally, the agency measured its success—or failure—by counting the numbers of illegal aliens apprehended *after* they crossed the border into America. Since 1988 these apprehension rates rose steadily from approximately 800,000 to 1.2 million illegal aliens in 1993. That year the Border Patrol in El Paso, Texas, a major illegal alien crossing point in western Texas along the Rio Grande River, tried a new tactic: preventing aliens from crossing the border *before* they crossed, instead of catching them afterwards. Apprehensions dropped by 72 percent as a result, compared to a mere 3 percent drop along the entire southwest border during the same time frame in the first half of 1994. Ironically, although this experiment should have been "a success story" and its "inventor" praised, the reverse was true; the Border Patrol Headquarters in Washington were angry about "this success."

The following short case tells the story of Silvestre Reyes, the head of the El Paso Border Patrol, who formulated this new strategy for reducing the flow of illegal immigrants and who was himself a grandchild of Mexican immigrants. The case recounts how he created this strategy in his district, implemented it, and then to his surprise found it greeted with hostility by his superiors in Washington, D.C. At first, he faced enormous pressures to reverse his new approach for protecting the border, but then later it became widely adopted along the southwestern U.S.-Mexican border.

In one sense, this case is a story of program implementation, but on a deeper level, it can be read as a study of public service motivation. What drove Mr. Reyes to risk his career and start this new, highly controversial strategy, in the face of severe public criticism and scorn from his superiors? Was it money? Was it fame? Was it a promise of a promotion? Hardly. Rather, as the case underscores, Reyes was simply motivated by the desire to perform his job better and to get the Border Patrol to see their work as stopping illegal entries into the United States, not merely generating "good" statistics of apprehension rates.

As you read this case, try to think about what it tells us about the contemporary motivational issues concerning public administration which were outlined in the foregoing essay by Perry and Wise:

What factors, in your view, motivated Mr. Reyes to "buck the system" and initiate this new strategy for reducing the flow of illegal aliens into El Paso?

Why did he suddenly face so much opposition to his new strategy from his superiors in Washington? Could he have anticipated this opposition better and "defused it" beforehand? How did he eventually overcome this criticism?

In what ways did his new approach change the way the Border Patrol ultimately judged its own program effectiveness?

Does the case support or contradict the Perry/Wise thesis concerning the uniqueness of public sector personnel motivation? Do you agree or disagree that motivational factors in the public service fundamentaly differ from those in business? And if so, why do these differences persist?

Can you think of any prior cases in this text where the uniqueness of public service motivation was also evident (hint: Case 7)?

A Success at the Border Earned Only a Shrug

JOEL BRINKLEY

EL PASO—Silvestre Reyes, chief of the Border Patrol here, accomplished something no other officer of the Immigration and Naturalization Service ever had. He got the border in his sector under control. Not just for a brief, flashy demonstration, but permanently.

El Paso had been the nation's second-busiest border crossing for illegal aliens. Every day, 8,000 or more people waded across the Rio Grande, then melted into the city's Hispanic neighborhoods. But in September 1993, Mr. Reyes devised a new border-control tactic. He positioned 400 of his officers right on the border, forming a blockade of sorts. It brought illegal immigration to a virtual halt.

The strategy has been in effect for a year now, and the border here remains generally quiet. With that, Mr. Reyes is dispelling the widely held belief that the nation's borders cannot be controlled without Draconian, police-state tactics.

His tactic may not work as effectively everywhere, but to the residents of El Paso, Chief Reyes is a hero. And in other immigration service offices around the country, employees who despair of a lack of leadership at headquarters see Mr. Reyes as a glimmer of hope.

"There's no strategic vision coming out of Washington, but that fellow in El Paso, he kind of revolutionized the thinking," said an assistant district director in the Los Angeles office. "He showed Washington that you *can* control the border."

But as the success of Mr. Reyes's strategy became clear a year ago, his superiors in Washington did not

Source: "A Rare Success at the Border Brought Scant Official Praise," by J. Brinkley from *The New York Times*, September 14, 1994. Copyright © 1994 by The New York Times Company. Reprinted by permission.

seem to see it that way. Rather than encourage or congratulate him, they greeted Mr. Reyes's achievement with skepticism at best, hostility at worst, depending on whose version is believed.

"We got caught behind the curve," grumbled James A. Puleo, who, as an executive associate commissioner in Washington, was one of Mr. Reyes's supervisors. The operation's surprising success raised questions by others in Government—irritating Mr. Puleo and others at I.N.S. headquarters because they were not immediately able to answer them.

Mr. Reyes said: "Their general attitude was, they were uncomfortable about being put in this position. It was like a Laurel and Hardy movie: 'This is a fine mess you've gotten us into, Ollie.'"

Chris Sale, the Deputy Commissioner, demurs. "That was not a message we deliberately sent," she said, "but I can see how that would occur."

Ms. Sale was acting commissioner at the time because the Clinton Administration had not yet appointed someone to lead the agency. During the first days of Mr. Reyes's operation, she said, "those of us in Washington, frankly politically leaderless, needed to make sure that we didn't end up in a situation that anyone at a policy level would regret."

Casting Doubt on the Old Way

There were other considerations. Mr. Reyes's approach threw into question the fundamental Border Patrol strategy of the last several decades: Let aliens cross the border, then try to catch them. That way, the Patrol could demonstrate to Congress that it was catching more and more aliens every year and request ever larger budgets.

The Mexican Government, meanwhile, had long

been contending that anything impinging on the free migration of Mexican laborers was an affront to the nation's sovereignty. Now Mexican political commentators were calling the El Paso operation another example of American "xenophobia."

Soon, Mexico filed a diplomatic protest, and that upset the State Department. As a result of that and other complaints, "I still have pockmarks on my rear end from being chewed out," said Doug Kruhm, acting chief of the Border Patrol.

Several I.N.S. officials said some of the service's leaders had tried to persuade Mr. Reyes to call off the operation. "When it came right down to it," a senior official said, "they were uncomfortable with the idea of controlling the border."

Ms. Sale and Mr. Kruhm deny that.

"There were a lot of questions," Mr. Kruhm said. "It could have been a real mess. But I don't personally remember anyone saying, Let's back off of this."

Still, he added, at one point Washington, trying to save money, told Mr. Reyes, " 'Maybe you'll have to pull it in some—not do so much.' "

Applause for a 'Celebrity'

Today, almost a year later, Mr. Reyes is a celebrity of sorts among immigration experts, who see his work as a model for the service. And officials from other border states, some of them angry because illegal immigration increased in their areas after the border in El Paso was closed, are demanding that the I.N.S. apply his strategy in their districts, too.

The Border Patrol maintains offices all along the border, administratively separate from the immigration service's district offices but co-equal with them. And now Congress is giving the I.N.S. money for new Border Patrol agents so the service can replicate Mr. Reyes's "extremely effective border patrol model" in other areas, as a House report puts it. In fact, several Government officials said they saw the El Paso operation as the immigration service's only real success in recent years.

Now some officials at I.N.S. headquarters are taking credit for the operation.

"All Silvestre Reyes did was put into effect what was already being discussed in concept here," Mr. Puleo said with a dismissive tone.

"Puleo said that?" Mr. Reyes responded. "That's an irony. I'm really surprised, especially since I kept getting hammered at the time."

The Idea

Stopping Trouble Before It Starts

Mr. Reyes, 49, is the grandchild of Mexican immigrants who fled the war and violence in Mexico 80 years ago. Silver, as he is known, grew up the eldest of 10 children in a suburb of El Paso. After college, he served in Vietnam, and when he returned home, he took several Civil Service exams. As he tells it now, the Border Patrol was the first Federal agency to call.

He rose through the patrol's ranks and was named head of the McAllen sector in 1984, becoming the Border Patrol's first Hispanic sector chief. And it was in McAllen, in the lower Rio Grande Valley, that Mr. Reyes got the idea for his new border strategy.

There, as elsewhere, Mexicans poured across the border every day. Border Patrol officers caught as many as they could and logged the apprehensions. After that, they packed the Mexicans onto buses and drove them back across the border. Many returned the next day.

But in about 1988, Mr. Reyes started noticing that many of the aliens were coming from Central America, and they had to be sent home by plane. That quickly grew expensive. So instead of seizing the illegal aliens, Mr. Reyes decided to keep them out of the country in the first place.

A Wall of Officers

To do that he redeployed his men right on the border—"the line," in Border Patrol parlance.

"I figured that if we blocked the line," Mr. Reyes explained, "it would back up the aliens on the Mexican side and start causing them problems over there."

He named his operation "Hold the Line," and it worked. "But I didn't have the resources to keep it up," he said.

The normal strategy, grabbing people after they crossed the border, allowed Mr. Reyes to keep as many, or as few, agents on duty at one time as the budget permitted. But "Hold the Line" required a constant presence of hundreds of agents, so the overtime expenses grew ruinous. He called the operation off after six weeks.

Then a year ago, Mr. Reyes was reassigned to El Paso, and he found the Border Patrol office there running out of control. Thousands of illegal aliens were streaming across the Rio Grande without constraint. Border Patrol officers were chasing them through the streets, backyards and parking lots. Often the officers grabbed El Paso residents by mistake and demanded proof that they were citizens.

There had been brawls and shootings, accusations of abuse, and loud public protests. The city had risen up in outrage, and a Federal judge had ordered the patrol to stop questioning people based solely on their appearance.

"The sector was in trouble," Mr. Reyes said. Officials in Washington said they had asked him to calm things. He decided a radical new approach was needed. Just as he had in McAllen, the new chief planned to redeploy his men along the river—close the border for 30 days, except at the legal crossing points. This time he called it "Operation Blockade."

The Pitch

'They Thought I Was Crazy'

Mr. Reyes sent a proposal for "Operation Blockade" to Mr. Kruhm in Washington, along with a request for $525,000 to pay for the expected overtime and for fence repairs.

"They turned me down flat," Mr. Reyes said.

Mr. Kruhm said: "We had no funding for that in the program. We'd started that year with a $10 million deficit."

Another senior I.N.S. officer who spoke on the condition that his name not be used recalled the thinking among officials in Washington this way: "They were saying: 'Why in the hell does he want to do this? We don't have any money.' "

"As far as I was concerned," the official said, "nothing was going to happen."

Stories differ about what happened next. A senior official said Mr. Reyes had then called an officer he knew in the immigration service's financial office to see if he could come up with the money on his own.

The financial officer offered him about $300,000 in end-of-the-budget-year money that had to be spent.

Mr. Reyes said that account was "factual and accurate," and he added that Mr. Kruhm was openly irritated when he heard about it.

But Mr. Kruhm says that's not true. "I got the money for him," he insisted.

Whatever the truth, after the money arrived, Mr. Reyes briefed his officers, and they made it clear that they did not like their new orders.

"They thought I was crazy," Mr. Reyes said. "But I told them: 'I'm not interested in apprehensions. I'm not interested in generating numbers. I'm interested in controlling the border.' "

Mr. Reyes said he had also made headquarters "promise that I would not be penalized if I didn't have big apprehension numbers."

The Blockade

A Sunday Surprise Sets Off Ripples

The new strategy went into effect last year on Sunday morning, Sept. 19. Every Sunday, more than 10,000 Mexicans waded across the river to El Paso so they could show up for work the next morning. But when the Mexicans looked across the river that Sunday, they saw a Border Patrol vehicle stationed every 100 yards or so along the entire border. More than 400 agents were waiting for them, stretching from one end of the town to the other and beyond.

They couldn't get through. The border was closed and would stay closed.

The next day, merchants in downtown El Paso began complaining that sales were down; the Mexicans were not coming in to shop. Many other city residents were upset because their employees had not shown up for work.

But within a few days the residents of El Paso began to see other effects. The police reported that the number of auto thefts and petty crimes had fallen. Merchants reported that shoplifting had dropped off. And everyone noted that city streets were largely free of beggars and windshield washers.

At the same time, many of the Mexican workers who had been crossing the border illegally because it was so easy started applying for border-crossing permits. As the permits were granted, the Mexicans—most of them maids and gardeners and in other service jobs—began returning to work, and merchants said sales started to pick up again.

'Mexico Was Calling'

"By the end of the week," said Al Giugni, district director for the I.N.S. in El Paso, "it had grown bigger than life itself. Radio and television and newspaper people were talking about nothing else. And they did polls." Though unscientific, the results were consistent: all of the polls showed public approval of 80 percent to 95 percent.

But to the Border Patrol in El Paso, Washington seemed unimpressed.

"The embassy in Mexico was calling," Ms. Sale, the Deputy Commissioner, said. "We got beaten up for not consulting the Mexican Government first. The Mexicans didn't like the name Operation Blockade, and certainly there were persons in the State Department who'd have been happier if it didn't happen."

At the time, the Administration was trying to win Congressional approval of the North American Free Trade Agreement, and the State Department was trying to be especially considerate of Mexican interests.

As a result, "we were asking a lot of questions" of Mr. Reyes, Mr. Kruhm added, "and I'm sure the people in El Paso felt we were not supporting them."

In calls to Mr. Reyes, officials familiar with the conversations said, his supervisors told him the operation was jeopardizing the trade agreement and causing other problems as well. During one conference call, two officials said, Mr. Reyes finally became exasperated and asked, Are you telling me to call this off?

If so, he went on to say, then he was going to hold a news conference and give out the name of the official at headquarters who had ordered him to do it.

Mr. Kruhm said: "He could have said that, but he was under a lot of pressure then. We were all under a lot of pressure."

The Aftermath

Changing a Name, And Some Minds

Even though he was getting little support from headquarters, when the 30 days were up Mr. Reyes decided to maintain the new border deployment permanently. He did make one concession. Since the Mexicans disliked the name Operation Blockade, he adopted another one, the one he had used for that first operation in McAllen: "Hold the Line."

Whatever their feelings in the early days, the officials at headquarters have given Mr. Reyes some new personnel this year to help him maintain the operation. And no matter how the service's leaders felt about Operation Blockade a year ago, it is clear that Mr. Reyes has brought changes in thinking at headquarters today.

"The operation was initiated by the chief," Mr. Kruhm says, "but now we have initiated similar operations in other areas, in South Texas. There was no fanfare, but they worked. They were very effective."

There has been another change, too.

"We are now trying to get away from using apprehensions as a measure of effectiveness," Mr. Kruhm said. "We really aren't getting anywhere when we go to Congress and say we made a million apprehensions last year.

"I think we should be saying how many people we prevented from coming in."

Chapter 11 Review Questions

1. In your own words, can you describe the Perry and Wise concept of rational, norm-based, affective motives? What do the authors mean by those terms?

What assumptions about human nature does their motivational concept rest upon? Do you believe these are valid assumptions?

2. Why do Perry and Wise argue that business motivational theories have limited application to the public sector? Do you agree or disagree? Why or why not?

3. Regarding the foregoing case study, "A Success at the Border Earned Only a Shrug," describe the various cross-pressures and multiple responsibilities that the head of the U.S. Border Patrol in El Paso, Texas, Silvestre Reyes, faced. Why do these persisting cross-pressures and responsibilities make it so difficult, if not impossible, to frame a clear, consistent motivational system for public officials like Mr. Reyes?

4. If indeed he "earned only a shrug" for his efforts, what can reward successful performance of an offical like Mr. Reyes? Do these motives come from rational, norm-based, affective motives that Perry and Wise's essay would theorize? Why or why not?

5. Given the difficult realities of the contemporary working environment of public administration today, how would you develop and implement an effective motivational system for a government agency? Assess some of the strengths and weaknesses of this system that you envisioned.

6. Select any one of the prior cases in this text and examine carefully the motivations of one or a few of the public officials in this case. How do these motives compare and contrast with those discussed in Case 11—are they the same or fundamentally different and why?

Key Terms

rational motives
norm-based motives
affective motives
normative orientation
renewal of public service

self-interested motives
"quiet crisis" in the federal service
advocacy of a special interest
loyalty to duty

Suggestions for Further Reading

Public personnel administration is a field of enormous complexity, specialization, and rapid change, and, therefore, looking at several basic introductory texts is necessary for a good overview: N. Joseph Cayer, *Public Personnel Administration in the U.S.,* Third Edition (New York: St. Martin's, 1996); Jonathan Beck, *Managing People in Public Agencies* (Boston: Little, Brown, 1984); Gilbert B. Siegel and Robert C. Myrtle, *Public Personnel Administration: Concepts and Practices* (Boston: Houghton Mifflin, 1991); Steven W. Hays and Richard C. Kearney, *Public Personnel Adminis-*

tration, Second Edition (Englewood Cliffs, N.J.: Prentice-Hall, 1990); Lloyd G. Nigro and Felix A. Nigro, *The New Public Personnel Administration,* Fourth Edition (Itasca, Ill.: F. E. Peacock Publishers, Inc., 1995); Carolyn Ban and Norma Riccucci, *Public Personnel Management* (New York: Longman, 1991); Donald Klinger and John Nalbandian, *Public Personnel Management,* Third Edition (Englewood Cliffs, N.J.: Prentice-Hall, 1993); and Dennis D. Riley, *Public Personnel Administration* (New York: Harper Collins, 1993). To supplement these introductions, students should further examine the basic *framing* documents of public personnel, such as the Civil Service Act of 1883, the Hatch Act, the Civil Service Reform Act of 1978, as well as several others contained in Frederick C. Mosher, ed., *Basic Documents of American Public Administration: 1776–1950* (New York: Holmes and Meier, 1976), and Richard J. Stillman II, ed., *Basic Documents of American Public Administration: Since 1950* (New York: Holmes and Meier, 1982).

For the best history of the American civil service system, see Paul Van Riper, *History of U.S. Civil Service* (New York: Harper & Row, 1958). For an insightful view of personnel practices at the local level, read Frank J. Thompson, *Personnel Policy in the City: The Politics of Jobs in Oakland* (Berkeley, Calif.: University of California Press, 1975); and for a view of its operation at the federal level, see Frederick C. Mosher, *Democracy and the Public Service,* Second Edition (New York: Oxford University Press, 1982); William I. Bacchus, *Staffing for Foreign Affairs* (Princeton: Princeton University Press, 1983); or Hugh Heclo, *A Government of Strangers: Executive Politics in Washington* (Washington, D.C.: The Brookings Institution, 1977). Articles contained in the two volumes of the "classics" series on personnel give readers a useful overview of the scope, diversity, and complexity of this field: Thomas H. Pattern, Jr., ed., *Classics of Personnel Management* (Chicago: Moore Publishing Co., 1979), and Frank J. Thompson, ed., *Classics of Public Personnel Policy,* Second Edition (Monterey, Calif.: Brooks/Cole, 1990), as well as a more contemporary set of readings in Patricia W. Ingraham and Barbara Romzek, eds., *Rethinking Public Personnel Systems* (San Francisco: Jossey-Bass, 1994), and part 6 of James L. Perry, *Handbook of Public Administration* (San Francisco: Jossey-Bass, 1989). "Further Readings" in chapters 6, 7, and 14 of this text offer additional references.

Among the articles on federal personnel, some of the more interesting ones include Benton G. Moeller, "What Ever Happened to the Federal Personnel System," *International Personnel Management,* 9 (Spring 1982), pp. 1–8; Bernard Rosen, "Uncertainty in the Senior Executive Service," *Public Administration Review,* 41 (March/April 1981), pp. 203–207; Norton E. Long, "S.E.S. and the Public Interest," *Public Administration Review,* 41 (May/June 1981), pp. 305–312; as well as the entire symposium on "The Public Service as an Institution," edited by Eugene B. McGregor, Jr., which contains several fine short essays on the subject, in *Public Administration Review,* 42 (July/August 1982), pp. 304–320. The Hudson Institute, *Civil Service 2000* (Washington, D.C.: U.S. Office of Personnel Management, 1988), offers interesting data on the future trends of public personnel, and Charles H. Levine and Rosslyn S. Kleeman, "The Quiet Crisis of the Civil Service" (Washington, D.C.: National Academy of Public Administration, 1988), are also useful.

For a comprehensive look that explains the state-of-the-art of public personnel labor relations see Richard C. Kearney, *Labor Relations in the Public Sector,* Second Edition (New York: Marcel Dekker, 1992); and Jack Rabin et al., eds., *Handbook of Public Sector Labor Relations* (New York: Marcel Dekker, 1994). One would also do well to skim current issues of *Public Administration Review, Harvard Business Review, Public Personnel Management, The Bureaucrat,* and *Public Management* for recent and fast-changing trends in the field of personnel.

One should not miss reading the Volcker Commission Report for an updated review of this topic, *Leadership for America* (Lexington, Mass.: Lexington Books, 1990); or for the local level, Frank J. Thompson, ed., *Revitalizing State and Local Government* (San Francisco: Jossey-Bass, 1993).

Endnotes in Perry/Wise essay give excellent sources for further readings on personnel motivation, also see chapters 6 and 7 in Hal G. Rainey, *Understanding and Managing Public Organizations* (San Francisco: Jossey-Bass, 1991) and Norma M. Riccucci's *Unsung Heroes* (Washington, D.C.: Georgetown University Press, 1995) offers good examples of what motivates outstanding federal executives.

CHAPTER 12

Public Budgeting: The Concept of Budgeting as Political Choice

The essence of budgeting is that it allocates scarce resources and hence implies choice between potential objects of expenditure. Budgeting implies balance and it requires some kind of decision-making process.

Irene S. Rubin

READING 12

Introduction

Budgets serve many important functions in government. In one sense, budgets are contracts annually agreed on by the executive and legislative branches that allow executive agencies and departments to raise and spend public funds in specified ways for the coming fiscal year (normally running in state and local governments from July 1 to June 30; changed at the federal level by the Congressional Budget Act of 1974 to end on September 30 and to begin October 1 each year). A budget imposes a mutual set of legal obligations between the elected and appointed officers of public organizations with regard to taxation and expenditure policies. A budget is, therefore, a legal contract that provides a vehicle for fiscal controls over subordinate units of government by the politically elected representatives of the people.

Budgets have other purposes as well: they can be planning devices used to translate presently scarce fiscal and human resources in the public sector into future governmental goals and programs. In this respect, budgets are vital instruments for directing what tasks government will perform and how human talent in society and public monies will be used.

In addition, budgets are forces for internal coordination and efficiency in public administration. Budget formulations annually impose choices concerning how public programs should be undertaken, interrelated, and measured in terms of their value, effectiveness, and worth to the general public. Related to the concept of budgets as a coordinating device is the idea that budgets are economic documents. In this role federal budgets are tools of fiscal policy, for they stimulate or slow down national economic growth through increased or decreased taxation or revenue expenditures.

Finally, budgets can also be viewed as political documents, reflecting through the allocation of funds the ultimate desires, interests, and power of various groups within the body politic as expressed by elected legislative bodies. In setting up an annual budget, various political participants engage in log rolling, compromises, and bargains to create a document that by and large mirrors the current priorities of the locality, state, or nation. The quality and quantity of government that the citizenry desires and will support at any given time is expressed by the budget.

Our conceptual understanding of these roles of the budget in modern government is comparatively new, being chiefly a twentieth-century phenomenon. In large part, our instituting formal budget documents began in the Progressive Era, when public budgets were developed as vehicles for governmental reform to produce improved economy and efficiency in the public sector and as instruments for imposing greater control over public spending. Many of these ideas and concepts were borrowed from the experience and practices of business management.

Although there remains a strong emphasis on the earlier notions of budgets as vehicles for imposing control, economy, and efficiency in government, a prominent current view of the role of budgets—and a perspective frequently held by political scientists, budgeting specialists, and public administration practitioners—is a political one: budgets are principally governed by considerations of compromise, strategy, and bargaining. Irene S. Rubin, a political scientist and prominent authority on public budgeting at Northern Illinois University, presents the political view of budget making in the opening chapter of her book *The Politics of Public Budgeting*. Rubin envisions government budgets as "not merely technical managerial documents" but rather "they are also intrinsically and irreducibly political." Her thesis is that although public budgets share many features of budgeting in general such as presenting choices over possible expenditures and problems of balancing revenues with expenditures, they differ in fundamental ways. The open environments within which budgets are developed, the variety of actors involved, the constraints imposed as well as the emphasis on public accountability, give budgets special and distinctive features in the public sector. These aspects add complexity and unique dilemmas to their formulation, operation, and conceptualization.

Professor Rubin's essay at the outset defines "what is budgeting" and the distinctive features of government budgets. From a local case of budget making in Dekalb, Illinois, she underscores the critical political dynamics of public budgeting processes and the variety of participants that are involved, even within the local setting. The elements of budgetary politics concern, in her view, "separate but linked" decision clusters, specifically five clusters dealing with the revenue process (How much income will be available and from where?); budget process (How to make the budget choices?); expenditure process (Which programs will get what?); the balance cluster (How revenues and expenditures will be balanced?); and budget implementation issues (How the budget will be put into operation?). Her essay concludes with an important distinction between understanding "macrobudgeting," or top-down budget viewpoints, versus "microbudgeting," which focuses on the specific actors and their strategies in putting together budgets.

As you read the following selection, keep in mind such questions as:

Why does Rubin stress throughout her writing the political over the technical or managerial aspects of public budgeting?

What differences are apparent from her perspective between government and business budget-making? Do you agree with her conclusions about these fundamental differences?

How do "macro" and "micro" points of view of budgets differ and yet why are *both* essential for a complete understanding of the budgetary process? What are the advantages and disadvantages of both ways of conceptualizing budgets? Do these perspectives on budgets relate to any of our earlier readings such as Charles Lindblom's "incremental decision-making model"?

Why does Rubin focus on understanding modern budgetary processes as "separate but linked decision clusters"? What are the major clusters of issues apparent in each?

The Politics of Public Budgets

IRENE S. RUBIN

Public budgets describe what governments do by listing how governments spend money. A budget links tasks to be performed with the amount of resources necessary to accomplish those tasks, ensuring that money will be available to wage war, provide housing, or maintain streets. Budgets limit expenditures to the revenues available, to ensure balance and prevent overspending. Most of the work in drawing up a budget is technical, estimating how much it will cost to feed a thousand shut-ins with a Meals on Wheels program or how much revenue will be produced from a 1 percent tax on retail sales. But public budgets are not merely technical managerial documents; they are also intrinsically and irreducibly political.

- Budgets reflect choices about what government will and will not do. They reflect general public consensus about what kinds of services governments should provide and what citizens are entitled to as members of society. Should government provide services that the private sector could provide, such as water, electricity, transportation, and housing? Do all citizens have a guarantee of health care, regardless of ability to pay? Are all insured against hunger? Are they entitled to some kind of housing?
- Budgets reflect priorities—between police and flood control, day care and defense, the Northeast and the Southwest. The budget process mediates between groups and individuals who want different things from government and determines who gets what. These decisions may influence whether the poor get job training or the police get riot training, both as a response to an increased number of unemployed.
- Budgets reflect the relative proportion of decisions made for local and constituency pur-

poses, and for efficiency, effectiveness, and broader public goals. Budgets reflect the degree of importance legislators put on satisfying their constituents and the legislators' willingness to listen to interest-group demands. For example, the Defense Department may decide to spend more money to keep a military base open because the local economy depends on it and to spend less money to improve combat readiness.

- Budgets provide a powerful tool of accountability to citizens who want to know how the government is spending their money and if government has generally followed their preferences. Budgeting links citizen preferences and governmental outcomes.
- Budgets reflect citizens' preferences for different forms of taxation and different levels of taxation, as well as the ability of specific groups of taxpayers to shift tax burdens to others. The budget reflects the degree to which the government redistributes wealth upward or downward through the tax system.
- At the national level, the budget influences the economy, so fiscal policy affects the level of employment—how many people are out of work at any time.
- Budgets reflect the relative power of different individuals and organizations to influence budget outcomes. Budgetary decision making provides a picture of the relative power of budget actors within and between branches of government, as well as the importance of citizens in general and specific interest groups.

In all these ways, public budgeting is political. But budgeting is not typical of other political processes and hence one example among many. It is both an important and a unique arena of politics. It is important because of the specific policy issues reflected in the budget: the scope of government, the distribution of wealth, the openness of government to interest groups, and the accountability of government to the public at large. It is unique

because these decisions have to take place in the context of budgeting, with its need for balance, its openness to the environment, and its requirements for timely decisions so that government can carry on without interruption.

Public budgets clearly have political implications, but what does it mean to say that key political decisions are made in the context of budgeting? The answer has several parts. First, what is budgeting? Second, what is public budgeting, as opposed to individual or family budgeting or the budgeting of private organizations? Third, what does *political* mean in the context of public budgeting?

What Is Budgeting?

The essence of budgeting is that it allocates scarce resources and hence implies choice between potential objects of expenditure. Budgeting implies balance, and it requires some kind of decision-making process.

Making Budgetary Choices

All budgeting, whether public or private, individual or organizational, involves choices between possible expenditures. Since no one has unlimited resources, people budget all the time. A young child makes a budget (a plan for spending, balancing revenues and expenditures) when she decides to spend money on a marshmallow rabbit rather than a chocolate one, assuming she has money enough for only one rabbit. The air force may choose between two different airplanes to replace current bombers. These examples illustrate the simplest form of budgeting because they involve only one actor, one resource, one time, and two straightforward and comparable choices.

Normally, budgeting does not take place by comparing only two reasonably similar items. There may be a nearly unlimited number of choices. Budgeting usually limits the options to consider by grouping together similar things that can be reasonably compared. When I go to the supermarket, I do not compare all the possible things I could buy, not only because I cannot absorb that number of comparisons, but because the comparisons would be meaningless and a waste of time. I do not go to the supermarket and decide to get either a turkey or a bottle of soda pop. I compare main dishes with main dishes, beverages with beverages, desserts with desserts. Then I have a common denominator for comparison. For example, I may look at the main course and ask about the amount of protein for the dollar. I may compare the desserts in terms of the amount of cholesterol or the calories.

There is a tendency, then, to make comparisons within categories where the comparison is meaningful. This is as true for governmental budgeting as it is for shoppers. For example, weapons might be compared with weapons or automobiles with automobiles. They could be compared in terms of speed, reliability, availability of spare parts, and so on, and the one that did the most of what you wanted it to do at the least cost would be the best choice. As long as there is agreement on the goals to be achieved, the choice should be straightforward.

Sometimes, budgeting requires comparison of different, and seemingly incomparable things. If I do not have enough money to buy a whole balanced meal, I may have to make choices between main dishes and desserts. How do I compare the satisfaction of a sweet tooth to the nourishment of a turkey? Or, in the public sector, how do I compare the benefits of providing shelters for the homeless with buying more helicopters for the navy? I may then move to more general comparisons, such as how clearly were the requests made and the benefits spelled out; who got the benefits last time and whose turn is it this time; are there any specific contingencies that make one choice more likely than the other? For example, will we be embarrassed to show our treatment of the homeless in front of a visiting dignitary? Or, are disarmament negotiations coming up in which we need to display strength or make a symbolic gesture of restraint? Comparing dissimilar items may require a list of priorities. It may be possible to do two or

more important things if they are sequenced properly.

Budgeting often allocates money, but it can allocate any scarce resource, for example, time. A student may choose between studying for an exam or playing softball and drinking beer afterward. In this example, it is time that is at a premium, not money. Or it could be medical skills that are in short supply, or expensive equipment, or apartment space, or water.

Government programs often involve a choice of resources and sometimes involve combinations of resources, each of which has different characteristics. For example, some federal farm programs involve direct cash payments plus loans at below-market interest rates, and welfare programs often involve dollar payments plus food stamps, which allow recipients to pay less for food. Federal budgets often assign agencies money, personnel, and sometimes borrowing authority, three different kinds of resources.

Balancing and Borrowing

Budgets have to balance. A plan for expenditures that pays no attention to ensuring that revenues cover expenditures is not a budget. That may sound odd in view of huge federal deficits, but a budget may technically be balanced by borrowing. Balance means only that outgo is matched or exceeded by income. The borrowing, of course, has to be paid off. Borrowing means spending more now and paying more in the future in order to maintain balance. It is a balance over time.

To illustrate the nature of budget balance, consider me as shopper again. Suppose I spend all my weekly shopping money before I buy my dessert. I have the option of treating my dollar limit as if it were more flexible, by adding the dimension of time. I can buy the dessert and everything else in the basket, going over my budget, and then eat less at the end of the month. Or I can pay the bill with a credit card, assuming I will have more money in the future with which to pay off the bill when it comes due. The possibility of borrowing against the future is part of most budget choices.

Process

Budgeting cannot proceed without some kind of decision process. Even in the simplest cases of budgeting, there has to be some limit set to spending, some order of decision making, some way to structure comparisons among alternatives, and some way to compare choices. Budget processes also regulate the flow of decisions so they are made in a timely manner.

Back to my shopping example: If I shop for the main course first, and spend more money than I intended on it because I found some fresh fish, there will be less money left for purchasing the dessert. Hence, unless I set a firm limit on the amount of money to spend for each segment of the meal, the order in which I do the purchasing counts. Of course, if I get to the end of my shopping and do not have enough money left for dessert, I can put back some of the items already in the cart and squeeze out enough money for dessert.

Governmental budgeting is also concerned with procedures for managing tradeoffs between large categories of spending. Budgeters may determine the relative importance of each category first, attaching a dollar level in proportion to the assigned importance, or they may allow purchasing in each area to go on independently, later reworking the choices until the balance between the parts is acceptable.

The order of decisions is important in another sense. I can determine how much money I am likely to have first and then set that as an absolute limit on expenditures, or I can determine what I must have, what I wish to have, and what I need to set aside for emergencies and then go out and try to find enough money to cover some or all of those expenditures. Especially in emergencies, such as accidents or other health emergencies, people are likely to obligate the money first and worry about where it will come from later. Governmental budgeting, too, may concentrate first on revenues and later on expenditures, or first on expenditures and later on income. Like individuals or families, during emergencies such as floods or hurricanes or wars, governments will commit the expenditures first and worry about where the money will come from later.

Governmental Budgeting

Public budgeting shares the characteristics of budgeting in general but differs from household and business budgeting in some key ways. First, in public budgeting, there are always people and organizations with different perspectives and different goals trying to get what they want out of the budget. In individual budgets, there may be only one person involved; and in family and business budgets, there may be only a limited number of actors and they may have similar views of what they want to achieve through the budget.

Second, public budgets are more open to the environment than budgets of families or businesses are. Not only are public budgets open to the economy but also to other levels of government, to citizens, to interest groups, to the press, and to politicians.

Third, budgets form a crucial link between citizen taxpayers and government officials. The document itself may be a key form of accountability. This function does not apply to businesses, families, or individuals.

Fourth, public budgeting is characterized by a variety of constraints, legal limits, perceived limits imposed by public opinion, rules and regulations about how to carry out the budget, and many more. Public budgeting is far more constrained in this sense than budgets of individuals or businesses.

Public budgeting has five particular characteristics that differentiate it from other kinds of budgeting. First, public budgeting is characterized by a variety of budgetary actors who often have different priorities and different levels of power over budget outcomes. These actors have to be regulated and orchestrated by the budget process. Second, in government there is a distinction between those who pay taxes and those who decide how money will be spent—the citizens and the elected politicians. Public officials can force citizens to pay taxes for expenditures they do not want, but citizens can vote politicians out of office. Third, the budget document is important as a means of public accountability. Fourth, public budgets are very vulnerable to the environment—to the economy, to changes in public opinion, to elections, to local contingencies such as natural disasters like floods, or political disasters such as the police bombing of MOVE headquarters in Philadelphia, which burned down part of a neighborhood. Fifth, public budgets are incredibly constrained. Although there is a built-in necessity to make budgets adaptable to contingencies, there are many elements of public budgets that are beyond the immediate control of those who draw up budgets.

A Variety of Actors

The first characteristic of public budgeting was the variety of actors involved in the budget and their frequently clashing motivations and goals. On a regular basis, bureau chiefs, executive budget officers, and chief executives are involved in the budget process, as are legislators, both on committees and as a whole group. Interest groups may be involved at intervals, sometimes for relatively long stretches of time, sometimes briefly. Sometimes citizens play a direct or indirect role in the budget process. Courts may play a role in budgets at any level of government at unpredictable intervals. When they do play a role in budgetary decisions, what are these actors trying to achieve?

Bureau Chiefs. Many students of budgeting assume that agency heads always want to expand their agencies, that their demands are almost limitless, and that it is up to other budget actors to curtail and limit their demands. The reasons given for that desire for expansion include prestige, more subordinates, more space, larger desks, more secretaries, and not incidentally, more salary. The argument presumes that agency heads judge their bureaucratic skills in terms of the satisfaction of their budget requests. Successful bureaucrats bring back the budget. Agency expansion is the measure of success.

Recent research has suggested that while some bureaucrats may be motivated by salaries, many feel that one of their major rewards is the opportunity to do good for people—to house the homeless, feed the hungry, find jobs for the unemployed, and send out checks to the disabled.[1] For these bureaucrats, efforts to expand agency budgets are the result of their belief in the programs they work for.

Recent research has also suggested that the bureaucracy has become more professional, which introduces the possibility of another motivation, the desire to do a good job, to do it right, to put in the best machinery that exists or build the biggest, toughest engineering project or the most complicated weapons.

The generalization that bureaucrats always press for budget increases appears to be too strong. Some agencies are much more aggressive in pushing for growth than others. Some are downright moribund. Sometimes agency heads refuse to expand when given the opportunity,[2] suggesting there are some countervailing values to growth. One of these countervailing values is agency autonomy. Administrators may prefer to maintain autonomy rather than increase the budget if it comes down to a choice between the two. A second countervailing value to growth is professionalism, the desire to get the job done, and do it quickly and right. Administrators generally prefer to hire employees who have the ability to get the job done, plus a little, spare amount of intelligence, motivation, and energy just in case they need to get some extra work done or do it fast in response to a political request.[3] Administrators may refuse to add employees if the proposed employees do not add to the agency's capacity to get things done.

A third countervailing value is program loyalty. Expansion may be seen as undesirable if the new mission swamps the existing mission, if it appears contradictory to the existing mission, or if the program requires more money to carry out than is provided, forcing the agency to spend money designated for existing programs on new ones or do a poor job.

A fourth countervailing value is belief in the chain of command. Many, if not all, bureaucrats believe that their role is to carry out the policies of the chief executive and the legislature. If those policies mean cutting back budgets, agency heads cut back the agencies. Agency heads may be appointed precisely because they are willing to make cuts in their agencies.[4]

Bureaucrats, then, do not always try to expand their agencies' budgets. They have other, competing goals, which sometimes dominate. Also, their achievements can be measured by other than expanded budgets. They may go for some specific items in the budget without raising totals, or may try for changes in the wording of legislation. They may strive to get a statutory basis for the agency and security of funding. They may take as a goal providing more efficient and effective service, rather than expanded or more expensive service.

The Executive Budget Office. The traditional role of the budget office has been to scrutinize requests coming up from the agencies, to find waste and eliminate it, and to discourage most requests for new money. The executive budget office has been perceived as the naysayer, the protector of the public purse. Most staff members in the budget office are very conscious of the need to balance the budget, to avoid deficits, and to manage cash flow so that there is money on hand to pay bills. Hence they tend to be skeptical of requests for new money.

In recent years, however, there has been a change in the role of budget office. At the national level under President Ronald Reagan, budgeting became much more top-down, with the director of the Office of Management and Budget (OMB) proposing specific cuts and negotiating them directly with Congress, without much scrutiny of requests coming up from departments or bureaus. OMB became more involved in trying to accomplish the policy goals of the President through the budget.[5] At state levels too, there has been an evolution of budget staff from more technical to more political and more policy-related goals. When the governor is looking for new spending proposals these may come from his budget office.

Chief Executive Officers. The role of chief executive officers (the mayor or city manager, the governor, the President) is highly variable, and hence these executives' goals in the budget process cannot be predicted without knowledge of the individuals. Some chief executives have been expansive, proposing new programs; others have been economy minded, cutting back proposals generated by the legislatures. Some have been efficiency oriented, reorganizing staffs and trying to maintain service levels without increases in taxes or expenditures.

Legislators. Legislators have sometimes been described as always trying to increase expenditures.[6] Their motivation is viewed as getting reelected, which depends on their ability to provide constituents services and deliver "pork"—jobs and capital projects—to their districts. Norms of reciprocity magnify the effects of these spending demands because legislators are reluctant to cut others' pork lest their own be cut in return. At the city level, a council member described this norm of reciprocity, "There is an unwritten rule that if something is in a councilman's district, we'll go along and scratch each other's back."[7]

For some legislators, however, getting reelected is not a high priority. They view elected office as a service they perform for the community rather than a career, and while they may be responsive to constituents' needs, they are simply not motivated to start new projects or give public employees a raise in order to get reelected. Also, some legislators feel secure about the possibility of reelection, and hence have no urgent need to deliver pork in order to increase their chances of reelections.[8]

Even assuming the motivation to get reelected, holding down taxes may be as important to reelection as spending on programs and projects. The consequence of tax reduction is usually curtailed expenditures. Legislators are bound to try to balance the budget, which puts some constraints on the desire to spend.

The tendency to provide pork is real, but there are counterbalancing factors. Some legislators are more immune to pressures from constituents because they are secure electorally, and legislators can organize themselves in such a way as to insulate themselves somewhat from these pressures. They can, for example, select more electorally secure representatives for key positions on appropriations committees; they can separate committees that deal extensively with interest groups from those that deal with expenditures; they can set up buffer groups to deal with interest groups; they can structure the budget process so that revenue limits precede and guide spending proposals.

Moreover, legislators have interests other than providing pork. Some legislators are deeply concerned about solving social problems, designing and funding defense and foreign aid systems, and monitoring the executive branch. The proportion of federal budget spent on pork-type projects has declined in recent years, despite reforms in Congress that decentralized control and allowed pressure for pork to increase.[9] "Congressmen are not single-minded seekers of local benefits, struggling feverishly to win every last dollar for their districts. However important the quest for local benefits may be, it is always tempered by other competing concerns."[10] The pull for local benefits depends on the program. Some, like water projects, are oriented to local payoffs; others, like entitlements programs for large numbers of people, are not. Programs with local pull account for smaller and smaller proportions of the budget[11] and the trend has accelerated since 1978.[12]

Interest Groups. Interest groups, too, have often been singled out as the driving force behind budget increases. They are said to want more benefits for their members and to be undeterred by concerns for overall budget balance or the negative effects of tax increases. Moreover, their power has been depicted as great. Well-funded interest groups reportedly wine and dine legislators and provide campaign funding for candidates who agree with their positions.

There is some truth to this picture, but it is over-simplified. Interest groups have other policy goals besides budget levels. In fact, most probably deal with the budget only when a crisis occurs, such as a threat to funding levels. Because they can be counted on to come to the defense of a threatened program, they reduce the flexibility of budget decision makers, who find it difficult to cut programs with strong interest-group backing. But many areas of the budget do not have strong interest-group backing. For example, foreign aid programs have few domestic constituencies. Agencies may even have negative constituencies, that is, interest groups that want to reduce their funding and terminate their programs. The American Medical Association sought for years to eliminate the Health Planning Program.

Often when there are interest groups, there are many rather than one, and these interest groups may have conflicting styles or conflicting goals, canceling one another out or absorbing energy in battles among themselves. A coalition of interest groups representing broad geographic areas and a variety of constituencies is likely to be more effective at lobbying.

Hence coalitions may form, but individual members of the coalition may not go along with measures supported by others, so the range of items lobbied for as a unified group may be narrow. Extensive negotiations and continual efforts are required to get two or more independent groups together for a lobbying effort, and the arrangement can then fall apart. In short, interest groups are often interested in maintaining their autonomy.

Individuals. Individuals seldom have a direct role in the budget process, as they did in the DeKalb case, but they often have an indirect role. They may vote on referenda to limit revenues, forbid some forms of taxation, or require budgetary balance. They voice their opinions also in public opinion polls, and more informally by calling or writing their elected representatives and giving their opinions. Their knowledge of the budget is not usually detailed, but their feelings about the acceptability of taxation are an important part of the constraints of public budgeting. Their preferences for less visible taxes and for taxes earmarked for specific approved expenditures have been an important factor in public budgeting.

The Courts. Another budget actor that plays an intermittent role in determining expenditures is the courts.[13] The courts get involved when other actors, often interest groups, bring a case against the government. Suits that affect the budget may involve service levels or the legality of particular forms of taxation. If a particular tax is judged unconstitutional, the result is usually lost revenues. If there are suits concerning levels of service, governments may be forced to spend more money on that service. There can also be damage suits against governments that affect expenditures. These suits are usually settled without regard to the government agencies' ability to pay. The result may be forced cuts in other areas of the budget, tax increases, or even bankruptcy. When the courts get involved, they may determine budget priorities. They introduce a kind of rigidity into the budget that says do this, or pay this, first.

Typical areas in which courts have gotten involved and mandated expenditures for state and local governments are prison overcrowding (declared cruel and unusual punishment) and deinstitutionalization of mentally ill and mentally handicapped patients. In each case, the rights of the institutionalized population required more services or more space, often involving expenditures of additional funds. From the perspective of the courts, the priority of rights outweighs immediate concerns for budget balances, autonomy of governmental units, and local priorities.

Power Differentials. These various actors not only have different and potentially clashing budgetary goals, but they typically have different levels of power. Thus, at times, the budget office may completely dominate the agencies; at times, the Congress may differ from the President on budgetary policy and pass its own preferences. The courts may preempt the decision making of the executive and the legislature. Some particular interest groups may always be able to get tax breaks for themselves.

The combination of different preferences and different levels of power has to be orchestrated by the budget process in such a way that agreement is reached, and the players stay in the game, continuing to abide by the rules. If some actors feel too powerless over the budget, they may cease to participate or become obstructionist, blocking any agreements or imposing rigid, nonnegotiable solutions. Why participate in negotiations and discussions if the decision will go against you regardless of what you do? If some actors lose on important issues, they may try to influence budget implementation to favor themselves. Or the actors with less budget power may try to change the budget process so that they have a better chance of influencing the outcomes.

The Separation of Payer and Decider

The second feature of public budgeting is that decisions about how money will be spent are made not by those providing the money but by their representatives. The payers and the deciders are two distinct groups. The payers are not given a choice about whether they want to pay or how much they want to pay. The power of the state may force them to pay. They may protest if they do not like how their money is being spent, and elect new representatives. They cannot, generally, take their money and do something else with it.

The distinction between the payers and the deciders leads to two crucial characteristics of public budgeting: public *accountability* and political *acceptability*. *Accountability* means to make sure that every penny of public money is spent as agreed, and to report accurately to the public on how money was spent. *Acceptability* means that public officials who make budget decisions are constrained by what the public wants. Sometimes they will do precisely what they think the public wants, even if the results are inefficient or inequitable, and sometimes they will present the budget so that it will be accepted by the public, even if they have not precisely followed public will. This effort may involve persuasion or deception.

Since public demands may not be clearly expressed, and since different segments of the public may make different and competing demands, and since public officials themselves may have priorities, officials may not be able or willing to be bound tightly to public opinion. Nevertheless, if politicians knowingly make decisions that differ from what the public wants, there is pressure to present the budget in a way that makes it appear acceptable. That pressure creates a tension between accountability, which requires nearly complete openness, and acceptability, which sometimes involves hiding or distorting information or presenting it in an unclear fashion.

The Budget Document and Accountability

Because of the separation of payer and decider, the budget document itself becomes an important means of public accountability. How did the public's representatives actually decide to spend taxpayer money? Did they waste it? Did they spend it on defense or police or on social services? The streets are in terrible shape—how much money did they spend on street repair? Citizens do not typically watch the decision making, but they and the press have access to the budget document and can look for the answers. They can hold the government accountable through the budget, to see that what officials promised them was actually delivered.

But budgets do not always present a complete and accurate picture. One example of how budgets can lose information happened recently in a state university. A university president decided to expand the big-time sports program, in an environment of overall financial scarcity. While some faculty members undoubtedly favored the action, many would have opposed it if they had been asked. The president did not ask their opinions, however; instead, the full costs of the program were disguised to make the budget appear acceptable. Because of progressive underestimates of

costs in the sports program, some pundits labeled the sports program the case of the disappearing budget.

To obscure the real costs, the president broke up the costs for the program and scattered them among different portions of the budget. To complicate the picture further, he drew on different pockets of revenue, including student athletic fees, bond revenues, and voluntary donations. When asked, he said money going to the athletic programs was earmarked and could not be spent on other programs, so that professors trying to get more money to teach history or biology would look elsewhere than to sports. The amount of money showing as costs in the athletic program remained constant every year, although the program costs were expanding. Fearing conflict and disapproval, the president hid the costs in the budget.

The more complicated the budget, the more different activities and accounts, the greater the discretion of the administrators. As one university president offered, "Not a day goes by when we do not wish we had a more complex budget." The complexity allows for choice of where to report expenditures, and which revenues to use, to highlight some expenditures and gloss over others.

It would be misleading to suggest that the tension between accountability and acceptability always leads to more distortion or more secrecy. Sometimes the balance tends toward more accountability and budgets become clearer and more representative of true costs. The federal budget, for example, has moved toward clearer and more comprehensive portraits of public expenditures in recent years. But the tension is always present, and each budget represents some degree of selectivity about what it will present and how. The art of selective revelation is part of public budgeting.

Openness to the Environment

Public budgets are open to the environment. The environment for budgeting includes a number of different factors including the over-all level of resources available (the amount of taxable wealth, the existing tax structure, current economic conditions); the degree of certainty of revenues; and a variety of emergencies such as very heavy snowfall, tornadoes, wars, bridge collapses, droughts, chemical explosions, and water pollution. The environment also includes rigidities resulting from earlier decisions, which may now be embodied in law. For example, rapid inflation in housing prices in California resulted in a citizen referendum to protect themselves from rapidly rising property taxes. The result of the referendum was incorporated in the state constitution, limiting the taxing options of local government. Constitutional restrictions to maintain a balanced budget or limit expenditures or put a ceiling on borrowing operate in a similar manner. Prior borrowing creates a legal obligation for future budgets, an obligation that may press other possible expenditures out of consideration or require higher levels of taxation. The environment in this sense may frame policy issues and limit alternatives. Public opinion is also part of the budgetary environment, and the perception of change in public opinion will be reflected in changing budgets.

The intergovernmental system is also a key part of the environment for budget actors. The legal sources of revenues, limits on borrowing, strings attached to grants, and mandated costs are but a few of the budgetary implications of the intergovernmental system. The requirement that some grants be spent on particular items or that a recipient match expenditures on grants may result in a pattern of spending different from what the state or local government would have preferred.

Budget Constraints

Openness to the environment creates the need for budgets to be flexible. Public officials have to be able to adapt quickly, reallocating funds to meet emergencies, spending more now and making up the difference later, cutting back expenditures during the year to meet sudden declines in revenues or increases in expenditures. But the same openness to the environment that creates the need for flexibility may simultaneously subject budgeting to numerous constraints.

For example, in California, a statewide referendum limited the rate of growth of local assessments, restraining the growth of property tax revenues. Federal grants provide budgetary constraints when they can be spent only on particular programs. The courts may create budgetary constraints by declaring programs inadequate or taxes illegal. Legal obligations to repay debt and maintain public businesses separate from the rest of the budget also create constraints.

The need for flexibility and the number of budgetary constraints contest with one another, creating patterns typical of public budgeting. For example, local officials may press for home rule, which gives more independence and autonomy to local governments to manage their own affairs and adapt to changing conditions. But state officials may erode home rule through continually mandating local costs. State universities may try to squirrel away contingency funds outside those appropriated by the legislature so that they can respond to emergencies; the legislature may then try to appropriate and hence control this new local source of revenues.

The Meaning of Politics in Public Budgeting

Public budgets have a number of special characteristics. These characteristics suggest some of the ways that the budget is political. Political is a word that covers a number of meanings, even when narrowed to the context of budgetary decision making. The purpose of this book is to clarify the meaning of politics in the context of budgeting by sorting out some key meanings and showing how these meanings apply to different parts of budgetary decision making.

Concepts of Politics in the Budget

The literature suggests at least five major ways of viewing politics in the budget: reformism, incrementalist bargaining, interest group determinism, process, and policy making.

- The first is a reform orientation, which argues that politics and budgeting are or should be antithetical, that budgeting should be primarily or exclusively technical, and that comparison between items should be technical and efficiency based. Politics in the sense of the opinions and priorities of elected officials and interest groups is an unwanted intrusion that reduces efficiency and makes decision making less rational. The politics of reform involves a clash of views between professional staff and elected officials over the boundary between technical budget decisions and properly political ones.

- The second perspective is the incrementalist view, which sees budgeting as negotiations among a group of routine actors, bureaucrats, budget officers, chief executives, and legislators, who meet each year and bargain to resolution. To the extent that interest groups are included at all in this view, they are conceived of in the pluralist model. The process is open, anyone can play and win, and the overall outcome is good; conflict is held down because everyone wins something and no one wins too much.

- The third view is that interest groups are dominant actors in the budget process. In its extreme form this argument posits that richer and more powerful interest groups determine the budget. Some interests are represented by interest groups and others are not, or are represented by weaker interest groups; the outcome does not approximate democracy. There may be big winners and big losers in this model. Conflict is more extensive than in the incrementalist model. This view of politics in budgeting raises the questions whether these interest groups represent narrow or broad coalitions, or possibly even class interest. To what extent do these interest groups represent oil or banking or the homeless, and to what extent do they represent business and labor more broadly?

- The fourth view of politics in the budget is that the budget process itself is the center and focus of budget politics. Those with particular budget goals try to change the budget process to favor their goals. Branches of government struggle with one another over budgetary power through the budget process; the budget process becomes the means of achieving or denying separation and balance between the branches of government. The degree of examination of budget requests, and the degree to which review is technical or political, cursory or detailed, is regulated by the budget process. The ability of interest groups to influence the budget, the role of the public in budget decisions, the openness of budget decision making—all these are part of the politics of process. In this view of politics, the individual actors and their strategies and goals may or may not be important, depending on the role assigned to individual actors in the budget process, and depending on whether the external environment allows any flexibility.

- The fifth view is that the politics of budgeting centers in policy debates, including debates about the role of the budget. Spending levels, taxing policies, and willingness to borrow to sustain spending during recessions are all major policy issues that have to be resolved one way or another during budget deliberations. Budgets may reflect a policy of moderating economic cycles or they may express a policy of allowing the economy to run its course. Each is a policy. Similarly, budgets must allocate funding to particular programs, and in the course of doing so, decide priorities for federal, state, and local governments. This view of politics in the budget emphasizes tradeoffs, especially those that occur between major areas of the budget, such as social services and defense or police. This view also emphasizes the role of the budget office in making policy and the format of the budget in encouraging comparisons between programs.

These five views of politics have been developed over time, and like an ancient document, the messages have been written over one another. Surely they are not all equally true, and certainly they often contradict each other. Parts of each may still be true, and they may be true of different parts of budgetary decision making, or true of budgetary decision making at different times or at different levels of government.

Budgetary Decision Making

The focus . . . is to explore the kind of politics that occurs in budgetary decision making. What is budgetary decision making like? We have already discovered that public budgeting is open to environmental changes and deals with policy conflicts. Policy conflicts can delay particular decisions or prevent them from being made at all; other budget decisions must be independent enough to be made without the missing pieces. They can be corrected later when missing pieces fall into place. Environmental emergencies can reorder priorities and alter targets that have already been determined. As a result, public budgeting must be segmental and interruptible. The need for segmentation and interruptibility is satisfied by dividing budgeting into separate but linked decision clusters: revenues, process, expenditures, balance, and implementation.

Decision making in each cluster proceeds somewhat independently while referring to decisions made in the other clusters, or in anticipation of decisions likely to be made in other clusters. These decision clusters are ultimately interdependent, but do not occur in a fixed sequence. The decision one needs to have in one decision cluster may not be made by another decision cluster in time to use. Then one may guess, or use an old figure, and then change when the new figure is determined. Sometimes decision-making cycles between estimates of revenues, estimates of expenditures, new estimates of revenues and new estimates of expenditures, in an iterative process.

The Revenue Cluster

Revenue decisions include technical estimates of how much income will be available for the following year, assuming no change in the tax structures, and policy decisions about changes in the level or type of taxation. Will taxes be raised or lowered? Will tax breaks be granted, and if so, to whom, for what purpose? Which tax sources will be emphasized, and which deemphasized, with what effect on regions, and economic classes, or on age groups? How visible will the tax burden be? Interest groups are intensely involved in the revenue cluster. The revenue cluster emphasizes the scarcity of resources that is an essential element in budgeting and illustrates the tension between accountability and acceptability that is a characteristic of public budgets. Revenues are also extremely sensitive to the environment because changes in the economy influence revenue levels and because the perception of public opinion influences the public officials' willingness to increase taxes.

The Budget Process

The process cluster concerns how to make budget decisions. Who should participate in the budget deliberations? Should the agency heads have power independent of the central budget office? How influential should interest groups be? How much power should the legislature have? How should the work be divided, and when should particular decisions be made? Normally the legislature takes a key role in establishing budget process, although the chief executive may propose desired changes. Interest groups play a minor role, if any role at all. The politics of process may revolve around individuals or groups trying to maximize their power through rearranging the budget process. This jockeying for power rises to importance when the competing parties represent the executive and legislative branches and involve the definition of the separation and balance between the branches of government. The politics of process may revolve around the policy issues of the level of spending and the ability of government to balance its budget.

The Expenditure Cluster

The expenditure cluster involves some technical estimates of likely expenditures, such as for grants that are dependent on formulas and benefit programs whose costs depend on the level of unemployment. But many expenditure decisions are policy relevant—which programs will be funded at what level, who will benefit from public programs and who will not, where and how cuts will be made, and whose interests will be protected. Agency heads are more involved in these decisions than in taxation or process decisions, and interest groups are also often active. This portion of the budget emphasizes the element of choice between items of expenditures in the definition of budgeting and illustrates the nature of the constraints on choices that is characteristic of public budgeting in particular.

The Balance Cluster

The balance cluster concerns the basic budgetary question whether the budget has to be balanced each year with each year's revenues, or whether borrowing is allowed to balance the budget, and if so, how much, for how long, and for what purposes. The politics of balance deals with questions whether balance should be achieved by increasing revenues, decreasing expenditures, or both, and hence reflects policies about the desirable scope of government. Sometimes the politics of balance emphasizes definitions, as the group in power seeks to make its deficits look smaller by defining them away. The balance cluster also deals with questions of how deficits should be eliminated once they occur and their amounts are pinned down. At the national level, because deficits may be incurred during recessions in an effort to help the economy recover, the ability to run a deficit is linked to policies favoring or opposing the role of the budget in controlling the economy and, in particular, the use of the budget to moderate unemployment. These issues—whether budgets should balance, the

proper scope of government and level of taxation, and the role of government in moderating unemployment—are issues that the general public cares about. Citizens may participate in this decision cluster through referenda and opinion polls; broad groups of taxpayers and interest-group coalitions representing broad segments of society may be involved in lobbying on this issue. Political parties may even include their policies toward deficits in their election platforms.

Budget Implementation

Finally, there is a cluster of decisions around budget implementation. How close should actual expenditures be to the ones planned in the budget? How can one justify variation from the budget plan? Can the budget be remade after it is approved, during the budget year? The key issues here revolve around the need to implement decisions exactly as made and the need to make changes during the year because of changes in the environment. The potential conflict is usually resolved by treating implementation as technical rather than policy related. Executive branch staff play the major role in implementation, wich much smaller and more occasional roles for the legislature. Interest groups play virtually no role in implementation. The allowance of technical changes does open the door to policy changes during the year, but these are normally carefully monitored and may cause open conflict when they occur.

Microbudgeting and Macrobudgeting

The five clusters of decision making outline the nature of the decisions actually being made, but tell little about how and why the decisions are made. On the one hand there are a number of budget actors, who all have individual motivations, who strategize to get what they want from the budget. The focus on the actors and their strategies is called *microbudgeting*. But the actors do not simply bargain with one another or with whomever they meet in the corridor. The actors are assigned budget roles by the budget process, the issues they examine are often framed by the budget process, and the timing and coordination of their decisions are often regulated by the budget process. The budget actors are not totally free to come to budget agreements in any way they choose. Individual actors are bound by environmental constraints. There are choices they are not free to make because they are against the law, or because the courts decree it, or because previous decision makers have bound their hands. The total amount of revenue available is a kind of constraint, as is popular demand for some programs and popular dislike of others. Budgetary decision making has to account not just for budgetary actors but also for budget processes and the environment. This more top-down and systemic perspective on budgeting is called *macrobudgeting*. Contemporary budgeting gives more emphasis to macrobudgeting than exclusively to microbudgeting.

One way of viewing the determinants of budgetary outcomes is as a casual model, depicted in Figure 12.1. In this schema, the environment, budget processes, and individuals' strategies all affect outcomes.

The environment influences budgetary outcomes directly and indirectly, through process and through individual strategies. The environment influences outcomes directly, without going through either budget process or individual strategies, when it imposes emergencies that reorder priorities. Thus a war or a natural disaster preempts normal budgetary decision making.

The environment influences the budget process in several ways. The level of resources available—both the actual level of wealth and the willingness of the citizens to pay their taxes—influences the degree of centralization of budgeting. When resources are especially scarce and there is apparent

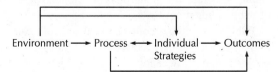

Figure 12.1 Decision making: Environment, process, and strategies

need to either cutback according to a given set of policies or make each dollar count toward specific economic goals, there is no room for bottom-up demands that result in compromises and a little bit of gain for everyone regardless of need. When resources are abundant, a more decentralized model of process may hold, with less emphasis on comparing policies and less competition between supporters of different policies.

The environment may influence the format of budget as well as the degree of centralization of decision making. When revenues are growing, there may be more emphasis on planning and on linking the budget to future community goals, to stimulate public demands for new spending. When there is little new money, the idea of planning may seem superfluous. Changing direction, or setting new goals, may seem impossible in the face of declining revenues that make current goals difficult to sustain.

Environment in the sense of the results of prior decisions may also influence process. If there is a huge accumulation of debt and little apparent way to control it, or if the budget has been growing very rapidly for reasons other than war, there may be attempts to change the budget process in an effort to control spending and debt. In contrast, if the environment suggests the need for additional spending, and the current budget process is delivering very slow growth, the process may be changed to make spending decisions quicker and easier.

The level of certainty of funding influences strategies as well. If whatever an agency was promised may never arrive, agency heads are likely to engage in continuous lobbying for their money, and continual rebudgeting internally every time circumstances change. Long-term or future agreements will be perceived as worthless; the possibility of toning down conflict by stretching out budget allocation times will disappear. Attention will focus on what is available now, and going after whatever it is, whether it is what you want or not, because what you really want may never show up and hence is not worth waiting for.

The intergovernmental grant structure is part of the environment that may influence strategies. Because some grant money may seem free, state and local governments may focus their energies on getting grants instead of raising local revenues. Or they may seek to decrease the amount of match required for a grant or increase their authority over how the money can be spent. Intergovernmental grants may make some expenditures relatively cheap, and some cutbacks relatively expensive, and hence frame constraints and choices for state and local budget officials.

The legal environment also influences strategies. For example, if public school teachers want tax raises to fund education and there is a provision in the state constitution forbidding income taxes, the teachers must either campaign for a constitutional revision (a time consuming and difficult task) or support a tax they know to be more burdensome to the poor. Thus the environment frames choices and influences strategies.

In Figure 12.1, the budget process influences strategies directly, and to a lesser extent, outcomes directly. But there is a double-headed arrow on the linkage between budget processes and strategies, suggesting that individuals' strategies also influence budget processes.

Budget processes influence strategies in some fairly obvious ways. If the budget structure allows for lengthy detailed budget hearings, open to the public and interest groups, at which decisions are often made, then various actors are likely to concentrate their efforts on making a good impression at these hearings. If the chief executive prepares the budget, which is subject to only superficial scrutiny and pro forma hearings before being approved by the legislature, anyone who wants to influence the budget—including the legislators themselves—must make their opinions heard earlier in the process, before the final executive proposal is put together. Informal discussion with department heads, or even telephone calls to the budget office, may be the route to influence. If the budget is made two or three times, with only the last one effective, then strategies may be to play out the first time or two with grandstanding—extreme positions to attract media attention—and more detailed and moderate positions later when the final decisions are made. The budget process orders the decisions in such a way that some of them are critical and de-

termine or influence those that come afterward. Budget strategies naturally gravitate to those key decisions no matter where they are located.

When budget outcomes contradict some group's preference, the group may try to change the budget process to help it get the outcomes it prefers. When coalitions of the dissatisfied can agree on particular changes, fairly substantial changes in process may result. A change in process will bring about a change in outcome if the change in process shifts power from one group of individuals who want to accomplish one goal to another group with different goals.

The final link in the figure is between the strategies of budget actors and outcomes. The effect of different strategies on the outcomes is hard to gauge. It seems obvious, however, that strategies that ignore the process or the environment are doomed to failure. Budget actors have to figure out where the flexibility is before they can influence how that flexibility will be used. Strategies that try to bypass superiors or fool legislators generally do not work; strategies that involve careful documentation of need and appear to save money are generally more successful.

Summary and Conclusions

Public budgeting shares the characteristics of all budgeting. It makes choices between possible expenditures, it has to balance, and it has a decision-making process. But public budgeting has a number of additional features peculiar to itself, such as its openness to the environment; the variety of actors involved in budgeting, all of whom come to it with different goals; the separation of taxpayers from budget decision makers; the use of the budget document as a means of public accountability; and the numerous constraints typical of public budgeting.

Public budgeting is both technical and political. Politics takes on some special meanings in the context of budgetary decision making. Budgetary decision making must be flexible, adaptive, and interruptible, which leads to a structure of five semi-independent strands of decision making, revenues, process, expenditures, balance, and implementation. Each such strand generates its own political characteristics.

Budget outcomes are not solely the result of budget actors negotiating with one another in a free-for-all; outcomes depend on the environment, and on the budget process as well as individual strategies. Individual strategies have to be framed in a broader context than simply perceived self-interest.

Budgeting is not well described as an annual process with little change from year to year. Budgetary decision making changes over time: interest group power waxes and wanes, competition in the budget increases and decreases, and the budget process itself varies over time. Changes in process take place in response to individuals, committees, and branches of government jockeying for power; in response to changes in the environment from rich to lean, or vice versa; in response to changes in the power of interest groups; and in response to scandals or excesses of various kinds.

Notes

1. Patricia Ingraham and Charles Barilleaux, "Motivating Government Managers for Retrenchment: Some Possible Lessons from the Senior Executive Service," *Public Administration Review* 43, no. 3 (1983): 393–402. They cite the Office of Personnel Management Federal Employee Attitude Surveys of 1979 and 1980, extracting responses from those in the Senior Executive Service, the upper ranks of the civil service and appointed administrators. In 1979, 99 percent of the senior executives said that they considered accomplishing something worthwhile was very important; 97 percent said the same in 1980. By contrast, in response to the question "How much would you be motivated by a cash award," only 45 percent said either to a great extent or a very great extent.

2. Twelve percent of LeLoup and Moreland's Department of Agriculture requests between 1946 and 1971 were for decreases. See Lance LeLoup, *Budgetary Politics,* 3d ed. (Brunswick, Ohio: King's Court, 1986), 83. For a more recent case study of an agency requesting decreases, see the case study of the Office of Personnel Management, in Irene Rubin, *Shrinking the Federal Government* (White Plains: Longman, 1985). See Irene Rubin, *Running in the Red: The Political Dynamics of Urban Fiscal Stress* (Albany: State University of New York Press, 1982) for an example of a department refusing additional employees.

3. For a good discussion of this phenomenon, see Frank Thompson, *The Politics of Personnel in the City* (Berkeley: University of California Press, 1975).

4. See Rubin, *Shrinking the Federal Government,* for examples during the Reagan administration.

5. U.S. Senate, Committee on Governmental Affairs, *Office of Management and Budget: Evolving Roles and Future Issues,* Committee Print 99–134, 99th Cong., 2d sess., prepared by the Congressional Research Service of the Library of Congress, February 1986.

6. See, for example, Kenneth Shepsle and Barry Weingast, "Legislative Politics and Budget Outcomes," in *Federal Budget Policy in the 1980s,* Gregory Mills and John Palmer, eds. (Washington, D.C.: Urban Institute Press, 1984), 343–367.

7. Rubin, *Running in the Red,* 56.

8. For a vivid account of the relationship between pork-barrel spending and building political coalitions, see Martin Shefter, "New York City's Fiscal Crisis: The Politics of Inflation and Retrenchment," *Public Interest* 48 (Summer 1977): 99–127.

9. See John Ellwood, "Comments," in Mills and Palmer, *Federal Budget Policy in the 1980s,* 368–378.

10. Douglas Arnold, "The Local Roots of Domestic Policy," in *The New Congress,*

Thomas Mann and Norman Ornstein, eds. (Washington, D.C.: American Enterprise Institute, 1981), 252, quoted by Ellwood, in Mills and Palmer.

11. Arnold, "Local Roots," 282.
12. Ellwood, in Mills and Palmer, 370.

13. Linda Harriman and Jeffrey Straussman, "Do Judges Determine Budget Decisions? Federal Court Decisions in Prison Reform and State Spending for Corrections," *Public Administration Review* 43, no. 4 (1983): 343–351.

☐ CASE STUDY 12

Introduction

Perhaps nothing is more vital to our understanding of public administration than how monies are budgeted to achieve public purposes. This subject, many believe, directly and decisively influences what policies are pursued and how management of public programs is achieved. For some, budgets in reality are what public administration is all about, namely the translation of public purposes into practical actions through the raising and expenditures of government monies. Rubin's foregoing essay therefore offers several stimulating insights into this critical process. It especially shows why this subject should not be viewed as merely a dry, technical document but as something that affects the central fabric of modern democratic society and the choices it faces.

Let's next turn to an actual example of what Rubin's selection addressed by studying the following case, "County Prison Overtime." This case study concerns a dispute over the amount and use of funds for the payment of overtime in a county correctional facility. At first glance, this may seem like a mundane and uninteresting problem. A county budget office staff prods an operating department to cooperate in a cost containment program to reduce the overall level of county spending (seemingly a trivial management task). But this routine administrative matter about overtime pay, which starts out as a simple exchange of memos, turns into an acrimonious confrontation between staff and line personnel and soon involves the county manager, the county board, and other local interests. County administrator George Truly finds himself in the middle of a battle over what Rubin called, "budget implementation decisions" that have important consequences for his workforce and the community at large.

As you read this case, you might reflect on the following points:

What was the basic nature of county government, its structure, workforce, and the politics of the whole community that contributed to the problems raised in this case?

Why is the case about what Rubin refers to in her essay as "budget implementation decisions"? What clusters of issues are involved?

How were these problems first raised in the case and what specific questions did the county administrator, George Truly, confront?

Can you outline the data, methods of analysis, understanding of the community, budgetary policies, and particular sensitivity of people that Truly required to make his decision? What alternatives were presented? Do you think he resolved the issue fairly, creatively, and effectively? Why or why not?

County Prison Overtime

TOM MILLS

Background

Franklin County is a suburban/rural county located in one of the Mid-Atlantic states; it adjoins a large eastern city. Franklin County has a land area of 650 square miles; a population of approximately 500,000; and 45 local governments that consist of boroughs, villages, and townships. The local governments have their own police forces but lack secure holding facilities for defendants arrested and bound over by local magistrates for trial in the county courts.

The county provides all criminal justice system services from the county courthouse located in Franklinville, the county seat. On a tract of county-owned land just outside of Franklinville, the county operates two detention facilities: a small medium-security facility for juveniles and a large, modern medium-security facility for both male and female adult detainees. The latter facility, called the county prison, has a capacity of approximately 340 inmates and is maintained and operated by a staff of 181 employees.

Franklin County's chief lawmaking and administrative authority is the elected county commission, which is vested with both executive and legislative powers. Voters also elect a number of administrative officers—including the sheriff, the controller, and the district attorney—and the judges of the county court, called the supreme court of common pleas.

The county commission consists of three members elected countywide for four-year terms. The county code requires that one of the three commissioners be a member of the opposing, or minority, party. The county is predominantly Republican, and members of that party regularly control the county-wide elective offices. The county commission, perhaps owing to its higher visibility, has occasionally

been controlled by a Democratic majority.

The county commissioners appoint a county administrator, all nonelected department heads, and the members of most county boards and commissions. The day-to-day operation of the county is the responsibility of the county administrator, who is a professional local government manager recruited and appointed on the basis of technical competence. The county boasts a commitment to professionalism. The county administrator recruits and hires his or her own staff and has been responsible for securing the appointments of the finance director, the personnel director, and the director of purchasing.

The county code constrains the county commissioners' powers of appointment in some instances. The power to appoint the director of the department of corrections, who oversees both the county prison and the juvenile rehabilitation center, is vested in a prison board. The prison board is composed of the president judge of the supreme court of common pleas or that judge's designee, the district attorney, the sheriff, the controller, and the three county commissioners. Five of the seven members of the board were Republicans at the time this case begins.

The Case

In the previous election, the Democratic party had won the majority of seats on the county commission by taking what proved to be the more popular position on a critical environmental issue. In hopes of re-election, the Democratic commissioners instituted a cost containment program that, if successful, would enable them to complete their term without raising taxes. The commissioners issued a directive to all department heads instructing them to implement economies wherever possible. The county administrator, George Truly, was given the principal responsibility for implementing the cost containment program. He, in turn, had charged the finance director, Donald Dexter, with much of the operating responsibility for the program.

After monitoring the expenditures of the county prison, Dexter was convinced that overtime expenditures were out of control. He had met on several occasions with Charles Goodheart, the director of corrections, and had called him almost weekly in an effort to reduce overtime costs. In Dexter's view, those contacts had been of little value, since overtime expenditures continued at what he regarded as an excessive rate. Somewhat reluctantly, he decided to go "on record." He dictated what was to be the first in a series of memorandums.

March 12
TO: Charles R. Goodheart, Director of
           Corrections
FROM: Donald D. Dexter, Finance Director
SUBJECT: Excessive Prison Overtime

Pursuant to the county commissioners' directive of January 8 establishing the cost containment program, my staff and I have been closely monitoring the overtime expenditures incurred in the operation of the county prison. We have had several meetings and numerous telephone conversations regarding this matter with both you and your key staff members—all to no avail. Overtime expenditures have continued to rise and might well exceed the budget allocation. This I find to be particularly distressing, since we had every hope that this was one area of your operation in which we could effect significant savings.

I would greatly appreciate it if you would provide me, at your first opportunity, with a detailed justification for the current rate of overtime usage and your plans to keep such expenditures to an absolute minimum.

cc: George S. Truly, County Administrator
      Frank Friendly, Personnel Director

Before sending this memorandum, Dexter had given the action considerable thought and had concluded that, even if the memorandum was a bit strong, it was warranted in this case.

In the weeks that followed, Dexter continued to scrutinize the prison payroll records but did not observe any reduction in the use of overtime. He was about to schedule yet another meeting with Goodheart when he received the following memorandum.

April 5
TO: Donald D. Dexter, Finance Director
FROM: Charles R. Goodheart, Director of
           Corrections
SUBJECT: Response to Your Request for
           Information Regarding Overtime
           Expenditures

You indicated in your memorandum of March 12 that you felt we were utilizing an excessive amount of overtime. I welcome the opportunity to explain what might appear to be excessive overtime usage, but which really is no more than prudent prison management.

You will recall that during the budget hearings last year, I shared with you information on overtime usage in the four surrounding counties. Each of these counties has a comparable prison system, and, as I noted then, each uses more overtime than we do.

You must remember that I requested $434,400 as an overtime allocation for the current fiscal year (including holiday overtime). The overtime figure that was allocated to this department was substantially less. When budget allocations were announced, there was no explanation for the reduced overtime figure other than a general statement—which certainly is appropriate for you as finance director to make—that times were difficult, money was tight, and every effort must be made to curtail unnecessary expenditures. Although I accept these comments in the spirit in which they were made, I still am held responsible and accountable to the prison board for operating a safe and secure correctional institution. Prisons are potentially very dangerous, and that danger can be averted only by keeping staffing levels at safe and realistic levels.

As we both know, there are many justifiable causes for overtime usage in a prison setting. In the following paragraphs I'll attempt to identify the major causes.

Turnover During last year and continuing into this year, we have experienced high levels of turnover among our correctional officers. When staff members leave we are required to fill their posts, which we do through the use of overtime. The problem continues during recruitment for replacements and during the three-week training course to which all recruits are sent. When you add the two-to-four-week delay in filling positions to the three-week training period, you can readily see that a considerable amount of overtime might be involved. Turnover is perhaps our most critical problem. Previously I sent you a detailed commentary on our turnover experience. Over the past several years, I have told everyone willing to listen that there is a strong relationship between turnover in a correctional institution and overtime expenditures.

First of all, entry-level correctional officers are poorly paid, and, as I've told the county commissioners at every budget hearing, that is certainly true in our case. Second, this is a very difficult profession, and prison personnel are continually required to work at very high stress levels. Finally, we enjoy very little public esteem, and the working conditions can on occasion be very unpleasant. Small wonder that there is high turnover not only in our prisons but in prisons all across this country. When a staff member leaves, the need to fill the post continues. Unless the prison board tells me that it does not want me to fill vacant posts, I will continue to do so, and I have no choice but to use overtime.

Hospital watches   Whenever an inmate requires inpatient treatment in a local hospital, I must provide the necessary security. Recently, two inmates were hospitalized. For each day of hospitalization, we provided two correctional officers per shift, three shifts per day, for a total of forty-eight hours of coverage. As you can see, the time mounts up rapidly. We have no fat in our shift complements; therefore, when a need like this arises, it must be covered with overtime.

Emergency situations   Whenever there is reason to believe that inmates might be planning an action that could endanger the security of the institution, I adopt an emergency plan that puts all supervisors on twelve-hour shifts. I do not place this institution on an emergency footing for any trivial or illusory cause. Those instances in which I have used emergency overtime have been fully justified, and I stand by my actions.

Sick leave   Our sick leave usage compares favorably with that of other county departments that enjoy less trying working conditions. Still, when a correctional officer calls in sick, his or her position must be filled, and it is usually filled by the use of overtime. We can't call in a replace-

ment on one hour's notice on the person's day off, upset his or her family life, and worsen a bad morale situation simply to cover an eight-hour shift. We feel that the use of overtime in these situations is the most sensible solution.

Workers' compensation   I have frequently remarked on this problem in the past. Today we are filling two posts that are vacant as a result of workers' compensation claims against the county. When an employee is injured on the job and a doctor certifies that he or she may not work, I have no choice but to utilize overtime to fill the post. I simply don't have any slack resources that would permit me to do otherwise.

Reserve duty   Under the laws of this state, all staff members who are members of bona fide military reserve units are authorized to take fifteen days of paid military leave annually. When they depart for their military training, their posts remain, and we are responsible for filling them. The problem is exacerbated by the tendency of both military leave and vacations to cluster in the summer months. Another aspect of military reserve duty also generates overtime. Our correctional officers are scheduled around the clock and frequently are scheduled to work on a weekend when they are expected to attend reserve drills. Under the policy adopted by the county commissioners, the reservists may take "no-pay" time and fulfill their reserve obligations. While the county saves their straight-time pay, I am forced to use overtime to fill their posts.

Vacations   We do make a concerted effort to schedule vacations so as not to result in overtime expenditures. Unfortunately, as a direct result of our lean staffing, on occasion we must resort to overtime to permit our correctional officers to enjoy the vacations they have earned.

Training programs   Compared to the standard advocated by national authorities, our training efforts are extremely modest. We provide equal employment opportunity training, particularly with respect to our female correctional officers, and some supervisory training. In addition, we provide training in interpersonal communication skills—training I regard as essential in an institution such as ours. Since our shift schedules contain no fat, personnel must be brought in for training on their days off, which, of course, results in overtime.

The major causes of our overtime expenditures are as noted above. I have brought these problems and their causes to the attention of the county commissioners at every budget hearing over the past nine years. Our staff utilization records and overtime documentation are available to anyone who wishes to review them. We have nothing to hide.

I don't mean to be flippant or discourteous, but frankly I'm no wizard. I cannot operate this institution without a reasonable overtime allocation any more than the Jews of antiquity could make bricks without straw. For you to insist that I do so strikes me as being every bit as unreasonable as was the order of the Pharaoh's overseer.

If you can provide specific suggestions regarding policies or methodologies that you feel will assist in overtime reduction without compromising safe and efficient operation of this institution, please be assured that we will be happy to work with you in implementing them. We are open to any thoughtful and constructive recommendations that you or your staff may have. In the meantime, you might consider funding a comprehensive study of our staffing needs, including the need for overtime, by a nationally recognized group specializing in the field of corrections.

cc: Members of the County Prison Board
     George S. Truly, County Administrator
     Frank Friendly, Personnel Director

Dexter read the memorandum twice, his feelings alternating between anger and frustration. He regarded Goodheart highly, knowing him to be a caring individual and a respected corrections professional. "But clearly," thought Dexter, "He's no administrator. I asked him for a detailed justification of his use of overtime and his plans to keep those expenditures to a minimum, and what did he do? He offered me a lesson in biblical history and tried to put the monkey on my back with that bit about 'any thoughtful and constructive recommendations' I might have—baloney!" Dexter noted that Goodheart had twice mentioned his accountability to the county prison board and had been ingracious enough to copy the prison board members on the memorandum. "That," thought Dexter sourly, "is just

a brazen example of saber rattling. Maybe he thinks that if he can broaden the controversy by bringing in the prison board, he can get me off his case. Not likely!" Still angry, he spun in his chair, picked up the mike of his recording machine, and dictated his reply.

Meanwhile, Jim Kirby, chair of the county commission, was enjoying his new role. He was no stranger to county government; he had been the minority commissioner for eight years under Republican administrations; but that, he felt, was essentially a "naysayer" role. Now, as chairman in a Democratic administration, he was in a position to take the lead on policy decisions, and he was enjoying it. He had founded a very successful business in the county and had called the shots there for more than thirty years. Although Kirby had often mused that government and business were much more different than alike—at least on paper—he relished his leadership role in the county.

Kirby prided himself on his capacity for work and made every effort to keep on top of things. He regretted that he had not read Goodheart's memorandum of April 5 before attending the monthly prison board meeting. He hated to be blindsided! The presiding judge of common pleas court, Harvey Strickland, who was also president of the prison board, had shown Kirby his copy of the memorandum as well as a copy of Dexter's memorandum of March 12, which had prompted Goodheart's reply. Strickland had been his usual amiable self, but Kirby knew from long experience that with him, you worried not about what he said but about what he left unsaid. The fact that Strickland had brought the memorandums with him to the meeting and his oblique references to "those in this life who are penny-wise and pound-foolish" convinced Kirby that trouble was brewing.

As soon as Kirby got back to his office, he called George Truly, the county administrator, and asked him to stop by. Truly was the perfect balance to Kirby. Kirby was "born to lead"—an activist by nature, full of ideas and restless energy and impatient with detail. Truly, on the other hand, was a "doer." A professional administrator with substantial background in local government, he disliked the publicity and pressure of policy leadership, preferring instead the satisfaction that came from making policies work and seeing that services were delivered. The two men understood each other and had developed an effective working relationship. Neither one worried about the line between policy and administration; each one understood the overlap between the two activities and freely advised the other about county problems.

As Truly walked through the doorway, Kirby asked him, "Are you familiar with Don Dexter's memo of March 12 and Charlie Goodheart's reply?"

Truly said that he was and that he had already spoken to Dexter about them but that he had been too late.

"What do you mean, too late?" Kirby asked. "This thing looks to me like it can still be salvaged."

"Then," Truly replied, "I guess you haven't seen Don's memorandum of April 7."

April 7
TO: Charles R. Goodheart, Director of
           Corrections
FROM: Donald D. Dexter, Finance Director
SUBJECT: Your Evasive Memorandum of April 5

In a sincere effort to implement the county commissioners' directive establishing a countywide cost containment program, I wrote to you on March 12. In my memorandum I asked you to provide me with a detailed justification for the current rate of overtime usage and your plans to keep such expenditures to an absolute minimum.

In reply, you gave me three pages of generalities and gratuitous comments. You're the prison expert, not me. If I had any good ideas on how you could run your operation more efficiently or economically, you can be sure I'd offer them. But as I see it, that's your job, not mine. My job is to see to the financial well-being of this county, and I can't do my job if I don't get cooperation. That's all I'm asking for—your cooperation in achieving the goals set for all of us by the county commissioners. Your knowledge of the Old Testament is doubtless better than mine, but I do know that the Pharaoh didn't pay overtime. As far as I am concerned, you can have all the straw you want, but cut down on the overtime.

cc: George S. Truly, County Administrator
      Frank Friendly, Personnel Director

The Decision Problem

After Kirby had finished reading Dexter's memo of April 7, he sighed wearily, laid it aside, looked up at Truly, and said, "I see what you mean. Any suggestions?"

Truly was a career administrator who had spent twenty-two years in a series of increasingly demanding city management jobs before being recruited by Kirby to serve as Franklin County administrator. He had been given carte blanche in the recruitment of his administrative staff, and he had picked, among others, Don Dexter. Dexter was extremely bright; he had been the controller for a large manufacturing firm in the county—quite an accomplishment for a man who was not yet thirty. "But," Truly reflected, "he's never swum in political waters before, and there's no question that he's in over his head."

As the two men reviewed the situation, they tried to define the problem specifically, to identify possible courses of action, and to anticipate the probable outcomes of those alternatives.

It was evident that whatever they did, they had to do it quickly. Strickland could not yet have seen Dexter's memorandum of April 7. If he had, he would have had it with him at the meeting, and he would not have been so affable.

The cost containment program was important to Kirby and the other Democrat on the county commission. It was probably their best hope of reelection. If they exempted the county prison from the program for fear of what the prison board might do, the program could be weakened throughout the county. After all, why should the other departments conform if the prison wasn't expected to do its part?

Under the county code, the prison board, not the county commission, was responsible for approving all prison-related expenditures. The board, with its Republican majority, could give Goodheart a blank check if they wanted to, and the commissioners would be able to do nothing about it. "Well not exactly 'nothing,'" groused Kirby. "We could direct the county solicitor to sue the prison board, but since the president of the board is also the presiding judge, that's more of a theoretical than a practical remedy."

In fact, it was much more likely that the prison board would wind up suing the county commissioners. If the board alleged that an imminent threat to public safety was created by the refusal of the commissioners and their agents to fund the county prison adequately, it could bring an action *in mandamus.* In that event, the prison board would not be likely to limit the action to the question of prison overtime but would, in all likelihood, open a Pandora's box of problems. Goodheart had documented many of these problems in his memorandum of April 5, and that memo would probably be Exhibit A at a trial. Issues most likely to be litigated included the needs for adequate prison staffing levels, proactive strategies to combat the high rate of turnover, and higher salaries for correctional officers.

Kirby knew that if political warfare broke out, the Republicans would move quickly to seize the high ground. They would allege that the Democrats were jeopardizing the safety and tranquility of the community for the sake of a few paltry dollars. Kirby was too old a hand to suppose that arguments of efficiency and economy would carry any weight with the public in such a debate—especially if people were convinced that they were going to be murdered in their beds.

Since all the elected officials in the county were Republicans with the exception of Kirby and the other Democratic commissioner, they could really make things untenable. So far, the elected officials had been cooperating in the cost containment program. If, however, they chose to support the prison board in a confrontation with the commission, the cost containment program would be thoroughly scuttled.

"Don Dexter really put us in a box," remarked Kirby.

"Yes, but he's young and bright; he won't make the same mistake again," replied Truly.

"If the presiding judge gets him in his sights, he won't have the opportunity," observed Kirby solemnly.

"Funny thing," Kirby continued, "Don was right; that memorandum from Charlie was evasive, but Don should have known better than to say so. More than that, he shouldn't have written at all. In a situation like that, you go to see the guy. Writing is a very incomplete, very limited way to communicate. It's a lot easier to talk tough to your dictating machine than to an adversary. My rules have always been, never write a letter if you can avoid it, and never throw one away."

After almost an hour of discussion, the two men had identified five alternative approaches to the problem. Unfortunately, none of them were without risk.

1. Exempt the prison from the cost containment program. Under this alternative, Kirby would contact Strickland informally and intimate that the commission would not be unduly concerned if the prison did not achieve its cost containment objectives. The justification offered would be that as a public safety and law enforcement agency, the prison ought not be held to the same standard of cost reduction as other agencies, lest public safety suffer. The main problem with this approach was that party loyalty was paramount in this county, and Strickland was certain to share this information with the other elected officials, especially the district attorney and the sheriff, who headed justice system agencies. Once the commissioners had yielded on the prison, it would be difficult for them to hold the line on other justice system agencies, and the cost containment program would be seriously jeopardized. The result could be that the majority commissioners would be branded as weak men of little resolve, and that could have serious spillover effects in other areas.

2. Fund an in-depth study of the prison by a nationally recognized group specializing in corrections. Since this was a solution proposed by the director of corrections, it would most likely gain the acceptance of the prison board. Apart from the cost of such a study, which could be considerable, its recommendations were not likely to be favorable to the county administration. Through long experience, Kirby and Truly had come to believe that special interest groups of whatever ilk rarely supported anything antithetical to their special interest. Worse yet, a comprehensive study might only document and verify the types of complaints that the director of corrections had been making for years. It was one thing to ignore his complaints; it would be something quite different were the county administration to ignore the studied recommendations of nationally recognized experts.

3. Conduct an in-house study of the need for

prison overtime. This alternative appeared to have a good deal to recommend it. The county had a small management analysis team that reported directly to the county administrator. The supervisor of the team was a thoroughly honest and objective career professional who had been a founding member of the Association of Management Analysts in State and Local Government (MASLIG) and was well respected both within the county and beyond its borders. The problem, of course, was one of credibility. Despite his excellent reputation, his objectivity might be questioned in the partisan political climate that prevailed in Franklin County. Moreover, the prison board might refuse to approve such a study. A study could be undertaken without the prison board's concurrence, as a prerogative of the majority commissioners, but in that event, the prison board might view the study as flawed.

4. Attempt to find an "honest broker" to conduct a study of prison overtime. "Honest" in this context meant someone who would be considered honest in the eyes of the prison board—someone they would perceive as having no ax to grind. Ideally, this person should already work for the county and be known by, and enjoy the confidence of, the prison board. But who? The downside of this alternative, assuming that such a person could be found, was that the "honest broker" might not be all that honest. Should such a person be selected with the prison board's concurrence, that person might very well take the prison board's side, to the considerable embarrassment of the county administration.

5. Invite Strickland to undertake the overtime study with members of his staff. The court's administrative staff included several career professionals in court administration who were graduates of the Institute for Court Management. They were undoubtedly capable of conducting the study, and Strickland and the prison board, which he clearly dominated, would certainly find them acceptable. The question, again, was one of objectivity. Truly favored this alternative, arguing that if, as he believed, they were really professionals, they would be objective. Kirby's response was in-

sightful: "I don't recall book and verse, but somewhere in the scripture it is written, 'Whose bread I eat, his song I sing,' and those fellows eat court bread."

What really was needed was a dispassionate review of prison overtime usage, the development of sound recommendations that would reduce overtime expenses without endangering the public, and an appraisal of the adequacy of the current budgetary allocation for prison overtime. This last point was particularly important. Goodheart continually reminded the prison board that his overtime request had been cut arbitrarily by the finance department without consultation or even explanation. True, there were other important questions that the study could appropriately consider, such as the adequacy of entry-level salaries for correctional officers and the appropriateness of current staffing levels. But solutions to both of these problems would be likely to cost the county more money. Given a choice, Kirby would prefer to postpone consideration of all problems that might result in increased cost to the county until after the next election.

Fortunately, the collective bargaining agreement with the local union that represented the correctional officers was due to expire in September. The study would certainly be completed well before then, and any recommendations requiring work-rule changes could be negotiated as part of the contract settlement.

Kirby turned to Truly and said, "George, give this some thought—and quickly! See what you can come up with."

Truly knew he had to work fast to answer two questions: (1) Which of the alternatives should be recommended? and (2) If a study were to be undertaken, what kind of person should be given the assignment?

The Aftermath

Truly's recommendation was a combination of alternatives 3, 4, and 5. He saw no reason to exempt the prison from measures that applied to all other parts of the county government, and he believed that the only way to obtain data for an objective approach to the issue was to commission a study, preferably by an "honest broker." After considering and rejecting several possibilities, Truly recommended that a study be conducted by a team to be headed by Geraldine Eager, administrative assistant to the minority commissioner. Eager was the daughter of the county chair of the Republican party. All of the Republican majority members of the prison board had known her since she was an infant, and all were beholden to her father. Eager had just completed her work for an M.P.A. degree and was looking forward to a career as a professional local government manager. She had interned in Truly's office, and he had established a mentoring relationship with her. She was relatively inexperienced, but that problem could be overcome by having the county's management analysis staff assist her in the study.

Kirby suggested the arrangement to minority commissioner Joe Finley, Eager's boss. He felt reasonably certain that Finley would jump at the idea. Kirby knew that Finley had promised Eager's father to give Eager responsible work and that Finley had thus far been unable to deliver on that promise. Kirby also knew from his own experience that in the commission form of government, minority commissioners, themselves, have little challenging and responsible work to do.

Finley agreed to propose the arrangement to the prison board. The board concurred in the study plan, imposing the condition at Strickland's suggestion that a member of the court administrative staff be on the study team.

The study team reviewed finance department and prison budget files, central payroll records, prison overtime expenditure reports, staffing plans, and shift staffing schedules. By using several different methods of calculating overtime budget estimates, the team determined that a reasonable overtime budget request from the prison would have ranged between $294,200 and $348,600, well below the $434,400 requested by the prison but in line with the finance department's allocation of $319,000.

The study team also found that the prison's estimate of overtime needed for holidays had been overstated by nearly $100,000 and that overtime costs had been inflated because higher-paid employees were working appreciably more overtime than their lower-paid co-workers. Finally, the study team found that 12.5 percent of all nonholiday overtime was occasioned by turnover, thus supporting Goodheart's contention that turnover was a serious problem.

In discussing possible solutions, the team came up with the concept of a correctional officer pool. Under this plan, twenty more correctional officers than were authorized in the budget would be recruited and sent to the three-week training program. On completing their training, they would be placed in a pool from which permanent appointments would be made as vacancies occurred. In the meantime, they would be on call to cover overtime assignments, but at a straight-time rate. In effect, until they achieved their permanent appointments, they would be per diem employees. The start-up costs of the pool were estimated at $16,152, and approval by the collective bargaining agent for the correctional officers was required, since this was a fundamental change in work rules.

The politics of the study worked out as well as the analysis did. The prison board accepted the study and endorsed the the pool concept, which was subsequently implemented. Kirby gave the prison board credit for the $50,000 in annual overtime savings realized by the pool arrangement. Potentially embarrassing aspects of the study were downplayed from the outset. The $100,000 overstatement of holiday overtime requirements was shrugged off by Goodheart with the quip that since he was sure that Dexter was going to cut his overtime request, it was just good budgetary strategy to build in a safety margin. This time, Dexter did not dispute his explanation.

Chapter 12 Review Questions

1. Why does Irene Rubin at the outset argue that "public budgets are not merely technical managerial documents that they are also intrinsically and irreducibly political"? Do you agree or disagree based on your reading of the case, "County Prison Overtime"?

2. In two or three sentences, summarize how Rubin defines "a public budget." How does it differ from the budget of a private firm?

3. Why does Rubin stress that the chief tension in public budgeting is between public accountability and public acceptability? What does she mean by those terms? Was that tension illustrated in the case study, "County Prison Overtime?"

4. Who are the major participants that Rubin believes are most involved in the public budgetary processes? What are they trying to achieve? Who was involved in the "County Prison Overtime" case and what were the positions they took as well as the strategies they used to achieve their goals?

5. List the five basic "budgetary decision-making clusters" that Rubin's essay outlines. Who are the key actors involved in each cluster? The special pattern of politics in each cluster? Did "County Prison Overtime" represent any one cluster? Does it "fit" Rubin's "cluster model" and if so, why? Or, why not?

6. What are the essential differences between microbudgeting and macrobudgeting according to Rubin? Why is it important to distinguish between the two? Did the case, "County Prison Overtime," represent either or both?

Key Terms

bureau chiefs

chief executive officers

power differentials

separation of payer and decider

open environment

budget constraints

reform orientation

incrementalist view

revenue cluster

expenditure cluster

balance cluster

budget implementation

microbudgeting

macrobudgeting

legal environment

intergovernmental grant structure

individual strategies

budget outcomes

fiscal year

policy choices

Suggestions for Further Reading

An excellent way to increase your understanding of budgets is to obtain a current city, county, state, or federal budget (usually the summary document provides all the important information) and read it carefully. Most summaries are written so that the layperson can understand their major contents and proposals. Also, now that public budgets are frequently the subjects of front-page headlines, read the major news coverage devoted to them, particularly in leading newspapers like the *New York Times, Washington Post, Christian Science Monitor, Los Angeles Times, St. Louis Post Dispatch,* and *Wall Street Journal* as well as in news magazines like *Time The Economist,* and *Newsweek.* The best up-to-date, scholarly survey of budgetary subjects is found in a thoughtfully edited journal, *Public Budgeting and Finance.* Each issue contains insightful articles by some of the leading experts in the field. Also do not neglect studying current issues of the *Public Administration Review* or *Governing,* as well as the annual volumes of *Setting National Priorities* published by the Brookings Institution in Washington, D.C.

Although they become dated quickly, introductory texts also offer a useful overview. For the best recent ones, see Robert D. Lee, Jr., and Ronald W. Johnson, *Public Budgeting Systems,* Fourth Edition (Baltimore: University Park Press, 1989); Donald Axelrod, *Budgeting for Modern Government,* Second Edition (New York: St. Martin's Press, 1995); Irene S. Rubin, *The Politics of Public Budgeting* (Chatham, N.J.: Chatham House, 1990); Albert C. Hyde, *Government Budgeting: Theory, Process, Politics,* Second Edition (Pacific Grove, Calif.: Brooks/Cole, 1992); Don A. Cozzetto, Mary G. Kweit, and Robert W. Kweit, *Public Budgeting* (New York: Longman, 1995); John L. Mikeskill, *Fiscal Administration* (Pacific Grove, Calif.: Brooks/Cole, 1995); Gerald J. Miller, *Government Financial Management Theory* (New York: Marcel Dekker, 1991); and Aaron Wildavsky, *The New Politics of the Budgetary Process,* Second Edition (New York: HarperCollins, 1992). For an outstanding historic collection of several of the best essays written on public budgeting, see Allen Schick, *Perspectives on Budgeting,* Revised Edition (Washington, D.C.: American Society for Public Administration, 1987). A handy, free guidebook that explains the difficult and arcane jargon of budgeting is *A Glossary of Terms Used in the Federal Budget Process* (Washington, D.C.: General Accounting Office, 1977). For a useful handbook of synthesizing essays by experts on various aspects of budgeting, see Jack Rabin, *Handbook on Public Budgeting* (New York: Marcel Dekker, 1992); and Allen Schick, *The Capacity to Budget* (Washington, D.C.: Urban Institute, 1990).

Undoubtedly, a profound impact on federal budgetary practices was made by the enactment of the 1974 Congressional Budget Reform Act, which is examined in several scholarly books, including Allen Schick, *Congress and Money* (Washington, D.C.: The Urban Institute, 1980); Dennis S. Ippolito, *Congressional Spending* (Ithaca, N.Y.: Cornell University Press, 1981); Lance T. LeLoup, *The Fiscal Congress* (Westport, Conn.: Greenwood Press, 1980); Rudolph G. Penner, ed., *The Congressional Budget Process After Five Years* (Washington, D.C.: American Enterprise Institute, 1981); and James P. Pfiffner, *The President, the*

Budget, and Congress (Boulder, Colo.: Westview Press, 1979). For two thoughtful case studies of federal budgetary politics, read Paul Light, *Artful Work: The Politics of Social Security Reform* (New York: Random House, 1985); and Irene S. Rubin, *Shrinking the Federal Government* (New York: Longman, 1985); and for an excellent look at where we are with the application of various budgetary systems, see George W. Downs and Patrick D. Larkey, *The Search for Government Efficiency* (New York: Random House, 1986), especially Chapters 4 and 5, as well as two insightful essays in the *Public Administration Review* 44 (March/April 1984): Hardy Wickwar, "Budgets One and Many," pp. 99–102, and Naomi Caiden, "The New Rules of the Federal Budget Game," pp. 109–117.

For two practical, "how-to" books on budgeting, refer to Edward A. Leham, *Simplified Government Budgeting* (Chicago, Ill.: Municipal Finance Officers Association, 1981), and Richard J. Stillman II, *Results-oriented Budgeting for Local Public Managers* (Columbia, S.C.: Institute of Governmental Research, University of South Carolina, 1982). Part five of James L. Perry, ed., *Handbook of Public Administration* (San Francisco: Jossey-Bass, 1989), offers several applied essays on public budgeting.

A remarkable inside look at modern federal budgeting is William Greider, *The Education of David Stockman and Other Americans* (New York: Dutton, 1981). Also read David Stockman's autobiography, *The Triumph of Politics: The Inside Story of the Reagan Revolution* (New York: Harper & Row, 1986).

Federal budgets today are driven by issues involving debt financing, indexing, and entitlements; three good books relating to these issues are: Robert Heilbroner and Peter Bernstein, *The Debt and the Deficit: False Alarms and Real Possibilities* (New York: W. W. Norton, 1989); R. Kent Weaver, *Automatic Government: The Politics of Indexation* (Washington, D.C.: Brookings, 1988); Peter G. Peterson and Neil Howe, *On Borrowed Time: How the Growth of Entitlement Spending Threatens America's Future* (San Francisco: Institute of Contemporary Studies, 1988); Daniel P.

Franklin, *Making Ends Meet: Congressional Budgeting in the Age of Deficits* (Washington, D.C.: CQ Press, 1992); and Donald F. Kettl, *Deficit Politics* (New York: Macmillan, 1992).

Several excellent overview essays on contemporary budgetary issues have appeared in recent years and among those by leading scholars in the field are: Robert D. Lee, "Developments in State Budgeting: Trends of Two Decades," *Public Administration Review* (May/June 1991), pp. 254–262; Irene S. Rubin, "Budget Theory and Budget Practice: How Good the Fit?" *Public Administration Review* (March/April 1990), pp. 179–189; Raphael Thelwell, "Gramm-Rudman-Hollings Four Years Later: A Dangerous Illusion," *Public Administration Review* (March/April 1990), pp. 190–198; Allen Schick, "Budgeting for Results: Recent Developments in Five Industrialized Countries," *Public Administration Review* (January/February 1990), pp. 26–34; Donald F. Kettl, "Expansion and Protection in the Budgetary Process," *Public Administration Review* (May/June 1989), pp. 231–239; Allen Schick, "Micro-Budget Adaptations to Fiscal Stress in Industrialized Democracies," *Public Administration Review* (January/February 1988), pp. 523–533; Aaron Wildavsky, "Political Implications of Budget Reform," *Public Administration Review* 52, (November/December 1992), pp. 594–599; Irene S. Rubin, "Who Invented Budgeting in the U.S.?" *Public Administration Review,* 53 (September/October 1993), pp. 438–444; and the entire symposium on "Public Debt," Jack Rabin, ed., in the *Public Administration Review,* 53 (January/February 1993), pp. 8–58.

Perhaps the best overview of where we are today with academic research in this field can be found in Naomi Caiden, "Public Budgeting in the United States: The State of the Discipline," in Naomi B. Lynn and Aaron Wildavsky, eds., *Public Administration: The State of the Discipline* (Chatham, N.J.: Chatham House, 1990).

CHAPTER 13

Implementation: The Concept of Optimal Conditions for Effectively Accomplishing Objectives

*L*egislators and other policy formulators can go a long way toward assuring
effective policy implementation if they see that a statute incorporates sound
theory, provides precise and clearly ranked objectives, and structures the implementation process in a wide number of ways so as to maximize the probability of target group compliance. In addition, they can take positive steps to
appoint skillful and supportive implementing officials, to provide adequate appropriations and to monitor carefully the behavior of implementing agencies
through the long implementation process, and to be aware of the effects of
changing socioeconomic conditions. . . .

Paul Sabatier and Daniel Mazmanian

READING 13

Introduction

From the very beginning of its conscious development as a field of study, public administration has stressed the importance of "good," "correct," "timely," and "efficient"
execution of public objectives. Sound implementation was and perhaps still is "the
bottom line" of what the administrative enterprise is all about. As Woodrow Wilson
wrote in "The Study of Administration," the first American essay on public administration in 1887, "The broad plans of government action are not administration; the detailed execution of such plans is administration."[1]

Although "detailed execution" may well have always been the central preoccupation of public administrators, the last two decades have witnessed an impressive emergence and growth of scholarship directed specifically at exploring this subject. Indeed,
by the 1980s implementation scholarship had become a distinct and separate subfield
of public administration, political science, and policy studies. Implementation scholarship now boasts its own considerable array of professional journals and dedicated

[1]Woodrow Wilson, "The Study of Administration," *Political Science Quarterly,* 2 (June 1887), p. 197.

scholars, as well as sizable conferences oriented toward discussing various intellectual viewpoints and new methodologies related to this subject.

Much of the original impetus to develop a conscious subfield of study concerning implementation came from what many perceived as the apparent failure of the Great Society Programs. In the mid-1960s President Lyndon B. Johnson succeeded in pushing through Congress in a relatively short period a vast range of new types of social programs designed to alleviate major social problems (such as hunger, delinquency, poverty, unemployment, racial discrimination, and urban decay) as well as other prominent social concerns of the day and aimed at building "The Great Society." As Robert T. Nakamura and Frank Smallwood write, "It was not long before disillusionment began to set in as it became apparent that it might be easier to 'legitimize' social policy by passing ambiguous legislation than to carry out such policy by means of effective program implementation."[2]

By the late 1960s and early 1970s students of public affairs began questioning the value of passing so many laws creating new social programs without paying adequate attention to whether these laws were effectively implemented or carried out at all. Theodore Lowi, in his *The End of Liberalism* (1969), popularized this attack on the broad expansion of governmental activities, which, he argued, had eroded clear standards for administrative accountability and consequently had led to a crisis of public authority over the role and purposes of government in society. As public programs grew into more and more abstract and complex activities, according to Lowi, "it became more difficult to set precise legislative guidelines for execution of public policy."[3] It also opened up government programs to chaotic pluralistic competition. Lowi termed this phenomenon *interest group liberalism*. His solution was to return to a more simplified structure in which Congress and the president make precise laws and the courts formulate strict judicial standards to guide administrative actions, thereby reducing administrative discretion to a minimum. Hence, implementation would become little if any problem for administrators because their choices would be restricted and their direction from policy makers would be well defined and specific.

Meanwhile, other scholars were by then also busily pointing out that the Great Society Programs were not working as planned. Several case studies appeared at this time making much the same point—namely, that the Great Society Social Programs, for various reasons, were not or could not be effectively implemented—such as Martha Derthick's *New Towns In-Town*[4] and Daniel P. Moynihan's *Maximum Feasible Misunderstanding*.[5] Jeffrey Pressman and Aaron Wildavsky's *Implementation* (1973)[6] especially sparked much of the serious academic interest in this topic. Pressman and Wildavsky wrote what was essentially a case study of the Economic Development Administration's effort in the late 1960s to provide jobs for the "hard-core" unemployed in Oakland, California. Their case turned out to be a study in how not to get things

---

[2]Robert T. Nakamura and Frank Smallwood, *The Politics of Policy Implementation* (New York: St. Martin's Press, 1980), p. 11.

[3]Theodore J. Lowi, *The End of Liberalism* (New York: W. W. Norton, 1969), p. 127.

[4]Martha Derthick, *New Towns In-Town* (Washington, D.C.: Urban Institute, 1972).

[5]Daniel P. Moynihan, *Maximum Feasible Misunderstanding* (New York: Free Press, 1970).

[6]Jeffrey L. Pressman and Aaron B. Wildavsky, *Implementation* (Berkeley: University of California Press, 1973).

done in government. At the end of their book they offered a prescriptive list of warnings about what should *not* be done to accomplish public policy objectives: "Implementation should not be divorced from policy"; "Designers of policy [should] consider the direct means for achieving their ends"; "Continuity of leadership is important"; "Simplicity in policies is much to be desired"; and so on.

After the appearance of the Pressman and Wildavsky book, Edwin C. Hargrove of the Urban Institute called implementation "the missing link" in social theory, and soon an impressive array of new methodological approaches began to search for "the missing link."[7] Several of the more prominent implementation theories that have been put forward during the past decade include the following:

> *Implementation as a linear process:* Donald S. Van Meter and Carl E. Van Horn, in an essay entitled "The Policy Implementation Process: A Conceptual Framework," which appeared in *Administration and Society* (1975), argue that implementation involves a linear process composed of six variables that link policy with performance: standards and objectives; resources; interorganizational communications and enforcement activities; characteristics of the implementing agencies; economic, social, and political conditions; and the disposition of the implementers.[8] Presumably relationships or changes in any one of these inputs ultimately, according to the authors, can influence the successful performance of the policy objectives.

> *Implementation as politics of mutual adaptation:* In a study of several federal programs by Milbrey McLaughlin in 1975 for the Rand Corporation, the writer concludes, "The amount of interest, commitment and support evidenced by the principal actors had a major influence on the prospects for success."[9] In other words, the political support from the top, according to McLaughlin, was the key to success or failure of program implementation.

> *Implementation as gamesmanship:* Eugene Bardach's *Implementation Game* (1977), as the book's title indicates, sees the subject essentially as a "game," "where bargaining, persuasion, and maneuvering under conditions of uncertainty occur"[10] to exercise control of outcomes. For Bardach, implementation therefore involves all the arts of gamesmanship: learning the rules of the game, devising tactics and strategy, controlling the flow of communications, and dealing with crises and uncertain situations as they arise.

> *Implementation as conditions for effectively accomplishing objectives:* Paul Sabatier and Daniel Mazmanian in "The Conditions of Effective Implementation: A Guide to Accomplishing Policy Objectives" (1979)[11] attempt to forecast what conditions promote or prevent policy implementation. They argue that the likelihood of implementation is enhanced by the existence of a favorable or "optimal" set of conditions. Conversely, in their view, implementation is impeded or alto-

[7]Edwin C. Hargrove, *The Missing Link* (Washington, D.C.: Urban Institute, 1975).

[8]Donald S. Van Meter and Carl E. Van Horn, "The Policy Implementation Process: A Conceptual Framework," *Administration and Society,* 6, no. 4 (February 1975), p. 449.

[9]Milbrey McLaughlin, "Implementation as Mutual Adaptation," in Walter Williams and Richard Elmore (eds.), *Social Program Implementation* (New York: Academic Press, 1976), pp. 167–180.

[10]Eugene Bardach, *The Implementation Game* (Cambridge, Mass.: M.I.T. Press, 1977), p. 56.

[11]Paul Sabatier and Daniel Mazmanian, "The Conditions of Effective Implementation: A Guide to Accomplishing Policy Objectives," *Policy Analysis,* 5, no. 4 (Fall 1979), pp. 481–504.

gether prevented when some or all of these conditions do not exist. Much of their essay is devoted to elaborating on the five conditions they consider necessary "that can go a long way toward assuring effective policy implementation if they are met."

Implementation as a circular policy leadership process: By comparison, Robert T. Nakamura and Frank Smallwood perceive implementation as a circular process intricately involved within the entire public policy-making process. In their book *The Politics of Policy Implementation* (1980), the authors argue, "Implementation is but one part of this [policy] process and is inextricably related to, and interdependent with, the other parts."[12] For Nakamura and Smallwood the critical element linking implementation to the rest of the policy process is leadership, which, in their words, is necessary "to coordinate activities in all three environments" (policy formulation, implementation, and evaluation) to achieve program goals.

Implementation as contingency theory: Ernest R. Alexander, by contrast, in "From Idea to Action," in *Administration and Society* (1985), develops a contingency model of policy implementation.[13] He views implementation as a complex "continuing interactive process," one that involves interactions with the environment, stimulus, policy, programs, and outcomes—all very much depending on the specific content, elements, and timing of these interactions.

Implementation as case analysis: As with the Pressman and Wildavsky book, case studies of a single implementation situation remain a popular approach to understanding this subject. They seek to draw specific "lessons" about right—or wrong—approaches to accomplishing public policies within a specific policy field. Charles S. Bullock III and Charles M. Lamb's *Implementation of Civil Rights Policy* (1986) presents a highly sophisticated case analysis of this sort.[14] It analyzes in depth five cases in the civil rights field and draws conclusions about the significance of ten specific variables involving the effective implementation of civil rights policies. The authors conclude that five variables in particular are critical for successful policy implementation: federal involvement, specific agency standards, agency commitment, support from superiors, and favorable cost/benefit ratios.

Today the debate among scholars continues over what constitutes the appropriate conceptual framework to best comprehend the implementation of public policy. It remains hardly a settled matter, with theories and counter-theories being put forward at a brisk pace. Certainly, as yet, scholars have not agreed on any *one* model to explain public implementation processes or how models work in government. Nevertheless, it would be worthwhile to look closely at one of the more prominent approaches to this topic to help clarify and understand this topic more thoroughly. The following conceptual framework for viewing implementation by two California-based policy analysts, Paul Sabatier and Daniel Mazmanian, "The Conditions of Effective Implementation: A Guide to Accomplishing Policy Objectives," reflects one of the major influential—not to mention controversial—approaches to appear in recent years. In their essay, Sabatier and

---

[12]Nakamura and Smallwood, *The Politics of Policy Implementation,* p. 21.

[13]Ernest R. Alexander, "From Idea to Action: Notes for a Contingency Theory of the Policy Implementation Process," *Administration and Society,* 16, no. 4 (February 1985), pp. 403–425.

[14]Charles S. Bullock III and Charles M. Lamb, *Implementation of Civil Rights Policy* (Monterey, Calif.: Brooks/Cole Publishing, 1986).

Mazmanian try to forecast what conditions promote or prevent policy implementation. They argue that the likelihood of implementation is enhanced by the existence of a favorable or "optimal" set of conditions. Conversely, in their view, implementation is impeded or prevented when some or all of these conditions do not exist. Much of their essay is spent elaborating on precisely what they consider the five essential conditions "that can go a long way toward assuring effective policy implementation if they are met." The writers also point out at the end of their essay how implementation can take place under less than ideal or "suboptimal conditions."

As you read this selection, keep the following questions in mind:

What assumptions do the authors make in building their conceptual model of optimal conditions for implementation? Do they assume, for example, that implementation activities take place in an open, democratic, and pluralistic society? One governed by laws? Or what? How do such assumptions shape the concept they put forward?

What implications does their model have for practicing public administrators? Can they use it successfully to predict when conditions are "ripe" for implementing programs or *how* to implement programs?

Are the two authors optimistic about the possibilities of shaping conditions to allow for successful implementation of public policies?

Would their ideas have proved useful for the policy makers and administrators designing a program in any of the previous case studies you have read in this text, such as "Dumping $2.6 Million on Bakersfield"? How so?

The Conditions of Effective Implementation

PAUL SABATIER AND DANIEL MAZMANIAN

. . . It is our contention that a statute or other major policy decision seeking a substantial departure from the status quo will achieve its objectives under the following set of conditions:

1. The program is based on a sound theory relating changes in target group behavior to the achievement of the desired end-state (objectives).

2. The statute (or other basic policy decision) contains unambiguous policy directives and structures the implementation process so as to maximize the likelihood that target groups will perform as desired.
3. The leaders of the implementing agencies possess substantial managerial and political skill and are committed to statutory goals.
4. The program is actively supported by organized constituency groups and by a few key legislators (or the chief executive) through-

out the implementation process, with the courts being neutral or supportive.

5. The relative priority of statutory objectives is not significantly undermined over time by the emergence of conflicting public policies or by changes in relevant socioeconomic conditions that undermine the statute's "technical" theory or political support.

The conceptual framework underlying this set of conditions . . . is based upon a (proto) theory of public agencies that views them as bureaucracies with multiple goals that are in constant interaction with interest (constituency) groups, other agencies, and legislative (and executive) sovereigns in their policy subsystem.

Before elaborating on each of these conditions, we should note that obtaining target group compliance is obviously much more difficult in some situations than in others. The greater the difficulty, the greater the legal and political resources that must be marshalled if compliance is to be achieved. In the terms of our framework, the required "strength" (or degree of bias) of the last four conditions is a function of several factors, including the amount of change required in target group behavior, the orientation of target groups toward the mandated change, and the diversity in proscribed activities of target groups. In other words, the greater the mandated change, the more opposed the target groups, and the more diverse their proscribed activities, the greater must be the degree of statutory structuring, the skill of implementing officials, the support from constituency groups and sovereigns, and the stability in socioeconomic conditions if statutory objectives are to be attained. Within this context, the set of five conditions should always be sufficient to achieve policy objectives. Moreover, each condition is probably necessary if the change sought is substantial and requires five to ten years of effort; in easier situations, however, it may be possible to omit one of the last three conditions.

Condition 1: The program is based on a sound theory relating changes in target group behavior to the achievement of the desired end-state (objectives).

Most basic policy decisions are based upon an underlying causal theory that can be divided into two components—the first relating achievement of the desired end-state(s) back to changes in target group behavior, the second specifying the means by which target group compliance can be obtained. Both the "technical" and the "compliance" components must be valid for the policy objective(s) to be attained.

At this point, we are concerned only with the former ("technical") component, as the remaining four conditions in our framework relate primarily to the latter. In particular, we wish to emphasize that target group compliance—and the costs involved in obtaining it—may be wasted if not correctly linked to the desired end-state. For example, the "technical" component of the theory underlying the 1970 Clean Air Amendments relates air quality levels back to emissions from various stationary and mobile sources (the target groups). It assumes that human activities are the major source of air pollutants and that pollutant emissions from various sources within an air basin can be related, via diffusion models, to air quality levels at specific locations. To the extent that nonhuman sources, such as volcanoes, constitute a major emission source or that little is known about pollutant interaction and transport in the atmosphere, target group compliance with legally prescribed emission levels will not achieve air quality objectives (or will do so only very inefficiently). Moreover, the administrative and other costs involved in obtaining compliance are likely to be resented—with a corresponding decline in political support for the program—to the extent that promised improvements in air quality are not at least approximated. In short, an invalid technical component has both direct and indirect effects on the (non)achievement of policy objectives.

We should note, however, that there are some programs for which target group compliance can be interpreted as *the* policy objective. In such instances, the absence of any explicit attempt to link target group behavior to some subsequent end-state means that the first of our five conditions would not apply (as the underlying "technical" component deals directly with that linkage). For example, the goal of desegregation policy in the South could be construed as the elimination of dual schools—in which case the compliance of local target groups (school boards) would be tantamount to successful implementation. Insofar, however, as the goal of desegregation was not simply the elimination of dual schools but also the improvement of black children's reading scores, the "technical" assumption that unified schools improve reading scores would have to be valid for the policy objective to be attained.

Condition 2: The statute (or other basic policy decision) contains unambiguous policy directives and structures the implementation process so as to maximize the likelihood that target groups will perform as desired.

This is the condition most under the control of policy formulators (such as legislators). Unfortunately, its importance has often been overlooked by behaviorally oriented social scientists. For these reasons, we will briefly examine its constituent parts.

(a) The policy objectives are precise and clearly ranked, both internally (within the specific statute) and in the overall program of implementing agencies. Statutory objectives that are precise and clearly ranked in importance serve as an indispensable aid in program evaluation, as unambiguous directives to implementing officials, and as a resource available to supporters of those objectives both inside and outside the implementing agencies. For example, implementing officials confronted with objections to their programs can sympathize with the aggrieved party but nevertheless respond that they are only following the legislature's instructions. Clear objectives can also serve as a resource to actors outside the implementing institutions who perceive discrepancies between agency outputs and those objectives (particularly if the statute also provides them formal access to the implementation process, such as via citizen suit provisions).

While the desirability of unambiguous policy directives within a given statute is normally understood, it is also important that a statute assigned for implementation to an existing agency clearly indicate the relative priority that the new directives are to play in the totality of the agency's programs. If this is not done, the new directives are likely to undergo considerable delay and be accorded low priority as they struggle for incorporation into the agency's operating procedures.

(b) The financial resources provided to the implementing agencies are sufficient to hire the staff and conduct the technical analyses involved in the development of regulations, the administration of permit/service delivery programs, and the monitoring of target group compliance. Although this condition is fairly obvious, ascertaining what constitutes "sufficient" resources presents enormous difficulties in practice. As a general rule, however, a threshold level of funding is necessary for there to be any possibility of achieving statutory objectives, and the level of funding above this threshold is (up to some saturation point) proportional to the probability of achieving those objectives. Financial resources are perhaps particularly problematic in labor-intensive service delivery programs and in regulatory programs with a high scientific or technological component, where implementing agencies often lack the funds to engage in the research and development necessary to examine critically the information presented by target groups and, in some cases, to develop alternative technologies.

(c) Implementation is assigned to agencies supportive of statutory objectives that will give the new program high priority. Any new program requires implementing officials who are not merely neutral but also sufficiently committed and persistent to develop new regulations and standard operating procedures and to enforce them in the face of resistance from target groups and from public officials reluctant to make the mandated changes.

Thus it is extremely important that implementation be assigned to agencies whose policy orientation is consistent with the statute and which will accord the new program high priority. This is most likely when a new agency is created with a clear mandate after an extensive political struggle, as the program will necessarily be its highest priority and the creation of new positions opens the door to a vast infusion of statutory supporters. Alternatively, implementation can be assigned to a prestigious existing agency that considers the new mandate compatible with its traditional orientation and is looking for new programs. In addition to selecting generally supportive agencies, a statute can sometimes stipulate that top implementing officials be selected from social sectors that generally support the legislation's objectives. Even if this cannot be done through legislation, legislative supporters can often play a critical role in the appointment of non-civil-service personnel within the implementing agencies.

In practice, however, the choice of implementing agencies and officials is often severely constrained. In many policy areas (such as education) there is little option but to assign implementation to existing agencies that may well be hostile or whose personnel may be so preoccupied with existing programs that any new mandate tends to get lost in the shuffle. In addition, most positions within any governmental agency are occupied by career civil servants who are often resistant to changes in existing procedures and programs and only moderately susceptible to the sanctions and inducements available to political appointees. In fact, the generally limited ability of policy formulators to assign implementation to agency officials committed to its objectives probably lies behind many cases of suboptimal correspondence of policy outputs with statutory objectives.

(d) The statute (or other basic policy decision) provides substantial hierarchical integration within and among implementing agencies by minimizing the number of veto/clearance points and by providing supporters of statutory objectives with inducements and sanctions sufficient to assure acquiescence among those with a potential veto. Surely one of the dominant themes in the implementation literature is the difficulty of obtaining coordinated action within any given agency and among the numerous semiautonomous agencies involved in most implementation efforts. The problem is particularly acute in federal statutes that rely on state and local agencies for carrying out the details of program delivery and for which some field-

level implementors and/or target groups display considerable resistance toward statutory directives. Thus one of the most important attributes of any statute (or other basic policy decision) is the extent to which it hierarchically integrates the implementing agencies. To the extent the system is only loosely integrated, there will be considerable variation in the degree of behavioral compliance among implementing officials and target groups— as each responds to the incentives for modification within its local setting—and thus a distinctly suboptimal attainment of statutory objectives.

The degree of hierarchical integration among implementing agencies is determined by the number of veto/clearance points involved in the attainment of statutory objectives and the extent to which supporters of statutory objectives are provided with inducements and sanctions sufficient to assure acquiescence among those with a potential veto. Veto/clearance points involve those occasions in which an actor has the capacity (quite apart from the question of legal authority) to impede the achievement of statutory objectives. Resistance from specific veto points can be overcome, however, if the statute provides sufficient sanctions and/or inducements to convince role occupants (whether implementing officials or target groups) to alter their behavior. In short, if these sanctions and inducements are great enough, the number of veto points can delay—but probably never ultimately impede—behavioral compliance by target groups. In practice, however, the compliance incentives are usually sufficiently modest that the number of veto/clearance points becomes extremely important. As a result, the most direct route to a statutory objective—such as a negative income tax to provide a minimum income—is often preferable to complex programs administered by numerous semiautonomous bureaucracies.

(e) The decision rules of implementing agencies are supportive of statutory objectives. In addition to providing unambiguous objectives, generally supportive implementing officials, few veto points, and adequate incentive for compliance, a statute (or other basic policy decision) can further bias the implementation process by stipulating the formal

decision rules of the implementing agencies. The decisions of implementing agencies are likely to be consistent with statutory objectives to the extent, for example, that the burden of proof in permit/ licensing cases is placed on the applicant and that agency officials are required to make findings fully consistent with statutory objectives. In addition, a statute can assign authority to make final decisions within implementing institutions to those subunits most likely to support statutory objectives. Finally, when multimembered commissions are involved, the statute can stipulate the majority required for specific actions. In the case of regulatory agencies that operate primarily through the granting of permits or licenses, decision rules that make the granting of a permit contingent upon substantial consensus, such as a two-thirds majority, are obviously conducive to stringent regulation.

(f) The statute (or other basic policy decision) provides ample opportunity for constituency (interest) groups and sovereigns supportive of statutory objectives to intervene in the implementation process through, for example, liberal rules of standing to agency and judicial proceedings and requirements for periodic evaluation of the performance of implementing agencies and target groups. While a statute can take steps to assure that implementing officials are generally supportive of statutory objectives and that the decision process involving implementing agencies and target groups contains few veto points, adequate incentives for compliance, and supportive formal rules, we nevertheless contend that implementing officials cannot necessarily be trusted to act in a manner consistent with statutory objectives. What is also required is constant oversight and intervention from supportive constituency groups and legislative (and executive) sovereigns.

A statute (or other basic policy decision) can take a number of steps to maximize the probability of such intervention. First, it can require opportunities for public input at numerous stages in the decision process of implementing agencies and even require that the agencies take positive steps to assure the participation of unorganized potential beneficiaries. Second, it can provide for liberal

rules of standing to appeal agency decisions to the courts. For example, the citizen suit provisions of the 1970 Clean Air Amendments have been used on several occasions to compel the U.S. Environmental Protection Agency to carry out statutorily mandated provisions that it had failed, for one reason or another, to do. Third, requirements for periodic reporting of agency performance to legislative and executive sovereigns and for evaluation studies by prestigious independent organizations (such as the National Academy of Sciences) are conducive to external oversight of the implementing agencies and probably to the achievement of statutory objectives.

In sum, a carefully formulated statute (or other basic policy decision) should be seen as a means by which legislators and other policy formulators can structure the entire implementation process and maximize the probability that the policy outputs of the implementing agencies and the behavior of target groups (whether outside or inside those agencies) will be consistent with statutory objectives. This requires, first, that they develop unambiguous policy objectives and incorporate a valid technical theory linking target group compliance with the desired impacts. In order to maximize the probability of such compliance, they should then assign implementation to supportive agencies, provide implementing officials with adequate financial resources, hierarchically integrate the implementation process through minimizing veto points and providing sufficient incentives to overcome resistance, bias the formal decision rules of implementing agencies, and provide opportunities for outsiders to participate in the implementation process and to evaluate accurately agency (and target group) performance.

But a statute, no matter how well it structures implementation, is not a sufficient condition for assuring target group compliance with its objectives. Assuring sufficient compliance to actually achieve those objectives normally takes at least three to five, and often ten to twenty, years. During this period, there are constant pressures for even supportive agency officials to lose their commitment, for supportive constituency groups and sovereigns to fail to maintain active political support, and for the entire process to be gradually undermined by changing socioeconomic forces. In short, while a statute can go a long way toward assuring successful implementation, there are additional conditions that must be fulfilled if its objectives are to be attained.

Condition 3: The leaders of the implementing agencies possess substantial managerial and political skill and are committed to statutory objectives.

As already indicated, legislators and other policy formulators can take a number of important steps—both in the drafting of a statute and in the subsequent appointment of non-civil-service personnel—to increase substantially the probability that the leaders of implementing agencies will be supportive of statutory objectives. In practice, however, statutory levers are often somewhat limited (except where creation of a new agency is feasible), and the process of appointing political executives is heavily dependent upon the wishes of the chief executive and important legislators—several of whom may well not be committed to implementation of the basic policy decision. In short, the support of top implementing officials is sufficiently important and problematic to warrant being highlighted as a separate condition for successful implementation.

Moreover, policy support is essentially useless if not accompanied by political and managerial skill in utilizing available resources. Political skill involves the ability to develop good working relationships with sovereigns in the agency's subsystem, to convince opponents and target groups that they are being treated fairly, to mobilize support among latent supportive constituencies, to present the agency's case adroitly through the mass media, and so forth. Managerial skill involves developing adequate controls so that the program is not subject to charges of fiscal mismanagement, maintaining high morale among agency personnel, and managing internal dissent in such a way that dissidents are convinced they have received a fair hearing.

Finally, there is some evidence that maintaining high morale, commitment, and perhaps even skill becomes increasingly difficult over time. Innovative policy initiatives often attract committed and skillful executives to implementing institutions, particularly in the case of new agencies. But such people generally become burned out and disillusioned with bureaucratic routine after a few years, to be replaced by officials much more interested in personal security and organizational maintenance than in taking risks to attain policy goals.

Condition 4: The program is actively supported by organized constituency groups and by a few key legislators (or the chief executive) throughout the implementation process, with the courts being neutral or supportive.

It is absolutely crucial to maintain active political support for the achievement of statutory objectives over the long course of implementation. If the first three conditions have been met, this essentially requires that sufficient support be maintained among legislative and executive sovereigns to provide the implementing agencies with the requisite financial resources annually, as well as assuring that the basic statute is not seriously undermined but instead modified to overcome implementation difficulties.

This seemingly rather simple requirement is, however, exceedingly difficult to accomplish, for a variety of reasons. First, the rather episodic issue-attention span of the general public and the mass media tends to undermine diffuse political support for any particular program among both the public and legislators. Second, there is a general tendency for organized constituency support for a wide variety of programs—including environmental and consumer protection, as well as efforts to aid the poor—to decline over time, while opposition from target groups to the costs imposed on them remains constant or actually increases. This shift in the balance of constituency support for such programs gradually becomes reflected in a shift in support among members of the legislature as a whole and the committees in the relevant subsystem(s). Third, most legislators lack the staff resources and/or the incentives to monitor program implementation actively. The exception is constituent casework, which tends to be heavily skewed towards complaints. Without active political support from a few key legislators, implementing officials supportive of the program find it difficult to overcome the constant drumbeat of constituent complaints, as well as the delay and resistance inherent in implementing any program requiring substantial behavioral change (except in those instances where target groups support such change).

Despite these difficulties, the necessary infusion of political support can be maintained if two factors are present. The first is the presence of a "fixer" (or fixers)—that is, an important legislator or executive official who controls resources important to other actors and who has the desire and the staff resources to closely monitor the implementation process, to intervene with agency officials on an almost continuous basis, and to protect the budget and the legal authority of the implementing agencies. Except in very unusual circumstances, however, any particular "fixer" is unlikely to occupy a crucial position and/or to maintain an interest throughout the long process of implementation. This brings us to the second, and ultimately the most important requirement, namely, the presence of an organized supportive constituency (interest) group that has the resources to monitor closely program implementation, to intervene actively in agency proceedings, to appeal adverse agency decisions to the courts and to the legislature, and to convince key legislators that the program merits their active support. For the paramount advantage of any organization over an individual is continuity. If the supportive constituency is present, "fixers" can generally be found and/or nurtured.

Programs involving intergovernmental relations, however, pose additional difficulties to the maintenance of political support. On the one hand, programs of intergovernmental "subordinates" (such as localities vis-à-vis states and the federal government) are often subject to revision and/or emasculation by superordinate units of government. Unless a program's representatives occupy important positions at the superordinate level, there is little that can be done to maintain its legal (and sometimes financial) integrity. Conversely, superordinate levels are usually confronted with substantial local variation in political support for program objectives and, consequently, in the compliance of local implementing officials with program directives. While such variation can, in principle, be overcome if the superordinate statute provides very substantial incentives for compliance and sufficient financial resources to enable superordinate officials essentially to replace local implementors, in practice the system is seldom structured to that degree, and thus superordinate officials are forced to bargain with recalcitrant local implementors. The result is greater sensitivity to local demands and generally a suboptimal achievement of statutory objectives.

The discussion thus far has focused on the need for political support among the legislative and executive sovereigns of implementing agencies. But one must not neglect the courts. In most cases, the contemporary deference of most federal and state courts to agency decision making means that they play a rather minor role in the implementation process except on procedural issues and to assure conformity with explicit statutory directives. But courts strongly opposed to a given statute have the authority to emasculate implementation through delay in enforcement proceedings, through repeatedly unfavorable statutory interpretations, and, in extreme cases, by declaring the statute unconstitutional. On the other hand, there have been some instances where courts have substantially strengthened programs through favorable rulings. Given the enormous potential role of the courts, we argue that successful implementation of statutory objectives requires that they be either neutral or supportive.

Condition 5: The relative priority of statutory objectives is not significantly undermined over time by the emergence of conflicting public policies or by changes in relevant socioeconomic conditions that undermine the statute's "technical" theory or political support.

Change is omnipresent in most contemporary societies, in part because most countries are immersed in an international system over which they have only modest control, in part because policy issues tend to be highly interrelated. Pollution control, for example, is linked to energy, to inflation and national monetary policy, to transportation, to public lands, and to numerous other issues. As a result of this continuous change, any particular policy decision is susceptible to an erosion of political support as other issues become relatively more important over time. Obvious examples would be the effect of the Vietnam War and inflation on many Great Society programs and the effect of the energy crisis and inflation on pollution control programs. Change can also be so extensive as essentially to undermine the technical assumptions upon which a policy is based, as when the migration of poor people from the South and Puerto Rico to northern industrial cities brought into serious question the ability of state and local governments to provide matching funds for welfare programs.

It is in responding to such changes that support for a particular program from key legislators, organized constituency groups, and implementing officials becomes crucial. If they are sensitive to the effects that changes in seemingly tangential policies and in technical assumptions can have on "their" program, they can take steps to see that these repercussions are addressed in any new legislation.

Policy Feedback and Evaluation

Thus far our attention has been focused on the extent to which implementing agencies and target groups act in a manner consistent with statutory objectives and ultimately on the extent to which those objectives are actually attained. In this respect we have mirrored the focus on formal goals of much of the literature on implementation assessment and program evaluation.

But if one is interested in the evolution of policy and particularly with the political feedback process, a much wider range of impacts (or outcomes) needs to be considered. Of particular importance are unintended impacts that affect political support for the program's objectives. For example, any assessment of the implementation of school desegregation policy should be concerned not only with the amount of desegregation achieved but also with the effect of desegregation on "white flight" and ultimately on the amount of political and financial support for the public schools. Moreover, there is some evidence that political feedback is based primarily upon perceived, rather than actual, impacts and that policy elites evaluate a program not in terms of the extent to which it achieves its legal mandate but rather in terms of its perceived conformity with their policy preferences.

The actual process of policy evaluation and feedback occurs continuously on an informal basis as the implementing agencies interact with concerned constituency groups, legislative (and executive) sovereigns, and the courts. At periodic intervals, however, the process normally becomes more formal and politically salient as attempts are made to revise substantially the basic statute. For example, major efforts to amend federal air pollution control law seem to occur every three to four years. Some of these revisions can be attributed to continued resistance from affected target groups, while others can be traced to significant changes in relevant social and economic conditions. Whatever the source of proposed changes, it is important that supporters of the original objectives provide for independent evaluation studies to accurately assess the actual impacts of the program. Such systematic evaluation serves both to correct imperfections in program design and performance and to counteract the tendency for complaints to dominate the informal feedback process.

Implementation Under Suboptimal Conditions

A frequently voiced criticism against both legislators and scholars is that they have been far more concerned with the passage of legislation than with its effective implementation. Over the past decade, however, a burgeoning interest in policy implementation and evaluation has occurred in the academic community. This has matched a corresponding shift of emphasis among legislators from the passage of major new policy initiatives to more effective implementation and oversight of existing programs. One of the principal purposes of this paper is to provide both communities an understanding of the conditions under which statutes (and other basic policy decisions) that seek to change the status quo can be effectively implemented—that is, can achieve their policy objectives.

Our discussion has shown that legislators and other policy formulators can go a long way toward assuring effective policy implementation if they see that a statute incorporates a sound technical theory, provides precise and clearly ranked objectives, and structures the implementation process in a wide number of ways so as to maximize the probability of target group compliance. In addition, they can take positive steps to appoint skillful and supportive implementing officials, to provide adequate appropriations and to monitor carefully the behavior of implementing agencies throughout the long implementation process, and to be aware of the effects of changing socioeconomic conditions and of new legislation (even in supposedly unrelated areas) on the original statute.

In practice, of course, even those legislators and other policy formulators concerned with effective implementation operate under substantial constraints that make it extremely difficult for them to perform all these tasks. Valid technical theories may not be available. Imperfect information, goal conflict, and multiple vetoes in legislative bodies make it very difficult to pass legislation that incorporates unambiguous objectives and coherently structures the implementation process. Implementation must often be assigned to agencies that are not supportive of the policy objectives. Supportive interest groups and legislators with the resources to serve as "fixers" may not be available or may go on to other things over the long course of implementation.

Nevertheless, even under such suboptimal conditions, several steps can be taken at least to increase the probability of effective implementation.

1. If a valid "technical" theory linking target group behavior to policy objectives is not available or is clearly problematic, then the authors of the statute should make a conscious effort to incorporate in it a learning process through experimental projects, extensive research and development, evaluation studies, and an open decision process involving as many different inputs as possible.
2. If the legislature insists on passing legislation with only the most ambiguous policy directives, then supporters of different points of view can initiate litigation in the hopes of finding a court that will invalidate the law as an unconstitutional delegation of (legislative) authority. While not very promising, this strategy has been employed successfully at least once in a California case, with subsequent legislation providing much clearer guidance to the agency.
3. If implementation cannot be assigned to strongly supportive agencies, then it is absolutely crucial to provide for intervention by outsiders through citizen suit provisions, periodic reporting to sovereigns, evaluation studies by prestigious and relatively independent outsiders, and perhaps special legislative oversight committees.
4. If there are no active supportive interest groups with the necessary resources to monitor implementation carefully, then identification and mobilization of such a group must be a major priority of supportive legislators and implementing officials—as any program is doomed in the long run without one. While it is occasionally possible to create new organizations from scratch, a more feasible strategy is to convince an existing organization with the requisite resources to expand its program to make program monitoring a major responsibility.

5. If a "fixer" is not readily available, then program supporters must make a major effort to find or develop one. This may involve convincing a competent new legislator to specialize in this area or convincing an existing legislator that constituents strongly support the program and thus require it being given higher priority. If legislators in the relevant committees having jurisdiction over the implementing agencies are apathetic (or, worse, hostile) toward the new program, then efforts should be made to reorganize committee jurisdictions or perhaps to create a special oversight committee with a program supporter as chairperson. Whatever the means, however, finding a "fixer" is of paramount importance for effective implementation.

In short, even if the conditions for effective implementation are not met at the time of the basic policy decision, policy formulators and other program supporters can still take a number of steps to approximate the ideal over time.

CASE STUDY 13

Introduction

As the foregoing essay by Paul Sabatier and Daniel Mazmanian indicates, serious scholars are spilling a lot of ink over the problems of public sector implementation. Theories about bureaucratic implementation, as a consequence, now abound in books and journals. But from the standpoint of the practicing public administrator on the firing line, how does a new program get developed, find support, and ultimately become implemented? How are governmental objectives achieved in practice? What are successful methods used for implementation and what are the real-life problems administrators encounter in the implementation process? Does the theory of implementation "square" with its actual practice from the standpoint of the flesh-and-blood public administrator?

The following case study, entitled "Dr. Barbara Levin and the Monroe Maternity Center, Inc.," by Jillian P. Dickert, who lectures at Harvard's Kennedy School of Government, describes the creation of a new method of obstetrical care in Monroe County, Tennessee. This was later extended throughout the State, thanks to the hard work and enterprising innovation of Dr. Barbara Levin, a physician certified in family practice medicine. The case in many ways is a "success story" about how Dr. Levin conceived of the Monroe County OB-GYN experiment, the first publicly funded, out-of-hospital, birthing center in the nation that was especially designed to care for poorer women who had little access to such services before. How Dr. Levin gained funding, gained political support, fended off criticisms, skillfully managed its operations, and ultimately expanded this innovative experiment throughout Tennessee is described in some detail. In order to succeed, Dr. Levin had to simultaneously—and artfully—struggle with numerous difficult issues, personalities, unforeseen problems, and organizational dilemmas—all of which demonstrate that effective program implementation is far more complex than the neat conceptual formulas often describe.

As you study this case, think about the following issues:

Why did Dr. Levin first develop this innovative experiment in Monroe County?

What were her chief problems of finding support for this project and in what ways did she deal with the opposition?

What prompted its extension throughout Tennessee, and how did Dr. Levin go about "strategizing" and "implementing" it statewide?

Did her work "square" with the ideas about implementation in the foregoing reading by Sabatier and Mazmanian? On the basis of this case, would you amend or add to their list of "conditions of effective implementation"?

Dr. Barbara Levin and the Monroe Maternity Center, Inc.

JILLIAN P. DICKERT

Throughout the 1980s, over 75 percent of Tennessee's 95 counties offered inadequate or no obstetrical delivery services. In the '90s, the situation showed few signs of improvement—indeed, some feared things were getting worse. Across the state, many practicing obstetricians—citing both low Medicaid reimbursement rates and skyrocketing malpractice insurance premiums—either refused to accept Medicaid patients (over half of Tennessee's population) or stopped delivering babies altogether. Financially strapped rural hospitals closed their costly obstetrical care units, forcing pregnant women to travel long distances for prenatal checkups. Most women ended up delivering in large, regional perinatal hospitals in urban centers where they received high-priced, "high-tech"—and often unnecessary—care. Tennessee's high rates of infant mortality—frequently resulting from inadequate prenatal care—in some areas surpassed those of the Third World.

By contrast, women in rural Monroe County, Tennessee saw their access to OB-GYN care improve dramatically during the same period—thanks to the enterprising public health officer, Dr. Barbara Levin, MD, MPH. Her creation of the Monroe Maternity

Center, Inc., the nation's first publicly funded, out-of-hospital "birthing center" and nurse-midwifery program, proved to be a viable response to the seemingly intractable problem of improving women's access to quality health care while containing its ever-escalating cost.

For the 1990s, Levin assumed an even greater challenge: the reproduction of her innovative birth center concept in communities throughout the state of Tennessee. In 1991, Levin had managed to establish a private, investor-owned maternity center in the eastern city of Knoxville. While the Knoxville center looked to be a profitable one, Levin wanted to see her birth center concept put on the public agenda. However, Levin's subsequent efforts to initiate a publicly funded birth center in Cumberland County that same year fell short of her goals: the region's Community Health Agency opted instead for one midwife operating under the aegis of the local hospital's existing obstetrical practice. While Levin was pleased with the CHA's interest in bringing midwifery to Cumberland County, the agency's program was quite a bit different from the community-based, freestanding birth center she had envisioned.

Monroe County, Tennessee

When Barbara Levin and her husband, Joshua Gettinger—both certified family practice physicians—completed their medical training in the late 1970s, their primary goal was to serve in an area "where

Source: Kennedy School of Government, Harvard University Case Program, No. C16-93-12180 and C16-93-12181

This case was written by Jillian P. Dickert for Henry Solano, Lecturer in Public Policy at the John F. Kennedy School of Government. Funds were provided by the Kennedy School's Innovations in State and Local Government Program. (0993)

[they] were needed most." The US National Health Service Corps pointed the couple in the direction of Monroe County. Situated on East Tennessee's North Carolina border in the foothills of the Great Smoky Mountains, the county had been identified by the state of Tennessee as a medical manpower shortage area. Its population of about 30,000—96% Caucasian—was considered economically "high risk." In 1979, 24.2% of its residents lived at or below the federal poverty line. Like much of Tennessee and the Appalachian region, more than half of Monroe County's residents had no medical insurance.

Upon their arrival in Monroe County in 1979, Levin and Gettinger set up a family practice at Sequoyah Health Services—the community clinic in Madisonville—and set out to accomplish their main objective: to establish what Levin describes as a "community-based, community-oriented health care system that could exist without [them]." Levin also took on the role of public health officer for the Monroe County Health Department.

Levin soon discovered that she had come to East Tennessee at a time when the entire region's maternal and child health care system was being stretched to its limits. During the latter part of the 1970s, the Tennessee Department of Health had developed a regionalized perinatal system to provide specialized "tertiary" care for high-risk pregnant women and infants. When the national medical malpractice crunch hit the Southeast in the early to mid-1980s, shutting down obstetrical practices throughout the region, the regional perinatal centers found themselves terribly overburdened, responsible not only for high-risk patients but many low-risk patients as well. For many women, obtaining maternity care had become, as Levin describes, "a nightmare": "If women are getting any care at all in Appalachia, they are getting it at these large public clinics where there are 300–400 other clients, with no consistency of providers." Meanwhile, local efforts to recruit additional obstetricians (OBs) proved fruitless.

In May 1982, the shortage of obstetrical care in Monroe County reached crisis levels when five of the area's seven practicing physicians stopped accepting patients for OB services. At the same time, a hospital seventeen miles away closed its OB practice and Medicaid-reimbursed and indigent OB care was halted in several adjacent counties. That left Drs. Levin and Gettinger as the only two physicians providing OB services for all of Monroe County and many indigent patients from surrounding counties as well.

That July, the state health commissioner, Dr. Eugene Fowinkle, held his annual three-day retreat for Tennessee's health officers and regional health directors. On the agenda for discussion was the new "Healthy Children Initiative," a statewide prenatal plan promoted by Governor Lamar Alexander and his wife, Honey Alexander, that promised "Honey Money" for prenatal care in every county. Levin recalls her reaction to the Alexander's plan: "It was definitely one of my more sarcastic moments, but I stood up at the meeting and said, 'I think it's all well and good that we provide prenatal care in every county, but there are no studies that show that prenatal care, in the absence of a place to deliver, makes any sense at all!' I thought it was stupid to put a prenatal plan into all these counties where there was no place to deliver. Were the mothers going to get prenatal care and then deliver in the street?" Levin's comment was met by a chorus of voices demanding, "Well, what are you going to do about it?" Surprising herself and many in the room, Levin responded, "I have a plan."

What Levin had in mind was a new, comprehensive women's health care system, central to which was the establishment of freestanding birth centers where certified nurse-midwives would provide family-centered OB-GYN care to "low-risk" women of all income levels.

Dr. Levin's Plan

About a month before the Tennessee health officers' meeting, Levin had—"on a whim," she says—attended a conference in Nashville entitled "How to Start a Birth Center" sponsored by the National Association of Childbearing Centers (NACC). NACC's promotion of freestanding birth centers had grown out of the 1970's alternative birth movement among women who viewed childbirth as a natural process, not a pathologic illness, and looked to the tradition of midwifery for a more personalized, family-centered, patient-controlled birthing experience. By 1982, over 100 birth centers had opened and were operating in the US[1]—virtually all of them targeting

---

[1]Although by 1992, there were about 150 birth centers in operation and another 40 or so in the development stages, the Health Insurance Association of America reported in 1989 that less than 0.5 percent of all deliveries in the US took place in birth centers. Midwives in general delivered less than 4% of all babies in the US that year. By contrast, about 80% of all babies born in Europe were delivered by midwives.

their services at upper-middle class women. Accordingly, care in most birth centers was provided in a home-like environment by certified nurse-midwives—registered nurses with advanced education in the profession of midwifery and certification by the American College of Nurse Midwives—rather than physicians.

As a public health officer, Levin was drawn to the concept of a birth center staffed by certified nurse-midwives (CNMs) for a different reason: Levin envisioned the concept working as part of a triage system within a comprehensive women's health care network coordinated with the regionalized perinatal centers already in place in the state. "In Tennessee, we have a high-risk system in the absence of a low-risk system," Levin explains. "The whole issue here is risk management. With a birth center, you have—since birth is a mostly natural event—more appropriately trained individuals providing the services at the appropriate level." In Levin's vision, CNMS operating under strict medical protocols could provide prenatal care and delivery at a birth center for the vast majority of women for whom childbirth involved no unusual risks. The CNMs could continually screen patients and refer those not meeting established low-risk criteria to specialized providers at nearby hospitals or at the regional perinatal center. Low-risk mothers-to-be remaining at the birth center could avail themselves to a full menu of services in one location, including prenatal clinics, parent education classes, nutrition counseling, delivery, postpartum, and Well-Woman gynecological care.

Levin projected that a birth center in Monroe County could handle approximately 100 births in its first year—about one-quarter of the county's annual birth total of 400. That would require two midwives and two birthing rooms. Since Levin viewed her plan as a solution to a public health problem, she assumed that the birth center should be publicly funded, even though that had never before been accomplished.[2] "I never thought of it any other way," says Levin. "I was a National Health Service Corps physician and I worked for the state of Tennessee. I had absolutely no private practice interests." Uncertain of the level of state support her idea could muster, Levin suggested that the birth center be fash-

ioned out of a double-wide trailer (40 feet across), which would cost less than $30,000. "In East Tennessee, a good 30% of the population lives in trailers, so that would still be a home-like birth for many people," Levin explains.

In August, Levin fleshed out her plan with Emily Ousley, a CNM practicing in Knoxville, and Larry Bowles, director of the Tennessee's Regional Health Department. While both Ousley and Bowles supported the birth center proposal, both agreed that Levin had a long, hard road ahead of her. Attracting state financial support would be no easy task, Bowles warned, and a public health project would need to jump through a series of bureaucratic hoops at local, regional and state levels—including the necessary approvals from the local Board of Health, the County Commission and the state licensing board. Clearing each of these hoops would require solid community support, including the endorsement of the medical community. Furthermore, Levin's proposal would involve dealing with prejudices about out-of-hospital births in an area where, in 1982, many people were only a generation away from a time when mothers gave birth at home, assisted by "granny midwives" with little formal childbirth training. It would mean changing deeply ingrained attitudes that did not differentiate between granny midwives and modern CNM professionals, and overcoming the widespread belief that only a doctor in a hospital could provide quality health care.

Garnering Support

Levin's first challenge was to secure public funding. With some apprehension, Levin and Bowles drove to Nashville in September, 1982, to meet with Health Commissioner Fowinkle. To everyone's surprise, Fowinkle—a twenty-year veteran as Tennessee's health commissioner—was immediately receptive. He approved the birth center as a demonstration project for Governor Alexander's "Healthy Children Initiative," and threw the entire weight of his support behind the project. That meant "real money" and an attractive, state-of-the-art birth facility—not the double-wide trailer Levin thought she would get. Fowinkle, Levin says, insisted on a "Cadillac" model: "As a model program, he wanted it to be recognizably permanent. He didn't want it to be something that could be wiped away by the next rainstorm." Now the birth center would be modeled

---

[2]Although many operated as non-profit organizations, all of the over 100 birth centers in the US at that time were privately funded and privately owned.

with two birthing rooms furnished like bedrooms but with all necessary equipment, a family quarters with a kitchen and living area, and plenty of space for general OB-GYN care and educational services.

Fowinkle offered $85,000 in state funds to build and equip the facility, $55,000 for two midwives' salaries, and an initial operating budget of $30,000.[3] Birth center patients would be charged a global fee of $1,250—less than half of what a normal hospital delivery cost in the area—including prenatal care, mandatory childbirth education classes, delivery and two follow-up home visits. (Medicaid would reimburse the birth center for the full $1,250.) A sliding fee scale would be offered for qualified women. It was expected that patient revenues would allow the birth center to become self-supportive within a few years.

Having secured financial arrangements for the birth center, Levin endeavored to build support for her ambitious project at the grassroots level. To start, Levin turned to a few close friends belonging to local women's organizations. Together the women held a series of "coffees," to which they invited the wife of each local board member whose approval Levin's plan would need in the coming weeks. (In 1982, all of the local boards and commissions were comprised entirely of male members.) At these coffees, Levin recounts, "the message went out very clearly, woman to woman, in a very 'human' way, that their husbands should support the birth center." The day before each board vote, Levin says, the women were telephoned and reminded to talk to their husbands. "We essentially developed a very personal lobby: the wife of the person about to vote," explains Levin. "It can be a powerful way to make things happen." Levin's strategy paid off. In October, 1982, the local Board of Health approved Levin's project, and in none of the required public forums was there ever a vote opposing the birth center.

In January, 1983, Levin won approval from the Monroe County Commission, which offered to donate land for the birth center and agreed to set aside $6,000 in the county budget to assist the birth center if necessary. Levin was also able to enlist the support of Charles Wilkins, the Monroe County

Executive, and Bob Harrill, the local representative for the state legislature. Their support proved invaluable in securing the required Certificate of Need, for which Levin would need an endorsement from the area medical community.

Overcoming Opposition

Initially, the medical community—both local and regional—saw Levin's proposal as radical, and warned of the potential risks of childbirth in an out-of-hospital setting. Dr. Steven Prinz, Director of Neonatology at Children's Hospital in Knoxville, describes the reaction he and his colleagues had to Levin's plan: "Quite frankly, we were worried about the concept of a birthing center and how we would interface with one. Personally, I was very concerned about the medical/legal-type risk and was doubtful that the midwives really would give good antenatal care. There's a tremendous potential for abuse [at a freestanding birth center] if you don't have people who are honest with themselves and who supervise what's done appropriately, because unfortunately, no matter what you do, there's always going to be the potential for problems arising anytime you have a delivery." Many believed that the physicians' concerns could stall the development of the birth center, or even block it entirely.

The support Levin had built among a few key people in the Monroe community kept the project moving forward despite these initial concerns. Wilkins, for one, personally arrived on the doorstep of every physician in the area with an "I support the birth center" petition in his hand. According to Dr. Levin, Wilkins proceeded to ask each physician two questions: "Are you going to deliver babies?" and "Are you going to support my birth center?" Wilkins then informed the physicians: "Well, basically you've got a choice: you can deliver babies or you can sign this petition supporting the birth center." All of the doctors chose the latter.

A similar tactic was employed to handle resistance from the director of the Department of OB-GYN at the University of Tennessee (UT)-Knoxville. According to Levin, he had written a letter to the American College of Obstetrics and Gynecology (ACOG) urging them to take a stand against the birth center plan. (ACOG opposed out-of-hospital births as a general rule.) This time Representative Harrill paid the director a personal visit. Harrill matter-

[3]Beginning in 1987, MMCI's operating budget and the midwives' salaries were replaced by an ongoing contract of $105,000 for maternity and Well-Woman care funded through the federal Maternal and Child Health Block Grant.

of-factly pointed out that although the university had received several million dollars from the state of Tennessee, not one of the thirty OB residents UT-Knoxville had graduated in the previous three years were practicing in any rural place in the state. Rep. Harrill then asked him a simple question: "Do you want me to discuss this on the Floor, or are you going to sign this letter of support for the maternity center?" and added, "and get this ACOG off my back!" The director obliged.

Scott Bowman, a prominent administrator for the local hospital in Sweetwater, publicly opposed the out-of-hospital birth center on the grounds that it would be "potentially unsafe in the event of a patient crisis," and, according to Levin, claimed his hospital board "would never be supportive" of such a center. Mindful of the devastating effect strong opposition from Sweetwater Hospital could have on her plans, Levin promptly arranged a meeting with the hospital board attorney, J. Michaels. But to her surprise, Michaels' eyes lit up when she told him the birth center would be staffed by CNMs; as it turned out, Michaels' own mother had worked as a midwife in the Monroe County area. "We just went straight from there!" Levin proclaims. "When Mr. Michaels told the board how things were, that's the way they were. We never had another problem with the hospital."

Also set against the birth center was Clifford Wilson, a lawyer and chairman of the board of Sequoyah Health Services—the community clinic where Levin and her husband, Dr. Gettinger, worked. According to Levin, Sequoyah's chairman thought the freestanding birth center was "a malpractice case about to happen," and believed Levin was "out of [her] bounds as a National Health Service Corps physician" since the board had not "instructed" her to set one up. As a result, Wilson fired her. This complicated matters, to say the least, since Levin, Gettinger, and a third, new Sequoyah physician (Dr. George Wiggins) had already agreed to work "on call" during each labor and delivery at the birth center, ready to serve as back-up physicians if any complications arose. (All three physicians had delivery privileges at Sweetwater Hospital.) Levin, Gettinger and Wiggins responded by forming a separate family practice corporation that would provide, among other services, back-up assistance for birth center patients falling outside the low-risk category. In a show of support for the birth center, Levin says, over half of Sequoyah's staff moved with her to the new practice, now known as Family Practice Associates, Inc.

With the medical community persuaded—at least on paper—that the birth center should be built, the East Tennessee Health Planning Council, representing sixteen East Tennessee counties, unanimously approved a Certificate of Need in June, 1983. Shortly afterward, the Tennessee Health Facilities Commission agreed to license the birth center as an "Ambulatory Surgery Center, with Practice Limited to Normal Obstetrics," and Levin and company were able to "break ground" in late June at a Madisonville site located six miles from Sweetwater Hospital. By December, the Monroe Maternity Center, Inc. (MMCI) was established as a "legislated non-profit corporation" under charter with the state of Tennessee and operated by a ten-member board of directors—two physicians, three county commissioners, a consumer representative, three laypersons, and the local state representative—appointed to three-year terms by the Monroe County Commission. Dr. Levin assumed the post of medical director, and the birth center's first baby was born in January, 1984.

Building the Case Load

Levin assumed that attracting patients to the birth center would be the easy part: "I felt that if women didn't have someplace to go then they'd obviously come here. I never even used the word marketing." Levin assumed that the level of need, together with the extensive newspaper coverage the birth center received thanks to the Alexanders' support, would assure a steady increase in MMCI's patient load. As it turned out, however, MMCI immediately encountered some of the old stereotypes about midwives. "Many think our CNMs are 'granny' midwives and don't realize the educational requirements necessary to become certified," explains Becky Bell, MMCI's administrator and marketing manager. Remarks like "they don't have real doctors there," and "you're good enough to go to a hospital" were whispered about the birth center that first year, Levin recalls. Bell adds that "when the center opened, most of the publicity focused on how the birth center would service the indigent population, so some people had the perception that 'this is where poor people go' and 'I can't go because I have insurance.'"

MMCI did manage 70 births in 1984—a significant portion of the county's birth total of 400—but fell short of the 100 births Levin had expected. In order to achieve self-sufficiency through patient revenues, the birth center would need to double its number of deliveries to 12 births per month. That, Levin concluded, would require an all-out community education campaign.

Convinced that their billboard and phone book advertisements were not sufficient, Levin and the MMCI staff took every opportunity to speak about the birth center to various groups and organizations in the Monroe County area, from bible studies and churches to schools and public health departments. They took pains to spread the word that the birth center was not for Medicaid patients only. "I made it real clear that this wasn't a Medicaid birth center because I think it gets the name and the agency feeling that would destroy it," says Levin. "People aren't going to fall in love with a Medicaid agency." Levin and the CNMs on staff offered to teach courses on public health and midwifery at local colleges, and Bell initiated a weekday parenting show on the local radio station. Levin also encouraged the use of MMCI as a community center, and opened its facilities for breastfeeding groups, baby showers, parenting fairs, and the like. Still, it was Levin's contention that MMCI's gentle, personalized midwifery care could bring enough word-of-mouth praise from satisfied customers to ensure a steady increase in new birth center patients.

Midwifery Care at MMCI

Apart from the provision of much-needed maternity care, Levin and her staff at the Monroe Maternity Center believed that they were offering a superior type of care—one that pampered the mother-to-be in a sensitive, family-centered environment. The idea was to make the client as comfortable as possible during her labor: she was permitted to walk around, watch TV, eat lightly, sit in the sun, take a warm bath—whatever she felt like doing. Throughout the labor, her family members and friends were permitted in the delivery room if she so desired. Viewing labor and childbirth as a "natural" process, MMCI staff kept medical interventions to a minimum.[4] The laboring woman was encouraged to deliver in the position best for her, using Lamaze techniques—rather than medication—to help her relax.[5] After a birth at MMCI, there was no separation of the mother and the baby; all infant care was done with the

mother in the room. The new mother was permitted to return home within 6–12 hours after delivery, and one of MMCI's two staff RNs then made two home visits during the first week after birth to physically assess both mother and baby and to provide information on newborn care, breastfeeding support, and general counseling. . . .

Results

MMCI's well-kept facility and its rare blend of low-cost, personalized care, public service and community involvement seemed to have succeeded in attracting a cross-section of women—not just the indigent—to the birth center. Drawing from five counties, MMCI's delivery load increased to a total of 116 births by 1991—over a quarter of all births by Monroe County residents, and Dr. Levin predicted that the birth total would reach 130 by 1992. While the majority of MMCI's clients were Medicaid or reduced-fee patients, more than 40% were privately insured or able to pay full fees. (Several major health insurers reimbursed MMCI 100% of their charges.) Upper-middle-class women from as far as Knoxville (40 miles away) drove to Madisonville to take advantage of MMCI's birthing program, and the wives of four area physicians gave birth at MMCI—a phenomenon that did not escape the notice of local clients.

MMCI experienced very good outcomes in the quality of services and client satisfaction consistent with the results of a national birth center study for non-economically high-risk populations and better than the statewide health rate indicators for Tennessee. Meanwhile, the cost of having a baby at MMCI—$2,400 in 1992—remained about half that of a traditional hospital delivery, with no service cutbacks. (In 1992, the Medicaid reimbursement rate for each delivery at MMCI increased to $2,400 from a rate of $1,390 in 1985.)

With such positive outcomes, MMCI was able to make believers of its many medical community critics. Dr. Steven Prinz of Children's Hospital in

---

[4]This also helped keep the birth center's costs down.

[5]Light pain medications such as Demerol, morphine, and local anesthetic were available when needed. The birth center would not, however, provide general anesthesia or an epidural, a regional anesthesia given in the lower part of a woman's back to numb the lower abdomen and upper legs during labor.

Knoxville now says: "I think that this sort of center can be of great benefit to many people that are underserved and other people that are looking for alternative, but safe, birthing methods." The local hospital in Sweetwater was also pleased to discover that MMCI's presence increased the total number of women staying in the county for delivery, and the hospital's maternity census did not suffer. At the same time, the increase in the number of women remaining in-county to give birth helped relieve some of the burden at the regional perinatal center at UT-Knoxville; while other rural counties had twice as many deliveries at UT in 1991 as they did five years earlier, the proportion of Monroe County births at UT remained stable.

Despite a change in Tennessee's gubernatorial administration, MMCI continued to receive about $100,000 annually from the state (in addition to Medicaid patient revenues). In 1990, approximately 60% of MMCI's $318,000 operating budget came from state sources. Monroe County extended its support for the birth center as well. Although the county was considered quite fiscally conservative, it contributed $45,000 to help pay for a $75,000 addition to MMCI's facility in 1991.[6] (The rest came from MMCI's cash reserves.) The Monroe County community also sustained its commitment to MMCI. Area residents regularly donated maternity and baby clothing and baby furniture for indigent patients using the birth center, while senior citizens contributed hand-stitched baby quilts and the local garden club maintained MMCI's landscaping. As Larry Bowles puts it: "I don't believe you could dynamite the maternity center out of Monroe County, it has so much deep-rooted community involvement and support."

Time to Reproduce

No one was more convinced of MMCI's success than Dr. Barbara Levin: "I'm no longer suggesting this as simply an alternative," Levin says of the birth center/nurse-midwifery concept. "I'm not even suggesting this as a stop-gap measure because we can't get obstetricians. With what I've seen—and I had to unlearn a whole lot that I learned in medical

school—I honestly feel that the care is better, that the patients' needs are more clearly met, that their risks are better handled, and that in the long run it's safer. This is the type of care that every single woman in America deserves." Since the birth center was conceived as a state demonstration project, Levin felt that by MMCI's fifth year—1989—it was time to transfer her innovation to another Tennessee locale. Her first opportunity arrived in East Tennessee's largest city: Knoxville.

Although not considered a medical manpower shortage area like Monroe, Knox County was nevertheless unable to escape the national obstetrical care crisis. In 1990, in a city where more than fifty percent of over 83,000 females between the ages of fifteen and forty-four qualified for Medicaid,[7] only three of Knoxville's twenty-nine OBs would accept Medicaid patients—and then only a limited number. As a result, the regional perinatal center for high-risk mothers at UT-Knoxville was flooded with indigent patients—both high- and low-risk—from Knox and its surrounding counties. Patients were forced to wait as long as three and four months for their first prenatal care visit. The only other place in Knoxville accepting Medicaid patients for prenatal care was the Knox County Health Department—even there, the waiting period for an appointment approached two months.

In 1989, while seeking an appointment for a high-risk MMCI patient, Dr. Levin ran up against UT's patient backlog. Concerned, Levin contacted Rita Hillhouse, East Tennessee's regional perinatal coordinator, who agreed that UT could no longer handle the swelling OB load. After looking at the numbers, both agreed that the region could benefit from a chain of birth centers like MMCI to care for the low-risk patients. The city of Knoxville alone would need three birth centers handling 300 deliveries each per year, they concluded.

Coincidentally, Levin attended an open house party two weeks later to celebrate Dr. Ray King's new gynecology/fertility clinic in Knoxville. (Dr. King had delivered two of Levin's four children.) Half jokingly, Levin asked King, "So, where's the room for my birth center?" Dr. King's response was, "It's downstairs." Levin soon discovered the King was serious; he had actually left office space on the lower level of his new practice for another physician. It was just large enough to accommodate a three-birthing-room maternity center.

[6]MMCI also hired a third midwife in 1992.

[7]In 1991, the state of Tennessee began covering obstetrical care for women at 185% of the federal poverty level.

The Maternity Center of East Tennessee

The Maternity Center of East Tennessee (MCET) was patterned after the Monroe County birth center with one major difference: the center would be private investor-funded. Levin says she and King "never tried to do a public center because the new state health commissioner [J.W. Luna] made it real clear that he would not do another birth center—he wanted a public-private enterprise." As far as Levin was concerned, "it was better than nothing. Private practice birth centers may lose some of that close provider-patient ratio, but in the long run, they'll still provide public access."

Levin and King designed MCET with a 50% Medicaid patient load in mind—even though it was Medicaid's low reimbursement rates that had in large part dissuaded many of Knoxville's already-overburdened private physicians from accepting any Medicaid patients at all. MCET's global fee for prenatal care, childbirth education classes, delivery, and two home visits was set to start at $2,500 with a Medicaid reimbursement rate of $2,200. Dr. King hoped MCET would demonstrate to the private sector that freestanding birth centers could be both financially and medically viable despite the large Medicaid clientele. To achieve that goal, MCET would have to simultaneously appeal to a large number of privately insured women, says Ed Pershing, Dr. King's accountant. "We felt like this was a chance to develop a model that would serve not only the uninsured but that would also be of such a quality that the upper-income, highly educated individual would want to choose it," Pershing explains. "We've seen that when you target a service to an indigent group, it often ends up getting stigmatized. We've tried to balance this one by making it attractive so that anyone from any socioeconomic background would come." It was expected that MCET would eventually handle 350 low-risk births per year (less than four percent of the total annual births in the area).

Not long after delivering its first babies in August, 1991, MCET encountered a second health care dilemma: now Knoxville *pediatricians* were refusing to accept Medicaid patients. Levin was shocked: "For MCET's first five babies, we found that we couldn't get them to pediatricians. I never had that problem in Monroe County. In Madisonville, once you got the babies born and gave them Medicaid cards, anyone would take them." But in Knoxville, Levin discovered, even the head of Children's Hospital could not find a pediatrician willing to accept Medicaid babies born at MCET. Levin's solution? Hire a family nurse practitioner to provide Well-Child care at MCET. "We now provide prenatal care, delivery, and two years of Well-Child care (physical exams, immunizations, etc.) in one location, with backup from the Children's Hospital emergency physician group. It's a crazy way to give Well-Child care, but it's better than no care at all!"

Securing private funders to invest in the birth center turned out to be problematic as well. After six months of operation, the maternity center in Knoxville remained undercapitalized by $75,000. "We capitalized for $300,000 with a 9 1/2% return on investment [ROI] over 5 years—that's a pretty reasonable return," argues Dr. King, who, along with his wife, personally invested $30,000 in the center. "But we presented that to numerous physicians and that was not enough return—they wanted 15% ROI. I was really disappointed in the physicians. There did not seem to be any benevolent spirit at all in this." Levin concurs: "You really need socially conscious investors. Maternity centers are not money-making 'McBirths.' They pay for themselves, but they are slow-growing, and it takes a while to convince people that they are going to realize the gain they will have." Nevertheless, before the end of its first year of operation, MCET was close to breaking even. As projected, 50% of MCET's revenues came from Medicaid reimbursement.

Levin was pleased with the transfer of her birth center concept in Knoxville, but she missed the extent of community involvement that the publicly-funded MMCI enjoyed. "I have always felt like [MCET] should have a community-owned board like at Monroe," Levin admits. "However, it's hard to tell someone to invest their money in a birth center and then give up control of it! But I advocated for that anyway, for the center's success. It would definitely be advantageous to their financial investment; the more the community feels a part of the center—in advocacy with it—the more rapidly the patient flow will increase, and as a result, the center will be successful." At the same time, Levin realized, "when you're a consultant, you've got to go with the flow."

The Stork Resort

Levin admits that it took some time for her to adjust to the role of consultant versus that of head administrator. She may not have fully adapted to that role when the prospect of reproducing the MMCI concept a second time arrived in Tennessee's Upper Cumberland region. In the fall of 1991, a crisis in OB care similar to that experienced by Monroe County in 1982 struck Cumberland County. Three of the area's family practice physicians (FPs) stopped delivering babies, leaving just two OBs and one FP (the FP planned to retire in 1992) responsible for delivering the 700 babies born each year in Cumberland and its two neighboring counties, Fentress and Bledsoe. Once again, recruiting physicians to the area seemed futile. In response to the crisis, the Upper Cumberland Community Health Agency (CHA)—a public, nonprofit, quasi-governmental agency—turned its attention to midwifery. Dr. Barbara Levin—now considered the regional expert on the subject—was consulted for advice.

In September, Levin was invited to speak at a board meeting held to discuss the issue. Levin seized the opportunity to push for another publicly funded, freestanding birth center as, Levin says, "a reasonable and cost-effective way to solve their problem." At first, the CHA seemed interested in a birth center modeled after MMCI, and in October, CHA staff paid a visit to the MMCI site along with a representative from the Cumberland Medical Center (the local hospital). The hospital owned a small house across the street from its facilities in Crossville, and initially, appeared open to the idea of turning the house into a birth center. Levin sought to promote her out-of-hospital birth center idea throughout the fall of '91, but much to her chagrin, the CHA telephoned her in December to inform her that they had decided instead to initiate a hospital-based midwife practice. Levin recalls that after the CHA made that decision, they no longer sought her advice.

The CHA's program, now known as the "Stork Resort," was scheduled to start accepting patients in July, 1992. It would involve revamping the hospital's OB wing to accommodate a two-room delivery suite for low-risk births. While the midwife's office would have its own entrance and waiting room, her services would be under the jurisdiction of the existing OB practice. The hospital's two OBs would provide backup assistance if necessary. The fee for the midwife service would start at $1,500—the same rate charged by Cumberland Medical Center physicians—and would include prenatal care, delivery, and postpartum care. However, this fee would not include the cost of the hospital stay (an additional $1,500–1,800 per day[8]) and any ancillary items, such as IVs; the hospital would bill the patient separately for these items.

To launch its midwifery program, the CHA would use public health monies from the state of Tennessee and a $37,500 Appalachian Regional Commission seed grant. Start-up costs were projected to reach $110,000 in order to purchase all necessary equipment and cover the salaries of both the midwife and one support staffperson.[9] The CHA intended to pay the midwife's salary until her practice reached its break-even point; subsequently, the midwife would begin repaying the CHA for all monies invested in her practice. After the CHA was repaid in full, the midwife would be free to continue her practice at the hospital. Sue Standifer, Executive Director of the Upper Cumberland CHA, explains the agency's motive: "We realize that there is money to be made there, but all we want to do is make sure the service is viable, that it gets going, and then we'll take the money that we recoup from there and start similar programs elsewhere." Standifer says the CHA felt this strategy would be more "cost-effective" than creating a separate birth center: "After we really got down and put the pencil to it, we felt that by starting small like this, we could actually save money by going into an existing office, utilizing the existing facilities in that community for delivery instead of going in and setting up something else. We believed that it was going to be more cost effective, and more efficient for the patients, to do it all in one practice—that way, [the patients] could see the physicians during their pregnancy if they needed to, without having to go to another facility." Standifer says safety was also a consideration: "For me, it's a plus to be able to have both the midwifery service and the comfort of knowing that you're in a hospital if there is a problem. I think most women feel safe in a hospital setting."

---

[8]During the program's first year of operation, the hospital stay for patients using the midwife service averaged two days for labor, delivery and recovery.

[9]Actual first-year costs turned out to be approximately $175,000.

Larry Bowles, now serving as a consultant for all CHAs in East Tennessee, feels that medical politics colored the CHA's decision to choose a hospital-based practice. "From the beginning, they probably thought that there would be physician opposition," Bowles speculates. "I don't think there would have been, but I think they felt like to avoid confrontational issues, just put it in a hospital." Levin saw other motives. "I don't think they wanted a birth center because I don't think the hospital wants to lose control of those births," Levin suggests, noting that "the hospital is going to earn money off of every delivery [the midwife] makes. The hospital could well afford to pay for this service; it doesn't have to come out of public money."

Louise Duncan, Director of Nursing at the Cumberland Medical Center, views the decision from another angle. "In a hospital our size that is community-based and determined to meet multiple levels of need in the community, it made only good sense to us to offer midwifery to patients that had the ability to select it when given a broader choice."

Chapter 13 Review Questions

1. How do you define the word "implementation"? In what ways does "implementation" differ from "management" or "administration"? What are the similarities and differences among these terms?

2. Can you outline how the concept of implementation draws on other ideas concerning decision making, communications, politics, budgeting, intergovernmental relations, public professional expertise, and the general environment that have been discussed earlier in this text? How does the concept of implementation both use and build on these other concepts?

3. Why has implementation become such a major concern for students and practitioners of public administration and public policy in recent decades? What was responsible for its development as a recent focus of scholarly research? Do you think there is a valid need for studying implementation in the public sector and, if so, why?

4. What are the essential elements of the implementation model that Sabatier and Mazmanian propose? What are its basic assumptions and utility for practicing public administrators? Can you define in your own words its basic processes? Is it applicable to all situations, such as in foreign affairs? Or, just in local issues? Do you see any limitations to this model?

5. From your reading of this case, what conditions contribute to complications in effective program implementation? What conditions help to support effective implementation?

6. Consider the key administrator in the case study and evaluate whether or not she was successful at implementing this program. By what standards can we judge Dr. Levin a success at the task of program implementation? In your opinion, what was the *most critical* ingredient for making her work successful?

Key Terms

conditions for implementation
target group behavior

unambiguous policy directives
sound technical theory

conflicting policy priorities
veto points
policy feedback

"fixers"
performance evaluation
constituency intervention points

Suggestions for Further Reading

The book that started much of the contemporary theorizing about this subject is now in its second edition and is still well worth reading, Jeffrey L. Pressman and Aaron B. Wildavsky, *Implementation,* Second Edition (Berkeley, Calif.: University of California Press, 1978) as well as several of the case studies that criticized the implementation of Great Society programs and also stimulated early research in this field, especially Martha Derthick, *New Towns In-Town* (Washington, D.C.: Urban Institute, 1972); Daniel P. Moynihan, *Maximum Feasible Misunderstanding* (New York: Free Press, 1969); Stephan K. Bailey and Edith K. Mosher, *ESEA: The Office of Education Administers a Law* (Syracuse: Syracuse University Press, 1968) as well as Beryl A. Radin, *Implementation, Change and the Federal Bureaucracy* (New York: Teachers College Press, 1977).

Serious students of implementation theory should review carefully the major conceptual approaches cited in the introduction to this chapter as well as other important contributions, such as Martin Rein and Francine F. Rabinovitz, "Implementation: A Theoretical Perspective," in Walter D. Burnham and Martha W. Weinberg, eds., *American Politics and Public Policy* (Cambridge, Mass.: MIT Press, 1978); and also in the same book, Michael M. Lipsky, "Implementation on Its Head"; Carl E. Van Horn, *Policy Implementation in the Federal System* (Lexington, Mass.: Lexington Books, 1979); A. Dunsire, *Implementation in Bureaucracy* (New York: St. Martin's Press, 1979); Walter Williams, *The Implementation Perspective* (Berkeley, Calif.: University of California Press, 1980); J. S. Larson, *Why Government Programs Fail* (1980); Helen M. Ingram and Dean E. Mann, eds., *Why Policies Succeed or Fail* (Los Angeles: Sage, 1980); R. D. Behn, "Why Murphy Was Right," *Policy Analysis* (Summer 1980); G. C. Ed-

wards, *Implementing Public Policy* (Washington, D.C.: Congressional Quarterly Press, 1980); Susan Barrett and Colin Fudge, eds., *Policy and Action: Essays on Implementation of Public Policy* (London: Methuen, Inc., 1981); Dennis J. Palumbo and Marvin A. Harder, eds., *Implementing Public Policy* (Lexington, Mass.: Lexington Books, 1981); Daniel A. Mazmanian and Paul A. Sabatier, eds., *Effective Public Policy Implementation* (Lexington, Mass.: Lexington Books, 1982); B. Hjern and D. O. Porter, "Implementation Structure," *Organization Studies* (1981); Randall B. Ripley and Grace A. Franklin, *Bureaucracy and Policy Implementation* (Homewood, Ill.: Dorsey Press, 1982); Walter William et al., *Studying Implementation: Methodological and Administrative Issues* (Chatham, N.J.: Chatham House, 1982); and B. Hjern and C. Hull, eds., "Implementation Beyond Hierarchy," Special Issue, *European Journal of Political Research.* For a helpful reader, see George C. Edwards III, ed., *Public Policy Implementation* (Greenwich, Conn.: JAI Press, 1989). For a recent review of techniques, strategies, and directions for further research, read David L. Weimer, "The Current Data of Design Craft: Borrowing, Tinkering and Problem Solving," *Public Administration Review,* 53 (March/April 1993), pp. 110–120, as well as Helen Ingram, "Implementation: A Review and Suggested Framework," Naomi B. Lynn and Aaron Wildavsky, eds., *Public Administration: The State of the Discipline* (Chatham, N.J.: Chatham House, 1990).

Additionally, greater attention is paid by scholars to careful case analysis of implementation within the context of particular policy fields such as M. K. Marvel, "Implementation and Safety Regulation: Varieties of Federal and State Administration Under OSHA," *Administration and Society* (May 1982); S. L. Yafee, *Prohibitive Policy: Im-*

plementing the Federal Endangered Species Act (Cambridge, Mass.: MIT Press, 1982); Donald C. Menzel, "Implementation of the Federal Surface Mining Control and Reclamation Act of 1977," *Public Administration Review* (March/April 1981); Dean E. Mann, ed., *Environmental Policy Implementation* (Lexington, Mass.: Lexington Books, 1982); Charles S. Bullock III and Charles M. Lamb, *Implementation of Civil Rights Policy* (Monterey, Calif.: Brooks/Cole, 1984); David L. Kirp and Donald N. Jensen, eds., *School Days, Rule Days* (Philadelphia, Pa.: Taylor & Francis, 1986); Gary C. Bryner, *Bureaucratic Discretion* (New York: Pergamon Press, 1987); Donald F. Kettl, *Government by Proxy* (Washington, D.C.: Congressional Quarterly Press, 1988); Joan W.

Allen et al., *The Private Sector in State Service Delivery: Examples of Innovative Practices* (Washington, D.C.: The Urban Institute, 1989); and Lester M. Salamon, ed., *Beyond Privatization: The Tools of Government Action* (Washington, D.C.: The Urban Institute, 1989). For an up-to-date summary of where we are today with implementation studies, read Malcolm L. Goggin, Ann O'M. Bowman, James P. Lester, and Laurence J. O'Toole, Jr., *Implementation Theory and Practice: Toward a Third Generation* (Glenview, Ill.: Scott, Foresman and Co., 1990); see especially its excellent bibliography, as well as Robert Stoker, *Reluctant Partners* (Pittsburgh: University of Pittsburgh Press, 1991).

PART THREE

Enduring and Unresolved Relationships: Central Value Questions, Issues, and Dilemmas of Contemporary Public Administration

P art Three focuses on three key persistent and pressing relationships in the field of public administration today: the problems of political-administrative relationships; the bureaucracy and the public interest; and ethics and the public service. All of these relational issues are new in the sense that they have come to the forefront of recent discussions and controversies in public administration. Yet, these issues have certainly been part of the problems and perplexities of public administration since its inception as an identifiable field of study after the turn of the twentieth century. Indeed, the topics of political-administrative relationships, the problems of ethics, and relationships between bureaucracy and the public interest were central themes of the writings of many early administrative theorists, such as Woodrow Wilson, Frederick Taylor, Luther Gulick, Louis Brownlow, and Leonard White. No doubt one could even trace the origins of these topics back to the classic writings of Plato, Aristotle, Moses, and Pericles. But for a variety of reasons, we are witnessing the reemergence of these older issues as very real dilemmas for public administrators today. Readings and cases in Part Three therefore address these critical issues:

CHAPTER 14

The Relationship Between Politics and Administration: *The Concept of Issue Networks* What are the current trends and practices in political oversight and control of administration? What are the implications for public administration and the governance of America?

CHAPTER 15

The Relationship Between Bureaucracy and the Public Interest: *The Concept of Public Sector Deregulation* What is the "public interest"? Is there such a thing that can serve as a guide to public administrators' work? How can it be applied as a meaningful concept to influence the direction and activities of government bureaucracies?

CHAPTER 16

The Relationship Between Ethics and Public Administration: *The Concept of Competing Ethical Obligations* How are ethical choices involved in contemporary decisions facing public servants? What is an appropriate conceptual model for understanding how ethical choices are involved in public administrators' choices? How can these choices be made in a more responsible manner?

CHAPTER 14

The Relationship Between Politics and Administration: The Concept of Issue Networks

*T*he iron triangle concept is not so much wrong as it is disastrously incomplete. And the conventional view is especially inappropriate for understanding changes in politics and administration during recent years. . . . Looking for the closed triangles of control, we tend to miss the fairly open networks of people that increasingly impinge upon government.

Hugh Heclo

READING 14

Introduction

Perhaps no issue has been more controversial or more discussed in public administration since its inception as a self-conscious field of study than the appropriate relationship between the politically elected representatives of the legislature and the permanent bureaucracy of the executive branch. Indeed, as was pointed out in Chapter 1, the first essay on the subject of public administration written in the United States, "The Study of Administration," prepared by a young political scientist named Woodrow Wilson in 1887, essentially wrestled with the problem of the proper relationship between these two spheres of government: politics and administration.[1] Wilson wrote his essay at a time when civil service reform had recently been instituted in the federal government (the Pendleton Act had been passed in 1883). Wilson sought to encourage the development of the newly established merit system and the emergence of a field of academic study—public administration—because in his words, "It is getting to be harder to run a constitution than to frame one." The new complexities of government—both in terms of widening popular participation of the citizenry in democratic government and the rising technological problems of organizing public programs—created, in Wilson's view, the urgent need for developing effective administrative services free from congressional "meddling."

---

[1]Woodrow Wilson, "The Study of Administration," *Political Science Quarterly,* 2 (June 1887), pp. 197–222.

Generally, the drift—both in terms of intellectual thought and institutional reform in the United States during the century after Wilson's writing—until the 1970s was toward a realization of the Wilsonian argument in favor of greater administrative independence from legislative oversight. War, international involvements, economic crises, and a host of other influences (including public administration theorists) supported the claims for administrative independence from detailed legislative control. In particular, as political scientist Allen Schick notes, three factors led to congressional acquiescence. The first factor was the massive growth in the size of government. "Big government weakened the ability of Congress to govern by controlling the details and it vested administration with more details over which to govern. In the face of bigness Congress could master the small things only by losing sight of the important issues." This was bolstered by the message of public administration theorists "that a legislature should not trespass on administrative matters inevitably registered on Congressional thinking about its appropriate role, especially because the theme was so attractively laced with the promise of order and efficiency in the public service and carried the warning that legislative intrusion would be injurious to good government."[2]

Nonpartisanship in foreign affairs also played a powerful role in checking congressional intrusion in executive affairs by conveying "the assurance that unchecked executive power would be applied benevolently in the national interest of the United States." Pluralism, a third factor in fostering congressional retreat, according to Schick, furthered administrative independence by the convincing certainty that wider administrative discretion over executive agencies would be in fact used "to provide benefits to powerful interests in society to the benefit of everyone."

In retrospect, perhaps these assumptions were naive, but they were generally accepted as truths until the early 1970s. Suddenly the abuses of Watergate, the disastrous consequences of Vietnam, the failure of numerous Great Society social programs, combined with an unusually high turnover of congressional seats, brought about a dramatic revival of congressional interest in the problems of Congress' control over executive activities. A variety of new laws were enacted to achieve more control: for example, widening the requirement of Senate approval of presidential appointees to executive offices; creation of the Congressional Budget Office to act as a legislative fiscal watchdog; the passage of the Freedom of Information Act to provide Congress and the general public with greater access to executive activities; and the War Powers Resolution, which restricted presidential initiative in foreign military involvements.

Concomitant with the rise of congressional oversight in the 1960s and 1970s, it became fashionable to argue that governmental policies emerged from *iron triangles*— three-way interactions involving elected members of Congress, particularly key committee and subcommittee chairpersons; career bureaucrats, particularly agency heads or senior staffers; and special interest lobbies, particularly powerful lobbies in specialized fields such as health, welfare, education, and defense. From this closed triad of interests, so the theory goes, governmental policies emerge by means of members of Congress writing and passing favorable legislation, bureaucrats implementing these

---

[2]Allen Schick, "Congress and the 'Details' of Administration," *Public Administration Review,* 36 (September/October 1976), pp. 516–528.

congressional mandates in return for bigger budgets, and special-interest groups backing (with re-election monies and other support) the helpful members of Congress: in all, a tidy and closed relationship.

Is this how the political-administrative relationships in government actually work today? In the following essay, Hugh Heclo (1944–   ), currently distinguished Robinson University professor at George Mason University, takes issue with the iron triangle conception of modern political-administrative relationships. He emphasizes, "The iron triangle concept is not so much wrong as it is disastrously incomplete." "Unfortunately," writes Heclo, "our standard political conceptions of power and control are not very well suited to the loose-jointed play of influence that is emerging in political administration. We tend to look for one group exerting dominance over another, for subgovernments that are strongly insulated from other outside forces in the environment, for policies that get 'produced' by a few 'makers.' " Instead, says Heclo, in "looking for the few who are powerful, we tend to overlook the many whose webs of influence provoke and guide the exercise of power. These webs, or what I will call 'issue networks,' are particularly relevant to the highly intricate and confusing welfare policies that have been undertaken in recent years."

Note that in Heclo's view of the *issue networks,* unlike the iron triangle concept, which assumed a small identifiable circle of participants, the participants are largely shifting, fluid, and anonymous. In fact, he writes, "it is almost impossible to say where a network leaves off and its environment begins." Whereas iron triangles are seen as relatively stable groups that coalesce around narrow policy issues, Heclo's issue networks are dispersed and numerous players move in and out of the transitory networks, without anyone being clearly in control over programs or policies. Although the "iron triangles at their roots had economic gain as an interest of all parties concerned," Heclo believes "any direct material interest is often secondary to intellectual or emotional commitment involving issue networks." Passion, ideas, and moral dedication replace, to a significant degree, material and economic gain from policy involvement.

The profound influence of the rise of these issue networks on government is manifold, Heclo thinks, especially in adding new layers of complexity to government. First, networks keep issues, potentially simple to solve, complex instead, primarily to gain power and influence by virtue of their own specialized expertise. Second, rather than fostering knowledge and consensus, issue networks push for argument, division, and contention to "maintain the purity of their viewpoints," which in turn sustain support from their natural but narrow public constituencies. Third, issue networks spawn true believers who become zealots for narrow interests rather than seekers of broad mandates of consensus, support, and confidence for public programs. Finally, rather than pushing for closure of debate, issue networks thrive by keeping arguments boiling and disagreements brewing. They survive by talking, debating, and arguing the alternatives, and not by finding common grounds for agreement and getting down to making things happen.

As you read this selection, keep the following questions in mind:

How does Heclo's issue network concept differ from the notion of iron triangles as the basis for political-administrative relationships?

What examples does Heclo give to support his new conceptualization of this relationship?

Do you find his arguments reasonable and correct on the basis of your experience or your reading of the case studies in this text?

What impact does the rise of issue networks have on democratic government in general and public administration in particular?

What new roles must public administrators assume, given the growth of issue networks today? Specifically, in your opinion, how can an administrator prepare or be trained for assuming these new roles?

Issue Networks and the Executive Establishment

HUGH HECLO

The connection between politics and administration arouses remarkably little interest in the United States. The presidency is considered more glamorous, Congress more intriguing, elections more exciting, and interest groups more troublesome. General levels of public interest can be gauged by the burst of indifference that usually greets the announcement of a new President's cabinet or rumors of a political appointee's resignation. Unless there is some White House "tie-in" or scandal (preferably both), news stories about presidential appointments are usually treated by the media as routine filler material.

This lack of interest in political administration is rarely found in other democratic countries, and it has not always prevailed in the United States. In most nations the ups and downs of political executives are taken as vital signs of the health of a government, indeed of its survival. In the United States, the nineteenth-century turmoil over one type of connection between politics and adminis-

"Issue Networks and the Executive Establishment" by Hugh Heclo from *The New Political System,* edited by Anthony King, 1978, pp. 87–124. Reprinted with permission of The American Enterprise Institute for Public Policy Research, Washington, D.C.

tration—party spoils—frequently overwhelmed any notion of presidential leadership. Anyone reading the history of those troubled decades is likely to be struck by the way in which political administration in Washington registered many of the deeper strains in American society at large. It is a curious switch that appointments to the bureaucracy should loom so large in the history of the nineteenth century, when the federal government did little, and be so completely discounted in the twentieth century, when government tries to do so much.

Political administration in Washington continues to register strains in American politics and society, although in ways more subtle than the nineteenth-century spoils scramble between Federalists and Democrats, Pro- and Anti-tariff forces, Nationalists and States-Righters, and so on. Unlike many other countries, the United States has never created a high level, government-wide civil service. Neither has it been favored with a political structure that automatically produces a stock of experienced political manpower for top executive positions in government.[1] How then does political administration in Washington work? More to the point, how might the expanding role of government be changing the connection between administration and politics?

Received opinion on this subject suggests that we already know the answers. Control is said to be vested in an informal but enduring series of "iron triangles" linking executive bureaus, congressional committees, and interest group clienteles with a stake in particular programs. A President or presidential appointee may occasionally try to muscle in, but few people doubt the capacity of these governments to thwart outsiders in the long run.

Based largely on early studies of agricultural, water, and public works policies, the iron triangle concept is not so much wrong as it is disastrously incomplete.[2] And the conventional view is especially inappropriate for understanding changes in politics and administration during recent years. Preoccupied with trying to find the few truly powerful actors, observers tend to overlook the power and influence that arise out of the configurations through which leading policy makers move and do business with each other. Looking for the closed triangles of control, we tend to miss the fairly open networks of people that increasingly impinge upon government.

To do justice to the subject would require a major study of the Washington community and the combined inspiration of a Leonard White and a James Young. Tolerating a fair bit of injustice, one can sketch a few of the factors that seem to be at work. The first is growth in the sheer mass of government activity and associated expectations. The second is the peculiar, loose-jointed play of influence that is accompanying this growth. Related to these two is the third: the layering and specialization that have overtaken the government work force, not least the political leadership of the bureaucracy.

All of this vastly complicates the job of presidential appointees both in controlling their own actions and in managing the bureaucracy. But there is much more at stake than the troubles faced by people in government. There is the deeper problem of connecting what politicians, officials, and their fellow travelers are doing in Washington with what the public at large can understand and accept. It is

on this point that political administration registers some of the larger strains of American politics and society, much as it did in the nineteenth century. For what it shows is a dissolving of organized politics and a politicizing of organizational life throughout the nation. . . .

Unfortunately, our standard political conceptions of power and control are not very well suited to the loose-jointed play of influence that is emerging in political administration. We tend to look for one group exerting dominance over another, for subgovernments that are strongly insulated from other outside forces in the environment, for policies that get "produced" by a few "makers." Seeing former government officials opening law firms or joining a new trade association, we naturally think of ways in which they are trying to conquer and control particular pieces of government machinery.

Obviously questions of power are still important. But for a host of policy initiatives undertaken in the last twenty years it is all but impossible to identify clearly who the dominant actors are. Who is controlling those actions that go to make up our national policy on abortions, or on income redistribution, or consumer protection, or energy? Looking for the few who are powerful, we tend to overlook the many whose webs of influence provoke and guide the exercise of power. These webs, or what I will call "issue networks," are particularly relevant to the highly intricate and confusing welfare policies that have been undertaken in recent years.

The notion of iron triangles and subgovernments presumes small circles of participants who have succeeded in becoming largely autonomous. Issue networks, on the other hand, comprise a large number of participants with quite variable degrees of mutual commitment or of dependence on others in their environment; in fact it is almost impossible to say where a network leaves off and its environment begins. Iron triangles and subgovernments suggest a stable set of participants coalesced to control fairly narrow public programs which are in the direct economic interest of each party to the alliance. Issue networks are almost the reverse image in each respect. Participants move in and out of the networks constantly. Rather than groups united in dominance over a program, no one, as far as one can tell, is in control of the policies and issues. Any direct material interest is often secondary to intellectual or emotional commitment. Network members reinforce each other's sense of issues as their interests, rather than (as standard political or economic models would have it) interests defining positions on issues.

Issue networks operate at many levels, from the vocal minority who turn up at local planning commission hearings to the renowned professor who is quietly telephoned by the White House to give a quick "reading" on some participant or policy. The price of buying into one or another issue network is watching, reading, talking about, and trying to act on particular policy problems. Powerful interest groups can be found represented in networks but so too can individuals in or out of government who have a reputation for being knowledgeable. Particular professions may be prominent, but the true experts in the networks are those who are issue-skilled (that is, well informed about the ins and outs of a particular policy debate) regardless of formal professional training. More than mere technical experts, network people are policy activists who know each other through the issues. Those who emerge to positions of wider leadership are policy politicians—experts in using experts, victuallers of knowledge in a world hungry for right decisions.

In the old days—when the primary problem of government was assumed to be doing what was right, rather than knowing what was right—policy knowledge could be contained in the slim adages of public administration. Public executives, it was thought, needed to know how to execute. They needed power commensurate with their responsibility. Nowadays, of course, political administrators do not execute but are involved in making highly important decisions on society's behalf, and they must mobilize policy intermediaries to deliver the goods. Knowing what is right becomes crucial, and since no one knows that for sure, going through the process of dealing with those who are

judged knowledgeable (or at least continuously concerned) becomes even more crucial. Instead of power commensurate with responsibility, issue networks seek influence commensurate with their understanding of the various, complex social choices being made. Of course some participants would like nothing better than complete power over the issues in question. Others seem to want little more than the security that comes with being well informed. As the executive of one new group moving to Washington put it, "We didn't come here to change the world; we came to minimize our surprises."[3]

Whatever the participants' motivation, it is the issue network that ties together what would otherwise be the contradictory tendencies of, on the one hand, more widespread organizational participation in public policy and, on the other, more narrow technocratic specialization in complex modern policies. Such networks need to be distinguished from three other more familiar terms used in connection with political administration. An issue network is a shared-knowledge group having to do with some aspect (or, as defined by the network, some problem) of public policy. It is therefore more well-defined than, first, a shared-attention group or "public"; those in the networks are likely to have a common base of information and understanding of how one knows about policy and identifies its problems. But knowledge does not necessarily produce agreement. Issue networks may or may not, therefore, be mobilized into, second, a shared-action group (creating a coalition) or, third, a shared-belief group (becoming a conventional interest organization). Increasingly, it is through networks of people who regard each other as knowledgeable, or at least as needing to be answered, that public policy issues tend to be refined, evidence debated, and alternative options worked out—though rarely in any controlled, well-organized way.

What does an issue network look like? It is difficult to say precisely, for at any given time only one part of a network may be active and through time the various connections may intensify or fade among the policy intermediaries and the executive and congressional bureaucracies. For example, there is no single health policy network but various sets of people knowledgeable and concerned about cost-control mechanisms, insurance techniques, nutritional programs, prepaid plans, and so on. At one time, those expert in designing a nationwide insurance system may seem to be operating in relative isolation, until it becomes clear that previous efforts to control costs have already created precedents that have to be accommodated in any new system, or that the issue of federal funding for abortions has laid land mines in the path of any workable plan.

The debate on energy policy is rich in examples of the kaleidoscopic interaction of changing issue networks. The Carter administration's initial proposal was worked out among experts who were closely tied in to conservation-minded networks. Soon it became clear that those concerned with macroeconomic policies had been largely bypassed in the planning, and last-minute amendments were made in the proposal presented to Congress, a fact that was not lost on the networks of leading economists and economic correspondents. Once congressional consideration began, it quickly became evident that attempts to define the energy debate in terms of a classic confrontation between big oil companies and consumer interests were doomed. More and more policy watchers joined in the debate, bringing to it their own concerns and analyses: tax reformers, nuclear power specialists, civil rights groups interested in more jobs; the list soon grew beyond the wildest dreams of the original energy policy planners. The problem, it became clear, was that no one could quickly turn the many networks of knowledgeable people into a shared-action coalition, much less into a single, shared-attitude group believing it faced the moral equivalent of war. Or, if it was a war, it was a Vietnam-type quagmire.

It would be foolish to suggest that the clouds of issue networks that have accompanied expanding national policies are set to replace the more familiar politics of subgovernments in Washington. What they are doing is to overlay the once stable political reference points with new forces that com-plicate calculations, decrease predictability, and impose considerable strains on those charged with government leadership. The overlay of networks and issue politics not only confronts but also seeps down into the formerly well-established politics of particular policies and programs. Social security, which for a generation had been quietly managed by a small circle of insiders, becomes controversial and politicized. The Army Corps of Engineers, once the picturebook example of control by subgovernments, is dragged into the brawl on environmental politics. The once quiet "traffic safety establishment" finds its own safety permanently endangered by the consumer movement. Confrontation between networks and iron triangles in the Social and Rehabilitation Service, the disintegration of the mighty politics of the Public Health Service and its corps—the list could be extended into a chronicle of American national government during the last generation. The point is that a somewhat new and difficult dynamic is being played out in the world of politics and administration. It is not what has been feared for so long: that technocrats and other people in white coats will expropriate the policy process. If there is to be any expropriation, it is likely to be by the policy activists, those who care deeply about a set of issues and are determined to shape the fabric of public policy accordingly. . . .

The Executive Leadership Problem

Washington has always relied on informal means of producing political leaders in government. This is no less true now than in the days when party spoils ruled presidential appointments. It is the informal mechanisms that have changed. No doubt some of the increasing emphasis on educational credentials, professional specialization, and technical facility merely reflects changes in society at large. But it is also important to recognize that government activity has itself been changing the informal mechanisms that produce political administrators. Accumulating policy commitments have become crucial forces affecting the kind of executive leadership that emerges. E. E. Schattschneider put it better when he observed that "new policies create new politics."[4]

For many years now the list of issues on the public agenda has grown more dense as new policy concerns have been added and few dropped. Administratively, this has proliferated the number of policy intermediaries. Politically, it has mobilized more and more groups of people who feel they have a stake, a determined stake, in this or that issue of public policy. These changes are in turn encouraging further specialization of the government's work force and bureaucratic layering in its political leadership. However, the term "political" needs to be used carefully. Modern officials responsible for making the connection between politics and administration bear little resemblance to the party politicians who once filled patronage jobs. Rather, today's political executive is likely to be a person knowledgeable about the substance of particular issues and adept at moving among the networks of people who are intensely concerned about them.

What are the implications for American government and politics? The verdict cannot be one-sided, if only because political management of the bureaucracy serves a number of diverse purposes. At least three important advantages can be found in the emerging system.

First, the reliance on issue networks and policy politicians is obviously consistent with some of the larger changes in society. Ordinary voters are apparently less constrained by party identification and more attracted to an issue-based style of politics. Party organizations are said to have fallen into a state of decay and to have become less capable of supplying enough highly qualified executive manpower. If government is committed to intervening in more complex, specialized areas, it is useful to draw upon the experts and policy specialists for the public management of these programs. Moreover, the congruence between an executive leadership and an electorate that are both uninterested in party politics may help stabilize a rapidly changing society. Since no one really knows how to solve the policy puzzles, policy politicians have the important quality of being disposable without any serious political ramifications (unless of course there are major symbolic implications, as in President Nixon's firing of Attorney General Elliot Richardson).

Within government, the operation of issue networks may have a second advantage in that they link Congress and the executive branch in ways that political parties no longer can. For many years, reformers have sought to revive the idea of party discipline as a means of spanning the distance between the two branches and turning their natural competition to useful purposes. But as the troubled dealings of recent Democratic Presidents with their majorities in Congress have indicated, political parties tend to be a weak bridge.

Meanwhile, the linkages of technocracy between the branches are indeliberately growing. The congressional bureaucracy that has blossomed in Washington during the last generation is in many ways like the political bureaucracy in the executive branch. In general, the new breed of congressional staffer is not a legislative crony or beneficiary of patronage favors. Personal loyalty to the congressman is still paramount, but the new-style legislative bureaucrat is likely to be someone skilled in dealing with certain complex policy issues, possibly with credentials as a policy analyst, but certainly an expert in using other experts and their networks.

None of this means an absence of conflict between President and Congress. Policy technicians in the two branches are still working for different sets of clients with different interests. The point is that the growth of specialized policy networks tends to perform the same useful services that it was once hoped a disciplined national party system would perform. Sharing policy knowledge, the networks provide a minimum common framework for political debate and decision in the two branches. For example, on energy policy, regardless of one's position on gas deregulation or incentives to producers, the policy technocracy has established a common language for discussing the issues, a shared grammar for identifying the major points of contention, a mutually familiar rhetoric of argumentation. Whether in Congress or the executive branch or somewhere outside, the "movers and shakers" in energy policy (as in health insurance, welfare reform, strategic arms limitation, occupational safety, and a host of other policy areas) tend to share an analytic repertoire for coping with the issues. Like experienced party politicians of earlier times, policy politicians in the knowledge networks may not agree; but they understand each other's way of looking at the world and arguing about policy choices.

A third advantage is the increased maneuvering room offered to political executives by the loose-jointed play of influence. If appointees were ambassadors from clearly defined interest groups and professions, or if policy were monopolized in iron triangles, then the chances for executive leadership in the bureaucracy would be small. In fact, however, the proliferation of administrative middlemen and networks of policy watchers offers new strategic resources for public managers. These are mainly opportunities to split and recombine the many sources of support and opposition that exist on policy issues. Of course, there are limits on how far a political executive can go in shopping for a constituency, but the general tendency over time has been to extend those limits. A secretary of labor will obviously pay close attention to what the AFL-CIO has to say, but there are many other voices to hear, not only in the union movement but also minority groups interested in jobs, state and local officials administering the department's programs, consumer groups worried about wage-push inflation, employees faced with unsafe working conditions, and so on. By the same token, former Secretary of Transportation William Coleman found new room for maneuver on the problem of landings by supersonic planes when he opened up the setpiece debate between pro- and anti-Concorde groups to a wider play of influence through public hearings. Clearly the richness of issue politics demands a high degree of skill to contain expectations and manage the natural dissatisfaction that comes from courting some groups rather than

others. But at least it is a game that can be affected by skill, rather than one that is predetermined by immutable forces.

These three advantages are substantial. But before we embrace the rule of policy politicians and their networks, it is worth considering the threats they pose for American government. Issue networks may be good at influencing policy, but can they govern? Should they?

The first and foremost problem is the old one of democratic legitimacy. Weaknesses in executive leadership below the level of the President have never really been due to interest groups, party politics, or Congress. The primary problem has always been the lack of any democratically based power. Political executives get their popular mandate to do anything in the bureaucracy secondhand, from either an elected chief executive or Congress. The emerging system of political technocrats makes this democratic weakness much more severe. The more closely political administrators become identified with the various specialized policy networks, the farther they become separated from the ordinary citizen. Political executives can maneuver among the already mobilized issue networks and may occasionally do a little mobilizing of their own. But this is not the same thing as creating a broad base of public understanding and support for national policies. The typical presidential appointee will travel to any number of conferences, make speeches to the membership of one association after another, but almost never will he or she have to see or listen to an ordinary member of the public. The trouble is that only a small minority of citizens, even of those who are seriously attentive to public affairs, are likely to be mobilized in the various networks.[5] Those who are not policy activists depend on the ability of government institutions to act on their behalf.

If the problem were merely an information gap between policy experts and the bulk of the population, then more communication might help. Yet instead of garnering support for policy choices, more communication from the issue networks tends to produce an "everything causes cancer" syndrome among ordinary citizens. Policy forensics among the networks yield more experts making more sophisticated claims and counterclaims to the point that the nonspecialist becomes inclined to concede everything and believe nothing that he hears. The ongoing debates on energy policy, health crises, or arms limitation are rich in examples of public skepticism about what "they," the abstruse policy experts, are doing and saying. While the highly knowledgeable have been playing a larger role in government, the proportion of the general public concluding that those running the government don't seem to know what they are doing has risen rather steadily.[6] Likewise, the more government has tried to help, the more feelings of public helplessness have grown.

No doubt many factors and events are linked to these changing public attitudes. The point is that the increasing prominence of issue networks is bound to aggravate problems of legitimacy and public disenchantment. Policy activists have little desire to recognize an unpleasant fact: that their influential systems for knowledgeable policy making tend to make democratic politics more difficult. There are at least four reasons.

Complexity

Democratic political competition is based on the idea of trying to simplify complexity into a few, broadly intelligible choices. The various issue networks, on the other hand, have a stake in searching out complexity in what might seem simple. Those who deal with particular policy issues over the years recognize that policy objectives are usually vague and results difficult to measure. Actions relevant to one policy goal can frequently be shown to be inconsistent with others. To gain a reputation as a knowledgeable participant, one must juggle all of these complexities and demand that other technocrats in the issue networks do the same.

Consensus

A major aim in democratic politics is, after open argument, to arrive at some workable consensus of views. Whether by trading off one issue against another or by combining related issues, the goal is agreement. Policy activists may commend this democratic purpose in theory, but what their issue networks actually provide is a way of processing dissension. The aim is good policy—the right outcome on the issue. Since what that means is disputable among knowledgeable people, the desire for agreement must often take second place to one's understanding of the issue. Trade-offs or combinations—say, right-to-life groups with nuclear-arms-control people; environmentalists and consumerists; civil liberties groups and anti-gun controllers—represent a kind of impurity for many of the newly proliferating groups. In general there are few imperatives pushing for political consensus among the issue networks and many rewards for those who become practiced in the techniques of informed skepticism about different positions.

Confidence

Democratic politics presumes a kind of psychological asymmetry between leaders and followers. Those competing for leadership positions are expected to be sure of themselves and of what is to be done, while those led are expected to have a certain amount of detachment and dubiety in choosing how to give their consent to be governed. Politicians are supposed to take credit for successes, to avoid any appearance of failure, and to fix blame clearly on their opponents; voters weight these claims and come to tentative judgments, pending the next competition among the leaders.

The emerging policy networks tend to reverse the situation. Activists mobilized around the policy issues are the true believers. To survive, the newer breed of leaders, or policy politicians, must become well versed in the complex, highly disputed substance of the issues. A certain tentativeness comes naturally as ostensible leaders try to spread themselves across the issues. Taking credit shows a lack of understanding of how intricate policies work and may antagonize those who really have been zealously pushing the issue. Spreading blame threatens others in the established networks and may raise expectations that new leadership can guarantee a better policy result. Vagueness about what is to be done allows policy problems to be dealt with as they develop and in accord with the intensity of opinion among policy specialists at that time. None of this is likely to warm the average citizen's confidence in his leaders. The new breed of policy politicians are cool precisely because the issue networks are hot.

Closure

Part of the genius of democratic politics is its ability to find a nonviolent decision-rule (by voting) for ending debate in favor of action. All the incentives in the policy technocracy work against such decisive closure. New studies and findings can always be brought to bear. The biggest rewards in these highly intellectual groups go to those who successfully challenge accepted wisdom. The networks thrive by continuously weighing alternative courses of action on particular policies, not by suspending disbelief and accepting that something must be done.

For all of these reasons, what is good for policy making (in the sense of involving well-informed people and rigorous analysts) may be bad for democratic politics. The emerging policy technocracy tends, as Henry Aaron has said of social science research, to "corrode any simple faiths around which political coalitions ordinarily are built."[7] Should we be content with simple faiths? Perhaps not; but the great danger is that the emerging world of issue politics and policy experts will turn John Stuart Mill's argument about the connection between liberty and popular government on its head. More informed argument about policy choices may produce more incomprehensibility. More policy intermediaries may widen participation among activists but deepen suspicions among unorganized nonspecialists. There may be more group involvement and less democratic legitimacy, more knowledge and more Know-Nothingism. Activists are likely to remain unsatisfied with, and nonactivists uncommitted to, what government is doing. Superficially this cancelling of forces might

seem to assure a conservative tilt away from new, expansionary government policies. However, in terms of undermining a democratic identification of ordinary citizens with their government, the tendencies are profoundly radical.

A second difficulty with the issue networks is the problem that they create for the President as ostensible chief of the executive establishment. The emerging policy technocracy puts presidential appointees outside of the chief executive's reach in a way that narrowly focused iron triangles rarely can. At the end of the day, constituents of these triangles can at least be bought off by giving them some of the material advantages that they crave. But for issue activists it is likely to be a question of policy choices that are right or wrong. In this situation, more analysis and staff expertise—far from helping—may only hinder the President in playing an independent political leadership role. The influence of the policy technicians and their networks permeates everything the White House may want to do. Without their expertise there are no option papers, no detailed data and elaborate assessments to stand up against the onslaught of the issue experts in Congress and outside. Of course a President can replace a political executive, but that is probably merely to substitute one incumbent of the relevant policy network for another.

It is, therefore, no accident that President Carter found himself with a cabinet almost none of whom were either his longstanding political backers or leaders of his party. Few if any of his personal retinue could have passed through the reputational screens of the networks to be named, for example, a secretary of labor or defense. Moreover, anyone known to be close to the President and placed in an operating position in the bureaucracy puts himself, and through him the President, in an extremely vulnerable position. Of the three cabinet members who were President Carter's own men, one, Andrew Young, was under extreme pressure to resign in the first several months. Another Carter associate, Bert Lance, was successfully forced to resign after six months, and the third, Griffin Bell, was given particularly tough treatment during his confirmation hearings and was being pressured to resign after only a year in office. The emerging system of political administration tends to produce executive arrangements in which the President's power stakes are on the line almost everywhere in terms of policy, whereas almost nowhere is anyone on the line for him personally.

Where does all this leave the President as a politician and as an executive of executives? In an impossible position. The problem of connecting politics and administration currently places any President in a classic no-win predicament. If he attempts to use personal loyalists as agency and department heads, he will be accused of politicizing the bureaucracy and will most likely put his executives in an untenable position for dealing with their organizations and the related networks. If he tries to create a countervailing source of policy expertise at the center, he will be accused of aggrandizing the Imperial Presidency and may hopelessly bureaucratize the White House's operations. If he relies on some benighted idea of collective cabinet government and on departmental executives for leadership in the bureaucracy (as Carter did in his first term), then the President does more than risk abdicating his own leadership responsibilities as the only elected executive in the national government; he is bound to become a creature of the issue networks and the policy specialists. It would be pleasant to think that there is a neat way out of this trilemma, but there is not.

Finally, there are disturbing questions surrounding the accountability of a political technocracy. The real problem is not that policy specialists specialize but that, by the nature of public office, they must generalize. Whatever an influential political executive does is done with all the collective authority of government and in the name of the public at large. It is not difficult to imagine situations in which policies make excellent sense within the cloisters of the expert issue watchers and yet are nonsense or worse seen from the viewpoint of ordinary people, the kinds of people political executives rarely meet. Since political executives themselves never need to pass muster with the electorate, the main source of democratic accountability must lie with the President and Congress. Given

the President's problems and Congress's own burgeoning bureaucracy of policy specialists, the prospects for a democratically responsible executive establishment are poor at best.

Perhaps we need not worry. A case could be made that all we are seeing is a temporary commotion stirred up by a generation of reformist policies. In time the policy process may reenter a period of detumescence as the new groups and networks subside into the familiar triangulations of power.

However, a stronger case can be made that the changes will endure. In the first place, sufficient policy-making forces have now converged in Washington that it is unlikely that we will see a return to the familiar cycle of federal quiescence and policy experimentation by state governments. The central government, surrounded by networks of policy specialists, probably now has the capacity for taking continual policy initiatives. In the second place, there seems to be no way of braking, much less reversing, policy expectations generated by the compensatory mentality. To cut back on commitments undertaken in the last generation would itself be a major act of redistribution and could be expected to yield even more turmoil in the policy process. Once it becomes accepted that relative rather than absolute deprivation is what matters, the crusaders can always be counted upon to be in business.

A third reason why our politics and administration may never be the same lies in the very fact that so many policies have already been accumulated. Having to make policy in an environment already crowded with public commitments and programs increases the odds of multiple, indirect impacts of one policy on another, of one perspective set in tension with another, of one group and then another being mobilized. This sort of complexity and unpredictability creates a hostile setting for any return to traditional interest group politics.

Imagine trying to govern in a situation where the short-term political resources you need are stacked around a changing series of discrete issues, and where people overseeing these issues have nothing to prevent their pressing claims beyond any resources that they can offer in return. Imagine too that the more they do so, the more you lose understanding and support from public backers who have the long-term resources that you need. Whipsawed between cynics and true believers, policy would always tend to evolve to levels of insolubility. It is not easy for a society to politicize itself and at the same time depoliticize government leadership. But we in the United States may be managing to do just this.

Notes

1. Hugh Heclo, *A Government of Strangers: Executive Politics in Washington* (Washington, D.C.: Brookings Institution, 1977).
2. Perhaps the most widely cited interpretations are J. Leiper Freeman, *The Political Process* (New York: Random House, 1965); and Douglass Cater, *Power in Washington* (New York: Vintage, 1964)
3. Steven V. Roberts, "Trade Associations Flocking to Capital as U.S. Role Rises," *New York Times,* March 4, 1978, p. 44.
4. E. E. Schattschneider, *Politics, Pressures and the Tariff* (Hamden: Archon, 1963), p. 288 (originally published 1935).
5. An interesting recent case study showing the complexity of trying to generalize about who is "mobilizable" is James N. Rosenau, *Citizenship Between Elections* (New York: The Free Press, 1974).
6. Since 1964 the Institute for Social Research at the University of Michigan has asked the question, "Do you feel that almost all of the people running the government are smart people, or do you think that quite a few of them don't seem to know what they are doing?" The proportions choosing the latter view have been 28 percent (1964), 38 percent (1968), 45 percent (1970), 42 percent (1972), 47 percent (1974), and 52 percent (1976). For similar findings on public feelings of lack of control over the policy process, see U.S. Congress, Senate, Subcommittee on Intergovernmental Relations of the Committee on Government Operations, *Confidence and Concern: Citizens View American Government,* committee print, 93d Cong., 1st sess., 1973, pt. 1, p. 30. For a more complete discussion of recent trends see the two articles by Arthur H. Miller and Jack Citrin in the *American Political Science Review* (September 1974).
7. Henry J. Aaron, *Politics and the Professors* (Washington, D.C.: Brookings Institution, 1978), p. 159.

☐ CASE STUDY 14

Introduction

Professor Heclo in the foregoing reading advances an important conceptualization, or rather reconceptualization, of political-administrative relationships, which some scholars suggest are central to the problems confronting modern public administration. However, from the standpoint of the practitioner of public administration, what personal attributes are most critical for individuals working within high-level policy making arenas? What characteristics are evident in those civil servants who perform well in top political-administrative positions? Are there special human abilities to be found in public officials who effectively do their jobs where politics and administration intersect?

In the following case, Norma M. Riccucci, an associate professor of public administration and policy at the Graduate School of Public Affairs, SUNY, Albany, New York, examines six high-level federal officials, whom she labels "execucrats." As she explains at the outset of her essay, Riccucci coined this new term "execucrat" because "bureaucrat" is "extremely pejorative and, hence, counterproductive." Thus she invents a new word for top-level career officials that combines both "executive" and "bureaucrat." The bulk of her essay sketches portraits of six successful "execucrats": their backgrounds, achievements, and the stories of how they accomplished their remarkable contributions to the public welfare within often highly charged political environments. On the basis of these six stories, Riccucci draws several interesting conclusions about what it takes to be a successful execucrat, indeed to survive and perform effectively in a hostile environment of interest groups and issue networks, as outlined previously by Hugh Heclo.

The following story is not *one* but rather *six* stories about some unique federal officials. In this respect, it is therefore *not* a case that recounts "the facts" of a single story, with a beginning and end, as is normally true of cases in this textbook. Instead, it contains six character sketches or stories of individual accomplishments from which the author draws some generalizations about the common traits they share, and which in turn, gave them the abilities to perform so well within high-level policy environments. Readers should pay special attention to the author's "study design" at the end of her essay to understand the methodology she used in order to select these six federal officials for her intensive investigation.

As you read about "Execucrats," try to think about several of the following issues:

Based upon these profiles of six successful federal officials, do you agree with the conclusions that Riccucci outlines? Or, based upon your own reading, would you add other traits that characterize these six individuals as "success" stories?

In your view, would the ingredients for successful performance at the federal level be the same for those who work in high-level policy posts at state and local levels? Or, would you modify those attributes as outlined by Professor Riccucci in certain ways to apply to "sub-national positions"?

From your perspective, how would you generalize about the best methods for knitting together "politics and administration"? Would your generalizations support or contradict Heclo's analysis of "issue networks" as the basis for understanding political-administrative relationships today? Or, would you suggest an alternative view?

"Execucrats"

NORMA M. RICCUCCI

Ever since the emergence of the politics-administration dichotomy, public administrationists and political scientists have grappled with the question

Source: "Execucrats" by Norma M. Riccucci, *Public Administration Review*, May/June 1995, Vol. 55, No. 3 pp. 218–230. Reprinted with permission from *Public Administration Review* © by the American Society for Public Administration (ASPA), 1120 G Street NW, Suite 700, Washington, D.C. 20005. All rights reserved.

of whether career servants participate, or ought to participate, in high-level decision and policy making in government. Although it is, by now, widely established that "execucrats," that is career *execu*tives/bureau*crats,* are indeed enmeshed in the public policy-making process, very little work has examined what it takes for them to be effective policy makers. (The term execucrat is introduced and used here instead of bureaucrat, which has become extremely pejorative and, hence, counterproductive.)

This article examines the ingredients of effective execucratic performance at the federal level of government. Through case studies, the accomplishments of six execucrats in different policy fields are analyzed to determine the significance of such factors as political and managerial skills for execucratic effectiveness.[1] Based on this analysis, inferences are made about what it takes to be a successful execucrat. . . .

Six Successful Execucrats

The "success stories" of the six execucrats included in this study are summarized in this section.

William Black and the Savings and Loan Debacle

Between 1980 and 1989, the savings and loan (S&L) or thrift industry was pillaged and plundered by fraud, mismanagement, and outright cupidity. The result has been one of the biggest financial crises in the history of this nation, perhaps second only to the Great Depression of the 1930s. It has been estimated that the cost of bailing out failed S&Ls will reach almost $200 billion, and that the American taxpayers will be footing about 80 percent of the bill.

It is difficult to pinpoint the exact beginning of the thrift industry's downfall, but there is some agreement that the spending around the Vietnam War as well as President Johnson's Great Society program spurred inflation, which in turn, spurred massive deregulation of the thrift industry, particularly by President Reagan in the early 1980s. It is perhaps these factors, along with the ensuing greed, corruption, and mismanagement on the part of S&L executives and politicians that ultimately resulted in the collapse of the S&L industry.

One of the persons instrumental in containing and redressing the S&L mess was William Black, who was hired in 1984 as the Litigation Director for the Federal Home Loan Bank Board, the quasi-independent federal agency which, up until 1989, regulated the thrift industry. In fact, it was Black, along with Ed Gray, Reagan's appointee to head the Bank Board in 1983, who was responsible for an im-

portant first step in containing the S&L fiasco—*rereg*-ulating the thrift industry. Black played a critical role because of his expertise in law, accounting, and economics. Specifically, Black was relied upon to write and enforce a new rule that would restrict direct investment powers of S&Ls. It was Gray's predecessor, Richard Pratt, who removed in the early 1980s various restrictions over what S&Ls could invest in. Pratt's move enabled S&Ls to invest in risky, fraudulent ventures.

In their efforts to reregulate the thrift industry, Black and Gray faced an incredible amount of resistance, not only from thrift owners but also from the Reagan administration, which was averse to *any* type of regulatory endeavor. In addition, Charles Keating, Jr., owner of Lincoln S&L in California, cashed in some chips with Congress, and persuaded enough members of the House of Representatives to sign a resolution which asked—but did not mandate—the Bank Board to delay implementation of the new direct investment rule. Gray and Black, however, refused to back off and began enforcing the new rule.

As the Bank Board began closing or taking over failed S&Ls, angry thrift operators turned up the heat on Congress to stop Black and Gray. The House Speaker at the time, Rep. Jim Wright (D-Tex), was particularly sympathetic to these pleas, since Texas S&Ls—where some of the most egregious forms of abuse were being committed—were the target of the Bank Board's crackdown. Wright responded by attempting to block Black's every move. Black, frustrated and left with no other alternative, responded by going to the media and exposing Wright's transgressions to the American people. This turned out to be an effective strategy for Black, because now the ugly secrets about the corruption, fraud, and cover-up of the extent of the S&L crisis were out. An investigation was ultimately led into Wright's improprieties concerning Texas S&Ls. On May 31, 1989, Wright resigned from Congress.

Keating's S&L was next on Black's list. The losses at Lincoln S&L were mounting. But Keating, aware of Black's crackdown on Texas S&Ls and Speaker Wright, did everything he could to keep his failing S&L open. One of Keating's major tactics was to muscle five U.S. senators to intervene on his behalf. The senators, who came to be known as "The Keating Five," had all received generous political contributions from Keating (DeConcini, D-Ariz., $55,000; Riegle, D-Mich., $76,000; McCain,

R-Ariz., $112,000; Glenn, D-Ohio, $200,000; and Cranston, D-Calif., $889,000) (Pizza, Fricker, and Muolo, 1989).

Black's strategy was to blow the whistle on the Keating Five. In fact, Black's courage and willingness to stand up to Keating and the five senators was a watershed in the S&L scandal. A major congressional investigation was launched into the extent of the S&L crisis, including into the role of the Keating Five. Keating was ultimately convicted of criminal racketeering by a federal court and was sentenced to twelve and a half years in prison, which is running concurrently with a ten-year, state prison sentence that Keating began serving in April 1992. Black's actions also triggered the 1989 reorganization of the federal home loan banking system, which was part of President Bush's bail-out plan.

Black made a lot of enemies as a result of his efforts, but he is also responsible for containing Americans' tab in bailing out the failed S&L industry. His courage, tenacity, and exceptional legal and financial skills contributed to his effectiveness. Ed Gray (1983) summed it up rather well when he said, "Bill Black deserves to be called a patriot in that he is a person who strongly cares about the public's well-being. Real patriotism is when you put the public interest ahead of your own. And this is exactly what Bill did."

Eileen Claussen and the Montreal Protocol

Sun bathing has become quite a popular ritual in many societies. For Americans, it continues to be a favorite pastime. Yet, little did we know that frolicking in the sun would carry such a high price tag. It has been estimated that by the year 2075, there will be over 150 million new cases of skin cancer in the United States, resulting in over 3 million deaths. It is also projected that there will be 18 million additional eye cataract cases in the United States, many resulting in blindness (U.S. Environmental Protection Agency, 1987).

Since the early 1970s, it has become evident that the ozone layer—the protective shield that screens out the sun's deadly ultraviolet rays—is losing its power. One of the biggest threats to the ozone layer are chlorofluorocarbons (CFCs), chemicals that, when released into the atmosphere, produce chlorine atoms which destroy ozone.[2]

In September of 1987 an international agreement was forged in Montreal, Canada, to curb the production of CFCs and other toxic chemicals. The Montreal Protocol on Substances that Deplete the Ozone Layer was signed by the United States and 23 other nations, industrialized as well as developing (Benedick, 1991; Roan, 1989). One of the persons instrumental in negotiating and implementing this accord and later renegotiating its terms is Eileen Claussen, Director of Atmospheric Programs of the U.S. Environmental Protection Agency (EPA), who has worked her entire career in the federal government.

Working in the international arena to forge agreement among diverse players over CFC reductions has certainly been a challenge to Claussen. Perhaps an even greater challenge was trying to get the Reagan administration to sign off on environmental regulation. In fact, after years of negotiations, and just prior to striking the international accord, the Reagan administration threatened to obstruct the entire agreement. It turned out that the Reagan White House was resistant to the U.S.'s role in regulating CFC production. A few of Reagan's political people devised a plan to nullify effectively the forthcoming international accord.

Interior Secretary Donald Hodel, Commerce Secretary Malcolm Baldrige, and White House Science Adviser William Graham advanced a "market-based" approach to curbing ozone depletion. They suggested to Claussen and her staff that people could wear hats and sunglasses and also use suntan lotion to protect themselves from the sun's ultraviolet rays! In an interview with the *Wall Street Journal,* Hodel went so far as to say, "People who don't stand out in the sun—it doesn't affect them" (Taylor, 1987). Hodel, Baldride, and Graham concluded that these steps, combined with advances in medical treatment, would eliminate the need to regulate CFCs.

Claussen was stunned! Recognizing that this so-called "Rayban Plan" was nothing more than an inane attempt by Reagan officials to eschew government regulation over CFCs, Claussen went on the offensive. An important strategy that she employed was to educate the public and garner its opposition to the administration's plan. The media were viewed as an obvious conduit here, and so the *Washington Post* was contacted. Over the next several days, political cartoons and editorials lampooning the administration's Rayban Plan appeared in the *Post* as well as other newspapers. Claussen was also successful in mobilizing support from environmental groups as well as key members of Congress.

Needless to say, the Rayban Plan failed. Ultimately, Claussen, along with her agency head, Lee Thomas, were able to bring the Reagan administration on board for the international accord, which was signed on Sept. 16, 1987.

A few years later, when the international negotiating teams called for greater CFC reduction measures, Claussen was once again rebuffed—this time by President Bush and his advisors. Not only did she have to deal with Bush's foot-dragging about environmental matters, but she also had to contend with the president's Chief of Staff, John Sununu. Mr. Sununu balked at the prospect of providing financial support to help developing countries phase out CFCs. Mr. Sununu, along with Office of Management and Budget (OMB) Director Richard Darman, announced that the United States *would not* provide funding for international environmental efforts that exceeded pre-existing limits. In effect, the U.S.'s role in this international endeavor would be severely hampered, thereby placing the entire accord in jeopardy.

Claussen would once again have to find a way to prevail over the administration. She found herself in countless meetings with White House officials to persuade them to provide financial backing for this endeavor. Claussen was also successful in encouraging other officials and groups—even industry—to press the Bush administration to provide funding. U.S. Senators, Democrats and Republicans alike, sent separate letters to President Bush, urging him to support the international environmental efforts so that the United States would maintain its leadership position within the world's environmental community. Prime Ministers Margaret Thatcher of Great Britain and Brian Mulrooney of Canada also put pressure on the Bush administration. Claussen's petitioning and lobbying efforts paid off. Sununu ultimately decided that the U.S. government would provide funding to assist developing countries eliminate ozone depleters.

Claussen has proven herself to be a world leader in environmental affairs. Her political, technical, and managerial skills, to name a few, have contributed to her success. As Vice President Gore (1993) observed, "Eileen Claussen provides invaluable expe-

rience and understanding of global environmental issues . . . to our Administration. She is talented, smart, committed, and tireless—a combination that ensures effectiveness and success."

Ambassador Edward Perkins: Helping to Change South Africa

April 29, 1994, marked a significant milestone for the Republic of South Africa. For the first time in the nation's history, blacks voted without restrictions in open, universal elections. As the world anticipated, they elected as their new president, Nelson Mandela, the most prominent leader of the anti-apartheid movement, who had served a 27-year prison term for conspiring to overthrow the government of South Africa. It was a remarkable event for South Africa where, for centuries, peoples' lives had been determined by the color of their skin; where whites have controlled the wealth and political power of the nation, despite the fact that they comprise only 15 percent of the population, and blacks and other nonwhites comprise 85 percent.

It was not until the mid to late 1980s that mounting internal and external pressures on the government gave way to formal, albeit slow, change in South Africa. Although no single person, group, country, or even event could ever be credited for the political, economic, and social changes, each actor has had some part in delivering South Africa to a place where racial oppression and repression of blacks would no longer be tolerated. Obviously, black South Africans have been pivotal in bringing about change to their nation. The persistent and formidable struggle of such prominent leaders as Nelson Mandela, despite his imprisonment, and Archbishop Desmond Tutu have also been critical to reform efforts.

In addition, there were the political dignitaries, entrusted with enforcing their countries' policies toward South Africa, who played an important role in the struggle to free black South Africa. One such person was Edward J. Perkins, U.S. ambassador to South Africa from 1986 to 1989. Ambassador Perkins—the first African-American ambassador to South Africa—is a career diplomat whose leadership, negotiation, and communication skills helped to promote positive change in South Africa.

It was a particularly challenging job for Perkins, before he even departed for his assignment. Congress, for example, was very concerned that Perkins, as a Reagan appointee, might not enforce the economic sanctions against South Africa, but, instead would adhere to Reagan's much-criticized "constructive engagement" policy, which called for "friendly," behind-the-scenes negotiations rather than open criticism and punitive (e.g., economic) sanctions. Ambassador Perkins also faced resistance from African Americans in the United States, who shared the fears of Congress. In addition, black as well as white South Africans were suspicious of Reagan's motives in appointing an African American to the post. Perhaps Perkins's chief supporters were high-level political appointees in the State Department, in particular George Shultz, Secretary of State at the time, and Chester Crocker, Assistant Secretary of State for African Affairs. (Indeed, Perkins would later work closely with Shultz and Crocker to help bring about change in South Africa.)

In short, Perkins was under close scrutiny from various camps, but he was unruffled by it. He plowed ahead with several incisive strategies. One was getting to know *everybody* in South Africa— whites, blacks, and even the leaders of banned black groups—and to develop clear and open lines of communication with them. This was a significant milestone for U.S. foreign policy in that no other U.S. ambassador before him was willing to work with the black community in South Africa. Because of his willingness to reach out and actually *listen* to them, black South Africans became very receptive to Perkins. Needless to say, this strategy was very unpopular with white South Africans.

In addition, Perkins lent his support to politically charged events in South Africa. One such event was an ecumenical protest by black South African bishops against a newly issued law that barred demonstrations against the government for its practice of mass detentions without a trial. At the time, some 30,000 people—mostly blacks, including an estimated 10,000 children—had been detained without a trial. Perkins was one of only three foreign ambassadors to participate in the protest. This brought worldwide attention to the U.S. ambassador. The *New York Times* ran an editorial which thanked and praised Perkins for his actions. It stated that "It's finally possible—how long has it been?—for Americans to take pride in some Reagan administration conduct in South Africa." It went on to say that Perkins's participation in the public protest against the new law "offers a new and welcome example for the Reagan administration. There may be hope yet that Pretoria will have to stop looking to Washington for comfort" (*New York Times,* 1987). The clear implication of the editorial was that the U.S.'s greatest weapon in dismantling apartheid was Ambassador Perkins.

Perkins's participation in this as well as other demonstrations was galvanizing. In particular, it established his credibility with black South African leaders and the black press. Further, it sent a very clear message to the white-controlled government of South Africa that a window was open for Americans to change the oppressive racial system through their ambassador; that Perkins would not, as ambassadors had done before him, "lower his voice" in deference to white leaders, but rather would make it known that change was on the horizon and that he would be an active participant in bringing it about.

Ultimately, it was these and other strategies,[3] along with Perkins's strong leadership and diplomatic skills, that helped chip away at South Africa's racist policies. Many have acknowledged Perkins's exceptional work in South Africa. Secretary Shultz (1993) summed it up in this concise fashion:

> Ed was very well qualified for the post, [because] he understood the issues, the problems and the opportunities [in South Africa]. And he understood American foreign policy so he could express that well. . . . In the end, Ed made a difference in South Africa because he is a first-class professional.

Stephen Marica and the Wedtech Scandal

Most of us probably remember Wedtech, the small manufacturing firm in the South Bronx which bilked the American taxpayers out of millions of dollars through fraud, deceit, bribery, and extortion. It was done through defense contracts, which were secured for Wedtech by corrupt business executives and politicians.

Steve Marica, Assistant Inspector General for the U.S. Small Business Administration (SBA), was one of the execucrats whose leadership skills and investigative expertise ultimately led to the indictment and conviction of the numerous business persons and political officials involved in the Wedtech scam.

His efforts also brought greater attention to corruption in general in the federal contracting business.

Wedtech's crimes were many. First, the company's owners lied on an application for the federal government's 8(a) "set-aside" program. While John Mariotta, founder, CEO, and Chair of Wedtech, qualified because of his Latino ancestry, he was not the "majority" owner of the business; rather, he and his partner, Fred Neuberger, each owned 50 percent. So, in order to qualify, the co-owners of Wedtech claimed that Mariotta owned two-thirds of the business, while Neuberger only a third.

In addition, Wedtech's owners forged close dealings with various congresspersons, including Mario Biaggi of the North Bronx and Robert Garcia of the South Bronx, who promised to use, for a certain fee, their influence in Washington on Wedtech's behalf. Also brought on board was San Francisco attorney, E. Robert Wallach, who happened to be a close friend of Edwin Meese III, then President Reagan's legal counselor in the White House. For a handsome monthly retainer, Wallach promised to use his influence with Meese to help Wedtech secure contracts under the 8(a) program. Others who used their political clout on behalf of Wedtech included U.S. Senator from New York, Alfonse D'Amato, Lyn Nofziger of Reagan's White House Office of Public Liaison, and Peter Neglia, the New York regional administrator of the SBA.

Other shady dealings of Wedtech included selling fraudulent stock to the American public, and illegally billing the government for Wedtech's contract work *before* it was actually completed. The irony is that, despite its wheeling and dealing, Wedtech was still failing financially precisely because of the large payoffs it was making to its political sponsors.

It was in 1986 that Steve Marica caught on to Wedtech. Marica had read a short *Wall Street Journal* article reporting that John Mariotta had been fired as CEO and chair of Wedtech's Board of Directors. Mariotta had become the scapegoat for the company's financial troubles and, so, he was fired. Marica, knowing that the firm was an 8(a) contractor realized that Wedtech would no longer qualify for the 8(a) program now that Mariotta was not the controlling interest in company. (Marica had no idea that Mariotta's initial application to the 8(a) program was fraudulent—or, for that matter, that Wedtech was engaged in so many other fraudulent, illegal ac-

tivities—because SBA's regional administrator, Neglia, had been covering up for Wedtech.)

When Wedtech did not withdraw from the 8(a) program, Marica's suspicions were raised, and so he launched an investigation into the firm's activities. No sooner was his investigation underway than Marica discovered that Wedtech was under investigation by a number of other authorities including the DA's Offices of Manhattan and the Bronx, the FBI, and Rudolph Giuliani, former U.S. Attorney in the Southern District of Manhattan. After learning this, Marica saw a strategic advantage to coordinating his investigation with that of Giuliani's. Mr. Giuliani, however, saw otherwise. Giuliani and his staff, like many others, believed that the SBA was somehow involved in the Wedtech scandal, since it was receiving such large government contracts under the 8(a) program. In short, Giuliani's staff felt that high-ranking management officials at Marica's agency could not be trusted. Marica assured the U.S. Attorney's office that he and his staff could be trusted. To prove this, Marica agreed to allow only certain members of his staff at the Office of Inspector General (OIG) to have access to Wedtech information. This was a difficult decision for Marica—and an unprecedented one for any manager at the OIG—yet it was a pivotal move because it ultimately demonstrated that his office could successfully participate in major cases as a trusted partner.

Another action that Marica took to improve the SBA's public image was to develop new training programs for SBA employees. One program was aimed at helping OIG investigators root out fraud and corruption. Marica also began training field managers on the recognition and reporting of internal weaknesses and program vulnerabilities identified by investigations.

In addition, Marica completely revitalized the Investigations Division (ID) of the OIG. He moved the direction of the ID into complex criminal investigations. Heretofore, the ID focused primarily on administrative cases, such as abuses to attendance and travel reimbursements.

Marica then took a variety of steps to improve the expertise, image, status and, hence, morale of the OIG's investigators. For example, Marica completely restructured the requirements and duties of the job. In line with the emphasis on criminal investigations, Marica initiated changes which allowed special agents to execute arrests and to carry firearms under certain conditions.

These and many other efforts helped to create a sense of identity and pride within the OIG and helped change the image of the SBA. In effect, the OIG was better prepared for criminal investigations into firms such as Wedtech. The Wedtech investigation, which eventually became an interjurisdictional effort, was a success, and many have credited Marica's strong leadership, managerial and investigative skills for the victory.

Dr. Vince Hutchins and Maternal and Child Health

Children are one of this nation's most valuable resources. They stand for hope, change, and a better tomorrow. Indeed, they are the future of this nation. Yet, for all our talk about how much we love our children, we have done poorly as a nation to invest properly in their health and well-being. Since the mid-1980s, there has been an upward trend in the percentage of babies born prematurely, and the infant mortality rate (death between birth and age 1) is once again on the rise. In fact, the infant mortality rate in the United States is about twice as high as in Japan and Sweden and a third higher than that of countries of comparable economic development (Miller, 1992; Sardell, 1990; Schlesinger and Kronebusch, 1990).

Maternal and child health (MCH) care is an area of public health that seeks to promote the health and well-being of all mothers and children, especially those who are unable to afford medical care and treatment. It is an extremely vital area of our public health system because it touches every American. Dr. Vince Hutchins, Director of the HHS's MCH Bureau from 1977 until his retirement in 1992, is a public health professional who has devoted his entire life to ensuring that mothers and children receive proper medical care and treatment. Just one of his many successful undertakings has been the establishment of the Healthy Mothers, Healthy Babies Coalition (HMHB), a public-private partnership devoted to promoting the health of mothers and children in this nation.

Reagan's cutbacks during the 1980s in health and human services, particularly those for mothers and children, created an extremely challenging situation for health care professionals. It was, indeed, a time for creative thinking. In order to avert the financial impact of Reagan's policies, Dr. Hutchins set about the task of identifying alternative approaches to financing MCH care programs. One of the programs that eventually emerged from Dr. Hutchins's resourceful and creative strategizing was the HMHB Coalition.

The HMHB Coalition represents the first national public-private effort around MCH care in the United States. Through preventive health education, the coalition's goal is to reduce infant mortality and low birth weight in the United States. A number of projects (e.g., around such areas as breastfeeding, adolescent pregnancy, and substance abuse) have been developed to reach mothers—especially those who are disadvantaged—through, for instance, outreach programs and the development of "culturally sensitive" public education materials.

Dr. Hutchins's primary strategy for establishing the coalition was to mobilize the MCH care constituency. Working with various public, private, and nonprofit groups, as well as members of Congress and a handful of key political appointees, Hutchins pieced together a partnership that would provide services to mothers and children.

The one group that Hutchins could not count on very much in this as well as other endeavors was the political folks. Granted, Hutchins enjoyed a good relationship with those political appointees who demonstrated some commitment to MCH matters (e.g., Madeleine Will of the Education Department's Office of Special Education and Rehabilitative Services). But, his relationship with other political appointees under both the Reagan and Bush administrations was marked by stress, mainly because of the regressive attitudes of those administrations toward MCH care issues.

Interestingly, Dr. Hutchins (1992) pointed out that there was a major difference in the relationship between career and political people under Reagan as compared to Bush. He said that "the relationship with political appointees under Bush was much worse than under Reagan. The Bush people were smarter, and so they knew how to stop things when the president wanted them stopped. They knew the system better . . . and, so they were able to get [Bush's] dirty work done."

Notwithstanding, Dr. Hutchins was successful in dealing with the conflict and avoiding the hurdles set up by political people in the executive branch under Bush and Reagan by working closely with members of Congress and MCH constituency groups. He said that overall, the support for his programs "has come more from the [MCH] constituency and the Hill than from the White House or the executive branch, except during the Carter years."

In addition to his ability to work effectively with Congress and the MCH constituency, a key reason Dr. Hutchins has been successful in influencing MCH care policies is risk taking. Hutchins said that "there is a philosophy that I believe in of not asking for permission to do something, but then being willing to have your hand slapped occasionally. . . . Risk-taking, within certain parameters, of course, is key. . . . Part of the fun of working in government is to see how far you are willing and able to go, even though we're rarely rewarded for risk-taking behavior. But you must be willing to put your wrist out and get it slapped. This is crucial if you want to get things to work in the federal government."

In short, the combination of his risk-taking behavior and his strong leadership and interpersonal skills allowed Dr. Hutchins to achieve major accomplishments around MCH care issues, an important one being the HMHB Coalition. It illustrates Dr. Hutchins's creativity and talents in maintaining services to mothers and children during a period of dwindling resources. He was a coalition- and consensus-builder and a team leader. He recognized the importance of relying on different players in and out of government and getting them to work together to accomplish the work around MCH care matters.

Dr. Helene Gayle and Worldwide AIDS Prevention

AIDS is an immune deficiency disorder which attacks and renders useless the body's immune system, thus leaving those affected by it prey to myriad diseases and infections. It is linked to a virus known as human immunodeficiency virus, or HIV. Like many viruses, the origins of HIV are unknown. Moreover, scientists and researchers are still uncertain as to exactly how HIV destroys the human immune system and whether it is alone responsible for AIDS (Shilts, 1988). Because there is still no cure for the disease, AIDS prevention has become a primary focus for public health officials.

One person who has played a critical role in AIDS prevention worldwide is Dr. Helene Gayle, an epidemiologist from the U.S. Centers for Disease Control and Prevention (CDC). Dr. Gayle can be credited for several accomplishments around AIDS prevention

efforts and public policy; two particularly stand out. One is bringing communities and community-based organizations that the U.S. federal government serves vis-à-vis AIDS more into the public policy process. She has been very instrumental in getting disparate groups, including minority, gay, and church communities, involved so that they have a better understanding of what the government does around AIDS. This has also fostered the CDC's ability to better understand and ultimately serve *their* needs.

One of the reasons why Dr. Gayle has been so successful at building bridges and fostering communications between the federal government and various communities is her interpersonal relations skills. Rashida Hassan, executive director of a nonprofit organization which provides services to African Americans on sexual health issues explains it in this fashion:

> Helene has been very effective in establishing a dialogue with community-based groups in order to keep us involved in the policy process [around AIDS]. And she is so effective because first and foremost, she has a personal commitment to the issue areas which goes beyond her government job. . . . Also, she was not afraid to make it clear to the federal government that they were not getting just a Dr. Helene Gayle, but they were getting a black female physician who was very dedicated to her work and the black community. We have been pleased to discover that the government has not neutralized her, that she still retains her African heritage and she has not relinquished this identity to the government bureaucracy. This has made a big difference to us and our clients, especially since there are very few women of color in government for us to talk to (Hassan, 1994).

Another important part of building bridges with community-based groups is cultivating good relationships with the other critical players in AIDS policy, particularly political appointees. Dr. James Curran, former associate director of CDC for AIDS, commented that Gayle works effectively with the political folks because

> she is not politically motivated. She is committed to the public's health and not any particular phi-

losophy of government. She is just doing her job and doing it very effectively and this is quite laudable (Curran, 1994).

A second area were Dr. Gayle has made a significant contribution to fighting AIDS internationally has been in the development of preventive tools and technologies for women's use (e.g., virucides and female condoms). When we consider the prevention tools that are currently available, they are all linked to male-controlled behaviors (e.g., the use of condoms). Obviously, as Gayle points out, "we can instruct women to ask their partners to use a condom, but for a variety of reasons this request is not always complied with. Likewise, we could instruct women to stick with one partner, but then if their partner doesn't abide by this, the woman again has no control over the transmission of HIV. So, developing new technologies more relevant to women is a high priority for us. It gives women some control over preventing the disease."

Dr. Gayle has demonstrated a strong commitment to working with and helping those afflicted with AIDS. She has proven to be an outstanding coalition builder, communicator, and manager in the field of AIDS policy. Dr. James Curran of the CDC summed up Dr. Gayle's commitment to the battle against AIDS in this fashion. He said that "the thing that men and women of all races and cultures should know about Helene is that she is an excellent example of a dedicated scientist and public servant. She truly enjoys working for the government and she has made enormous contributions to our efforts to fight AIDS" (Curran, 1994).

Ingredients of Effective Execucratic Performance

Table 1 provides a summary of the execucrats' specific accomplishments and the skills and attributes that contributed to their successful performance. As we can see, there are some commonalties between and among the six execucrats in the various skills and attributes categories. For example, they all demonstrated such management and leadership skills as good planning, organizing, and communication, attributes we would expect *any* effective manager to possess. On this same dimension, they were all goal-oriented and exhibited good interpersonal skills, which, as Stewart and Garson (1983; 63) have said, fit the "ideal profile of an effective leader."

Likewise, there were several personality traits which were common to all six execucrats. For example, each execucrat was very honest, trustworthy, and determined, and each exhibited high moral and ethical standards. As noted earlier, these attributes have been deemed important ingredients for successful execucratic performance.

Not surprisingly, there was some overlap between personality traits and management/leadership skills. That is to say, the execucrats were effective managers and leaders in part because of their personalities. For example, all six of the execucrats were described as being honest and trustworthy and this represents one reason why the execucrats were effective managers and leaders. Similarly, Black, Claussen, and Hutchins were variously described as being risk takers or "gutsy," and this personality trait contributed in part to their managerial effectiveness. This is not to say, of course, that risk taking will always lead to successful managerial performance. Rather, it happened to work for these execucrats in large part because of the particular circumstances and situations they faced.

It would appear that personality traits interact with not just management and leadership skills to explain effective execucratic performance but also with situational factors. A good example can be seen with Dr. Helene Gayle, whose strong identification to her African heritage has proven to be an effective attribute, given the circumstances surrounding her job (i.e., working with various community-based groups that the government serves *vis-à-vis* AIDS).

The interaction of certain skills and attributes, then, informs us about execucratic success.[5] Perhaps the more important point to be made here is that execucrats must truly know and understand the intricacies of the environments they work in and must also have insight into whether their style will fit or clash with their milieu. A number of other attributes of successful execucratic performance are presented in Table 1. For example, the specific strategies that the six execucrats employed also contributed to their success. Claussen's use of the media, Marica's attention to improving the credibility of his agency, and Perkins's decision to go into the black South African townships are examples of particular strategies that these execucrats deliberately employed to attain their goals.

Also making a difference was the execucrats' technical expertise in such areas or fields as medicine (Gayle and Hutchins), public health (Gayle and Hutchins), law (Marica and Black), foreign affairs/international relations (Perkins), environmental science (Claussen), and accounting and economics (Black). So, too, did their experience in government, which not only contributed to their expertise and knowledge of the technical and administrative workings of the federal government but also provided them with a cognitive map of the Washington establishment.

Perhaps the most interesting set of observations emerging from this research revolve, not surprisingly, around political skills. While political skill takes on a host of meanings, they all revolve around the different ways in which execucrats are involved in policy making. For example, some are involved directly via iron triangles or issue networks[6] (Claussen and Hutchins), and others, while working within a highly charged political milieu, affect policy by, for example, interpretation of law (Marica, Black, and Perkins), developing and implementing programs (Gayle, Black, Marica, and Perkins), law enforcement (Marica and Black), and direct advice to the President (Perkins).

Because they are involved in policy making in different ways, they secure their power from different sources or policy players and as a corollary, they must employ or exercise their political skills in different ways. Their success ultimately hinges upon their knowledge of the policy and political workings of their domains. The best illustration of this point revolves around the different types of relationships that the execucrats developed with various policy players, particularly political appointees. For example, as we can see from Table 1, all six execucrats had good relationships with political appointees. In some fashion, they were brought into the execucrats' policy-making circles. However, cultivating good relation- ships was much more deliberate as well as extensive for some as compared to other execucrats. For instance, Ambassador Edward Perkins had an excellent working relationship with many political appointees in the State Department including the Secretary of State, George Shultz, and the Assistant Secretary of State, Chester Crocket. Support from such persons is critical, because in a policy area such as foreign affairs, where the policies are very sensitive to national security as well as global harmony, congenial, cooperative relationships between execucrats and political ap-

pointees are imperative (Warwick, 1975).

On the other hand, the more critical constituents or players in Eileen Claussen's and Dr. Vince Hutchins's policy-making environments were legislators, interest groups, other execucrats, and even the media. This being the case, they had relatively few ties to political appointees, and these ties were not necessarily essential to their successful performance. Dr. Hutchins, for example, had a good working relationship with a few key political appointees in the Reagan and Bush administrations. These were persons who happened to be very committed to promoting MCH care. However, the overall relationship between political appointees and career execucrats, including Hutchins, was very strained, particularly during the Bush administration. Notwithstanding, Hutchins was able to get his job done because, like Claussen, he bypassed or did end runs around the political folks who tried to prevent him from responding to the needs of mothers and children in our society.

In short, the manifestations of effective political skills differ from execucrat to execucrat because they are involved in policy making in different ways and, as such, they must interact with and rely on different policy players in order to effect change to their policy areas. Their success is ultimately contingent upon their knowledge of the policy and political workings of their domains. As we have seen, these six execucrats certainly possess such knowledge. They knew the right people to interact with, were skillful at working with them, and they knew what types of behaviors would or would not work to get the job done in their policy milieu.

Conclusions

There are several ingredients to effective execucratic performance. A number of factors emerged from this study and certainly additional research would help to inform us better about the complexities of execucratic behavior and what it takes to be successful. The execucrats do not fit a unique mold, nor is there "one best way" for effecting positive change to any policy area. In any case, this study was never intended to prescribe attributes of successful execucratic performance. Instead, it helps us to understand better the intricacies of execucratic life and the tools, skills, and strategies execucrats employ in their efforts to make our lives a little better.

Table 1 The Successful Performance of Six Federal Execucrats and the Goals They Accomplished

Execucrat, agency, and accomplishment	Political skills	Management and leadership skills	Situational factors
William Black Office of Thrift Supervision Helped break & clean up S&L mess	Good* relationship with key political appointee (Ed Gray); knowledgeable of Washington, D.C., establishment; good political instincts	Good communicator; goal oriented; good insight; sound decision maker; honest; strong sense of commitment to equity & fairness; pragmatic; good writing & analytical skills; good debater & recorder; risk taker; good interpersonal skills; good role model; good listener; good planner & coordinator	Political roadblocks set up by members of Congress (e.g., Rep. Wright) & political appointees (e.g., Danny Wall & Lee Henkel); muscled & harassed by S&L executives
Eileen Claussen Environmental Protection Agency (EPA) Negotiated & renegotiated Montreal Protocol	Effective player in "iron triangle" (i.e., good working skills & relationship with Congress, interest groups & other execucrats); good relationship with EPA heads (Lee Thomas & William Reilly) & other political appointees at EPA	Visionary; politically astute; good interpersonal skills; good negotiator & mediator; pragmatic; sound decision maker; focused; innovative; good listener; goal oriented; open-minded; participative management style; good motivator; inspires followership; good planner & coordinator; political risk taker; honest; expedient	Obstacles set up by Reagan (e.g., Rayban Plan) & Bush White Houses; chilly, hostile climate created by Reagan & Bush officials; challenges by powerful business communities (in U.S. & abroad)
Edward Perkins State Department Helped break down system of apartheid in South Africa	Good relationship with President Reagan & political appointees (George Shultz & Chester Crocker); good political instincts	Good diplomacy skills; good negotiator & mediator; sound decision maker; good listener & communicator; fair; open-minded; good planner & organizer; approachable; good interpersonal skills; credible; honest; good speaker; sound insight; focused; goal oriented; emphasis on professionalism	Heated tensions because of opposition to Reagan's constructive engagement policy; black South Africans very suspicious of this African-American Reagan-appointee; under close scrutiny by African Americans; attacks by white South Africans under President Botha
Stephen Marica Small Business Administration (SBA) Helped break Wedtech scandal	Good relationship with political appointees & career staff; good political insight	Sound decision maker; good negotiator & mediator; good communicator; sound analytical skills; strong sense of commitment to equity & fairness; high moral & ethical standards; creative; responsive & sensitive to employees' needs; dedicated to staff; good motivator; inspires loyalty; inspires followership; establishes climate of trust; creates opportunities for job satisfaction & career development; emphasis on professionalism; good planner & organizer; goal oriented	Low public image of SBA's Office of Inspector General (OIG); staff shortages
Vince Hutchins Bureau of Maternal & Child Health (HHS) Developed Healthy Mothers, Healthy Babies Coalition	Effective player in "iron triangle" (i.e., good working skills & relationship with Congress, interest groups, & other execucrats); good relationship with key political appointees; knows lay-of-the-land & people nationwide in maternal & child health (MCH) care; good political instincts	Visionary; politically astute; good interpersonal skills; sound decision maker; risk taker; innovative & creative; goal oriented; resourceful; good planner, coordinator, & organizer; good communicator; collaborative; commitment to equity & fairness; respectful of employees; good mentoring skills; inspires loyalty; inspires followership; high moral & ethical standards; sensitive & responsive to needs of clients; optimist	Cutbacks in MCH care funding; tensions with some Reagan & Bush officials; Reagan & Bush administrations' chilly attitude toward MCH care (e.g., as expressed in Bush's definition of "family")
Helene Gayle Centers for Disease Control & Prevention (HHS) Working to stop spread of AIDS	Knows her way around international AIDS scene; good working relationships with interest groups and political appointees	Good negotiator & mediator; good communicator; good interpersonal skills; good planner & organizer; collaborative; sensitive & responsive to needs of clients; sensitive to & respects cultural differences (can walk in others' shoes, i.e., is able to empathize); open-minded; politically savvy; good mentoring skills; goal-oriented; strong identification to her African heritage	Challenges posed by AIDS "hysteria" (grounded in perception that it is a gay disease); working with disease that currently has no cure; addressing behavioral change in different cultural settings

*The more neutral term "good" is used here instead of such terms as "excellent" and "outstanding."

Table 1 The Successful Performance of Six Federal Execucrats and the Goals They Accomplished (*cont.*)

Execucrat, agency, and accomplishment	Government experience	Technical expertise	Strategy	Personality
William Black Office of Thrift Supervision Helped break & clean up S&L mess	College internship with federal government; contract work as lawyer for federal government; relatively new to government employment at time of S&L scandal	Law, economics, & accounting	Regulating S&L industry; heavy reliance on law; directly confronting corrupt politicians & S&L executives; use of media; whistleblowing	Strong sense of ethics, morality & integrity; self-assured; gutsy; aggressive; intense; courageous; determined; strong sense of perseverance; good sense of humor; maverick
Eileen Claussen Environmental Protection Agency (EPA) Negotiated & renegotiated Montreal Protocol	Entire career in federal government; worked her way up federal government hierarchy	Environmental science	Use of media; coalition building with members of Congress & interest groups (business & public); inclusive of all interests; compromising when necessary; sought incremental change in CFC reduction	Assertive; trustworthy; honest; credible; vociferous; self-assured; determined & firm; dogged; open-minded; self-starter; maverick; good-humored; gutsy; gregarious & lively
Edward Perkins State Department Helped break down system of apartheid in South Africa	Entire career in federal government; worked his way up federal government hierarchy	Public administration, public policy & international relations	Keeping Americans informed; listening to *all* sides; reaching out & establishing dialogue with black South Africans, including banned groups; public support of black South Africans & their efforts to end apartheid (e.g., participation in demonstrations); firm with white government officials; vigorously enforcing economic sanctions in South Africa	Unflappable; self-starter; charismatic; dignified; poised; self-disciplined & self-controlled; determined & resolute; quiet; low-key; resilient; honest; trustworthy; methodical
Stephen Marica Small Business Administration (SBA) Helped break Wedtech scandal	Entire career in federal government; worked his way up federal government hierarchy	Law enforcement & criminal investigations	Improving credibility of SBA's OIG; complete overhaul of OIG; development of training programs for OIG employees; boosting employee morale; personnel "housecleaning"	High morale & ethical character; level headed; straight-forward & honest; strong-willed; firm; determined; self-assured; even tempered; people-oriented
Vince Hutchins Bureau of Maternal & Child Health (HHS) Developed Healthy Mothers, Healthy Babies Coalition	Second half of career in federal government; worked his way up federal government hierarchy; retired from federal service	General medicine, pediatrics, & public health	Develop public-private partnerships; coalition building; maintain open, on-going dialogue with persons & groups in MCH care	Charismatic; humble & unassuming; honest & trustworthy; high sense of integrity & morality; kind, gentle & compassionate; low-key; accommodating & understanding; people-oriented; determined; even-tempered; gutsy; good sense of humor; playfully mischievous
Helene Gayle Centers for Disease Control & Prevention (HHS) Working to stop spread of AIDS	Relatively new to federal government service; fast-tracking her way up federal government hierarchy	General medicine, pediatrics, & public health	Coalition building; fostering open dialogue with disparate groups & people	Charismatic; understanding & compassionate; open-minded; persistent, determined & firm; good sense of humor; infectious smile; honest & forthcoming; strong sense of cultural identity; people oriented; maverick

One can also gather from this study, particularly the larger version of it, that execucrats do make positive contributions to our society. Each execucrat in his or her own way accomplished some major feat which ultimately promoted the public good. Yet, they have received modest praise, if any, for their efforts. Indeed, their names are probably unfamiliar to most. It seems to be the case, as many have said, that execucrats are brought into the public's eye only when someone is to be blamed for something gone wrong (Goodsell, 1985). This study painted a different picture of government workers. It called attention to just a few of the "unsung heroes" who have made important contributions to our society in a host of policy domains.

• • •

Study Design

In selecting execucrats for this study, several criteria were relied upon. First, *federal* execucrats were chosen to participate because the policy focus at this level is broader and has wider applicability. In addition, there was an interest in locating execucrats who were presumed to be successful or have made an important contribution to society. Also, because the study has a current rather than historical focus, the accomplishment for which the execucrats are responsible had to have taken place in roughly the last ten years. Finally, it was also important to select execucrats from across agencies rather than from a single agency.

Given these criteria, a sample of execucrats was selected from several sources, including the list of recipients of the U.S. Presidential Rank Awards, which are made annually by the president to "exceptional" senior career executives. In addition, approximately 600 members of the Council for Excellence in Government (CEG), a nonprofit organization committed to promoting excellence in the federal service, were surveyed and asked to nominate noteworthy execucrats. Mark Abramson, former President of CEG and currently president of Leadership Inc., was instrumental in this endeavor. About 30 viable names emerged from this undertaking, and after interviewing each of them, six execucrats were selected for in-depth profiles.

The study is limited to only six execucrats because, in the book version of this study, *Unsung Heroes* (Georgetown University Press), there was a desire to provide as much detail as possible on the stories of each execucrat—what they accomplished and how—and the various factors that contributed to their success. The rich profiles provide a better, more comprehensive picture of what it takes to be a successful execucrat.

Through interviews with these and other execucrats, as well as senators, congresspersons, rank-and-file employees, interest group representatives and other relevant players, and use of any media coverage that may have accompanied the event, the accomplishments of execucrats in their respective fields are analyzed to ascertain the relative significance of the seven factors on their effectiveness. Inferences are then made about ingredients for effective execucratic performance.

Notes

This article is based on Riccucci's *Unsung Heroes: Federal Execucrats Making a Difference*, from Georgetown University Press.

1. A distinction is sometimes drawn between management and leadership, but for the purposes here, no such distinction is drawn. It should further be noted that effective leaders can exist anywhere in an organization's hierarchy.
2. CFCs have been used for a variety of purposes, including as a foaming agent for styrofoam products, e.g., fast food containers at McDonald's and Burger King. CFCs have also been used as the propellant for aerosol sprays. While the EPA was successful in banning virtually all aerosol uses of CFCs in the late 1970s, it has been less than successful in banning nonaerosol uses of CFCs.
3. For example, Perkins vigorously enforced the economic sanctions mandated by the U.S. Congress against South Africa and also made certain that American businesses operating there did not abuse the employment rights of black South Africans.
5. It is important to stress that the skills and attributes cannot be placed on an ordinal scale. That is to say, one skill is not necessarily more important than another, but rather it is the combination of skills and their interaction that contributes to execucratic success.

6. For a discussion of issue networks, see Levine, Peters, and Thompson (1990) and Heclo (1978).

References

Benedick, Richard, 1991. *Ozone Diplomacy: New Directions in Safeguarding the Planet.* Cambridge: Harvard University Press.

Cayer, N. Joseph, 1989. "Qualities of Successful Program Managers." In Robert E. Cleary and Nicholas Henry, eds., *Managing Public Programs.* San Francisco: Jossey-Bass, Inc., pp. 121–142.

Cooper, Terry L. and N. Dale Wright, eds., 1992. *Exemplary Public Administrators.* San Francisco: Jossey-Bass.

Curran, James, 1994. Personal interview with author (February 8).

Denhardt, Robert, 1993. *The Pursuit of Significance.* Belmont, CA: Wadsworth.

Doig, Jameson W. and Erwin C. Hargrove, eds., 1987. *Leadership and Innovation: A Biographical Perspective on Entrepreneurs in Government.* Baltimore, MD: Johns Hopkins University Press.

Faerman, Sue R., Robert E. Quinn, Michael P. Thompson, and Michael McGrath, 1990. *A Framework for Excellence.* Albany, NY: Governor's Office of Employee Relations.

Gerth, H.H. and C. Wright Mills, 1946. *From Max Weber: Essays in Sociology.* New York: Oxford University Press, p. 232.

Goodsell, Charles T., 1985. *The Case for Bureaucracy: A Public Administration Polemic,* 2nd ed., Chatham, NJ: Chatham House Publishers, Inc.

Gore, Al, 1993. Statement from Vice President Gore (May 28).

Gray, Ed, 1993. Personal interview with author. (March 3).

Greenstein, Fred I., 1975. *Personality and Politics.* New York: W.W. Norton and Company.

Hassan, Rashida, 1994. Personal interview with author. (February 23).

Heclo, Hugh, 1977. *A Government of Strangers.* Washington, DC: Brookings Institution.

———, 1978. "Issue Networks and the Executive Establishment." In Anthony King, ed., *The New American Political System.* Washington, DC: American Enterprise Institute, pp. 87–124.

Holzer, Marc, 1989. "Minnowbrook II: Conclusions." *Public Administration Review,* vol. 49 (March/April), pp. 221–222.

Hutchins, Vince, 1992. Personal interview with author (July 21).

Levine, Charles H., B. Guy Peters, and Frank J. Thompson, 1990. *Public Administration: Challenges, Choices and Consequences.* Glenview, IL: Scott, Foresman and Co.

Lewis, Eugene, 1980. *Public Entrepreneurship.* Bloomington, IN: Indiana University Press.

Lipsky, Michael, 1980. *Street-Level Bureaucracy: Dilemmas of the Individual in Public Services.* New York: Russell Sage Foundation.

Lynn, Laurence E. Jr., 1984. "The Reagan Administration and the Renitent Bureaucracy." In Lester M. Salamon and Michael S. Lund, eds., *The Reagan Presidency and the Governing of America.* Washington, DC: The Urban Institute Press, pp. 339–379.

———, 1987. *Managing Public Policy.* Boston: Little, Brown and Company.

Meier, Kenneth J., 1993. *Politics and the Bureaucracy,* 3rd ed. Pacific Grove, CA: Brooks/Cole.

Miller, C. Arden, 1992. "Policy for Maternal and Infant Health: Where We Stand." In Jonathan B. Kotch, Craig H. Blakely, Sarah S. Brown, and Frank Y. Wong, eds., *A Pound of Prevention. The Case for Universal Maternity Care in the U.S.* Washington, DC: American Public Health Association, pp. xi–xviii.

Nachmias, David and David H. Rosenbloom, 1980. *Bureaucratic Government, USA.* New York: St. Martin's Press.

New York Times, 1987. "Ambassador Perkins's Prayer." (April 15), p. A26.

Perry, James L., 1989. "The Effective Public Administrator." In James L. Perry, ed., *Handbook of Public Administration.* San Francisco: Jossey-Bass, Inc., pp. 619–627.

Peters, B. Guy, 1989. *The Politics of Bureaucracy,* 3rd ed., New York: Longman.

Pizzo, Stephen, Mary Fricker, and Paul Muolo, 1989. *Inside Job: The Looting of America's Savings and Loans.* New York: McGraw-Hill.

Roan, Sharon, 1989. *Ozone Crisis.* New York: John Wiley & Sons, Inc.

Rosenbloom, David H., 1989. *Public Administration: Understanding Management, Politics, and Law in the Public Sector,* 2nd ed., New York: Random House.

Rourke, Francis E., 1976. *Bureaucracy, Politics, and Public Policy,* 2nd ed., Boston: Little, Brown and Co.

Sardell, Alice, 1990. "Child Health Policy in the U.S." *Journal of Health Politics, Policy, and Law,* vol. 15 (Summer), pp. 271–304.

Schlesinger, Mark and Karl Kronebusch, 1990. "The Failure of Prenatal Care Policy for the Poor." *Health Affairs,* vol. 9 (Winter), pp. 91–111.

Shultz, George, P., 1993. Personal interview with author (November 24).

Shilts, Randy, 1988. *And the Band Played On.* New York: Penguin Books.

Starling, Grover, 1993. *Managing the Public Sector.* Belmont, CA: Wadsworth Publishing Co.

Stewart, Debra W. and G. David Garson, 1983. *Organization Behavior and Public Management.*

New York: Marcel Dekker.

Taylor, R.E., 1987. "Advice on Ozone May Be: 'Wear Hats and Stand in Shade.' " *Wall Street Journal* (May 29), p. 8.

U.S. Environmental Protection Agency, 1987. "An Assessment of the Risks of Stratospheric Modification." (January) Washington, DC.

Warwick, Donald P., 1975. *A Theory of Public Bureaucracy: Politics, Personality and Organization in the State Department.* Cambridge: Harvard University Press.

Yin, Robert D., 1984. *Case Study Research.* Beverly Hills, CA: Sage Publications.

Chapter 14 Review Questions

1. How does Heclo conceptualize the current relationship between politics and administration? What are the basic elements of his *issue network* idea and how does the idea differ from the *iron triangle* notion of political-administrative relations?

2. Heclo primarily applied the issue network notion to the federal level of government. Is it possible to apply it to state and local levels as well? Describe why or why not.

3. In what ways does the issue network concept pose serious dilemmas for democratic government in general and public administration in particular? Does the case offer "answers" to this issue?

4. What implications does the issue network theory hold for the practical functions and training of public administrators? Does it essentially alter the types of jobs, tasks, and roles they perform? Think about what the case study tells us about preparing students for these kinds of jobs.

5. Did you find this issue network concept evident in the six "success stories" in the foregoing case study? If so, in what ways? If not, how would you conceptualize the political-administrative relationships as reflected in these six profiles?

6. On the basis of your analysis of the foregoing reading and case study, what general recommendations would you make to improve the relationships between administration and politics in America? Be sure to think carefully about the *value implications* of any new reform measures you may advocate.

Key Terms

politics-administration dichotomy
issue networks

iron triangles
policy makers

proliferation of interests	issue specialization
think tanks	issue watchers
technopols	single-issue organizations
trade and professional associations	presidential appointees
public policy processes	professional-bureaucratic complex

Suggestions for Further Reading

You would do well to compare and contrast Heclo's ideas with those of earlier theorists who argued for a clearer, more distinct separation of politics and administration (what is termed the political-administrative dichotomy), especially Woodrow Wilson, "The Study of Administration," *Political Science Quarterly,* 2 (June 1887), pp. 197–222; Frank J. Goodnow, *Politics and Administration* (New York: Macmillan, 1900); or the later writers who discovered the interest groups involved with administrative processes and gave roots to the iron triangle concept, particularly Paul H. Appleby, *Policy and Administration* (University, Ala.: University of Alabama Press, 1949); E. Pendelton Herring, *Public Administration and the Public Interest* (New York: Russell and Russell, 1936); and David B. Truman, *The Governmental Process* (New York: Alfred A. Knopf, 1951).

Of course, because of the sheer size, complexity, and power of American government, more complicated political-administrative relationships have arisen in the last three decades, described by several astute observers, including Hugh Heclo, *A Government of Strangers: Executive Politics in Washington* (Washington, D.C.: The Brookings Institution, 1977); Don K. Price, *The Scientific Estate* (Cambridge, Mass.: Harvard University Press, 1965); Frederick C. Mosher, *Democracy and the Public Service,* Second Edition (New York: Oxford University Press, 1982); Christopher H. Foreman, Jr., *Signals from the Hill* (New Haven, Conn.: Yale University Press, 1988); Emmette S. Redford, *Democracy in the Administrative State* (New York: Oxford University Press, 1969); Francis E. Rourke, *Bureaucracy, Politics and Public Policy,* Third Edition (Boston: Little, Brown, 1984); Harold Seidman and Robert Gilmour, *Politics, Po-*

sition and Power, Fourth Edition (New York: Oxford University Press, 1986); Lawrence C. Dodd and Richard L. Schott, *Congress and the Administrative State* (New York: John Wiley & Sons, 1979); Louis Fisher, *The Politics of Shared Power: Congress and the Executive* (Washington, D.C.: Congressional Quarterly Press, 1981); and Herbert Kaufman, *The Administrative Behavior of Federal Bureau Chiefs* (Washington, D.C.: The Brookings Institution, 1981).

The *National Journal, Governing,* and *Congressional Quarterly* serve to provide timely insiders' views of this topic. You should give particular attention to the writers who discuss the changes in the 1990s that have decisively altered political-administrative relationships: see David M. Ricci, *The Transformation of American Politics* (New Haven, Conn.: Yale University Press, 1993); Donald F. Kettl, *Sharing Power* (Washington, D.C.: The Brookings Institution, 1993); James Q. Wilson, *Bureaucracy* (New York: Basic Books, 1989); Paul C. Light, *Thickening Government* (Washington, D.C.: The Brookings Institution, 1995); and James H. Svárá, *Official Leadership in the City* (New York: Oxford University Press, 1990).

Several excellent book-length case examinations of various policy fields provide further insights into this subject. See Robert J. Art, *The TFX Decision* (Boston: Little, Brown, 1968); Stephen Bailey and Edith K. Mosher, *ESEA: The Office of Education Administers a Law* (Syracuse, N.Y.: Syracuse University Press, 1968); A. Lee Fritschler, *Smoking and Politics* (Englewood Cliffs, N.J.: Prentice-Hall, 1975); Richard J. Stillman II, *The Integration of the Negro in the U.S. Armed Forces* (New York: Praeger Publishers,

1968); Daniel P. Moynihan, *The Politics of the Guaranteed Income* (New York: Random House, 1973); Milton D. Morris, *Immigration: The Beleaguered Bureaucracy* (Washington, D.C.: The Brookings Institution, 1985); Charles L. Schultze, *The Politics and Economics of Public Spending* (Washington, D.C.: The Brookings Institution, 1968); I. M. Destler, *U.S. Foreign Economic Policy-Making* (Washington, D.C.: The Brookings Institution, 1978); Martha Derthick, *Policy-Making for Social Security* (Washington, D.C.: The Brookings Institution, 1978); Barbara J. Nelson, *Making an Issue of Child Abuse* (Chicago: University of Chicago Press, 1984); Paul Light, *Artful Work: The Politics of Social Security Reform* (New York: Random House, 1985); Frederick C. Mosher, *A Tale of Two Agencies* (Baton Rouge, La.: Louisiana State University Press, 1984); and Gerald Garvey, *Facing the Bureaucracy* (San Francisco: Jossey-Bass, 1993). For a good collection of essays, many dealing with various aspects of this topic, read Francis E. Rourke, *Bureaucratic Power in National Policy Making,* Fourth Edition (Boston: Little, Brown, 1986). See also several of the essays contained in the bicentennial issue of the *Public Administration Review* (January/February 1987), edited by Richard J. Stillman, II; particularly, Chester A. Newland, "Public Executives: Imperium, Sacerdotium, Collegium? Bicentennial Leadership Challenges"; James P. Pfiffner, "Political Appointees and Career Executives: The Democracy-Bureaucracy Nexus in the Third Century"; and James D. Carroll, "Public Administration in the Third Century of the Constitution: Supply-Side Management Privatization or Public Investment." See also John Nalbandian, "Reflections of a 'Pracademic' on the Logic of Politics and Administration," *Public Administration Review,* 54 (November/December 1994), pp. 531–536; as well as several broad philosophical essays such as Dwight Waldo, "A Theory of Public Administration Means in Our Time a Theory of Politics Also"; James W. Fesler, "The State and Its Study: The Whole and the Parts"; Herbert Kaufman, "The End of an Alliance"; and Charles T. Goodsell, "Emerging Issues in Public Administration," all contained in Naomi B. Lynn and Aaron Wildavsky, eds., *Public Administration: The State of the Discipline* (Chatham, N.J.: Chatham House, 1990). For a good survey of academic models of legislative/administrative relationships, read Jeff Gill, "Formal Models of Legislative/Administrative Interaction," *Public Administration Review,* 55 (January/February 1995), pp. 99–106.

CHAPTER 15

The Relationship Between Bureaucracy and the Public Interest: The Concept of Public Sector Deregulation

To do better, we have to deregulate the government. If deregulation of a market makes sense because it liberates the entrepreneurial energies of its members, then it is possible that deregulating the public sector may also help energize it.

James Q. Wilson

READING 15

Introduction

Since the advent of public administration as an identifiable field, considerable scholarly debate has ensued over the question of public interest. Is there such a thing? How can it serve to guide the work of practicing public administrators? From where does the concept of public interest derive? How can it be applied as a meaningful concept in public agencies to influence the direction of administrative decisions?

Thoughtful administrative theorists have wrestled with these questions throughout the twentieth century but have arrived at very different "answers." Much of the dialogue on this subject turns ultimately on what "image" or "identity" theorists support for the field or how they define its substance and boundaries as an academic and applied field of practice. Three major perspectives have been put forward by scholars.

First, there are those administrative scientists who identify public administration essentially as a "tool" or "technique" in order to produce this or that most "efficient," "economical," or "effective" result. These writers tend to be highly positivist and rational in their thinking about the field. They view the emergence of "the public interest" from the application of the "right value-free tool of analysis" that will automatically achieve "correct results" for the general welfare. Writings by Frederick Taylor, the father of scientific management, or Herbert Simon, one of the founders of the behavioral movement within contemporary administrative sciences, advance such points of view. Listen to Herbert Simon's perspective on this topic:

The theory of administration is concerned with how an organization should be constructed and operated in order to accomplish its work efficiently. A fundamental principle of administration, which follows almost immediately from the rational character of 'good' administration, is that among several alternatives involving the same expenditure, the one should always be selected which leads to the greatest accomplishment of administrative objectives; and among several alternatives that lead to the same accomplishment the one should be selected which involves the least expenditure.[1]

By contrast to this "rational machine model," whereby administrators become like "cogs" or "robots," the field of public administration is seen by other writers as central to the governance of America's constitutional democracy. They give public administrators key, creative leadership role(s) in promoting "the public interest." There is a long tradition of reformist literature in the field, dating from Woodrow Wilson's classic 1887 essay (refer to Chapter 1), which advance this viewpoint, namely that public administration is essential in order "to run the constitution." By placing public administration at the center of constitutional governance, administrative discretion and influence are enhanced, and "the public interest" consequently becomes equated with trained, enlightened public administration that advances broad community interests through the wise application of expertise and problem-solving skills. Influential authors such as Paul Appleby, Norton Long, Emmette Redford, and Merle Fainsod have advocated this perspective, but perhaps Carl Friedrich most forcefully articulated it:

> A modern administrator is in many cases dealing with problems so novel and complex that they call for the highest creative ability. This need for creative solutions effectively focuses attention upon the need for action. The pious formulas about the will of the people are all very well, but when it comes to these issues of social maladjustment the popular will has little content. . . .
> . . . throughout the length and breadth of our technical civilization there is arising a type of responsibility on the part of the permanent administrator, the man who is called upon to seek and find the creative solutions for our crying technical needs, which cannot be effectively enforced except by fellow-technicians who are capable of judging his policy in terms of the scientific knowledge bearing upon it.[2]

If Friedrich's view sees "good government" derived from the professionalism, expertise, training, ethical standards as well as the creativity of the public service, a third set of influential writers such as Arthur Bentley, David Truman, and Robert Dahl view the "public interest" as mainly the product of the pulling and hauling of various group interests in society. For these political scientists, there is no such "absolute" as "the public interest," but rather "it" is merely a "process" or the resultant of the contest among special interests as codified in law, rules, and informal agreements. Public administrators thus become much less important figures in shaping "the public interest." Among group theorists' writings, public administrators are viewed as "people-in-the-middle" for resolving competing interests or as catalysts through which varied interests are transmuted and represented. David Truman describes the administrator's mediatory role as follows:

The administrator is called upon to resolve the difficulties that were too thorny for the legislature to solve, and he must do so in face of the very forces that were acting in the legislature, though their relative strength may have changed. Note that it is not the ambiguities in the law that make difficult the question of what groups shall have privileged access to an administrator. Almost all legislative declarations are ambiguous in part. It is rather the causes of the ambiguity that make the difference. If the administrator holds out for an interpretation of these controverted ambiguous provisions that is not in itself a compromise, he invites the affected groups either to denounce his 'dictatorial' methods and his 'unscrupulous assumption of powers not granted to him' or to expose his 'sell-out' of the 'public interest.'[3]

In the following selection from his recent book, *Bureaucracy,* James Q. Wilson, the James Collins Professor of Management at the University of California, Los Angeles, and 1990 recipient of the James Madison Award of the American Political Science Association, examines this subject in light of the operations of public agencies in the late 20th century. His book drew upon a wide range of contemporary studies of the U.S. Army, FBI, DEA, CIA, Social Security, and other public entities and tried to provide a comprehensive analysis, as the book's subtitle suggests, of "what government agencies do and why they do it." In his last chapter, Wilson offers his appraisal of how public agencies can be made more responsible and responsive to "the public interest." While he does not define what the "public interest" is, Wilson begins by making the assumption that "the daily incentives operating in the political work encourage a very different course of action" by bureaucrats which often is contradictory to achievement of their own "public purposes." In other words, the incentive structures within which bureaucrats must operate often confounds or prevents attainment of "the public interest." Wilson outlines why this happens and what, in his view, can be done about it. His reforms are modest, but they are argued compellingly.

As you read Wilson's essay, you should think about:

What assumptions does he make about the nature of public administration which in turn shape his understanding about "what is the public interest"?

How do you evaluate his proposed reforms? Their pluses? Negatives?

In what ways does Wilson's thinking compare and contrast with the three historic perspectives on the public interest and public administration which were outlined in this introduction? Does Wilson offer us a fourth alternative model? Since most of Wilson's argument is derived from federal examples, does this apply to state/local levels?

Notes

1. Herbert A. Simon, *Administrative Behavior: A Study of Decision-Making Processes in Administrative Organization* (New York: Free Press, 1947), p. 38.
2. Carl J. Friedrich, "Public Policy and the Nature of Administrative Responsibility," in Friedrich and Mason, eds., *Public Policy* (Cambridge: Harvard University Press, 1940), p. 12.
3. David B. Truman, *The Governmental Process* (New York: Alfred A. Knopf, 1951), p. 443.

Bureaucracy and the Public Interest

JAMES Q. WILSON

The German army beat the French army in 1940; the Texas prisons for many years did a better job than did the Michigan prisons; Carver High School in Atlanta became a better school under Norris Hogans. These successes were the result of skilled executives who correctly identified the critical tasks of their organizations, distributed authority in a way appropriate to those tasks, infused their subordinates with a sense of mission, and acquired sufficient autonomy to permit them to get on with the job. The critical tasks were different in each case, and so the organizations differed in culture and patterns of authority, but all three were alike in one sense: incentives, culture, and authority were combined in a way that suited the task at hand. . . . [But,] the daily incentives operating in the political world encourage a very different course of action.

Armies

Though the leadership and initiative of field officers and noncoms is of critical importance, the Pentagon is filled with generals who want to control combat from headquarters or from helicopters, using radios to gather information and computers to process it. Though the skill of the infantryman almost always has been a key to military success, the U.S. Army traditionally has put its best people in specialized units (intelligence, engineering, communications), leaving the leftovers for the infantry.[1] Though it has fought wars since 1945 everywhere except in Europe, the army continues to devote most of its planning to big-tank battles on the West German plains.

Prisons

. . . many observers gave the most favorable attention to prison executives who seemed to voice the best intentions (rehabilitation, prisoner self-governance) rather than the best accomplishments (safe, decent facilities).

Schools

Especially in big cities, many administrators keep principals weak and teachers busy filling out reports, all with an eye toward minimizing complaints from parents, auditors, interest groups, and the press. Teachers individually grumble that they are treated as robots instead of professionals, but collectively they usually oppose any steps—vouchers, merit pay, open enrollment, strengthened principals—that in fact have given teachers a larger role in designing curricula and managing their classrooms. . . . politically, extra resources . . . go to all schools "equally" rather than disproportionately to those schools that were improving the most.

These generals, wardens, administrators, and teachers have not been behaving irrationally; rather, they have been responding to the incentives and constraints that they encounter on a daily basis. Those incentives include the need to manage situations over which they have little control on the basis of a poorly defined or nonexistent sense of mission and in the face of a complex array of constraints that seems always to grow, never to shrink. Outside groups—elected officials, interest groups, professional associations, the media—demand a voice in the running of these agencies and make that demand effective by imposing rules on the agencies and demanding that all these rules be enforced all of the time.

Moreover, habitual patterns of action—the lessons of the past, the memories of earlier struggles, the expectations of one's co-workers—narrow the area within which new courses of action are sought.

Bureaucrats often complain of "legislative micromanagement," and indeed it exists. . . . with respect to the armed forces, there has been a dramatic increase in the number of hearings, reports, investigations, statutory amendments, and budgetary adjustments with which the Pentagon must deal.[2] But there also has been a sharp increase in presidential micromanagement. Herbert Kaufman notes that for a half century or more the White House has feared agency independence more than agency paralysis, and so it has multiplied the number of presidential staffers, central management offices, and requirements for higher-level reviews. Once you start along the path of congressional or White House control, the process acquires a momentum of its own. "As more constraints are imposed, rigidities fixing agencies in their established ways intensify. As a result, complaints that they do not respond to controls also intensify. Further controls, checkpoints, and clearances are therefore introduced."[3] Much the same story can be told with respect to the growing involvement of the courts in agency affairs.

With some conspicuous exceptions the result of this process has been to deflect the attention of agency executives away from how the tasks of their agencies get defined and toward the constraints that must be observed no matter what the tasks may be. Who then decides what tasks shall be performed? In a production agency with observable outputs and routinized work processes, the answer is relatively simple: The laws and regulations that created the agency also define its job. But in procedural, coping, and craft agencies, the answer seems to be nobody in particular and everybody in general. The operating-level workers define the tasks, occasionally by design, as in those cases where operator ideology makes a difference, but more commonly by accident, as in those instances where prior experiences, professional norms, situational and technological imperatives, and peer-group expectations shape the nature of the work.

From time to time a gifted executive appears at a politically propitious time and makes things happen differently. He or she creates a new institution that acquires a distinctive competence, a strong sense of mission, and an ability to achieve socially valued goals. The Army Corps of Engineers, the Social Security Administration, the Marine Corps, the Forest Service, the FBI: For many years after they were created, and in many instances still today, these agencies, along with a few others that could be mentioned, were a kind of elite service that stood as a living refutation of the proposition that "all bureaucrats are dim-witted paper-shufflers." And these are only the federal examples; at the local level one can find many school systems and police departments that have acquired a praiseworthy organizational character.

But one must ask whether today one could create from scratch the Marine Corps, or the FBI, or the Forest Service; possibly, but probably not. Who would dare suggest that a new agency come into being with its own personnel system (and thus with fewer opportunities for civil servants to get tenure), with a single dominant mission (and thus with little organizational deference to the myriad other goals outsiders would want it to serve), and with an arduous training regime designed to instill *esprit de corps* (and thus with less regard for those niceties and conveniences that sedentary people believe to be important)? Or how optimistic should we be that today we could organize a Social Security Administration in a way that would bring to Washington men and women of exceptional talent? Might not many of those people decide today that they do not want to risk running afoul of the conflict-of-interest laws, that they have no stomach for close media and congressional scrutiny, and that they would not accept the federal pay levels pegged to the salaries of members of Congress fearful of raising their own compensation?

It would be a folly of historical romanticism to

imagine that great agencies were created in a golden age that is destined never to return, but it would be shortsighted to deny that we have paid a price for having emphasized rules and constraints to the neglect of tasks and mission. At the end of her careful review of the problems the SSA has had in managing disability insurance and supplemental security income, Martha Derthick makes the same point this way: "If the agencies repeatedly fall short, one ought at least to consider the possibility that there is a systematic mismatch between what they are instructed to do and their capacity to do it."[4] In recent years, when Congress has been creating new programs and modifying old ones at a dizzying rate, often on the basis of perfunctory hearings (or, as with the Senate's consideration of the 1988 drug bill, no hearings at all), a government agency capable of responding adequately to these endless changes would have to be versatile and adaptable, "capable of devising new routines or altering old ones very quickly." These qualities, she concludes, "are rarely found in large formal organizations."[5] I would only add that government agencies are far less flexible than formal organizations generally.

Things are not made much better by our national tendency to engage in bureaucrat-bashing. One has to have some perspective on this. It is true that bureaucracies prefer the present to the future, the known to the unknown, and the dominant mission to rival missions; many agencies in fact are skeptical of things that were "NIH"—Not Invented Here. Every social grouping, whether a neighborhood, a nation, or an organization, acquires a culture; changing that culture is like moving a cemetery: it is always difficult and some believe it is sacrilegious. It is also true, as many conservatives argue, that the government tries to do things that it is incapable of doing well, just as it is true, as many liberals allege, that the government in fact does many things well enough. As Charles Wolf has argued, both markets and governments have their imperfections; many things we might want to do collectively require us to choose between unsatisfactory alternatives.[6]

A Few Modest Suggestions That May Make a Small Difference

To do better we have to deregulate the government.* If deregulation of a market makes sense because it liberates the entrepreneurial energies of its members, then it is possible that deregulating the public sector also may help energize it. The difference, of course, is that both the price system and the profit motive provide a discipline in markets that is absent in non-markets. Whether any useful substitutes for this discipline can be found for public-sector workers is not clear, though I will offer some suggestions. But even if we cannot expect the same results from deregulation in the two sectors we can agree at a minimum that detailed regulation, even of public employees, rarely is compatible with energy, pride in workmanship, and the exercise of initiative. The best evidence for this proposition, if any is needed, is that most people do not like working in an environment in which every action is second-guessed, every initiative viewed with suspicion, and every controversial decision denounced as malfeasance.

James Colvard, for many years a senior civilian manager in the navy, suggests that the government needs to emulate methods that work in the better parts of the private sector: "a bias toward action, small staffs, and a high level of delegation which is based on trust."[7] A panel of the National Academy of Public Administration (NAPA), consisting of sixteen senior government executives holding the rank of assistant secretary, issued a report making the same point:

> Over many years, government has become entwined in elaborate management control systems and the accretion of progressively more

---

*I first saw this phrase in an essay by Constance Horner, then director of the federal Office of Personnel Management: "Beyond Mr. Gradgrind: The Case for Deregulating the Public Sector," *Policy Review* 44 (Spring 1988): 34–38. It also appears in Gary C. Bryner, *Bureaucratic Discretion* (New York: Pergamon Press, 1987), 215.

detailed administrative procedures. This development has not produced superior management. Instead, it has produced managerial overburden. . . . Procedures overwhelm substance. Organizations become discredited, along with their employees. . . . The critical elements of leadership in management appear to wither in the face of a preoccupation with process. The tools are endlessly "perfected"; the manager who is expected to use these tools believes himself to be ignored. . . . Management systems are not management. . . . The attitude of those who design and administer the rules . . . must be reoriented from a "control mentality" to one of "how can I help get the mission of this agency accomplished."[8]

But how can government "delegate" and "trust" and still maintain accountability? If it is a mistake to foster an ethos that encourages every bureaucrat to "go by the book," is it not an equally serious problem to allow zealots to engage in "mission madness," charging off to implement their private versions of some ambiguous public goal? (Steven Emerson has written a useful account of mission madness in some highly secret military intelligence and covert-action agencies.[9]) Given everything we know about the bureaucratic desire for autonomy and the political rewards of rule making, is there any reason to suppose that anybody will find it in his or her interest to abandon the "control mentality" and adopt the "mission accomplishment" mentality?

Possibly not. But it may be worth thinking about what a modestly deregulated government might look like. It might look as it once did, when some of the better federal agencies were created. At the time the Corps of Engineers, the Forest Service, and the FBI were founded much of the federal government was awash in political patronage, petty cabals, and episodic corruption. Organizing an elite service in those days may have been easier than doing so today, when the problems are less patronage and corruption than they are officiousness and complexity. But the keys to organizational success have not changed. The agencies were started

by strong leaders who were able to command personal loyalty, define and instill a clear and powerful sense of mission, attract talented workers who believed they were joining something special, and make exacting demands on subordinates.

Today there is not much chance to create a new agency; almost every agency one can imagine already has been created. Even so, the lessons one learns from changing agencies confirm what can be inferred from studying their founding.

First: Executives should understand the culture of their organizations—that is, what their subordinates believe constitute the core tasks of the agency—and the strengths and limitations of that culture. If members widely share and warmly endorse that culture the agency has a sense of mission. This permits the executive to economize on scarce incentives (people want to do certain tasks even when there are no special rewards for doing it); to state general objectives confident that subordinates will understand the appropriate ways of achieving them; and to delegate responsibility knowing that lower-level decisions probably will conform to higher-level expectations.

A good executive realizes that workers can make subtle, precise, and realistic judgments, but only if those judgments refer to a related, coherent set of behaviors. People cannot easily keep in mind many quite different things or strike reasonable balances among competing tasks. People want to know what is expected of them; they do not want to be told, in answer to this question, that "on the one hand this, but on the other hand that."

In defining a core mission and sorting out tasks that either fit or do not fit with this mission, executives must be aware of their many rivals for the right to define it. Operators with professional backgrounds will bring to the agency their skills but also their biases: Lawyers, economists, and engineers see the world in very different ways. You cannot hire them as if they were tools that in your skilled hands will perform exactly the task you set for them. Black and Decker may make tools like that, but Harvard and MIT do not. Worker peer groups also set expectations to which operators conform, especially when the operators work in a threatening, unpredictable, or confrontational environment. You may design the ideal patrol officer or school-teacher, but unless you understand the demands made by the street and the classroom, your design will remain an artistic expression destined for the walls of some organizational museum.

These advantages of infusing an agency with a sense of mission are purchased at a price. An agency with a strong mission will give perfunctory attention, if any at all, to tasks that are not central to that mission. Diplomats in the State Department will have little interest in embassy security; intelligence officers in the CIA will not worry as much as they should about counterintelligence; narcotics agents in the DEA will minimize the importance of improper prescriptions written by physicians; power engineers in the TVA will not think as hard about environmental protection or conservation as about maximizing the efficiency of generating units; fighter pilots in the USAF will look at air transport as a homely stepchild; and navy admirals who earned their flag serving on aircraft carriers will not press zealously to expand the role of minesweepers.

If the organization must perform a diverse set of tasks, those tasks that are not part of the core mission will need special protection. This requires giving autonomy to the subordinate tasks subunit (for example, by providing for them a special organizational niche) and creating a career track so that talented people performing non-mission tasks can rise to high rank in the agency. No single organization, however, can perform well a wide variety of tasks; inevitably some will be neglected. In this case, the wise executive will arrange to devolve the slighted tasks onto another agency, or to a wholly new organization created for the purpose. Running multitask conglomerates is as risky in the public as in the private sector. There are limits to the number of different jobs managers can manage. Moreover, conglomerate agencies rarely can develop a sense of mission; the cost of trying to do everything is that few things are done well. The turf-conscious executive who stoutly refuses to surrender any tasks, no matter how neglected, to another agency is courting disaster; in time the

failure of his or her agency to perform some orphan task will lead to a political or organizational crisis. Long ago the State Department should have got out of the business of building embassies. Diplomats are good at many things, but supervising carpenters and plumbers is not one of them. Let agencies whose mission is construction—the Army Corps of Engineers or the navy's Seabees—build buildings.

Second: Negotiate with one's political superiors to get some agreement as to which are the *essential* constraints that must be observed by your agency and which the marginal constraints. This, frankly, may be impossible. The decentralization of authority in Congress (and in some state legislatures) and the unreliability of most expressions of presidential or gubernatorial backing are such that in most cases you will discover, by experience if not by precept, that all constraints are essential all of the time. But perhaps with effort some maneuvering room may be won. A few agencies obtained the right to use more flexible, less cumbersome personnel systems modeled on the China Lake experiment, and Congress has the power to broaden those opportunities. Perhaps some enlightened member of Congress will be able to get statutory authority for the equivalent of China Lake with respect to procurement regulations. An executive is well advised to spend time showing that member how to do it.

Third: Match the distribution of authority and the control over resources to the tasks your organization is performing. In general, authority should be placed at the lowest level at which all essential elements of information are available. Bureaucracies will differ greatly in what level that may be. At one extreme are agencies such as the Internal Revenue Service or maximum-security prisons, in which uniformity of treatment and precision of control are so important as to make it necessary for there to be exacting, centrally determined rules for most tasks. At the other extreme are public schools, police departments, and armies, organizations in which operational uncertainties are so great that discretion must be given to (or if not given will be taken by) lower-level workers.

A good place in which to think through these

matters is the area of weapons procurement. The overcentralization of design control is one of the many criticisms of such procurement on which all commentators seem agreed. Buying a new aircraft may be likened to remodeling one's home: You never know how much it will cost until you are done; you quickly find out that changing your mind midway through the work costs a lot of money; and you soon realize that decisions have to be made by people on the spot who can look at the pipes, wires, and joists. The Pentagon procures aircraft as if none of its members had ever built or remodeled a house. It does so because both it and its legislative superiors refuse to allow authority to flow down to the point where decisions rationally can be made.

The same analysis can be applied to public schools. As John Chubb and Terry Moe have shown, public and private schools differ in the locus of effective control.[10] At least in big cities, decisions in private schools that are made by headmasters or in Catholic schools that are made by small archdiocesan staffs are made in public schools by massive, cumbersome headquarters bureaucracies. Of course, there are perfectly understandable political reasons for this difference, but not very many good reasons for it. Many sympathetic critics of the public schools believe that the single most useful organizational change that could be made would be to have educational management decisions—on personnel, scheduling, and instructional matters—made at the school level.[11]

Fourth: Judge organizations by results. This [essay] has made it clear that what constitutes a valued result in government usually is a matter of dispute. But even when fairly clear performance standards exist, legislatures and executives often ignore them with unhappy results. William E. Turcotte compared how two state governments oversaw their state liquor monopolies. The state that applied clear standards to its liquor bureaucrats produced significantly more profit and lower administrative costs than did the state with unclear or conflicting standards.[12]

Even when results are hard to assess more can be done than is often the case. If someone set out to evaluate the output of a private school, hospital, or security service, he or she would have at least as much trouble as would someone trying to measure the output of a public school, hospital, or police department. Governments are not the only institutions with ambiguous products.

There are two ways to cope with the problem in government. One is to supply the service or product in a marketlike environment. Shift the burden of evaluation off the shoulders of professional evaluators and onto the shoulders of clients and customers, and let the latter vote with their feet. The "client" in these cases can be individual citizens or government agencies; what is important is that the client be able to choose from among rival suppliers.

But some public services cannot be supplied, or are never going to be supplied, by a market. We can imagine allowing parents to choose among schools, but we cannot imagine letting them choose (at least for most purposes) among police departments or armies. In that case one should adopt the second way of evaluating a public service: carry out a demonstration project or conduct a field experiment. (I will use the two ideas interchangeably, though some scholars distinguish between them.[13]) An experiment is a planned alteration in a state of affairs designed to measure the effect of the intervention. It involves asking the question, "if I change X, what will happen to Y, having first made certain that everything else stays the same?" It sounds easy, but it is not.

A good experiment (bad ones are worse than no experiment at all) requires that one do the following: First, identify a course of action to be tested; call it the treatment. A "treatment" can be a police tactic, a school curriculum, or a welfare program. Second, decide what impact the treatment is intended to have; call this the outcome. The outcome can be a crime rate, an achievement score, a work effort, a housing condition, or an income level. Third, give the treatment to one group (the experimental group) and withhold it from another (the control group). A group might be a police precinct, a class of students, the tenants in a housing project, or people who meet some eligibility requirement (say, having low incomes). It is quite important how the membership in these groups is determined. It should be done randomly; that is, all eligible precincts, schools, tenants, or people should be randomly sorted into experimental and control groups. Random assignment means that all the characteristics of the members of the experimental and control groups are likely to be identical. Fourth, assess the condition of each group before and after the treatment. The first assessment describes the baseline condition, the second the outcome condition. This outcome assessment should continue for some time after the end of the treatment, because experience has shown that many treatments seem to have a short-term effect that quickly disappears. Fifth, make certain that the evaluation is done by people other than those providing the treatment. People like to believe that their efforts are worthwhile, so much so that perhaps unwittingly they will gather data in ways that make it look like the treatment worked even when it did not.*

The object of all this is to find out what works. Using this method we have discovered that tripling the number of patrol cars on a beat does not lower the crime rate; that foot patrol reduces the fear of crime but not (ordinarily) its incidence; and that arresting spouse-beaters reduces (for a while) future assaults more than does counseling the assaulters.[14] We have learned that giving people an income supplement (akin to the negative income tax) reduces work effort and in some cases encourages families to break up.[15] We have learned that giving special job training and support to welfare mothers, ex-offenders, and school drop-outs produces sizable gains in the employment records of the welfare recipients but no gain for the ex-offenders and school

drop-outs.[16] We have learned that a housing allowance program increases the welfare of poor families even though it does not improve the stock of housing.[17] We have learned that more flexible pay and classification systems greatly benefit the managers of navy research centers and improve the work atmosphere at the centers.[18]

There also have been many failed or flawed management experiments. In the 1930s, Herbert Simon carried out what may have been the first serious such experiment when he tried to find out how to improve the performance of welfare workers in the California State Relief Administration. Though elegantly designed, the experimental changes proved so controversial and the political environment of the agency so unstable that it is not clear that any useful inferences can be drawn from the project.[19] The attempt to evaluate educational vouchers at Alum Rock was undercut by the political need to restrict participation by private schools. There are countless other "studies" that are evaluations in name only; in reality they are self-congratulatory conclusions written by program administrators. The administrative world is a political world, not a scientific laboratory, and evaluators of administration must come to terms with that fact. Often there are no mutually acceptable terms. But where reasonable terms can be struck, it is possible to learn more than untutored experience can tell us about what works.

Such dry and dusty research projects probably seem thin fare to people who want Big Answers to Big Questions such as "How can we curb rampant bureaucracy?" or "How can we unleash the creative talents of our dedicated public servants?" But public management is not an arena in which to find Big Answers; it is a world of settled institutions designed to allow imperfect people to use flawed procedures to cope with insoluble problems.

The fifth and final bit of advice flows directly from the limits on judging agencies by their results. All organizations seek the stability and comfort that comes from relying on standard operating procedures—"SOPs." When results are unknown or equivocal, bureaus will have no incentive to alter

---

*Matters are, of course, a bit more complicated than this summary might suggest. There is a small library of books on evaluative research that go into these matters in more detail; a good place to begin is Richard P. Nathan, *Social Science in Government* (New York: Basic Books, 1988). On the political aspects of evaluation, see Henry J. Aaron, *Politics and the Professors* (Washington, D.C.: The Brookings Institution, 1978). On the technical side see Thomas D. Cook and Donald T. Campbell, *Quasi-Experimentation* (Chicago: Rand McNally, 1979). There is even a journal, *Evaluation Review*, specializing in these issues.

those SOPs so as better to achieve their goals, only an incentive to modify them to conform to externally imposed constraints. The SOPs will represent an internally defined equilibrium that reconciles the situational imperatives, professional norms, bureaucratic ideologies, peer-group expectations, and (if present) leadership demands unique to that agency. The only way to minimize the adverse effect of allowing human affairs to be managed by organizations driven by their autonomous SOPs is to keep the number, size, and authority of such organizations as small as possible. If none of the four preceding bits of advice work, the reader must confront the realization that there are no solutions for the bureaucracy problem that are not also "solutions" to the government problem. More precisely: All complex organizations display bureaucratic problems of confusion, red tape, and the avoidance of responsibility. Those problems are much greater in government bureaucracies because government itself is the institutionalization of confusion (arising out of the need to moderate competing demands); of red tape (arising out of the need to satisfy demands that cannot be moderated); and of avoided responsibility (arising out of the desire to retain power by minimizing criticism).

In short, you can have less bureaucracy only if you have less government. Many, if not most, of the difficulties we experience in dealing with government agencies arise from the agencies being part of a fragmented and open political system. If an agency is to have a sense of mission, if constraints are to be minimized, if authority is to be decentralized, if officials are to be judged on the basis of the outputs they produce rather than the inputs they consume, then legislators, judges, and lobbyists will have to act against their own interests. They will have to say "no" to influential constituents, forgo the opportunity to expand their own influence, and take seriously the task of judging the organizational feasibility as well as the political popularity of a proposed new program. It is hard to imagine this happening, partly because politicians and judges have no incentive to make it happen and partly because there are certain tasks a democratic government must undertake even if

they cannot be performed efficiently. The greatest mistake citizens can make when they complain of "the bureaucracy" is to suppose that their frustrations arise simply out of management problems; they do not—they arise out of governance problems.

Bureaucracy and the American Regime

The central feature of the American constitutional system—the separation of powers—exacerbates many of these problems. The governments of the United States were not designed to be efficient or powerful, but to be tolerable and malleable. Those who devised these arrangements always assumed that the federal government would exercise few and limited powers. As long as that assumption was correct (which it was for a century and a half) the quality of public administration was not a serious problem except in the minds of those reformers (Woodrow Wilson was probably the first) who desired to rationalize government in order to rationalize society. The founders knew that the separation of powers would make it so difficult to start a new program or to create a new agency that it was hardly necessary to think about how those agencies would be administered. As a result, the Constitution is virtually silent on what kind of administration we should have. At least until the Civil War thrust the problem on us, scarcely anyone in the country would have known what you were talking about if you spoke of the "problem of administration."

Matters were very different in much of Europe. Kings and princes long had ruled; when their authority was captured by parliaments, the tradition of ruling was already well established. From the first the ministers of the parliamentary regimes thought about the problems of administration because in those countries there was something to administer. The centralization of executive authority in the hands of a prime minister and the exclusion (by and large) of parliament from much say in executive affairs facilitated the process of controlling the administrative agencies and bending them to some central will. The constitutions of many European states easily could have been written by a school of management.

Today, the United States at every level has big and active governments. Some people worry that a constitutional system well-designed to preserve liberty when governments were small is poorly designed to implement policy now that governments are large. The contrast between how the United States and the nations of Western Europe manage environmental and industrial regulation is illuminating: Here the separation of powers insures, if not causes, clumsy and adversarial regulation; there the unification of powers permits, if not causes, smooth and consensual regulation.

I am not convinced that the choice is that simple, however. It would take another book to judge the advantages and disadvantages of the separation of powers. The balance sheet on both sides of the ledger would contain many more entries than those that derive from a discussion of public administration. But even confining our attention to administration, there is more to be said for the American system than many of its critics admit.

America has a paradoxical bureaucracy unlike that found in almost any other advanced nation. The paradox is the existence in one set of institutions of two qualities ordinarily quite separate: the multiplication of rules and the opportunity for access. We have a system laden with rules; elsewhere that is a sure sign that the bureaucracy is aloof from the people, distant from their concerns, and preoccupied with the power and privileges of the bureaucrats—an elaborate, grinding machine that can crush the spirit of any who dare oppose it. We also have a system suffused with participation: advisory boards, citizen groups, neighborhood councils, congressional investigators, crusading journalists, and lawyers serving writs; elsewhere this popular involvement would be taken as evidence that the administrative system is no system at all, but a bungling, jerry-built contraption wallowing in inefficiency and shot through with corruption and favoritism.

That these two traits, rules and openness, could coexist would have astonished Max Weber and continues to astonish (or elude) many contemporary students of the subject. Public bureaucracy in this country is neither as rational and predictable as Weber hoped nor as crushing and mechanistic as he feared. It is rule-bound without being overpowering, participatory without being corrupt. This paradox exists partly because of the character and mores of the American people: They are too informal, spontaneous, and other-directed to be either neutral arbiters or passionless Gradgrinds. And partly it exists because of the nature of the regime: Our constitutional system, and above all the exceptional power enjoyed by the legislative branch, makes it impossible for us to have anything like a government by appointed experts but easy for individual citizens to obtain redress from the abuses of power. Anyone who wishes it otherwise would have to produce a wholly different regime, and curing the mischiefs of bureaucracy seems an inadequate reason for that. Parliamentary regimes that supply more consistent direction to their bureaucracies also supply more bureaucracy to their citizens. The fragmented American regime may produce chaotic government, but the coherent European regimes produce bigger governments.

In the meantime we live in a country that despite its baffling array of rules and regulations and the insatiable desire of some people to use government to rationalize society still makes it possible to get drinkable water instantly, put through a telephone call in seconds, deliver a letter in a day, and obtain a passport in a week. Our Social Security checks arrive on time. Some state prisons, and most of the federal ones, are reasonably decent and humane institutions. The great majority of Americans, cursing all the while, pay their taxes. One can stand on the deck of an aircraft carrier during night flight operations and watch two thousand nineteen-year-old boys faultlessly operate one of the most complex organizational systems ever created. There are not many places where all this happens. It is astonishing it can be made to happen at all.

Notes

1. Arthur T. Hadley, *The Straw Giant* (New York: Random House, 1986), 53–57, 249–52.
2. CSIS, *U.S. Defense Acquisition: A Process in Trouble* (Washington, D.C.: Center for Strategic and International Studies, March 1987), 13–16.
3. Herbert Kaufman, *The Administrative Behavior of Federal Bureau Chiefs* (Washington, D.C.: The Brookings Institution, 1981), 192.
4. Martha Derthick, *Agency Under Stress: The Social Security Administration and American Government* (Washington, D.C.: Brookings Institution, forthcoming).
5. Ibid., chap. 3.
6. Charles Wolf, Jr., *Markets or Governments: Choosing Between Imperfect Alternatives* (Cambridge, Mass.: MIT Press, 1988).
7. James Colvard, "Procurement: What Price Mistrust?" *Government Executive* (March 1985): 21.
8. NAPA, *Revitalizing Federal Management: Managers and Their Overburdened Systems* (Washington, D.C.: National Academy of Public Administration, November 1983), vii, viii, 8.
9. Steven Emerson, *Secret Warriors* (New York: G. P. Putnam's Sons, 1988).
10. John E. Chubb and Terry M. Moe, "Politics, Markets, and the Organization of Schools," *American Political Science Review* 82 (1988): 1065–87.
11. Chester E. Finn, Jr., "Decentralize, Deregulate, Empower," *Policy Review* (Summer 1986): 60; Edward A. Wynne, *A Year in the Life of a School* (forthcoming).
12. William E. Turcotte, "Control Systems, Performance, and Satisfaction in Two State Agencies," *Administrative Science Quarterly* 19 (1974): 60–73.
13. Richard P. Nathan, *Social Science in Government: Uses and Misuses* (New York: Basic Books, 1988), chap. 3.
14. These projects were all done by the Police Foundation and are described in James Q. Wilson, *Thinking About Crime,* rev. ed. (New York: Basic Books, 1983).
15. See Joseph A. Pechman and P. Michael Timpane, eds., *Work Incentives and Income Guarantees* (Washington, D.C.: Brookings Institution, 1975); and R. Thayne Robson, ed., *Employment and Training R&D* (Kalamazoo, Mich.: Upjohn Institute for Employment Research, 1984).
16. Nathan, *Social Science,* chap. 5; and Manpower Demonstration Research Corporation, *Summary and Findings of the National Supported Work Demonstration* (Cambridge, Mass.: Ballinger, 1980).
17. See studies cited in chap. 19.
18. See references to China Lake research cited in chap. 8.
19. Clarence E. Ridley and Herbert A. Simon, *Measuring Municipal Activities* (Chicago: International City Managers' Association, 1938).

☐ CASE STUDY 15

Introduction

On December 6, 1994, Orange County, California, having 2.3 million residents, was forced to file for bankruptcy under Chapter 9 of the Bankruptcy Code. The move came after Robert Citron, the County Treasurer, admitted that Orange County's $7.7 billion investment pool that he managed on behalf of 187 local communities and agencies in the County had lost $1.5 billion since January 1, 1994.

Ironically, Orange County has one of the richest per-capita incomes among American counties, and Mr. Citron's 17-year career was nationally recognized as having one of the best municipal fund management records. Indeed, only a few months before, both Standard and Poor's and Moody's Bond Rating Services had assigned their highest short-term bond ratings to Orange County's last big issuance of $110 million debt.

Then suddenly on December 6, when Orange County failed to come up with the cash plus collateral it owed of $1.25 billion, CS First Boston—one of several Wall Street firms that had lent the county cash to buy bonds—quickly seized $2 billion of securities it had been holding as collateral and dumped them on the market at a significant loss to the county. The rise in interest rates since Spring 1994 had shrunk the county's liquid assets from $2.2 billion to $350 million, or a mere fraction of what they owed creditors in December. When word went out about the county's insolvency, there was soon "a run on" the county's remaining cash reserves and the county had no recourse other than to seek bankruptcy protection from its creditors.

However, Orange County came close to preventing its historic insolvency from occurring. The following *Wall Street Journal* article by staff writer Laura Jereski recounts the remarkable eleventh-hour attempt to save the county's investment fund from default. It is a tale of secret codes and of all-night frantic efforts set amid a siege mentality and an odd kind of governmental arrangement—the sort of stuff of spy novels, not municipal administration. Through the hard work of the assistant county treasurer, Matthew Raabe, his staff, lawyers, and investment bankers, "a rescue package" was designed to "save the County fund." However, the arcane structure and rules of operation imposed severe—and ultimately fatal—restrictions upon the county commissioners in dealing effectively *and* quickly with the fiscal nightmare.

As you read this relatively brief, though fascinating, case, reflect upon what it says in relationship to Wilson's foregoing essay:

How did the Orange County "incentive structures" inhibit the commissioners from preventing the default?

Why were these structures created in the first place?

What would you recommend to reform the governmental structures so as to permit the county managers "to manage" future crises such as these more effectively *and* quickly? (You might think about some of Wilson's recommendations.) Where else in this book might Wilson's prescriptions for reform work effectively?

But No Cigar: How a Rescue Mission Failed, Just Barely, in Orange County

LAURA JERESKI

Early in the morning of Dec. 6, just hours before Or-

"But No Cigar: How a Rescue Mission Failed, Just Barely, in Orange County" by Laura Jereski from *The Wall Street Journal*, December 22, 1994. Reprinted by permission of *The Wall Street Journal*, © 1994 Dow Jones & Company, Inc. All Rights Reserved Worldwide.

ange County's final financial collapse, local officials came within a penstroke of preventing the largest municipal bankruptcy in U.S. history.

A rescue mission, operating in secret in New York and Santa Ana, had hammered out a plan to restructure the county's toppling investment fund and avoid default. Time was critical. The fund was hemorrhaging cash, with losses at $1.5 billion and mounting. To avoid tipping off financial markets about any plans, the team coded its cellular-phone messages: Orange County was "Oscar."

After four days of round-the-clock meetings, the rescue team of county finance officials, consultants and Wall Street experts was within sight of its goal. To prevent a messy and costly liquidation of the fund's $20 billion portfolio, one of four big investment banks would be chosen to restructure the fund's debts and stop further losses. All that was needed was a green light from the county government.

A Beleaguered Board

That wasn't going to be easy, however. Unlike many jurisdictions, Orange County had no chief executive to whom the rescue team could turn. Instead, crucial decisions rested with a board of five elected supervisors—a former policeman, a social worker, a former business-school professor and two career politicians near retirement.

Despite a population of 2.6 million and one of the highest per-capita incomes in the nation, the county retains a system of government devised in simpler times, the 1870s. Its government is "clearly a 19th-century artifact struggling to cope with the emerging 21st century," says Peter Detwiler, staff director to the California Senate local-government committee.

The five individuals are isolated by laws inhibiting them from meeting freely, without 24 hours' public notice. In contrast to practices elsewhere, they can't override these "sunshine" laws even in emergencies. To keep informed, the supervisors were forced to rely heavily on an outside law firm whose own interests, in part, diverged from theirs, say people involved in the county's debacle. Burdened by conflicting advice, the supervisors ultimately left the county's fate to market forces.

Asking for Their Money

Not until mid-November, in fact, when those market forces began squeezing the fund, did the supervisors first realize the depth of their problem. Sensing trouble, the fund's participants—more than 180 local governmental bodies—started clamoring for their

money. "We were told there was a liquidity problem," recalls Supervisor Roger Stanton, the former professor.

Through its bond counsel at LeBoeuf, Lamb, Greene & MacRae, a New York law firm, the county hired Capital Market Risk Advisors (CMRA), a New York consulting firm, last month to do some sleuthing in the portfolio. At that point, the county simply wanted to find out what the portfolio contained.

What CMRA found was far worse than anyone imagined. For years, the fund's manager, County Treasurer Robert L. Citron, had been chalking up high yields by borrowing heavily from Wall Street brokers to buy even more bonds. That worked fine when interest rates were falling, but when rates turned back up this year, losses mounted. Instead of calling it quits, Mr. Citron doubled up.

Demands for Collateral

As the portfolio's value continued to slide, the lenders demanded that he put up more collateral. Those demands drained the fund of almost $900 million by Dec. 1, leaving it with only $350 million of quickly available money—just a fraction of what was needed to meet additional collateral payments of $1.25 billion falling due the following Tuesday, Dec. 6.

Before the county officials could fully come to grips with the CMRA analysis, word of the fund's difficulties was spreading fast. So, the county called a news conference on Dec. 1 to announce a $1.5 billion "paper loss," roughly 20% of the value of the fund's principal.

The news conference was a grueling public debut for Matthew Raabe, the county's assistant treasurer. Mr. Citron, who was soon to be forced out of office, sat despondently in the background while Mr. Raabe explained the situation and fielded questions.

The earnest 38-year-old accountant had been Mr. Citron's deputy since 1987. But stepping into his boss's shoes would be problematical. Despite Mr. Raabe's years in the treasurer's office, he had made none of the critical investment decisions, according to colleagues and reports by the county auditor, Steven Lewis.

At first, Mr. Raabe's lack of knowledge of the fund's investments made it hard for him to understand how bleak the situation really was, his colleagues and outside consultants say. In a telephone conference call that Friday morning with Moody's Investors Service, Mr. Raabe couldn't answer some basic questions. For example, he said he didn't know how $900 million in cash had left the fund in six weeks, say several participants in the call, or about the fund's huge unhedged holdings of "inverse floaters," volatile bonds that dropped sharply in value as interest rates rose. Mr. Raabe's attorney declined to make him available for comment.

The CMRA consultants, by contrast, recognized all the markings of impending financial collapse. The disclosure of Orange County's loss meant the county's once-accommodating brokers would quit bankrolling the tottering fund. In particular, Tuesday's $1.25 billion collateral payment loomed with chilling urgency.

If the fund couldn't meet that commitment, its lenders probably would seize its collateral and dump it to recover their money. Those fire sales could rack up big additional losses for the fund. And the fund's participants would undoubtedly step up demands for their money.

Reversing the fund's existing losses was out of the question, of course. But raising much-needed cash would give the fund some breathing room to reorganize its finances and head off bankruptcy. The potential long-term costs of bankruptcy were considerable. As New York City's brush with insolvency in the 1970s showed, the bond market can be very unforgiving. For a multibillion-dollar bond issuer such as Orange County, the lasting drag on its financing costs would be immense.

Exploring the Options

On Friday, the CMRA consultants contacted every Wall Street firm that had avoided doing business with Mr. Citron to explore the fund's options and negotiate a workout. Four stepped up: J.P. Morgan & Co., Goldman, Sachs & Co., Salomon Inc. and Swiss Bank Corp. They were coded as "Joe," "Golf," "Sierra" and "White Cross."

At 8 o'clock Saturday morning, CMRA and TSA Capital Management, a bond firm specializing in exotic securities, met with bankers in a suite at the Regency Hotel in New York. They shuffled half-hour spots to accommodate the christening of one

banker's child. By the time the Goldman bankers left, shouldering tuxedos on the way to their annual dinner, about 100 experts were filtering through the fund's financial data.

None of the firms was told which others had been consulted. J.P. Morgan was so anxious to prevent word from seeping out to its trading desks that it rewired conference rooms for computers to quarantine its Orange County experts.

Meanwhile, in Santa Ana, the task of coordinating the county's rescue had fallen to Mr. Raabe. He and three other members of the county staff set up a "war room" on the third floor of the Orange County Hall of Administration, an ultramodern inverted pyramid of white stone in the city's civic center. They spent all Saturday on the phone with the consultants in New York, racing in turn to retrieve trading records and other statistics on the portfolio from the treasury building 50 yards away.

A Ray of Hope

On Saturday night, over dinner at a local grill, Mr. Raabe told other members of the county's staff and two lawyers from LeBoeuf Lamb that he expected to be able to present some possible solutions to board members the following day.

That same night, the LeBoeuf Lamb lawyers called the Securities and Exchange Commission, trying to throw the fund on its mercy and pleading that the agency ask for appointment of a receiver, according to SEC officials and a LeBoeuf Lamb lawyer. However, the supervisors say they weren't told until the next day.

But "the only basis to intervene would have been to allege that there was a fraud, that it was continuing and that there was going to be imminent damage to the public interest," William McLucas, the SEC's chief of enforcement, says now. Only if those conditions were met could the SEC ask a federal court for permission to appoint a receiver.

The LeBoeuf Lamb attorneys may have had reasons of their own for this bold initiative. The fund's dire condition posed a knotty problem: Just a few months before, the law firm had cleared a $600 million county bond issue whose proceeds went into the investment fund. The offering documents, registered at the SEC, disclosed none of the fund's burgeoning problems and, indeed, cited its good track record.

The fund's imminent collapse could make the firm vulnerable to bondholder lawsuits.

"The point here was to salvage the situation. We went to the SEC for the county and the bondholders," says Taylor Briggs, a LeBoeuf Lamb partner. Mr. Briggs denies that there could be any conflict between the interests of the bondholders seeking payment from Orange County and those of the cash-strapped county itself or between the county and the law firm. "At the time that we were advising the county, our interests were not adverse to the county," he says. Indeed, not until Orange County filed for bankruptcy on Dec. 6 did LeBoeuf Lamb concede that the firm would face a conflict if it continued to represent the county.

Bankruptcy Specialist Consulted

As the lawyers talked over the weekend with the SEC, they also began consulting with Carl Eklund, their bankruptcy specialist in Denver, Mr. Eklund says.

Back in New York, J.P. Morgan offered the best hope to avert bankruptcy. The two sides set up a meeting for 4 a.m. Sunday to nail down details. In a boardroom at Morgan's headquarters in a deserted Lower Manhattan, the consultants met with some 18 investment bankers, many in business suits despite the odd hour.

The Morgan bankers proposed to take the fund's nearly $5 billion face value of unencumbered holdings off the county's hands. Those assets mainly consisted of risky derivative securities, whose market value had been hammered by rising short-term rates to less than $4.5 billion.

J.P. Morgan agreed to stand by to purchase the fund's bonds as its cash needs required, up to a total outlay of $4.4 billion. Assuming the market didn't move against the bank, Morgan stood to make up to $100 million, says a person familiar with the bid. Armed with this commitment, the consultants dashed to make a 6:50 a.m. flight to Orange County.

Early Sunday afternoon, Supervisor William Steiner was watching a Los Angeles Rams game when he got a call. Could he immediately go to his office for an important briefing, a staffer asked.

He and the other supervisors rushed to the Hall of Administration for a 1 p.m. meeting with members of Mr. Raabe's team and Terry Andrus, the county counsel, who represents the board of supervisors.

The supervisors had to wait alone in their office suites while staffers ran from office to office to brief each in turn.

There was a lot of news, all of it bad.

Mr. Stanton and other supervisors recall being told at those meetings that the SEC, which had begun an investigation of the fund, might freeze the assets. Moreover, the SEC probably would sue Mr. Citron for fraud. And "in a general sense," says Supervisor Stanton, "we were told there was an attempt to get cooperation from Wall Street firms."

A 'Stunned' Supervisor

Supervisor Steiner, who headed a home for abused children until he was appointed to the board by California Gov. Pete Wilson last year, felt broadsided. "We were stunned" by the news, he recalls.

But because of the sunshine laws, it was illegal for the supervisors to confer that day. "This is the most inefficient form of government you can imagine," says Supervisor Gaddi Vasquez, the former cop. To satisfy the sunshine law, the board couldn't meet before midafternoon Monday, at the earliest. The delay, Mr. Andrus says, "turned out to be a definite impediment to effective decision-making."

Monday morning, without telling Mr. Raabe and the county staff, Mr. Andrus began consulting with LeBoeuf Lamb's Mr. Eklund about the county's filing for bankruptcy, Mr. Eklund recalls.

At a closed-door session of the board on Monday afternoon, the conflicting agendas of the county staff and the board's advisers at last collided. In a letter to the board the following day, Mr. Raabe summarized what took place: Mr. Raabe presented the details of the Wall Street workout plan. He explained that at least one firm stood ready to make a bid for the entire portfolio. (Indeed, J.P. Morgan had already begun pricing the bonds in the market.)

The main snag, Mr. Raabe wrote, was that he wasn't empowered to hire a fiduciary to oversee the sell-off. As he explained, no investment bank would risk bidding for the portfolio without a fiduciary on hand to ensure proper pricing.

At the Monday meeting, the county staff, which works directly for the supervisors, seconded Mr. Raabe's recommendation that a fiduciary be hired. Unexpectedly, however, LeBoeuf Lamb objected, throwing the meeting into disarray.

According to Supervisor Stanton, the lawyers still hoped to get the SEC to take over the fund. So, anything that side-stepped the possibility of fraud—as the Wall Street plan did—might threaten the lawyers' own hopes of SEC intervention.

Wall Street Plan Blocked

In the meeting, the LeBoeuf Lamb lawyers, joined by Mr. Andrus, the county counsel, blocked the Wall Street plan by throwing up two legal hurdles. First, they argued the fund's legal status was so unclear that they couldn't say who actually owned the assets. What's more, Mr. Andrus balked at indemnifying the fiduciary against any lawsuits that might arise over the sale of the portfolio.

Faced with conflicting advice, the supervisors adjourned. After they left, the lawyers continued bickering with the staff long into the night, staff members say.

At 2:45 a.m., at Mr. Andrus's suggestion, the staff dispatched police cars to rouse the supervisors to reconsider the issue. Mr. Raabe "was frantic," Supervisor Steiner says. The staff "had a siege mentality." Again, discussions with the supervisors took place one on one.

As Mr. Steiner recalls, "We were told that potentially the entire pool would melt down, with a loss far in excess of $1.5 billion, and there was J.P. Morgan poised" to buy the portfolio. Mr. Stanton recalls that bankruptcy and bringing in the SEC "were the two options, the two viable options." He stresses that "no other recommendation was presented to us."

However, Mr. Raabe made a last desperate plea for the plan. "I implore you to consider the devastating outcome if this request is not approved," he wrote in his summary, noting on the document the hour: 3 o'clock on Tuesday morning.

The board and its lawyers turned him down. "We were under incredible pressure to make a decision for the other investors" in the fund, Mr. Steiner says. "They would never forgive us."

Later Tuesday, unable to meet its collateral demands, the county and its fund sought refuge in bankruptcy court. At that point, LeBoeuf Lamb, admitting a conflict of interest, turned the case over to bankruptcy specialists at Stutman, Treister & Glatt, a Los Angeles law firm.

On Tuesday and Wednesday, the fund's lenders rushed to unload some $11.4 billion of its bonds. Late Wednesday, the county hired Salomon Brothers—one of the Wall Street white knights, which had been prepared to buy $1.5 billion of bonds from the county just the day before—to auction off the fund's remaining assets. Already, the fund's losses exceed $2 billion, while the yoke of bankruptcy court will hamper Orange County for years to come.

Chapter 15 Review Questions

1. Sum up in a few sentences James Q. Wilson's approach to improving bureaucratic responsiveness to the public interest. How does his perspective compare and contrast to the three approaches outlined in the introduction to this chapter?
2. What are some of the basic unstated assumptions about public bureacracy and public interest implicit in Wilson's argument? Are these assumptions valid in your view?
3. In the Orange County case study, list the central problems that you found led to the county filing Chapter 9 bankruptcy.
4. Given your list, what specific recommendations by James Q. Wilson might prevent this problem from reoccurring in the future?
5. Would you add any other reforms, other than those outlined by Wilson? And if so, why?
6. What might be some of the difficulties of implementing these proposed reforms?

Key Terms

deregulate government
culture of the organization
control mentality
mission accomplishment
balancing distribution of
    authority with program tasks
overcentralization of control

judging agencies by results
separation of powers
paradoxical bureaucracy
legislative micromanagement
presidential micromanagement
turf-conscious administrator

Suggestions for Further Reading

The proper role of government in serving the public interest is one that has been considered and debated for decades. Certainly with the founding of the United States, one need only turn to the Federalist papers to read about the concerns for the role of government. Specifically, "Publius" [James Madison], The Federalist No. 10," (New York Packet, November 23, 1787) serves as a starting point for understanding the interests and intensity of the citizen's desires for assuring a "public voice" in government matters. Readings that continue to propagate the debate of government's relationship with the public can be found in John Stuart Mill's, *On Liberty* (London: J.W. Parker and Son, 1859) and *Consideration on Representative Government* (London: Parker, Son and Bourn, 1861) and Georg Wilhelm Friedrich Hegel, *The Philosophy of Right* (Berlin: In der Kicolaischen Buchhandlung, 1821). The results of these discussions did not prove to be futile, and, in fact, the move toward ensuring a democratic administration became stronger with time. For an introductory discussion of democratic administration, one should read Paul H. Appleby's *Big Democracy* (New York: Alfred A. Knopf, 1945), as well as *Policy and Administration* (University: University of Alabama Press, 1949) and *Morality and Administration in Democratic Government* (Baton Rouge: LSU Press, 1952). Appleby clearly is one of the most influential authors on the subject of administrative democracy. For further interpretations of his essays, a helpful compilation is included in Roscoe C. Martin's, ed., *Public Administration and Democracy:*

Essays in Honor of Paul H. Appleby (Syracuse, N.Y.: Syracuse University Press, 1965).

The essence of the discussion on bureaucracy and the public interest is obviously discovered when one explores the notion of political bureaucracy. For an overview of the requirements for serving the public interest from a bureaucratic standpoint, one should read Lewis C. Mainzer, *Political Bureaucracy* (Glenview, Ill.: Scott, Foresman and Co., 1973), and Peter Woll, *American Bureaucracy* (New York: W. W. Norton and Co., 1963). Additionally, for an essay in defense of the "administrative machinery's" ability to respond to the public interest, Norton Long, *The Polity* (Chicago: Rand McNally and Co., 1962) argues the vitality of "the administration" in serving the public interest. On the other hand, Peter Blau, *The Dynamics of Bureaucracy* (Chicago: University of Chicago Press, 1955), argues that bureaucracy and democracy are incompatible and are incapable of successfully coexisting.

The next level for discussion on bureaucracy and the public interest takes us to the notion of representative bureaucracy. Much of the literature argues for its importance as a democratic ideal. Steven G. Koven's chapter, "The Bureaucratic-Democratic Conundrum: A Contemporary Inquiry into the Labyrinth," in *Handbook of Bureaucracy*, Ali Farazmand, ed. (New York: Marcel Dekker, Inc., 1994), pp. 79–96; and Brian J. Cook, "The Representative Function of Bureaucracy: Public Administration in Constitutive Perspective," *Administration & Society*, 23, 4 (February 1992), pp.

403–429, provide a valuable "first-look" at the significance of representative bureaucracy. Further, Charles M. Wiltse, "The Representative Function of Bureaucracy," *American Political Science Review,* 35 (June 1941), pp. 510–516 should be reviewed for discussion on bureaucracy's role in assisting Congress in fulfilling its constitutional obligation of providing representation. Students of public administration should also be familiar with Norton E. Long, "Bureaucracy and Constitutionalism," *American Political Science Review,* 46 (September 1952), pp. 808–818, and Charles Merriam, *Political Power* (New York: McGraw-Hill, 1934). A more recent theoretical exploration is offered by Samuel P. Krislov, *Representative Bureaucracy* (Englewood Cliffs, N.J.: Prentice-Hall, 1974), and Harry Kranz, *The Participatory Bureaucracy* (Lexington, Mass.: Lexington Books, 1976). Further readings should include Morris Janowitz, Deil Wright, and William Delany, *Public Administration and the Public—Perspectives Toward Government in a Metropolitan Community,* no. 36 in University of Michigan, Michigan Governmental Studies (Ann Arbor: Bureau of Government, Institute of Government Administration, University of Michigan, 1958).

The challenge to representative bureaucracy, however, is in maintaining a level of accountability to the public. One should read Bernard Rosen's *Holding Government Bureaucracies Accountable* (New York: Praeger Publishers, 1982) for a basic overview of the techniques developed to hold bureaucracies accountable. The challenge in doing this, however, is defined in M. Shamsul Haque's chapter, "The Emerging Challenges to Bureaucratic Accountability: A Critical Perspective," in *The Handbook of Bureaucracy,* Ali Farazmand, ed. (New York: Marcel Dekker, 1994), pp. 265–286.

The debate over the meaning of a "representative bureaucracy" continued with Norton E. Long, "Bureaucracy and Constitutionalism," *American Political Science Review,* 46 (September 1952), pp. 808–818. Further, J. Donald Kingsley, *Representative Bureaucracy: An Interpretation of the British Civil Service* (Yellow Springs, Ohio: An-

tioch Press, 1944), introduced representative bureaucracy to class and racial makeup. One may also want to briefly examine the role of public personnel in a democratic regime. Be sure to review Frederick C. Mosher's *Democracy and the Public Service* (New York: Oxford University Press, 1968). And more specifically, it would be helpful to examine the public administrator as a link with the public interest. Peter deLeon calls for "participatory policy analysis" in "The Democratization of the Policy Sciences," *Public Administration Review,* 52, 2 (March/April 1992), pp. 125–129. Other excellent readings include Richard C. Box, "The Administrator as Trustee of the Public Interest: Normative Ideals and Daily Practice," *Administration & Society,* 24, 3 (November 1992), pp. 323–345; John Clayton Thomas, "Public Involvement and Governmental Effectiveness: A Decision-Making Model for Public Managers," *Administration & Society,* 24, 4 (February 1993), pp. 444–469, and Philip Selznick, *TVA and the Grass Roots* (New York: Harper & Row, 1949). Norton E. Long provides a standard for evaluating the outcomes, management structures, and processes, programs, and policies in "Conceptual Notes on the Public Interest for Public Administration and Policy Analysts," *Administration & Society,* 22, 2 (August 1990), pp. 170–181. Finally, the argument that public administration is the "mechanism" whereby decisions are made in compatibility with the basic tenets of democracy is found in Emmette S. Redford, *Democracy in the Administrative State* (New York: Oxford University Press, 1969).

"The public" is defined in numerous ways: first, the so-called "active citizen" is often characterized as being on the receiving end of public goods. For an interesting essay on the active citizenship, read Camilla Stivers, "The Public Agency as Policy: Active Citizenship in the Administrative State," *Administration & Society,* 22, 1 (May 1990), pp. 86–105. Also, it may be worthwhile to read Norton E. Long's "Seeking the Polity's Bottom Line: A Conceptual Note," *Administration & Society,* 24, 2 (August 1992), pp. 107–114. One of the most famous evaluations of how American pluralism works at the local level where elitist theory is discarded for a more activity citizenry in urban policies is Robert A. Dahl's *Who Governs? Democracy and Power in an American City* (New Haven: Yale University Press, 1961).

No discussion is complete without examining the role of public interest groups in the American bureaucratic regime. A "must-read" on this topic is E. Pendleton Herring, *Group Representation before Congress* (Baltimore: Johns Hopkins Press, 1929) and *Public Administration and the Public Interest* (New York: McGraw Hill, 1936). Others worth scanning include Allan J. Cigler and Burdett A. Loomis, eds., *Interest Group Politics* (Washington, D.C.: Congressional Quarterly Press, 1983); V.O. Key, Jr., *Politics, Parties, and Pressure Groups* (New York: Thomas Y. Crowell Co., 1942); and David B. Truman, *The Governmental Process* (New York: Alfred A. Knopf, 1951). Another author advocating the value of interest groups is David B. Truman, *The Governmental Process* (New York: Alfred A. Knopf, 1951). For discussions citing the problems associated with pressure groups, read Theodore Lowi's *The End of Liber-*

alism (New York: W. W. Norton and Co., 1969); an examination of the usefulness of special interests to the public good can be found in Grant McConnell's *Private Power and American Democracy* (New York: Alfred A. Knopf, 1966).

The public interest is defined beyond the interests of pressure groups. Public opinion is also another valuable aspect for defining the public's interest. For a discussion on public opinion and the means for directing it toward democratic values, one should read Harold D. Lasswell, *Democracy Through Public Opinion* (Menasha, Wisconsin: George Banta Publishing Co., 1941). Others interested in the information-source of public opinion include V. O. Key, Jr., *Public Opinion and American Democracy* (New York: Alfred A. Knopf, 1961); Water Lippmann, *Public Opinion* (New York: Harcourt, Brace, and Co., 1922); Angus Campbell, Philip E. Converse, Warren E. Miller, and Donald Stokes, *The American Voter* (New York: John Wiley and Sons, 1960); and Herbert Kaufman, *Administrative Feedback* (Washington, D.C.: The Brookings Institution, 1973).

CHAPTER 16

The Relationship Between Ethics and Public Administration: The Concept of Competing Ethical Obligations

The twentieth century has hardly been distinguished either by its observance of agreed moral codes or by its concentration on ethical inquiry. On the contrary, it has been distinguished by a 'decay' of traditional moral codes, a widespread feeling that morality is 'relative' if not utterly meaningless, and a disposition to regard ethical inquiry as frivolous, irrelevant. These currents of thought and feeling have been associated with a 'falling away' from religious belief and a concomitant rise of 'belief' in science and its philosophical—or antiphilosophical—aura.

Dwight Waldo

READING 16

Introduction

Leading thinkers in public administration long ago recognized that the critical issues of government ultimately involved moral choices. The definitive policy decisions made by public officials often have at their base conflicting ethical issues, such as whether to give precedence to the public interest or to the narrower demands of profession, department, bureau, or clientele. The ambivalent position in which public officials often find themselves has led some sensitive administrative theorists like Chester Barnard to say that the chief qualification of an executive is the ability to resolve these competing ethical codes—legal, technical, personal, professional, and organizational codes. In Barnard's view, the strength and quality of an administrator lies in his or her capacity to deal effectively with the moral complexities of organizations without being broken by the imposed problems of choice: ". . . neither men of weak responsibility nor those of limited capability," writes Barnard, "can endure or carry the burden of many simultaneous obligations of different types. If they are 'overloaded' either ability, responsibility, or morality or all three will be destroyed. Conversely, a condition of complex morality, great activity, and high responsibility cannot endure without commensurate ability."[1]

For Paul Appleby, another administrative theorist, the institutional arrangements in government provide the most effective safeguards for ensuring ethical administrative behavior. Appleby, in his book *Morality and Administration in Democratic Government,*[2] contends, however, that the traditional constitutional arrangements, such as checks and balances, federalism, or the Bill of Rights, do not supply this protection against immorality. Rather, two institutional safeguards are the best guarantees of administrative morality: (1) the ballot box and (2) hierarchy. By means of the *ballot box* the electorate judges direct the performance of government at periodic intervals. Through *hierarchy* important decisions are forced upward in the administrative structure where they can receive broader, less technical, and more political review. Appleby equates the application of broad, disinterested, and political judgment with responsible and ethical administration.

In another selection written as a memorial essay to Appleby, "Ethics and the Public Service," Stephen K. Bailey draws on Appleby's writings to develop some further insights into the essential qualities of moral behavior in the public service. At the core of Bailey's essay is his emphasis on three moral qualities in public administration: "optimism, courage, and fairness tempered by charity." Optimism, in the author's view, is the ability of a public servant to deal with morally ambiguous situations confidently and purposefully. Courage is the capacity to decide and act in the face of situations when inaction, indecision, or agreement with the popular trend would provide the easy solution. Fairness tempered by charity allows for the maintenance of standards of justice in decisions affecting the public interest.[3]

Bailey emphasizes the high ethical content of most important public questions. He points out how the varied complexities of public service add enormous complications to moral behavior so that the resolution of public issues can never be black or white. The "best solution," writes Bailey, "rarely is without its costs. . . . And one mark of moral maturity is in the appreciation of the inevitability of untoward and often malignant effects of benign moral choices." A strain of pessimism appears in Bailey's writing, for he observes that public policies rarely lead to a total victory for the "right" and a total defeat for the "wrong." Indeed, policy solutions themselves often create new policy problems.

Is ethical conduct in the public service the result of Barnard's thesis of an administrator's creative ability to resolve "competing ethical codes"? Or, Appleby's "institutional safeguards"? Or, Bailey's essential "moral qualities"?

In the following selection by Dwight Waldo, "Public Administration and Ethics," the author attempts to "map" the difficult and complicated terrain of the relationship between public administration and ethics. As Waldo asserts at the beginning: ". . . moral

---

[1]Chester I. Barnard, *The Functions of the Executive* (Cambridge, Mass.: Harvard University Press, 1938), p. 272.

[2]Paul H. Appleby, *Morality and Administration in Democratic Government* (Baton Rouge, La.: Louisiana State University Press, 1952).

[3]Stephen K. Baily, "Ethics and the Public Service," in Roscoe C. Martin, ed., *Public Administration and Democracy* (Syracuse, N.Y.: Syracuse University Press, 1965).

or ethical behavior in public administration is a complicated matter, indeed *chaotic.*" In order to elaborate on the reasons for this current complexity, he proceeds to sketch briefly the historical backdrop of how the distinction between "public" and "private" morality evolved and the relationship between "the state and higher law." Here we are treated to a concise 2000-year overview of political theories that brought us to our present late 20th century dilemmas. He thus provides us with a thoughtful intellectual background for comprehending our contemporary confused scene. Waldo then develops further perspectives on the present by what he calls "a map—of sorts" or an outline "of the sources and types of ethical obligations to which the public administrator is expected to respond." He identifies a dozen ethical obligations, ranging from the broadest "Obligations to the Constitution" and "To Religion and to God" to the narrowest, "To Self" and "To Family and Friends." He defends this "mapping project" in the subsequent sections on "A Need for Maps" and "A Need for Navigation Instruments" because "If we are going to talk about ethics in public life it would be useful to know what we are talking about." In the end, Waldo offers no easy answers but rather concludes with six thought-provoking "observations and reflections" on this topic concerning "some of the matters that would be worthy of attention in a more serious and systematic way."

A word about Dwight Waldo (1913–   ): This selection you are about to read came from one of his eleven out-of-course lectures that he delivered before he retired as the Albert Schweitzer Distinguished Service Professor from the Maxwell School of Citizenship and Public Affairs, Syracuse University. Together these lectures were published as a book, *The Enterprise of Public Administration: A Summary View,* in which Waldo attempted to sum up his four decades of involvement both as a practitioner and as an academic within the field. Waldo served in the Bureau of the Budget during World War II, as director of the Institute of Governmental Studies at the University of California at Berkeley in the 1950s, as editor-in-chief of the *Public Administration Review* for twelve years in the 1960s and 1970s, and as president of the National Schools of Public Affairs and Administration in the 1970s. However, he made his lasting mark on the field by his seminal writings, such as *The Administrative State, The Study of Public Administration, Perspectives on Administration, The Novelist on Organization and Administration,* and many others. Waldo's contributions were deemed so important to the advancement of the field by his peers that the American Society for Public Administration named its annual prize for lifetime academic achievement The Dwight Waldo Award.

When you read his essay, you will no doubt gain an appreciation of why Waldo's contributions are regarded so highly by administrative scholars. Few others write with such stylistic grace, raise such profound questions, or provide the historical context to present-day issues in public administration. In particular, try to think about these questions as you read the essay:

Why does Waldo argue we need "maps" and "navigation instruments" to guide us through this subject? What does he mean by those terms and do you concur with his rationale for advancing this thesis?

Do you agree with his list of twelve "ethical obligations"? Would you add or delete any on his list?

Why does he contend that "the twentieth century has hardly been distinguished either by its observance on agreed moral codes or by its concentration on ethical inquiry"? The sources for this decay of morality?

From your reading of Waldo, what practical advice does his essay offer the public administrator on-the-firing-line in sorting out the ethical dilemmas that he or she faces?

Public Administration and Ethics: A Prologue to a Preface

DWIGHT WALDO

"No process has been discovered by which promotion to a position of public responsibility will do away with a man's interest in his own welfare, his partialities, race, and prejudices."—James Harvey Robinson

"You are welcome to my house; you are welcome to my heart . . . my personal feelings have nothing to do with the present case. . . . As George Washington, I would do anything in my power for you. As President, I can do nothing."—George Washington, to a friend seeking an appointment

"There is not a moral vice which cannot be made into relative good by context. There is not a moral virtue which cannot in peculiar circumstances have patently evil results."—Stephen Bailey

"The big organization dehumanizes the individual by turning him into a functionary. In doing so it makes everything possible by creating a new kind of man, one who is morally unbounded in his role as func-

tionary. . . . His ethic is the ethic of the good soldier: take the order, do the job, do it the best way you know how, because that is your honor, your virtue, your pride-in-work."—F. William Howton

"It seems to be inevitable that the struggle to maintain cooperation among men should destroy some men morally as battle destroys some physically."—Chester Barnard

"The raising of moral considerations in any discussion on organizations usually causes discomfort. . . . Nonetheless, if morality is about what is right and wrong, then behavior in organizations is largely determined by such considerations."—David Bradley and Roy Wilkie

"The first duty of a civil servant is to give his undivided allegiance to the State at all times and on all occasions when the State has a claim on his service."—Board of Inquiry, United Kingdom, 1928

The subtitle of this presentation and the several heterogeneous epigraphs are directed toward emphasizing the central theme of this presentation, namely, that moral or ethical* behavior in public administration is a complicated matter, indeed, *chaotic.* While some facets of the matter have been treated with insight and clarity, nothing in the way of a comprehensive and systematic treatise exists—or if so I am unaware of it.[1] This situation may not reflect just accident or lack of interest. What may be reflected is the fact that a systematic treatise is impossible, given the scope, complexity, and intractability of the material from which it would have to be constructed and given an inability to find acceptable or defensible foundations of ideas and beliefs on which it could be grounded.

In this discussion I hope to indicate some of the subjects that might be given attention in a systematic treatise. I appreciate that even this hope may represent pretentiousness.

Public Morality and Private Morality

An appropriate beginning is to note a distinction between public and private morality and the possibility of a conflict between them.[2] This is a very elementary distinction, but much evidence indicates that it is little understood. As presented in the media, including the columns of the pundits, morality in public office is a simple matter of obeying the law, being honest, and telling the truth. *Not so.*

Public morality concerns decisions made and action taken directed toward the good of a collectivity which is seen or conceptualized as "the public," that is, as an entity or group larger than immediate social groups such as family and clan. Conventionally, "the public" in the modern West is equated with "the nation," or "the country." Thus when decisions are made and actions taken vis-à-vis other nations or countries a public interest is presumed to be in view. Similarly, when the decision or action is directed inward toward the affairs of the nation-state, a public or general interest is presumed to come before private or group interests.

In either case a decision or action justified as moral because it is judged to be in the interest of the public may be immoral from the standpoint of all, or nearly all, interpretations of moral behavior for individuals. The most common example is killing. When done by an individual it is, commonly, the crime of homicide. When done in warfare or law enforcement on behalf of the public it is an act of duty and honor, perhaps of heroism—presuming the "correct" circumstances. All important governments have committed what would be "sins" if done by individuals, what would be "crimes" if done under their own laws by individuals acting privately.

Those in government who decide and act on behalf of the public will from time to time, of *necessity* as I see it, be lying, stealing, cheating, killing. What must be faced is that all decision and action in the public interest is inevitably morally complex, and that the price of any good characteristically entails some bad. Usually the bad is not as simple and stark as the terms just listed signify; but sometimes it *is,* and honesty and insight on our part can begin with so acknowledging.

Ironically, the concept of "the public" is regarded, and I believe properly, as a good and even precious thing. It is a heritage from Greek and Roman antiquity. Its projection, elaboration, nurture, and defense are generally represented as the work of inspired thinkers, virtuous statesmen, and brave warriors. How can this be, when sins and crimes are committed in the name of the public? The answer is twofold. First, my favorite question: Compared to what? Assuming government is desirable, or at least inevitable, what legitimating concept is better? At least the idea of government in the name of a public advances that enterprise beyond purely personal and often tyrannical rule. Second, once in motion, so to speak, the concept of the public becomes invested with, a shelter for, and even a source of, goods that we identify with words such as citizenship, security, justice, and liberty.

---

*Strictly speaking, *moral* signifies right behavior in an immediate and customary sense; *ethical* signifies right behavior as examined and reflected upon. But no warranty is given that this distinction is always made in what follows.

The State and Higher Law

To see the matter of public and private morality in perspective it is necessary to understand the complicated relationship of both moralities to the concept of *higher law*. The concept of higher law, simply put for our purposes, holds that there is a source and measure of rightness that is above and beyond both individual and government. In our own history it is represented prominently in the justification of the Revolution against the government of George III, and it inspired the Declaration of Independence.

The classical Greek philosophers, from whom much of our tradition of political thought derives, sought a moral unity. Are the good man and the good citizen the same? Both Plato and Aristotle answered the question affirmatively, though Plato more certainly than Aristotle. In the comparatively simple world of the city-state this answer could be made plausible, given the Greek conviction of superiority and the elitist nature of citizenship: the polity creates citizens in its admirable image and is thus the source of man's morality; there can be no legitimate appeal from what it holds to be right.

But as Sophocles' *Antigone* signifies, the idea of a higher law—in this case the laws of Zeus as against those of the king, Creon—existed even in Athens. During the Hellenistic period, after the decline of the city-state, the idea of a natural law above and beyond the mundane world was elaborated, especially by the Stoics. A sense of personhood apart from the polity, and of the essential equality of humans *as* humans was developing, and this was accompanied by a growing belief that right and wrong rested on foundations beyond the polity. As Sabine put it in his history of political theory; "Men were slowly making souls for themselves." With Christianity these ideas were of course broadened and deepened. The idea of God's law, or natural law—and characteristically the two became conflated—was to become a powerful force in relation to both private and public morality.

For more than a millennium after the fall of Rome, during a period in which government all but disappeared in the West, the relationship of the two powers, the sacred and the secular—for most purposes to be equated with Church and secular authority—was at the center of political philosophy and political controversy; but the theoretical and logical supremacy of the higher law was seldom questioned. With the emergence of the modern state a new era opened. The authority of a state, even a secular state, to determine right and wrong for its citizens was powerfully asserted by political theorists, notably Machiavelli and Hobbes. On the other hand, the long era of higher-law thinking had left an indelible imprint on thought and attitude. That there is something to which one's conscience gives access and which provides guidance on right and wrong remains a strong feeling even among those who regard themselves as completely secular.

The discussion of higher law has indicated that the initial duality of public morality and private morality was simplistic. There *is* an important, and insufficiently appreciated, distinction between the two, as I hope was demonstrated. But two important matters are now apparent. One is that higher law does not equate with or relate only to private morality as against public. Its sanction can be claimed by the polity if the polity represents the sacred as well as the secular, that is, if there is no separation of church and state—or perhaps even if there is.

The other matter is that the public-private distinction is but one example, albeit a crucial one for our purposes, of a class of relationships that can be designated *collectivity-person*. The biological person is of course distinguishable from any collectivity: nation, party, union, family, whatever. But whether the person can have or should have moral standing apart from the collectivities that have created him and given him meaning is a large part of what ethics is about; for all collectivities of any durability and significance will claim, explicitly or implicitly, to be the source of moral authority. While the state may well, and in some cases inevitably will, claim moral supremacy, the individual will have to weigh its claims against his or her interpretations of competing claims of other collectivities *and* the claims of higher law and "conscience."

Plainly, the ethical landscape is becoming very cluttered and complex. More to this shortly. But first a few words on *reason of state.* Reason of state is public morality at its extreme reach. Plainly put, it is conduct that violates all or nearly all standards of right conduct for individuals; this in the interests of the creating, preserving, or enhancing state power, and rationalized by "the ends justify the means" logic. A few years ago I had occasion to review the literature on this subject in Political Science in the United States. Significantly, what I found was very little, and this mostly by émigré scholars. Unbelievably, there is no entry for this important subject in the seventeen-volume *International Encyclopedia of the Social Sciences,* even though it was planned and executed during the moral-ethical hurricane of the Vietnam War. A number of historical factors, beyond exploring here, have led us to gloss over and even deny the complexities and contradictions that exist when public and private morality conflict, as inevitably they sometimes will.

A Map—of Sorts

A few years ago, attempting to address the subject "Ethical Obligations and the Public Service," I made a rough sketch of the ethical obligations of the public administrator as seen from one point of view. Later, this sketch was somewhat elaborated and refined in collaboration with Patrick Hennigan in a yet unpublished essay. It will serve present purposes to indicate the nature of this endeavor.

The sketch, or "map," as we called it, is of ethical obligations of the public administrator with special reference to the United States. The perspective taken is that of the *sources* and *types* of ethical obligations to which the public administrator is expected to respond. We identify a dozen, but as we indicate, the list is capable of indefinite expansion and does not lend itself to logical ordering.

FIRST. OBLIGATION TO THE CONSTITUTION.

This is a legal obligation of course, but it is also a source of ethical obligations, which may be symbolized and solemnized by an oath to uphold and defend the Constitution. The upholding of regime and of regime values is a normal source of public-service obligation, and the Constitution is the foundation of regime and of regime values for the United States. But note: not an unambiguous foundation. A great deal of our history, including a civil war, can be written in terms of different interpretations of the Constitution.

SECOND. OBLIGATION TO LAW.

Laws made under the Constitution are a source not just of legal obligation but also of ethical obligations, as public-service codes of ethics normally underscore. Note again the ambiguities and puzzles. What if the law is unclear? What if laws conflict? What if a law seems unconstitutional, or violates a tenet of higher law? What is the ethical status of regulations made under the law?

THIRD. OBLIGATION TO NATION OR COUNTRY.

By most interpretations, a nation or country or people is separable from regime, and plainly this sense of identity with a nation, country, or people creates ethical obligations. Indeed, in many situations the obligation to country—Fatherland, Motherland, Homeland, however it may be put—overrides the obligation to regime. Lincoln, justifying his actions in 1864: "Was it possible to lose the nation, and yet preserve the constitution?"

FOURTH. OBLIGATION TO DEMOCRACY.

As indicated in previous discussions, this is separable from obligation to Constitution, granted that the relationship is complicated and arguable. Whatever the intent of the Framers—and I do not expect agreement on that, ever—democracy happened: it came to be accepted as an ideology or ethic and as a set of practices that somewhat overlie and somewhat intertwine with the Constitution. The emotional and intellectual acceptance of democracy creates obligations that are acknowledged and usually felt by the public administrator. But again, note the ambiguities: Is the will of the people *always* and *only* expressed in law? If in other ways, how? And how legitimated? Is the *will* of the people, however expressed, to be put ahead of the *welfare* of the people as seen by a public official with information not available to the people?

FIFTH. OBLIGATION TO ORGANIZATIONAL-BUREAUCRATIC NORMS.

These may be logically divided between those that are *generic* and those that are *specific*. The generic obligations are deeply rooted, perhaps in human nature, certainly in history and culture. They are associated with such terms as loyalty, duty, and order, as well as, perhaps, productivity, economy, efficiency. Specific obligations will depend upon circumstance: the function, the clientele, the technology.

SIXTH. OBLIGATION TO PROFESSION AND PROFESSIONALISM.

The disagreements among sociologists as to what precisely *profession* entails may be disregarded here. All would agree that a profession, indeed a well-developed occupation, has an ethos that acts to shape the values and behavior of members. This ethos concerns actions pertaining to fellow professionals, clients, patients, employers, and perhaps humanity in general. We have become much more aware of the strength and effects of professional values and behavior in public administration since the publication of Frederick Mosher's *Democracy and the Public Service.*

SEVENTH. OBLIGATION TO FAMILY AND FRIENDS.

Obligation to family is bedrock in most if not all morality. But in countries shaped by the Western political tradition it is formally accepted that *in principle* obligation to country and/or regime as well as to the public is higher than that to family. While the newspaper on almost any day will indicate that the principle is often breached, we are very clear and insistent on the *principle,* and on the

whole we believe that the principle prevails. But in countries in which the concept of public is recent and inchoate and in which family or other social group remains the center of loyalty and values, the principle is breached massively, so much so that the creation of an effective government may be impossible.

Friendship is less than family, but shares with it the immediate, personal bond; and friendship as well as family is honored in moral tradition. To indicate the ethical problems that may arise from this source one has only to set forth a name: Bert Lance.

EIGHTH. OBLIGATION TO SELF.

Yes, to self: this is a respectable part of our moral tradition, best epitomized in the Shakespearean "This above all, to thine own self be true." Selfishness and egocentrism are by general agreement bad. The argument for *self* is that self-regard is the basis for other-regard, that proper conduct toward others, doing one's duty, must be based on personal strength and integrity. But, granting the principle, how does one draw the line in practice between proper self-regard and a public interest?

NINTH. OBLIGATION TO MIDDLE-RANGE COLLECTIVITIES.

In view here is a large and heterogeneous lot: party, class, race, union, church, interest group, and others. That these are capable of creating obligations felt as moral is quite clear, and that these obligations are carried into public administration is also quite clear. When, and how, is it proper for such obligations to affect administrative behavior, to influence public decisions?

TENTH. OBLIGATION TO THE PUBLIC INTEREST OR GENERAL WELFARE.

This obligation is related to Constitution, to nation, to democracy. But it is analytically distinct. It is often explicitly embodied in law, but also has something of a separate existence. The concept is notoriously difficult to operationalize, and has been repeatedly subject to critical demolition. But presumably anyone in public administration must take it seriously, if only as a myth that must be honored in certain procedural and symbolic ways.

ELEVENTH. OBLIGATION TO HUMANITY OR THE WORLD.

It is an old idea, and perhaps despite all a growing idea, that an obligation is owed to humanity in general, to the world as a total entity, to the future as the symbol and summation of all that can be hoped. All "higher" religions trend in this direction, however vaguely and imperfectly. It is certainly an ingredient in various forms of one-world consciousness, and it figures prominently in the environmental ethic and in ecological politics.

TWELFTH. OBLIGATION TO RELIGION, OR TO GOD.

Immediately one must ask, are these two things or the same thing? The answer is not simple. But that obligations are seen as imposed by religion or God is not doubted even by atheists. One could quickly point to areas of public administration in which these felt obligations are at the center of "what's happening"—or possibly not happening.

A Need for Maps

Obviously, this listing of sources and types of ethical obligations involved in public administration is rough. The number, twelve, is plainly arbitrary. Perhaps some of the items were wrongly included, or should be combined. Perhaps some should be further divided and refined. Certainly other items might be included: *science,* for example, since science is interpreted not just to require a set of proper procedures but to be an ethos with accompanying ethical imperatives. As we know, *face-to-face groups* develop their own norms and powerfully influence behavior, but were not even mentioned. And what of *conscience*? Is it to be regarded as only a passive transmitter of signals or as in part at least an autonomous source of moral conduct?

You will have noticed that I did not attempt to order the twelve types of obligations, that is, list them in order of importance or ethical imperative. This was neither an oversight nor—I believe—a lack of intelligence on my part, but rather reflected the untidiness of the ethical universe. Perhaps the list included incommensurables. In any event, we lack the agreed beliefs which would enable us to construct an order of priority, one to twelve, with the higher obligation always superior to the lower.

How are we to proceed? How can we achieve enough clarity so that we can at least discuss our differences with minimum confusion, the least heat and the most light? My own view is that a desirable, perhaps necessary, preliminary activity is to construct more and better maps of the realm we propose to understand. Granted that this expectation may reflect only the habits of academia; professors are prone to extensive preparation for intellectual journeys never undertaken. But I do not see how we can move beyond a confused disagreement until there is more agreement on what we are talking about.

If I am essentially correct, then what would be useful would be a serious and sizable mapmaking program. We need various types of maps, analogous to maps that show physical features, climatic factors, demographic data, economic activity, and so forth. We need maps of differing scale, some indicating the main features of a large part of the organizational world, some detailing particular levels, functions, and activities. Despite common elements, presumably—no, certainly—the ethical problems of a legislator are significantly different from those of a military officer, those of a regulatory commissioner different from those of a police chief, those of a first-line supervisor from those of a department head.

Simply put: If we are going to talk about ethics in public life it would be useful to know what we are talking about.

A Need for Navigation Instruments

The metaphor of maps may not have been the most apt, but I now use one that may be less felicitous, that of navigation instruments. But at least the second metaphor is complementary: given maps, how do we navigate? How do we find our way through what the maps show us? Let me indicate the nature of some navigation equipment that would be of use.

First, it would be useful to have an instrument to guide us through the historical dimensions of our ethical problems in public administration. Above all, it would be useful to have an explication of the implications and consequences of the disjunction, noted in earlier discussions, between the rise of political self-awareness and the rise of administrative self-awareness. Both as a part of that inquiry and independently, what do we know about the rise and growth of administrative morality, of notions of stewardship, duty and obligations, reciprocal or unilateral? With respect to estate management, which has been so large a part of administrative history, have rules of proper conduct been widely divergent, or has the nature of the function disposed toward uniformity? Since estate management has been centrally involved in royal governance, from Sumer to the Sun King—and beyond—what effect has this had on bureaucratic morality? Perhaps it is worth more than mere mention that *estate* and *state* are cognates, both derived from the Latin *stare:* "to be *or* stand"; the essential notion in both cases is of substance, firmness, an organizing center.

Second, it would be useful to have instruments provided by the social sciences or derived from a survey of them. Immediately, we face the fact indicated in the epigraph from Bradley and Wilkie at the head of this chapter: "The raising of moral considerations in any discussion on organizations usually causes discomfort." In addressing organizational behavior as in contemporary social science generally, ethics is not just a neglected interest, it is a rejected interest. I shall return to this point; but what I have in mind presently need not cause serious discomfort, though it no doubt would strike many as a peculiar interest and a waste of energy. What I have in view is not an addressing of ethical issues as such, but rather a survey to determine what the several social sciences have to say about ethical matters, either directly or indirectly. For example, are ethical issues present in disguise—morality pretending to be science? We can see that the *yes* answer has often been true in the past, and not a few claim it is true now. What would the most

honest, nonideological view reveal? Aside from this question, do the paradigms and tools of the several social sciences offer any handles for ethical inquiry?

Political Science, presumably, would be most centrally involved. And that brings me, inevitably, back to the theme of disjunction: what are the consequences for both Political Science and Public Administration, more broadly, *politics* and *administration,* of the fact that politics reached self-awareness in classical Greece and administration not until the late nineteenth century—this despite the fact that, even (especially?) in small and simple polities, politics and administration were inevitably intermingled.

The other social sciences, even Anthropology, need also to be surveyed. "Even Anthropology?"—an argument could be made that its determined lack of normativeness plus its comparativeness make it particularly germane. Sociology—beginning with its ancestry in Montesquieu and others, and certainly decisively in Comte, Spencer, Durkheim, Weber, Parsons, and other major figures—is rich with relevant material; whether in spite of or because of its scientific stance is hard to say. And Economics? One should not, of course, be put off with its scientific aura and impressive technical apparatus. Adam Smith, in his own view and that of his contemporaries, was a moral philosopher; and Irving Kristol has recently reminded us that Smith's *An Inquiry into the Nature and Causes of the Wealth of Nations* was not intended as a defense of the *morality* of free enterprise. Economics, both in what it attends to and in what it refuses to attend to, in the behavior it licenses and in the behavior it forbids, is very central to any inquiry into ethical conduct in administration: As a random illustration, the recent realization that noxious waste chemicals simply have been dumped in tens of thousands of locations. What sins are committed in the name of externalities and exogenous variables?

Third, ethics as a self-aware enterprise, together with the philosophic matrices from which differing ethical theories are derived, needs to be searched and ordered for the purposes of ethical analysis and judgment in public administration. It may be thought peculiar, to say the least of it, that only well into this discussion ethical theory as such is brought to the fore. But as I view the matter it deserves no high priority. For ethics has little attended to proper behavior in large-scale organization. Its central interests have been elsewhere, tending to oscillate between the probing of traditional relationships such as those of family and friendships and rather abstract and bloodless general principles of conduct. While there is to be sure a great deal in the literature that is relevant, its relevance becomes clear only by extrapolation and application.

Fourth, religion also needs to be surveyed with the object of determining what instruments of navigation it can provide. For our purposes attention should be centered on the Judeo-Christian stream of religious thought and practice, but all major religions should be included. Among the many subjects on which I am not expert are theology and religious history. However, it takes only a little knowledge and understanding to appreciate three things. The first is that theology as such, like ethics to which it is linked in many ways, has attended very little to proper conduct in formal organizations, at least those not religious. Second, as with ethics, there is in theology a great deal that can be made relevant by extrapolation and application. In fact, the writings of Reinhold Niebuhr moved vigorously in this direction; and perhaps I do less than justice to others of whose work I may be unaware. Third, the history and effect of religious institutions and the second, third and X-order effects of religious thought and practice are of so great import for organizational life that one could devote a career to the matter without doing more than explore a few areas. The point is made simply by referring to the work under the heading of Protestant Ethic.

The Pyramid Puzzle

Not surprisingly, many of the most interesting and significant questions concerning administration and ethics concern the theory and practice of hierarchy. Some of these questions are generic, in the sense that they apply to business and nonprofit private organizations as well as to public administration. But some have a special relevance to public administration, as they concern governmental institutions and political ideology. It will be instructive to focus briefly on this pyramid puzzle in the public context.

Central, at least to my own interest, is the fact that hierarchy is represented both as a force for morality and a source of immorality. Both cases are familiar to us, though perhaps not in the context of ethics.

The affirmative case has it that hierarchy is a force that works both for the soft values of democracy and the hard values of effectiveness, efficiency, and economy; indeed, that the achievement of the soft and hard values is complementary, not two things but a single thing. This is a central theme of old-line Public Administration, and the reasoning and conclusions are familiar: Democracy is, realistically, achievable only if power is concentrated so that it can be held accountable, and this is possible only through hierarchy. Otherwise, responsibility bleeds into the social surround. The devices for focusing citizen attention so that it could be made effective—devices such as the short ballot and party reform—were part of the old-line package. Responsibility was viewed as owed upward, subordinate to superordinate, to the top of the pyramid, then bridged over by the electoral principle to the people. Authority was viewed as moving the other direction, upward from the people through their elected representative, then bridged over to the top of the pyramid and descending, echelon by echelon, to every officer and employee.

That this way of viewing things has considerable logic and force strikes me as self-evident. It is plausibly, though hardly unarguably, based on Constitution and history, and can be bolstered with much evidence. It can be, and has been, buttressed by arguments from foreign experience and from business practice. Able and honorable persons have supported the main tenets of the argument. Thus Paul Appleby in his *Morality and Administration in Democratic Government:*[3] The hierarchical principle forwards effective government, but above all it is necessary to democratic government, insuring through its operation the triumph of the general interest over special interests. Thus Marver Bernstein in "Ethics in Government: The Problems in Perspective,"[4] arguing that serious ethical irregularities as well as inefficiencies are all but assured through the absence of hierarchical control in the arrangements for some regulatory agencies, which create conflicts of interest or in effect make the regulatory agencies captives of the interests to be regulated. Thus Victor Thompson in his *Without Sympathy or Enthusiasm: The Problem of Administrative Compassion,*[5] where he argues that the prescriptions for participation equal an invitation for the unauthorized to steal the "tool" of administration from its "owners," the public.

The case against hierarchy in turn has considerable logic and force. It also has roots in Constitution and history, and can be bolstered with much evidence. In this case persons who are able and honorable have stressed the contradictions involved in using hierarchy as a means of promoting democracy, the limitations of hierarchy as a means of achieving effectiveness and efficiency, and its complicity in forwarding immorality. Thus Vincent Ostrom in this *The Intellectual Crisis in American Public Administration,*[6] arguing the spuriousness of the case for centralization, and the greater democracy achievable by organizing public administration into smaller units more in accord with "consumer" will and control. Thus the advocates of a New Public Administration,[7] who take social equity as guiding principle and seek to achieve it "proactively," through client-oriented and client-involving devices. Thus F. William Howton—quoted in one of the epigraphs[8]—who speaks for many who believe that hierarchy with its accustomed corollaries creates deformed humans with deadened consciences. Thus Frederick Thayer in his *An End to Hierarchy! An End to Competition!*[9] who finds hierarchy implicated in immorality as well as promoting inefficiency, and necessarily to be abolished if there is to be a tolerable future—indeed, perhaps, a *future.*

My aim is not to weigh the arguments, much less render a verdict, but rather to emphasize the tangle of ethical problems in and related to the principle and practice of hierarchy; this by way of illustrating the central position of ethical concerns in our professional business—whether or not we care to attend to them *as* ethical questions. But before passing on, let me pose one question that many would regard as the paramount one: What difference does democracy make with respect to the morality of actions taken by government? Rousseau, if I understand him correctly, argued that while the people can be *mistaken,* they cannot be *wrong.* Two examples to ponder, the first from history, the second hypothetical. (1) If the bombing of Haiphong was "immoral," was the firebombing of Hamburg and Dresden—which was massively greater—also immoral? If not, why not? (2) If the Holocaust had been carried out under a democratic government rather than a dictatorship, would an Eichmann have been any more or less immoral? In reflecting on this, bear in mind Herman Finer's notable essay on "Administrative Responsibility in Government,"[10] in which he holds with regard to the public servant: "The first commandment is subservience."

Observations and Reflections

The spirit and nature of this discussion was indicated by the [essay] subtitle, A Prologue to a Preface. At most I can hope to point to some of the matters that would be worthy of attention in a more serious and systematic inquiry. In conclusion, the following further observations and reflections. I shall proceed discontinuously, serially.

FIRST

The twentieth century has hardly been distinguished either by its observance of agreed moral codes or by its concentration on ethical inquiry. On the contrary, it has been distinguished by a "decay" of traditional moral codes, a widespread feeling that morality is "relative" if not utterly meaningless, and a disposition to regard ethical inquiry as frivolous, irrelevant. These currents of thought and feeling have been associated with a "falling away" from religious belief and a concomitant rise of "belief" in science and its philosophical—or anti-philosophical—aura.

These developments have coincided with the Organizational Revolution: an unprecedented increase in the variety, number, size, and power of organizations, at the center of which is government, public administration. It has coincided also, and relatedly, with the arrival of administrative self-awareness, with a new type of "scientific" interest in administrative study and a resulting increase in administrative technology.

So we confront this historical situation: Just at the time the organizational world is thickening and thus the need for ethical guidance increasing, not only does old morality erode but no serious effort is made to create new codes of conduct appropriate to the new situation; and the scientific mentality that is largely responsible for the Organizational Revolution simultaneously makes it difficult to take ethical matters seriously.

SECOND

In no country does the level of conscious ethical conduct in government reach the level of complex reality, but the United States may have one problem to an unusual degree. It has often been observed that Americans tend to view morality very heavily if not exclusively in sexual and pecuniary terms: in the public area, Elizabeth Rays on payrolls and Tongsun Parks passing envelopes of currency behind closed doors.

As I see it, a concern for *public* morality must indeed include a concern with the ordinary garden varieties of sexual and pecuniary misconduct within or affecting public life; we would have to be ignorant of history and oblivious to contemporary political life to think otherwise. However, as even my few shallow probes indicate, the matter of ethically proper conduct reaches far, far beyond the popular images of sex and money. It presents problems of conduct for which traditional morality, growing in and shaped to simpler times, provides little guidance. Or worse, it provides *mis*guidance.

THIRD

Some of the better writings bearing on our subject emphasize the prevalence, perhaps even the necessity, of "moral ambiguity" in organizational life. Thus Stephen Bailey in his "Ethics and the Public Service";[11] I refer back to the epigraph from this essay emphasizing the "contextuality" of good and evil. Thus Melville Dalton in his *Men Who Manage,*[12] who concluded that persons from a middle-class background are more likely to become successful managers than persons from a working-class background, not because of superior ability or technical skill but because of a socialization that better prepares them to cope with moral ambiguity.

If we cannot *clarify* the ethics of the organizational world, perhaps it will help if we can advance *understanding* of the complexity and confusion. If ambiguity cannot be eliminated, then a "tolerance for ambiguity" becomes an essential operating skill. A *moral* quality as well as an operating skill? I shall not try to answer that.

FOURTH

The following seems to be true, almost axiomatically: Moral complexity increases as memberships in organizations increase; persons in formal organizations in addition to traditional/nonformal organizations face greater moral complexity than those only in the latter; those in formal *public* organizations face more moral complexity than those in nonpublic organizations; and moral complexity increases as responsibilities in an administrative hierarchy increase.

If this is a correct view, then high-placed administrators (managers, executives) in public organizations are at the very center of ethical complexity. In this connection I refer you to the probing of morality in relation to administration in Chester Barnard's *The Functions of the Executive*[13]—from which comes the epigraph at the head of this chapter. *The Functions* is of course widely and correctly viewed as a seminal work. But it is a commentary on the interests of the past generation that this discussion of morality has been generally ignored.

Barnard believed that "moral creativeness" was an essential executive function. As the quoted sentence indicates, he believed also that the burden assumed could lead to moral breakdown. In a similar vein Stephen Bailey, in the essay cited in observation Third above, uses the metaphor "above the timber line" to signify the severe moral climate in which the high executive must operate and the dangers to which he is exposed.

FIFTH

We have recently seen, and we presently see, the growth of a gray area, an area in which any clear distinction between the categories of *public* and *private* disappears, disappears in a complex and subtle blending of new organizational modes and legal arrangements. In this gray area, hierarchy is diminished, but does not disappear; new lateral and diagonal relationships grow up and operate along with it, making it formally and operationally difficult to answer the question: Who's in charge here?

As I view it, our ethical problems are compounded in this growing gray world. Who will be responsible for what to whom? In what will duty consist and by what can honesty be judged? One view is that, with hierarchy relaxed and freedom increased, the way is open for the development of authentic *personal* morality. Harlan Cleveland seeks a solution in the hope and prescription that managers in the "horizontal"[14] world that is emerging will regard themselves as "public managers"—because in fact they will be. I confess that on most days I find it hard to share either of these two varieties of optimism.

SIXTH

As the epigraph from David Bradley and Roy Wilkie indicates, "the raising of moral considerations" in the study of organizations has not been popular. Indeed, the chapter on Morality and Organizations in their *The Concept of Organization*[15] is, to my knowledge, without a parallel in the scores of general treatments of organizational behavior or theory.

A number of factors, some pertaining to American public affairs and without need of mention, and some pertaining to the general climate of our intellectual life that are beyond explicating here,

suggest that there may be a change in the situation, that we will begin to address seriously the ethical dimensions of our organizational world—here I allow myself a bit of optimism. This may be best done—perhaps it can be done only—by working from the empirical base legitimated in recent social science. It might begin, for example, with map-making, along the lines suggested earlier. Later, just possibly, we may be able to address the ethical as such.

One point of view has it that ethical inquiry is dangerous. Samuel Butler put it this way: "The foundations of morality are like all other foundations: if you dig too much about them, the superstructure will come tumbling down." But in our case, the digging has been done; the superstructure is already down. But then, the old superstructure was not to our purpose anyway. Perhaps on a new foundation we can use some of the fallen materials to build a superstructure that *is* to our purpose?

Notes

1. Certainly Robert T. Golembiewski's *Men, Management, and Morality: Towards a New Organizational Ethic* (New York: 1965) is an able and useful work, and I do not wish to demean it. But the picture in my mind is of a work even broader in scope, one taking into account developments of the past decade. Neither do I mean to slight the useful work of Wayne A. R. Leys, done when ethics was *really* unfashionable: *Ethics and Social Policy* (New York: 1946), and *Ethics for Policy Decisions: The Art of Asking Deliberative Questions* (New York: 1952).

2. The analysis set forth in this section is a brief version of that in my "Reflections on Public Morality" (*6 Administration and Society* [November 1974], pp. 267–282).

3. Paul Appleby, *Morality and Administration in Democratic Government* (Baton Rouge, La.: 1952).

4. Marver Bernstein, "Ethics in Government: The Problems in Perspective" (*61 National*

Civic Review [July 1972], pp. 341–347).

5. Victor Thompson, *Without Sympathy or Enthusiasm: The Problem of Administrative Compassion* (University, Ala.: 1975).

6. Vincent Ostrom, *The Intellectual Crisis in American Public Administration* (University, Ala.: 1973).

7. See the symposium, H. George Frederickson, ed., "Social Equity and Public Administration" (*34 Public Administration Review* [January/February 1974], pp. 1–51).

8. F. William Howton, *Functionaries* (Chicago: 1969).

9. Frederick C. Thayer, *An End to Hierarchy! An End to Competition! Organizing the Politics and Economics of Survival* (New York: 1973).

10. Herman Finer, "Administrative Responsibility in Democratic Government" (*1 Public Administration Review* [Summer 1941], pp. 335–350).

11. Stephen Bailey, "Ethics and the Public Service" (*23 Public Administration Review* [December 1964], pp. 234–243).

12. Melville Dalton, *Men Who Manage* (New York: 1959).

13. Chester Barnard, *The Functions of the Executive* (Cambridge, Mass.: 1947). See especially Chapter 17, The Nature of Executive Responsibility.

14. Harlan Cleveland, *The Future Executive: A Guide for Tomorrow's Managers* (New York: 1972).

15. David Bradley and Roy Wilkie, *The Concept of Organization: An Introduction to Organizations* (Glasgow: 1974).

☐ CASE STUDY 16

Introduction

Dwight Waldo's foregoing essay treated readers to a broad-brush overview of the modern complicated ethical terrain confronting public administrators. Rather than *one* code, he "maps" a dozen (or more) competing ethical obligations to which administrators must be loyal. How in fact does an administrator choose among these codes and decide which one or several to adhere to? How do administrators juggle these competing demands? Prioritize them? Decide which one or several that they owe their ultimate allegiance to? Especially when "the answers" are not clear-cut, nor even the "questions," as is true in many difficult administrative problems?

In the following interesting case study by Professor Douglas F. Morgan of Lewis and Clark College, we can see in a concrete way the central ethical dilemmas of modern public administration that Waldo's essay outlined in theory. The case recounts the moral quandary posed for public librarians because of vocal complaints from patrons over the circulation of a book, Madonna's *Sex*. Professor Morgan outlines how the controversy began and describes the three different kinds of responses to this issue made by libraries across America. He stresses how the librarians' professional association, the American Library Association, especially its Office of Intellectual Freedom, played a critical role shaping the choices made by individual libraries. As he concludes:

> The Madonna controversy provides us with an important lesson to ponder about the problem of administrative role ambiguity. This problem cannot be solved without some way of ordering the multiplicity of claims that are made upon our career

public servants. Librarians in the Madonna case and in other censorship efforts have been largely successful in undertaking this ordering process. They have done so by relying on a strong professional ethos, an organizational standard bearer to help educate its members into first principles, and concrete administrative strategies for translating first principles into plans of action.

As you review this case study, consider some of these questions:

Why is it difficult for librarians to develop clear-cut policies for dealing with the circulation of books like Madonna's *Sex*?

What were the three varieties of administrative responses libraries around the United States used in handling this issue? Their criteria for dealing with it and your evaluation of the applied administrative criteria?

How did the official librarian professional association, the ALA, help individual libraries sort out their choices? Why were professional standards so influential in this case?

Which of Waldo's ethical codes were used to resolve this problem? Does Waldo's point about the emphasis upon "sex" and "money" in ethical considerations in the public sector, particularly in America, have relevance to this case study? And if so, why do both topics tend to stir up intense controversies?

Madonna's *Sex*

DOUGLAS F. MORGAN

"Some are born great; some achieve greatness; some have greatness thrust upon them." It is in this way that librarians have become a censor of literature. . . . Books that distinctly commend what is wrong, that teach how to sin and how pleasant sin is, sometimes with and sometimes without the added sauce of impropriety, are increasingly popular, tempting the author to imitate them, the publishers to produce, the bookseller to exploit. Thank Heaven they do not tempt the librarian (quoted in ALA, Manual, p. xvi).

—*Arthur E. Bostwick, ALA President, 1908*

"Madonna's *Sex*" by Douglas F. Morgan from *Administrative Theory & Praxis*, 15 (2), 1993. Copyright © 1993 by Public Administration Theory Network (PAT-Net). Reprinted by permission.

Susan Miller was completing the final routines of the day at the library circulation desk when she was suddenly confronted by an angry father accompanied by his 14-year old son who had just picked up a book held on reserve in his name.

"What's going on here?", the patron asked as he thrust the book into the face of the librarian. "Don't you restrict things like this from circulating to minors? Why is this kind of book even in the library in the first place? It clearly is unfit reading!"

This is not what you needed to hear at this time of day. As the Head of Public Services, two of your clerks failed to appear for work because of icy road conditions. That did not seem to stop the hoards of school children who flocked to the library to pass the time of day. As a result of having to work without a rest-break checking out books all day at the circulation desk, you will have to spend the evening completing your budget request for the next fiscal year in order to meet the 8:00 AM deadline set by your Library Director.

As a children's librarian by training, you deeply resent all of the endless administrative work that takes you away from what you most enjoy and have been best prepared to carry out—selecting and recommending good literature to children and their parents. Increasingly, you've been having second thoughts about whether you are really cut out for your current environment. There is just too much time spent on keeping track of clerical routines, doing budget preparation, undertaking personnel evaluations, and responding to patrons' complaints. As you fantasized about what it might be like to work in a larger library system where you could make more use of the professional knowledge and skills for which you have been trained, you are suddenly jolted out of your fantasizing by a distraught parent who insists that you, not he, should make the choices about what is suitable reading for his son.

You notice that the book is a copy of Madonna's *Sex,* a series of personal poses taken by a well-known photographer who erotically captures the pop star's sexual fantasies. The photo album has been on the *New York Times* best seller list for the past four weeks and there is a backlog of 57 reserve requests. You've dealt with this kind of situation before, so you politely give the Library's standardized response:

> "We encourage parents to help their children select material that is appropriate to their interests and level of reading skill. Could I help you find a more suitable book?" "That's not the point. The public tax dollars should not be used to support this kind of material. It contains graphic pornographic illustrations and encourages a lifestyle that is socially devastating. Moreover, you have a special responsibility to protect our young people from getting access to this kind of material at the taxpayer's expense."

As the line of patrons waiting to check out books begins to build, you see that your efforts are not going to prevail. So you resort to another technique that has usually worked in the past. You ask the angry patron to formally file his objections on a special complaint form the library has prepared for this purpose.

That did not end the matter. The following week the Director of the Library hands you the completed complaint form from Charles Jones, the angry father who had confronted you about Madonna's *Sex.* The Director requests you to draft a reply that can be sent out under the Library Director's signature.

As you think about what to do, all kinds of questions begin to run into a swirling eddy in your mind. Is the complaint from Jones a part of an organized campaign within the community to determine what the library purchases? Does the new Director wish to have such complaints handled the same way they have been handled in the past? How should the occasion be used to edify two new members of the Board that have recently been appointed? Is it really time to move, even though not a particularly good time in terms of the economy and your personal family situation?

You go to your file drawer and pull out a copy of the last letter the former director sent to an angry patron under similar circumstances. What should you do?

Administrative Fantasies and Role Ambiguity

Sue Miller's moral dilemma is fertile ground for those concerned with the ethical basis of administrative discretion. The practical consequences of deciding whether to purchase a book like Madonna's *Sex* and how to make it available to patrons provides a pedagogically rich opportunity to explore the meaning of integrity (Benjamin, 1990; Dobel, 1990), and the conflict among personal, professional, and organizational claims. For some library employees Madonna's *Sex* presented them with the moral dilemma of facilitating the circulation of material they found personally objectionable. Some even requested alterations in their work assignments, using as leverage the employer's legal requirement to make "reasonable accommodations". These circumstances provide rich fodder to explore questions of prudence, integrity, compromise, exit, voice, and loyalty. In short, they provide an opportunity to examine the appropriate substantive standards that ought to guide the exercise of administrative discretion. However, in this [essay] I am primarily interested in using the Madonna controversy to explore the institutional conditions (both organizational and professional) necessary to translate principles of right action into effective administrative practice. For the remainder of this [essay], I will assume that the professional librarian is not in doubt about the professional moral standards (hereafter referred to as stewardship principles) that ought to guide the exercise of her discretion and that these standards are not in conflict with her personal ethical beliefs.

Even when a career administrator is confident about the "right thing to do", frequently there is a large abyss between the cup of stewardship belief and the lip of institutional action. For example, under the circumstances described above, libraries and their administrative agents have a variety of options that may be equally consistent with stewardship principles. Some may use the controversy to avoid organizational risk, to temporize and forestall, or to shift decision making responsibility somewhere else in the administrative and political process. Others may choose to mobilize constituency support, or to redefine the universe of moral discourse, or to educate and edify citizens within the community. Choices about which of these courses of action best reflect the responsible exercise of one's stewardship obligations greatly depend on the influence of mediating organizational and professional conditions.

Much of the recent literature on administrative ethics agrees on the need to ground the exercise of bureaucratic discretion on some larger stewardship principles (Kass, 1991; Rohr, 1986, 1989; Morgan and Kass, 1991; Spicer & Terry, 1993; Stivers, 1993). While helping to clarify the content and locus of stewardship obligation, this literature does not help us understand the social, organizational, and professional mediating processes that enable these principles to be translated into effective action. On the other hand, those who have shed light on the conditions for effective moral action within social and organizational settings, tend to leave career administrators at sea about the higher stewardship obligations these conditions are intended to serve (Hummel, 1982; McGregor, 1967; Likert, 1961; Weisband & Frank, 1975). The role of librarians in the Madonna controversy allows us to explore this linkage between stewardship principles and the mediating conditions for effective moral practice.

There are at least three reasons why librarians and local public libraries are particularly useful in exploring the linkage between principles of "right thinking" and the conditions for "right action". First, libraries, along with schools, reflect as well as shape the social construction of meaning within local communities. Second, professional librarians participate in this process of "making social meaning" with the kind of formal professional training that does not differ in significant respects from that received by most public sector career administrators. Finally, both librarians and libraries are greatly influenced by the American Library Association's growing role in shaping the meaning of censorship controversies in cases like Madonna's *Sex*.

Local libraries, especially in smaller communities, are about as close as we get today to the politics of the Greek agora. They are the chief organizational venues for reading programs, communal forums, and cultural activities that foster a commonly shared sense of community. They occupy a morally tender place in the soul of a community and depend on the financial sustenance of local citizens to keep them in operation. It is not surprising, then, that they occasionally become the lightening rod within local communities for differences of opinion about the meaning of democratic governance.

Over the last several years local differences of opinion over what books libraries should purchase and to whom they should be made available have dramatically increased. From September 1, 1990 through April 15, 1993, the Office of Intellectual Freedom of the American Library Association received 1,577 reports of challenges to library materials. In the 1991 calendar year there were 512 reported cases. This grew to 653 cases in calendar year 1992, a 28% increase. In the first four months of 1993, there were 253 reported cases (ALA, Office of Intellectual Freedom, May 1990). If that pace continues throughout 1993, reported challenges will have doubled within the past two years. How much of this increase is a result of increased reporting and how much from increases in attempts to censor is impossible to determine. However, library professionals agree that attempts by community groups to censor the purchase and dissemination of local library materials have sharply increased in recent years.

Since libraries are expected to reflect the needs of their citizens and protect the right of access to ideas for all users, they cannot easily hide from disgruntled patrons who do not like the books they purchase. Since a library can not remain a library without purchasing books, and since no library has unlimited financial resources to purchase everything that is published, choices have to be made. Why shouldn't community acceptability be a key book selection standard, especially when the majority of the community foots the bill? The answer is not so easy and so obvious as is reflected in the responses of libraries in the Madonna controversy. Institutional responses to complaints about the acquisition of *Sex* have ranged all the way from not purchasing the book, to removing it once purchased, to vigorously defending the purchase in the face of protracted public opposition, to making alterations in priorities (if not policies) in order to enable parents to have more control over what their children read.

A second reason the controversy over Madonna's *Sex* is so interesting to students of administrative discretion is that librarians are like most trained professionals. They graduate from professional school, having spent more time learning the techniques and skills of good librarianship than acquiring a clear understanding of the ends these skills are intended to serve. Like most career bureaucrats, they arrive at positions of discretionary administrative authority without much prior training and education about their larger leadership role within and to the local communities they serve. But by virtue of living within a local glass house, in the words of Alan Bostwick, they have the opportunity for greatness to be "thrust upon them". In fact, they frequently are unable to avoid this opportunity.

Finally, professional librarians carry out their work under the guiding mantel of the First Amendment, the principles of which are reflected in a Library Bill of Rights which simultaneously opposes censorship and aggressively promotes the acquisition and dissemination of materials that provide "for the interest, information, and enlightenment of all people of the community the library serves" (ALA, Manual, p. 3). Taken literally, these words seem to make even a smidgen of community interest sufficient justification for the purchase, display, and dissemination of library resources, however unpopular they may be. Yet local libraries, like schools, are political entities controlled and funded by officials who are selected with an expectation that they will be responsive to the will of the community. This expectation has taken on greater poignancy in recent years as taxpayers have become ever more vigilant in guarding their tax dollars. A group of citizens who threaten to withhold its support in the next levy election until Madonna's *Sex* or some other objectionable material is removed from the Library has to be taken seriously! In doing so, there are at least two questions of interest to students of administrative discretion. What influence does a professional association standard like the Library Bill of Rights have on shaping the universe of local moral discourse? Second, what lessons can be learned from this controversy about rendering various notions of "constitutional stewardship" useful practical guides to the exercise of administrative discretion?

Madonna's *Sex:* Patterns of Administrative Response

The controversy began on October 21, 1992 when Madonna's much publicized *Sex* was released for sale. The book was a mylar-wrapped, spiral-bound series of photographs portraying the sexual fantasies of the exhibitionist pop star in revealing and erotic poses. Advance reviews of the book were non existent, since no pre-publication copies were released. With a hefty price tag of $49.95 and a fragile binding, librarians were compelled to decide whether or not to purchase the book based on the publicity surrounding it and/or patron requests. In many places, such requests were extremely large, as tends to be the case with most highly publicized best sellers. But in the case of *Sex*, more often than not requests for the book were accompanied by an equal number of requests to remove or restrict it (ALA Newsletter, Jan. 1993, p. 1). The administrative dilemma this presented for local librarians was nicely summarized by Judith Krug, Director of the ALA, Office of Intellectual Freedom. If libraries refused to buy the book, it would appear to be censorship, since there was surely patron demand; if they bought a lot of copies for circulation, however, these might be stolen or damaged. Many libraries chose to buy just one or two copies to keep on reserve, but this often sparked as much opposition and criticism as if the library had purchased dozens of copies to satisfy demand (ALA Newsletter, Jan. 1993, p. 1). Libraries responded to this dilemma with three different patterns of administrative action.

1. "Just Say No" or Emptio Interuptus

Ironically, Madonna's home town of Rochester Hills, Michigan, was one of the cities where the decision not to purchase *Sex* did not raise a controversy. "We don't see it as an essential purchase," said public library director Christine Hage, "and because of the cost we wouldn't just buy it without the interest. We meet public demand; if the public is curious, this is a good use of public money. I guess the public isn't interested" (American Libraries, December, 1992).

But what should a library director do when confronted with a large public demand for the book? To what extent should demand be tempered by considerations of whether a book passes some kind of cost-benefit or good buy test, an external consensus about quality, or the appropriateness of the content for the collection? Typical of many library directors facing these kind of questions, Ralph Edwards, Director of the Phoenix public library waited until reviews of the book began to appear and then decided the book wasn't worth buying. "If you've read the reviews, you know they're all bad. We decided it didn't have sufficient artistic quality or content quality to make it worth spending $50 a shot on" (Phoenix Gazette, October 29, 1993). In Scottsdale, Arizona, library director Linda Saferite concluded that the spiral binding would not survive repeated circulations (Scottsdale Progress, October 30, 1992). In Glendale, Arizona, library director Rodeane Widom reported that she didn't have the budget to spend on a photo book whose photographer "is not anyone who was given any real acclaim" (Arizona Republic, October 29, 1993).

In Mesa, Arizona the book provoked substantial controversy after library director Vince Anderson revealed that he had placed an order for it. After receiving hundreds of complaints about the decision, the library director canceled the order at the request of Mesa Mayor Willie Wong. The mayor reported that when he got up October 27th and saw a newspaper story about the library purchase, he thought, "My career is over. I'm dead meat. I had to take the community into consideration, although I'm a strong supporter of the First Amendment. My feeling is that the community is not in support of Madonna's book. So I canceled the order." Asked why he did not refer the book to the review committee, Wong said, "I'm not really sure how we purchase books. All I know is this particular book is very controversial" (Mesa Tribune, October 27, 28, 1992).

The chair of the Mesa Library Advisory Board, Fred Missel, complained "that a precedent has been set regarding censorship and the library. . . . I will abide by [Wong's] decision, but there is a broader issue at work here. I'm concerned that the process of the community evaluating itself had been taken away" (Mesa Tribune, October 29, 1992).

In Colorado Springs, Colorado, after three days of answering over 400 angry telephone calls, Pikes Peak Library officials decided to cancel the library's order for the Madonna book. Many callers threatened to vote against a November 3rd bond issue that would raise $8 million for physical improvements at a library branch. Following its normal protocol the library had ordered the book after four patrons requested it. After the order was placed, an additional 73 patrons requested the book before the order was cancelled.

Library director Bernie Margolis said that officials didn't buckle under to pressure from "any narrowly focused perspective", but he did acknowledge that the scores of irate callers influenced the decision. "Certainly," he said, "the calls help us gauge the importance of the items to the community." Margolis claimed that the bond issue was not a factor in the decision. "I think we would have sacrificed the winning of a bond issue to stand up for the First Amendment," he said. "In my personal view, this book is not worth fighting for. I believe, personally, that it's pornography." Margolis said the book was rejected because it did not meet the library's purchasing criteria (Colorado Springs Gazette-Telegraph, October 20, 21, 23, 1992). The library bond issue did not pass.

2. Making Madonna's *Sex* Safe

Some libraries were willing to permit Madonna's *Sex* to enter the library doors, but not to allow its easy exit. Some of the justification for restricted access was based on the fragile quality of the book's binding and some was based on the appropriateness of the contents for minors. Most libraries restrict circulation of various materials, including reference books, expensive art portfolios, and similar items that are expensive and/or have heavy short-term demand. However, restricted access, as opposed to noncirculation, is undertaken less frequently, usually because of the need to pass First Amendment tests.

The controversy over restricted access was especially heated in Houston and Austin, Texas. In Houston, a group called Citizens Against Pornography (CAP) began to mobilize when it became known that the library had ordered four copies of the controversial book for its main branch, using an anonymous donation. Two copies of the book were to be shelved in the Fine Arts section and available for circulation. The other two copies were to be shelved in the reference section for library use only. Citing a 1978 City Council Resolution on community standards, CAP President, Geneva Kirk Brooks called on Mayor Bob Lanier to halt the purchase. The group also called for the resignation of Library Director, David Henington. "Some of the worst pornography is in our libraries and schools," Brooks declared.

On November 24 Brooks led about a dozen people to a City Council meeting where they angrily called on lawmakers to remove the book or face recall. "If some slut performed the same acts on the streets of Houston, she'd be arrested, so why should we let Madonna perform the same vulgarity on the shelves of our public library?" asked one of the participants. Another observed that "the likes of Thomas Jefferson, James Madison, et al. never in their wildest imaginations envisioned a foul-mouthed, trashy woman masturbating with a crucifix," and concluded by calling on the city's vice squad to shut the library down (Houston Chronicle, November 11, 25, 27, 1992).

As the demonstrators cajoled the council, a review of the book by a special library committee was already underway, following receipt of a formal request to reconsider it. On December 2, the committee decided and Library Director Henington agreed to restrict in-library access to adults only (Houston Chronicle, December 2, 1992).

In Austin, library officials were compelled to restrict access to *Sex* after Travis County Attorney Ken Oden issued an opinion declaring that it was illegal for minors to see the book. Prior to this opinion the Austin libraries had added *Sex* to their collections on November 12. Library Director, Brenda Branch had decided to limit access to Madonna's *Sex* by keeping copies behind the circulation desk and requiring reviewers to present a photo identification listing their address in order to prevent theft or damage to the book. Her decision drew protests from the community, including Mayor Bruce Todd, who said he objected to minors having access to the book "because these types of publications exploit women." The next day, Library Director Branch changed her opinion, saying the library would review its open access policy with respect to Madonna's work. That review was rendered moot by County Attorney Oden's opinion.

Oden issued an opinion on the legality of circulating Madonna's *Sex* to minors after Austin police vice officers asked whether the book could be classified as pornography. Oden responded to the police request with an official opinion, declaring that "in our community this publication is legal for adults, but it is not legal for sale, distribution or display to children unless the child is accompanied by a consenting parent or guardian. . . . There is really no distinction between public libraries or private businesses. The government has no greater right to sell, display or distribute this material than private businesses have. . . . We would prosecute any public or private organization which chose after notice of the grand jury ruling to continue to provide the publication to children." (Austin American-Statesman, November 26, December 1, 1992).

In Ingham County, Michigan, restricted access has been raised to a highly developed administrative art. Parents can fill out a form requesting specific titles or subjects that are approved for their children. If staff are in doubt, they must call the parent and receive explicit permission for the material to be checked out. These forms must be filed in each of the system's five separate branches and renewed each year.

3. Unrestricted Access: Madonna's *Sex* May Be Had for the Price of a Library Card

Many libraries throughout the United States relied on their existing selection policies and principles of unrestricted access to purchase Madonna's *Sex* and circulate it to anyone with a library card. Some of these libraries have faced spirited challenges from angry patrons. One of the most extreme attacks occurred in Monroe County, Michigan. In the face of angry citizens demanding the removal of Madonna's *Sex* after it had been ordered and placed on unrestricted access, the Monroe County Library Board voted to retain the Madonna book, supporting unrestricted access. Both the library Director, Gordon Conable, and the library board chair, Judith See, were asked to resign and received threatening and harassing phone calls both at their homes and places of work from angry members of the community. There were even terrorist threats to the library, which resulted in evacuation and temporary closure (Office of Intellectual Freedom, "Memorandum," March 1993).

One of the more bizarre twists on the Monroe County tale is that the Board Chair, Judith See, an employee of the Agricultural Extension Service and a program director of local 4-H programs, was pressured by her employer/supervisor to submit her resignation as Board Chair. After doing so, pressure was exerted by high level sources within national Republican Party circles on local county board commissioners to refuse to accept Judith See's resignation. They did so and Judith See continued as Board Chair. But there is an uneasy peace in Monroe County. The elected District Attorney has threatened to issue an opinion similar to the one prepared by the County Prosecutor in Austin, Texas, which classifies Madonna's *Sex* as pornographic, thus making it illegal to disseminate to minors under 18 without explicit parental consent ("Interview with Gordon Conable", Director, Monroe County Library, April 2, 1993).

Impact of ALA's Office of Intellectual Freedom

When faced with the extreme attacks and hard-ball political pressures described in the above section, library directors and their Boards turned to lawyers for official legal opinions. Most of these opinions indicated that Madonna's *Sex* did not meet the constitutional standard of obscenity for minors. However, these opinions did not necessarily improve the librarian's ability to carry on a dialogue with angry members of the community, or for that matter, stand tall in the face of strident community opposition. Of greater assistance in this regard was the American Library Association's Office of Intellectual Freedom.

Throughout the Madonna controversy, the Office of Intellectual Freedom provided its local members with information, guidance, and, most important of all, an ethical compass from which to take and keep their bearing. Through a variety of communication sources the American Library Association and its affiliated offices have constantly reminded its members that their primary mission is to promote and defend intellectual freedom against all forms of censorship.

Compared to most other public professions, this stewardship responsibility is well-developed and reasonably well defined. While the profession's basic reference source recognizes that the philosophy of intellectual freedom is too young to be rooted in tradition, . . . it has gained recognition as the substance of the total philosophy shaping library service in the United States. . . . From the standpoint of intellectual freedom, the library's role in our society is not based on the principle of majority rule, but on the principle embodied in the First Amendment, that minority points of view have a right to be heard, no matter how unpopular with or even detested by the majority. (American Library Association, Intellectual Freedom Manual, xxxv, 12, hereafter cited as Manual).

This commitment to intellectual freedom is reflected in the Library Bill of Rights first adopted in 1939 and an Intellectual Freedom Committee (IFC) created in 1940 to recommend policies to safeguard these rights.

Library Bill of Rights

The Library Bill of Rights consists of the following six provisions:

1. Books and other library resources should be provided for interest, information, and enlightenment of all people of the community the library serves. Materials should not be excluded because of origin, background, or views of those contributing to their creation.
2. Libraries should provide materials and information presenting all points of view on current and historical issues. Materials should not be proscribed or removed because of partisan or doctrinal disapproval.
3. Libraries should challenge censorship in the fulfillment of their responsibility to provide information and enlightenment.

4. Libraries should cooperate with all persons and groups concerned with resisting abridgment of free expression and free access to ideas.
5. A person's right to use a library should not be denied or abridged because of origin, age, background, or views.
6. Libraries which make exhibit spaces and meeting rooms available to the public they serve should make such facilities available on an equitable basis, regardless of the beliefs or affiliations of individuals or groups requesting their use.

The Bill of Rights is accompanied by more than 125 pages of interpretive guidelines governing the application of the rights under varying circumstances. These include placing the responsibility on parents for controlling access to materials by minors; opposing labeling or expurgation of library materials; preventing restrictions on access which may place a heavy burden on the homeless, the elderly, the physically handicapped, and other classes with special needs; protecting patron's rights of privacy over law enforcement needs, unless accompanied by a court order; etc.

Taken together the Library Bill of Rights and Interpretative Guidelines promote an absolutist interpretation, or what the *Manual* characterizes as a "purist approach" (xviii), to a reading of the First Amendment to the Constitution. The justification for this interpretation is based on the First Amendment language which states that "Congress shall make no law . . . abridging freedom of speech, or of the press." The *Manual* concedes that there are exceptions to this "purist approach," such as fighting words, obscenity, etc. but the ALA takes the position that the courts and not libraries or their agents should assume responsibility for making these exceptions (Manual, p. 61 ff.).

Office of Intellectual Freedom

What intellectual freedom means in practice is not left to the unguided discretion of individual librarians. In 1967 an Office of Intellectual Freedom (OIF) was established to serve as the educational arm of the IFC. The Office of Intellectual Freedom bears responsibility for educating librarians and the general public on the importance of intellectual freedom, using ALA policies as a guide. The OIF has become a powerful organizational force in cultivating national conformity among librarians to the tenants of intellectual freedom.

The philosophy of the *Office of Intellectual Freedom* is based on the premise that if librarians are to appreciate the importance of intellectual freedom they must first understand the concept as it relates to the individual, the institution, and the functioning of society. Believing that with understanding comes the ability to teach others, OIF maintains a broad program of information publications, projects, and services (Manual, pp. xxii–xxiii).

The OIF publishes a bimonthly *Newsletter on Intellectual Freedom* and a monthly *OIF Memorandum*. In addition, the office prepares special materials, including the *Banned Books Week Resource Kit; The Bill of Rights Bicentennial: A Resource Book,* prepared for use during the 1991 bicentennial celebration of the Bill of Rights; issue-oriented monographs such as *Censorship and Selection: Issues and Answers for Schools;* and *Confidentiality in Libraries: An Intellectual Freedom Modular Education Program.* Each year the OIF publishes a list of books that have been challenged or banned from public and school libraries through local community action. In addition to preparing publications, the OIF consults with librarians confronting potential or actual censorship activities.

Within the scope of this study, it has not been possible to determine the causal significance of the various OIF activities mentioned above in socializing members of the library profession into the meaning of stewardship. For example, at an individual level it would be interesting to examine the impact of the OIF on both the form and substance of the decisions made by individual librarians during the Madonna controversy. At institutional level it would be interesting to examine the number of successful censorship efforts in relationship to the number of library boards that have explicitly adopted the Library Bill of Rights as official board policy. However, there is one measure of impact that is worth mentioning and about which we have some empirical evidence.

According to the Office of Intellectual Freedom, development of a materials selection policy is one of the central factors in helping to fend off censorship attempts by members of the local community.

While "[t]he primary purpose of a materials selection or collection development program is to promote the development of a collection based on institutional goals and user needs . . . , the secondary purpose is service in defending the principles of intellectual freedom (ALA, Manual, 207)." In a recent examination of seven variables affecting successful censorship attempts of local school boards, Dianne McAfee concluded that the use of a materials selection policy "is found most consistently to predict retention" (Hopkins, 1993, p. 66). In another report of these findings, Hopkins recommended what the Office of Intellectual Freedom has been advising library selection specialists for years: "have a board approved materials selection policy which is followed when a challenge occurs; seek support when material is challenged; and before material is reviewed, be sure to have the complaint submitted in writing (ALA, Newsletter, January, 1992, pp 1, 20)."

There are several characteristics of a materials selection policy which strengthen a librarian's ability to fend off censorship attempts. First, the development of the policy and frequent re-examination of what it means provides an opportunity for the organization to educate both its employees and new board members as to the nature of the institution's larger stewardship obligations. This can be especially important for library board members who may be indirectly appointed to their positions, with little prior experience or instruction in the exercise of governmental authority. Second, a concrete selection policy enables abstract principles of stewardship to be institutionalized into the day-to-day routines of the organization, thereby facilitating the transformation of abstract principles into tradition. Third, when disputed cases arise, a materials selection policy helps to structure the universe of discourse away from what is offensive to a particular patron to the contributions of the selection policy to the good of the larger community.

Through its various publications, model policies, and legal support, the Office of Intellectual Freedom has provided those exercising administrative discretion with a mediating institutional structure for defining the meaning of stewardship by linking library policy with constitutional principles. Without this institutional linkage . . . the core philosophy of intellectual freedom could [not] have developed over the past 40 years into the rooted tradition it presently enjoys in the library profession.

Conclusion

The Madonna controversy provides us with an important lesson to ponder about the problem of administrative role ambiguity. This problem cannot be solved without some way of ordering the multiplicity of claims that are made upon our career public servants. Librarians in the Madonna case and in other censorship efforts have been largely successful in undertaking this ordering process. They have done so by relying on a strong professional ethos, an organizational standard bearer to help educate its members into first principles, and concrete administrative strategies for translating first principles into plans of action. The chief lesson we can learn from the Madonna controversy is the need to go beyond our concern for defining the proper catechism for administrative practice and pay equal attention to the mediating social, organizational, and professional structures that transform this catechism into meaningful moral action.

Endnotes

1. Without abandoning responsibility for sins of omission and commission, I wish to especially thank Candace Morgan, Deputy Director, Community Library Services, Fort Vancouver Regional Library, and Chair of the ALA Intellectual Freedom Committee, for her thoughtful comments and corrections of factually inaccurate representations.
2. "Madonna Book Found Legal by Illinois Attorney General", Library Hotline, American Library Association, vol. 22:2. (May 24, 1993).

References

American Library Association, Office of Intellectual Freedom, *Intellectual Freedom Manual,* 4th Edition (Chicago, 1992), p. xvi.

American Library Association, Office of Intellectual Freedom, *Newsletter on Intellectual Freedom,* published bimonthly.

American Library Association, Office of Intellectual Freedom, *Memorandum,* published monthly.

Dobel, J. P. (1990). "Integrity in the public service", *Public Administration Review,* 50(May/June), 354–364.

Hopkins, D. M. (1993). "A conceptual model of factors influencing the outcome of challenges to library materials in secondary school settings." *Library Quarterly,* 63(1), 40–72.

Hummel, R. P. (1987). *The Bureaucratic Experience.* (2nd ed.) New York: St. Martin's Press.

Kass, H. D. (1990). "Stewardship as a fundamental element in images of public administration." In H. D. Kass and B. L. Catron (Eds.), *Images and Identities in Public Administration.* Newbury Park, CA: Sage.

Likert, R. (1961). *New Patterns of Management.* New York: Harper.

McGregor, D. (1967). *The Professional Manager.* New York: McGraw Hill.

Martin, B. (1990). *Splitting the Difference: Compromise and Integrity in Ethics and Politics.* Lawrence, KS: University of Kansas Press.

Morgan, C. (1990). "Whose on first?", *ALKI.* Washington State Library Association: 6: 86.

Morgan, D. & Kass, H. D. (1991). "Legitimizing administrative discretion through constitutional stewardship." In J. S. Bowman (Ed.), *Ethical Frontiers in Public Management.* San Francisco: Jossey-Bass Publishers.

Morgan, D. (1990). "Administrative phronesis: discretion and the problem of administrative legitimacy in our constitutional system." In H. D. Kass and B. L. Catron, ed., *Images and Identities in Public Administration.* Newbury Park, CA: Sage.

Morgan, D. (1993). The public interest. In T. Cooper (Ed.), *Handbook of Public Administration,* 125–146, New York: Marcel Dekker, forthcoming.

Rohr, J. (1986). *To Run a Constitution: The Legitimacy of the Administrative State.* Lawrence, KS: University of Kansas Press.

Rohr, J. (1989). *Ethics for Bureaucrats: An Essay on Law and Values.* (2nd, ed.), New York: Marcel Dekker.

Spicer, M. W. & Terry, L. D. (1993). "Legitimacy, history, and logic: public administration and the constitution." *Public Administration Review,* (May/June), 239–246.

Stiver, C. (1991). *Gender Images in Public Administration: Legitimacy and the Administrative State.* Newbury Park, CA: Sage.

Weisband, E., & Frank, T. M. (1975). *Resignation in Protest: Political and Ethical Choices Between Loyalty to Team and Loyalty to Conscience in American Public Life.* New York: Grossman.

Wildavsky, A. (1984). *The Politics of the Budgetary Process.* 4th ed. Boston, MA: Little Brown.

Chapter 16 Review Questions

1. How would you sum up the advice about ethical behavior in the public office suggested in Waldo's essay? How do his views on the subject differ from those of Chester Barnard, Stephen Bailey, or Paul Appleby, to which the introduction of this chapter refers? Whose approach to ethics in government do you find the more persuasive? Explain your answer.

2. What factors caused Madonna's *Sex* to pose an ethical dilemma for librarians? How did they deal with these problems? What norms or values influenced their actions? Which were the *most* influential and why? Were their choices fundamentally moral and ethical? Why or why not?

3. On the basis of your reading of the case study, would you add any points to Waldo's essay regarding other criteria or standards for correct moral behavior by public officials?

4. Why do issues that arise in government always contain at least some degree of ethical or moral choice? In your opinion, are similar moral choices apparent in decision making in the private sector? Explain your answer.

5. Some observers argue that it is impossible to teach individuals who are preparing for public service careers to be moral and ethical—in other words, family background, religion, personal attitudes, and upbringing have more to do with a person's ethical orientation than does formal educational training. Do you agree? Or, are there ways formal education can inculcate ethical behavior in those persons who may someday fill government posts?

6. Compare and contrast Case Study 1, "The Blast in Centralia No. 5," with Case Study 16 from the standpoint of their ethical lessons for public administrators. Can you extract from the cases a specific list of important lessons for practicing public administrators?

Key Terms

public versus private morality
higher law
ethical obligations
moral complexity

reason of state
the pyramid puzzle
metaphor of maps
ethical theory

Suggestions for Further Reading

Despite the enormous concern recently expressed about this topic, perhaps the most sensitive treatments remain those by earlier theorists: Chester Barnard, *The Functions of the Executive* (Cambridge, Mass.: Harvard University Press, 1938)—especially Chapter 17; Paul H. Appleby, *Morality and Administration in Democratic Government* (Baton Rouge, La.: Louisiana State University Press, 1952); and Frederick C. Mosher, *Democracy and the Public Service,* Second Edition (New York: Oxford University Press, 1982)—especially Chapter 8.

The classic scholarly debate over this subject (though it is couched in terms of responsibility instead of ethics) is between Carl J. Friedrich, "Public Policy and the Nature of Administrative Responsibility," *Public Policy,* 1 (Cambridge, Mass.: Harvard University Press, 1940), pp. 3–24; and Herman Finer, "Administrative Responsibility in Democratic Government," *Public Administra-*

tion Review, 1 (Summer 1941), pp. 335–350. Along with the Friedrich-Finer arguments, which remain highly germane even today, you should also read John M. Gaus, "The Responsibility of Public Administration," in Leonard D. White, *The Frontiers of Public Administration* (Chicago: University of Chicago Press, 1936), pp. 26–44, as well as Arthur A. Maass and Laurence I. Radway, "Gauging Administrative Responsibility," *Public Administration Review,* 9 (Summer 1949), pp. 182–192. For a useful overview of where we are today with research on this topic, read John A. Rohr, "Ethics in Public Administration: A State-of-the-Discipline Report," in Naomi B. Lynn and Aaron Wildavsky, eds., *Public Administration: The State of the Discipline* (Chatham, N.J.: Chatham House, 1990).

For more recent writings that have addressed this subject with varying degrees of success or failure, see John Rohr, *Ethics for Bureaucrats,* Second

Edition (New York: Marcel Dekker, 1988); Sissela E. Bok, *Lying* (New York: Random House, 1979), and *Secrets* (New York: Pantheon, 1983); John P. Burke, *Bureaucratic Responsibility* (Baltimore: The Johns Hopkins Press, 1986). Terry L. Cooper, *An Ethic of Citizenship for Public Administration* (Englewood Cliffs, N.J.: Prentice Hall, 1991); William L. Richter et al., *Combating Corruption/Encouraging Ethics: A Sourcebook for Public Service* (Washington: D.C.: American Society for Public Administration, 1990); Terry L. Cooper, *The Responsible Administration: An Approach to Ethics for the Administrative Role,* Third Edition (San Francisco: Jossey-Bass, 1990); Gerald M. Pops and Thomas J. Paulak, *The Case for Justice* (San Francisco: Jossey-Bass, 1991); David H. Rosenbloom and James D. Carroll, eds., *Towards Constitutional Competence: A Casebook for Public Administrators* (Englewood Cliffs, N.J.: Prentice Hall, 1990); Kathryn G. Denhardt, *The Ethics of Public Service: Resolving Moral Dilemmas in Public Organizations* (New York: Greenwood, 1988); and James Q. Wilson, *The Moral Sense* (New York: Free Press, 1993). In addition, there are several excellent essays, such as Mark T. Lilla, "Ethos, 'Ethics' and Public Service," *The Public Interest,* 63 (Spring 1981), pp. 3–17, or, in the same issue, Thomas C. Schelling, "Economic Reasoning and the Ethics of Policy," pp. 37–61. For other essays, see York Wilbern, "Types and Levels of Public Morality," *Public Administration Review,* 44 (March/April 1984), pp. 102–108; Barbara S. Romzek and Melvin J. Dubnik, "Accountability in the Public Sector: Lessons from the Challenger Tragedy," *Public Administration Review,* 47 (May/June 1987), pp. 227–238; Terry L. Cooper, "Hierarchy, Virtue, and the Practice of Public Administration: A Perspective for Normative Ethics" *Public Administration Review,* 47 (July/August, 1987), pp. 320–328; Dennis F. Thompson, "The Possibility of Administrative Ethics," *Public Administration Review,* 45 (September/October 1985), pp. 555–561; James S. Bowman, "Ethics in Government, A National Survey of Public Administration," *Public Administration Review,* 50 (May/June 1990), pp. 345–353;

J. Patrick Dobel, "Integrity in the Public Service," *Public Administration Review,* 50 (May/June 1990) pp. 354–366; Lloyd G. Nigro and William D. Richardson, "Between Citizen and Administration: Administrative Ethics and *PAR,*" *Public Administration Review,* 50 (November/December 1990), pp. 623–635; Richard T. Green, "Character Ethics and Public Administration," *International Journal of Public Administration,* 17 (1994), pp. 2137–2164; Debra Stewart, "Theoretical Foundations of Ethics in Public Administration: Approaches to Understanding Moral Action," *Administration and Society,* 23 (November 1991), pp. 357–373; Philip H. Jos and Samuel M. Hines, Jr., "Care, Justice and Public Administration," *Administration and Society,* 25 (November 1993), pp. 373–392; Lewis Mainzer, "Vulgar Ethics for Public Administration," *Administration and Society,* 23 (May 1991), pp. 3–28; Louis C. Gawthrop, "The Ethical Foundations of American Public Administration," *International Journal of Public Administration,* 16 (1993), pp. 139–163; Dennis Wittmer, "Ethical Sensitivity and Managerial Decision-Making: An Experiment," *Journal of Public Administration Research and Theory,* 2 (1992), pp. 443–462; Frank Marini, "The Use of Literature in the Exploration of Public Administration Ethics: The Example of Antigone," *Public Administration Review,* 52 (September/October 1992), pp. 420–426; as well as the entire issue of *The Annals* (January 1995) devoted to essays on "Ethics in American Public Service."

Any in-depth review of this subject should include study of the Ethics in Government Act of 1978, as well as the enabling legislation and debates over such seminal oversight mechanisms as the War Powers Resolution of 1973, Freedom of Information Act 1967 (with 1974 amendments), Privacy Act (1974), the Inspector General's Office (1976), and the various ombudsman offices instituted within state and local governments. For many of these recent documents, see Richard J. Stillman II, ed., *Basic Documents of American Public Administration Since 1950* (New York: Holmes and Meier, 1982).

Many novels focus on the role of ethics in public life. For an excellent discussion of how they contribute to our understanding of the subject, see Dwight Waldo, *The Novelist on Organization and Administration: An Inquiry into the Relationship Between Two Worlds* (Berkeley, Calif.: Institute of Governmental Studies, June 1968), or Marc Holzer, Kenneth Morris, and William Ludwin, *Literature in Bureaucracy* (Wayne, N.J.: Avery Publishing, 1979).

For two useful applied casebooks on this topic, read William M. Timmins, *A Casebook of Public Ethics and Issues* (Monterey, Calif.: Brooks/Cole, 1990), and Mark H. Moore and Malcolm K. Sparrow, *Ethics in Government: The Moral Challenge of Public Leadership* (Englewood Cliffs, N.J.: Prentice-Hall, 1990).

Topic Index

Citizens' Rights and Participation

Communications in Administration

The Legislature and Congress

Decision Making

Ethical Issues

Health and Human Services

Implementation

Intergovernmental Programs and Policies

National Defense and International Relations

Personnel and Civil Service

Planning and Policy Development

Power and Politics in Administration

Presidency

Regulation, Rule Enforcement, and Law Enforcement

State and Local Government

The Study of Public Administration as a Discipline

Third-party Government

Index